I0603830
CHICKEN MERRY
HAWK DE NEAR.
Jamiaca

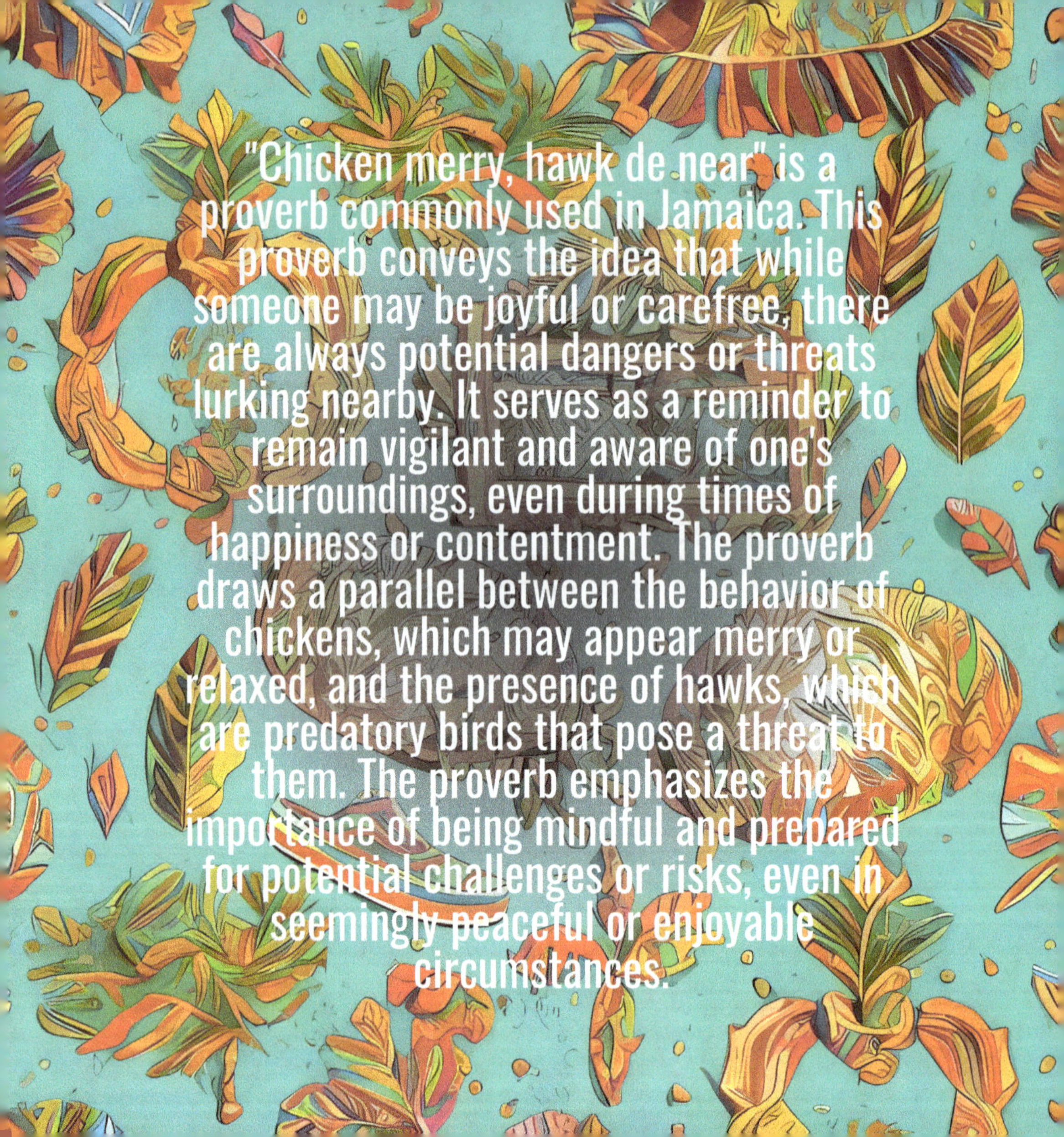

"Chicken merry, hawk de near" is a proverb commonly used in Jamaica. This proverb conveys the idea that while someone may be joyful or carefree, there are always potential dangers or threats lurking nearby. It serves as a reminder to remain vigilant and aware of one's surroundings, even during times of happiness or contentment. The proverb draws a parallel between the behavior of chickens, which may appear merry or relaxed, and the presence of hawks, which are predatory birds that pose a threat to them. The proverb emphasizes the importance of being mindful and prepared for potential challenges or risks, even in seemingly peaceful or enjoyable circumstances.

As I hold this collection of proverbs from Europe, Africa, Latin America, South Asia, East Asia, the Caribbean, and Arabia in my hands, I am reminded of the immense wisdom and cultural richness that these small yet powerful phrases hold. Proverbs are not just words; they are the threads that connect generations, weaving together the tapestry of our shared human experience. Passed down from elders to children, from one mouth to another, these proverbs offer an alternative and wise perspective on life's complexities.

Each proverb in this collection is matched with an intricate pattern as its background, meticulously crafted to reflect the traditional patterns of the country or region it originates from. These patterns pay homage to the rich cultural heritage and artistic traditions that have shaped these proverbs. They serve as a visual reminder of the diverse tapestry of our world, where wisdom and beauty intertwine.

What is truly fascinating is how these proverbs, despite originating from different corners of the globe, often cross over and share striking similarities. They remind us of the interconnectedness of humanity and the universal themes that resonate across cultures. Through these proverbs, we catch glimpses of the values, beliefs, and attitudes that shape societies, offering a window into the hearts and minds of people around the world.

Please note that while this collection labels proverbs with countries, it is important to recognize that many proverbs are associated with multiple cultures. The origins of proverbs are often elusive, as they flow through oral traditions, transcending borders and boundaries. Proverbs embody the collective wisdom of humanity, and their true power lies in their ability to transcend cultural boundaries and speak to the shared human experience.

In our fast-paced and ever-evolving world, proverbs are a beautiful lost art that deserves to be rediscovered and appreciated. They offer us a connection to our roots, a bridge between past and present, and a reminder of the timeless values that have guided humankind for centuries. As you explore this collection, arranged in a randomized order, let it signify the multicultural and unified world we inhabit, where wisdom knows no borders.

May these proverbs enlighten our minds, touch our hearts, and inspire us to reflect, grow, and embrace the beauty of our shared humanity.

A WISE ENEMY IS
BETTER THAN A
FOOLISH FRIEND.
Hindi

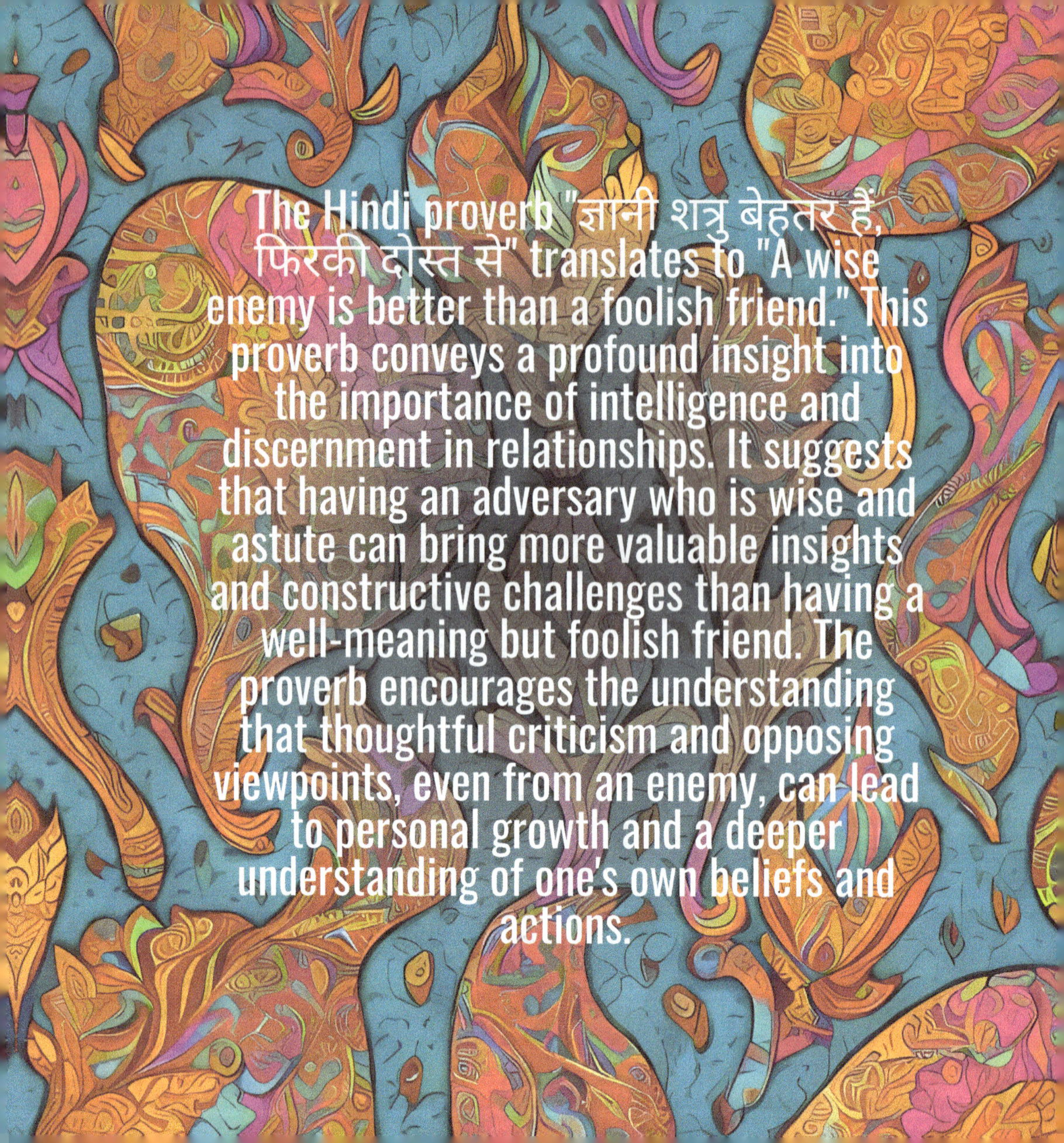
The Hindi proverb "ज्ञानी शत्रु बेहतर हैं, फिरकी दोस्त से" translates to "A wise enemy is better than a foolish friend." This proverb conveys a profound insight into the importance of intelligence and discernment in relationships. It suggests that having an adversary who is wise and astute can bring more valuable insights and constructive challenges than having a well-meaning but foolish friend. The proverb encourages the understanding that thoughtful criticism and opposing viewpoints, even from an enemy, can lead to personal growth and a deeper understanding of one's own beliefs and actions.

WHOEVER DOESN'T RESPECT THE PENNY ISN'T WORTH THE DOLLAR.
Germany

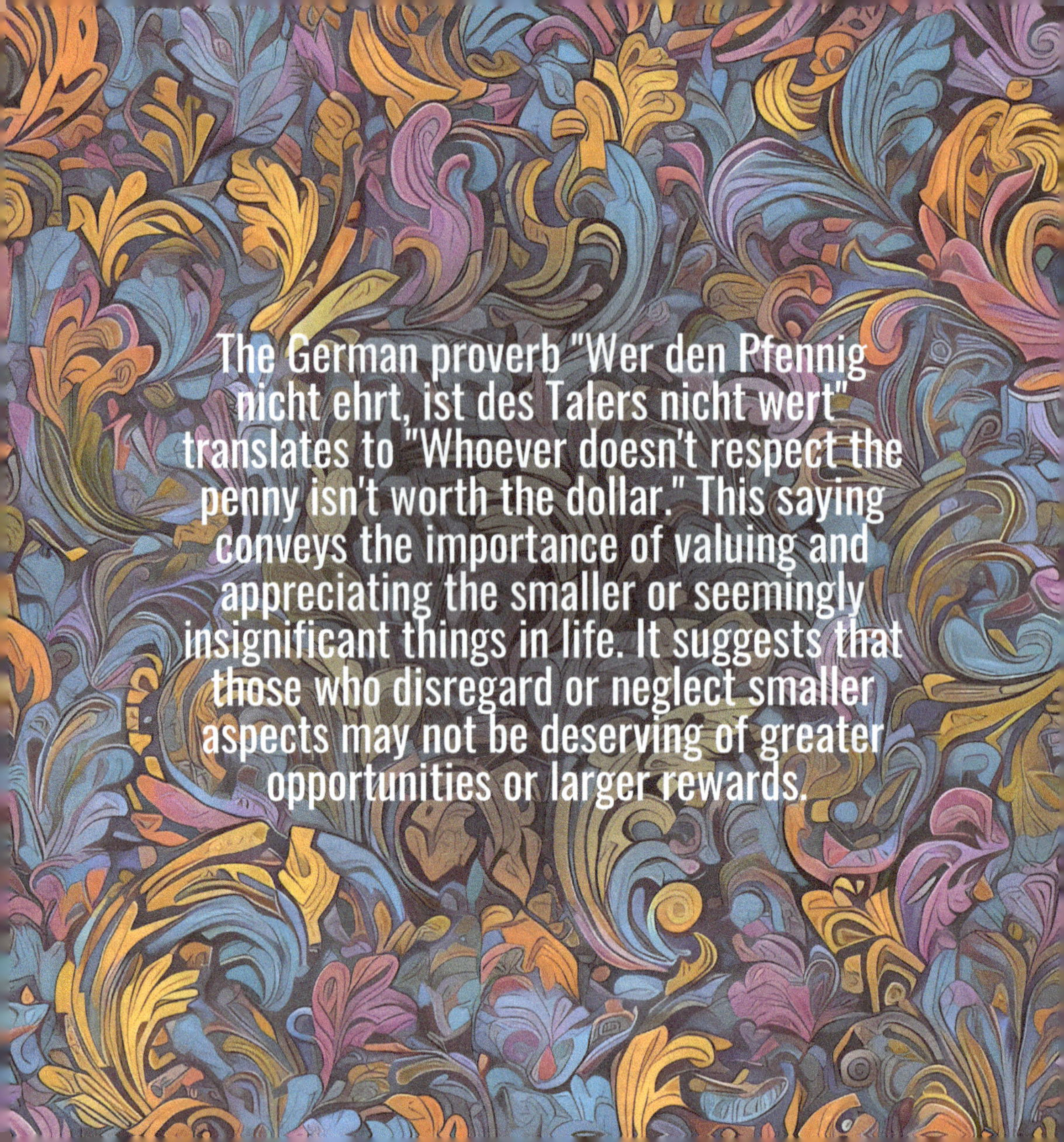

The German proverb "Wer den Pfennig nicht ehrt, ist des Talers nicht wert" translates to "Whoever doesn't respect the penny isn't worth the dollar." This saying conveys the importance of valuing and appreciating the smaller or seemingly insignificant things in life. It suggests that those who disregard or neglect smaller aspects may not be deserving of greater opportunities or larger rewards.

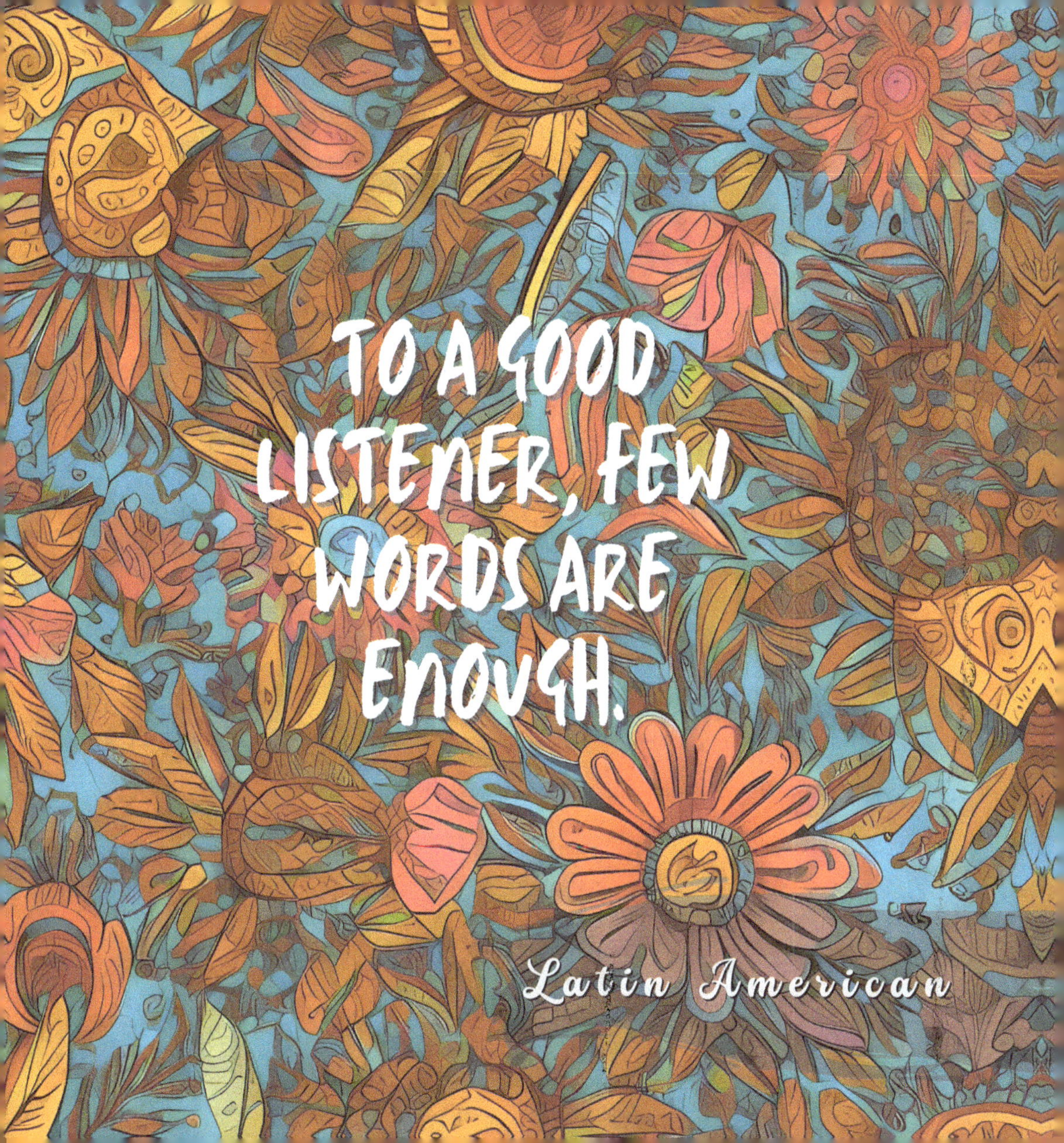
TO A GOOD LISTENER, FEW WORDS ARE ENOUGH.
Latin American

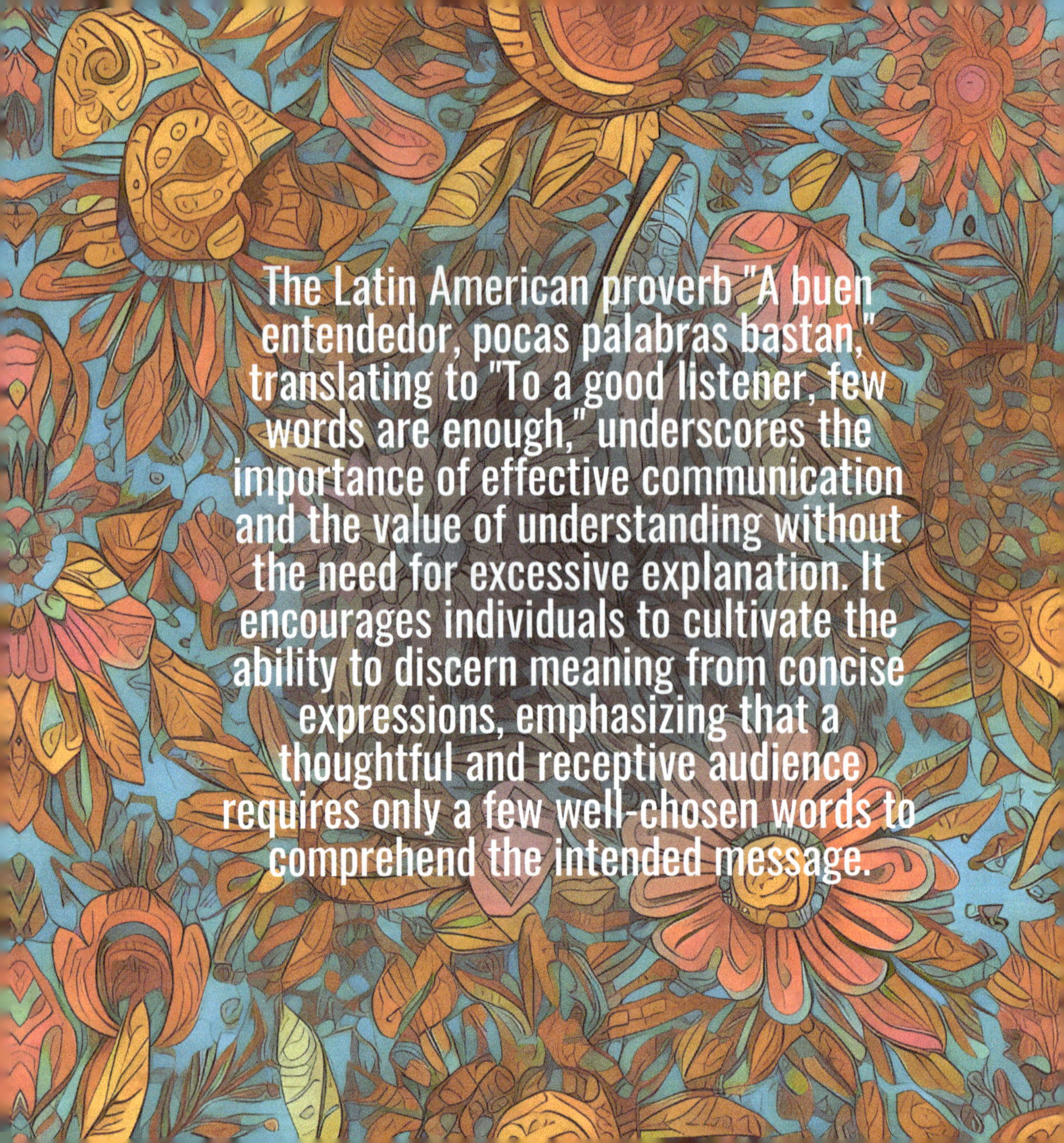
The Latin American proverb "A buen entendedor, pocas palabras bastan," translating to "To a good listener, few words are enough," underscores the importance of effective communication and the value of understanding without the need for excessive explanation. It encourages individuals to cultivate the ability to discern meaning from concise expressions, emphasizing that a thoughtful and receptive audience requires only a few well-chosen words to comprehend the intended message.

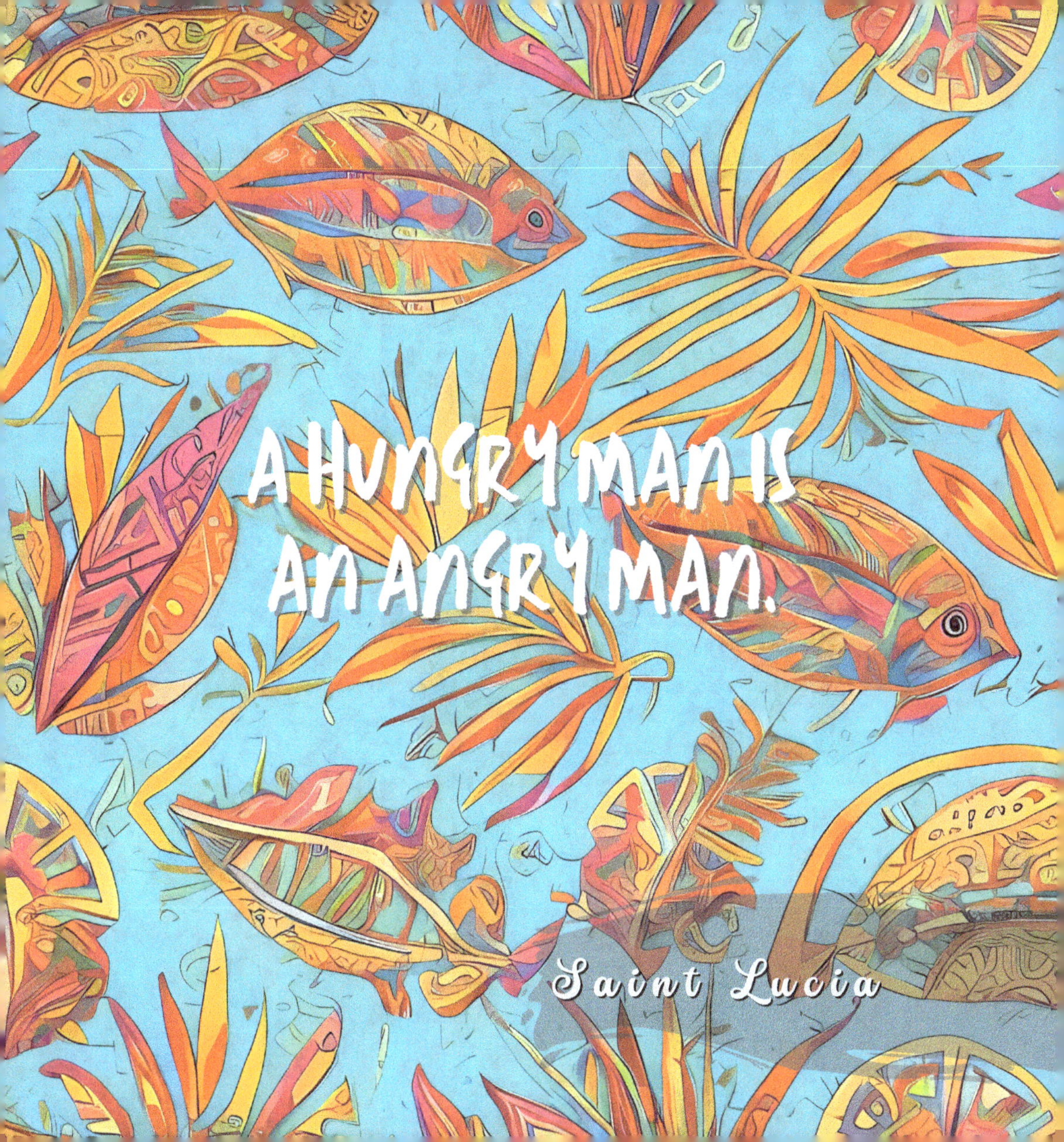
A Hungry man is
an angry man.
Saint Lucia

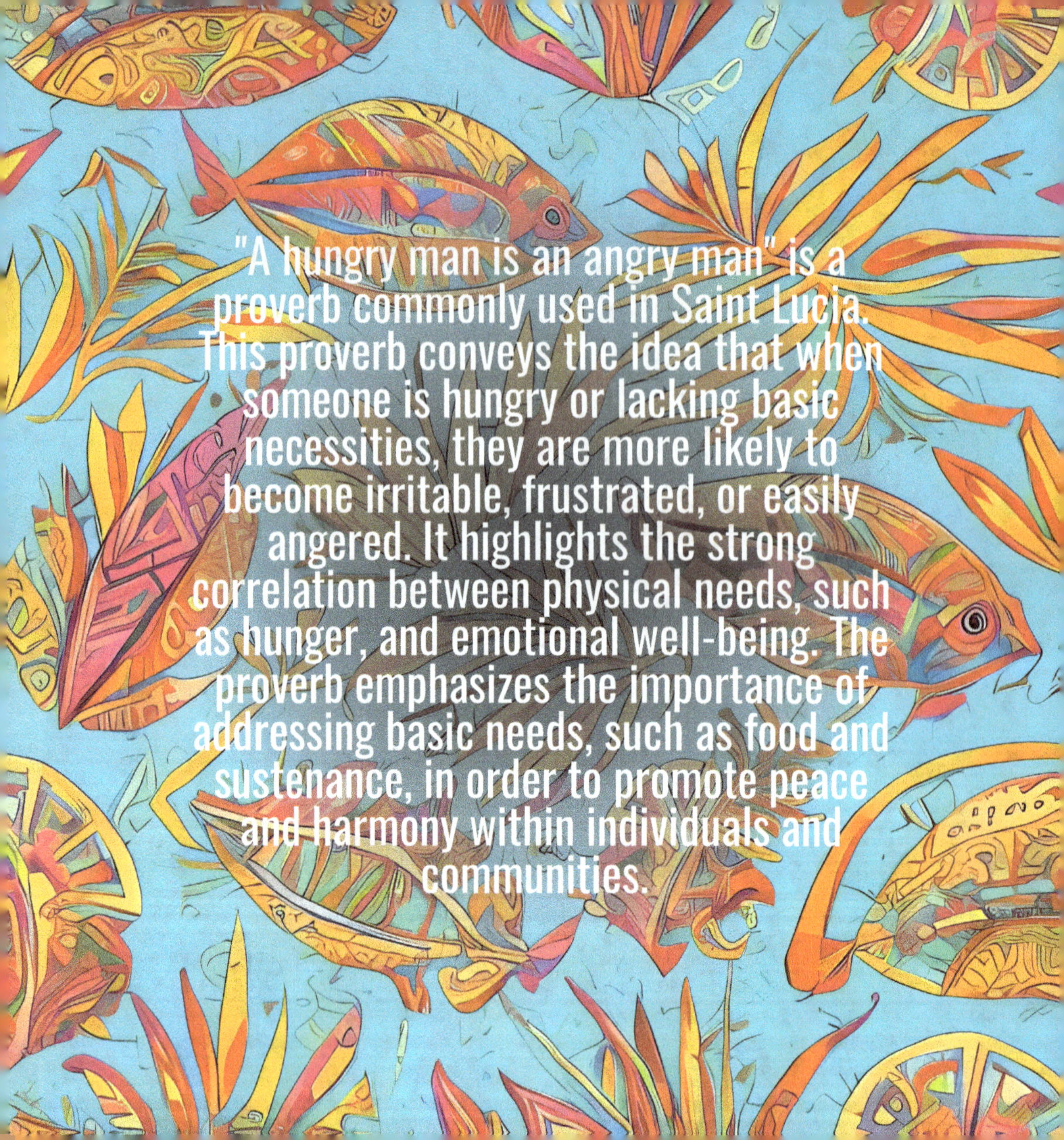
"A hungry man is an angry man" is a proverb commonly used in Saint Lucia. This proverb conveys the idea that when someone is hungry or lacking basic necessities, they are more likely to become irritable, frustrated, or easily angered. It highlights the strong correlation between physical needs, such as hunger, and emotional well-being. The proverb emphasizes the importance of addressing basic needs, such as food and sustenance, in order to promote peace and harmony within individuals and communities.

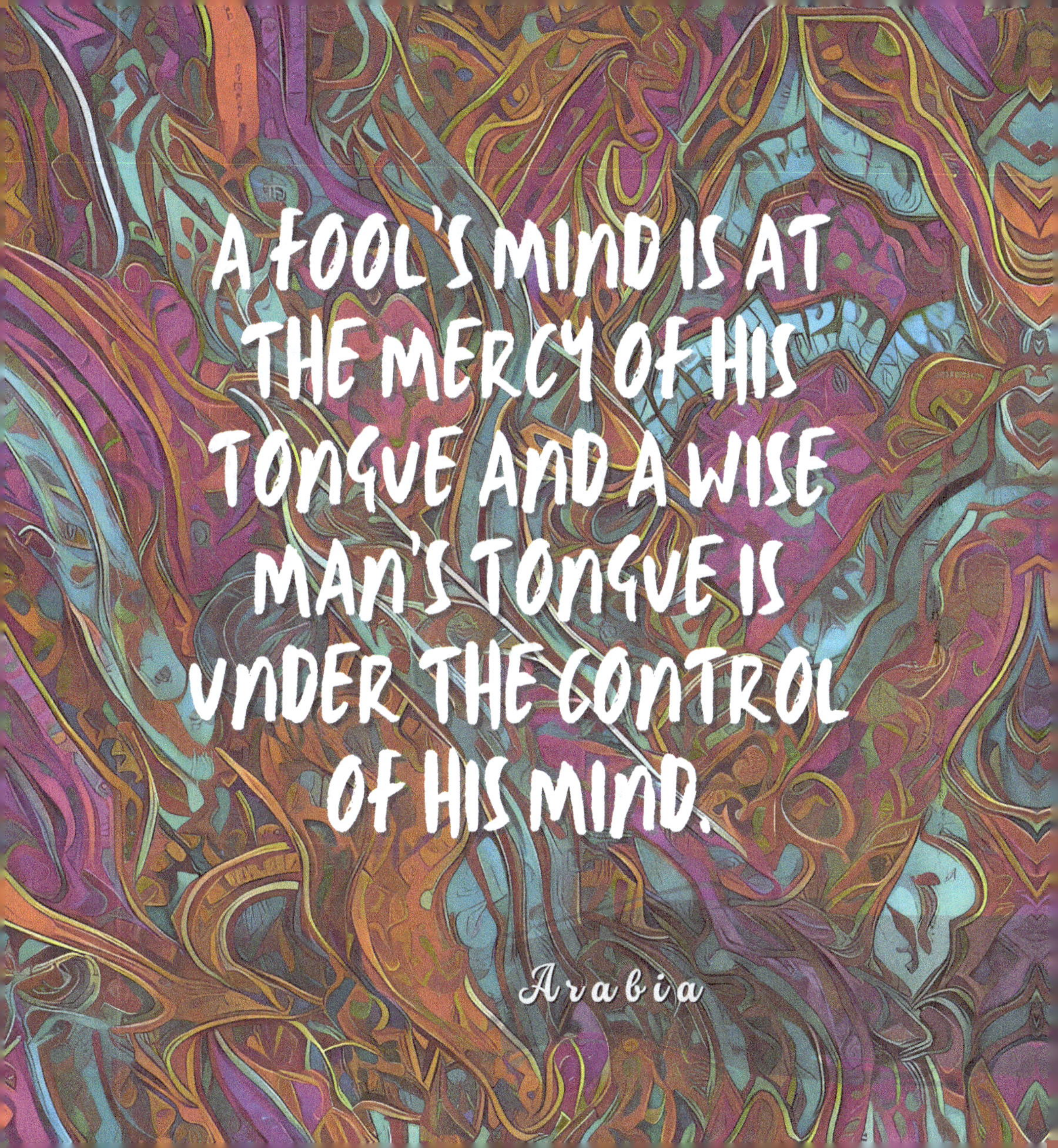
A FOOL'S MIND IS AT
THE MERCY OF HIS
TONGUE AND A WISE
MAN'S TONGUE IS
UNDER THE CONTROL
OF HIS MIND.
Arabia

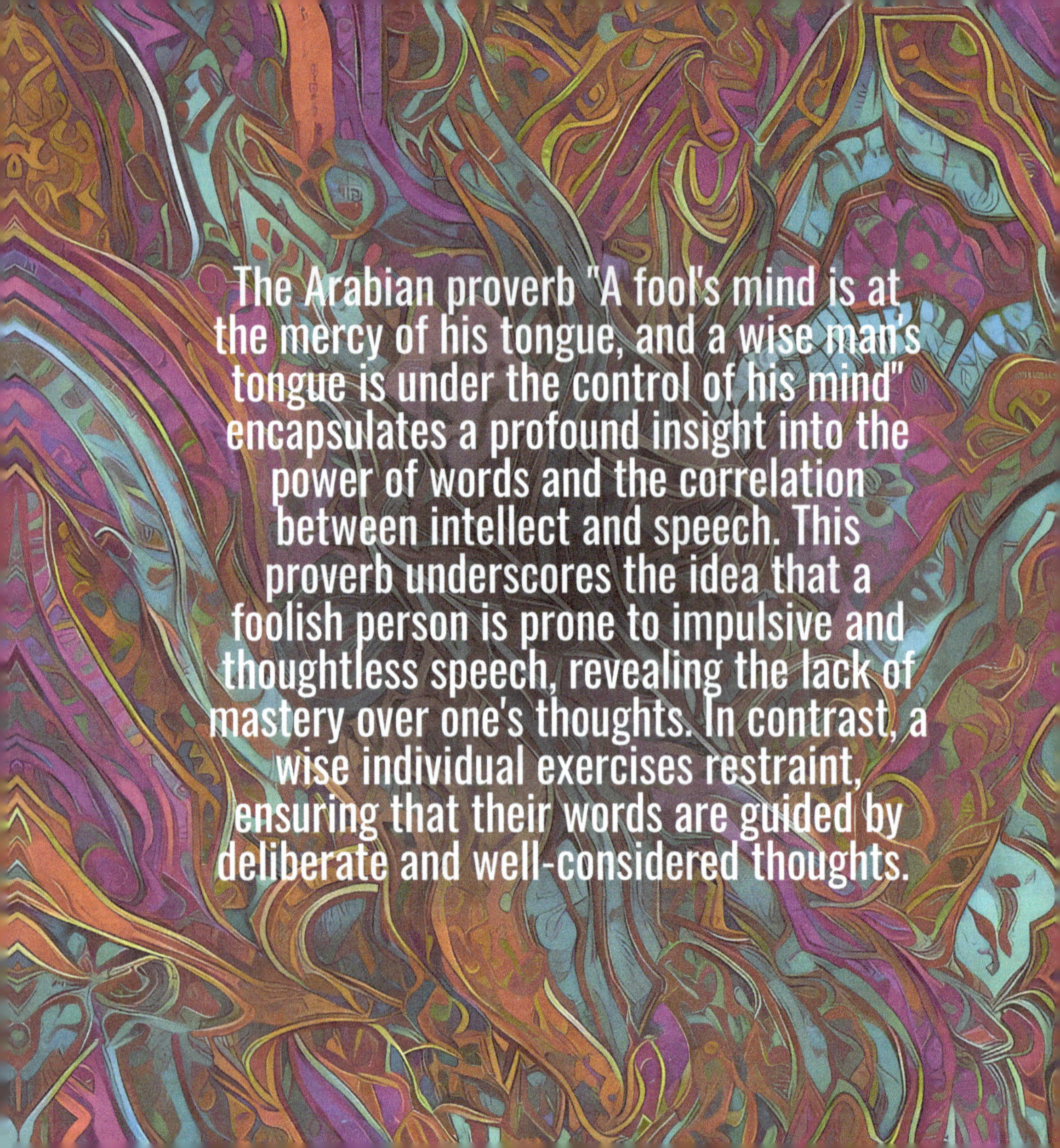
The Arabian proverb "A fool's mind is at the mercy of his tongue, and a wise man's tongue is under the control of his mind" encapsulates a profound insight into the power of words and the correlation between intellect and speech. This proverb underscores the idea that a foolish person is prone to impulsive and thoughtless speech, revealing the lack of mastery over one's thoughts. In contrast, a wise individual exercises restraint, ensuring that their words are guided by deliberate and well-considered thoughts.

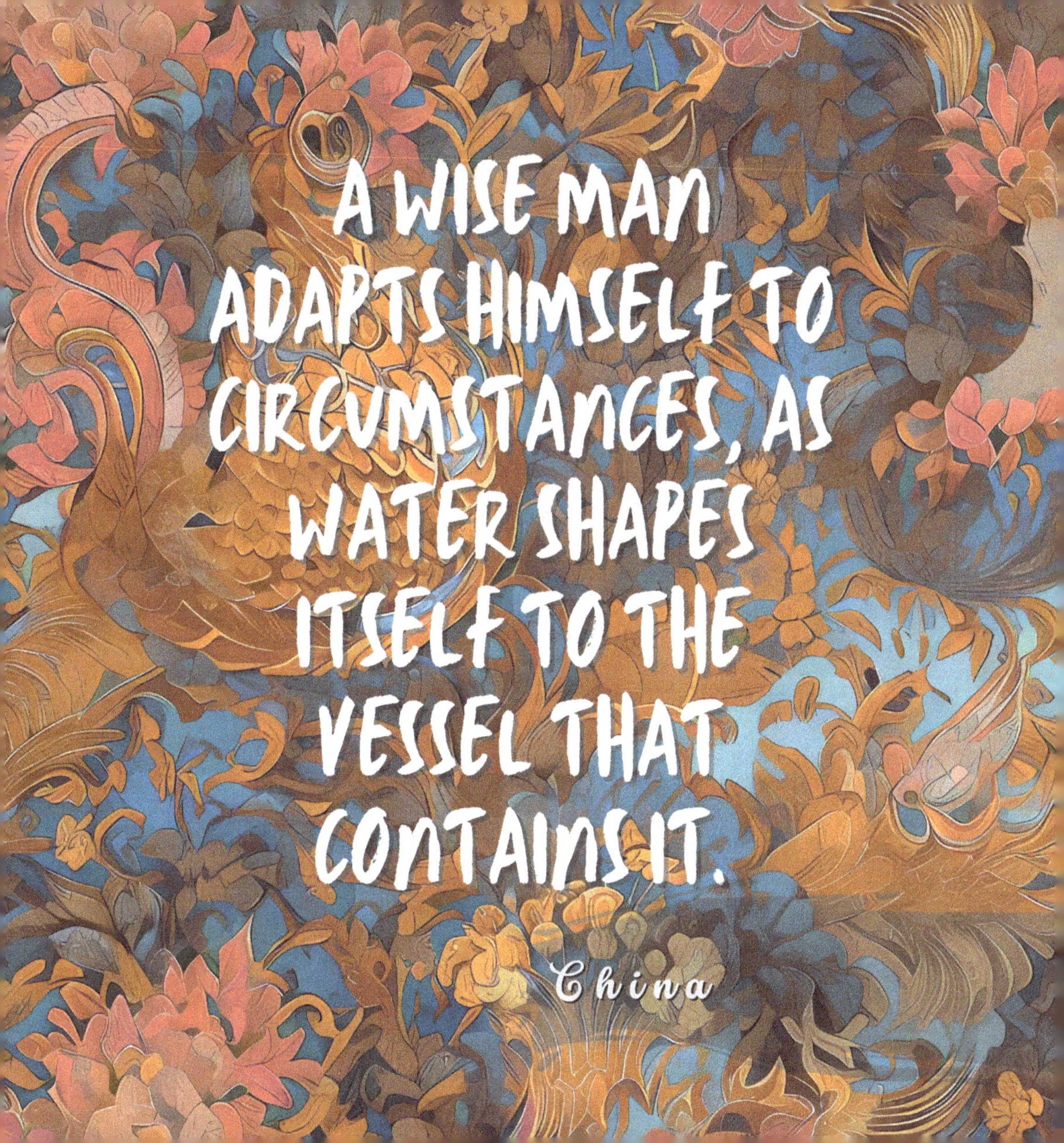
A WISE MAN
ADAPTS HIMSELF TO
CIRCUMSTANCES, AS
WATER SHAPES
ITSELF TO THE
VESSEL THAT
CONTAINS IT.
China

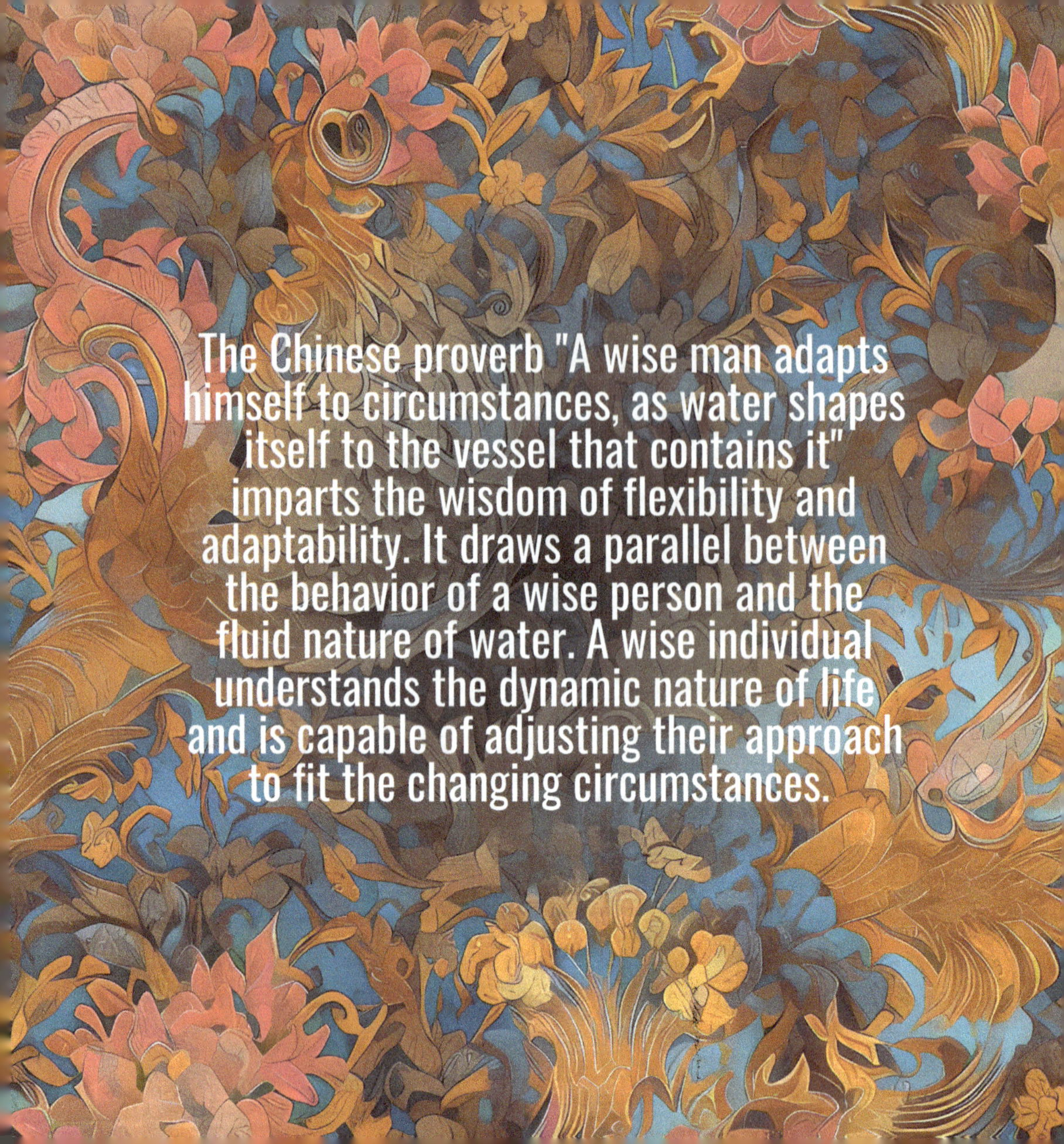

The Chinese proverb "A wise man adapts himself to circumstances, as water shapes itself to the vessel that contains it" imparts the wisdom of flexibility and adaptability. It draws a parallel between the behavior of a wise person and the fluid nature of water. A wise individual understands the dynamic nature of life and is capable of adjusting their approach to fit the changing circumstances.

A WEALTHY PERSON
IS NOT KNOWN BY
HIS WEALTH BUT BY
HIS BEHAVIOR.
Somalia

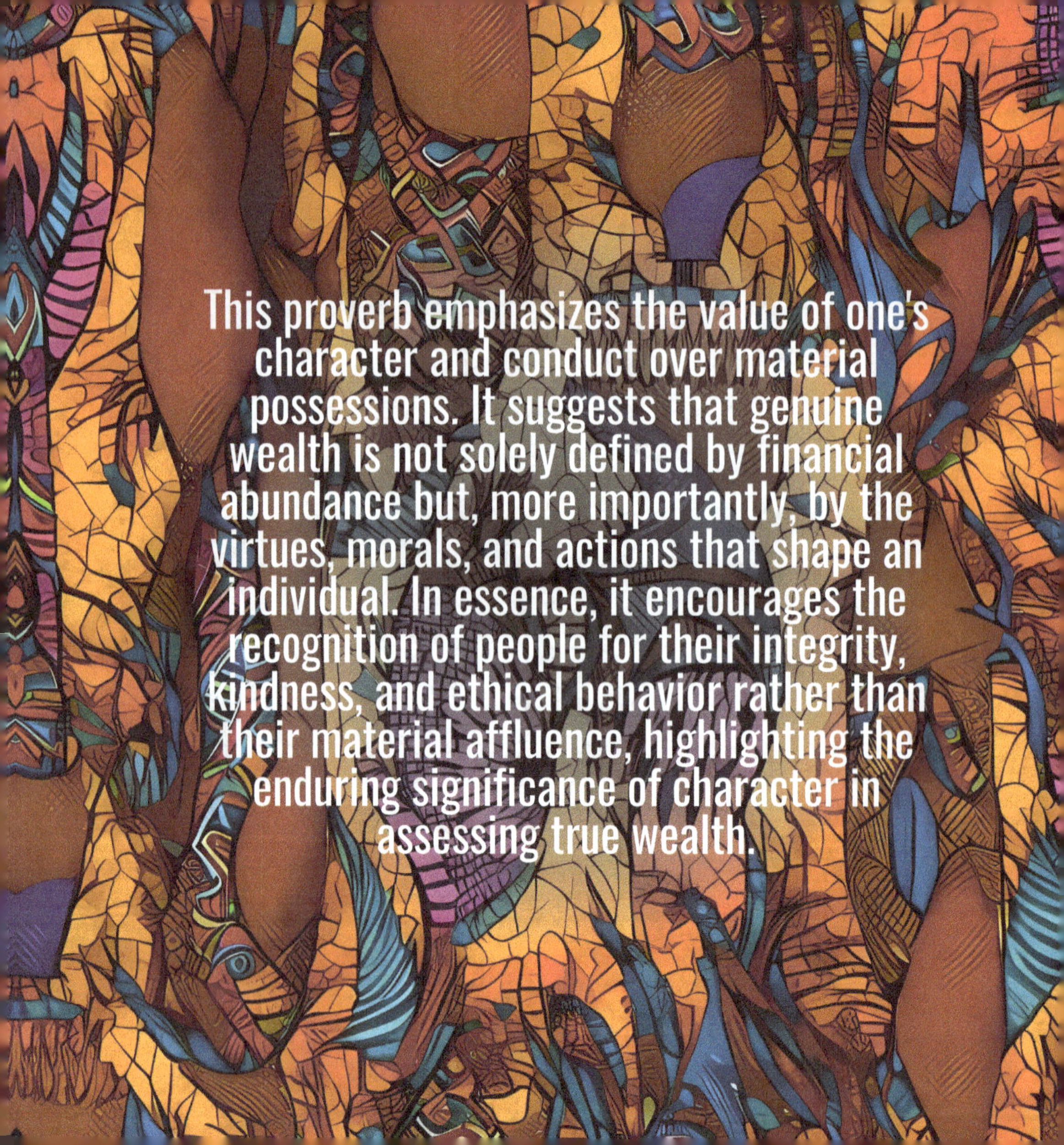

This proverb emphasizes the value of one's character and conduct over material possessions. It suggests that genuine wealth is not solely defined by financial abundance but, more importantly, by the virtues, morals, and actions that shape an individual. In essence, it encourages the recognition of people for their integrity, kindness, and ethical behavior rather than their material affluence, highlighting the enduring significance of character in assessing true wealth.

A SMALL HOUSE
CAN HOLD AS MUCH
HAPPINESS AS A BIG
ONE.
India

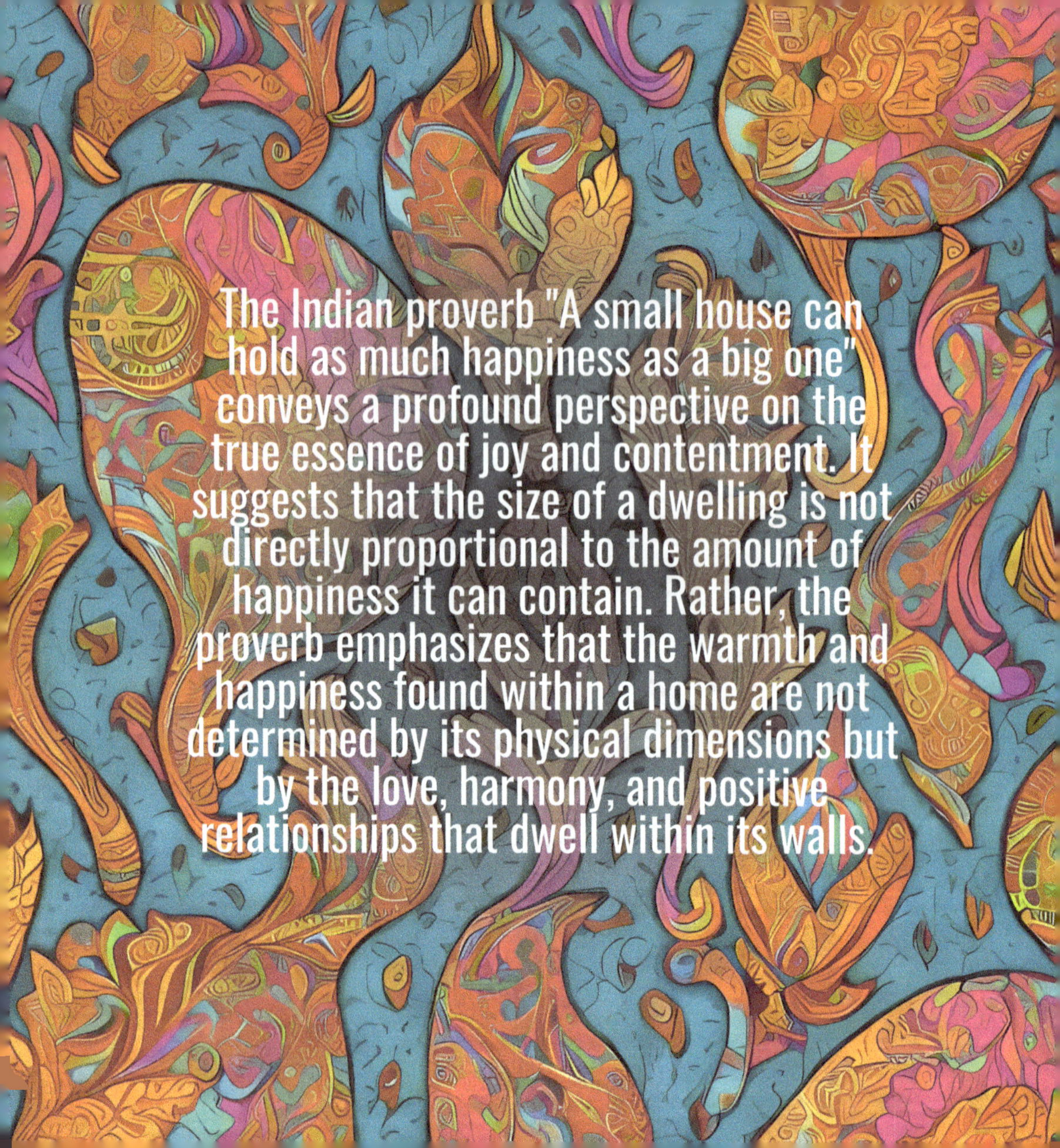

The Indian proverb "A small house can hold as much happiness as a big one" conveys a profound perspective on the true essence of joy and contentment. It suggests that the size of a dwelling is not directly proportional to the amount of happiness it can contain. Rather, the proverb emphasizes that the warmth and happiness found within a home are not determined by its physical dimensions but by the love, harmony, and positive relationships that dwell within its walls.

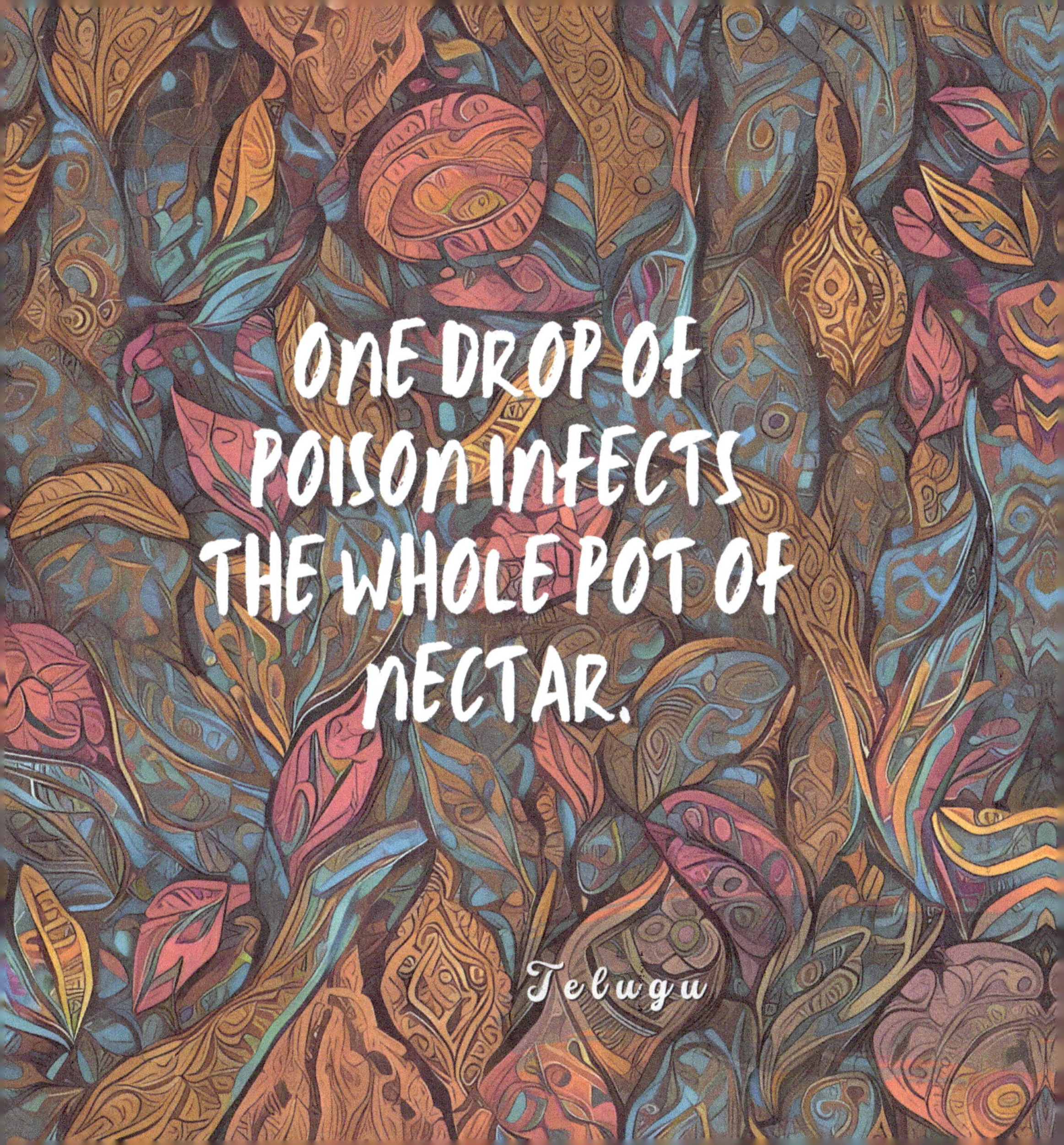
ONE DROP OF POISON INFECTS THE WHOLE POT OF NECTAR.
Telugu

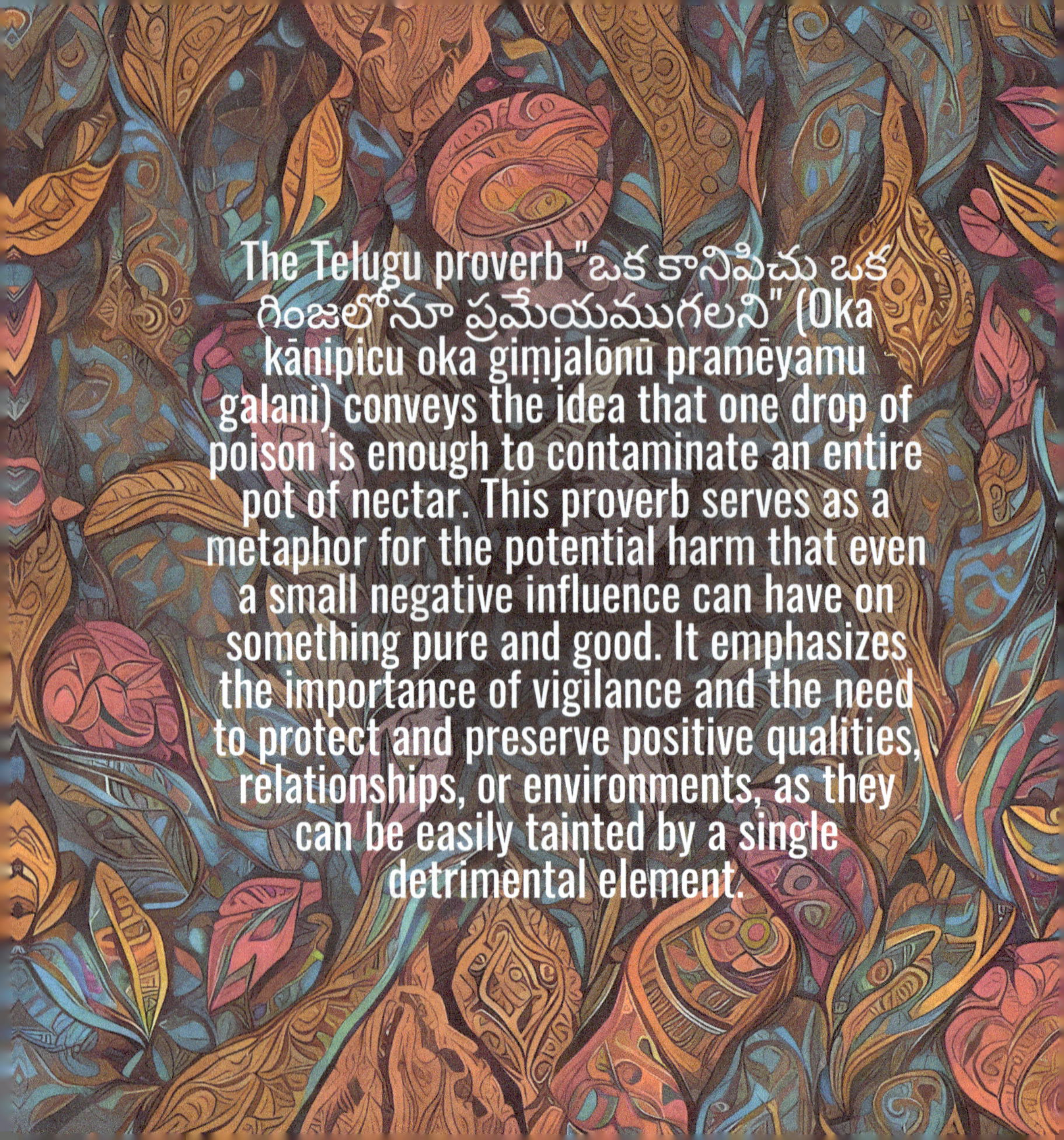

The Telugu proverb "ఒక కానిపిచు ఒక గింజలోనూ ప్రమేయముగలని" (Oka kānipicu oka giṃjalōnū pramēyamu galani) conveys the idea that one drop of poison is enough to contaminate an entire pot of nectar. This proverb serves as a metaphor for the potential harm that even a small negative influence can have on something pure and good. It emphasizes the importance of vigilance and the need to protect and preserve positive qualities, relationships, or environments, as they can be easily tainted by a single detrimental element.

YOU CAN'T RUN
WITH THE HARE
AND HUNT WITH
THE HOUNDS.
England

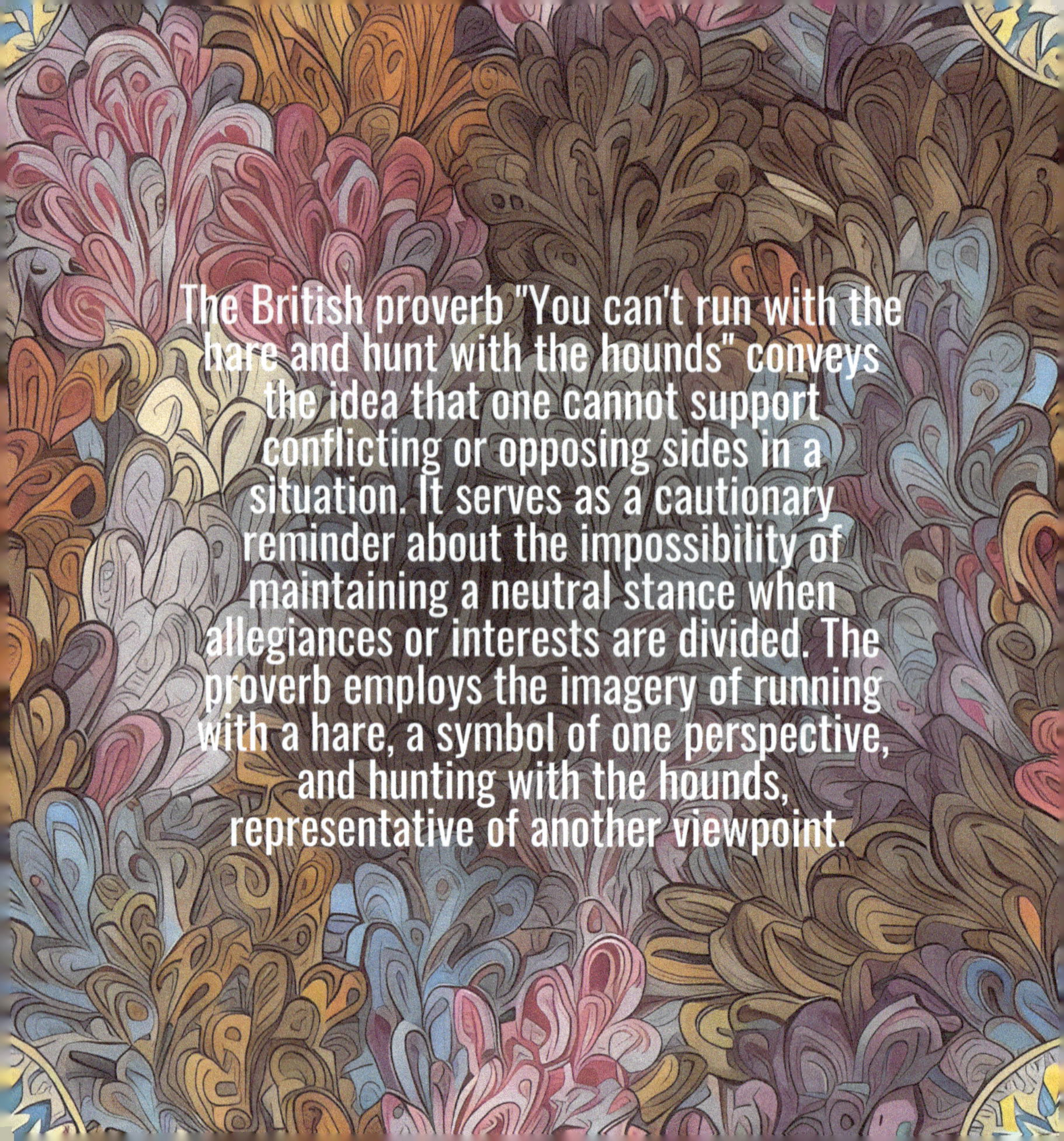
The British proverb "You can't run with the hare and hunt with the hounds" conveys the idea that one cannot support conflicting or opposing sides in a situation. It serves as a cautionary reminder about the impossibility of maintaining a neutral stance when allegiances or interests are divided. The proverb employs the imagery of running with a hare, a symbol of one perspective, and hunting with the hounds, representative of another viewpoint.

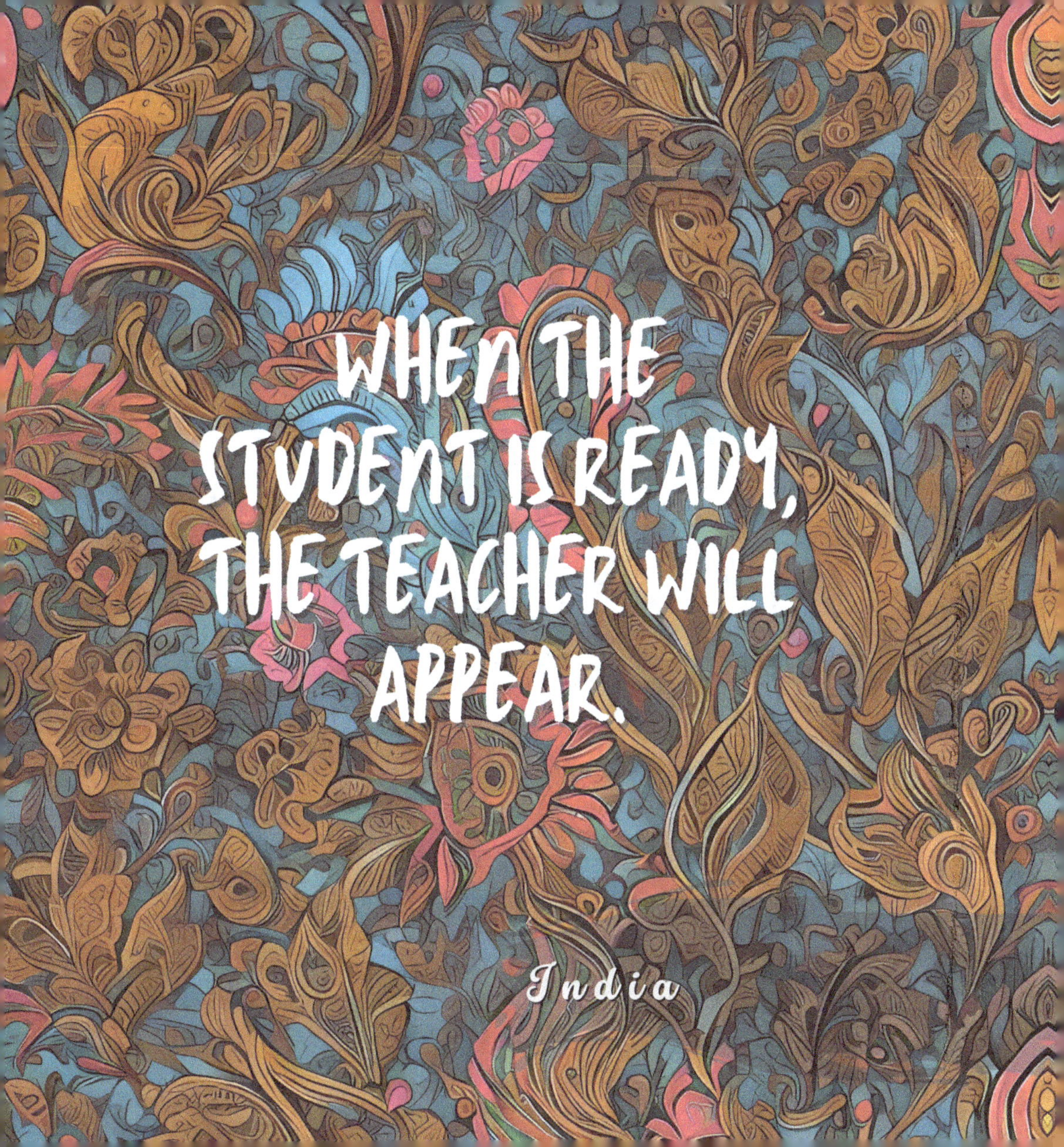
WHEN THE
STUDENT IS READY,
THE TEACHER WILL
APPEAR.
India

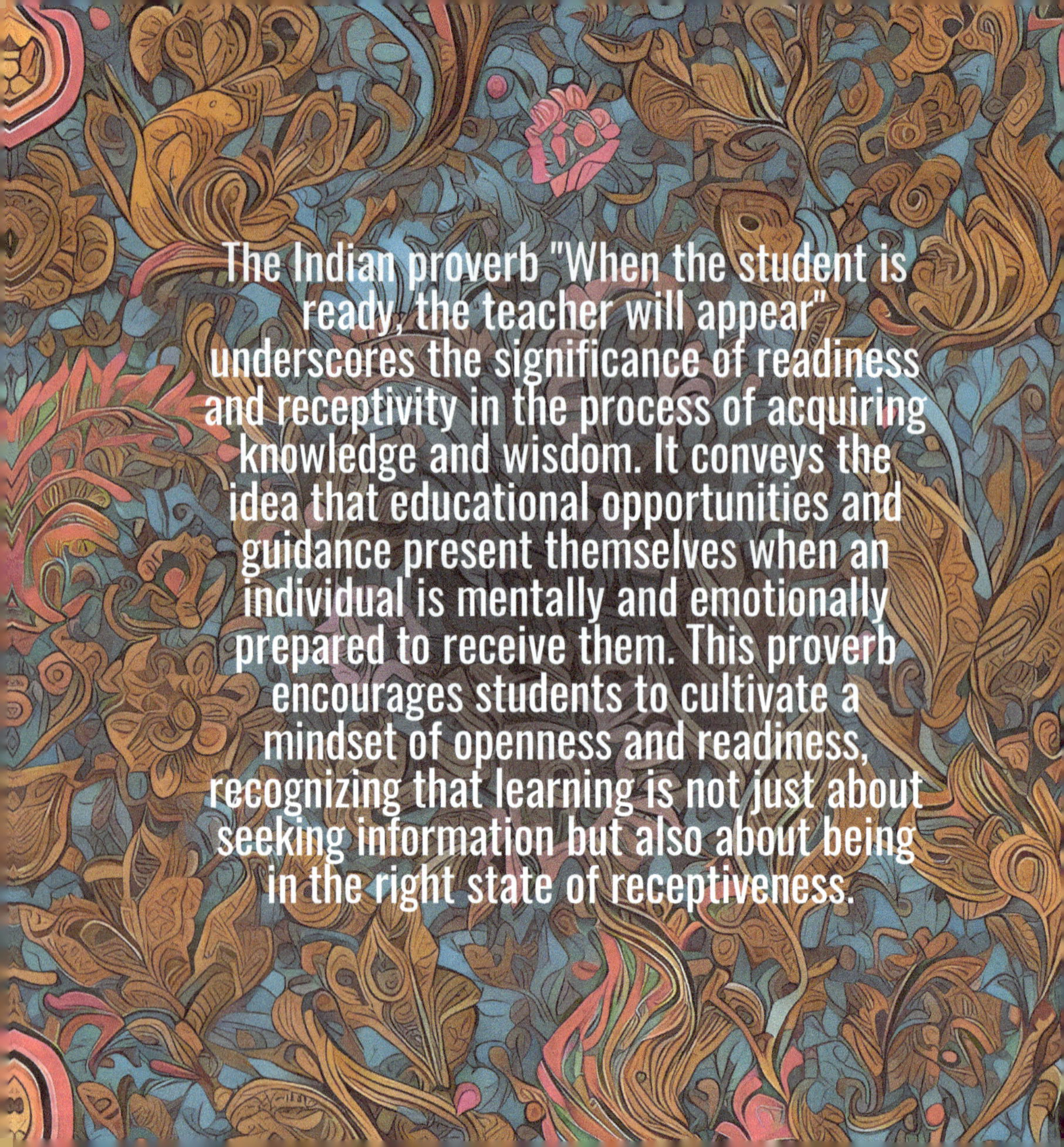

The Indian proverb "When the student is ready, the teacher will appear" underscores the significance of readiness and receptivity in the process of acquiring knowledge and wisdom. It conveys the idea that educational opportunities and guidance present themselves when an individual is mentally and emotionally prepared to receive them. This proverb encourages students to cultivate a mindset of openness and readiness, recognizing that learning is not just about seeking information but also about being in the right state of receptiveness.

THE DOVE THAT
DOESN'T FLY
SHOULDN'T
COMPLAIN ABOUT
THE AIR.
Latin American

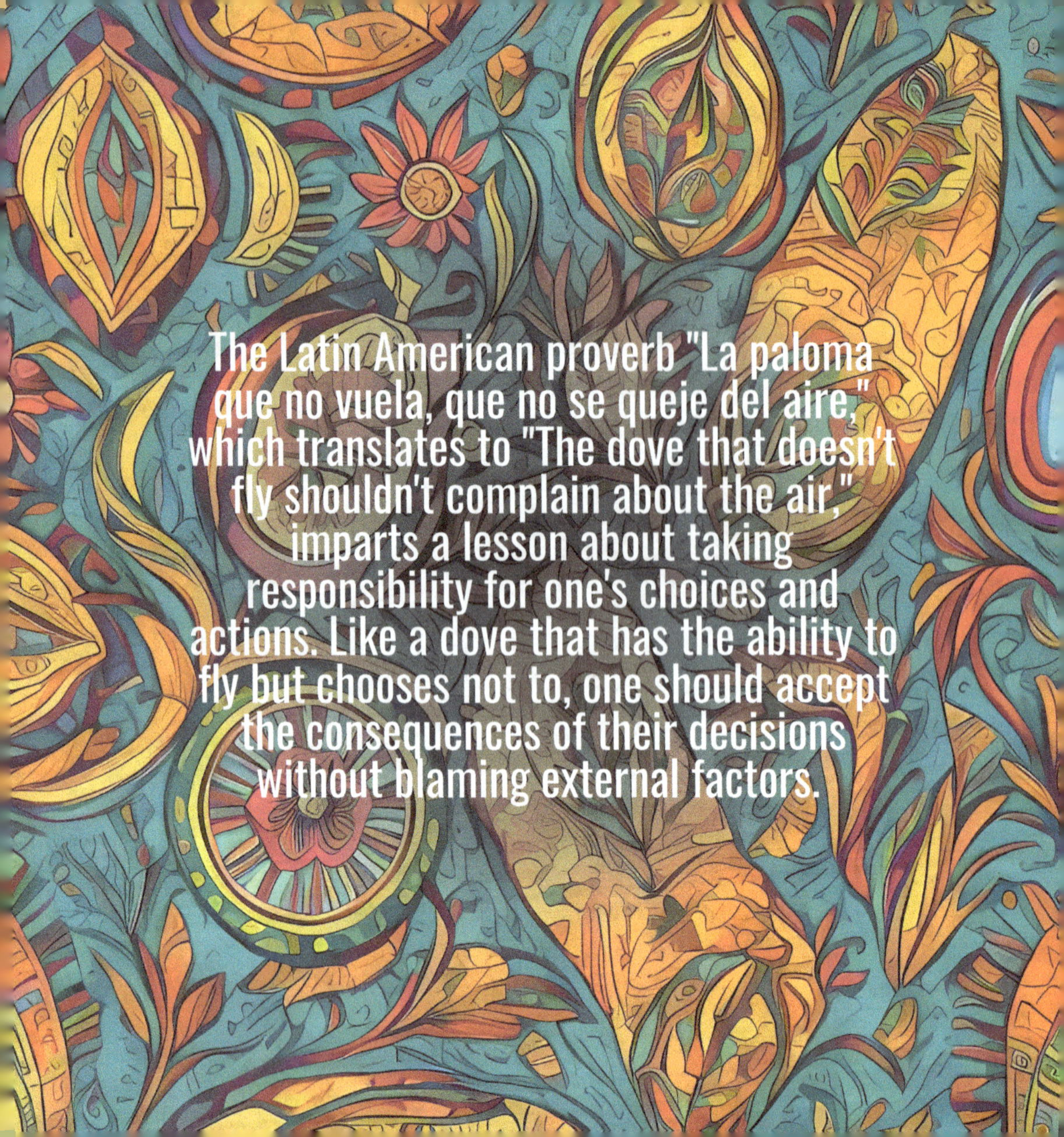

The Latin American proverb "La paloma que no vuela, que no se queje del aire," which translates to "The dove that doesn't fly shouldn't complain about the air," imparts a lesson about taking responsibility for one's choices and actions. Like a dove that has the ability to fly but chooses not to, one should accept the consequences of their decisions without blaming external factors.

NOT ALL TEETHY
'SMILES' ARE LAUGHS
Grenada

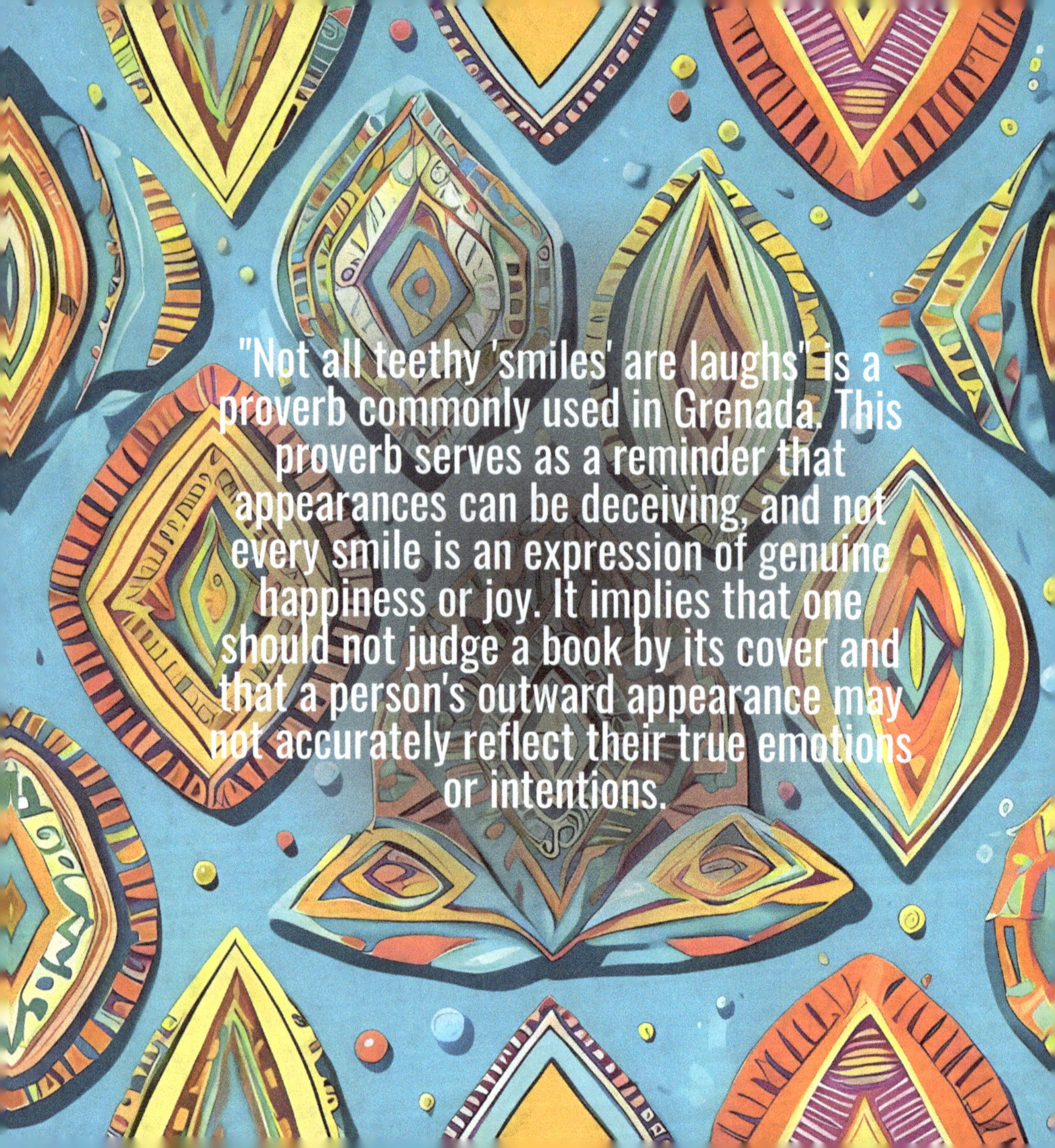

"Not all teethy 'smiles' are laughs" is a proverb commonly used in Grenada. This proverb serves as a reminder that appearances can be deceiving, and not every smile is an expression of genuine happiness or joy. It implies that one should not judge a book by its cover and that a person's outward appearance may not accurately reflect their true emotions or intentions.

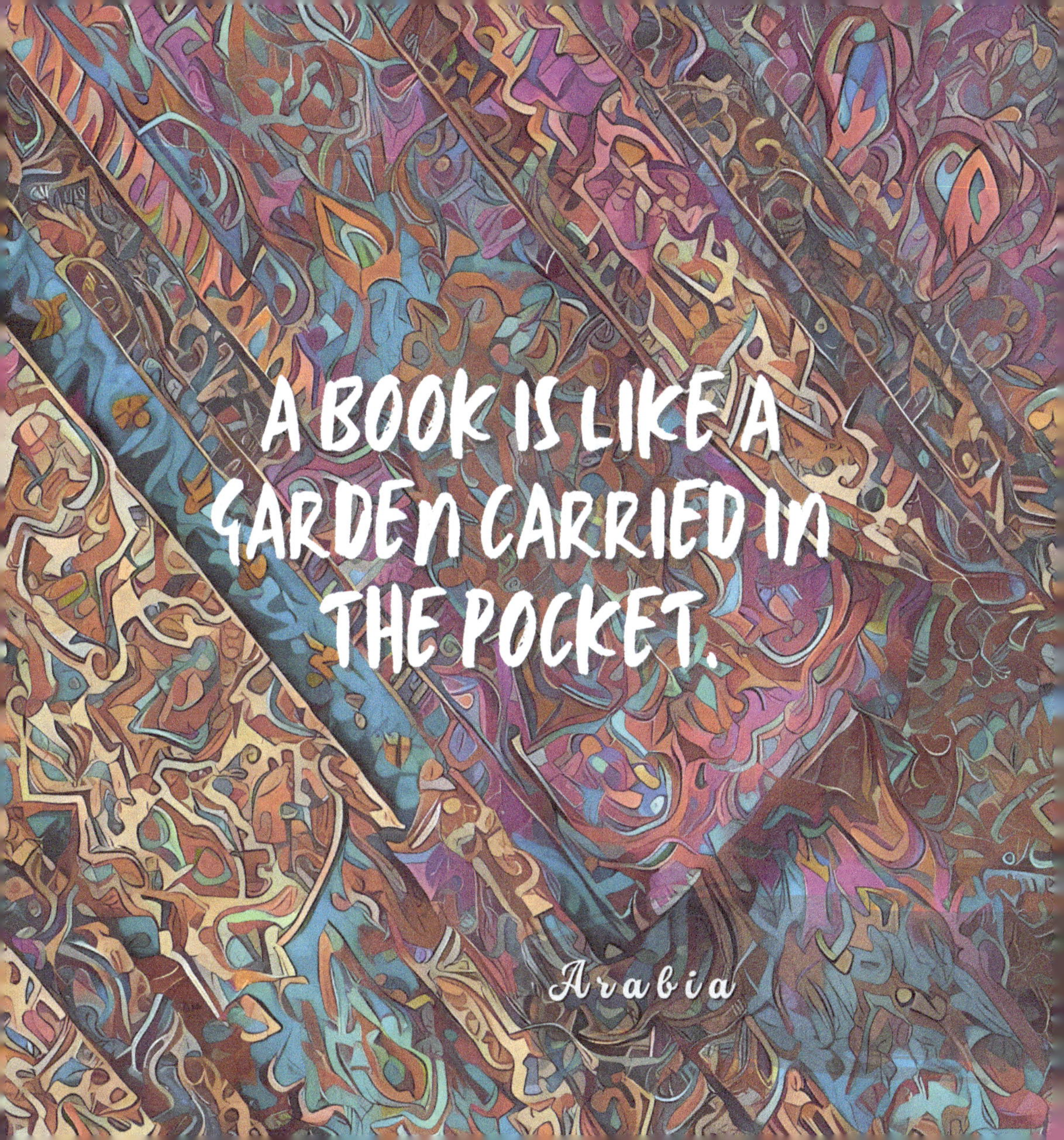
A BOOK IS LIKE A GARDEN CARRIED IN THE POCKET.
Arabia

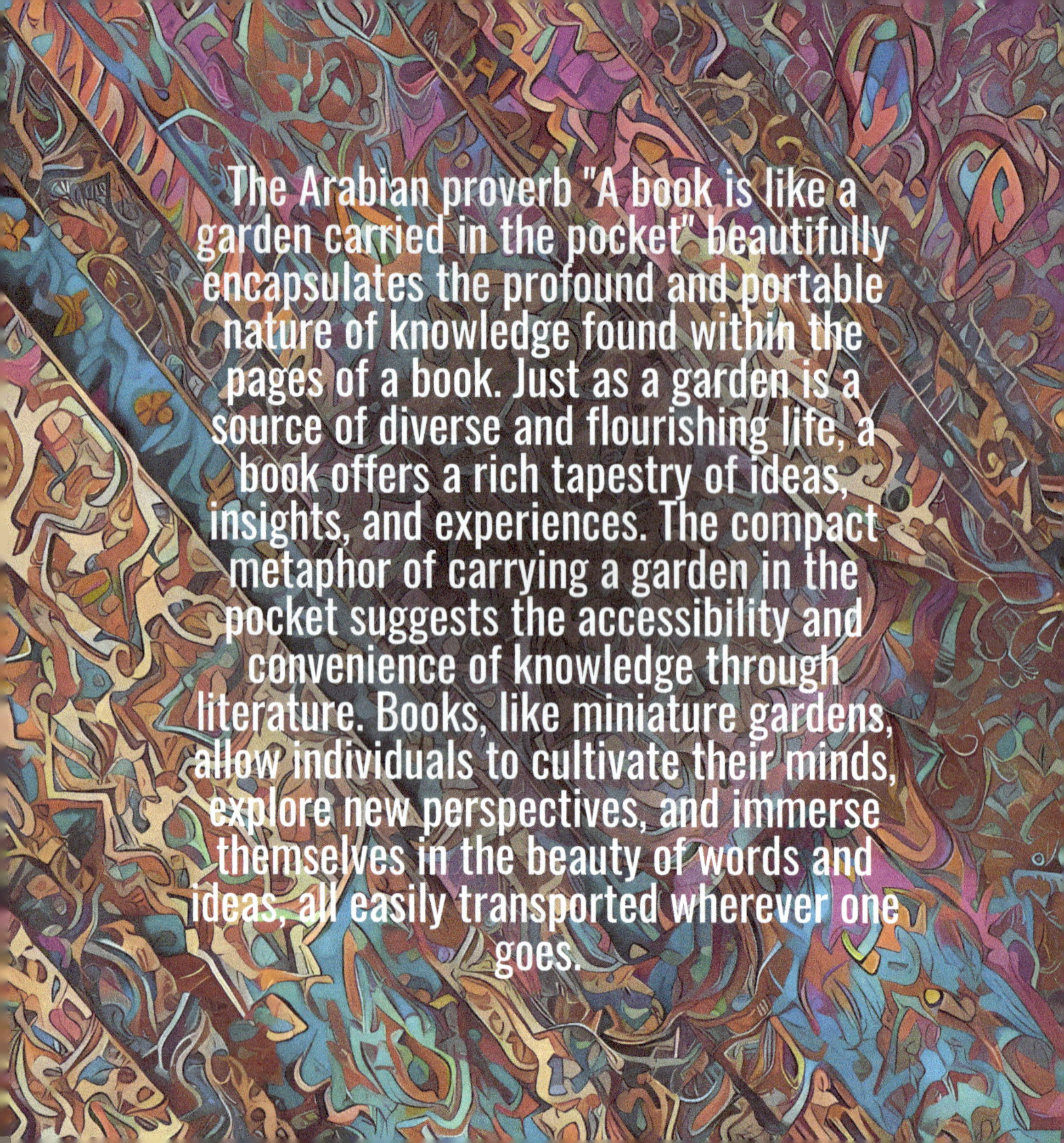

The Arabian proverb "A book is like a garden carried in the pocket" beautifully encapsulates the profound and portable nature of knowledge found within the pages of a book. Just as a garden is a source of diverse and flourishing life, a book offers a rich tapestry of ideas, insights, and experiences. The compact metaphor of carrying a garden in the pocket suggests the accessibility and convenience of knowledge through literature. Books, like miniature gardens, allow individuals to cultivate their minds, explore new perspectives, and immerse themselves in the beauty of words and ideas, all easily transported wherever one goes.

BETTER TO BE THE
HEAD OF A DOG
THAN THE TAIL OF
A LION.
Vietnam

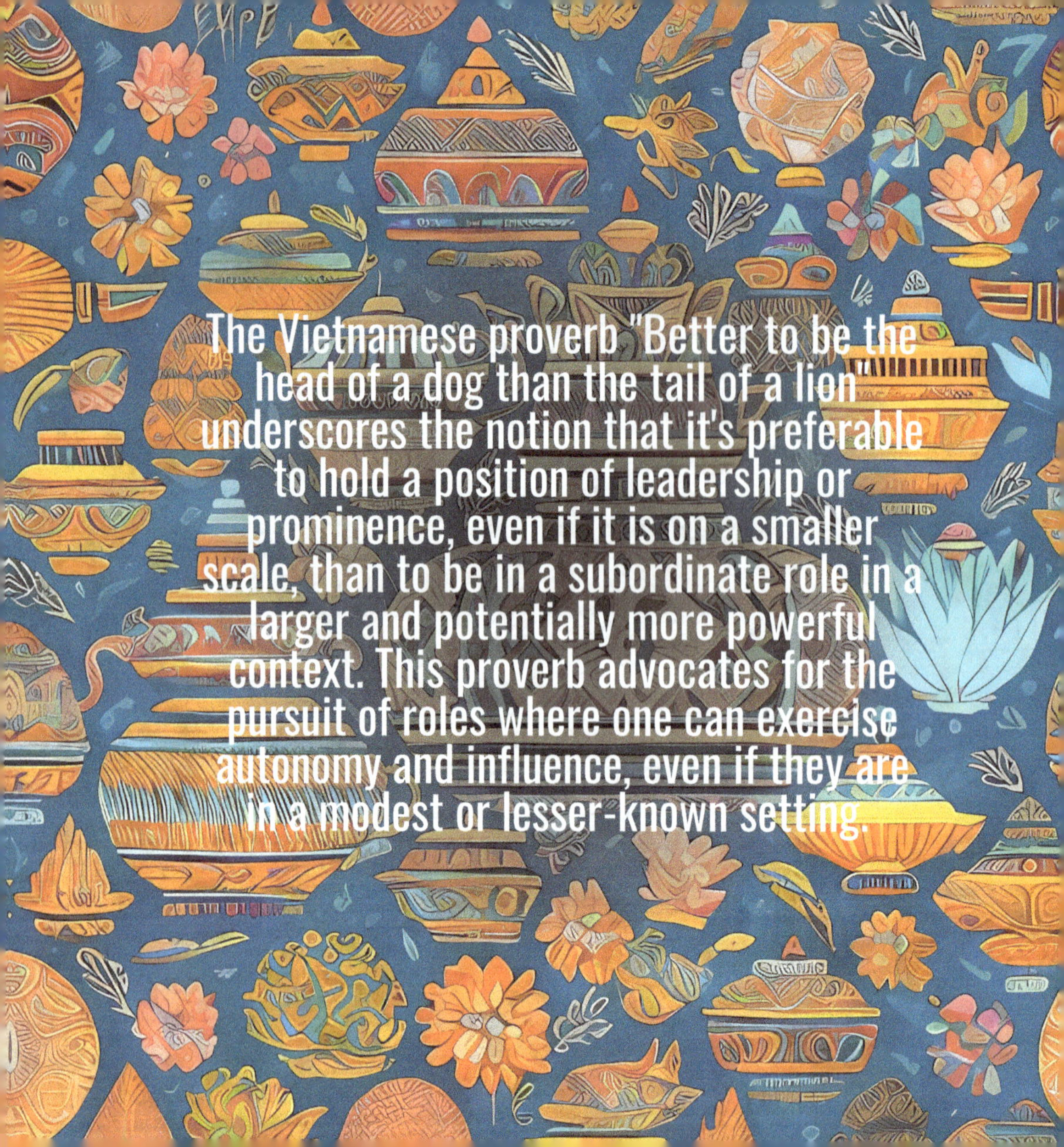
The Vietnamese proverb "Better to be the head of a dog than the tail of a lion" underscores the notion that it's preferable to hold a position of leadership or prominence, even if it is on a smaller scale, than to be in a subordinate role in a larger and potentially more powerful context. This proverb advocates for the pursuit of roles where one can exercise autonomy and influence, even if they are in a modest or lesser-known setting.

DON'T LET PEOPLE
TURN YOU INTO A
PUPPET SHOW.
Jamaica

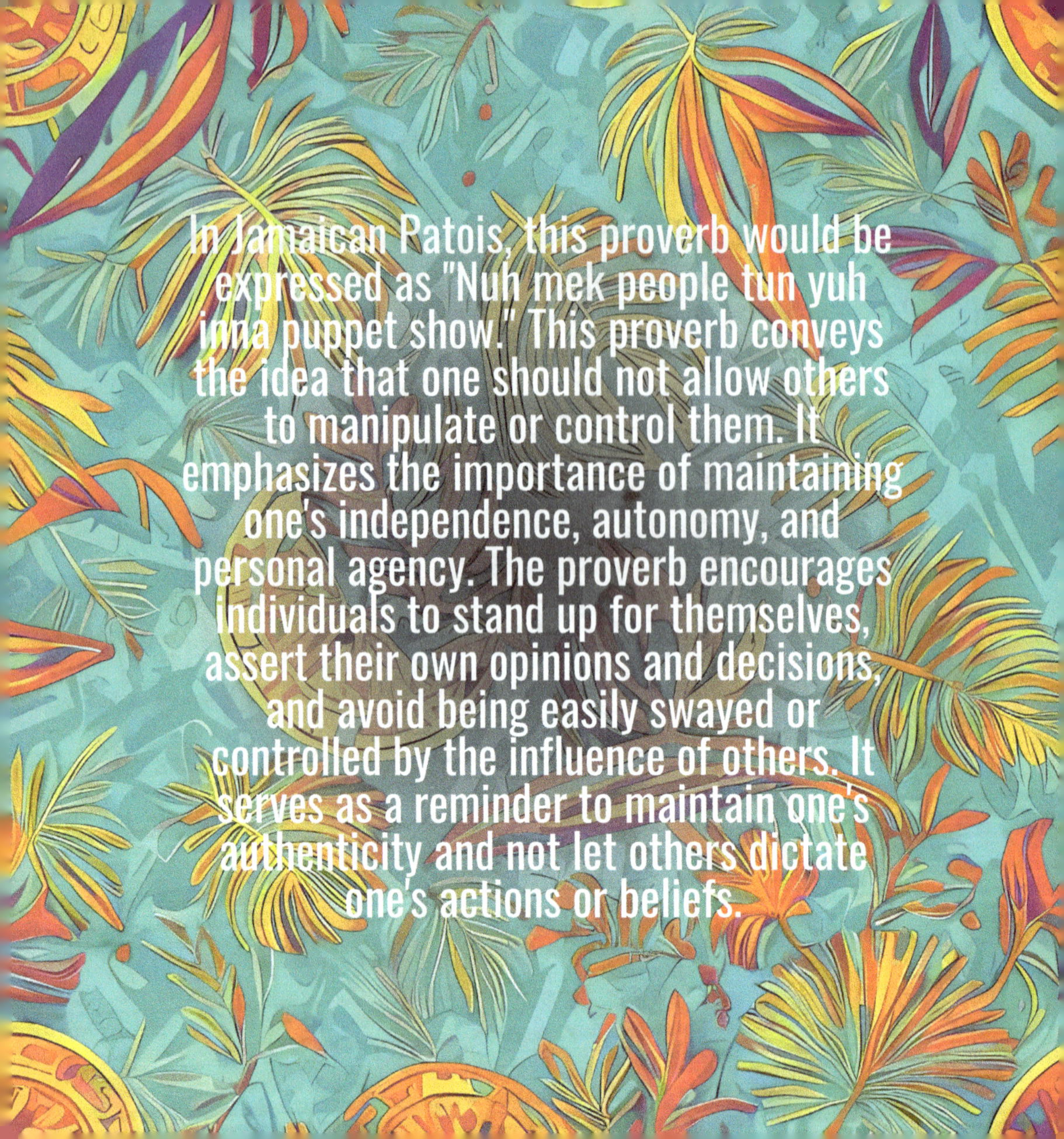
In Jamaican Patois, this proverb would be expressed as "Nuh mek people tun yuh inna puppet show." This proverb conveys the idea that one should not allow others to manipulate or control them. It emphasizes the importance of maintaining one's independence, autonomy, and personal agency. The proverb encourages individuals to stand up for themselves, assert their own opinions and decisions, and avoid being easily swayed or controlled by the influence of others. It serves as a reminder to maintain one's authenticity and not let others dictate one's actions or beliefs.

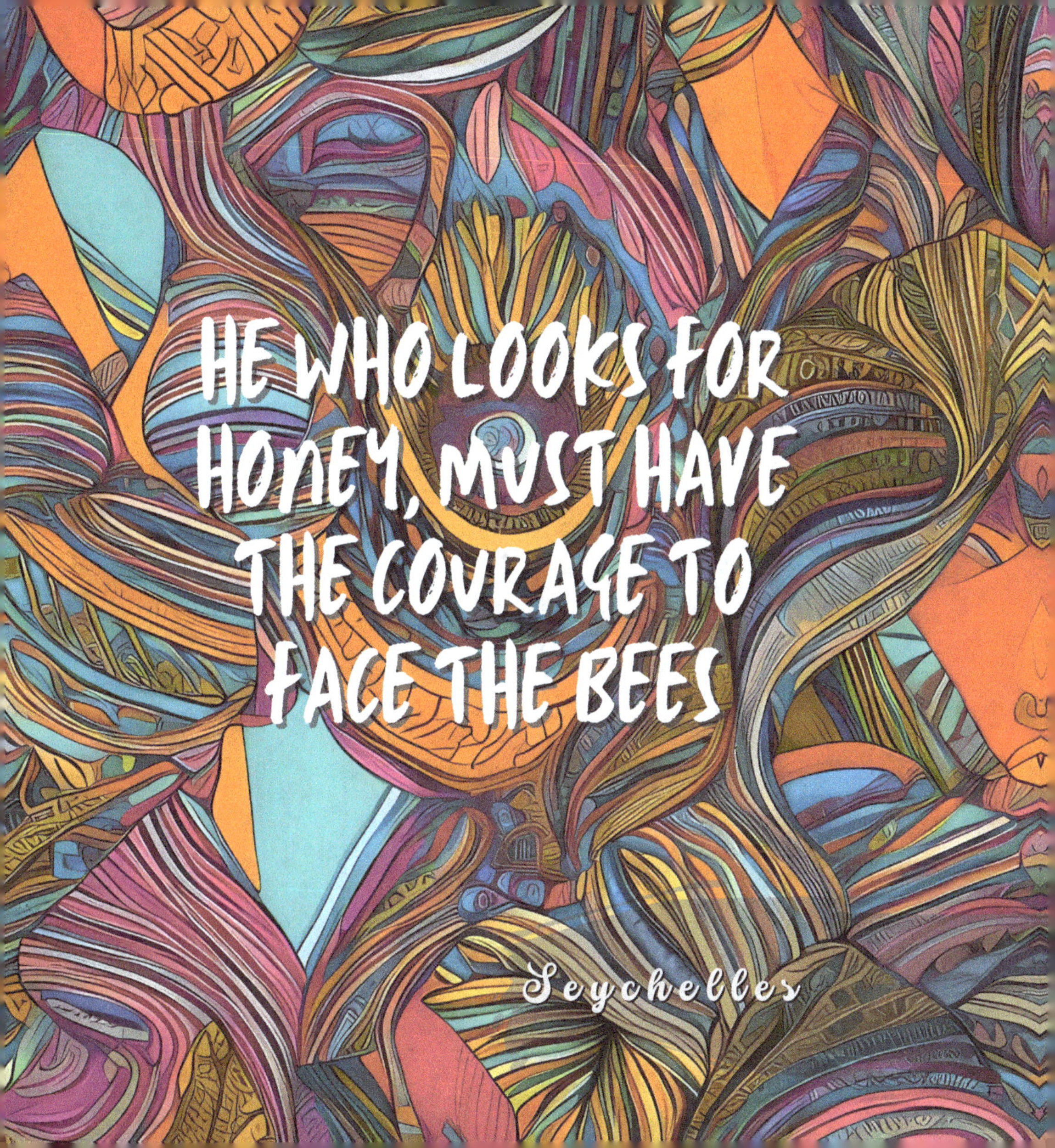
HE WHO LOOKS FOR HONEY, MUST HAVE THE COURAGE TO FACE THE BEES
Seychelles

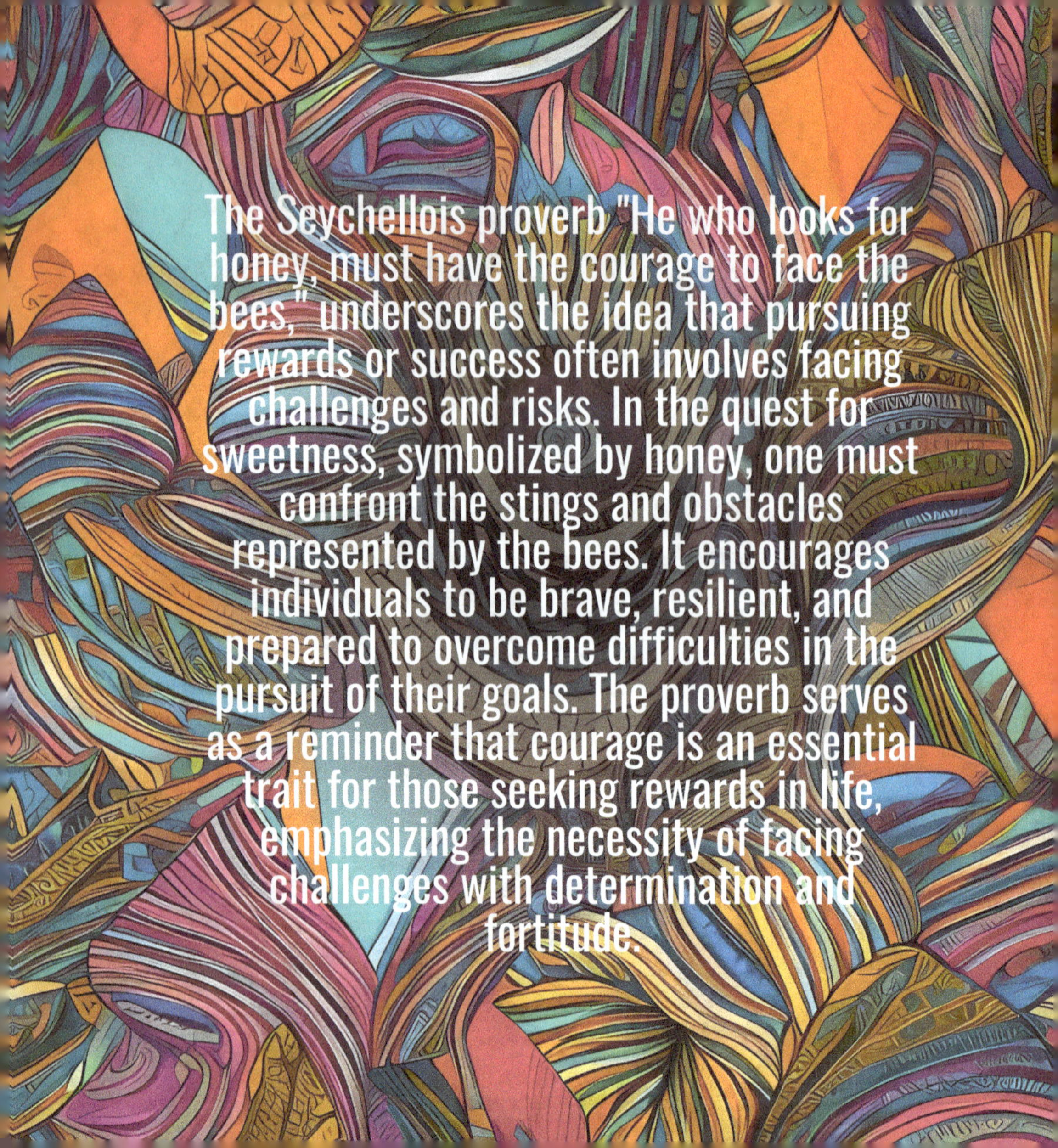

The Seychellois proverb "He who looks for honey, must have the courage to face the bees," underscores the idea that pursuing rewards or success often involves facing challenges and risks. In the quest for sweetness, symbolized by honey, one must confront the stings and obstacles represented by the bees. It encourages individuals to be brave, resilient, and prepared to overcome difficulties in the pursuit of their goals. The proverb serves as a reminder that courage is an essential trait for those seeking rewards in life, emphasizing the necessity of facing challenges with determination and fortitude.

A SMALL POT IS
SOON HOT.
Tamil

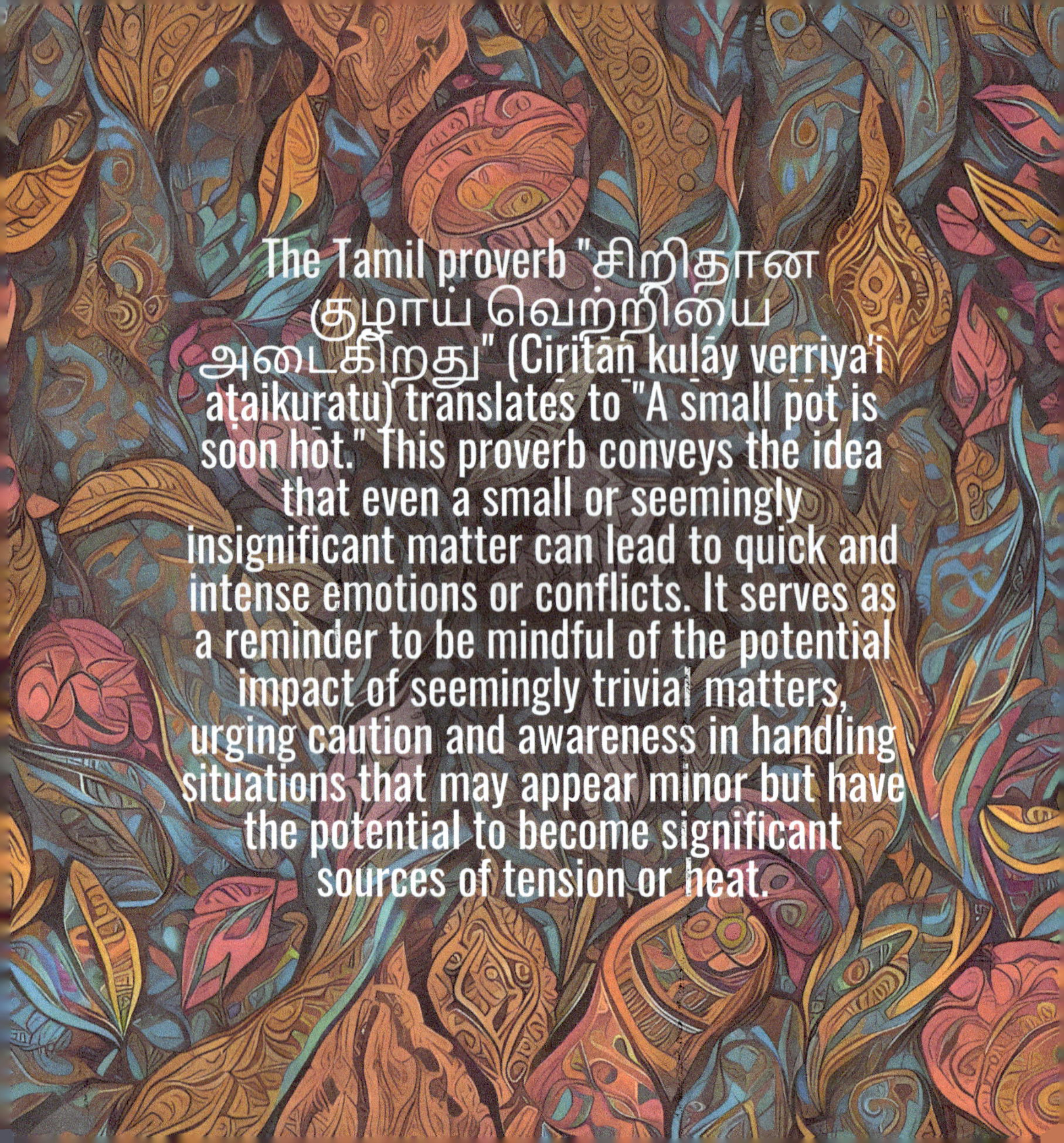
The Tamil proverb "சிறிதான குழாய் வெற்றியை அடைகிறது" (Ciritāṉ kuḻāy veṟṟiya'i aṭaikuṟatu) translates to "A small pot is soon hot." This proverb conveys the idea that even a small or seemingly insignificant matter can lead to quick and intense emotions or conflicts. It serves as a reminder to be mindful of the potential impact of seemingly trivial matters, urging caution and awareness in handling situations that may appear minor but have the potential to become significant sources of tension or heat.

THE BIGGER THEY ARE, THE HARDER THEY FALL.
England

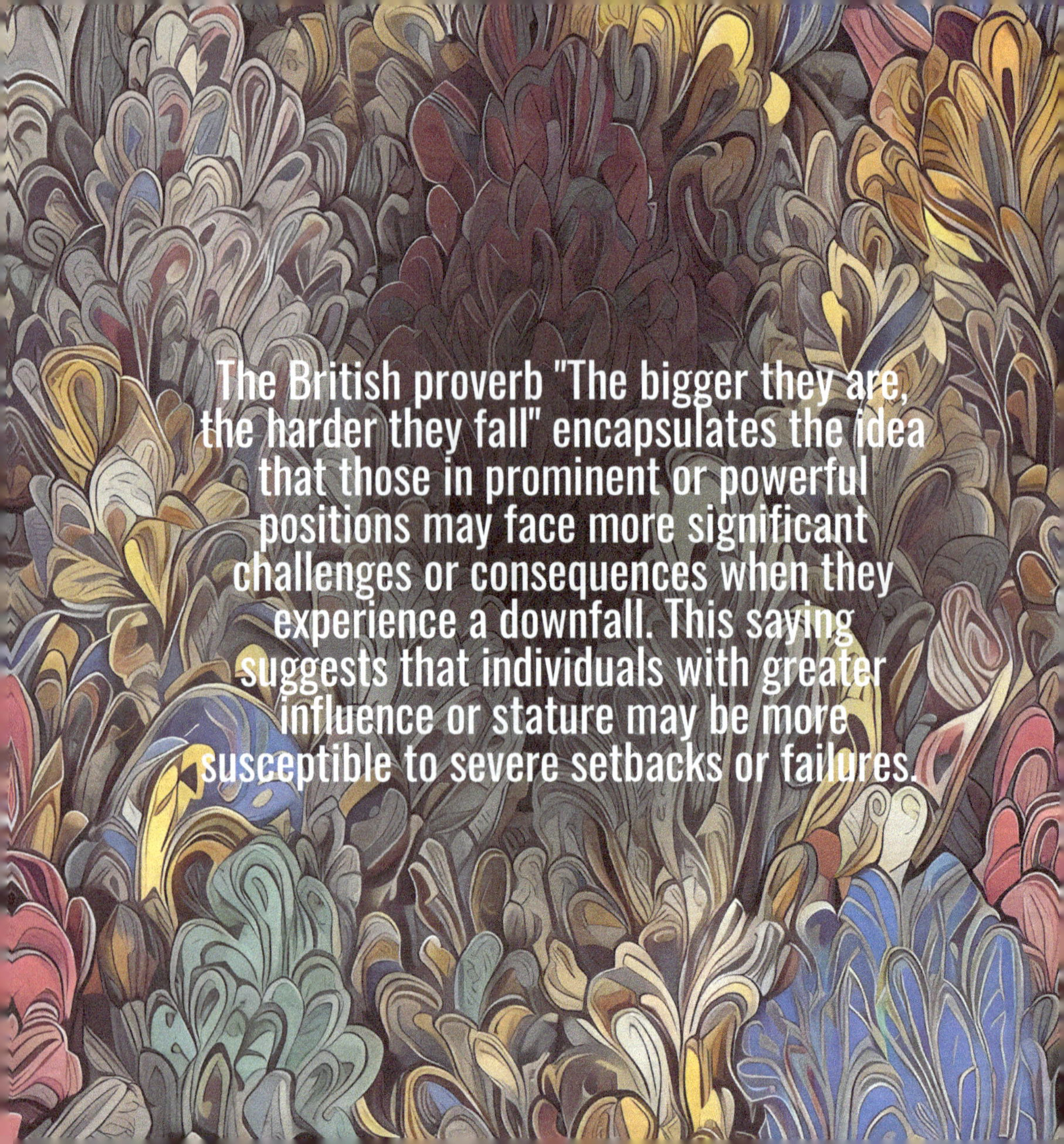

The British proverb "The bigger they are, the harder they fall" encapsulates the idea that those in prominent or powerful positions may face more significant challenges or consequences when they experience a downfall. This saying suggests that individuals with greater influence or stature may be more susceptible to severe setbacks or failures.

GOD HELPS THOSE
WHO RISE EARLY.
Latin American

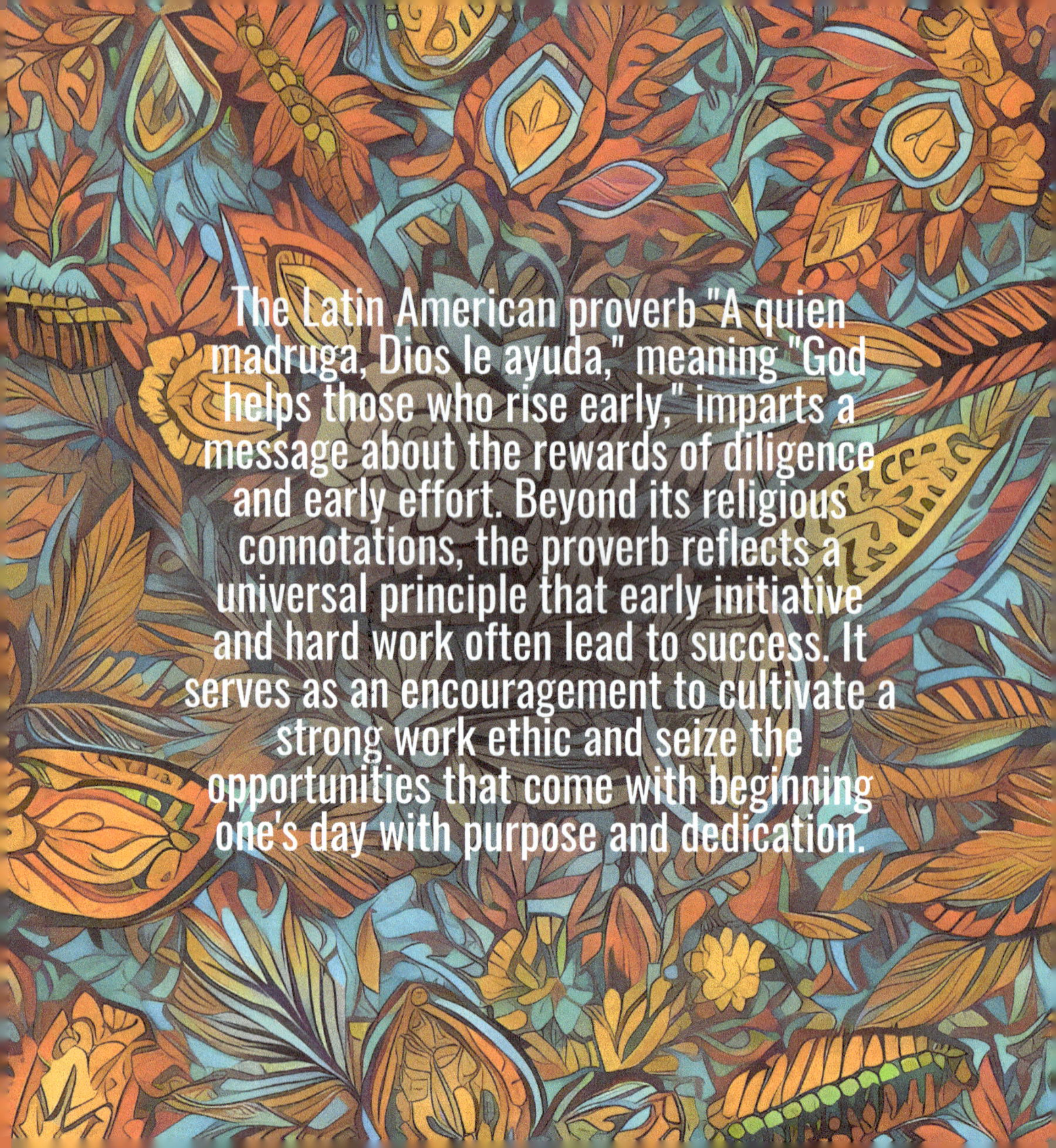
The Latin American proverb "A quien madruga, Dios le ayuda," meaning "God helps those who rise early," imparts a message about the rewards of diligence and early effort. Beyond its religious connotations, the proverb reflects a universal principle that early initiative and hard work often lead to success. It serves as an encouragement to cultivate a strong work ethic and seize the opportunities that come with beginning one's day with purpose and dedication.

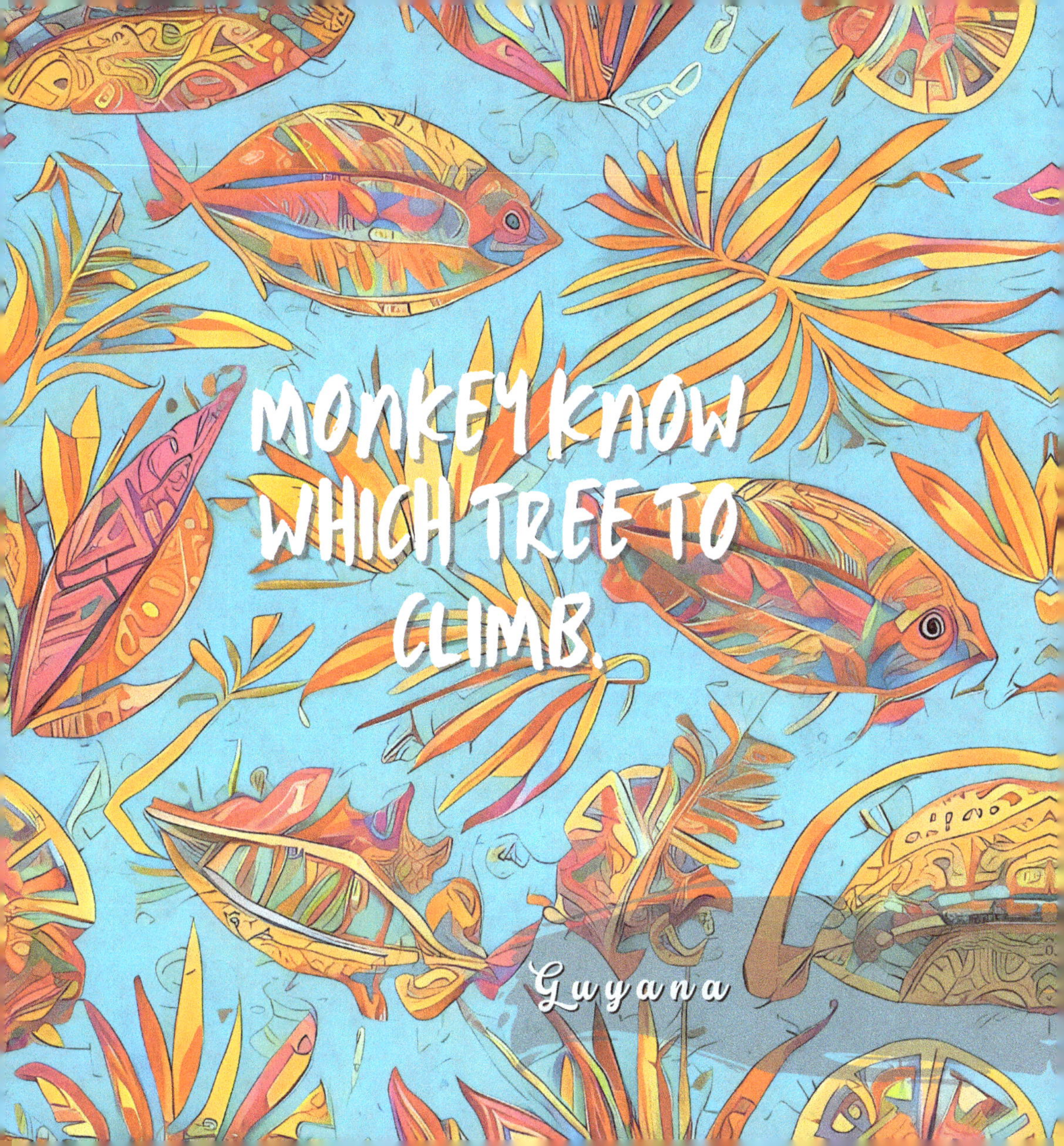
MONKEY KNOW WHICH TREE TO CLIMB.
Guyana

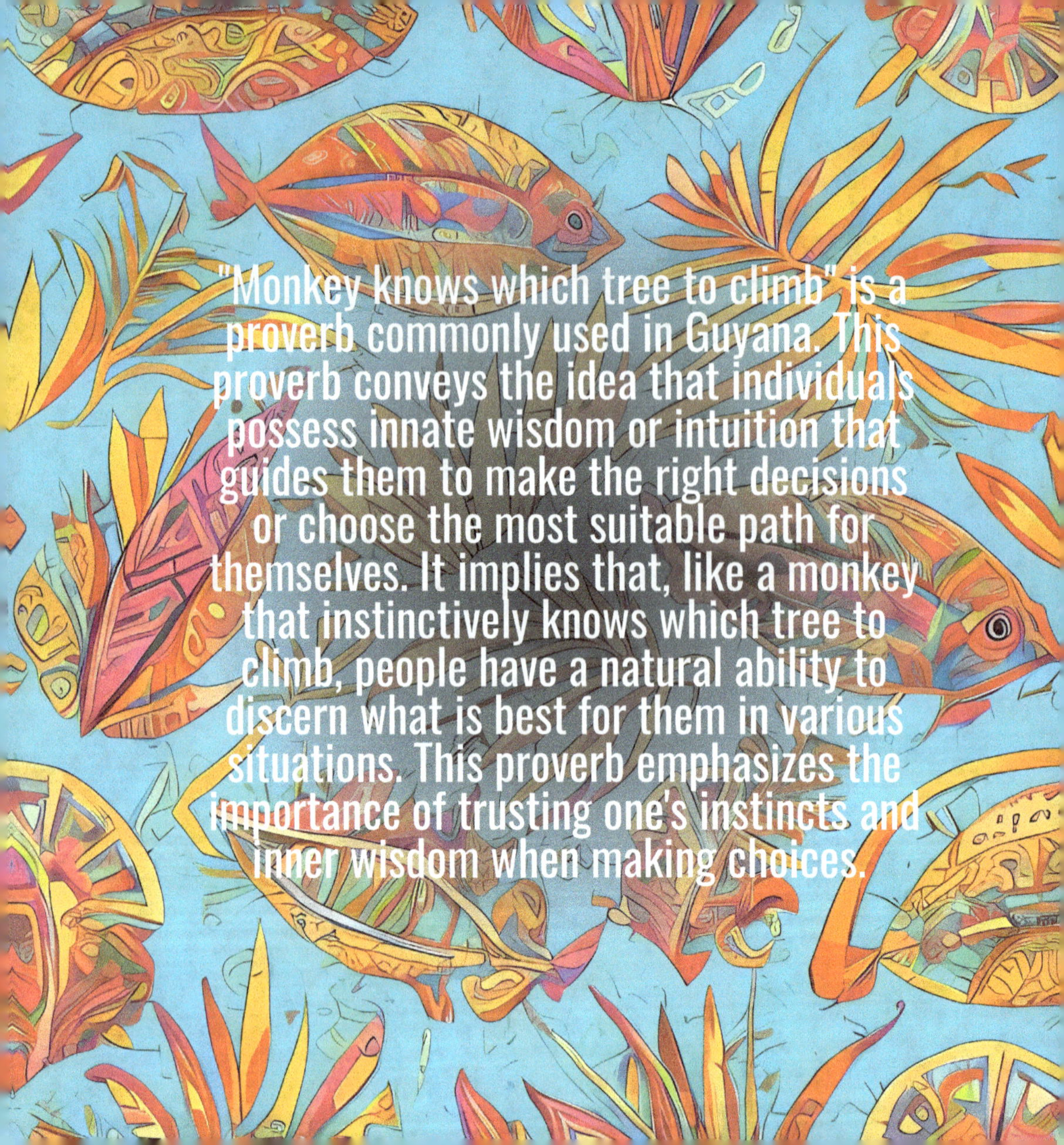

"Monkey knows which tree to climb" is a proverb commonly used in Guyana. This proverb conveys the idea that individuals possess innate wisdom or intuition that guides them to make the right decisions or choose the most suitable path for themselves. It implies that, like a monkey that instinctively knows which tree to climb, people have a natural ability to discern what is best for them in various situations. This proverb emphasizes the importance of trusting one's instincts and inner wisdom when making choices.

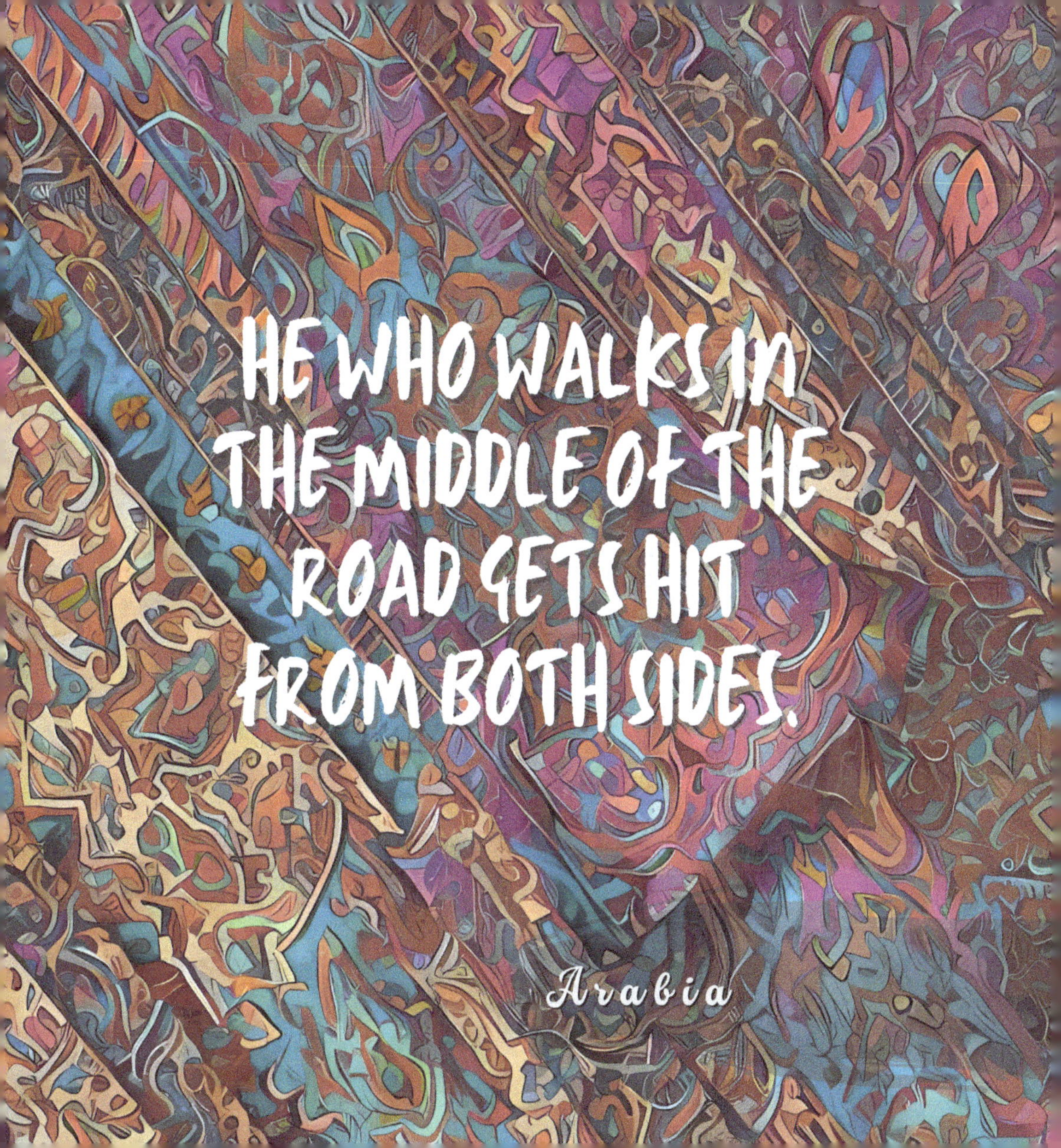
HE WHO WALKS IN
THE MIDDLE OF THE
ROAD GETS HIT
FROM BOTH SIDES.
Arabia

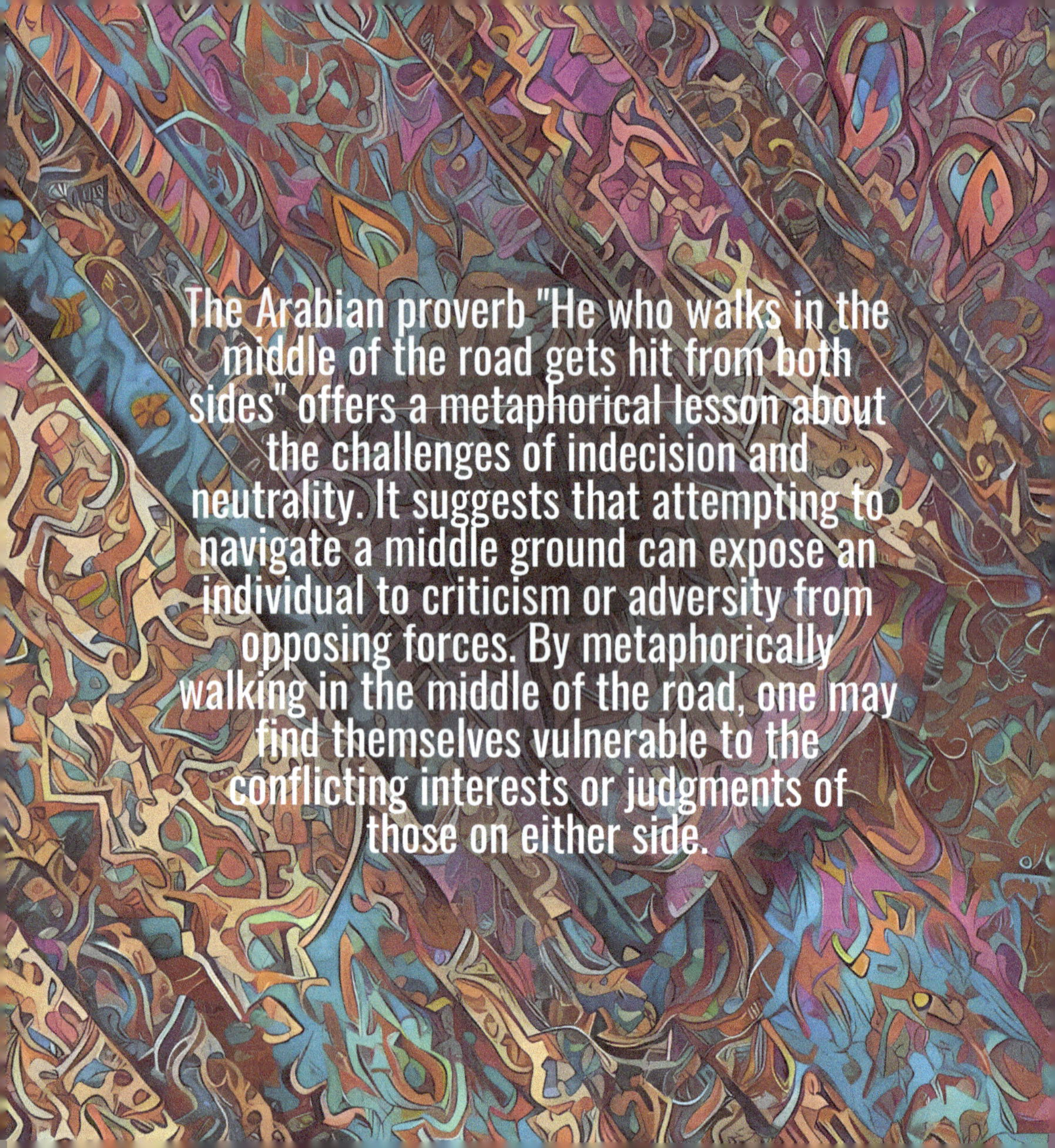

The Arabian proverb "He who walks in the middle of the road gets hit from both sides" offers a metaphorical lesson about the challenges of indecision and neutrality. It suggests that attempting to navigate a middle ground can expose an individual to criticism or adversity from opposing forces. By metaphorically walking in the middle of the road, one may find themselves vulnerable to the conflicting interests or judgments of those on either side.

IT DOES NOT MATTER HOW SLOWLY YOU GO AS LONG AS YOU DO NOT STOP.
China

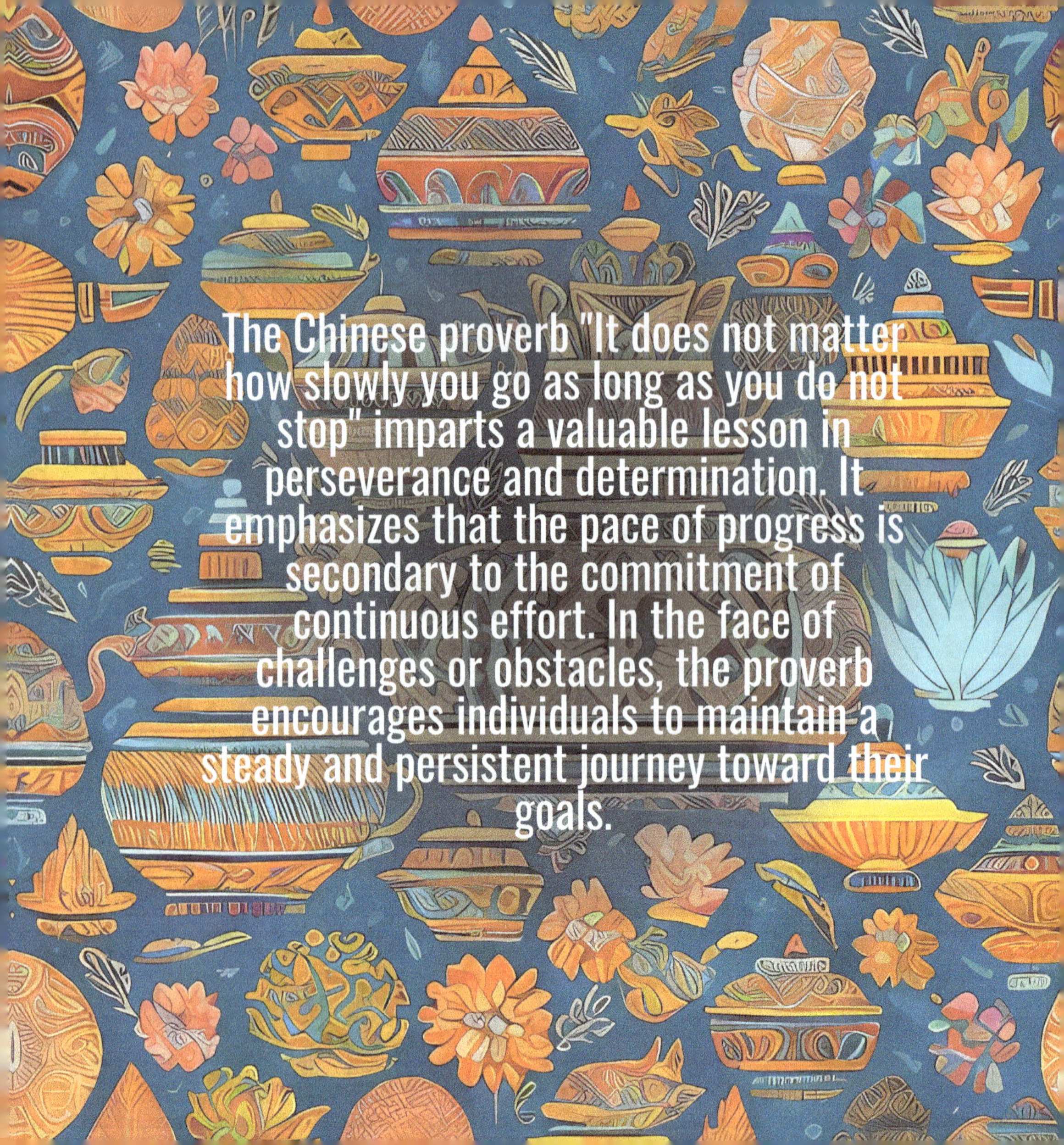
The Chinese proverb "It does not matter how slowly you go as long as you do not stop" imparts a valuable lesson in perseverance and determination. It emphasizes that the pace of progress is secondary to the commitment of continuous effort. In the face of challenges or obstacles, the proverb encourages individuals to maintain a steady and persistent journey toward their goals.

DO NOT CONFINE
YOUR CHILDREN TO
YOUR OWN
LEARNING, FOR
THEY WERE BORN
IN ANOTHER TIME.
Mongolia

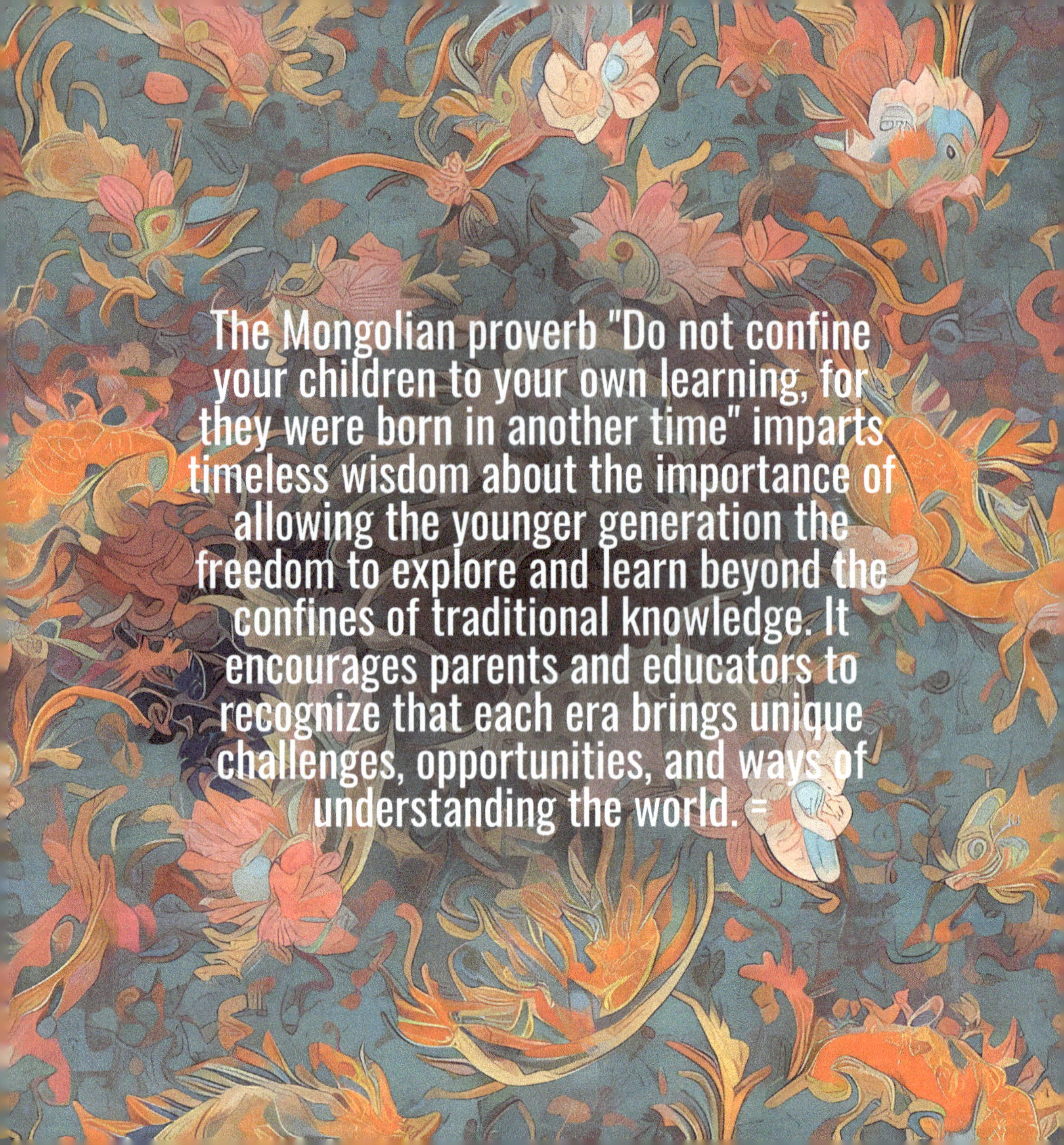

The Mongolian proverb "Do not confine your children to your own learning, for they were born in another time" imparts timeless wisdom about the importance of allowing the younger generation the freedom to explore and learn beyond the confines of traditional knowledge. It encourages parents and educators to recognize that each era brings unique challenges, opportunities, and ways of understanding the world.

DON'T THROW
STONES IF YOU LIVE
IN A GLASS HOUSE.
Norway

The Norwegian proverb "Bedre med en god nabo enn en fjern venn" translates to "Better a good neighbor than a distant friend." This saying reflects a universal truth about the importance of close, reliable connections in one's immediate community. It emphasizes the practical advantages of having a supportive neighbor over a friend who is physically distant.

NO EVIL LASTS A HUNDRED YEARS.
Latin American

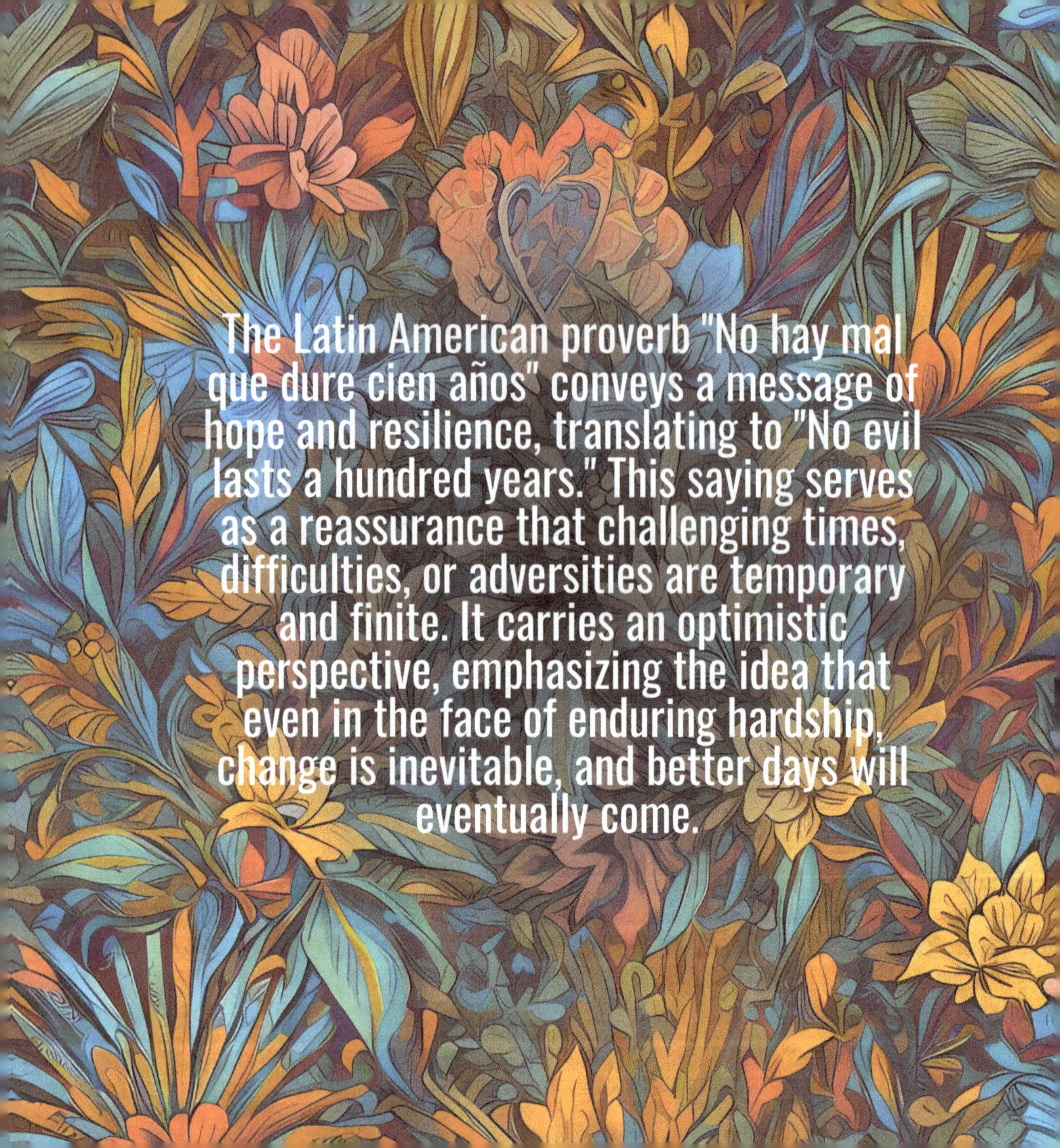

The Latin American proverb "No hay mal que dure cien años" conveys a message of hope and resilience, translating to "No evil lasts a hundred years." This saying serves as a reassurance that challenging times, difficulties, or adversities are temporary and finite. It carries an optimistic perspective, emphasizing the idea that even in the face of enduring hardship, change is inevitable, and better days will eventually come.

RAIN FALL BUT
WE'RE TOUGH.
Grenada

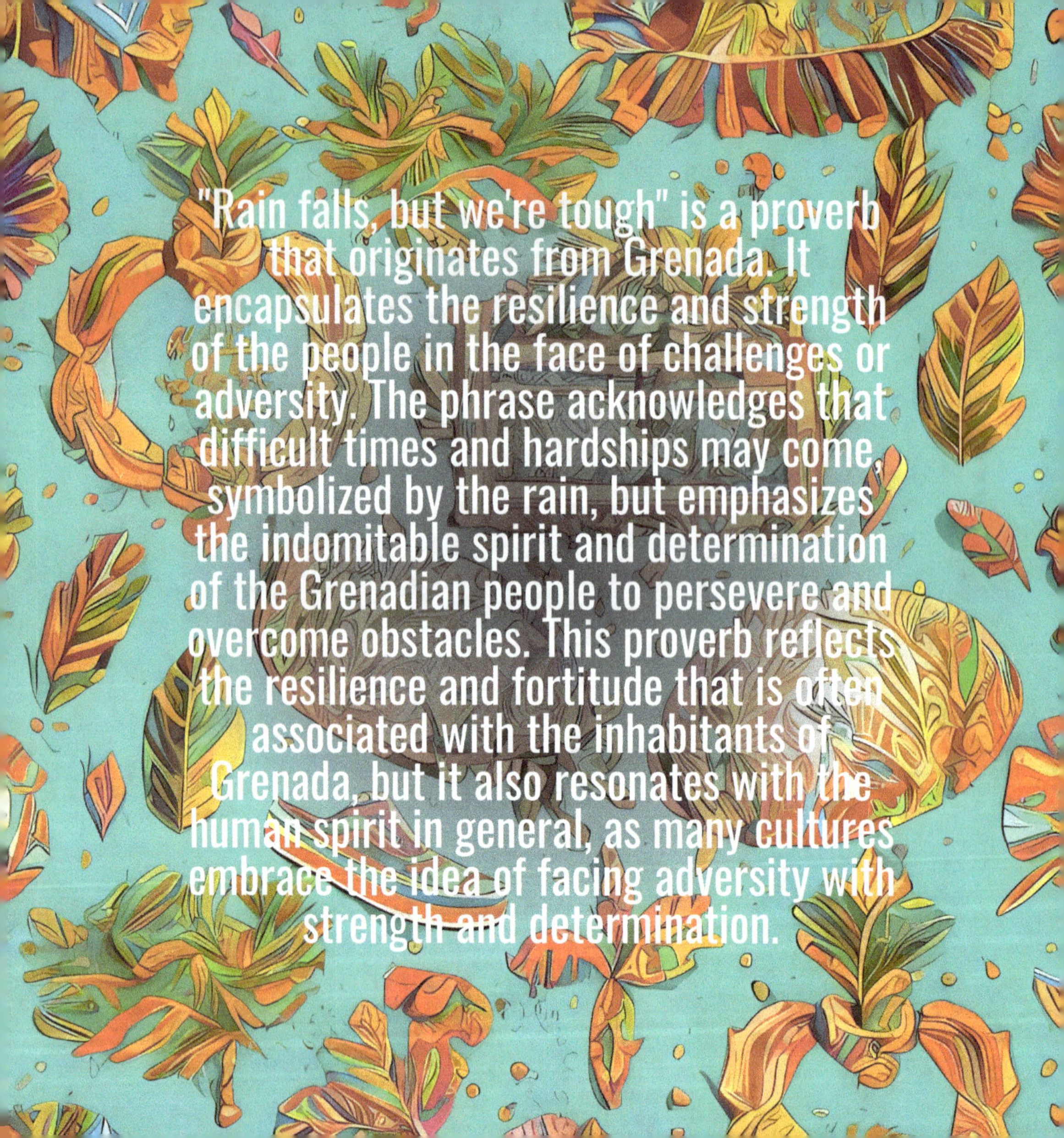

"Rain falls, but we're tough" is a proverb that originates from Grenada. It encapsulates the resilience and strength of the people in the face of challenges or adversity. The phrase acknowledges that difficult times and hardships may come, symbolized by the rain, but emphasizes the indomitable spirit and determination of the Grenadian people to persevere and overcome obstacles. This proverb reflects the resilience and fortitude that is often associated with the inhabitants of Grenada, but it also resonates with the human spirit in general, as many cultures embrace the idea of facing adversity with strength and determination.

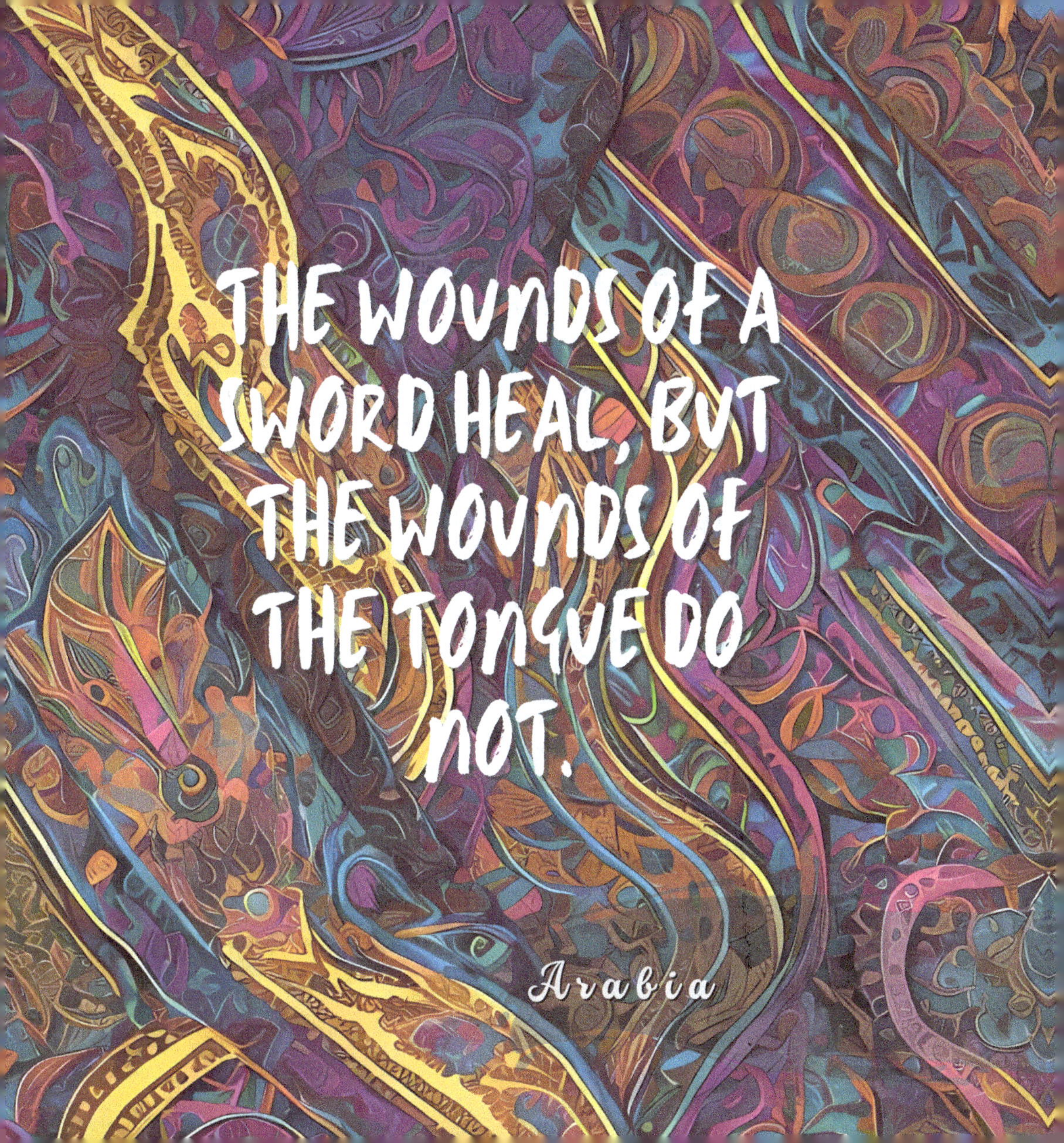
THE WOUNDS OF A SWORD HEAL, BUT THE WOUNDS OF THE TONGUE DO NOT.
Arabia

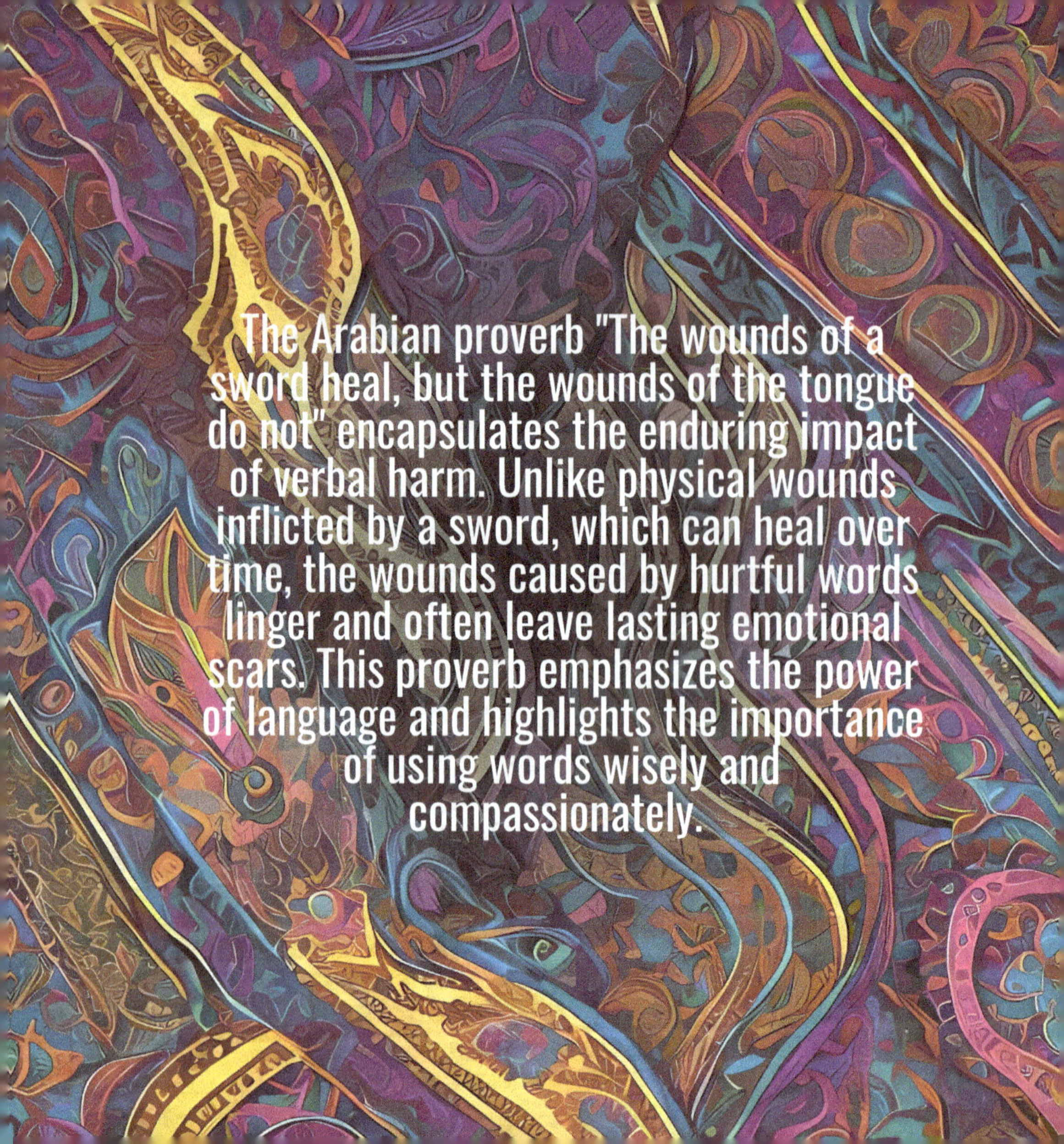

The Arabian proverb "The wounds of a sword heal, but the wounds of the tongue do not" encapsulates the enduring impact of verbal harm. Unlike physical wounds inflicted by a sword, which can heal over time, the wounds caused by hurtful words linger and often leave lasting emotional scars. This proverb emphasizes the power of language and highlights the importance of using words wisely and compassionately.

BETTER TO BE A
BROKEN PIECE OF
JADE THAN AN
INTACT PIECE OF
POTTERY.
China

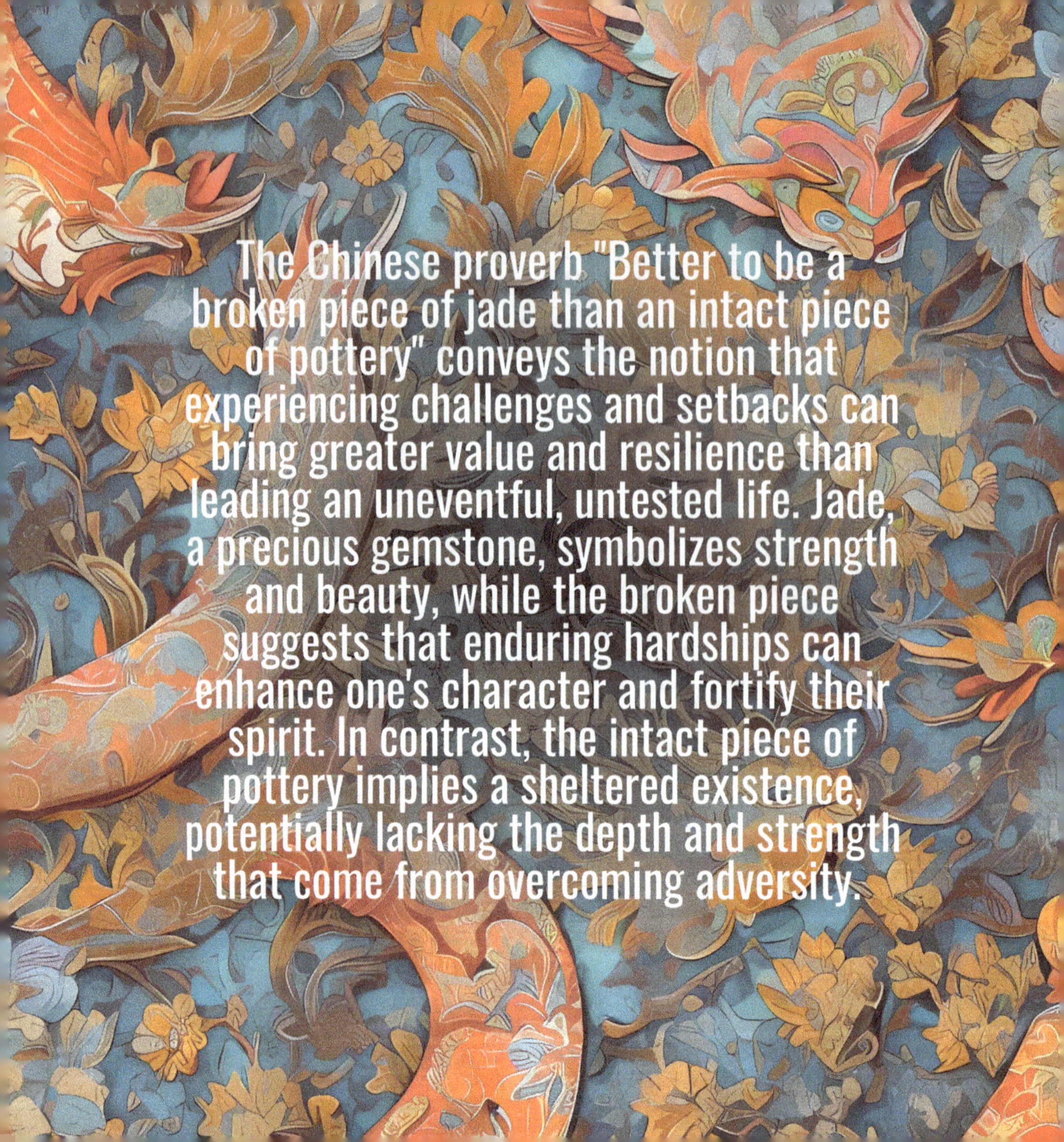

The Chinese proverb "Better to be a broken piece of jade than an intact piece of pottery" conveys the notion that experiencing challenges and setbacks can bring greater value and resilience than leading an uneventful, untested life. Jade, a precious gemstone, symbolizes strength and beauty, while the broken piece suggests that enduring hardships can enhance one's character and fortify their spirit. In contrast, the intact piece of pottery implies a sheltered existence, potentially lacking the depth and strength that come from overcoming adversity.

YOU HAVE TO TAKE BAD SITUATIONS AND MAKE JOKES.
Jamaica

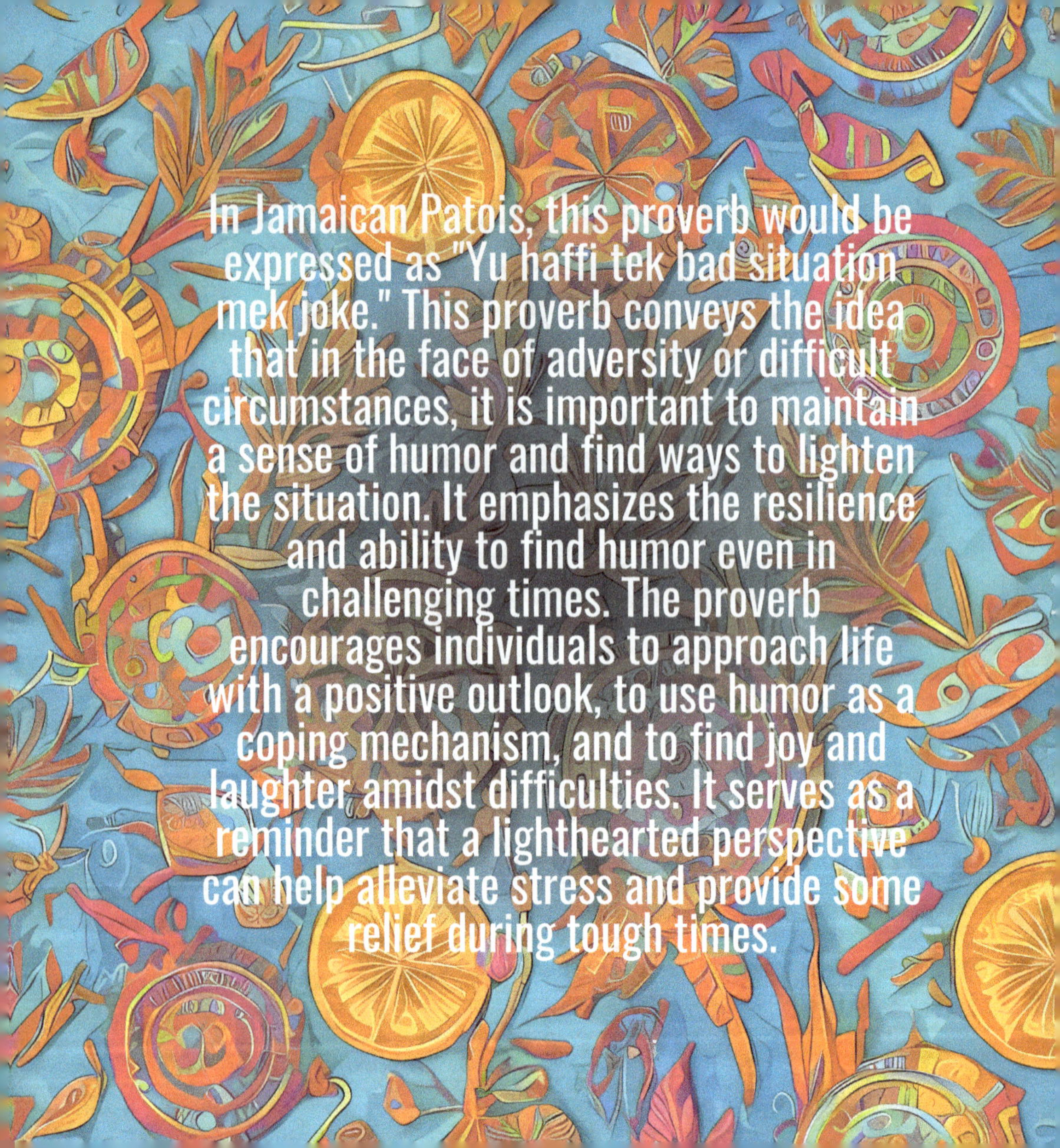

In Jamaican Patois, this proverb would be expressed as "Yu haffi tek bad situation mek joke." This proverb conveys the idea that in the face of adversity or difficult circumstances, it is important to maintain a sense of humor and find ways to lighten the situation. It emphasizes the resilience and ability to find humor even in challenging times. The proverb encourages individuals to approach life with a positive outlook, to use humor as a coping mechanism, and to find joy and laughter amidst difficulties. It serves as a reminder that a lighthearted perspective can help alleviate stress and provide some relief during tough times.

ONE FALSEHOOD SPOILS A THOUSAND TRUTHS.
Tanzania

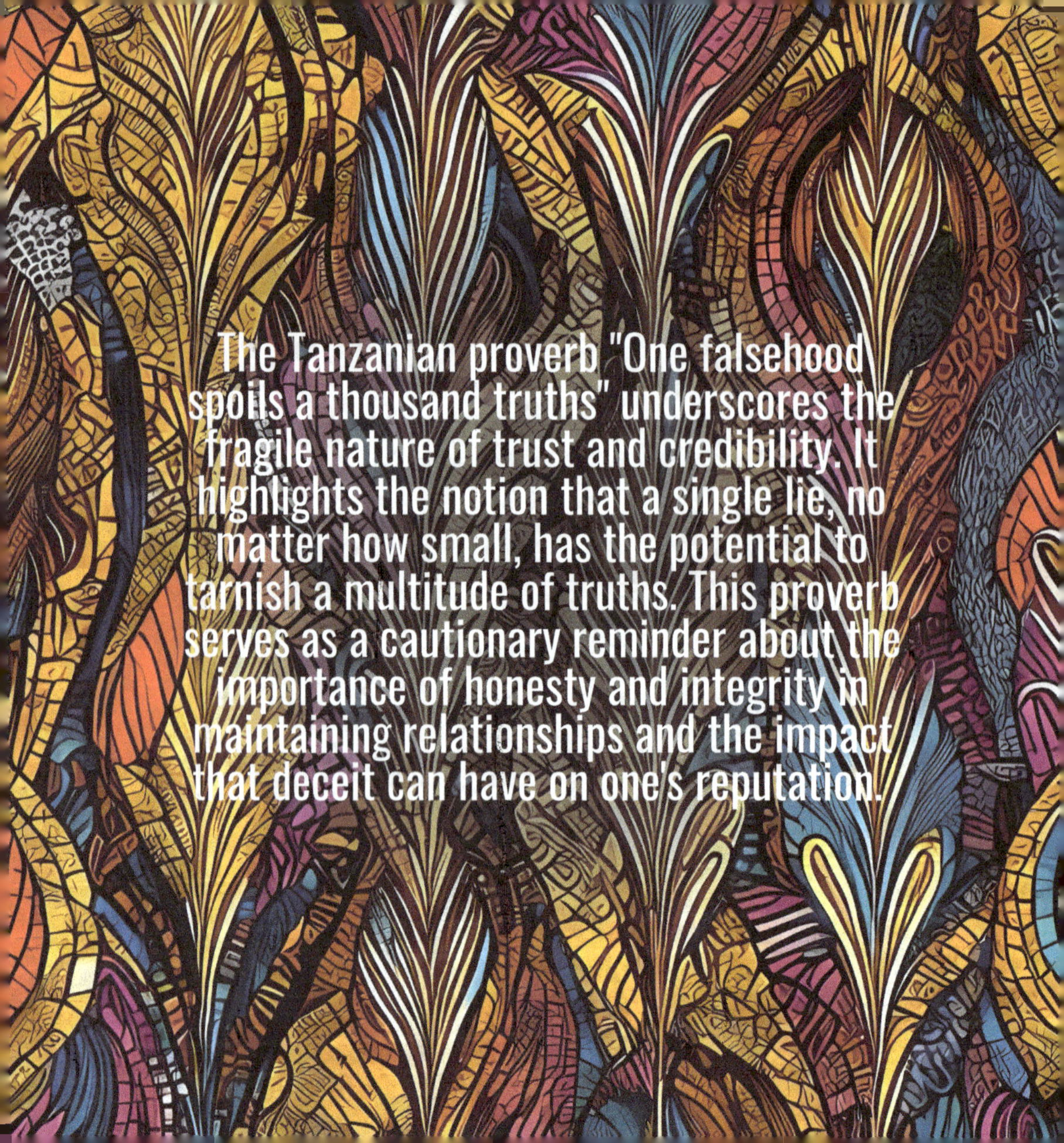

The Tanzanian proverb "One falsehood spoils a thousand truths" underscores the fragile nature of trust and credibility. It highlights the notion that a single lie, no matter how small, has the potential to tarnish a multitude of truths. This proverb serves as a cautionary reminder about the importance of honesty and integrity in maintaining relationships and the impact that deceit can have on one's reputation.

A GOOD REPUTATION IS MORE VALUABLE THAN MONEY
Bengali

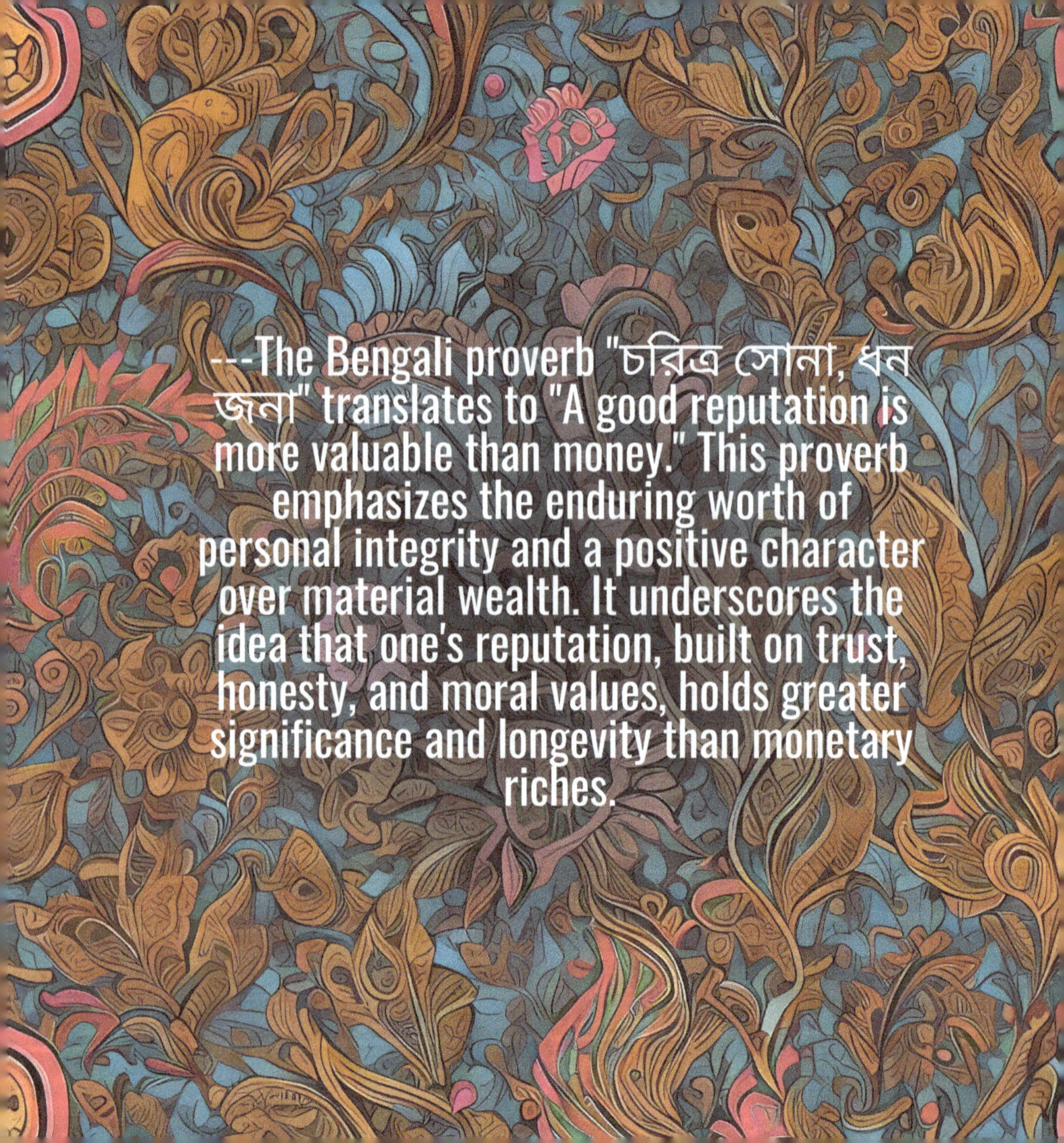

---The Bengali proverb "চরিত্র সোনা, ধন জনা" translates to "A good reputation is more valuable than money." This proverb emphasizes the enduring worth of personal integrity and a positive character over material wealth. It underscores the idea that one's reputation, built on trust, honesty, and moral values, holds greater significance and longevity than monetary riches.

A JACKAL DOES NOT SMELL ITS OWN STENCH.
Malayalam

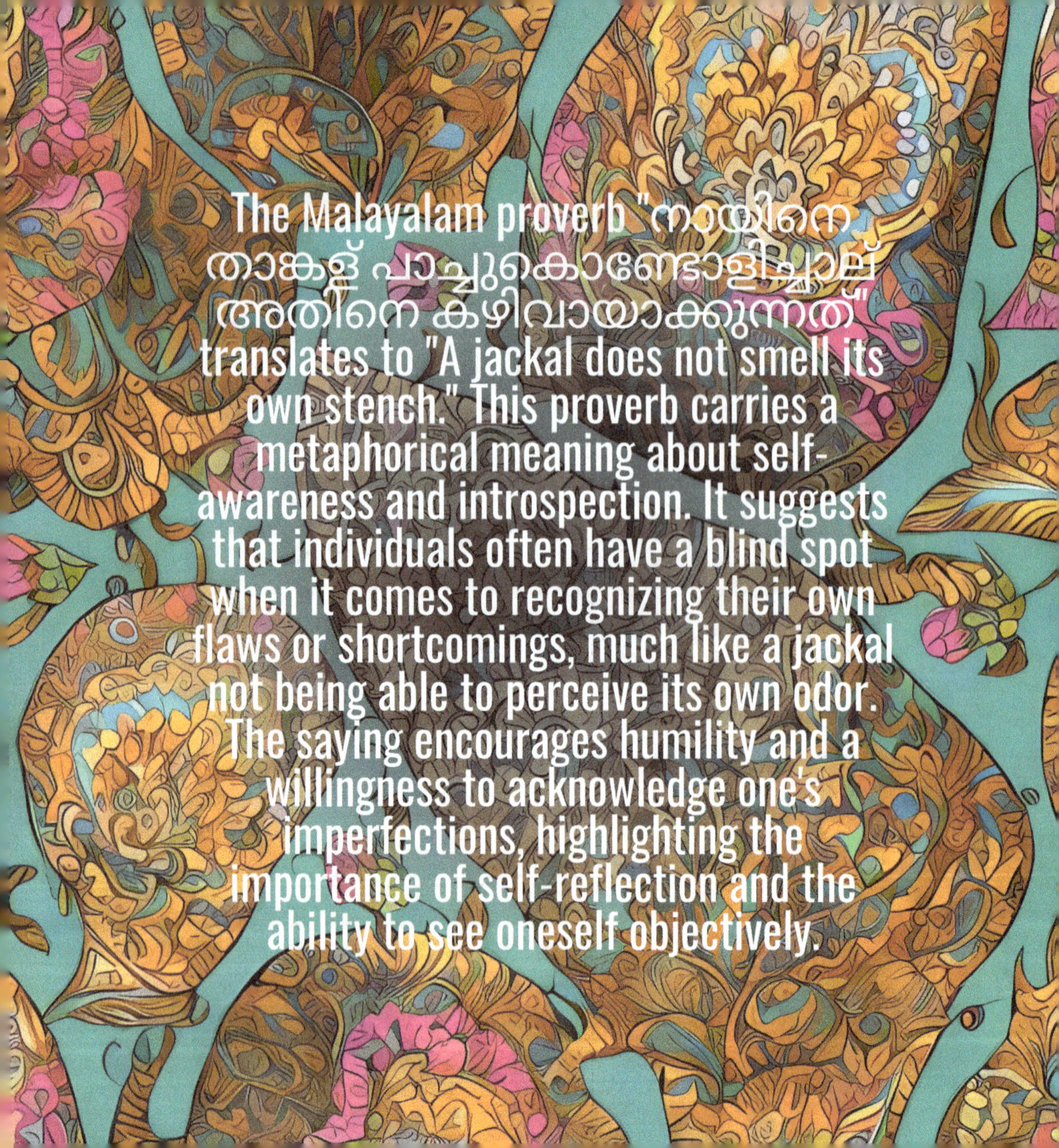

The Malayalam proverb "നായിനെ താങ്കള് പാച്ചുകൊണ്ടോളിച്ചാല് അതിനെ കഴിവായാക്കുന്നത്" translates to "A jackal does not smell its own stench." This proverb carries a metaphorical meaning about self-awareness and introspection. It suggests that individuals often have a blind spot when it comes to recognizing their own flaws or shortcomings, much like a jackal not being able to perceive its own odor. The saying encourages humility and a willingness to acknowledge one's imperfections, highlighting the importance of self-reflection and the ability to see oneself objectively.

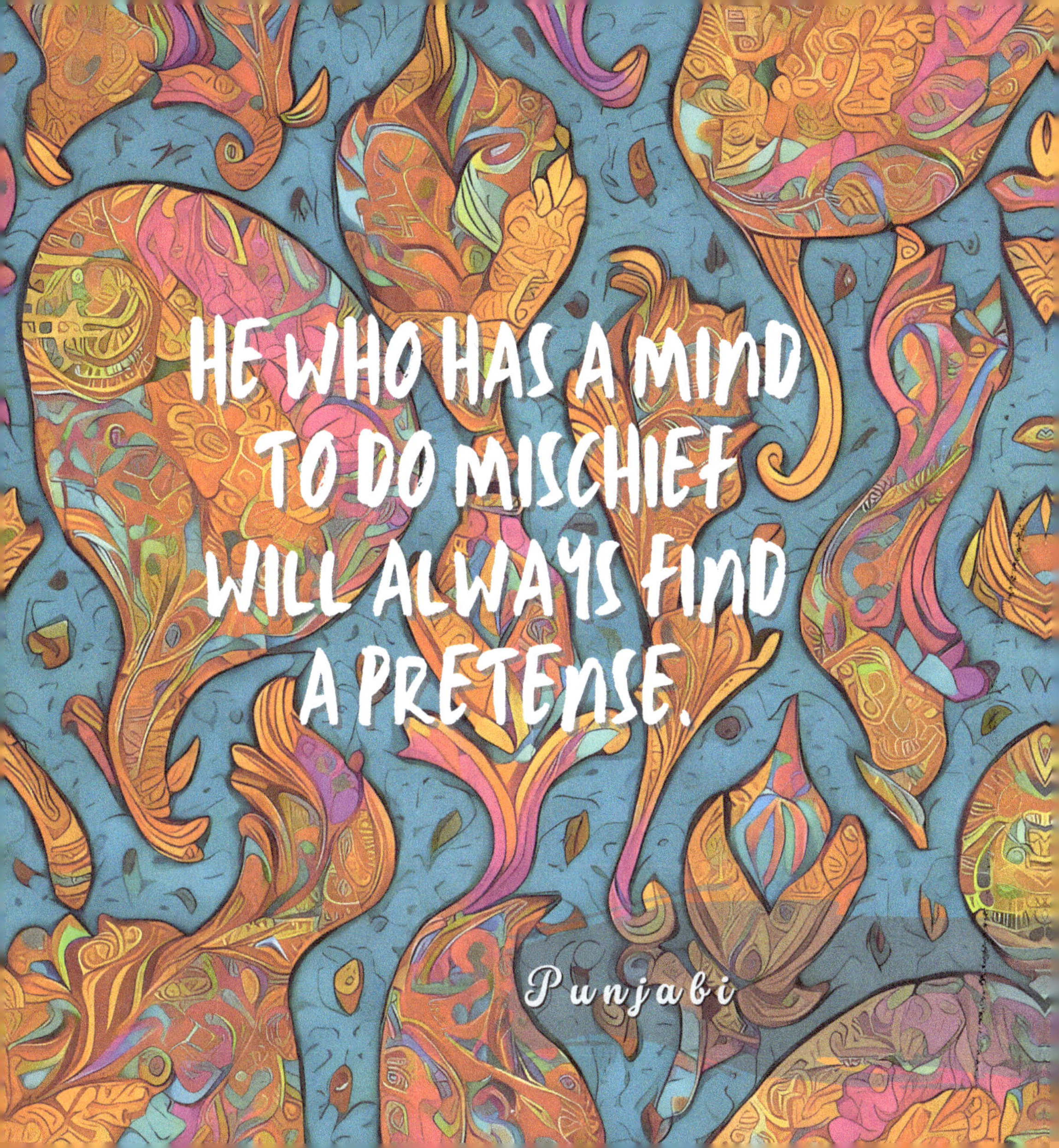
HE WHO HAS A MIND
TO DO MISCHIEF
WILL ALWAYS FIND
A PRETENSE.
Punjabi

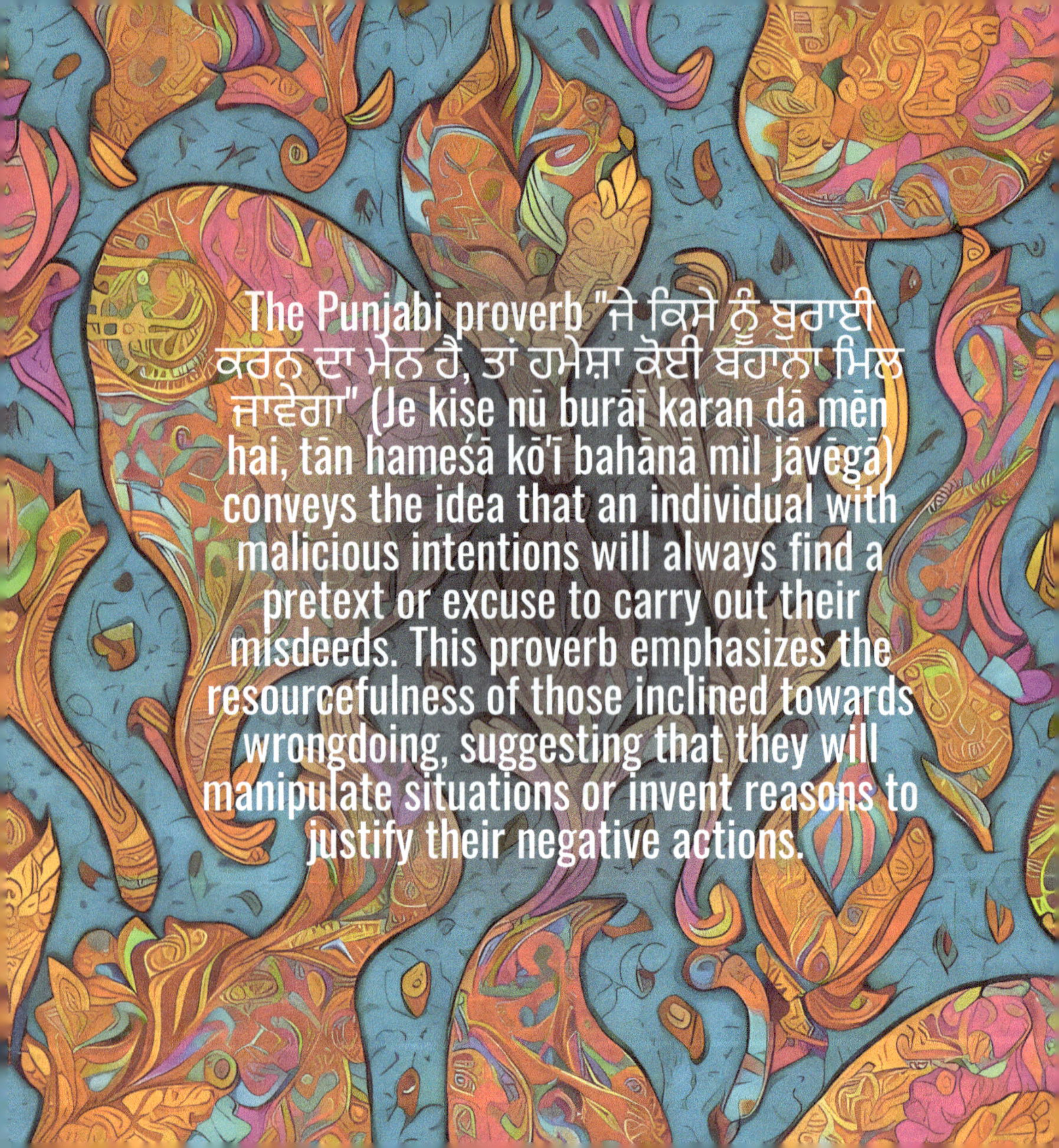

The Punjabi proverb "ਜੇ ਕਿਸੇ ਨੂੰ ਬੁਰਾਈ ਕਰਨ ਦਾ ਮੇਨ ਹੈ, ਤਾਂ ਹਮੇਸ਼ਾ ਕੋਈ ਬਹਾਨਾ ਮਿਲ ਜਾਵੇਗਾ" (Je kise nū burāī karan dā mēn hai, tān hameśā kō'ī bahānā mil jāvēgā) conveys the idea that an individual with malicious intentions will always find a pretext or excuse to carry out their misdeeds. This proverb emphasizes the resourcefulness of those inclined towards wrongdoing, suggesting that they will manipulate situations or invent reasons to justify their negative actions.

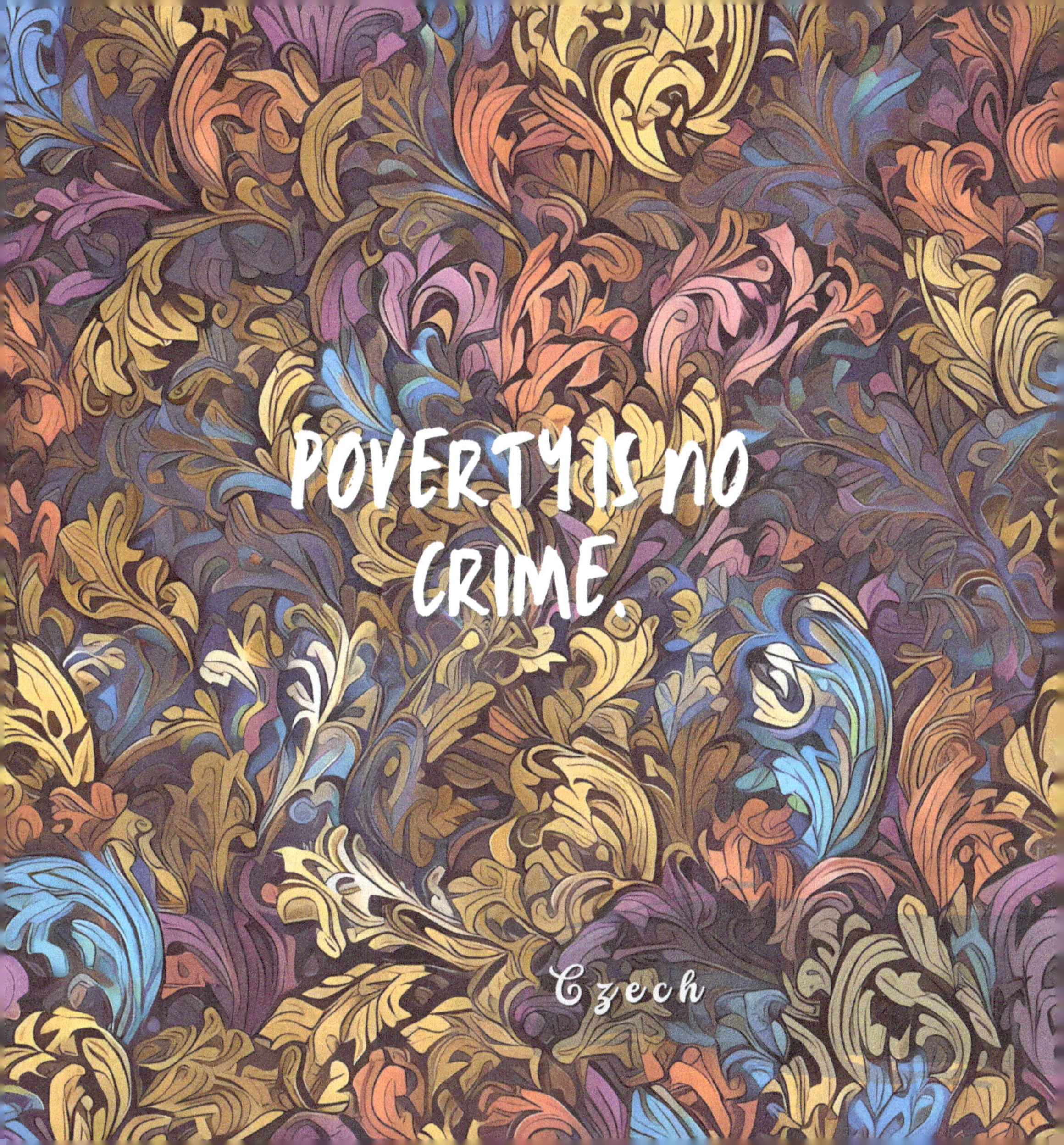
POVERTY IS NO CRIME.
Czech

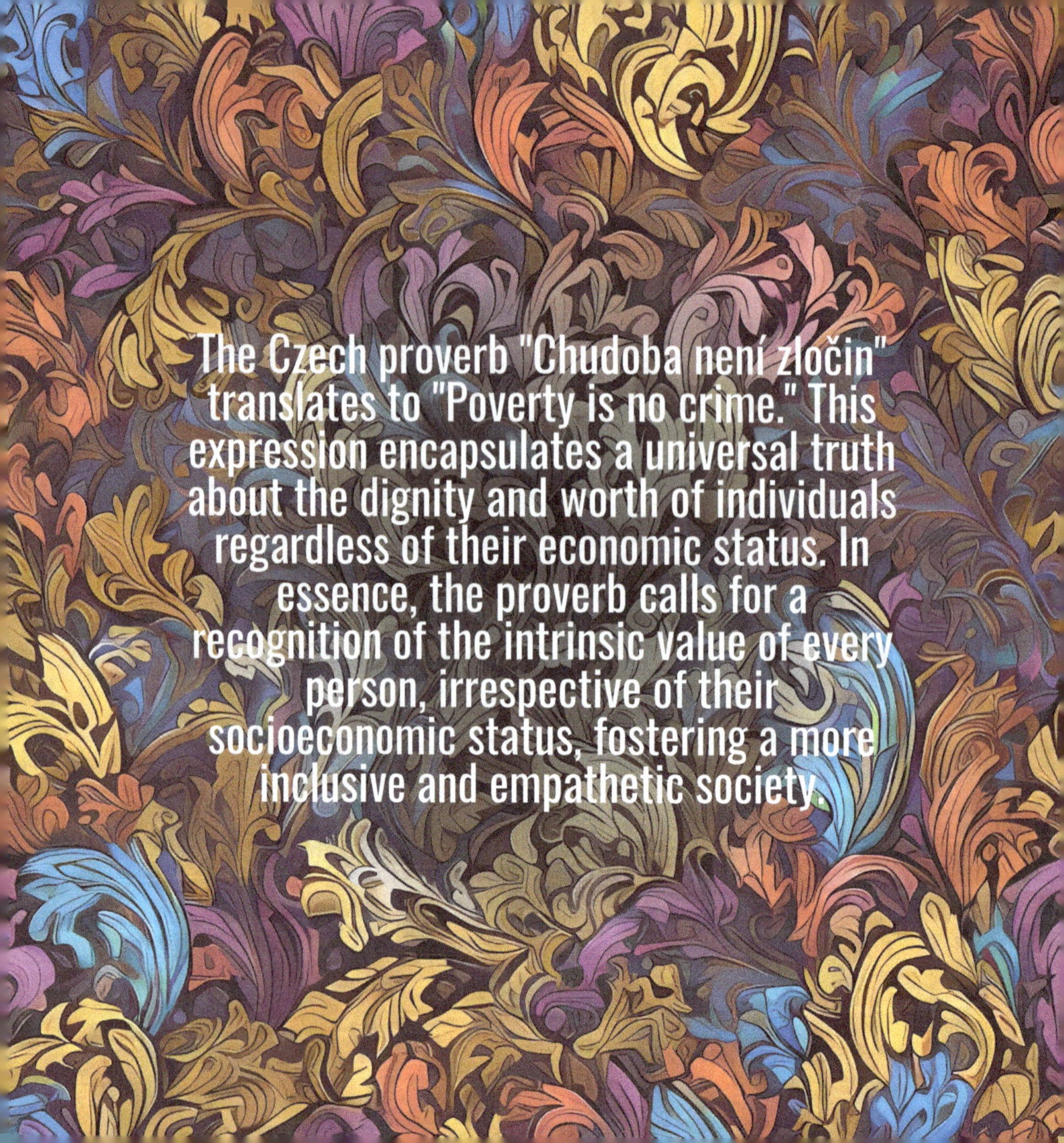

The Czech proverb "Chudoba není zločin" translates to "Poverty is no crime." This expression encapsulates a universal truth about the dignity and worth of individuals regardless of their economic status. In essence, the proverb calls for a recognition of the intrinsic value of every person, irrespective of their socioeconomic status, fostering a more inclusive and empathetic society.

WHERE LOVE REIGNS, THE IMPOSSIBLE MAY BE ATTAINED.
India

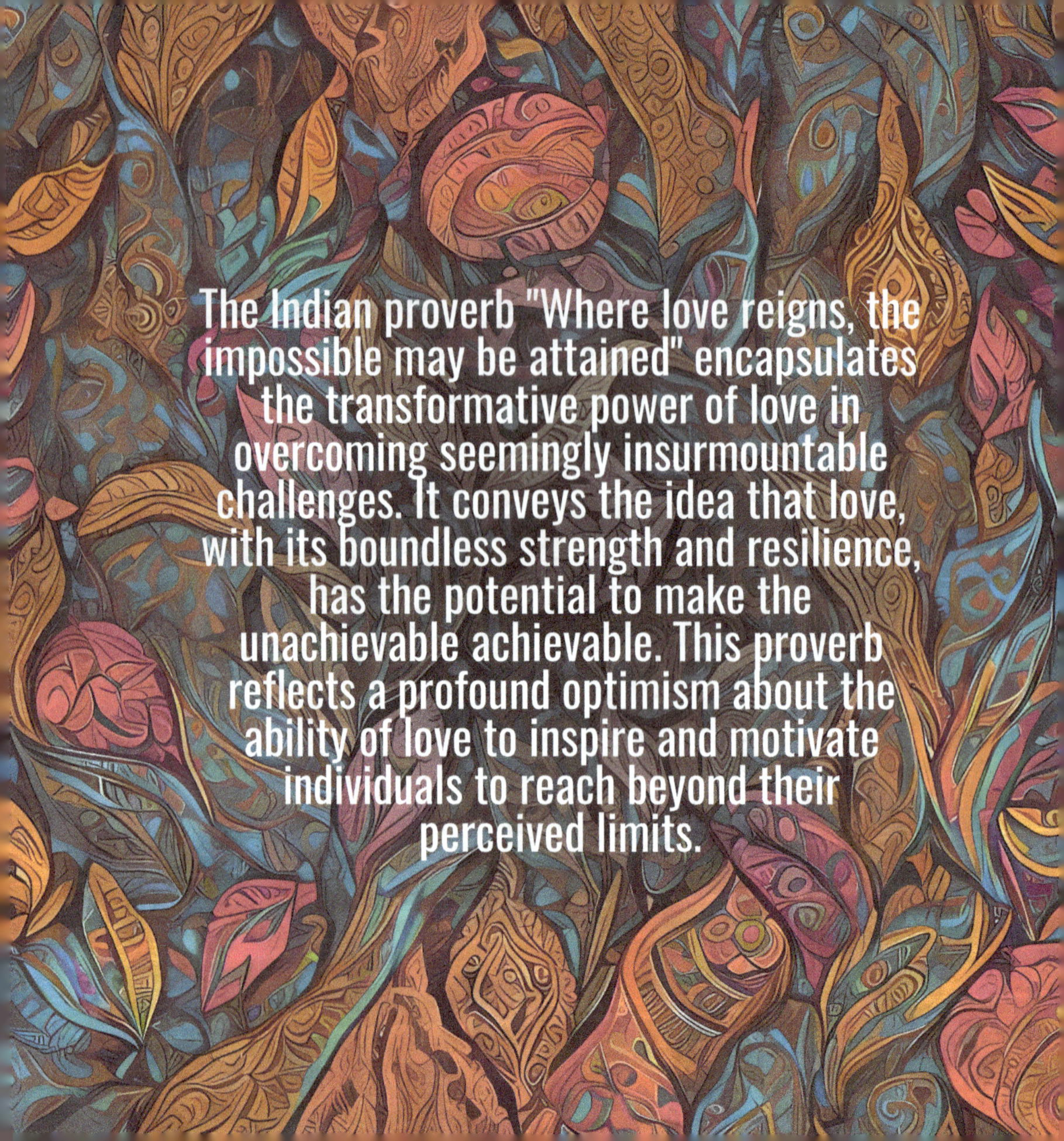

The Indian proverb "Where love reigns, the impossible may be attained" encapsulates the transformative power of love in overcoming seemingly insurmountable challenges. It conveys the idea that love, with its boundless strength and resilience, has the potential to make the unachievable achievable. This proverb reflects a profound optimism about the ability of love to inspire and motivate individuals to reach beyond their perceived limits.

THE DARKEST HOUR
HAS ONLY SIXTY
MINUTES.
England

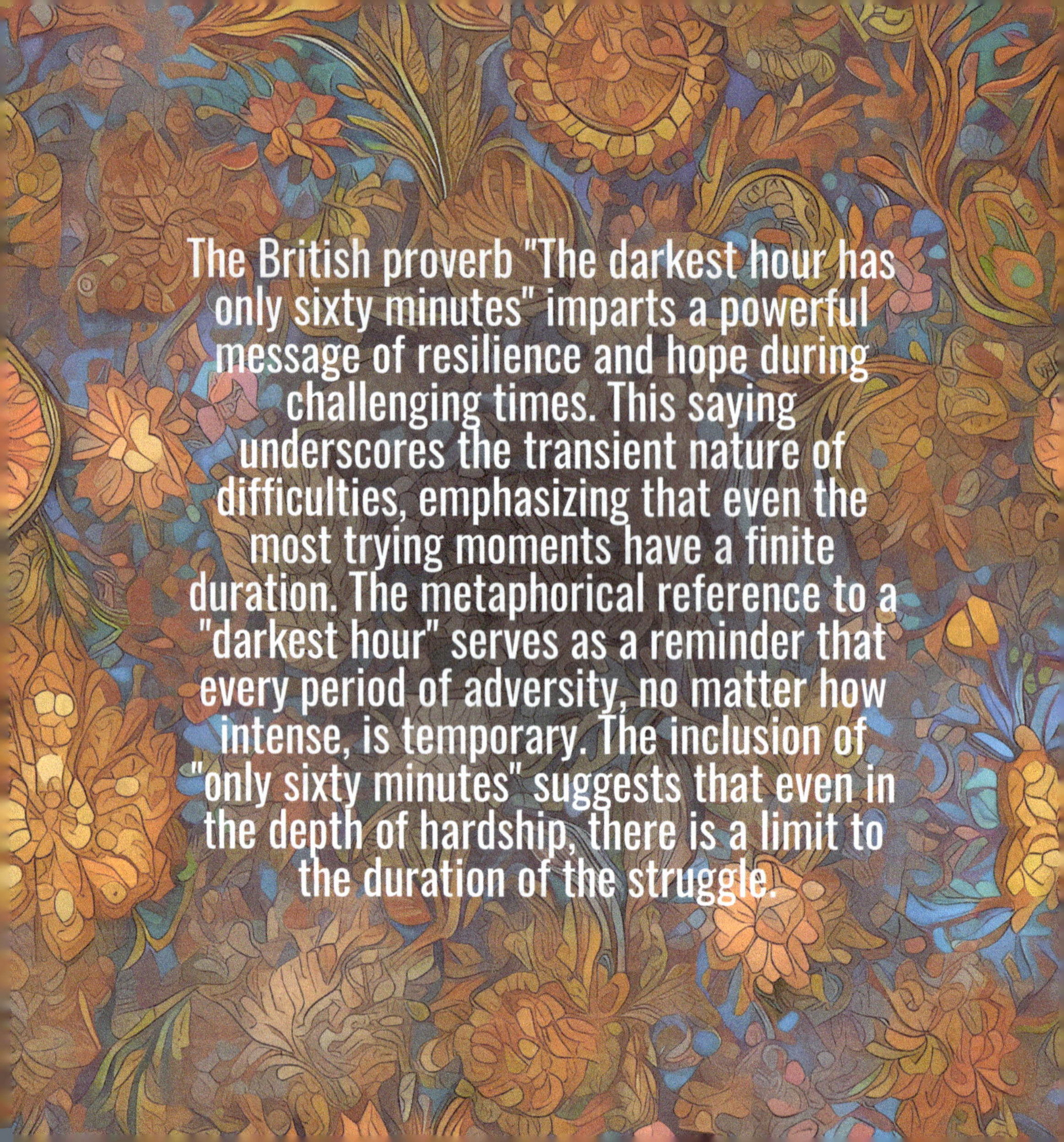

The British proverb "The darkest hour has only sixty minutes" imparts a powerful message of resilience and hope during challenging times. This saying underscores the transient nature of difficulties, emphasizing that even the most trying moments have a finite duration. The metaphorical reference to a "darkest hour" serves as a reminder that every period of adversity, no matter how intense, is temporary. The inclusion of "only sixty minutes" suggests that even in the depth of hardship, there is a limit to the duration of the struggle.

WHERE THERE'S
SMOKE, THERE'S
FIRE.
Italy

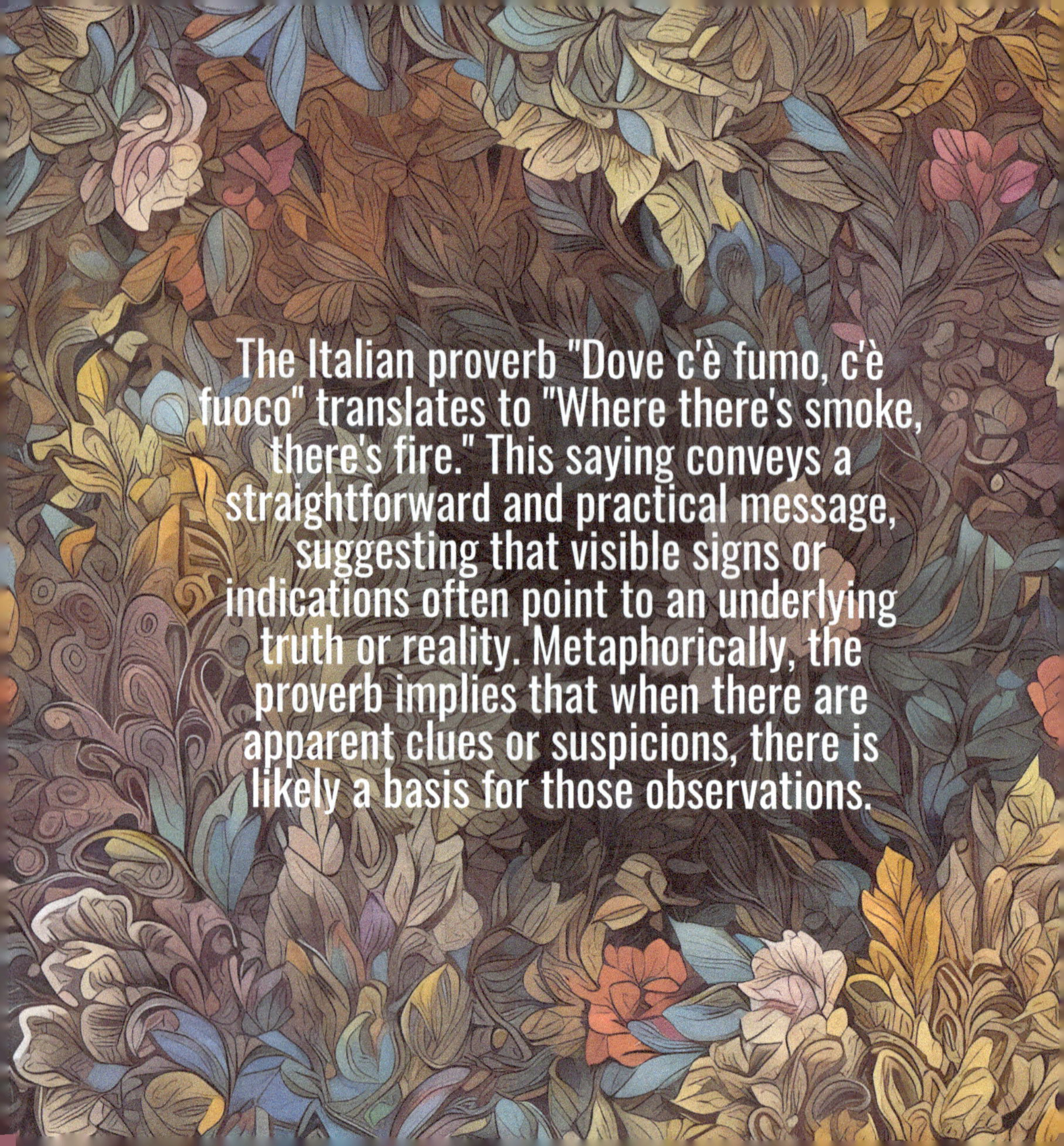

The Italian proverb "Dove c'è fumo, c'è fuoco" translates to "Where there's smoke, there's fire." This saying conveys a straightforward and practical message, suggesting that visible signs or indications often point to an underlying truth or reality. Metaphorically, the proverb implies that when there are apparent clues or suspicions, there is likely a basis for those observations.

WHO DOESN'T RISK,
DOESN'T CROSS THE
RIVER.
Latin American

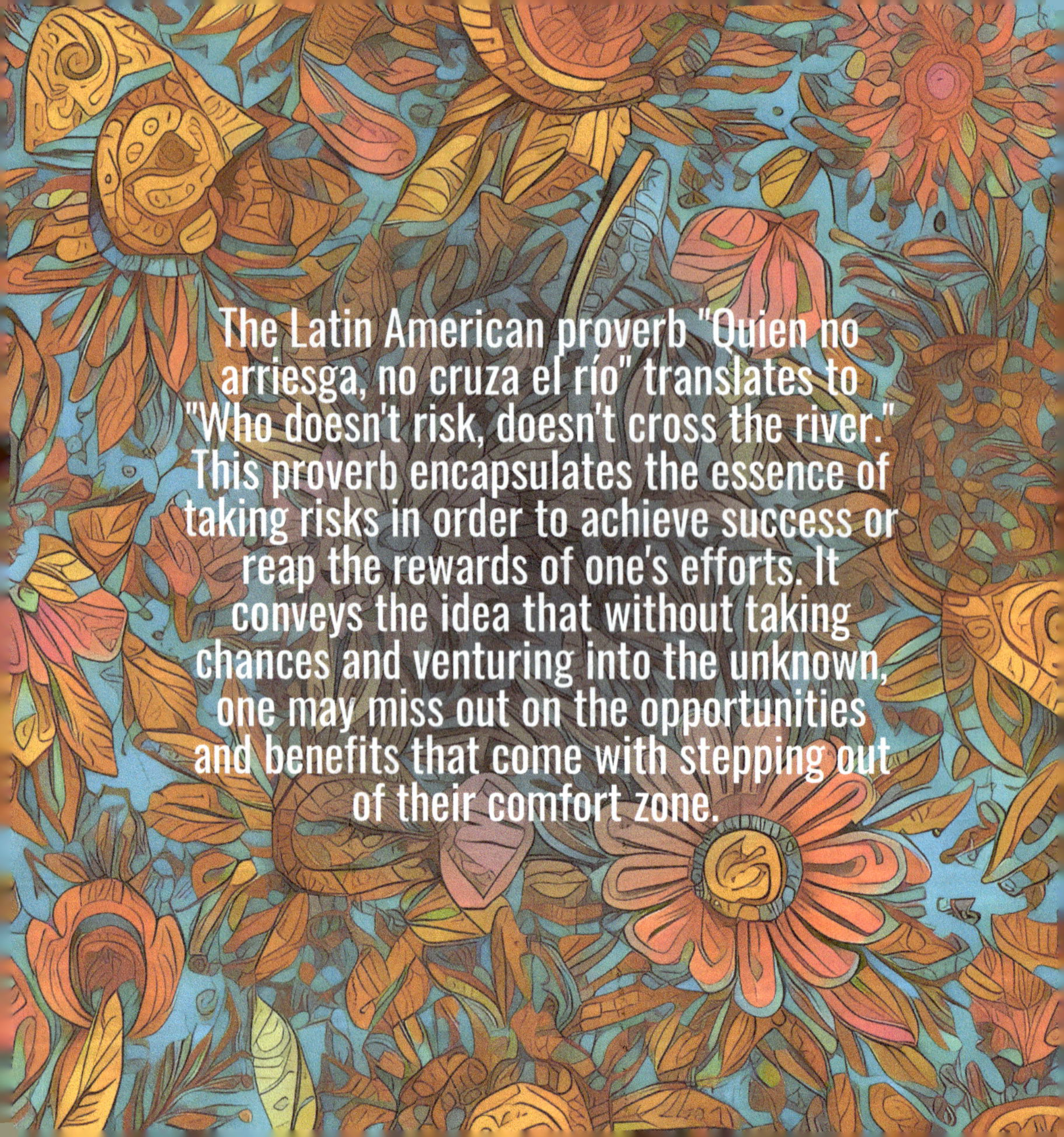
The Latin American proverb "Quien no arriesga, no cruza el río" translates to "Who doesn't risk, doesn't cross the river." This proverb encapsulates the essence of taking risks in order to achieve success or reap the rewards of one's efforts. It conveys the idea that without taking chances and venturing into the unknown, one may miss out on the opportunities and benefits that come with stepping out of their comfort zone.

OUT OF THE FRYING PAN AND INTO THE FIRE.
England

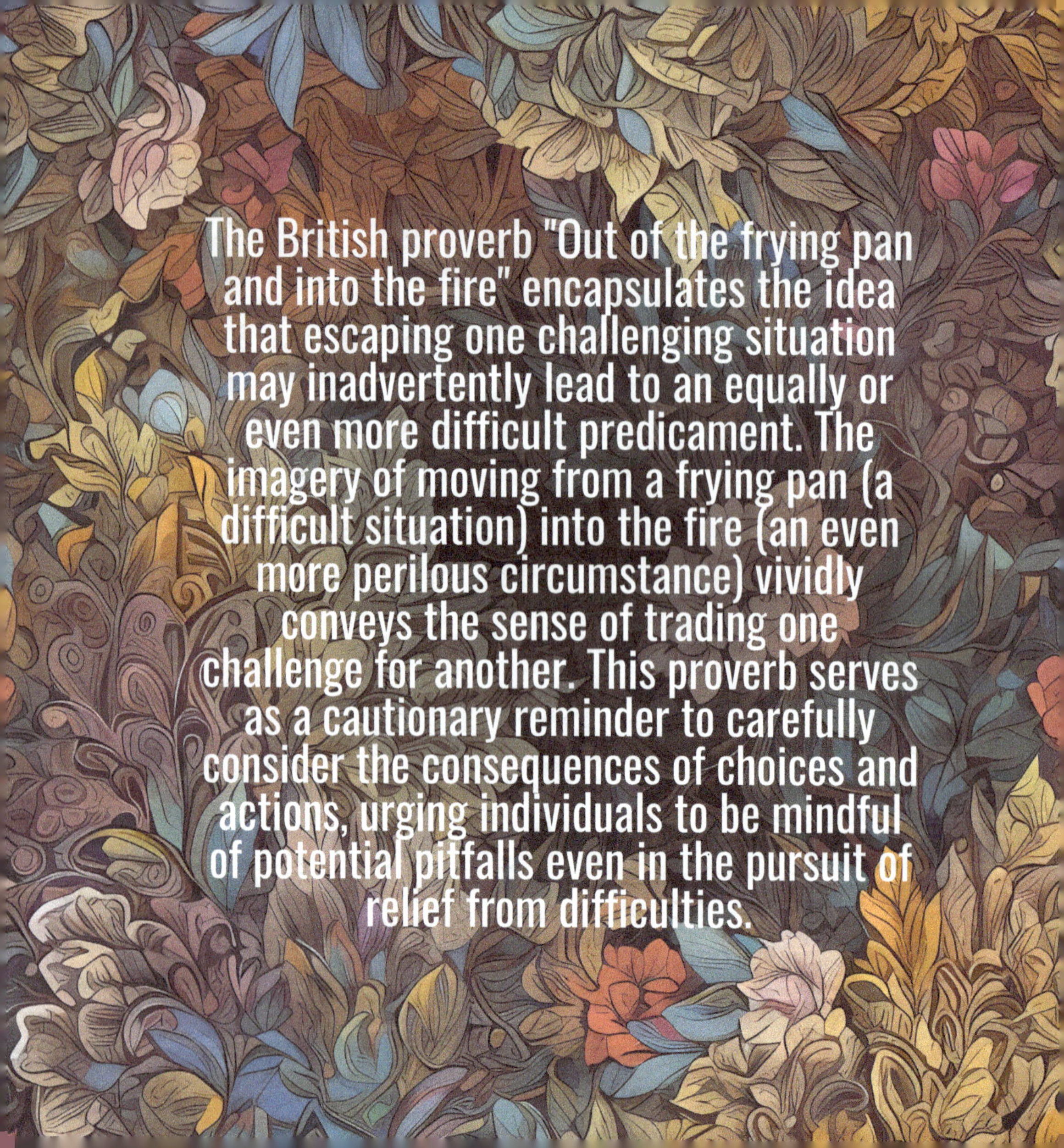
The British proverb "Out of the frying pan and into the fire" encapsulates the idea that escaping one challenging situation may inadvertently lead to an equally or even more difficult predicament. The imagery of moving from a frying pan (a difficult situation) into the fire (an even more perilous circumstance) vividly conveys the sense of trading one challenge for another. This proverb serves as a cautionary reminder to carefully consider the consequences of choices and actions, urging individuals to be mindful of potential pitfalls even in the pursuit of relief from difficulties.

DON'T LOOK A GIFT
HORSE IN THE
MOUTH
Latin American

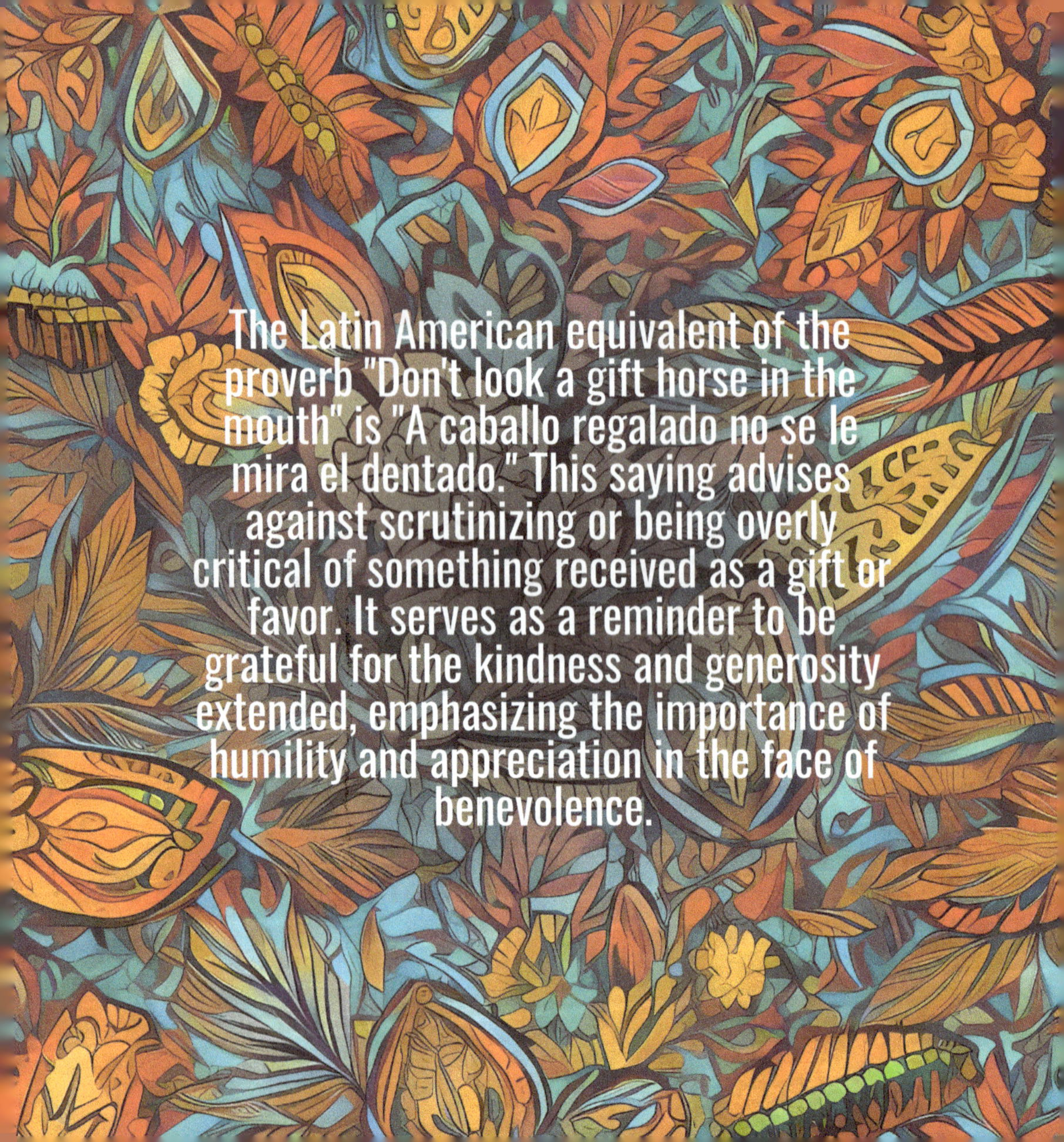

The Latin American equivalent of the proverb "Don't look a gift horse in the mouth" is "A caballo regalado no se le mira el dentado." This saying advises against scrutinizing or being overly critical of something received as a gift or favor. It serves as a reminder to be grateful for the kindness and generosity extended, emphasizing the importance of humility and appreciation in the face of benevolence.

DO NOT SPEAK OF
MY DEBTS UNLESS
YOU MEAN TO PAY
THEM.
Spain

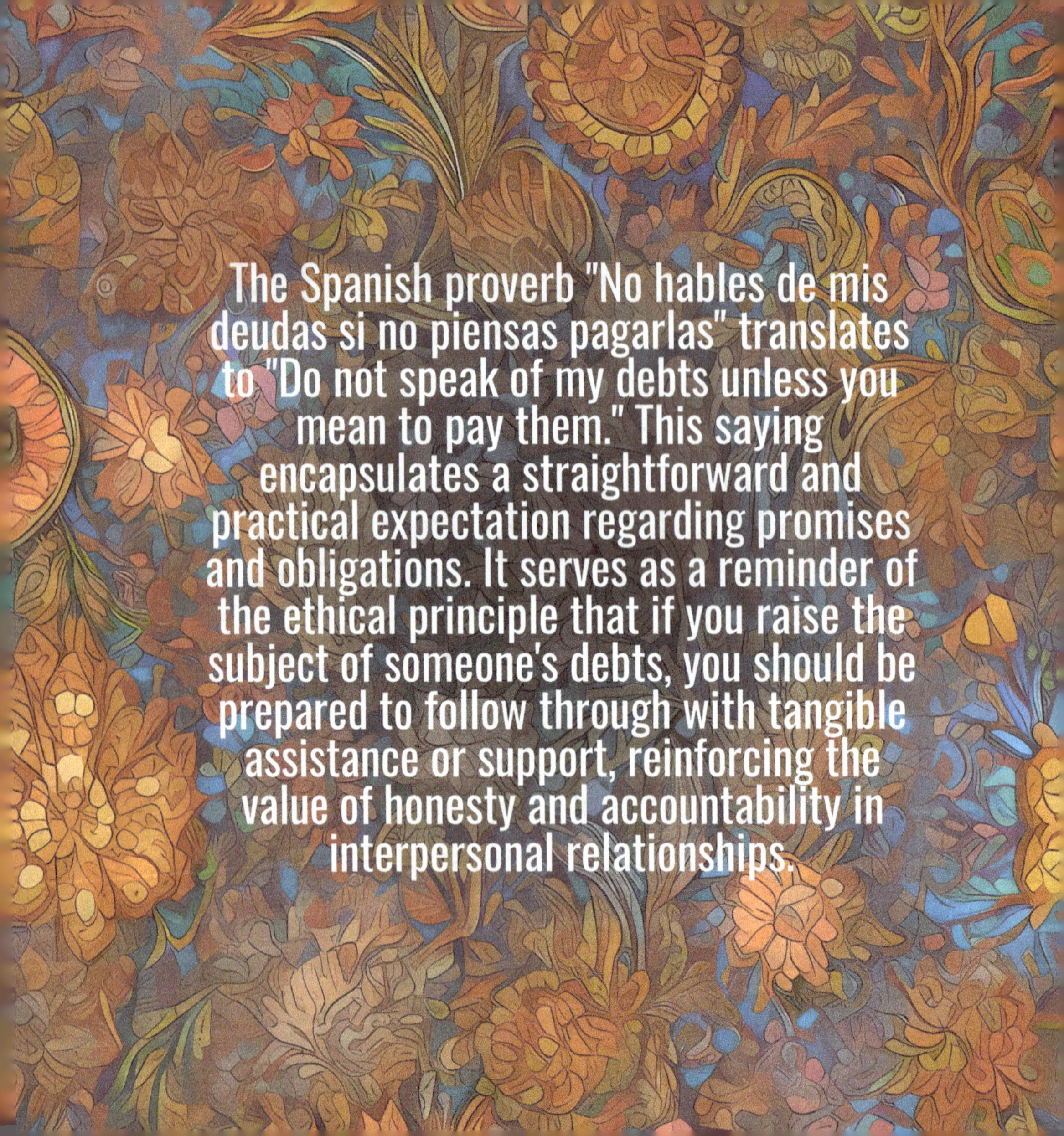

The Spanish proverb "No hables de mis deudas si no piensas pagarlas" translates to "Do not speak of my debts unless you mean to pay them." This saying encapsulates a straightforward and practical expectation regarding promises and obligations. It serves as a reminder of the ethical principle that if you raise the subject of someone's debts, you should be prepared to follow through with tangible assistance or support, reinforcing the value of honesty and accountability in interpersonal relationships.

DON'T LEAVE FOR
TOMORROW WHAT
YOU CAN DO TODAY.
Latin American

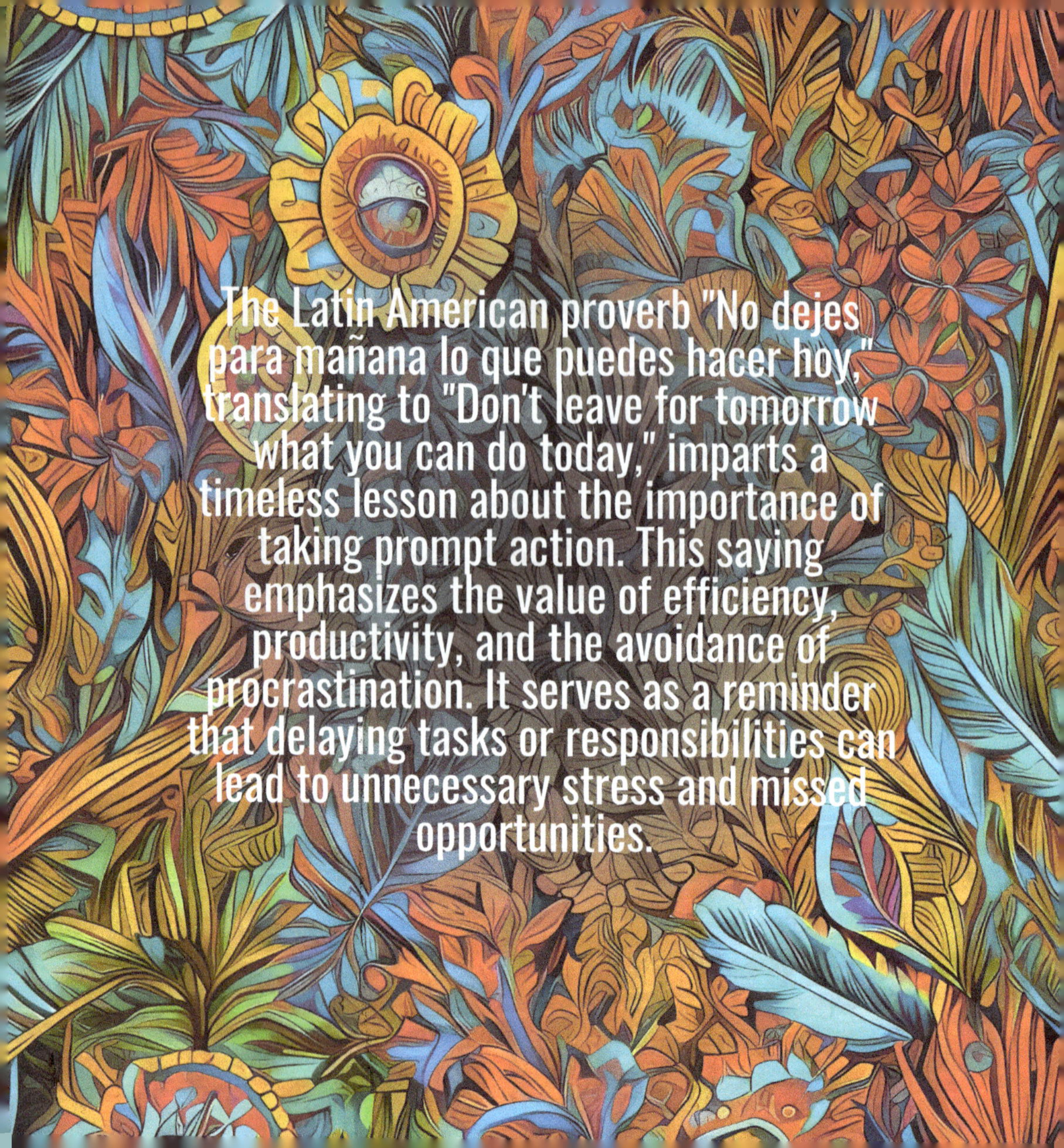
The Latin American proverb "No dejes para mañana lo que puedes hacer hoy," translating to "Don't leave for tomorrow what you can do today," imparts a timeless lesson about the importance of taking prompt action. This saying emphasizes the value of efficiency, productivity, and the avoidance of procrastination. It serves as a reminder that delaying tasks or responsibilities can lead to unnecessary stress and missed opportunities.

DON'T SELL THE
BEAR'S SKIN
BEFORE YOU'VE
KILLED IT.
France

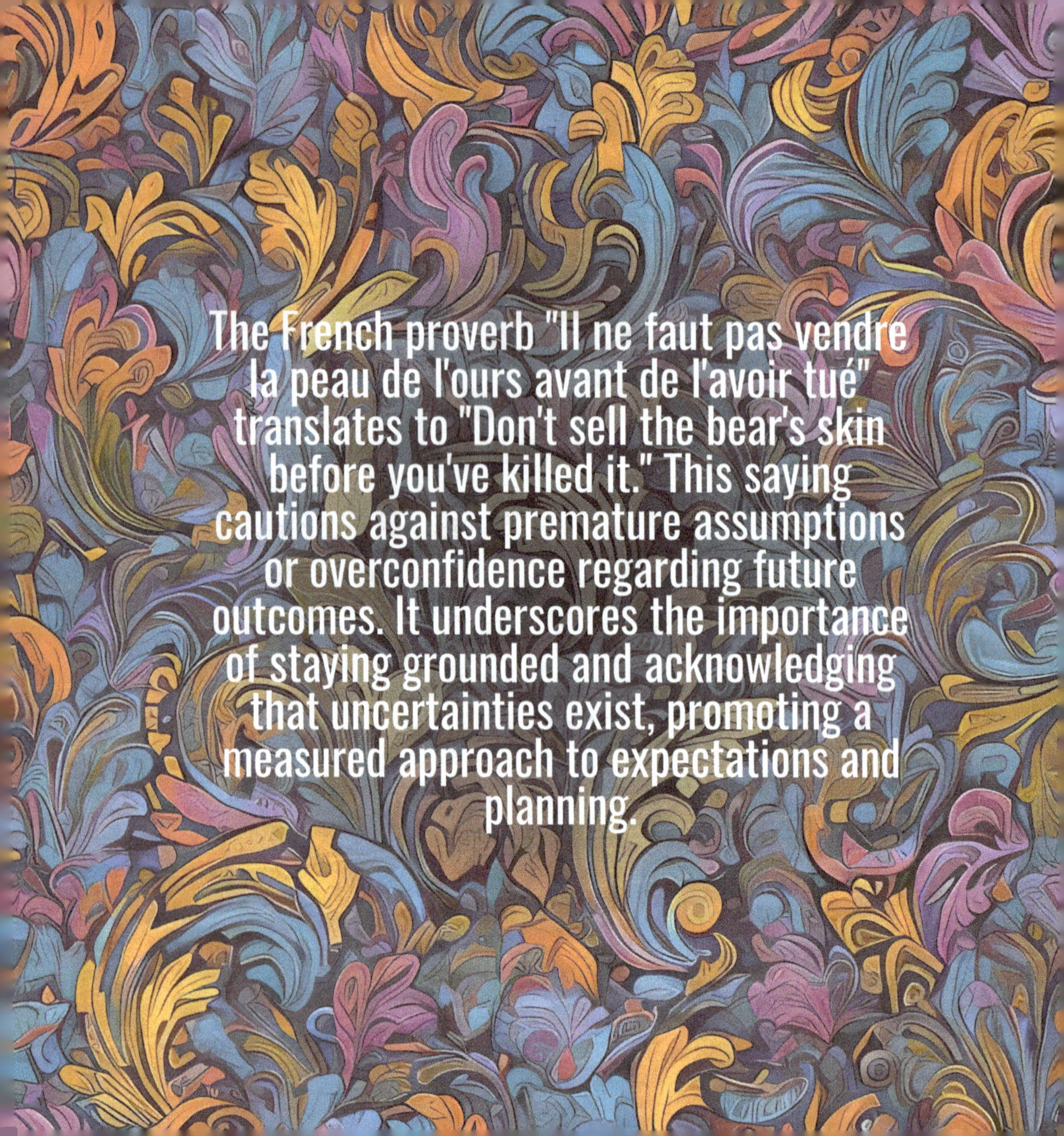
The French proverb "Il ne faut pas vendre la peau de l'ours avant de l'avoir tué" translates to "Don't sell the bear's skin before you've killed it." This saying cautions against premature assumptions or overconfidence regarding future outcomes. It underscores the importance of staying grounded and acknowledging that uncertainties exist, promoting a measured approach to expectations and planning.

THE SUN DOES NOT FORGET A VILLAGE.
Antigua & Barbuda

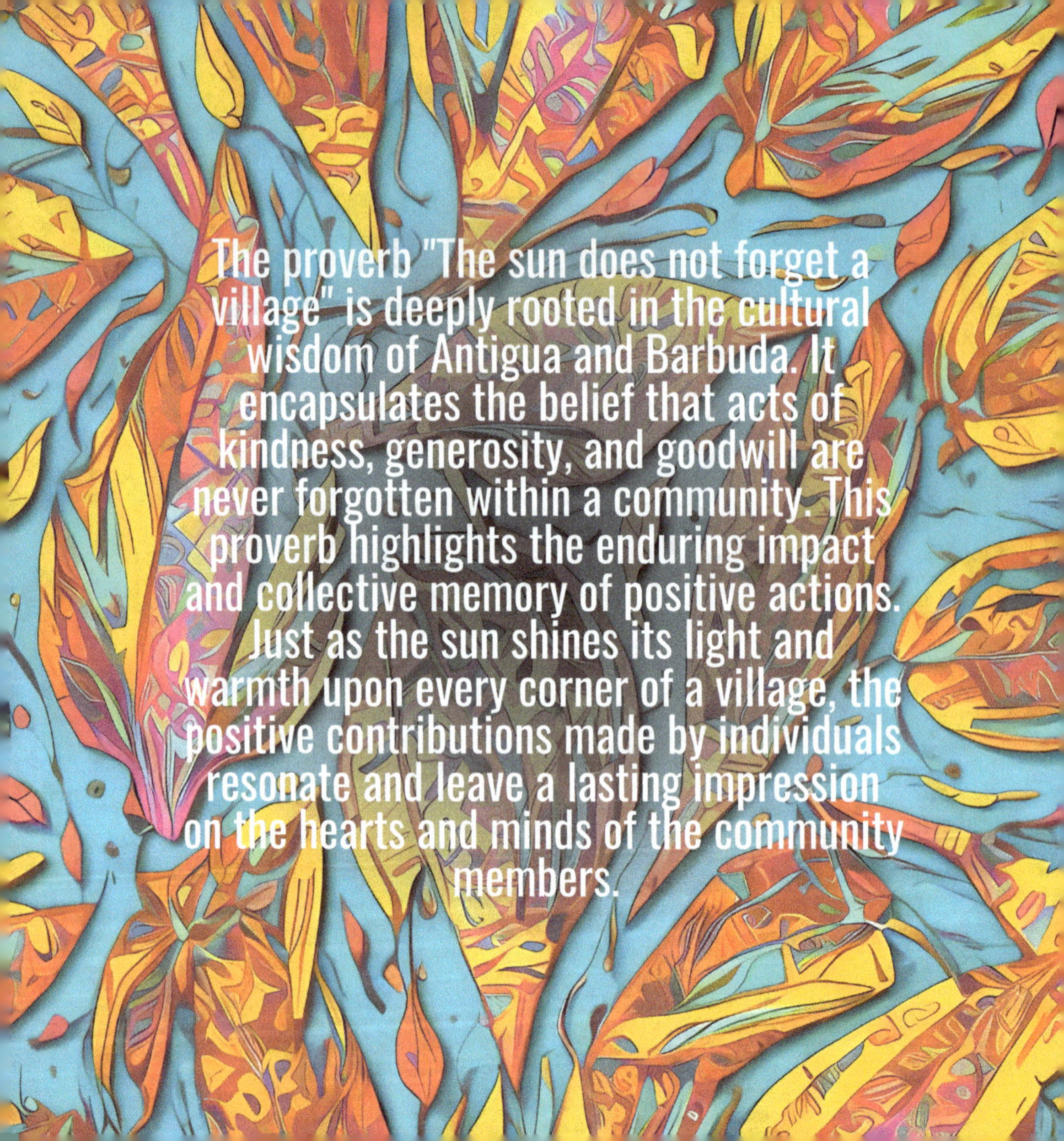

The proverb "The sun does not forget a village" is deeply rooted in the cultural wisdom of Antigua and Barbuda. It encapsulates the belief that acts of kindness, generosity, and goodwill are never forgotten within a community. This proverb highlights the enduring impact and collective memory of positive actions. Just as the sun shines its light and warmth upon every corner of a village, the positive contributions made by individuals resonate and leave a lasting impression on the hearts and minds of the community members.

When you're in trouble, even a child's shirt will fit you.
Jamaica

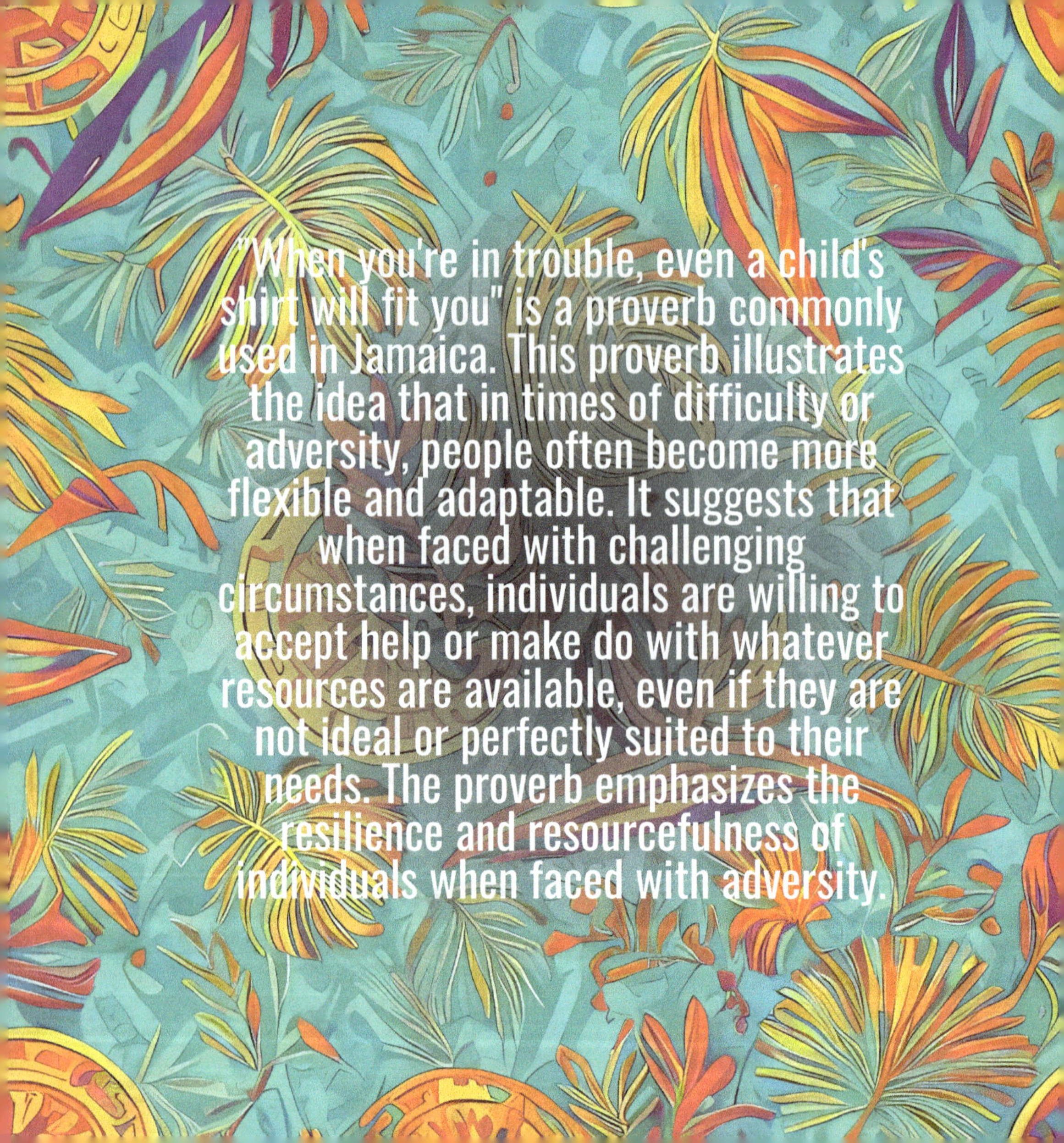
"When you're in trouble, even a child's shirt will fit you" is a proverb commonly used in Jamaica. This proverb illustrates the idea that in times of difficulty or adversity, people often become more flexible and adaptable. It suggests that when faced with challenging circumstances, individuals are willing to accept help or make do with whatever resources are available, even if they are not ideal or perfectly suited to their needs. The proverb emphasizes the resilience and resourcefulness of individuals when faced with adversity.

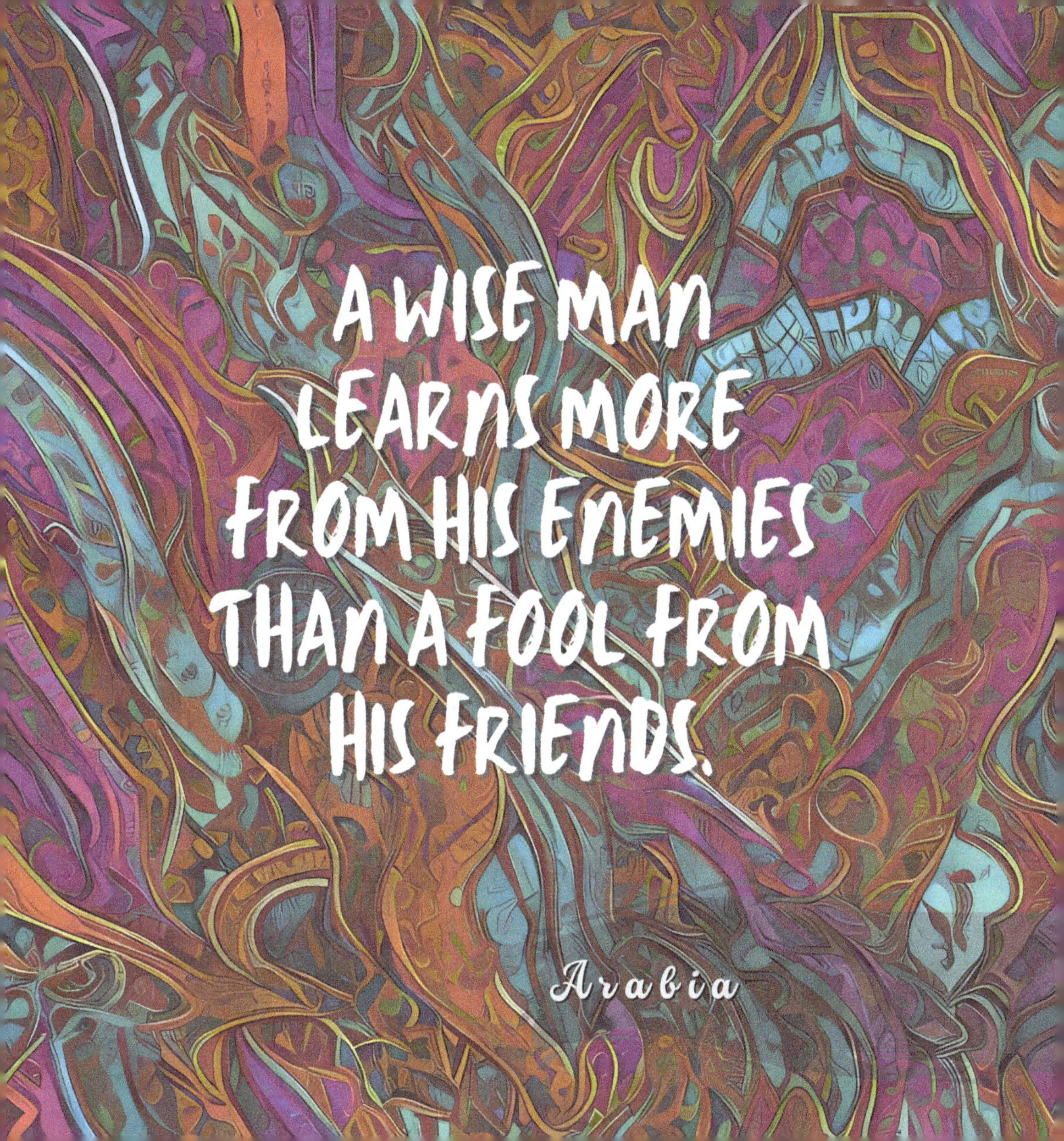
A WISE MAN
LEARNS MORE
FROM HIS ENEMIES
THAN A FOOL FROM
HIS FRIENDS.
Arabia

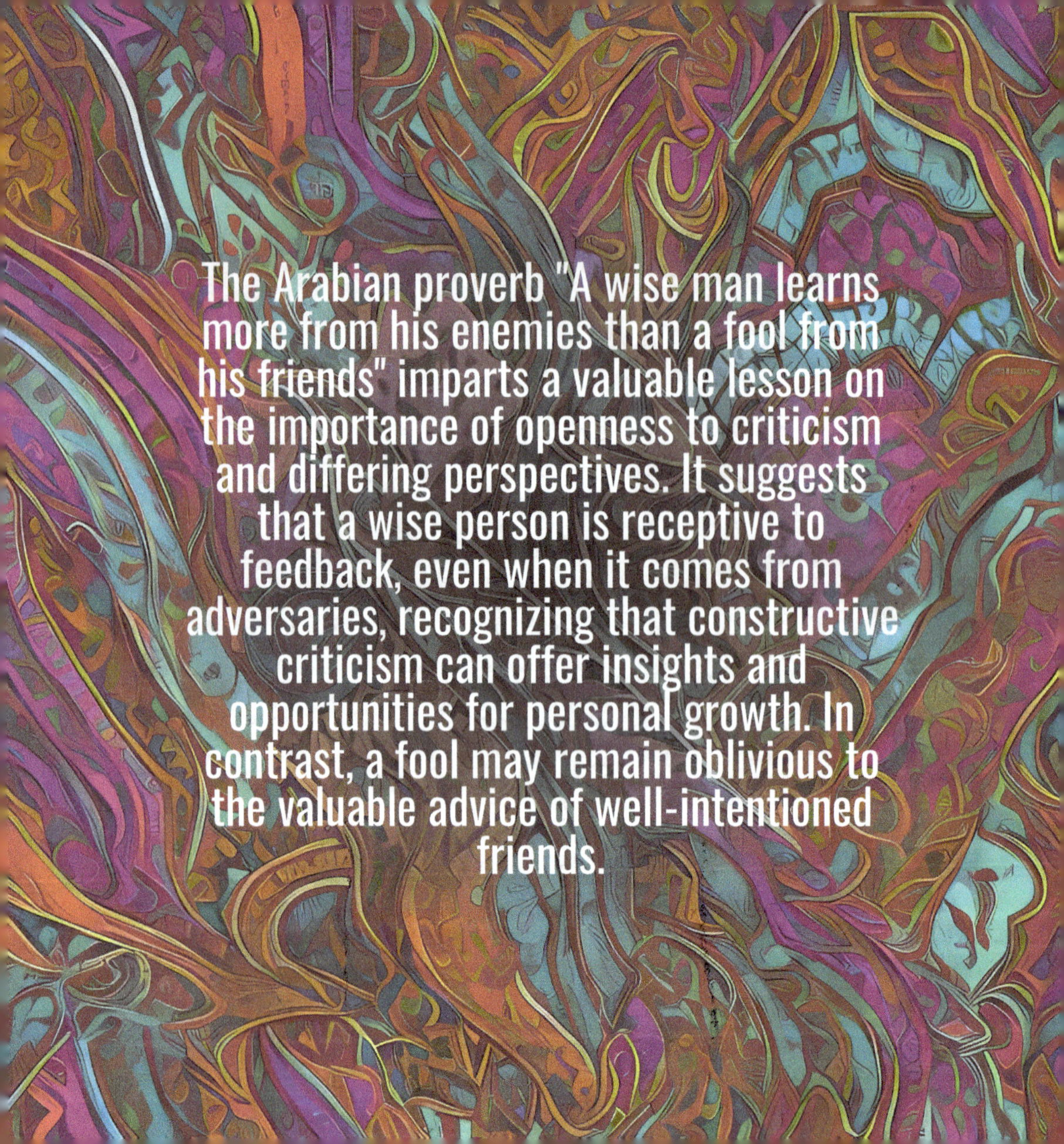
The Arabian proverb "A wise man learns more from his enemies than a fool from his friends" imparts a valuable lesson on the importance of openness to criticism and differing perspectives. It suggests that a wise person is receptive to feedback, even when it comes from adversaries, recognizing that constructive criticism can offer insights and opportunities for personal growth. In contrast, a fool may remain oblivious to the valuable advice of well-intentioned friends.

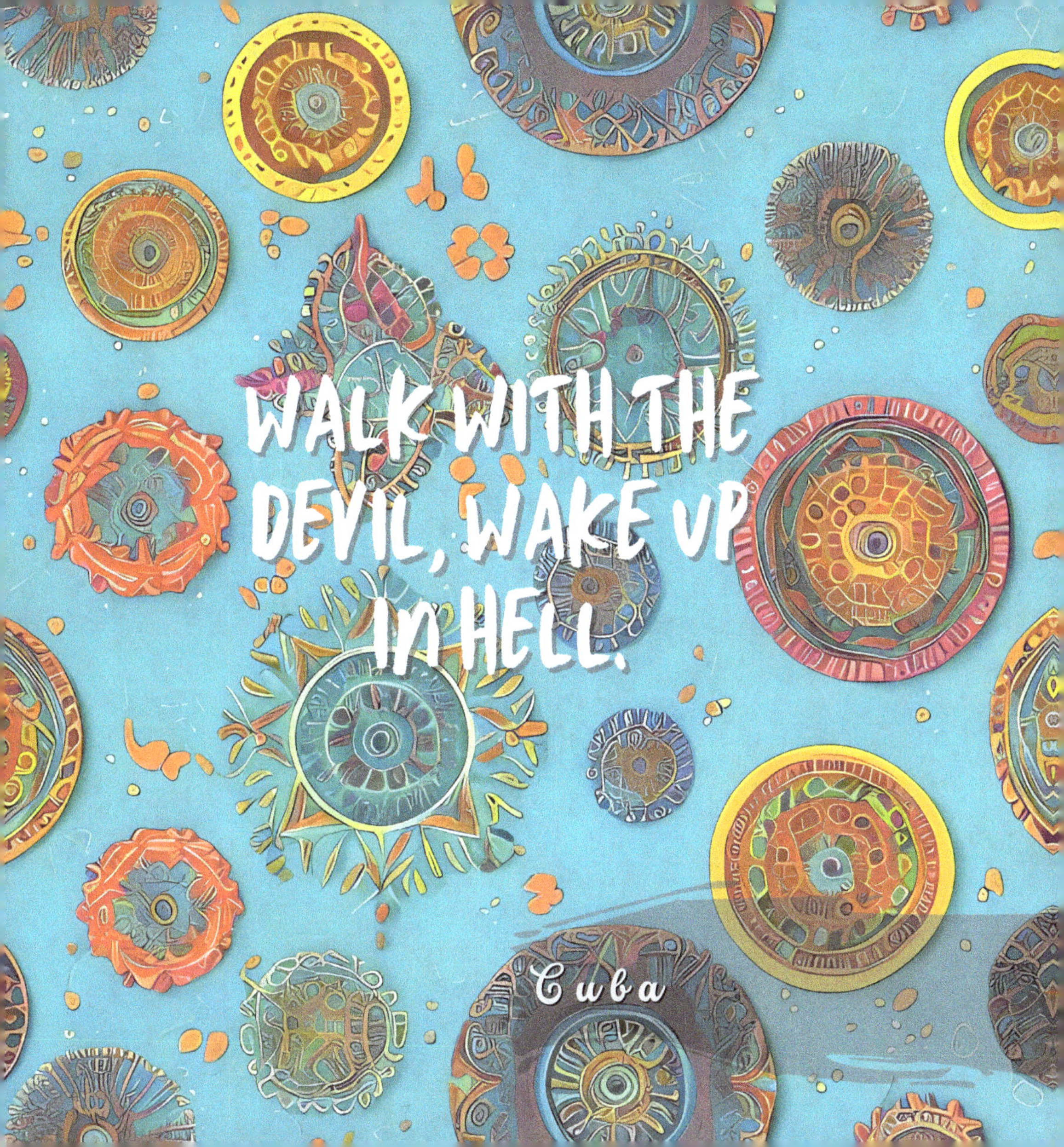
WALK WITH THE
DEVIL, WAKE UP
IN HELL.
Cuba

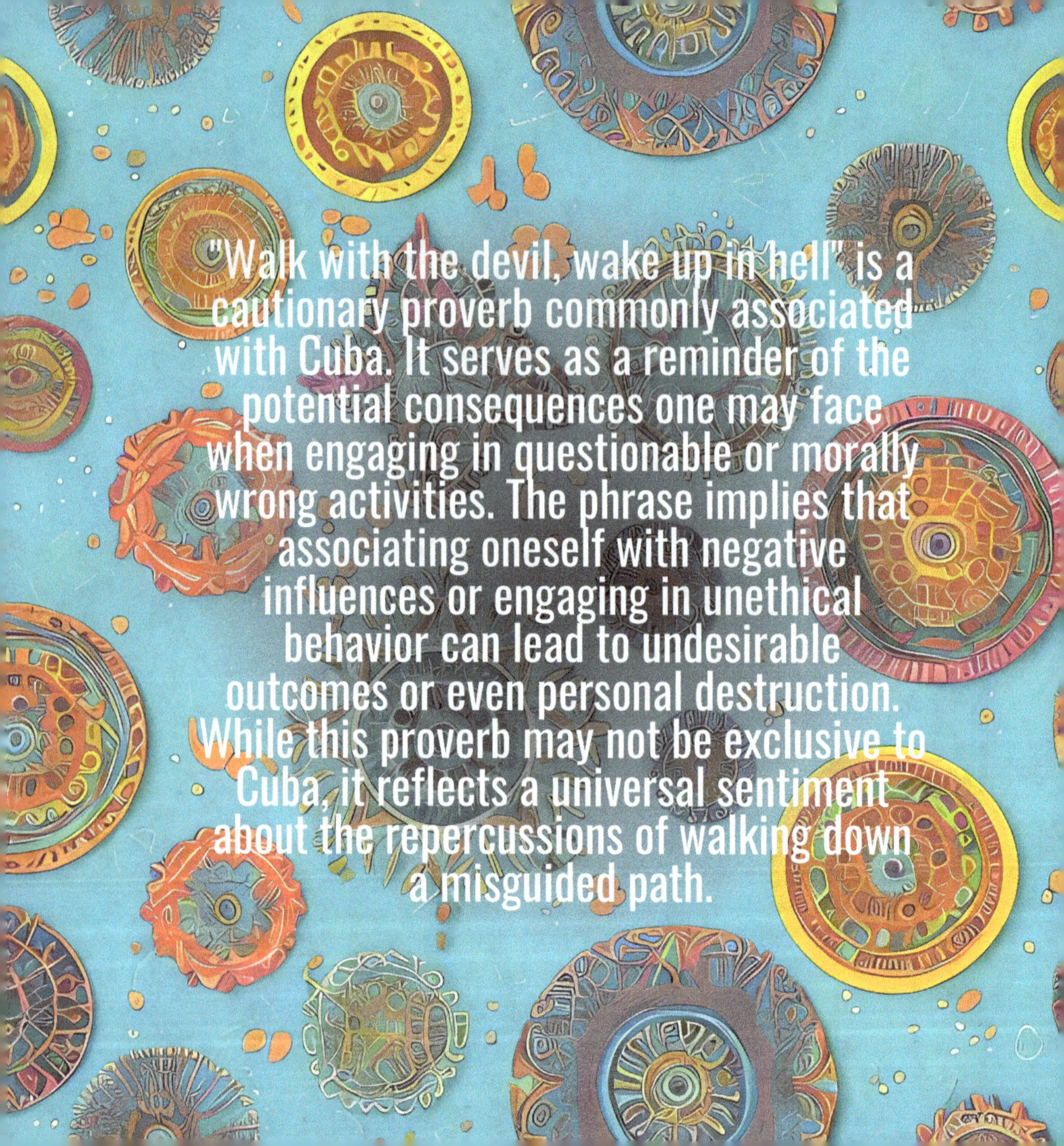
"Walk with the devil, wake up in hell" is a cautionary proverb commonly associated with Cuba. It serves as a reminder of the potential consequences one may face when engaging in questionable or morally wrong activities. The phrase implies that associating oneself with negative influences or engaging in unethical behavior can lead to undesirable outcomes or even personal destruction. While this proverb may not be exclusive to Cuba, it reflects a universal sentiment about the repercussions of walking down a misguided path.

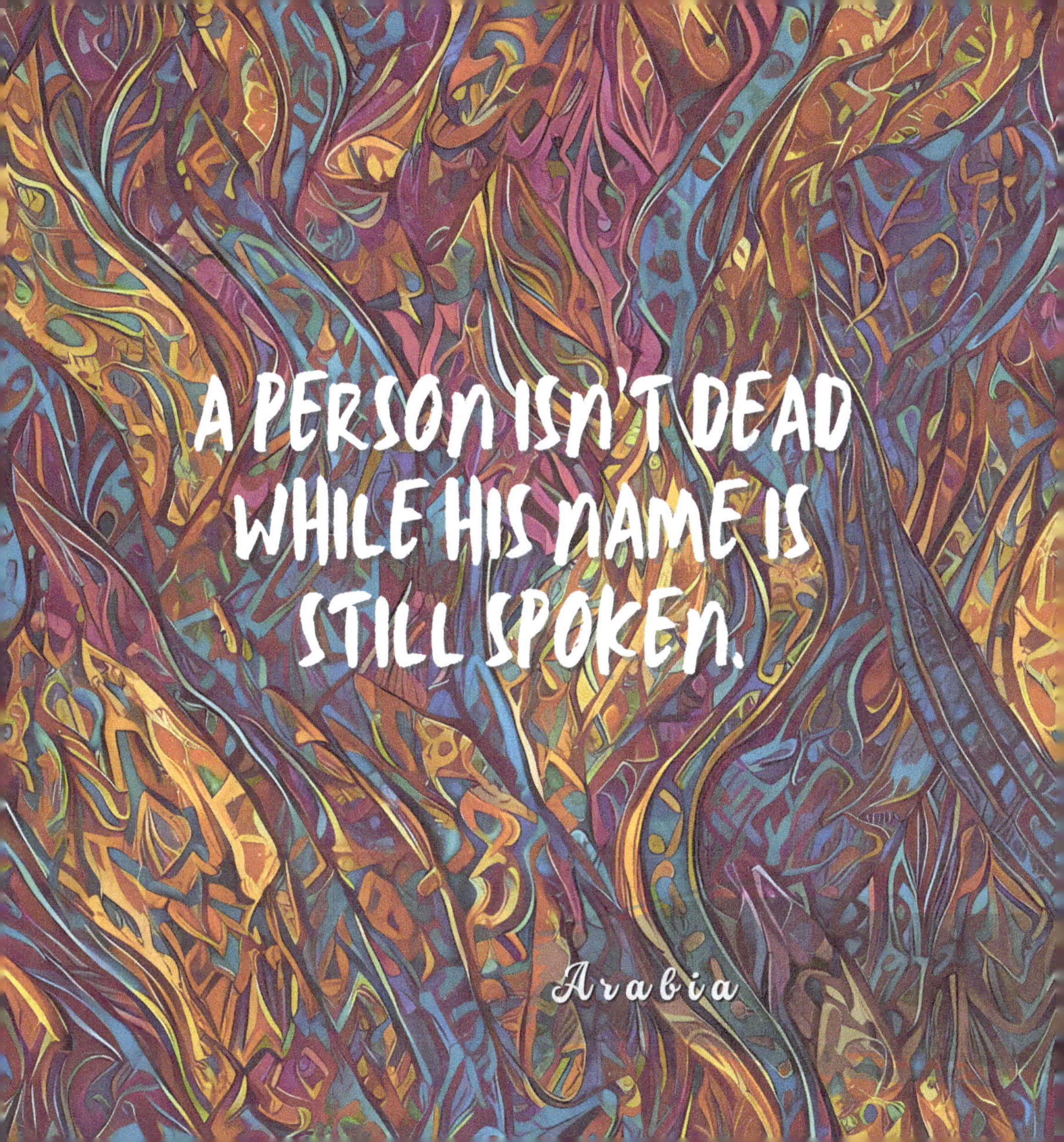
A PERSON ISN'T DEAD
WHILE HIS NAME IS
STILL SPOKEN.
Arabia

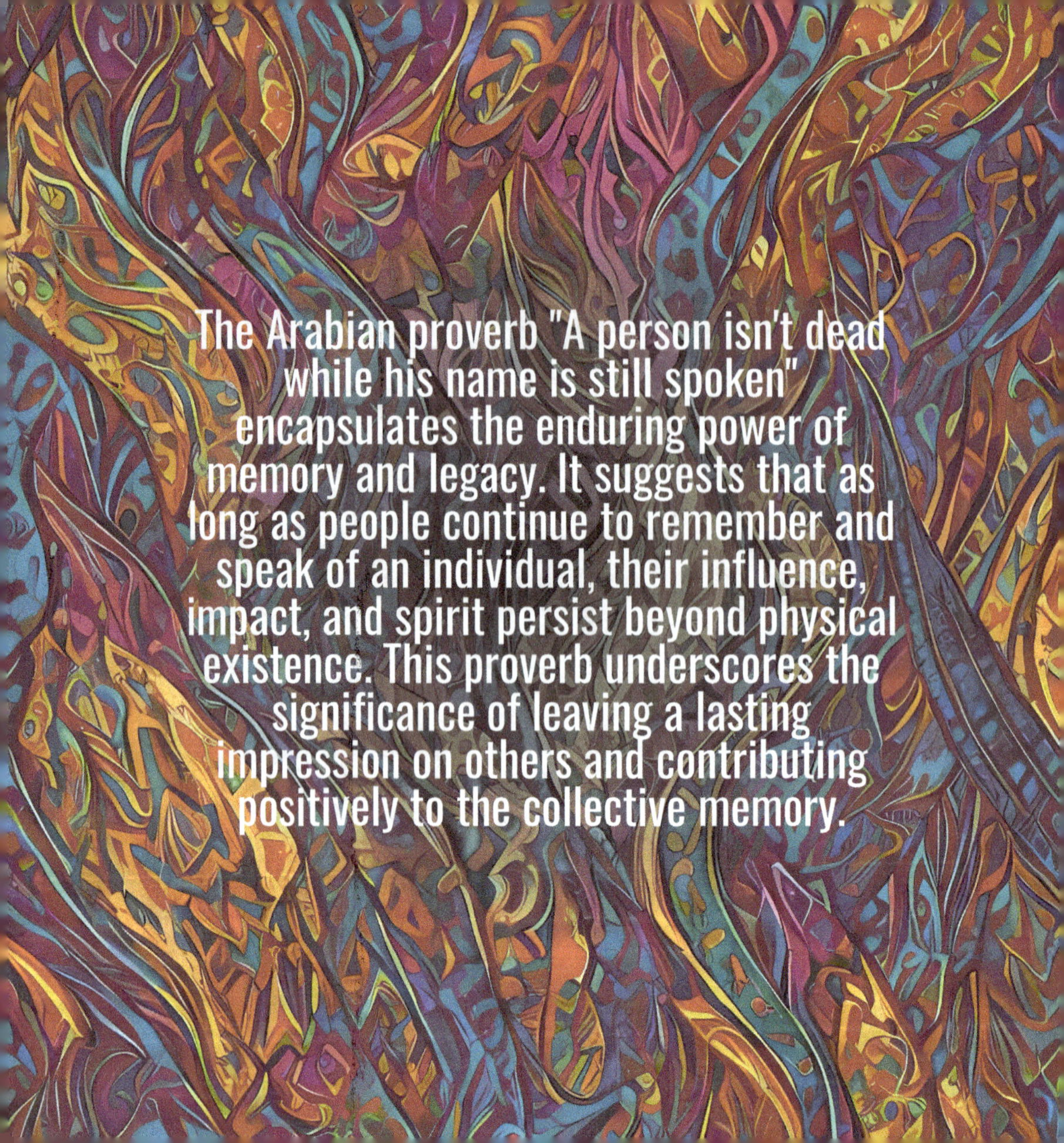
The Arabian proverb "A person isn't dead while his name is still spoken" encapsulates the enduring power of memory and legacy. It suggests that as long as people continue to remember and speak of an individual, their influence, impact, and spirit persist beyond physical existence. This proverb underscores the significance of leaving a lasting impression on others and contributing positively to the collective memory.

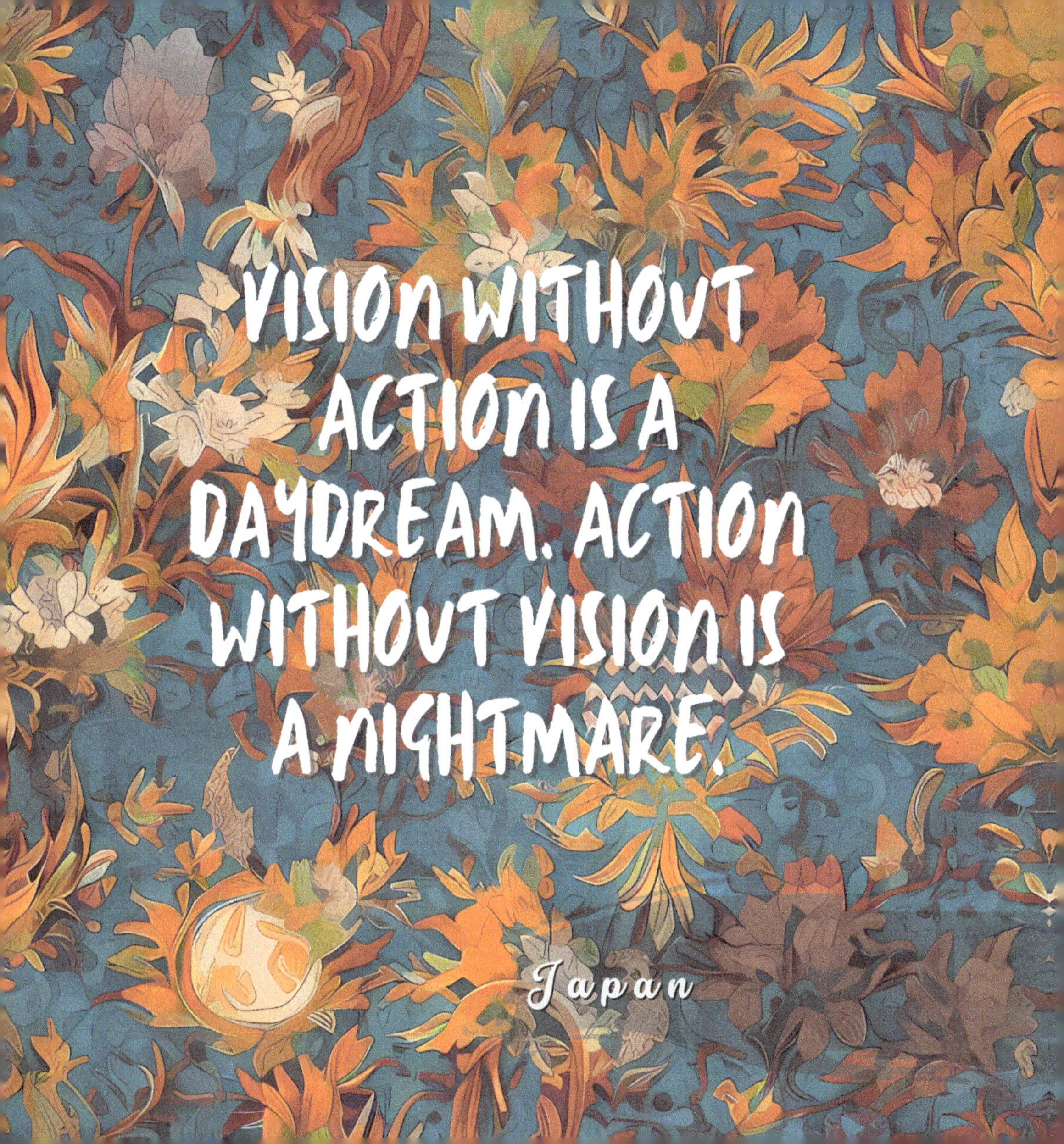
VISION WITHOUT ACTION IS A DAYDREAM. ACTION WITHOUT VISION IS A NIGHTMARE.
Japan

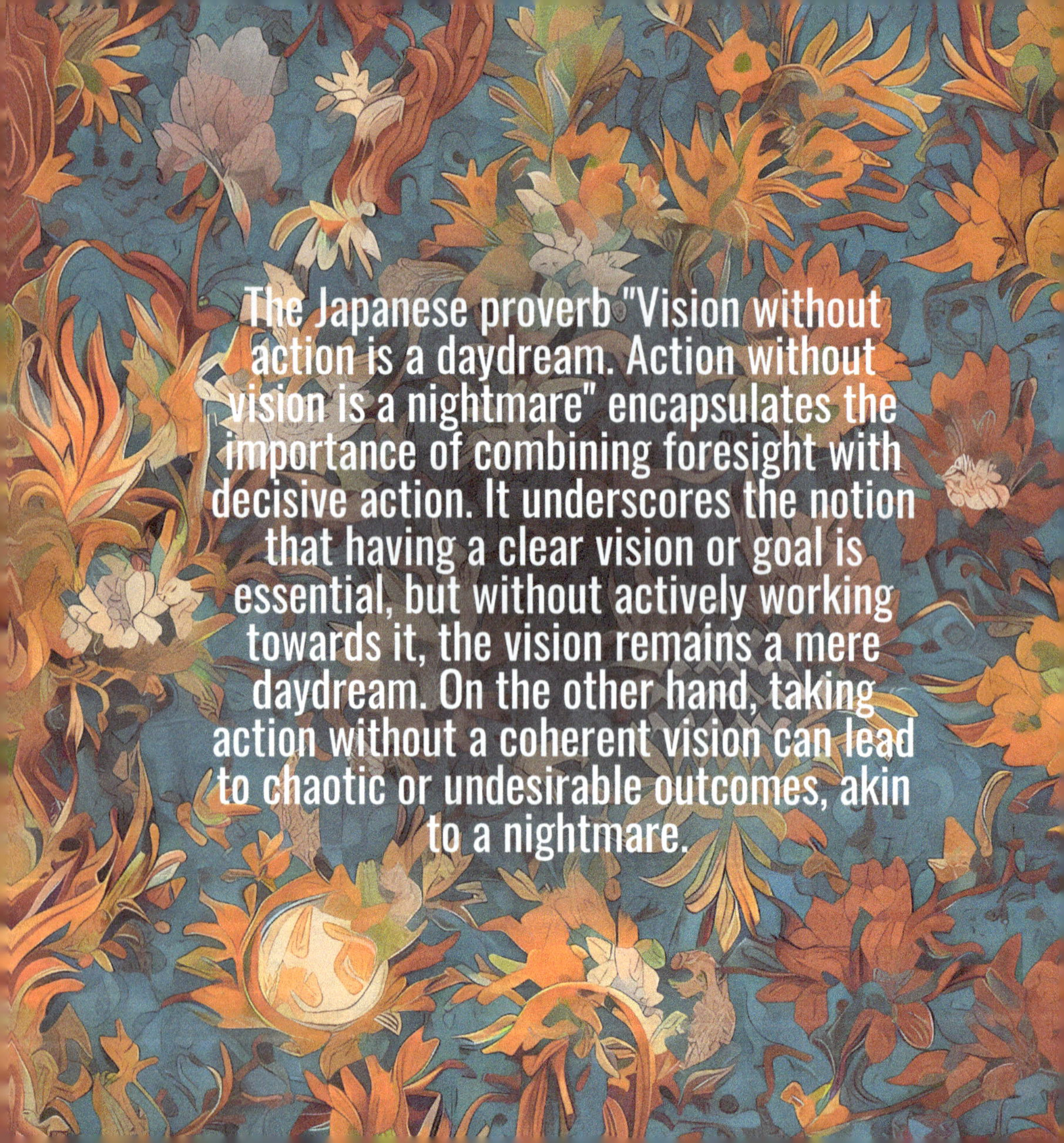

The Japanese proverb "Vision without action is a daydream. Action without vision is a nightmare" encapsulates the importance of combining foresight with decisive action. It underscores the notion that having a clear vision or goal is essential, but without actively working towards it, the vision remains a mere daydream. On the other hand, taking action without a coherent vision can lead to chaotic or undesirable outcomes, akin to a nightmare.

DO GOOD AND
THROW IT IN
THE SEA.
Arabia

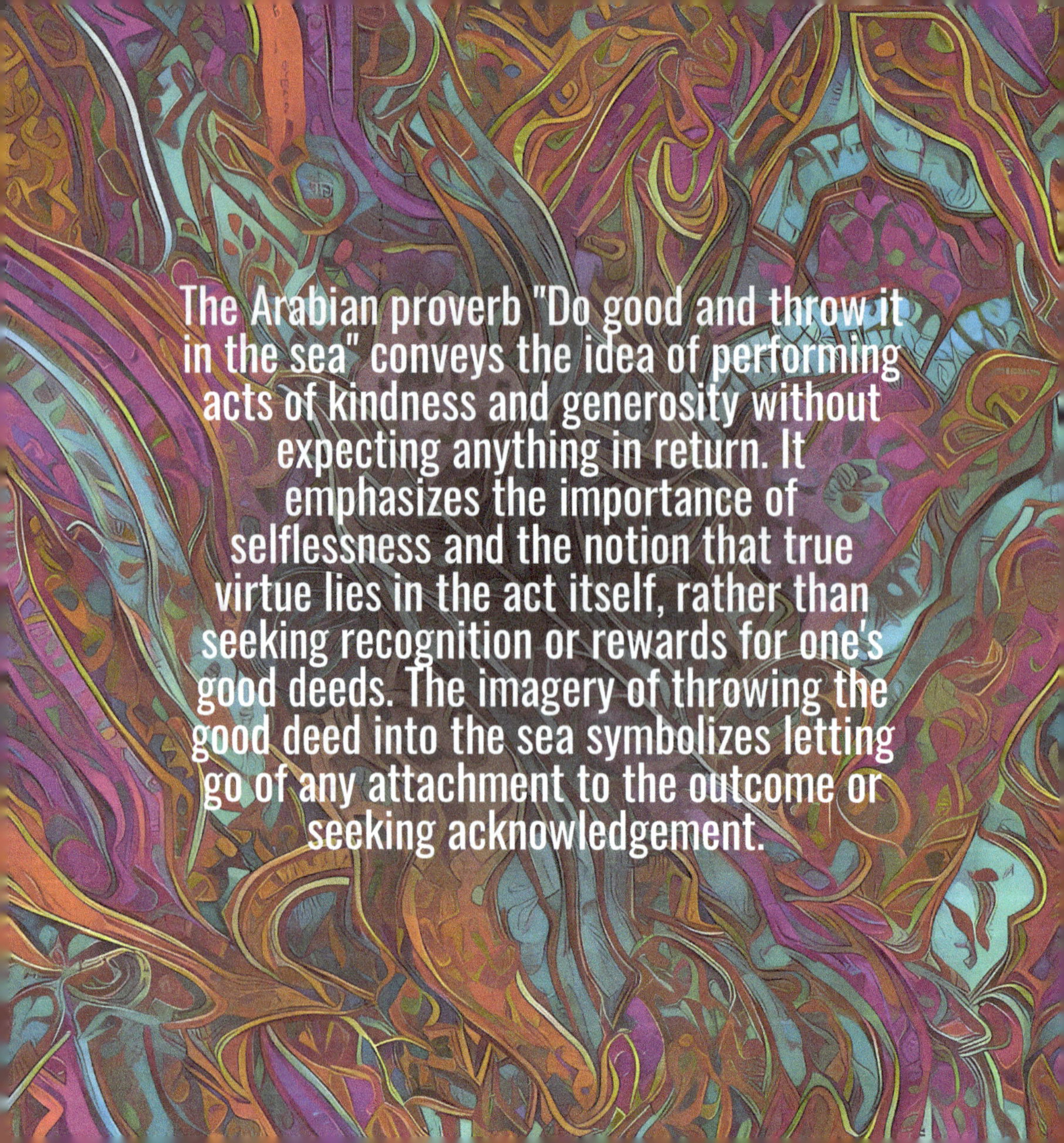

The Arabian proverb "Do good and throw it in the sea" conveys the idea of performing acts of kindness and generosity without expecting anything in return. It emphasizes the importance of selflessness and the notion that true virtue lies in the act itself, rather than seeking recognition or rewards for one's good deeds. The imagery of throwing the good deed into the sea symbolizes letting go of any attachment to the outcome or seeking acknowledgement.

EVEN A DOG CAN DISTINGUISH BETWEEN BEING STUMBLED OVER AND BEING KICKED.
Mongolia

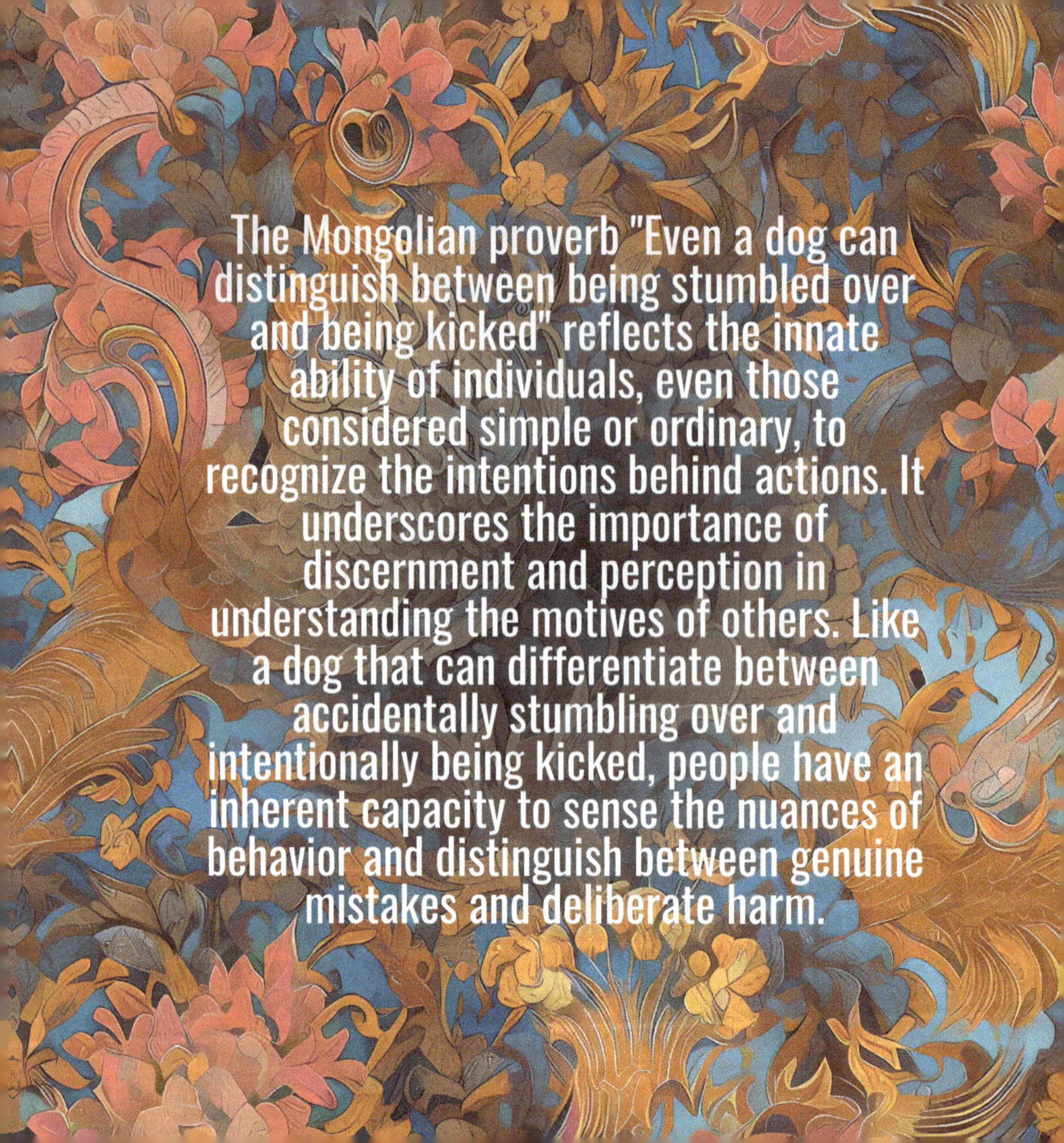

The Mongolian proverb "Even a dog can distinguish between being stumbled over and being kicked" reflects the innate ability of individuals, even those considered simple or ordinary, to recognize the intentions behind actions. It underscores the importance of discernment and perception in understanding the motives of others. Like a dog that can differentiate between accidentally stumbling over and intentionally being kicked, people have an inherent capacity to sense the nuances of behavior and distinguish between genuine mistakes and deliberate harm.

THE CHILD WHO IS NOT EMBRACED BY THE VILLAGE WILL BURN IT DOWN TO FEEL ITS WARMTH.
African

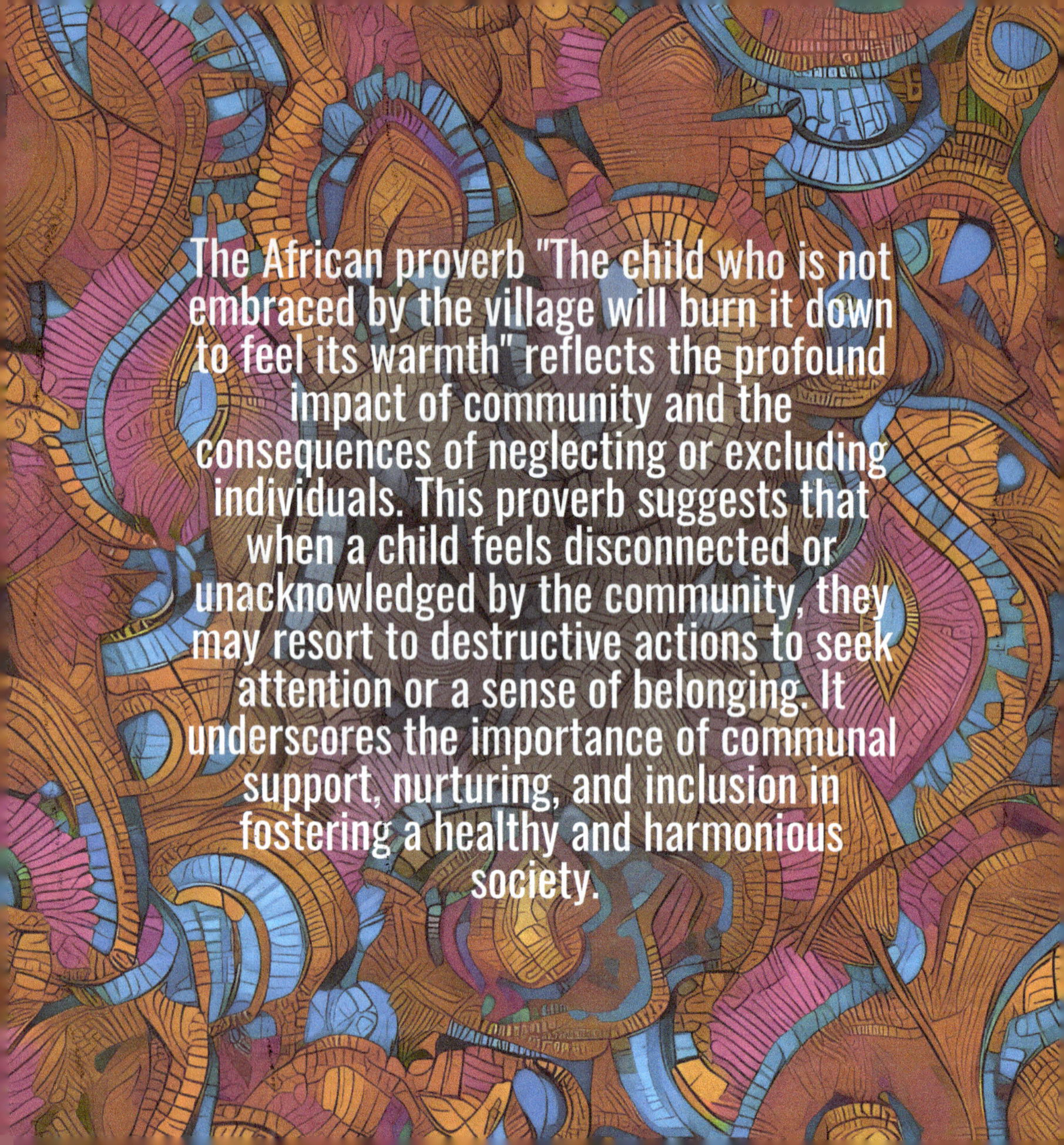
The African proverb "The child who is not embraced by the village will burn it down to feel its warmth" reflects the profound impact of community and the consequences of neglecting or excluding individuals. This proverb suggests that when a child feels disconnected or unacknowledged by the community, they may resort to destructive actions to seek attention or a sense of belonging. It underscores the importance of communal support, nurturing, and inclusion in fostering a healthy and harmonious society.

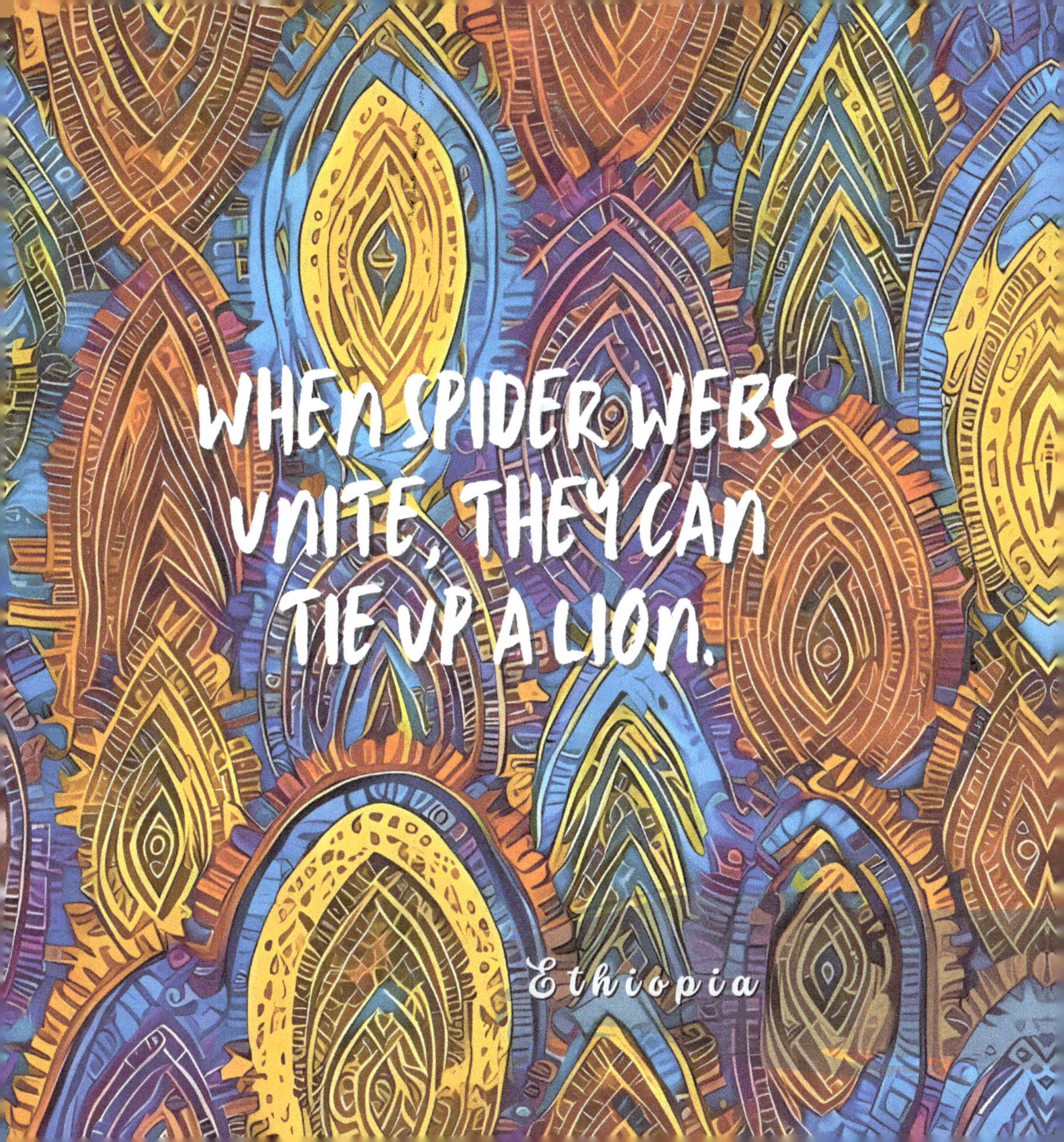
WHEN SPIDER WEBS UNITE, THEY CAN TIE UP A LION.
Ethiopia

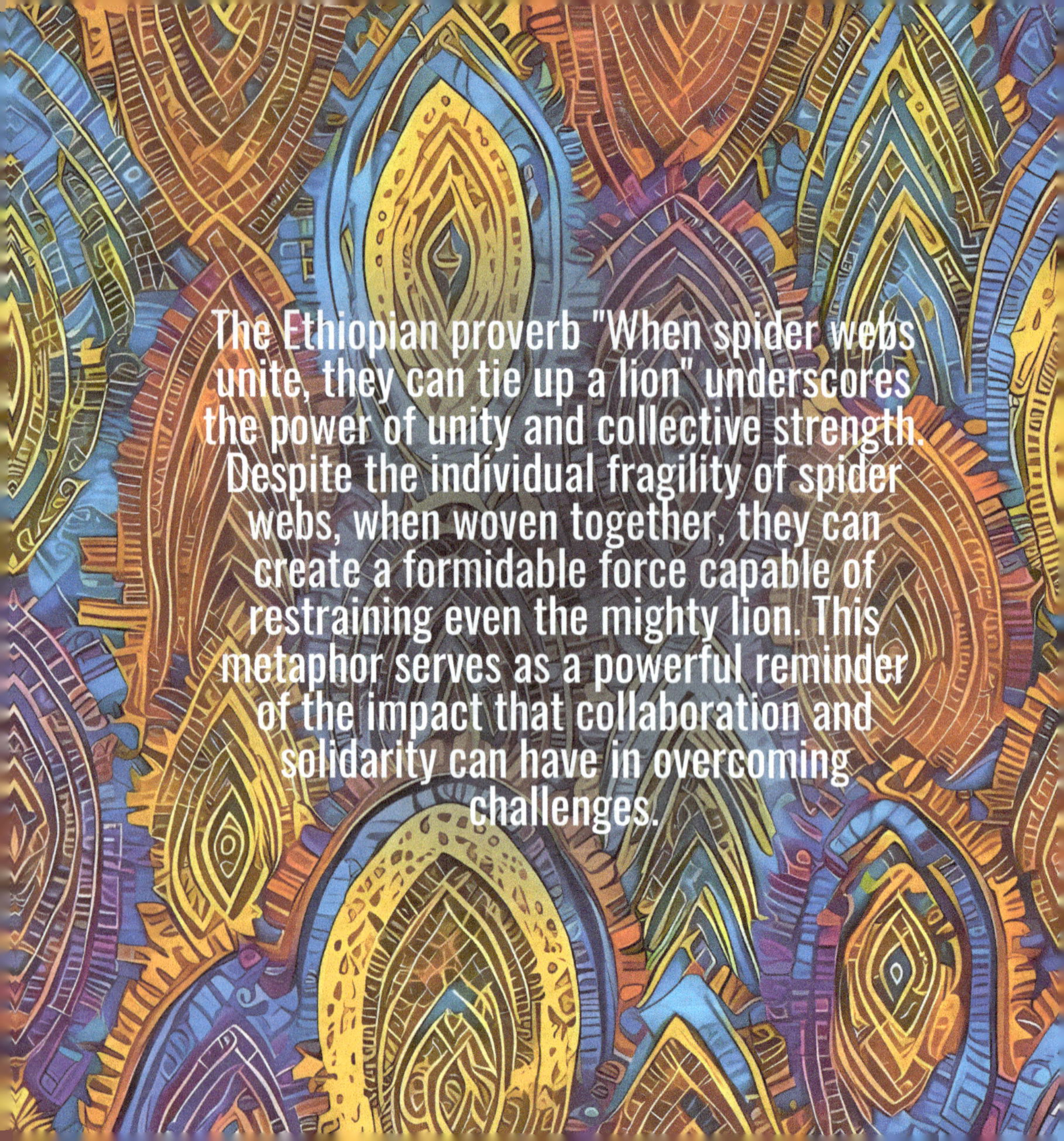

The Ethiopian proverb "When spider webs unite, they can tie up a lion" underscores the power of unity and collective strength. Despite the individual fragility of spider webs, when woven together, they can create a formidable force capable of restraining even the mighty lion. This metaphor serves as a powerful reminder of the impact that collaboration and solidarity can have in overcoming challenges.

ONE KIND WORD
CAN WARM THREE
WINTER MONTHS.
Taiwan

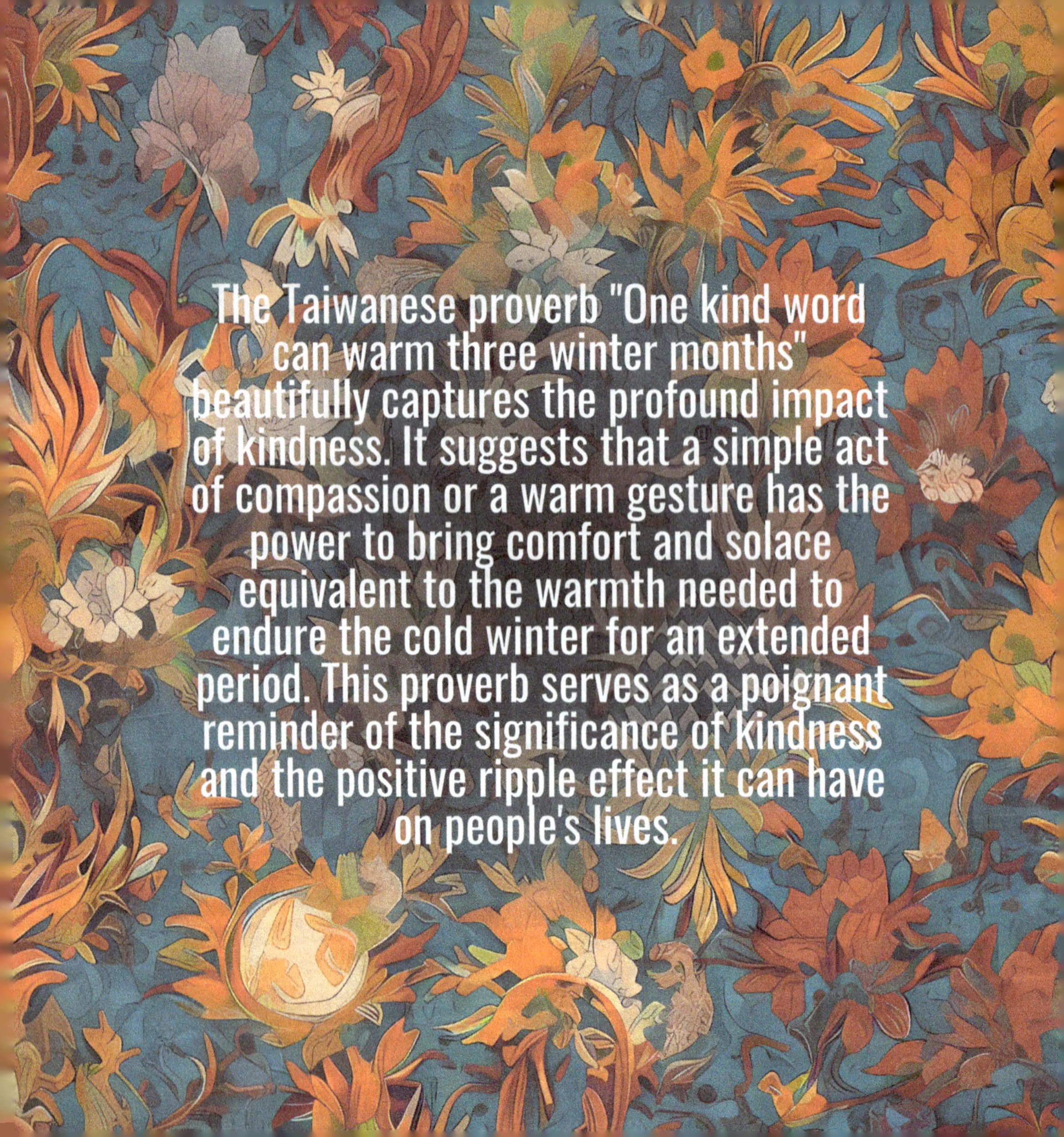

The Taiwanese proverb "One kind word can warm three winter months" beautifully captures the profound impact of kindness. It suggests that a simple act of compassion or a warm gesture has the power to bring comfort and solace equivalent to the warmth needed to endure the cold winter for an extended period. This proverb serves as a poignant reminder of the significance of kindness and the positive ripple effect it can have on people's lives.

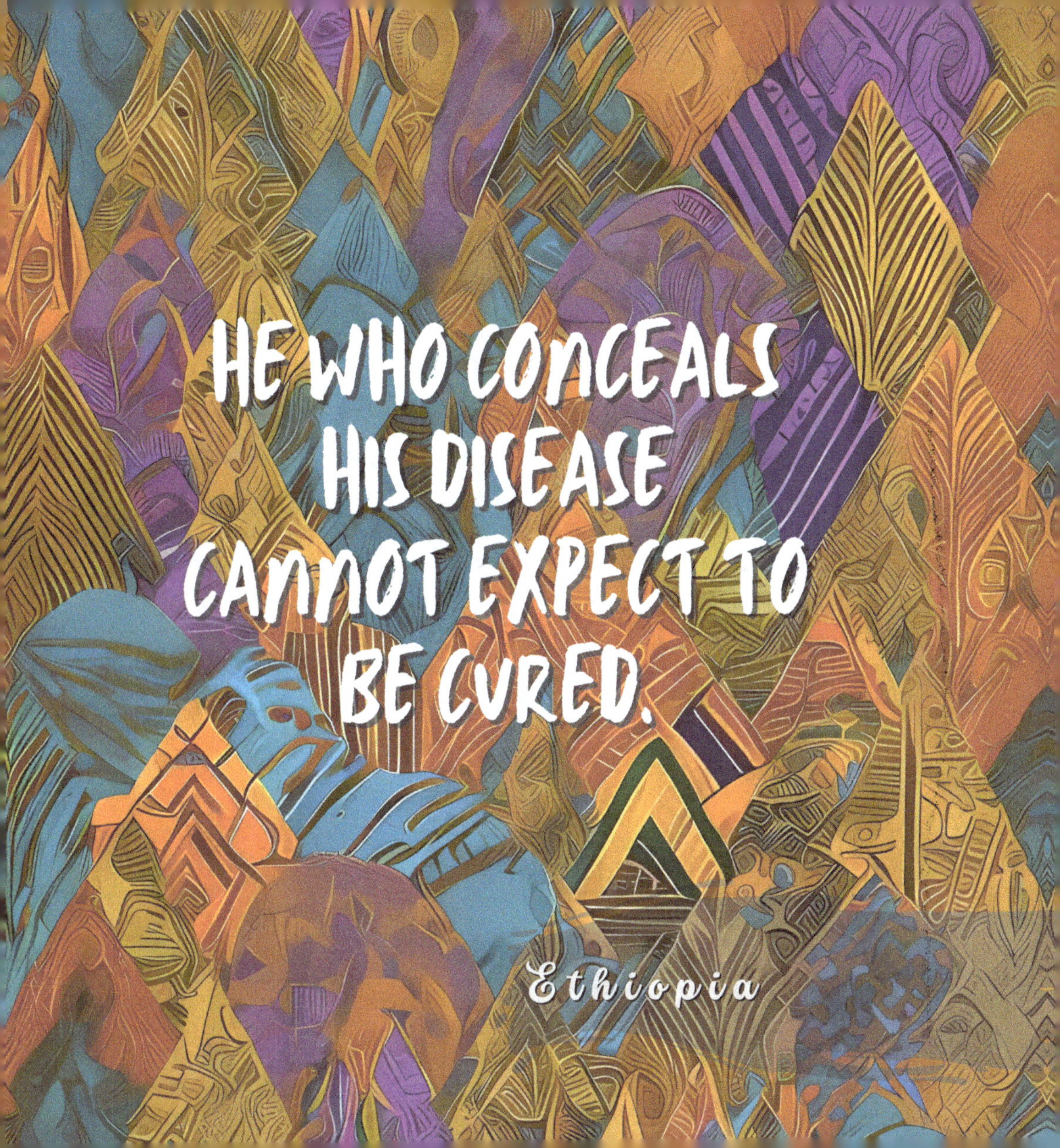
HE WHO CONCEALS
HIS DISEASE
CANNOT EXPECT TO
BE CURED.
Ethiopia

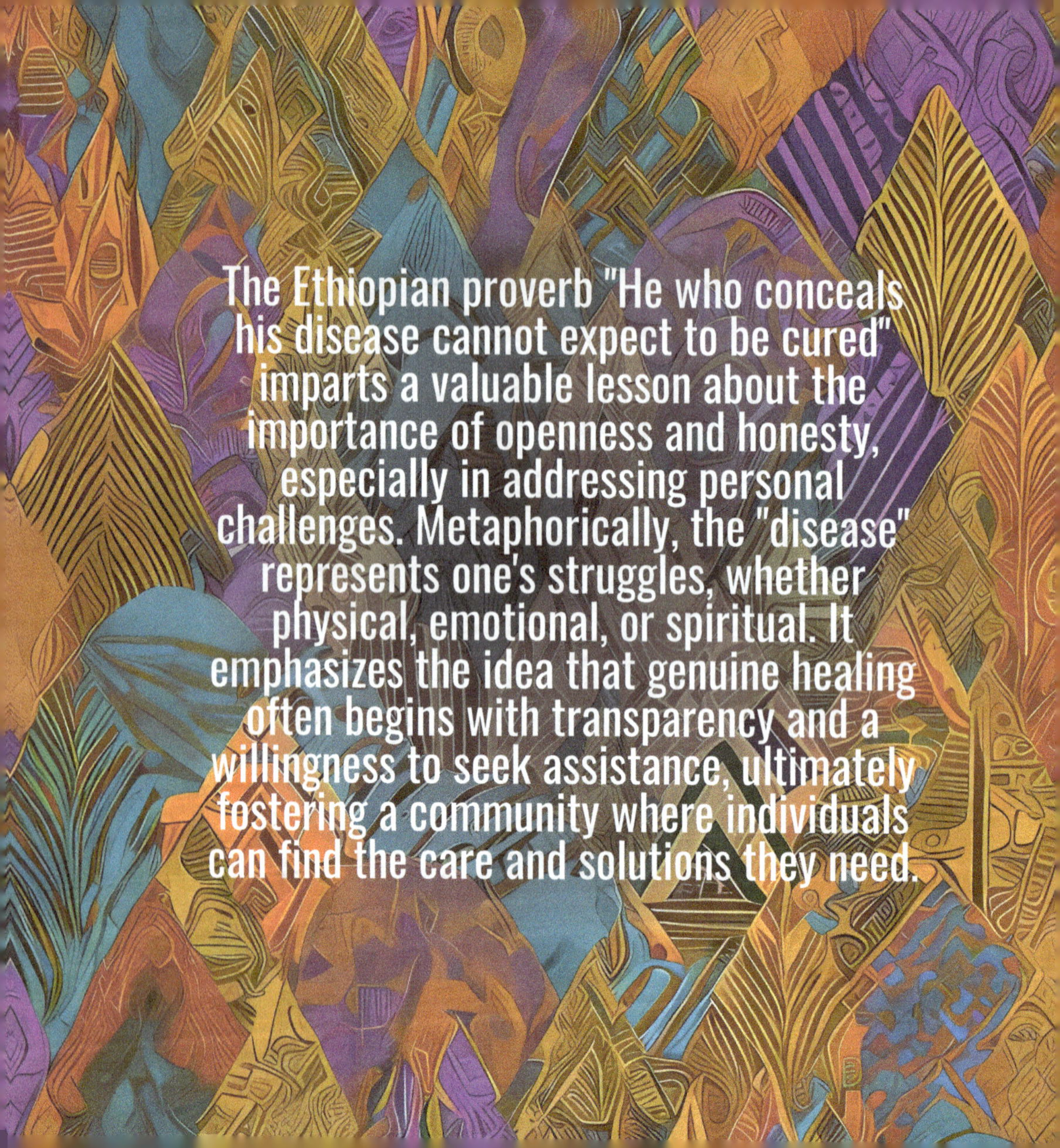
The Ethiopian proverb "He who conceals his disease cannot expect to be cured" imparts a valuable lesson about the importance of openness and honesty, especially in addressing personal challenges. Metaphorically, the "disease" represents one's struggles, whether physical, emotional, or spiritual. It emphasizes the idea that genuine healing often begins with transparency and a willingness to seek assistance, ultimately fostering a community where individuals can find the care and solutions they need.

A WISE MAN WHO KNOWS PROVERBS RECONCILES DIFFICULTIES.
Senegal

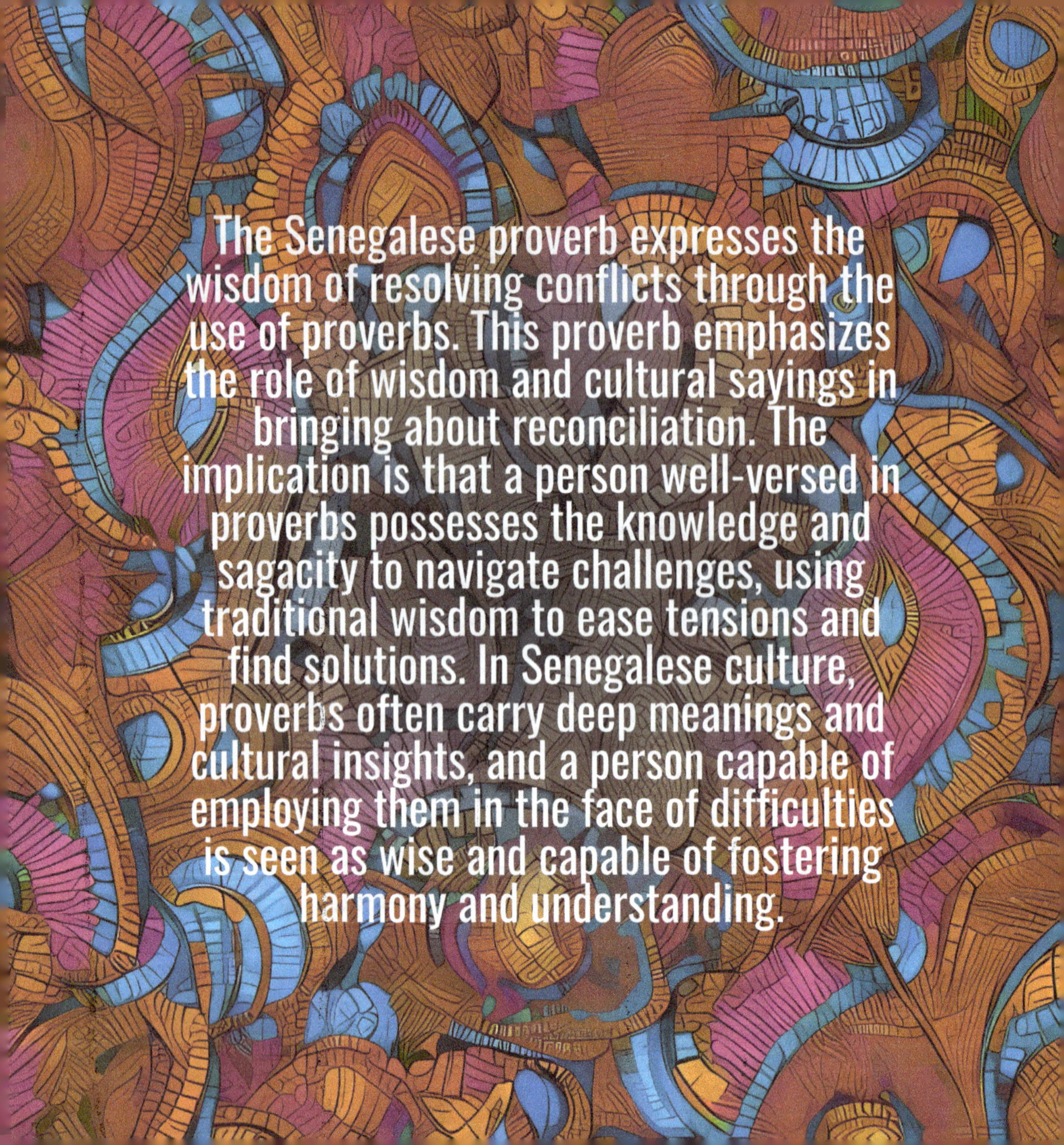

The Senegalese proverb expresses the wisdom of resolving conflicts through the use of proverbs. This proverb emphasizes the role of wisdom and cultural sayings in bringing about reconciliation. The implication is that a person well-versed in proverbs possesses the knowledge and sagacity to navigate challenges, using traditional wisdom to ease tensions and find solutions. In Senegalese culture, proverbs often carry deep meanings and cultural insights, and a person capable of employing them in the face of difficulties is seen as wise and capable of fostering harmony and understanding.

ONE COCONUT AT A TIME FILLS THE BASKET.
Jamaica

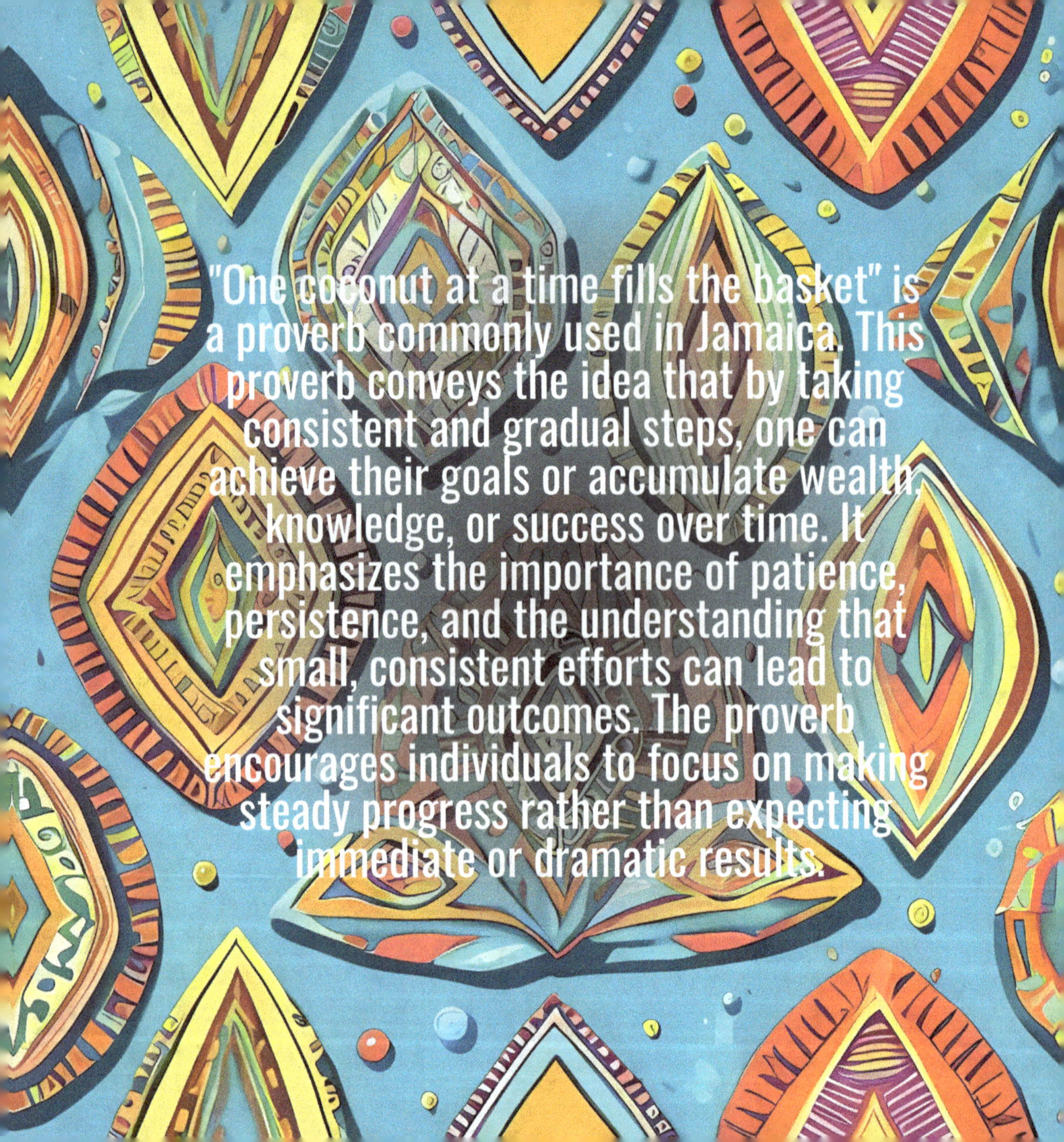
"One coconut at a time fills the basket" is a proverb commonly used in Jamaica. This proverb conveys the idea that by taking consistent and gradual steps, one can achieve their goals or accumulate wealth, knowledge, or success over time. It emphasizes the importance of patience, persistence, and the understanding that small, consistent efforts can lead to significant outcomes. The proverb encourages individuals to focus on making steady progress rather than expecting immediate or dramatic results.

A BIRD DOES NOT
CHANGE ITS
FEATHERS BECAUSE
THE WEATHER IS
BAD.
Nigeria

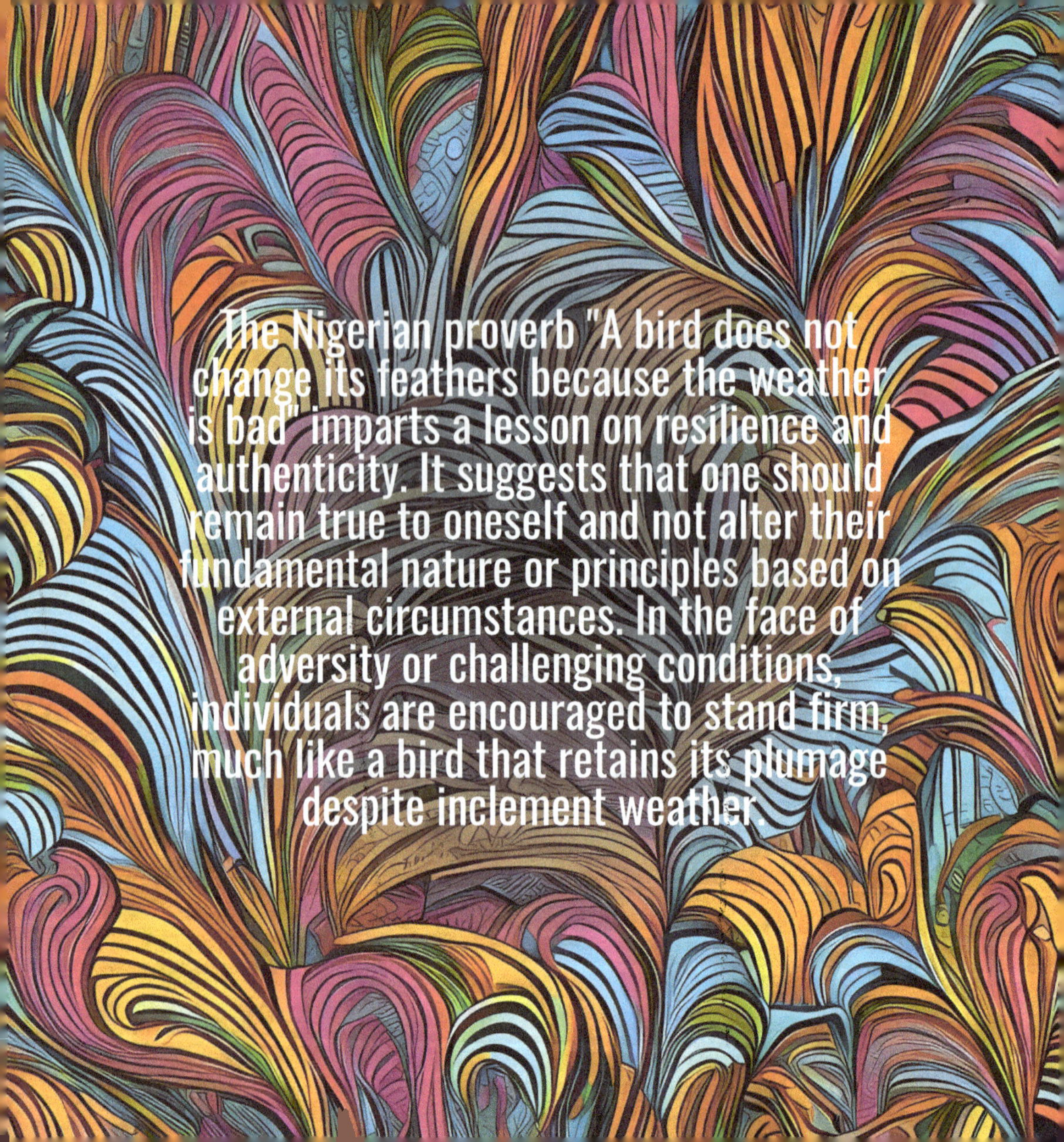
The Nigerian proverb "A bird does not change its feathers because the weather is bad" imparts a lesson on resilience and authenticity. It suggests that one should remain true to oneself and not alter their fundamental nature or principles based on external circumstances. In the face of adversity or challenging conditions, individuals are encouraged to stand firm, much like a bird that retains its plumage despite inclement weather.

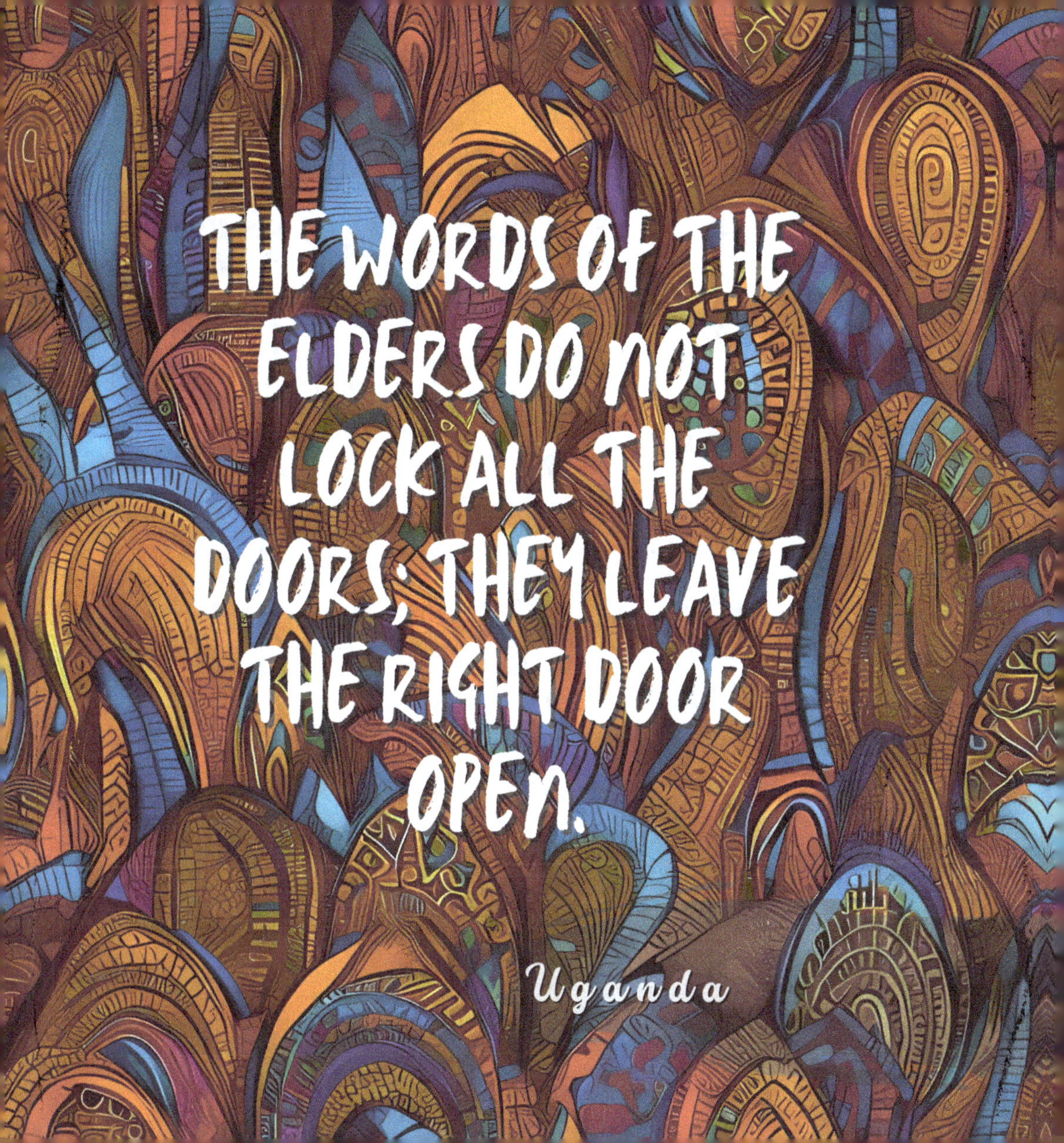
THE WORDS OF THE ELDERS DO NOT LOCK ALL THE DOORS; THEY LEAVE THE RIGHT DOOR OPEN.
Uganda

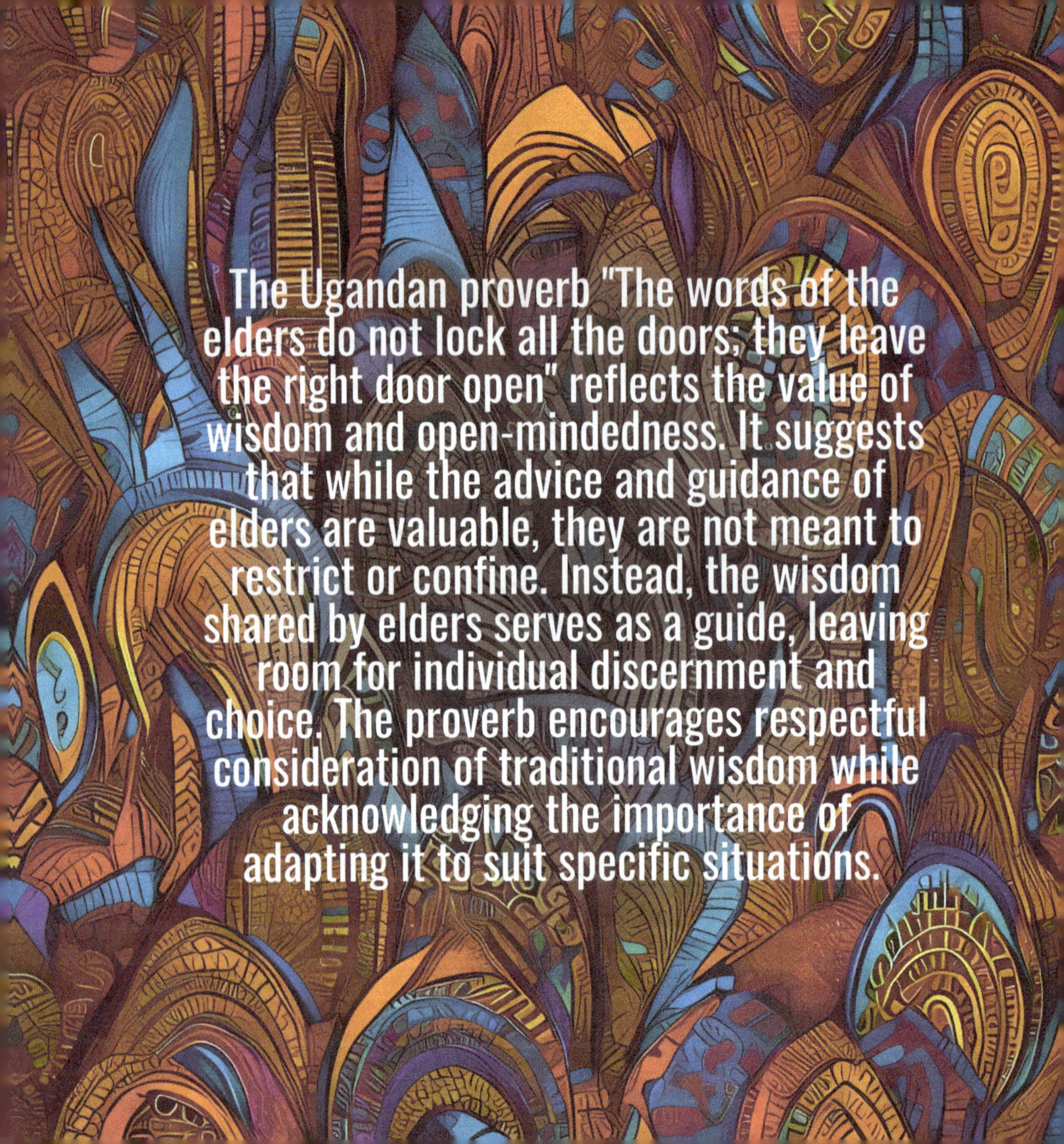

The Ugandan proverb "The words of the elders do not lock all the doors; they leave the right door open" reflects the value of wisdom and open-mindedness. It suggests that while the advice and guidance of elders are valuable, they are not meant to restrict or confine. Instead, the wisdom shared by elders serves as a guide, leaving room for individual discernment and choice. The proverb encourages respectful consideration of traditional wisdom while acknowledging the importance of adapting it to suit specific situations.

THE FOOLISH PERSON DOES NOT LEARN FROM HIS MISTAKES.
Bengali

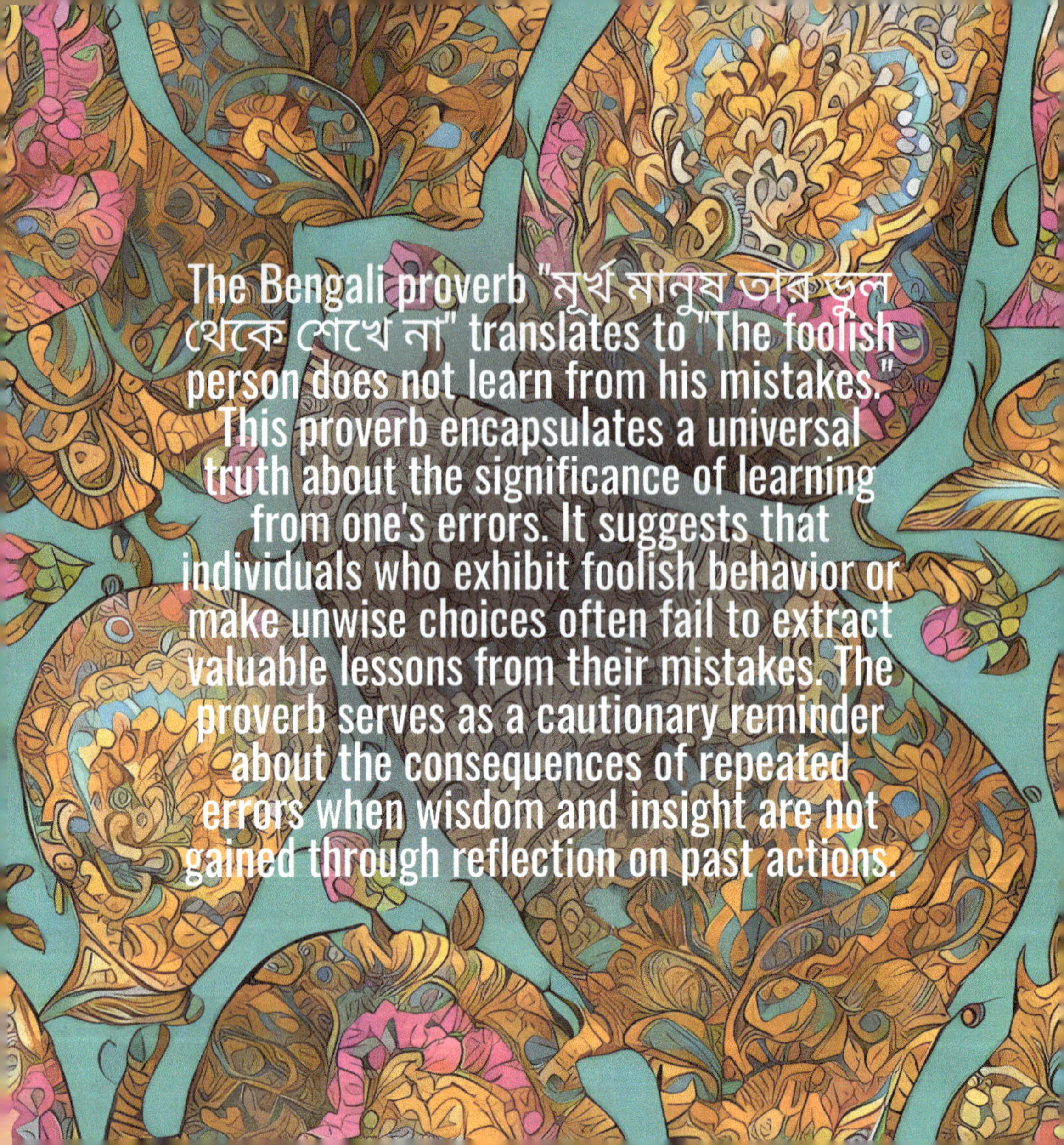

The Bengali proverb "মূর্খ মানুষ তার ভুল থেকে শেখে না" translates to "The foolish person does not learn from his mistakes." This proverb encapsulates a universal truth about the significance of learning from one's errors. It suggests that individuals who exhibit foolish behavior or make unwise choices often fail to extract valuable lessons from their mistakes. The proverb serves as a cautionary reminder about the consequences of repeated errors when wisdom and insight are not gained through reflection on past actions.

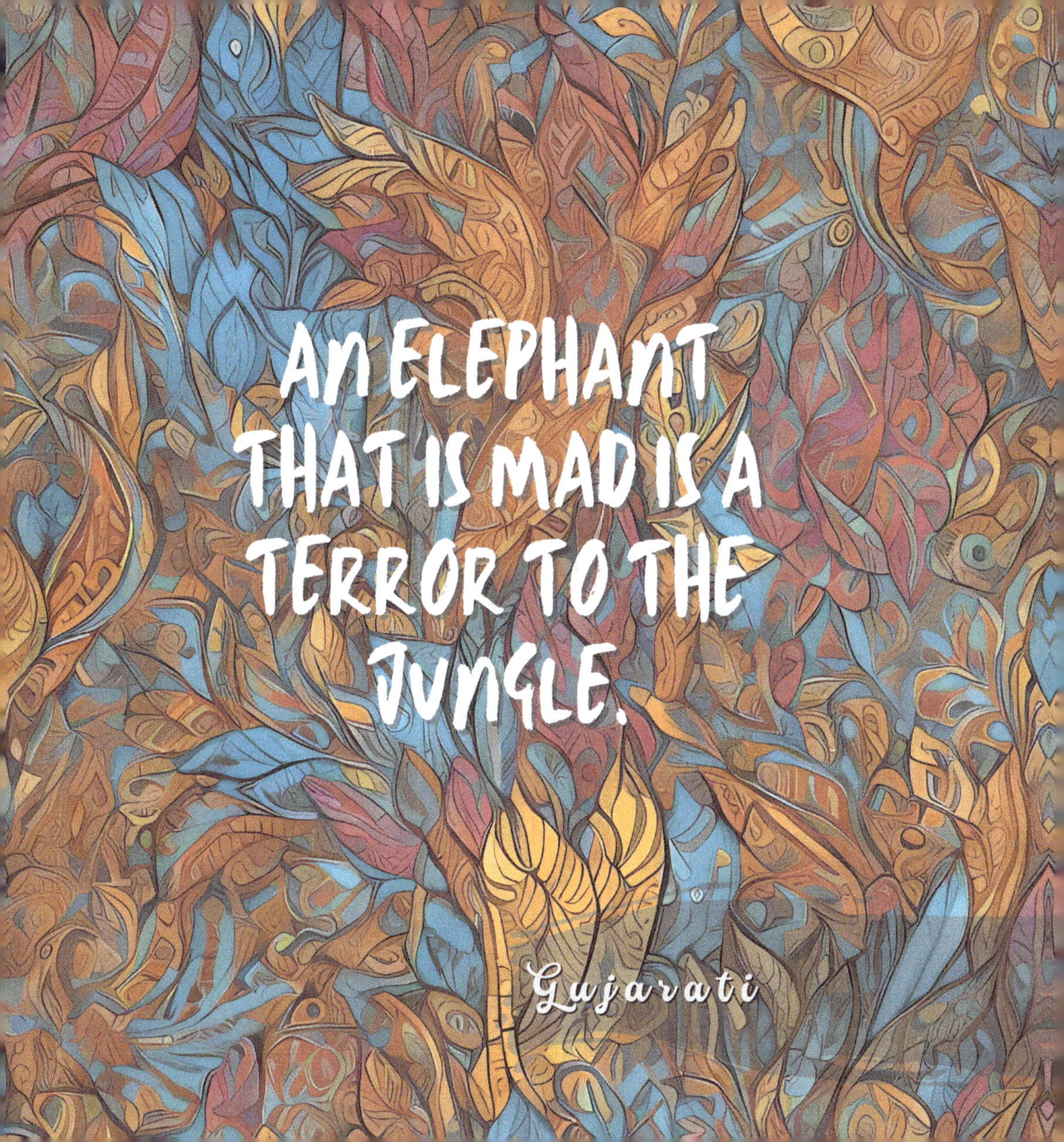
AN ELEPHANT
THAT IS MAD IS A
TERROR TO THE
JUNGLE.
Gujarati

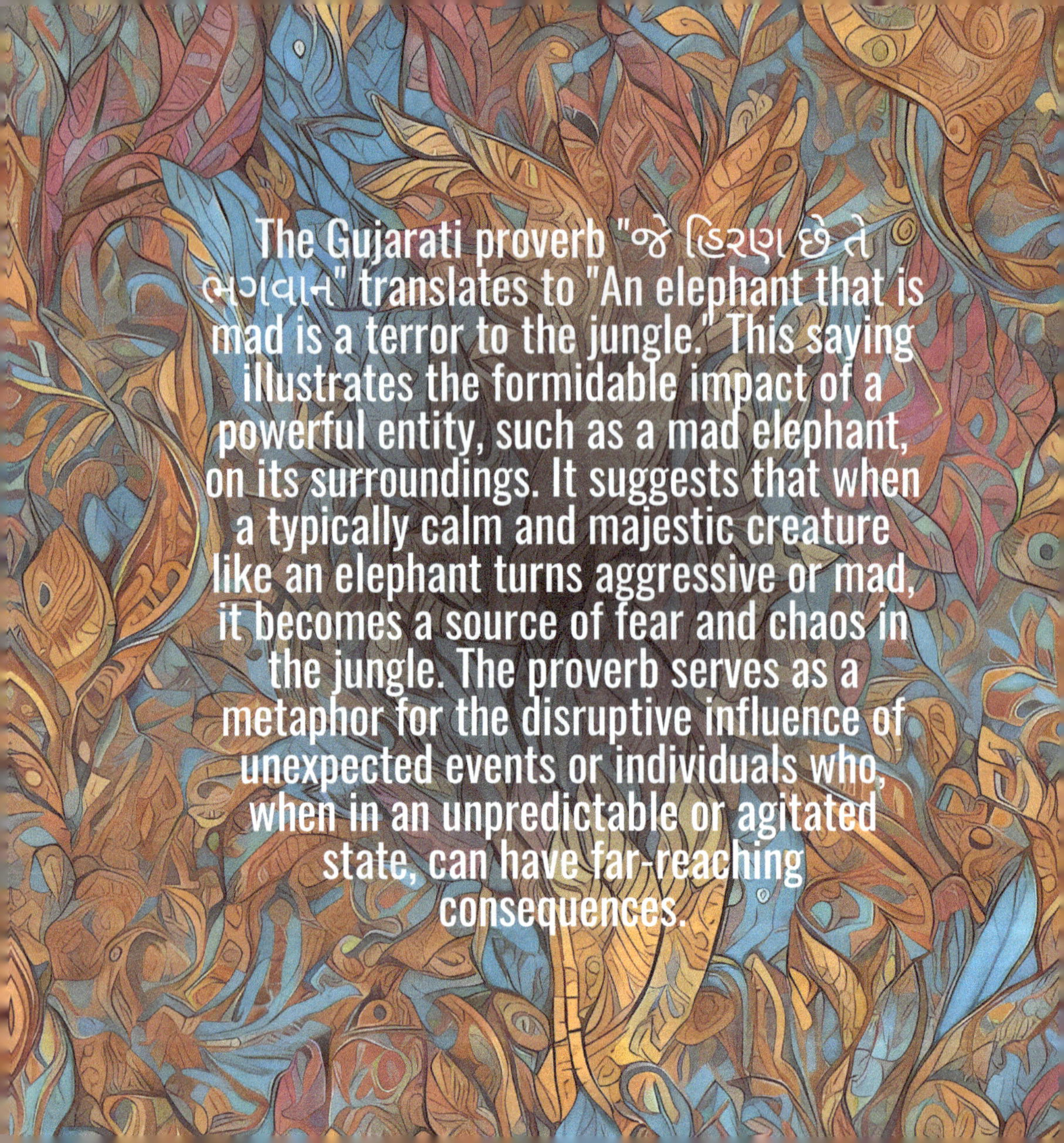
The Gujarati proverb "જે હિરણ છે તે ભગવાન" translates to "An elephant that is mad is a terror to the jungle." This saying illustrates the formidable impact of a powerful entity, such as a mad elephant, on its surroundings. It suggests that when a typically calm and majestic creature like an elephant turns aggressive or mad, it becomes a source of fear and chaos in the jungle. The proverb serves as a metaphor for the disruptive influence of unexpected events or individuals who, when in an unpredictable or agitated state, can have far-reaching consequences.

A GOOD BULL IS RECOGNIZED IN ITS OWN HERD.
Kannada

The Kannada proverb "ಒಳ್ಳೆಯ ಎಮ್ಮೆ ತನ್ನ ಹೊರಡಿಲಿಯಲ್ಲಿ ಗುರುತಿಸಲಾಗುತ್ತದೆ" translates to "A good bull is recognized in its own herd." This proverb speaks to the notion that true worth and excellence are often most apparent and appreciated within familiar surroundings. The saying implies that the exceptional qualities of a valuable individual, symbolized by the 'good bull,' become evident and recognized by those who are closest and most familiar with the person. It emphasizes the importance of being acknowledged and valued within one's own community or circle, suggesting that genuine recognition often comes from those who intimately understand and appreciate the qualities and contributions of the individual in their natural environment.

EVEN THE MOON
HAS SPOTS.
Marathi

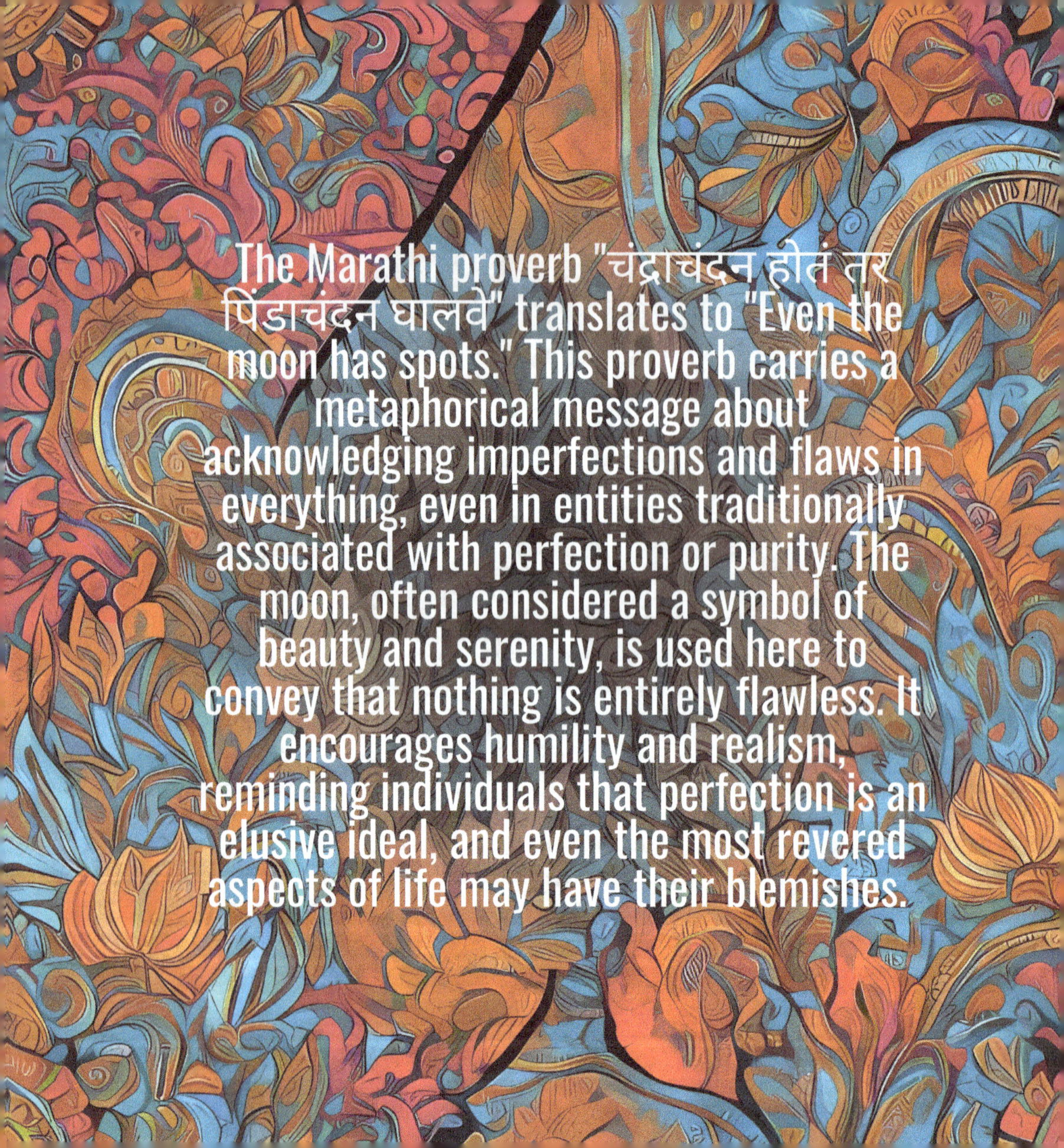

The Marathi proverb "चंद्राचंदन होतं तर पिंडाचंदन घालवे" translates to "Even the moon has spots." This proverb carries a metaphorical message about acknowledging imperfections and flaws in everything, even in entities traditionally associated with perfection or purity. The moon, often considered a symbol of beauty and serenity, is used here to convey that nothing is entirely flawless. It encourages humility and realism, reminding individuals that perfection is an elusive ideal, and even the most revered aspects of life may have their blemishes.

EVERY MAN IS THE ARCHITECT OF HIS OWN FORTUNE.
Ancient Rome

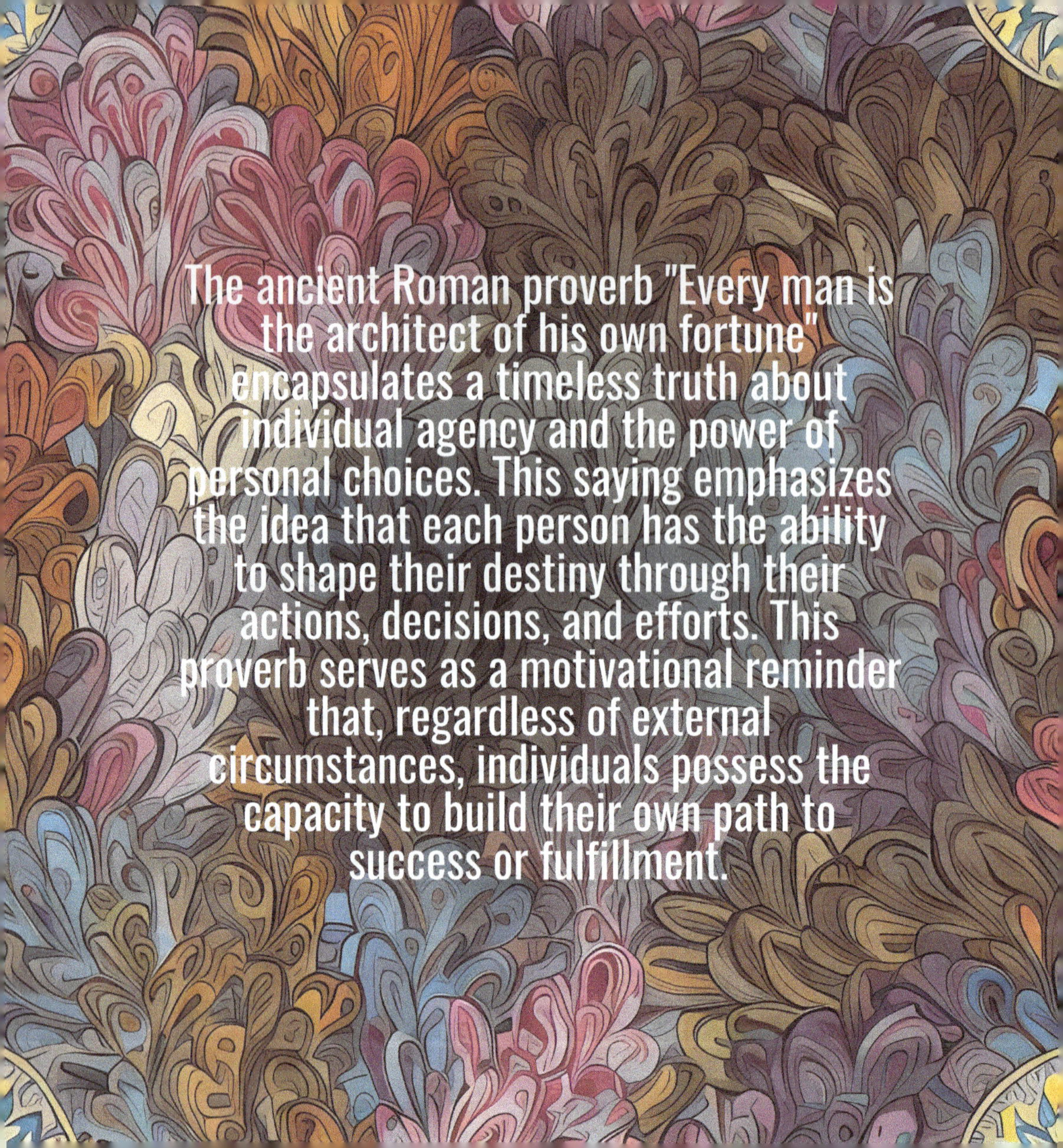
The ancient Roman proverb "Every man is the architect of his own fortune" encapsulates a timeless truth about individual agency and the power of personal choices. This saying emphasizes the idea that each person has the ability to shape their destiny through their actions, decisions, and efforts. This proverb serves as a motivational reminder that, regardless of external circumstances, individuals possess the capacity to build their own path to success or fulfillment.

CUT YOUR COAT
ACCORDING TO
YOUR CLOTH.
England

The British proverb "Cut your coat according to your cloth" imparts a practical and prudent piece of advice about managing resources wisely. It serves as a reminder to exercise prudence and avoid overextending oneself, promoting a balanced and responsible approach to decision-making and goal-setting.

A SNAKE DOES NOT
GIVE BIRTH TO A
DOVE.
Assamese

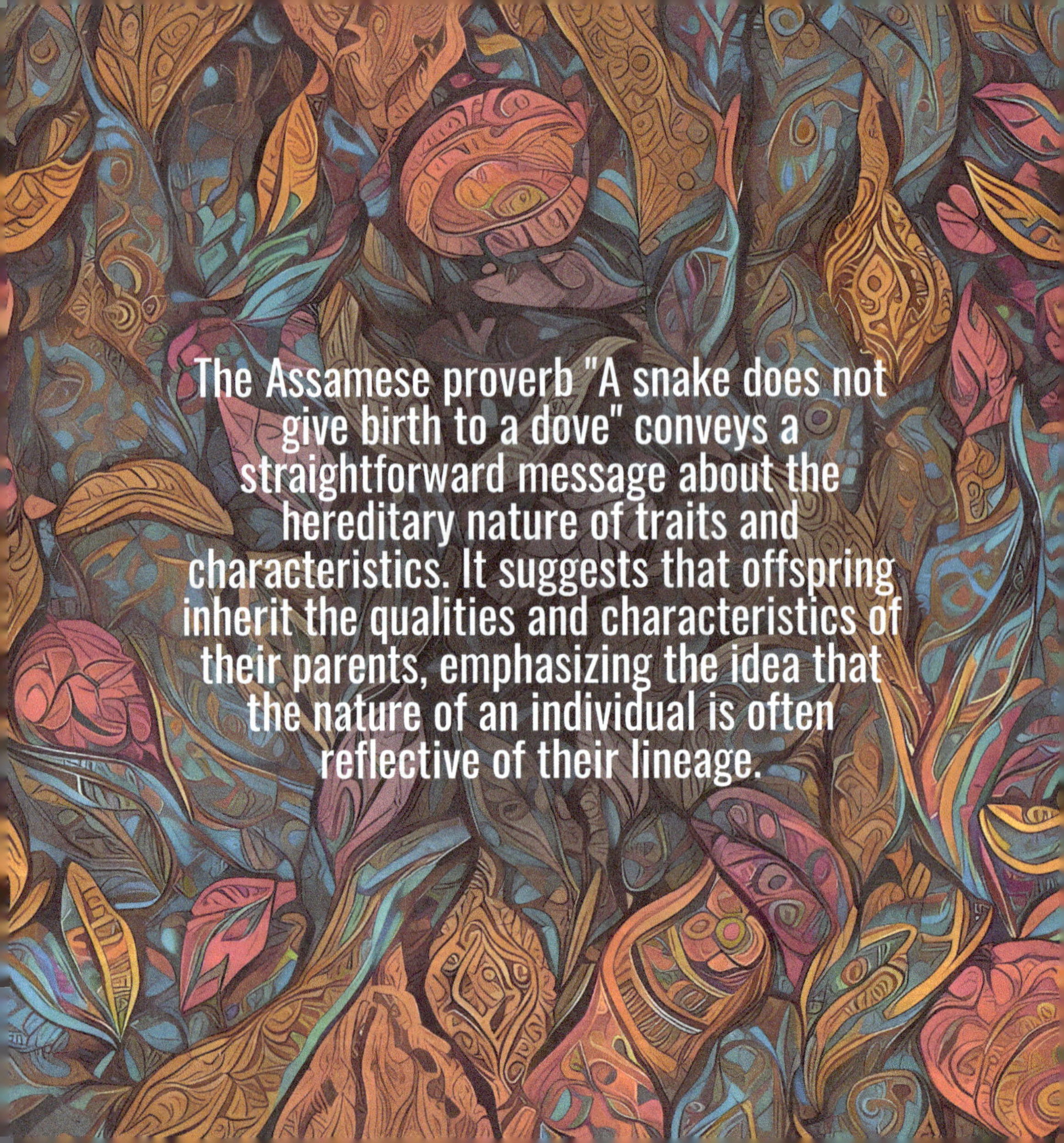

The Assamese proverb "A snake does not give birth to a dove" conveys a straightforward message about the hereditary nature of traits and characteristics. It suggests that offspring inherit the qualities and characteristics of their parents, emphasizing the idea that the nature of an individual is often reflective of their lineage.

WHAT YOU SOW,
YOU REAP.
Kannada

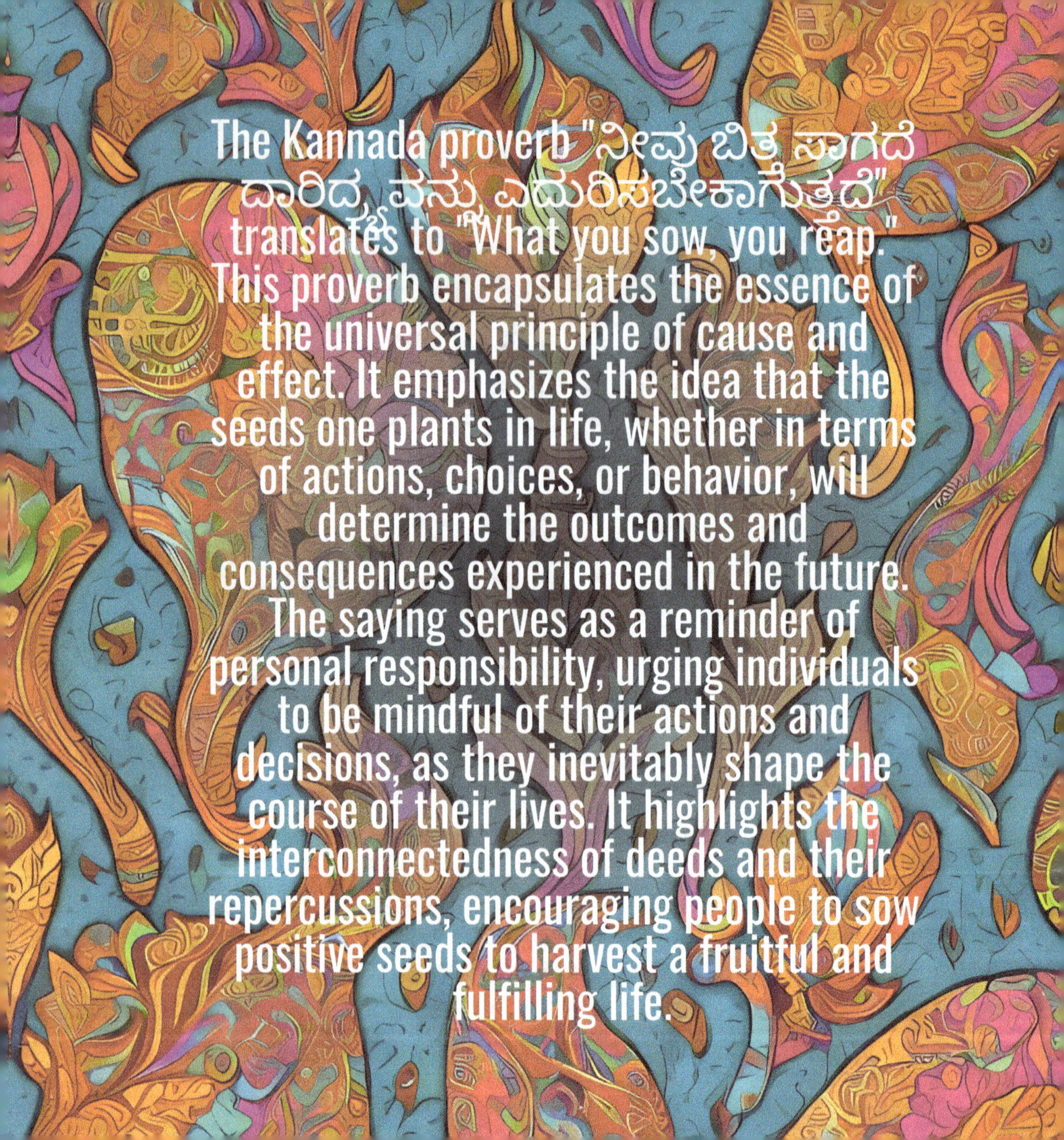
The Kannada proverb "ನೀವು ಬಿತ್ತ ಸಾಗದೆ ದಾರಿದ, ವನ್ನು ಎದುರಿಸಬೇಕಾಗುತ್ತದೆ" translates to "What you sow, you reap." This proverb encapsulates the essence of the universal principle of cause and effect. It emphasizes the idea that the seeds one plants in life, whether in terms of actions, choices, or behavior, will determine the outcomes and consequences experienced in the future. The saying serves as a reminder of personal responsibility, urging individuals to be mindful of their actions and decisions, as they inevitably shape the course of their lives. It highlights the interconnectedness of deeds and their repercussions, encouraging people to sow positive seeds to harvest a fruitful and fulfilling life.

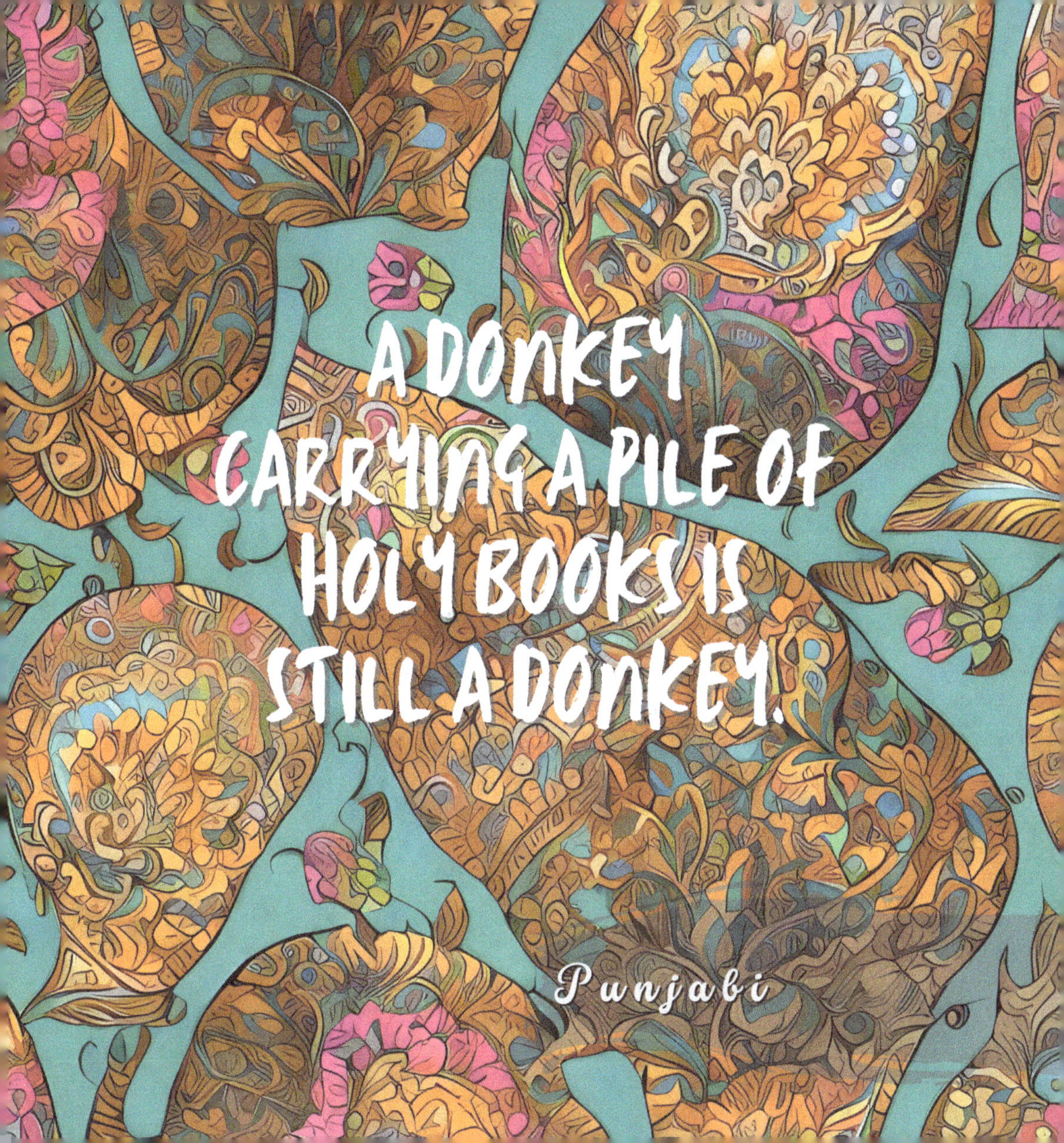
A DONKEY
CARRYING A PILE OF
HOLY BOOKS IS
STILL A DONKEY.
Punjabi

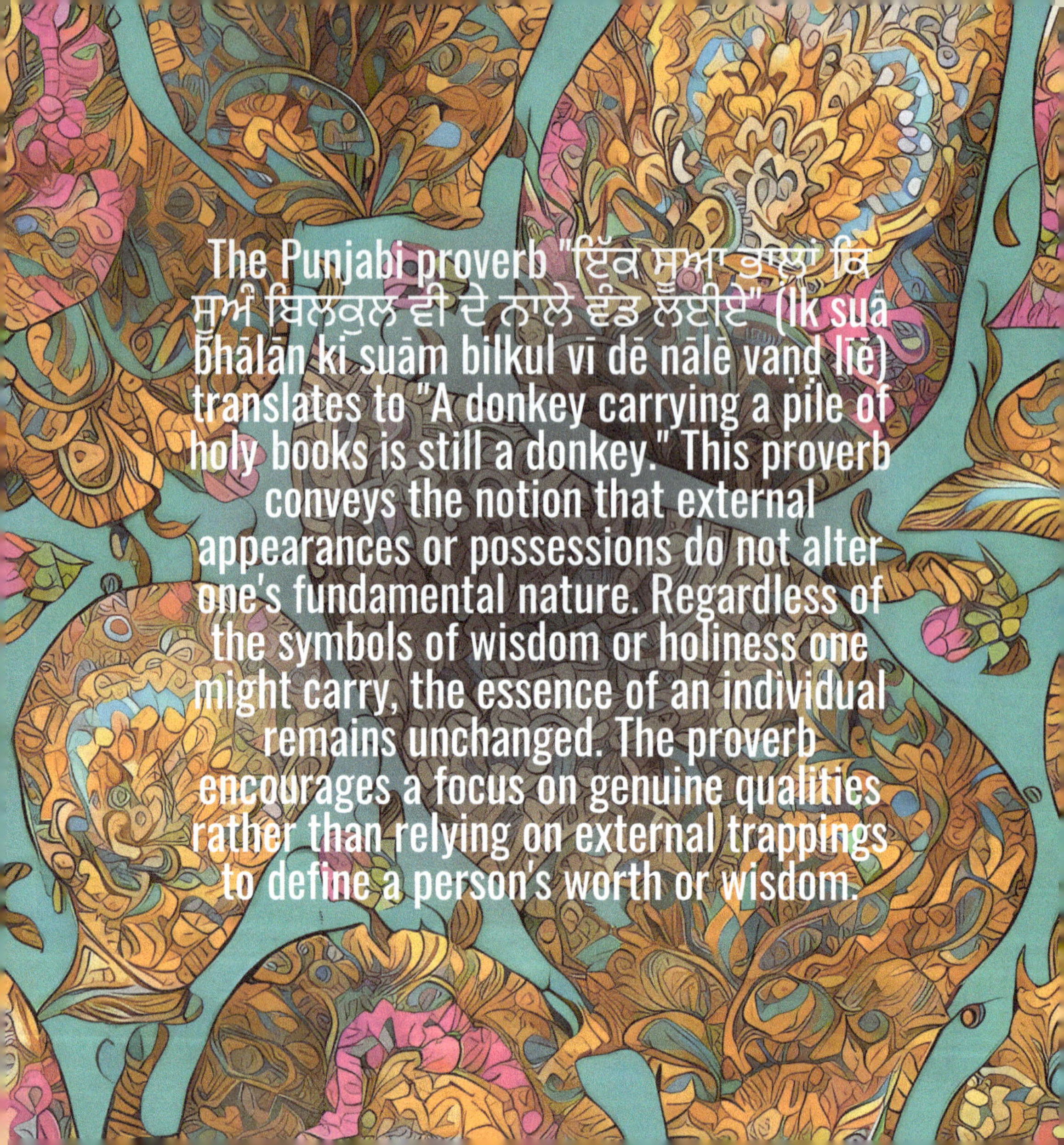

The Punjabi proverb "ਇੱਕ ਸੂਆ ਭਾਲ਼ਾਂ ਕਿ ਸੂਐਂ ਬਿਲਕੁਲ ਵੀ ਦੇ ਨਾਲੇ ਵੰਡ ਲੱਈਏ" (Ik suā bhālān ki suām bilkul vī dē nālē vanḍ līē) translates to "A donkey carrying a pile of holy books is still a donkey." This proverb conveys the notion that external appearances or possessions do not alter one's fundamental nature. Regardless of the symbols of wisdom or holiness one might carry, the essence of an individual remains unchanged. The proverb encourages a focus on genuine qualities rather than relying on external trappings to define a person's worth or wisdom.

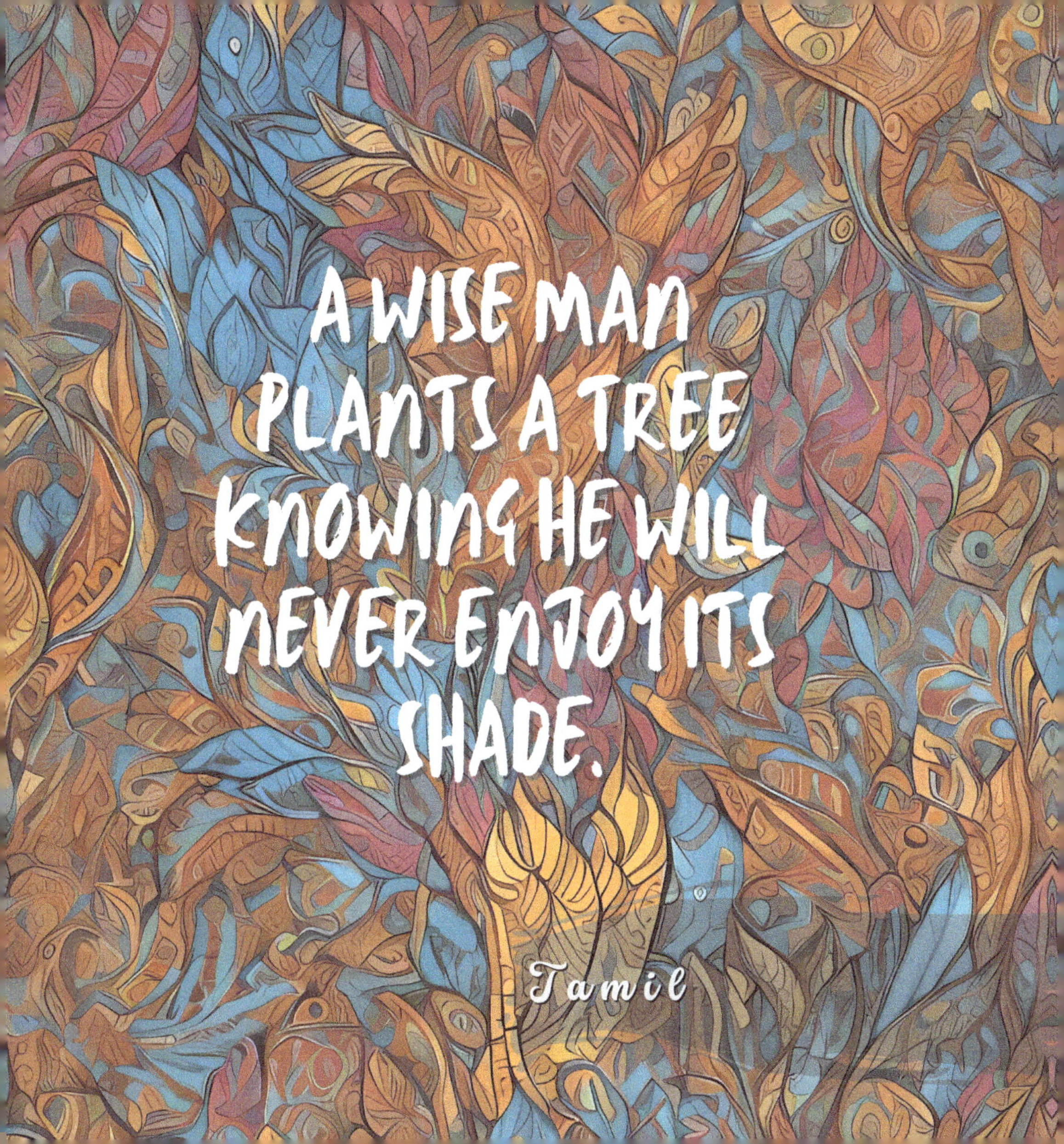
A WISE MAN
PLANTS A TREE
KNOWING HE WILL
NEVER ENJOY ITS
SHADE.
Tamil

The Tamil proverb "அறிவாளி அரசு விளக்கி வாழ்ந்தான் காடுக்குள்" (Aṟivāḷi arasu viḷakki vāḻntāṉ kāṭukkuḷ) conveys the wisdom of a person who plants a tree fully aware that they may never personally benefit from its shade. This proverb encapsulates the selfless and forward-thinking nature of wise individuals who contribute to the well-being of future generations without expecting immediate rewards. It encourages the cultivation of knowledge, growth, and positive contributions to society, emphasizing the importance of actions that have enduring and far-reaching benefits, even if the individual may not witness the fruits of their efforts in their lifetime.

ONE WHO DOES NOT
LISTEN TO ADVICE,
WILL LEARN
THROUGH
EXPERIENCE.
Marathi

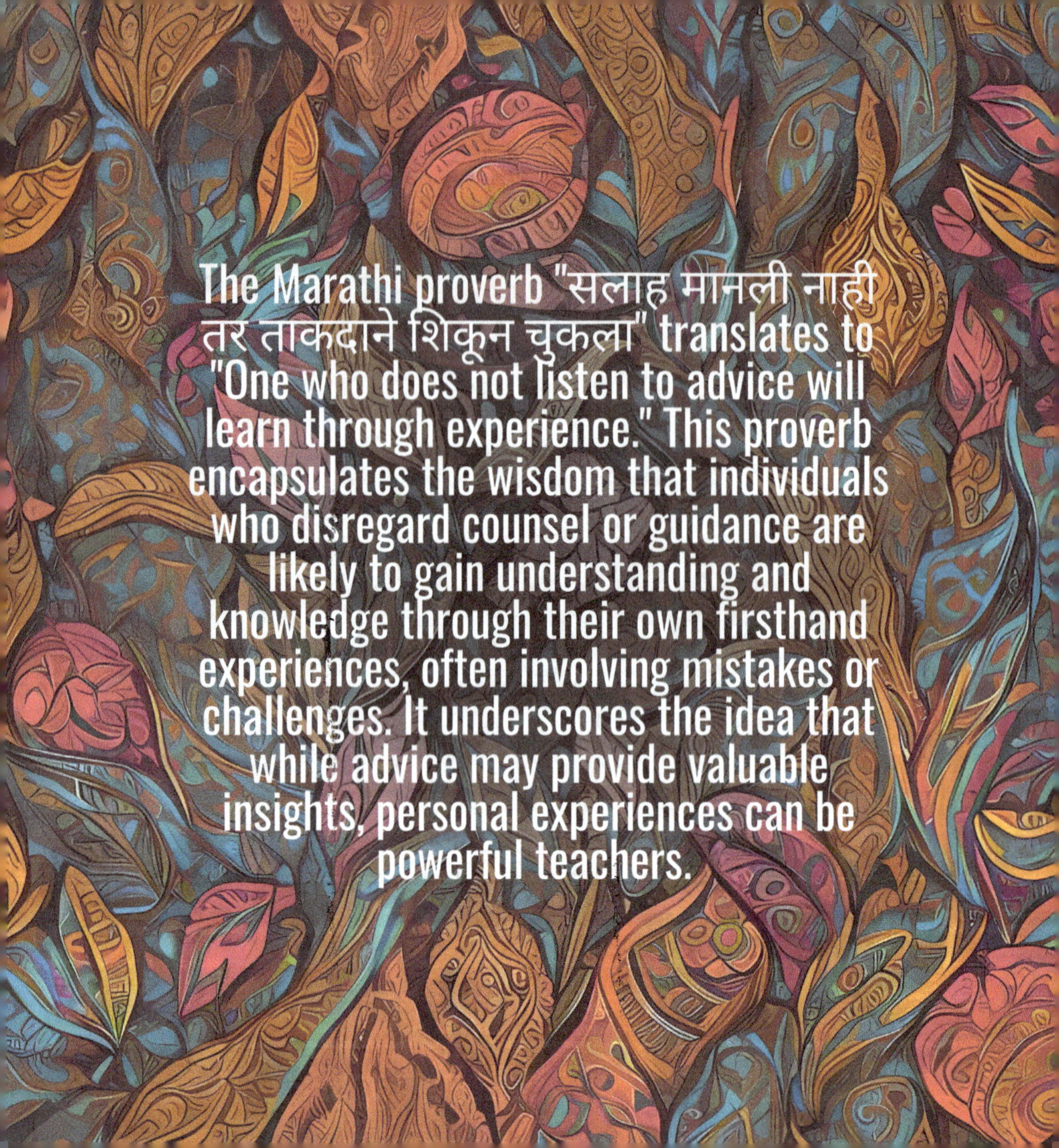

The Marathi proverb "सलाह मामली नाही तर ताकदाने शिकून चुकला" translates to "One who does not listen to advice will learn through experience." This proverb encapsulates the wisdom that individuals who disregard counsel or guidance are likely to gain understanding and knowledge through their own firsthand experiences, often involving mistakes or challenges. It underscores the idea that while advice may provide valuable insights, personal experiences can be powerful teachers.

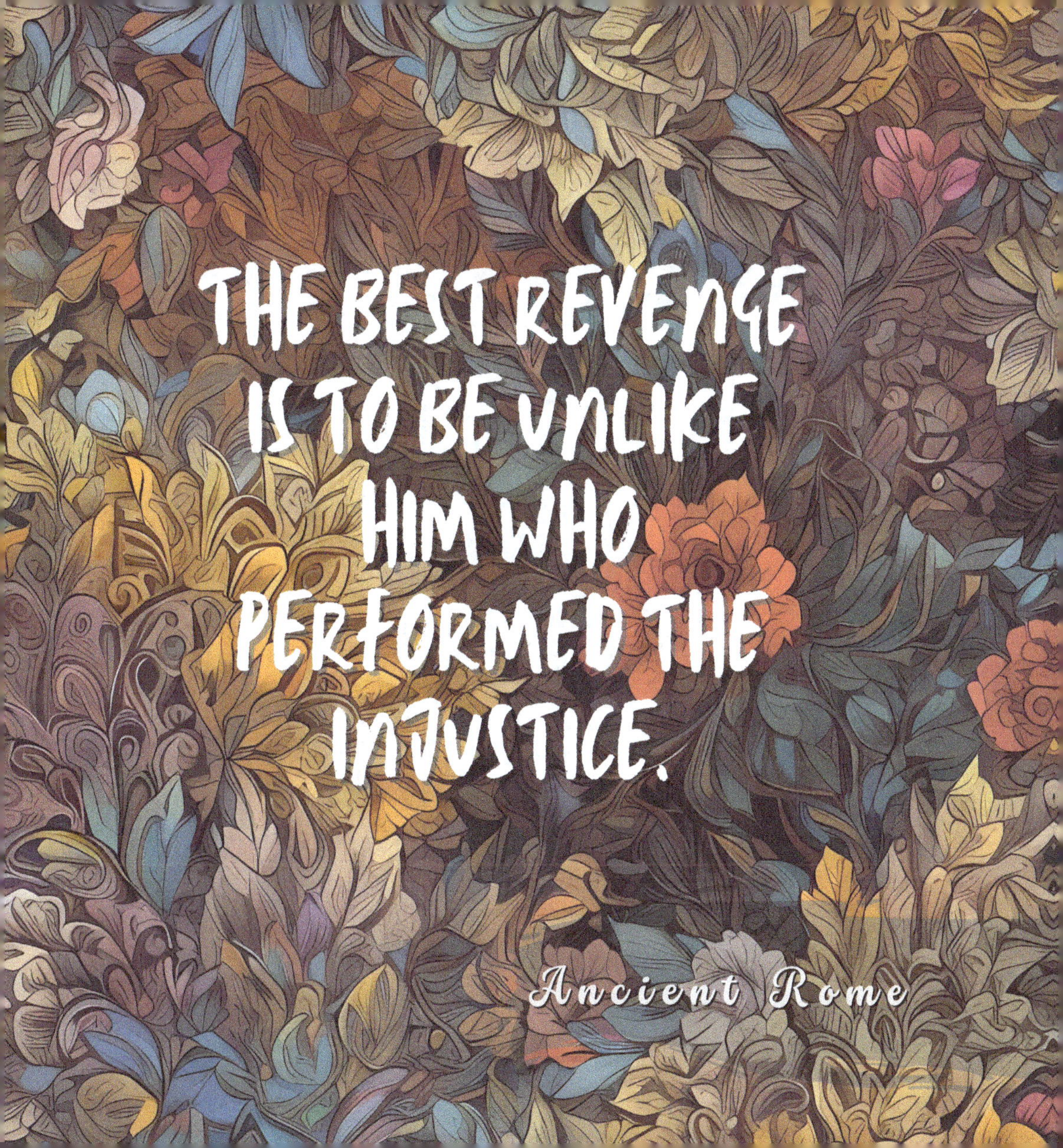
THE BEST REVENGE
IS TO BE UNLIKE
HIM WHO
PERFORMED THE
INJUSTICE.
Ancient Rome

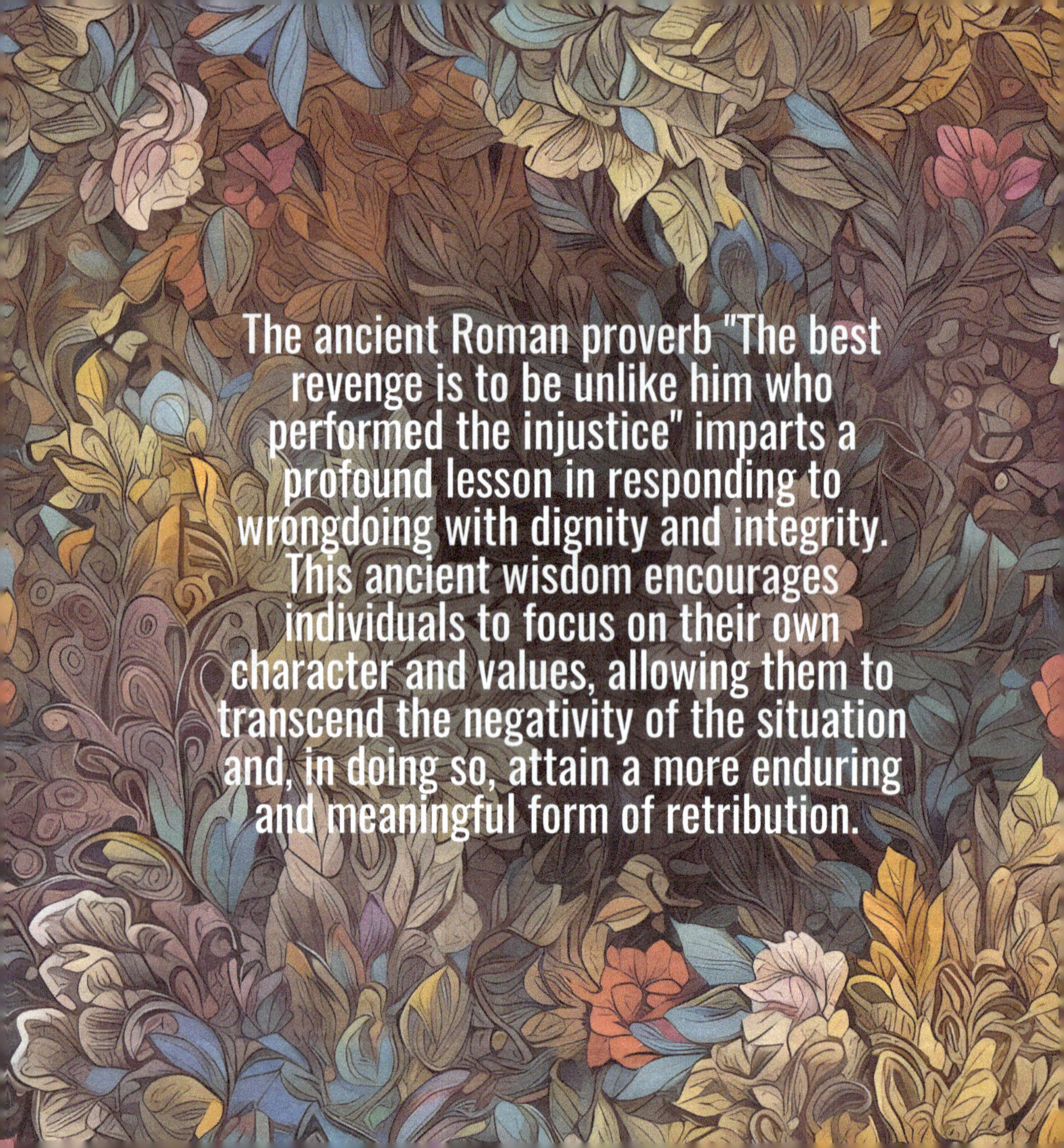
The ancient Roman proverb "The best revenge is to be unlike him who performed the injustice" imparts a profound lesson in responding to wrongdoing with dignity and integrity. This ancient wisdom encourages individuals to focus on their own character and values, allowing them to transcend the negativity of the situation and, in doing so, attain a more enduring and meaningful form of retribution.

THE GREATEST WEAKNESS OF ALL WEAKNESSES IS TO FEAR TOO MUCH TO APPEAR WEAK.
Czech

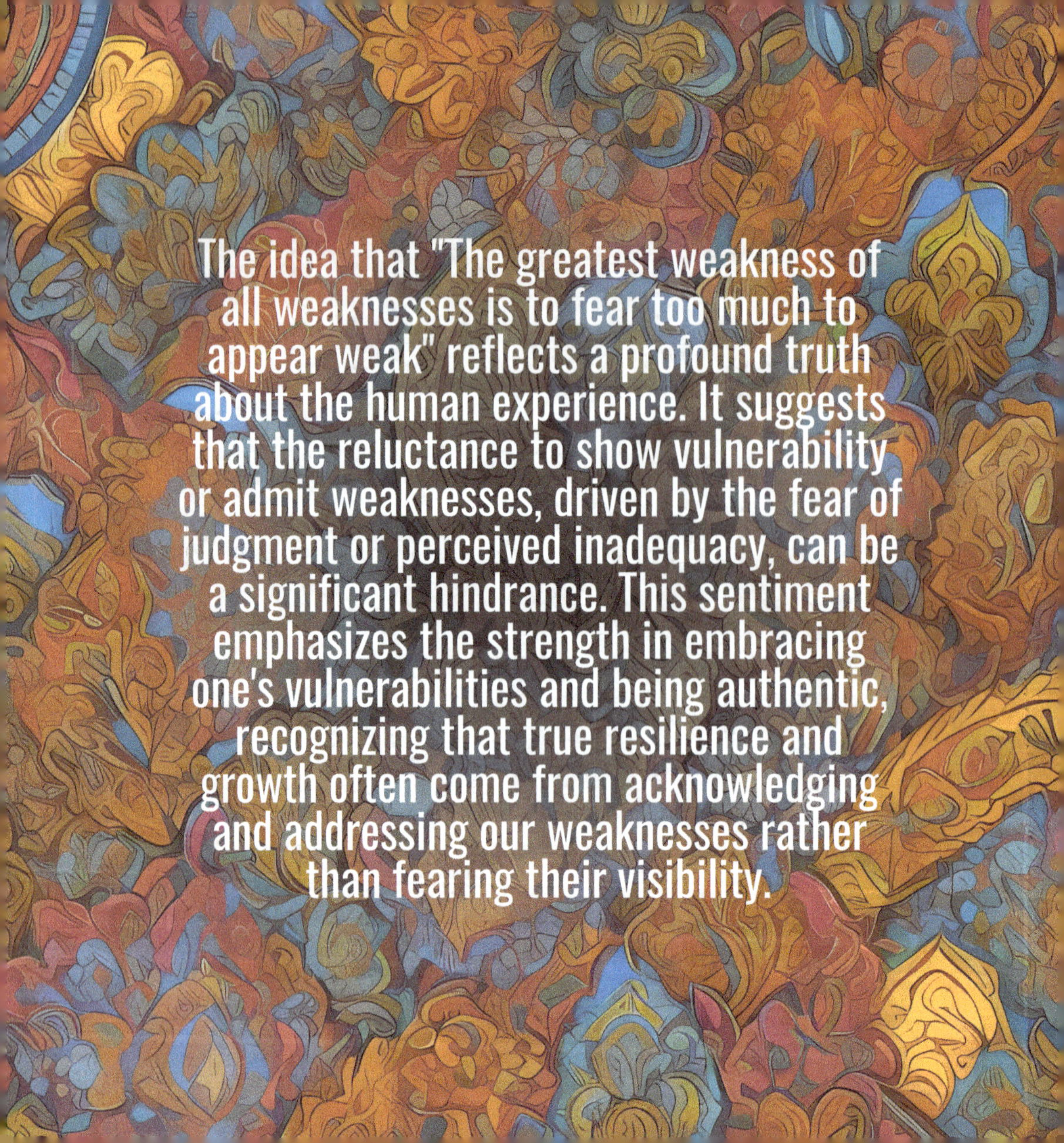

The idea that "The greatest weakness of all weaknesses is to fear too much to appear weak" reflects a profound truth about the human experience. It suggests that the reluctance to show vulnerability or admit weaknesses, driven by the fear of judgment or perceived inadequacy, can be a significant hindrance. This sentiment emphasizes the strength in embracing one's vulnerabilities and being authentic, recognizing that true resilience and growth often come from acknowledging and addressing our weaknesses rather than fearing their visibility.

A SMOOTH SEA
NEVER MADE A
SKILLED SAILOR.
England

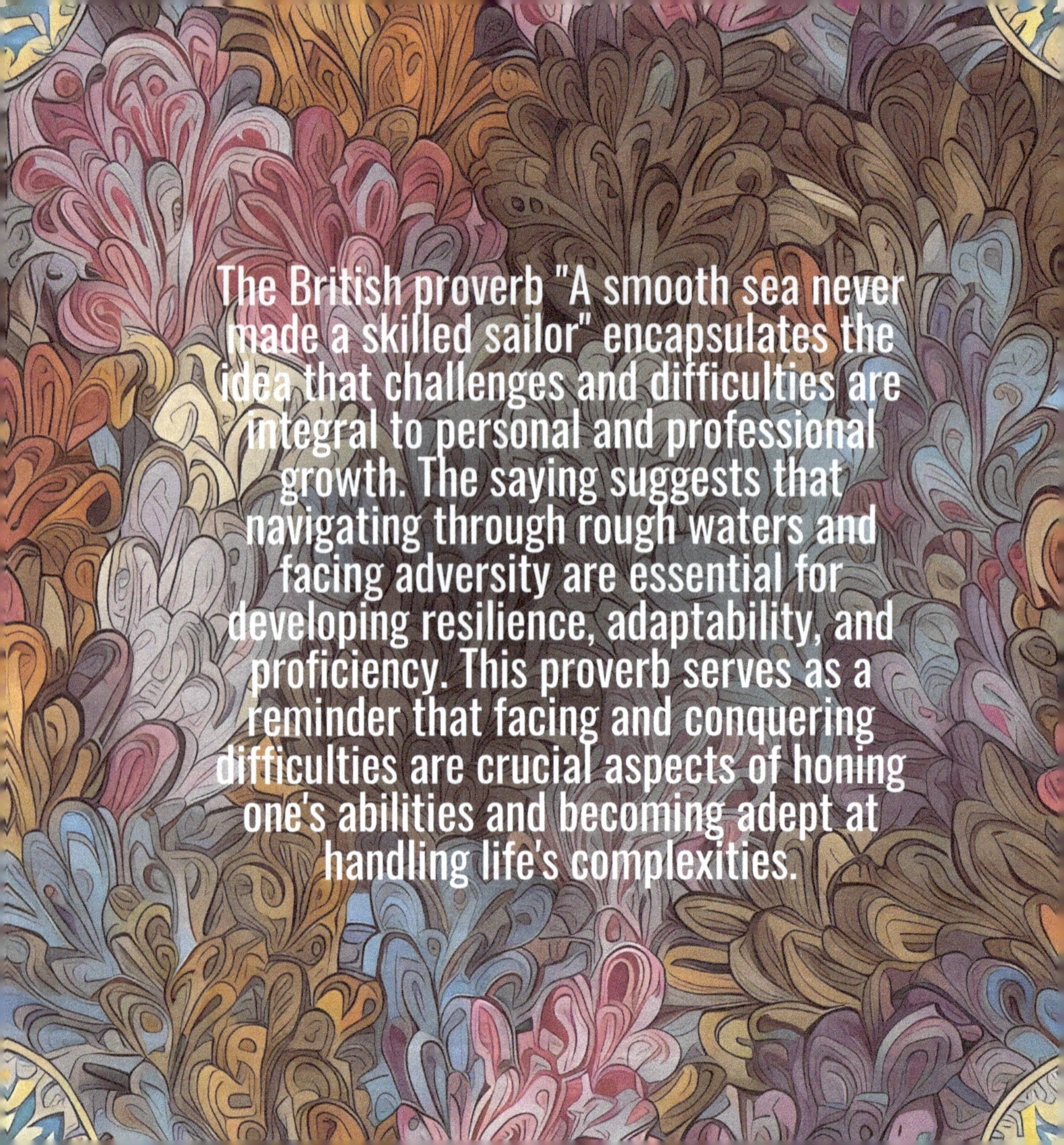

The British proverb "A smooth sea never made a skilled sailor" encapsulates the idea that challenges and difficulties are integral to personal and professional growth. The saying suggests that navigating through rough waters and facing adversity are essential for developing resilience, adaptability, and proficiency. This proverb serves as a reminder that facing and conquering difficulties are crucial aspects of honing one's abilities and becoming adept at handling life's complexities.

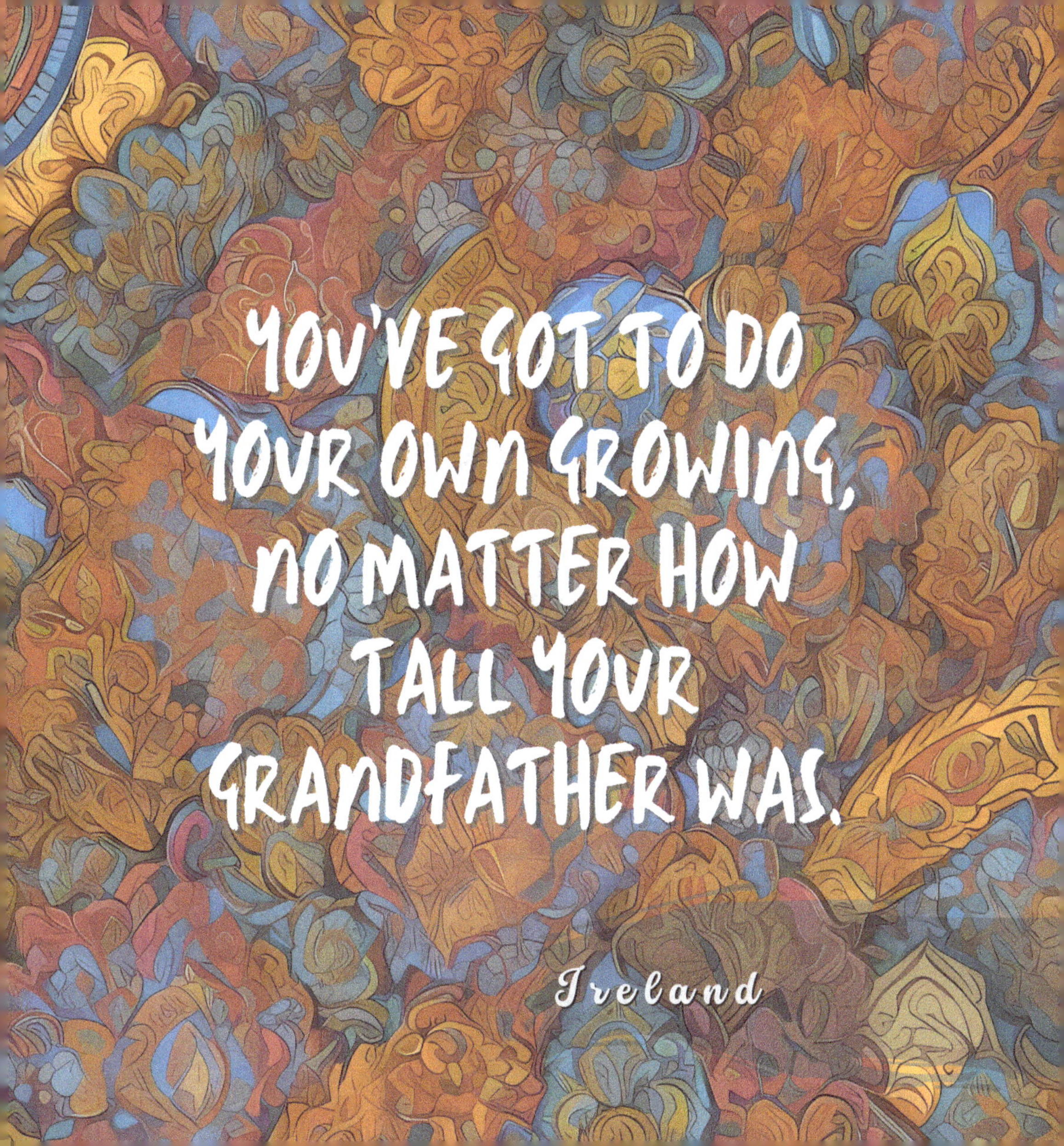
YOU'VE GOT TO DO
YOUR OWN GROWING,
NO MATTER HOW
TALL YOUR
GRANDFATHER WAS.
Ireland

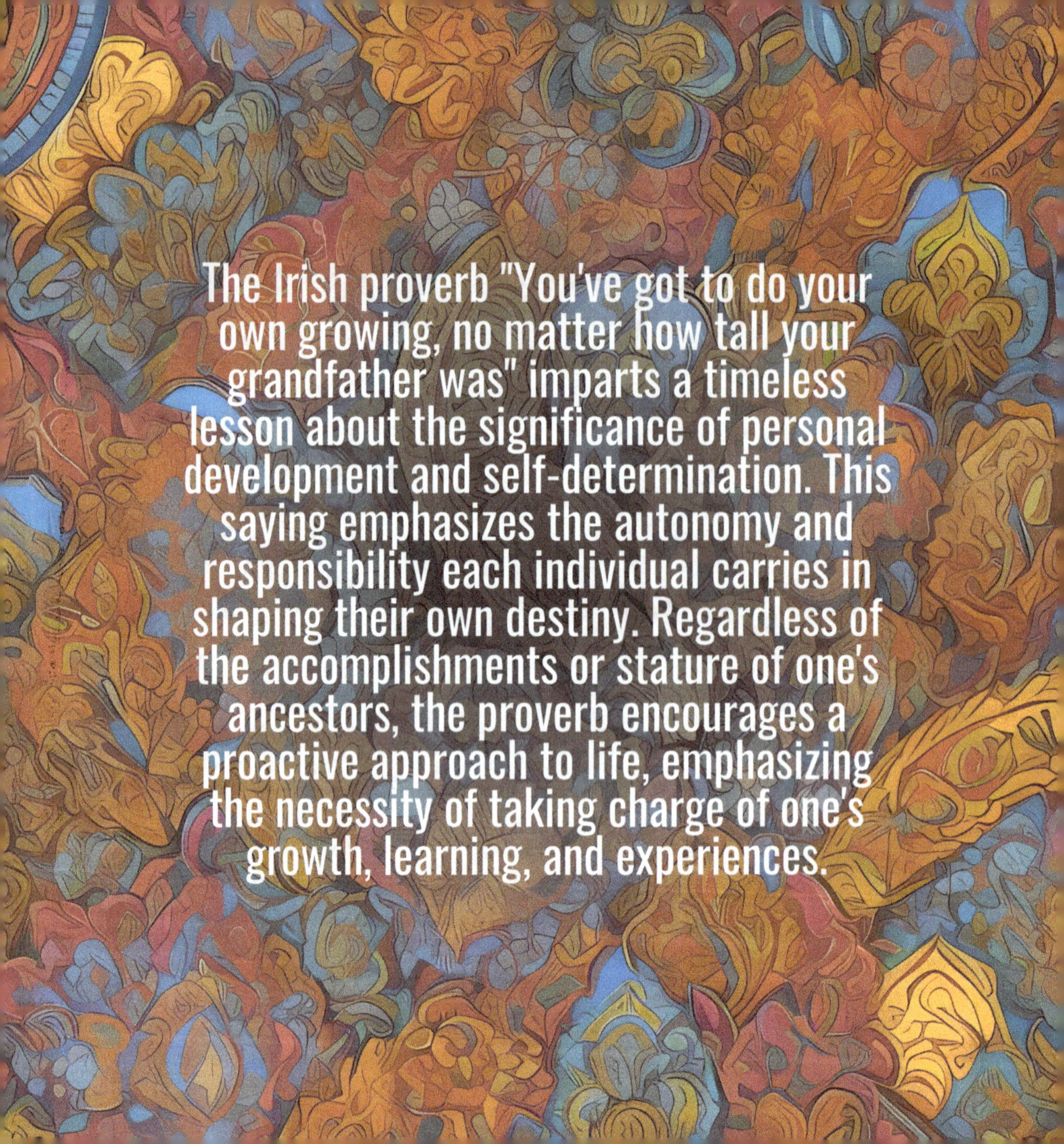

The Irish proverb "You've got to do your own growing, no matter how tall your grandfather was" imparts a timeless lesson about the significance of personal development and self-determination. This saying emphasizes the autonomy and responsibility each individual carries in shaping their own destiny. Regardless of the accomplishments or stature of one's ancestors, the proverb encourages a proactive approach to life, emphasizing the necessity of taking charge of one's growth, learning, and experiences.

WHEN IN ROME, DO AS THE ROMANS DO.
Latin

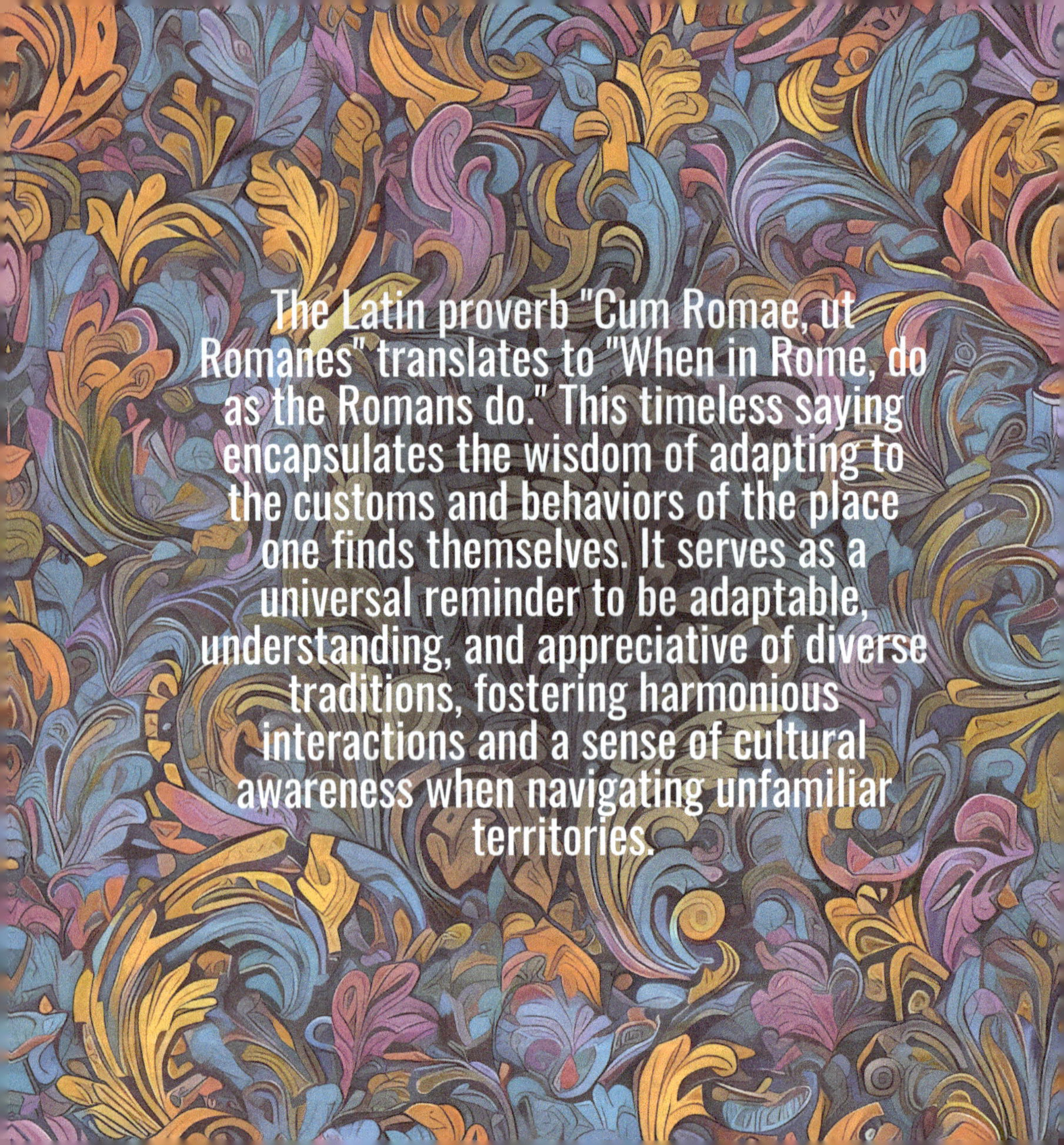
The Latin proverb "Cum Romae, ut Romanes" translates to "When in Rome, do as the Romans do." This timeless saying encapsulates the wisdom of adapting to the customs and behaviors of the place one finds themselves. It serves as a universal reminder to be adaptable, understanding, and appreciative of diverse traditions, fostering harmonious interactions and a sense of cultural awareness when navigating unfamiliar territories.

THERE IS NO EVIL
THAT DOESN'T
BRING SOME GOOD.
Latin American

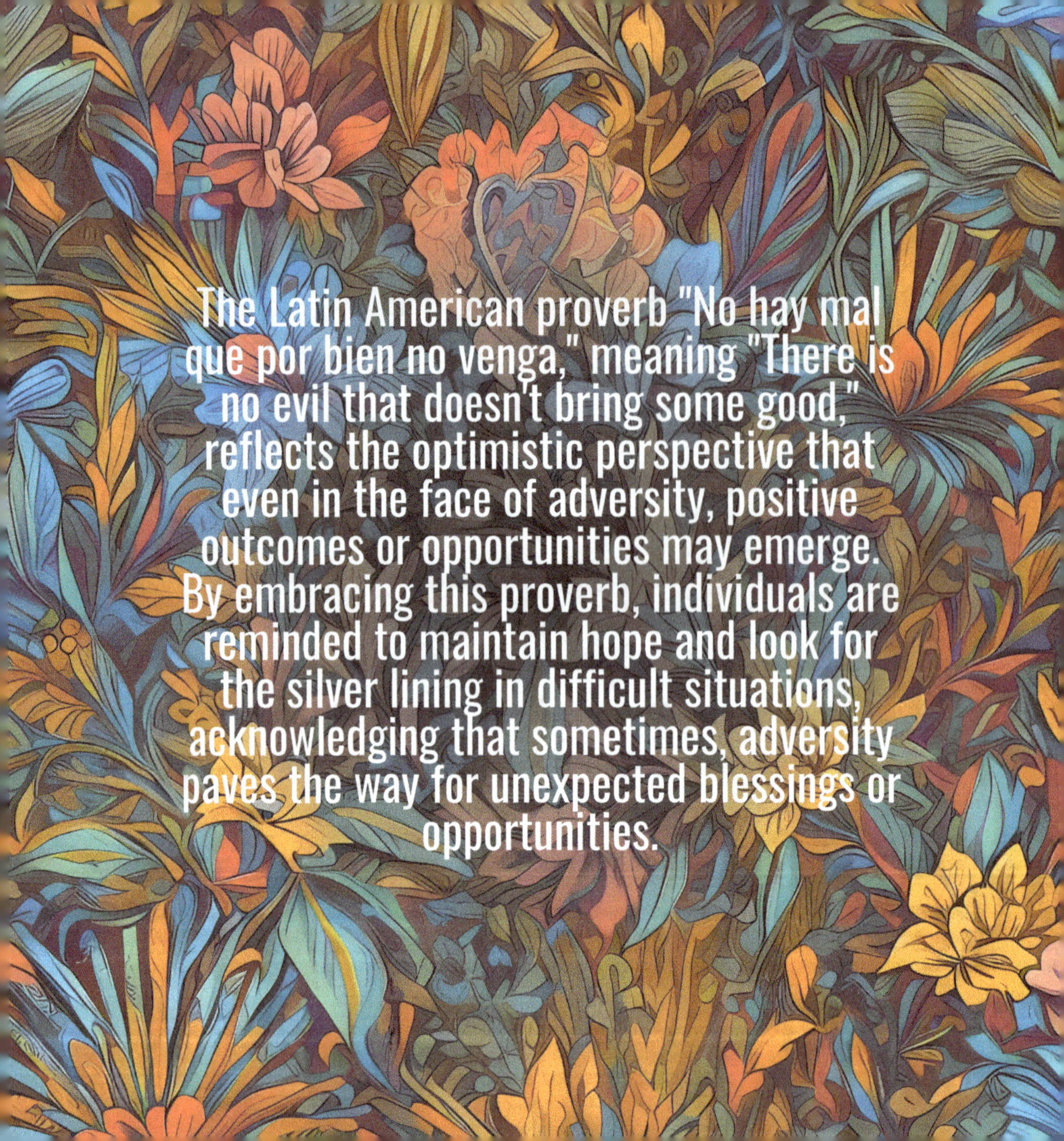
The Latin American proverb "No hay mal que por bien no venga," meaning "There is no evil that doesn't bring some good," reflects the optimistic perspective that even in the face of adversity, positive outcomes or opportunities may emerge. By embracing this proverb, individuals are reminded to maintain hope and look for the silver lining in difficult situations, acknowledging that sometimes, adversity paves the way for unexpected blessings or opportunities.

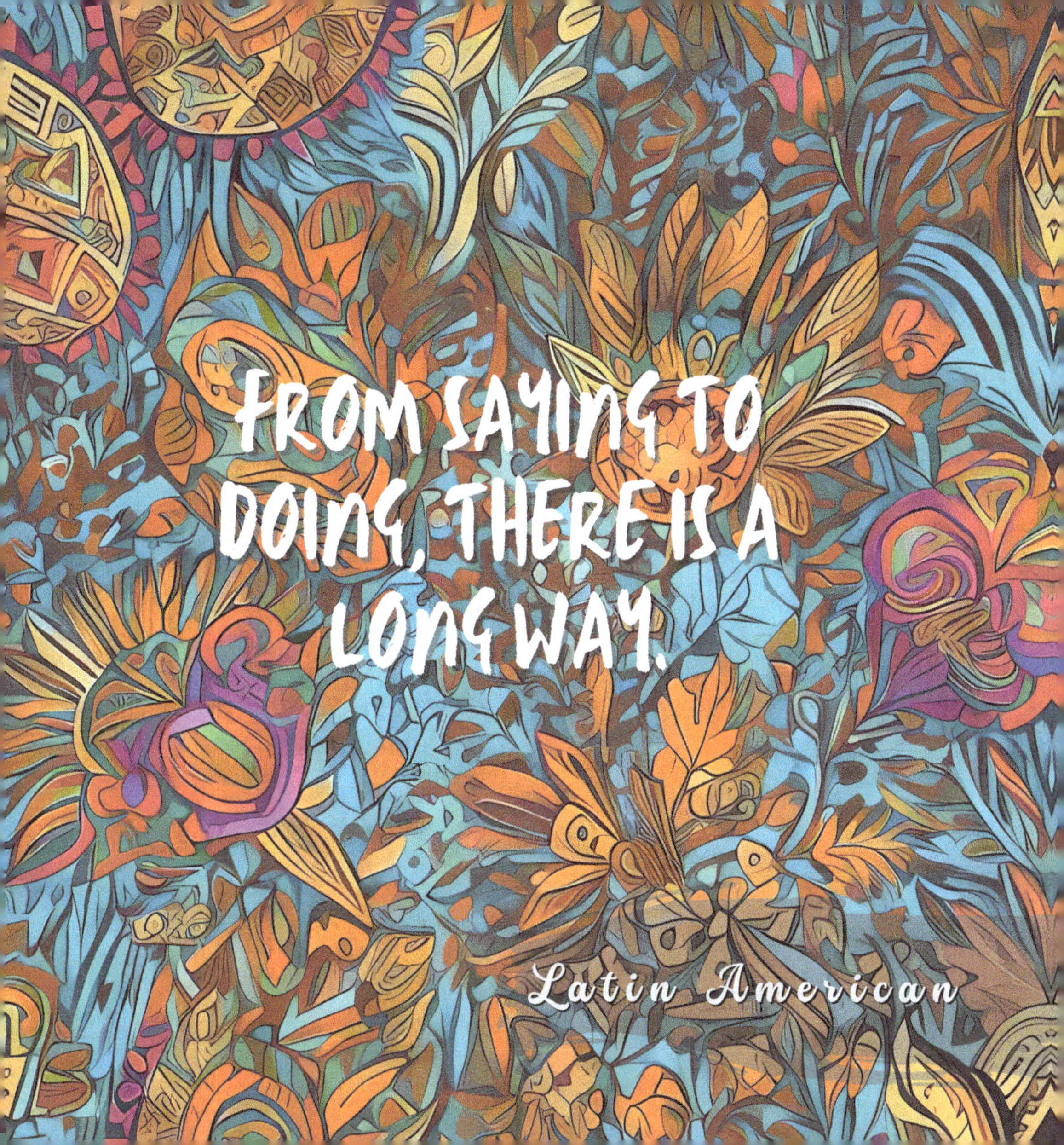
FROM SAYING TO DOING, THERE IS A LONG WAY.
Latin American

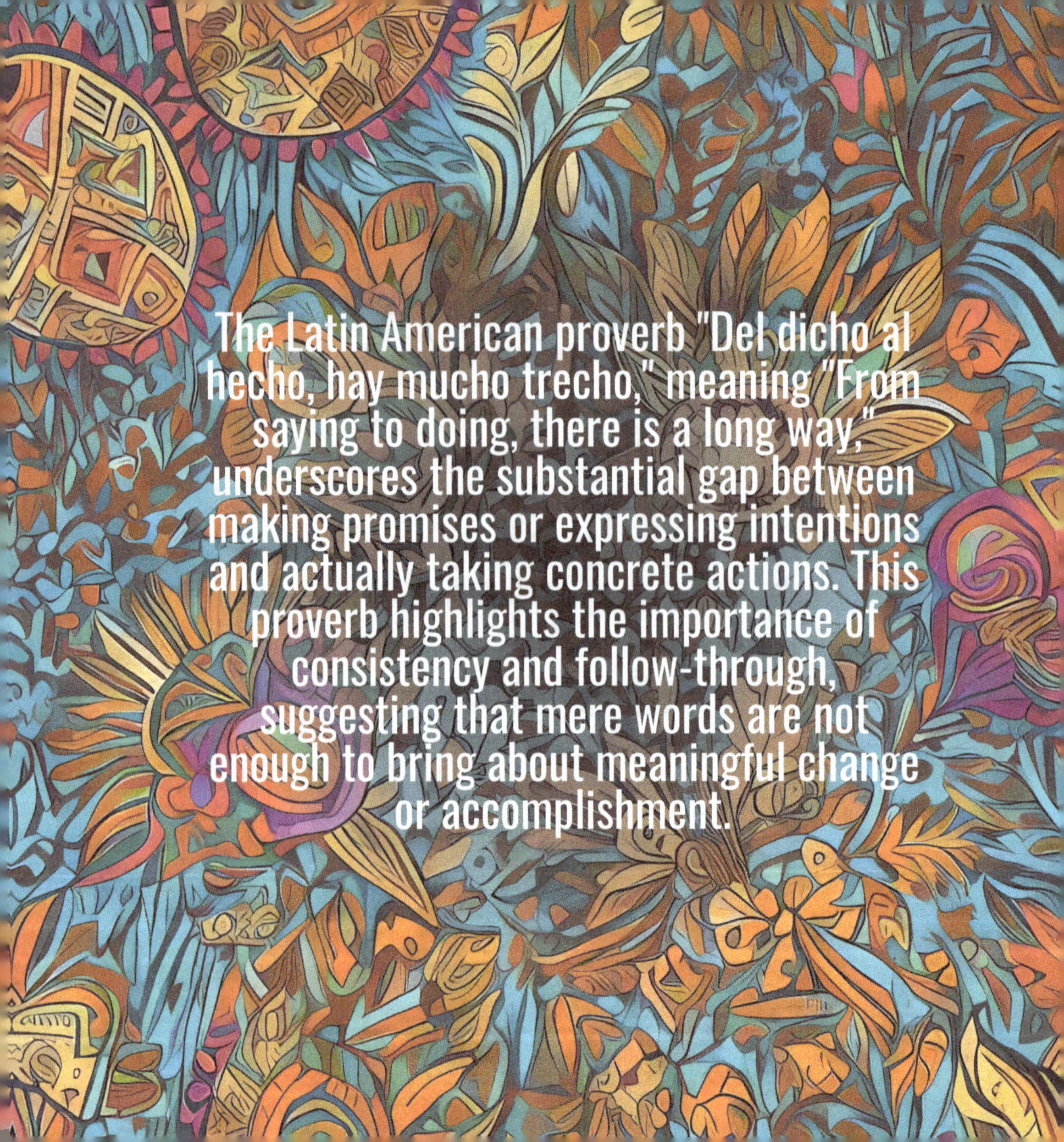

The Latin American proverb "Del dicho al hecho, hay mucho trecho," meaning "From saying to doing, there is a long way," underscores the substantial gap between making promises or expressing intentions and actually taking concrete actions. This proverb highlights the importance of consistency and follow-through, suggesting that mere words are not enough to bring about meaningful change or accomplishment.

TOO MANY COOKS
SPOIL THE BROTH.
Germany

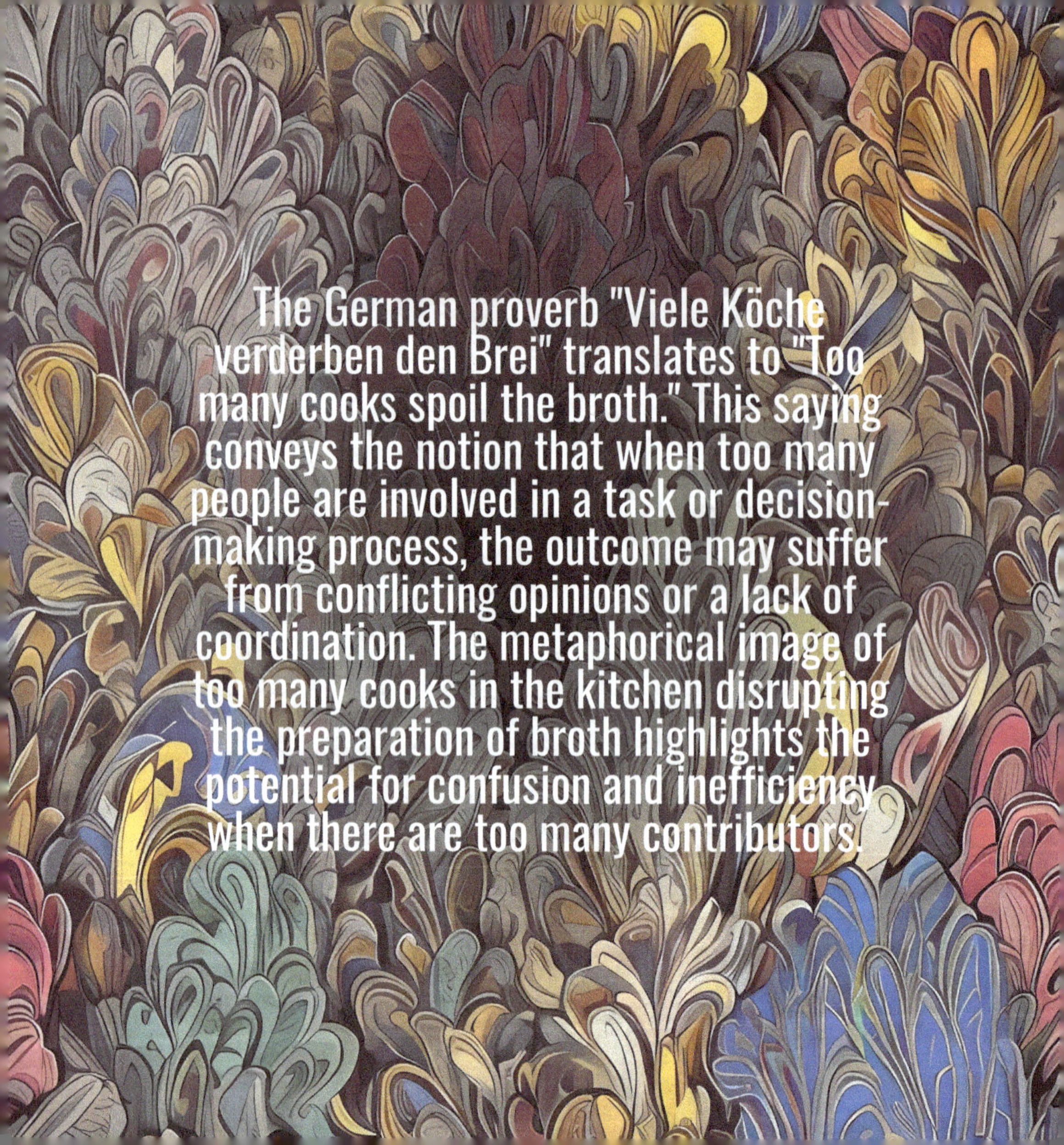

The German proverb "Viele Köche verderben den Brei" translates to "Too many cooks spoil the broth." This saying conveys the notion that when too many people are involved in a task or decision-making process, the outcome may suffer from conflicting opinions or a lack of coordination. The metaphorical image of too many cooks in the kitchen disrupting the preparation of broth highlights the potential for confusion and inefficiency when there are too many contributors.

LIES HAVE SHORT LEGS.
Latin American

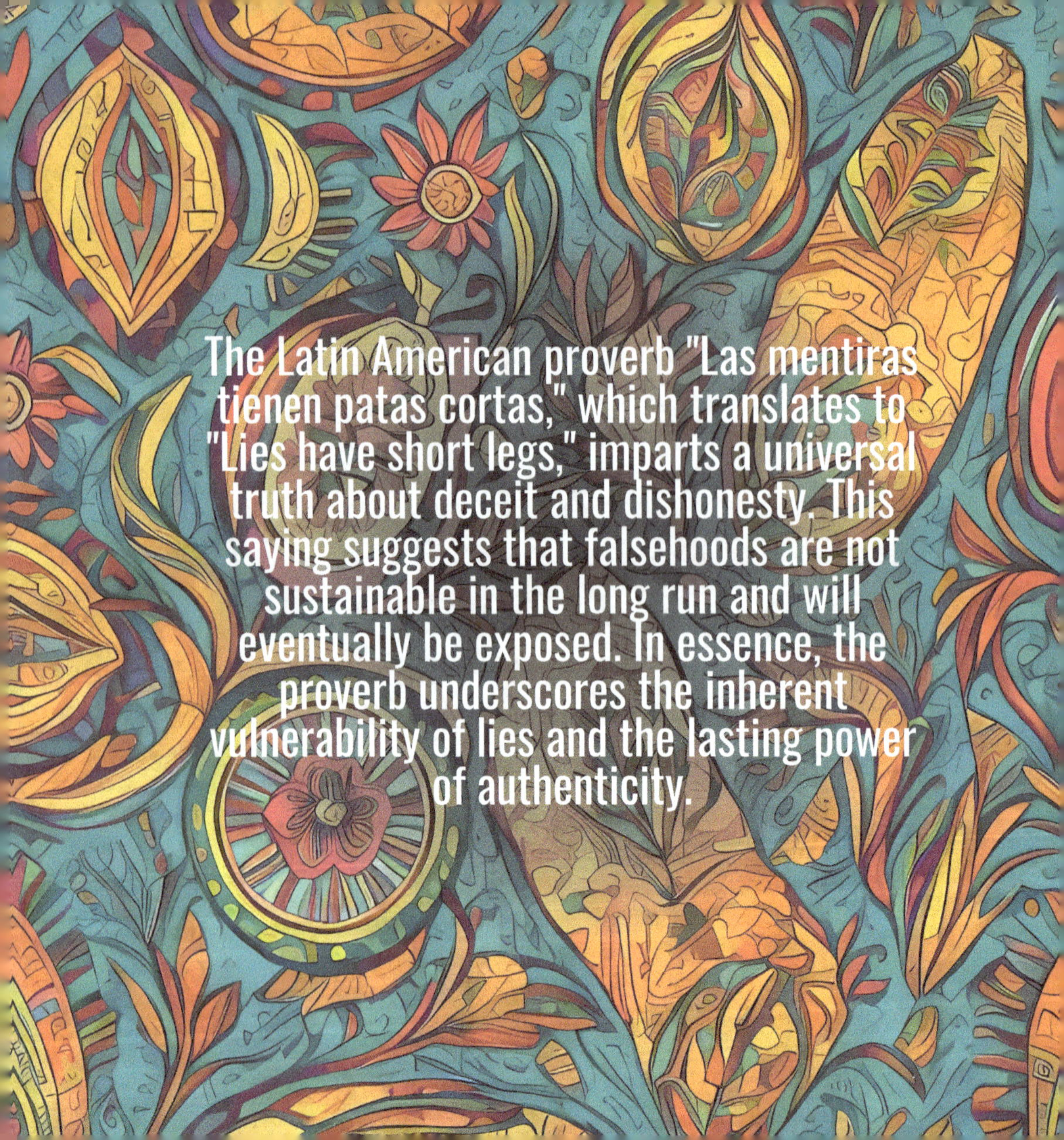
The Latin American proverb "Las mentiras tienen patas cortas," which translates to "Lies have short legs," imparts a universal truth about deceit and dishonesty. This saying suggests that falsehoods are not sustainable in the long run and will eventually be exposed. In essence, the proverb underscores the inherent vulnerability of lies and the lasting power of authenticity.

YOU COULD CALL ME
ANYTHING, BUT
LATE FOR DINNER.
Bahamas

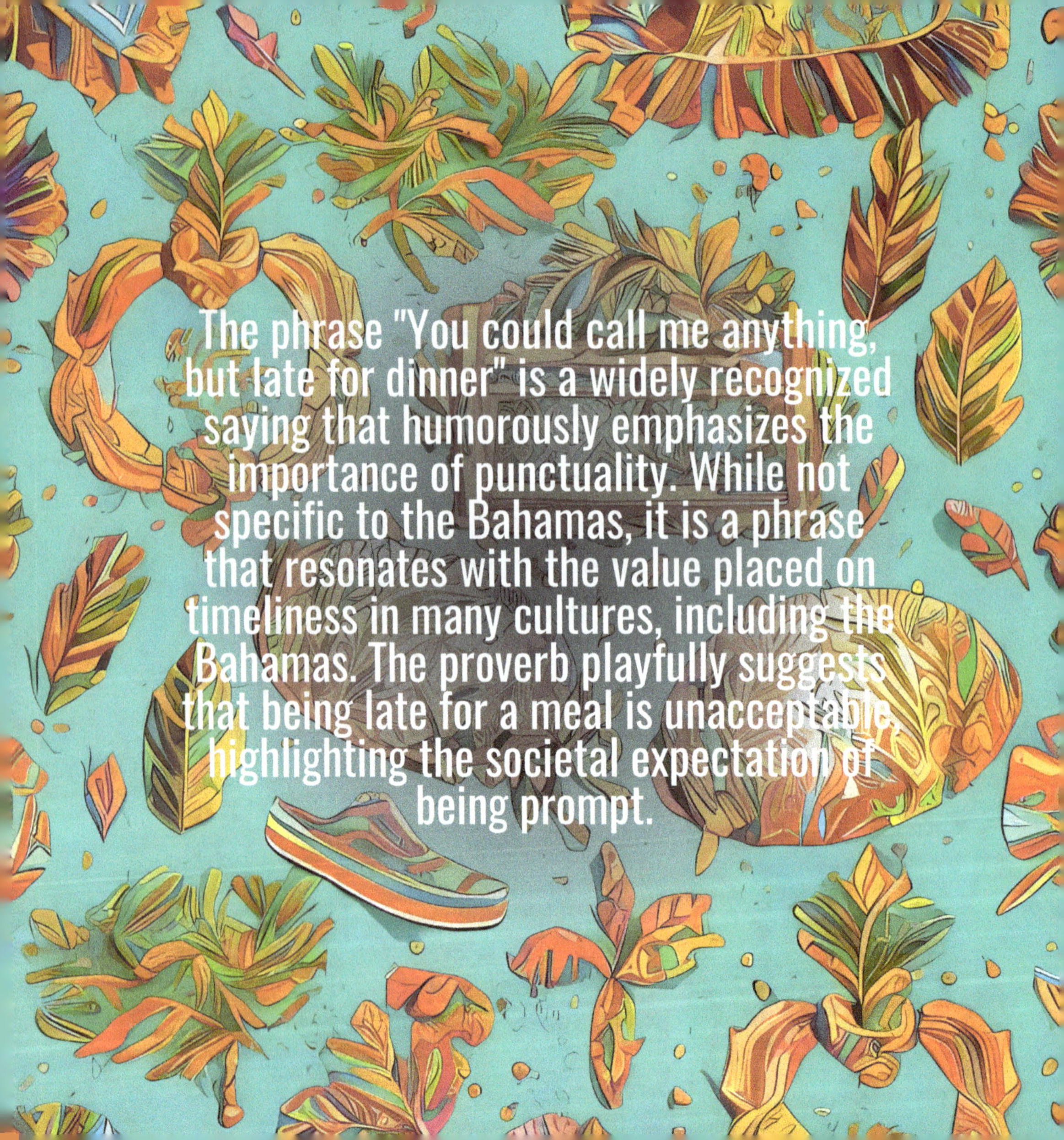
The phrase "You could call me anything, but late for dinner" is a widely recognized saying that humorously emphasizes the importance of punctuality. While not specific to the Bahamas, it is a phrase that resonates with the value placed on timeliness in many cultures, including the Bahamas. The proverb playfully suggests that being late for a meal is unacceptable, highlighting the societal expectation of being prompt.

ONE HAND CYAN'T CLAP.
Guyana

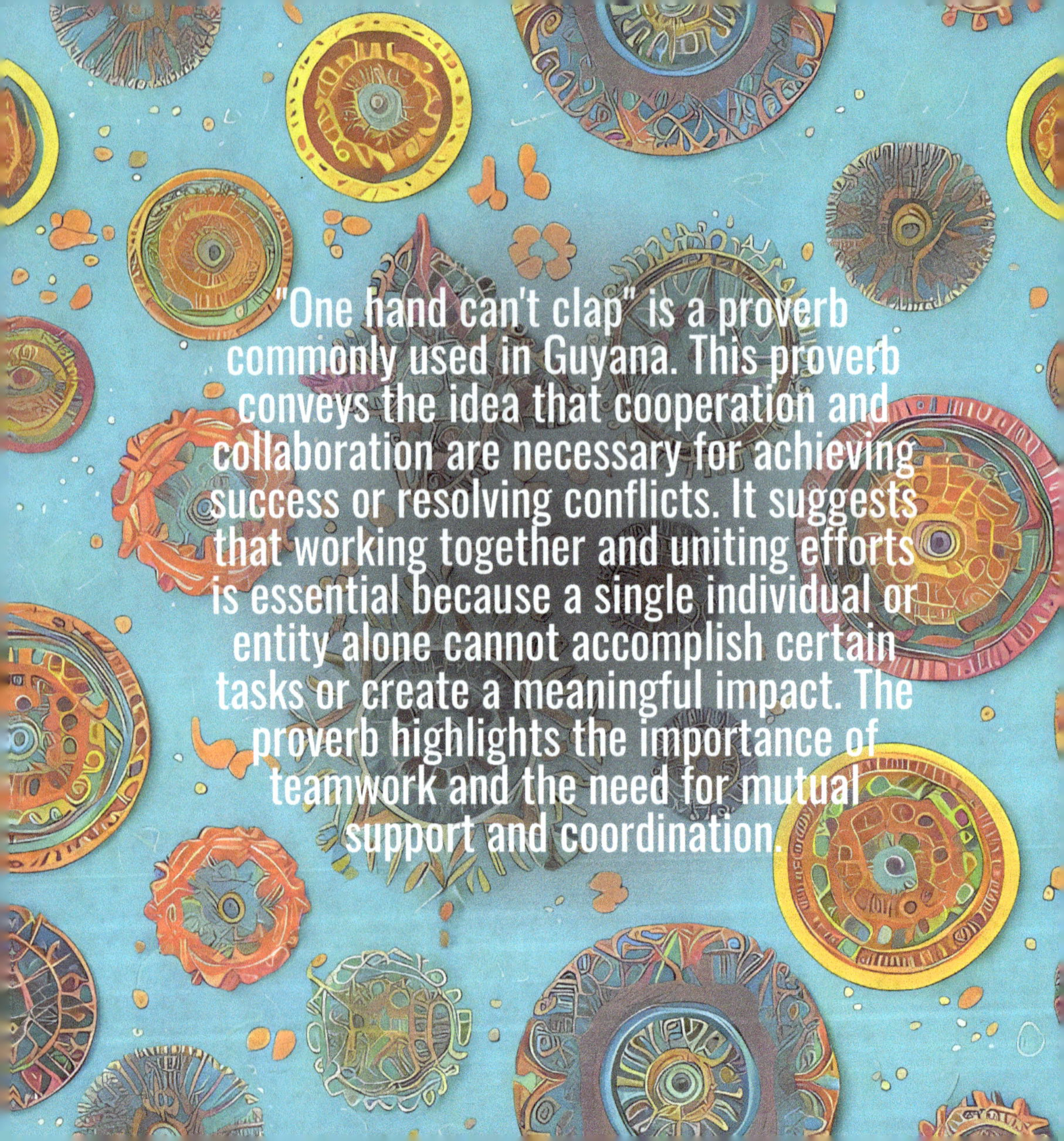
"One hand can't clap" is a proverb commonly used in Guyana. This proverb conveys the idea that cooperation and collaboration are necessary for achieving success or resolving conflicts. It suggests that working together and uniting efforts is essential because a single individual or entity alone cannot accomplish certain tasks or create a meaningful impact. The proverb highlights the importance of teamwork and the need for mutual support and coordination.

DON'T WATCH ME,
WATCH YOU.
Jamaica

"Don't watch me, watch you" is a proverb commonly used in Jamaica. This proverb carries a message of self-reflection and personal accountability. It implies that individuals should focus on their own actions, behavior, and responsibilities instead of being overly concerned or judgmental about others. It encourages individuals to prioritize self-improvement and self-awareness, emphasizing the importance of minding one's own business rather than being preoccupied with the actions or opinions of others. This proverb promotes individual growth and self-accountability.

THERE IS NO BAD
WEATHER, ONLY
BAD CLOTHES.
Sweden

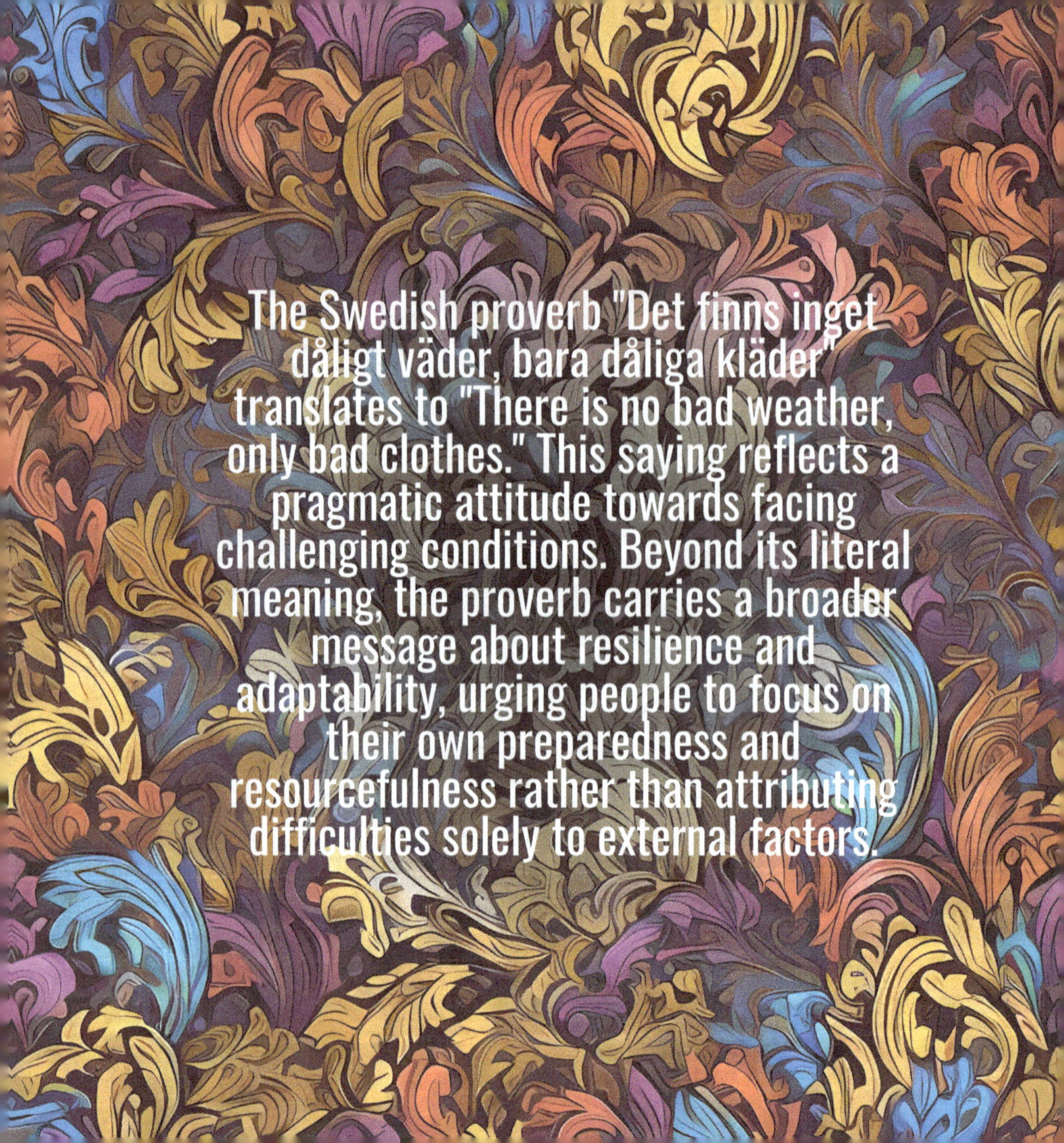

The Swedish proverb "Det finns inget dåligt väder, bara dåliga kläder" translates to "There is no bad weather, only bad clothes." This saying reflects a pragmatic attitude towards facing challenging conditions. Beyond its literal meaning, the proverb carries a broader message about resilience and adaptability, urging people to focus on their own preparedness and resourcefulness rather than attributing difficulties solely to external factors.

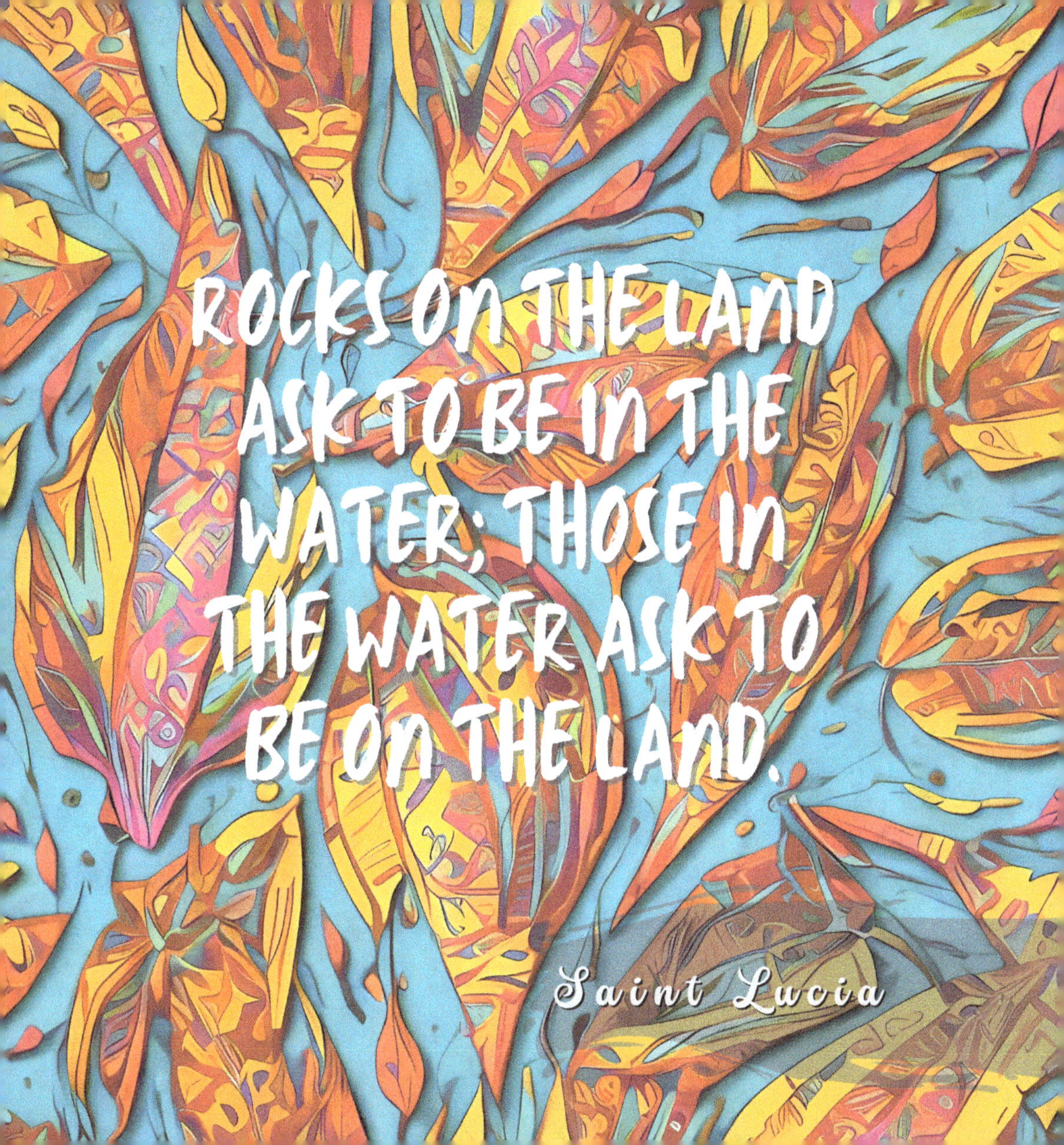
ROCKS ON THE LAND ASK TO BE IN THE WATER; THOSE IN THE WATER ASK TO BE ON THE LAND.
Saint Lucia

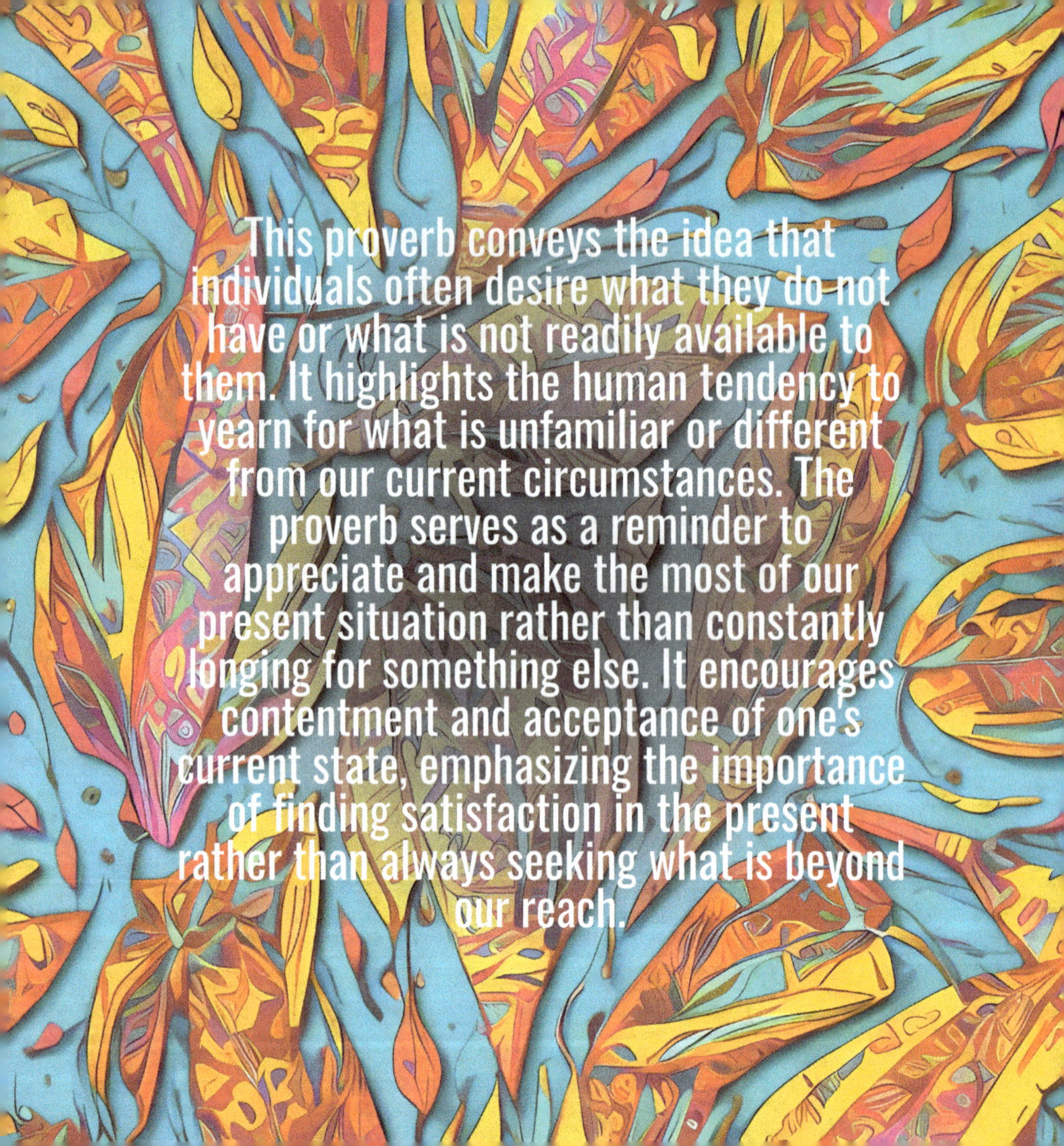

This proverb conveys the idea that individuals often desire what they do not have or what is not readily available to them. It highlights the human tendency to yearn for what is unfamiliar or different from our current circumstances. The proverb serves as a reminder to appreciate and make the most of our present situation rather than constantly longing for something else. It encourages contentment and acceptance of one's current state, emphasizing the importance of finding satisfaction in the present rather than always seeking what is beyond our reach.

WHAT MISSES YOU,
WAS SUPPOSED TO
GO PAST YOU.
Trinidad &
Tobago

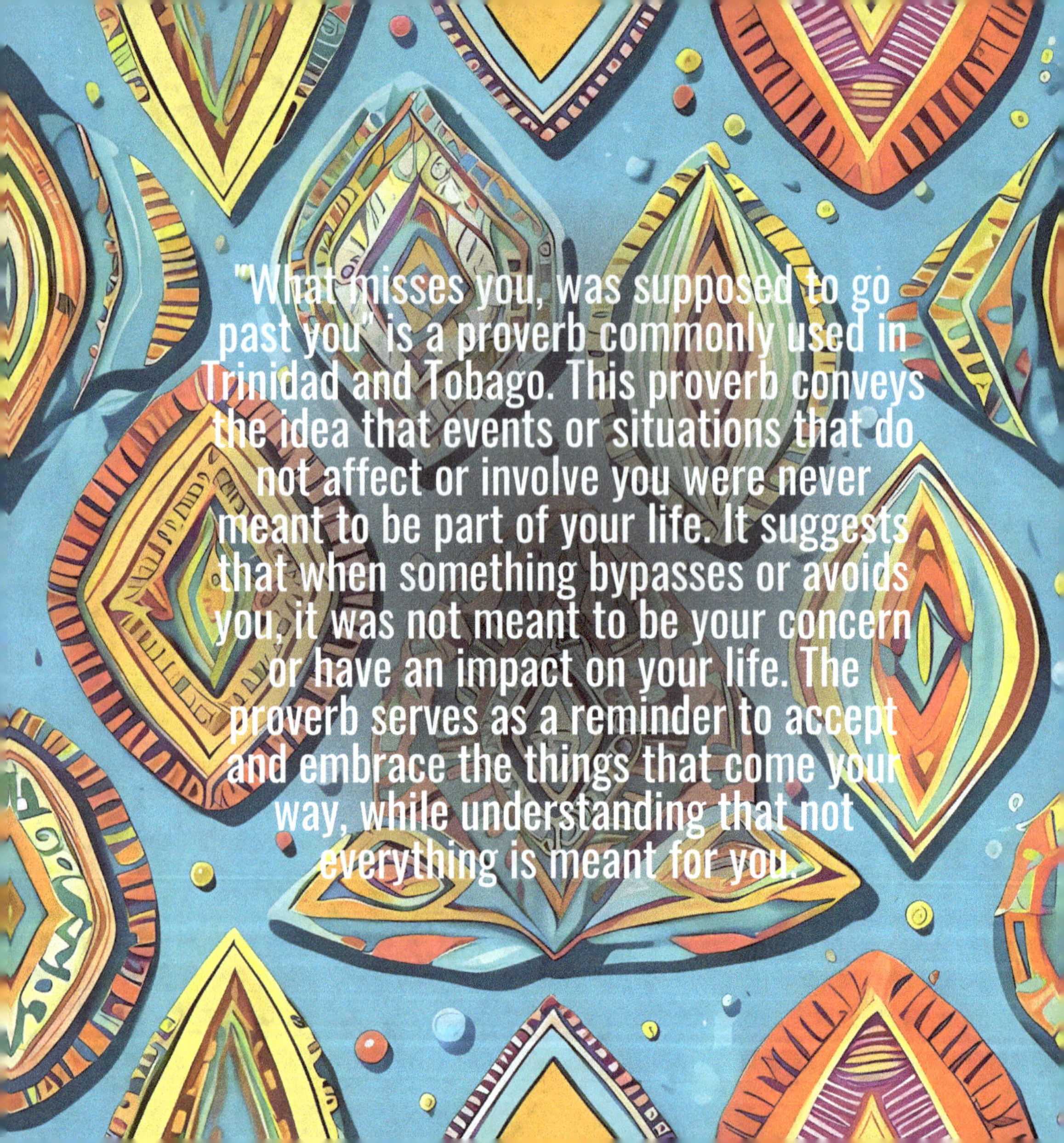
"What misses you, was supposed to go past you" is a proverb commonly used in Trinidad and Tobago. This proverb conveys the idea that events or situations that do not affect or involve you were never meant to be part of your life. It suggests that when something bypasses or avoids you, it was not meant to be your concern or have an impact on your life. The proverb serves as a reminder to accept and embrace the things that come your way, while understanding that not everything is meant for you.

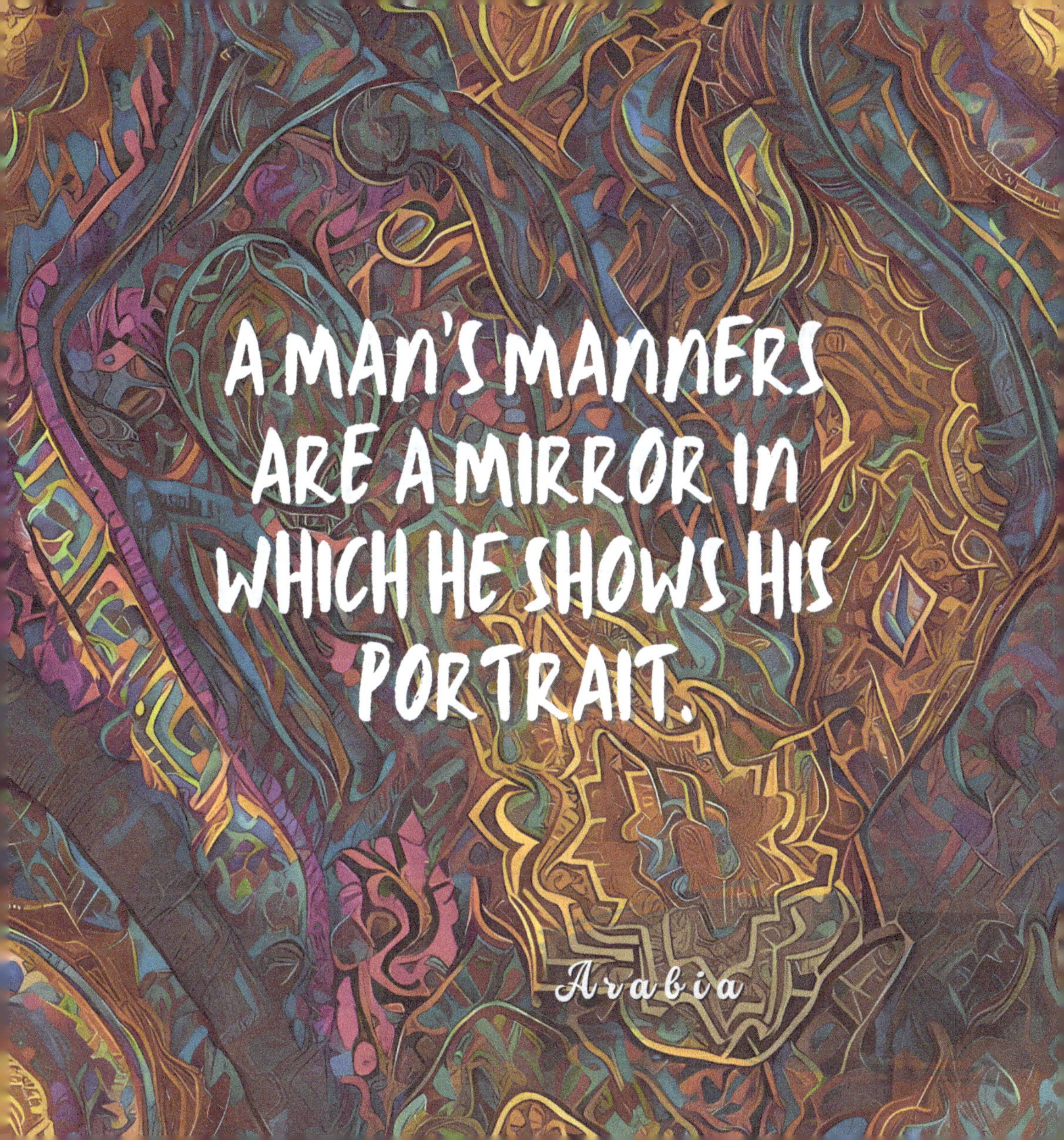
A MAN'S MANNERS ARE A MIRROR IN WHICH HE SHOWS HIS PORTRAIT.
Arabia

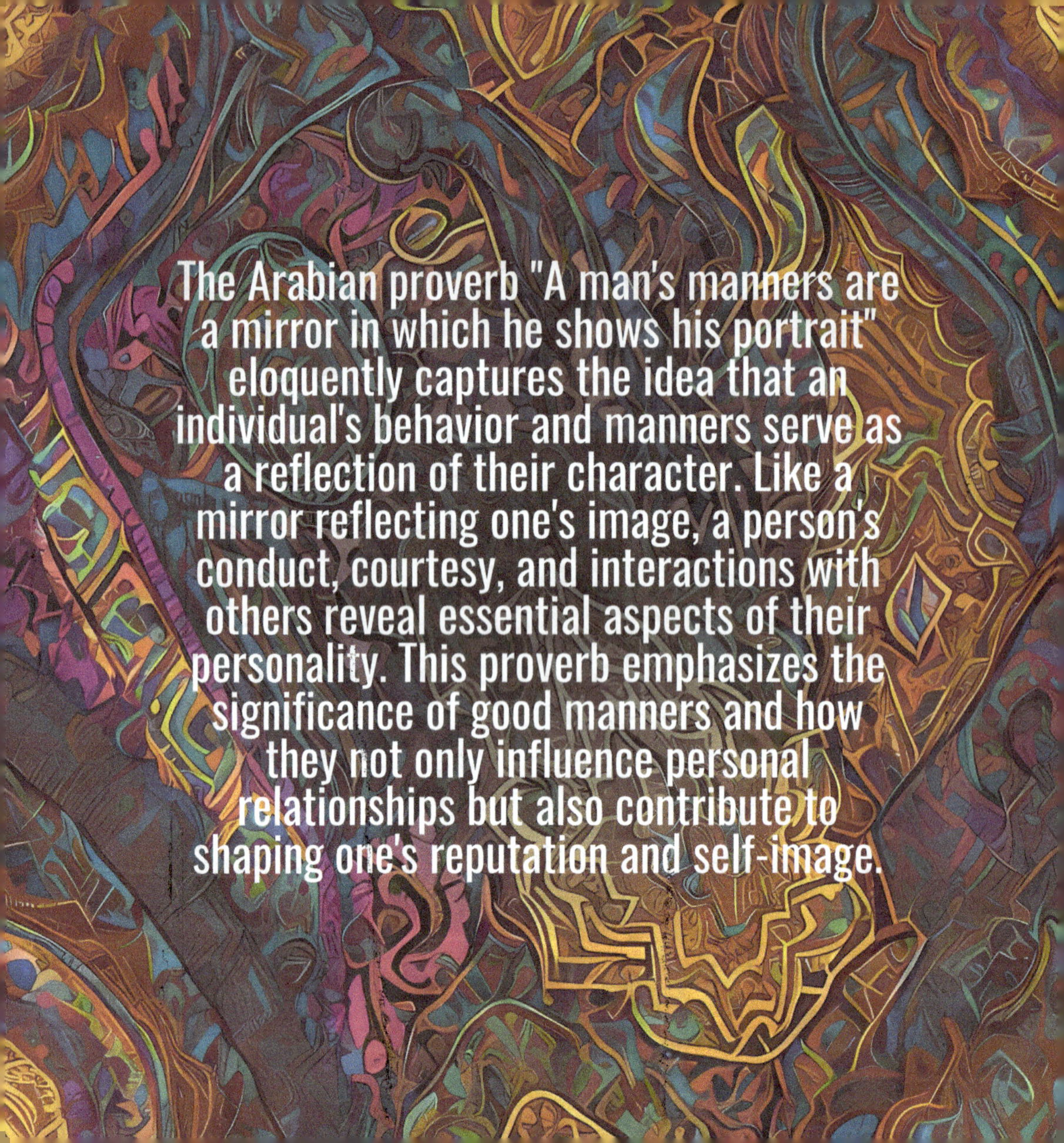

The Arabian proverb "A man's manners are a mirror in which he shows his portrait" eloquently captures the idea that an individual's behavior and manners serve as a reflection of their character. Like a mirror reflecting one's image, a person's conduct, courtesy, and interactions with others reveal essential aspects of their personality. This proverb emphasizes the significance of good manners and how they not only influence personal relationships but also contribute to shaping one's reputation and self-image.

THE FRUIT OF
SILENCE IS
TRANQUILITY.
Arabia

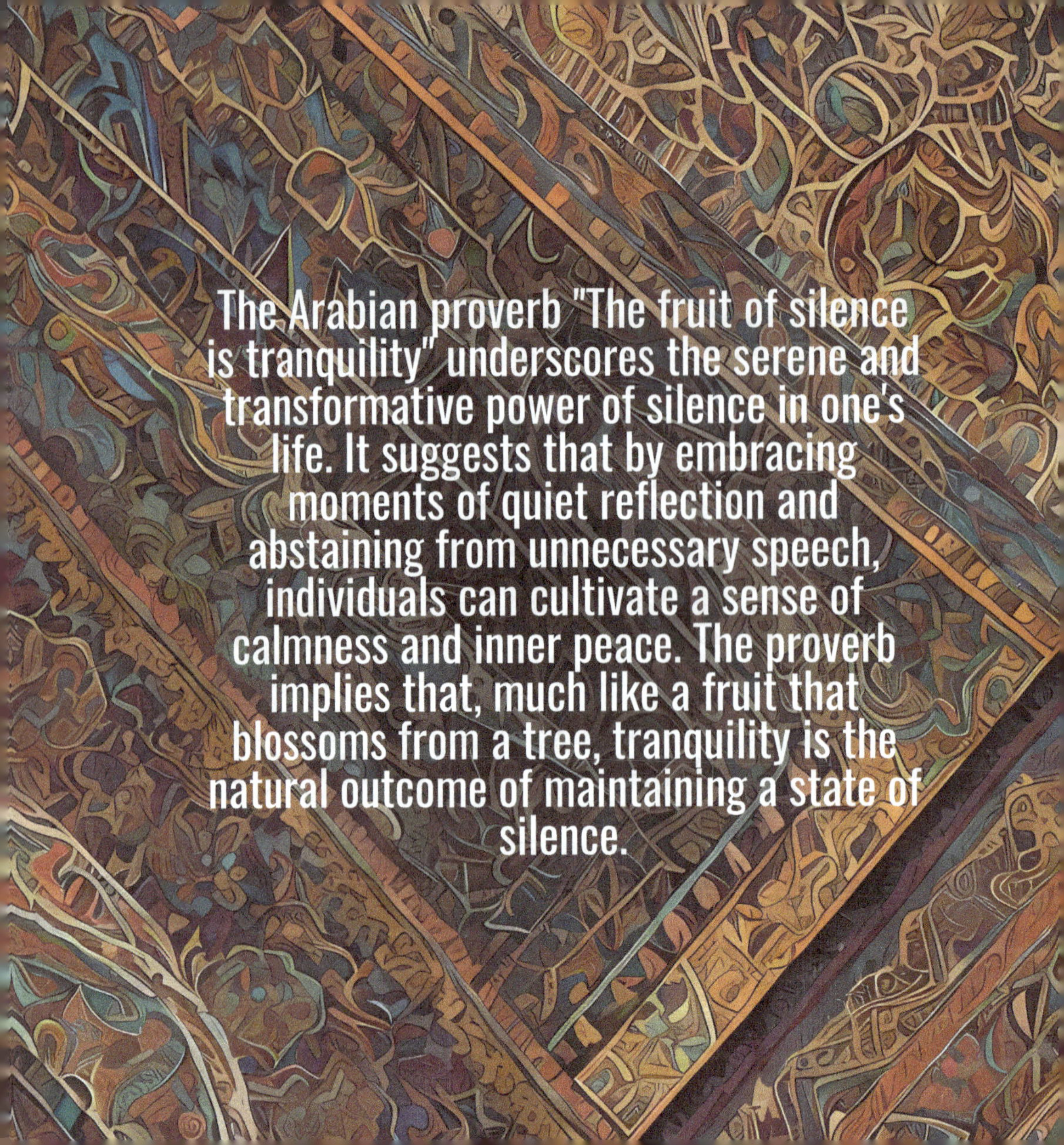

The Arabian proverb "The fruit of silence is tranquility" underscores the serene and transformative power of silence in one's life. It suggests that by embracing moments of quiet reflection and abstaining from unnecessary speech, individuals can cultivate a sense of calmness and inner peace. The proverb implies that, much like a fruit that blossoms from a tree, tranquility is the natural outcome of maintaining a state of silence.

HE WHO SPEAKS
MUCH MAKES
MISTAKES.
Arabia

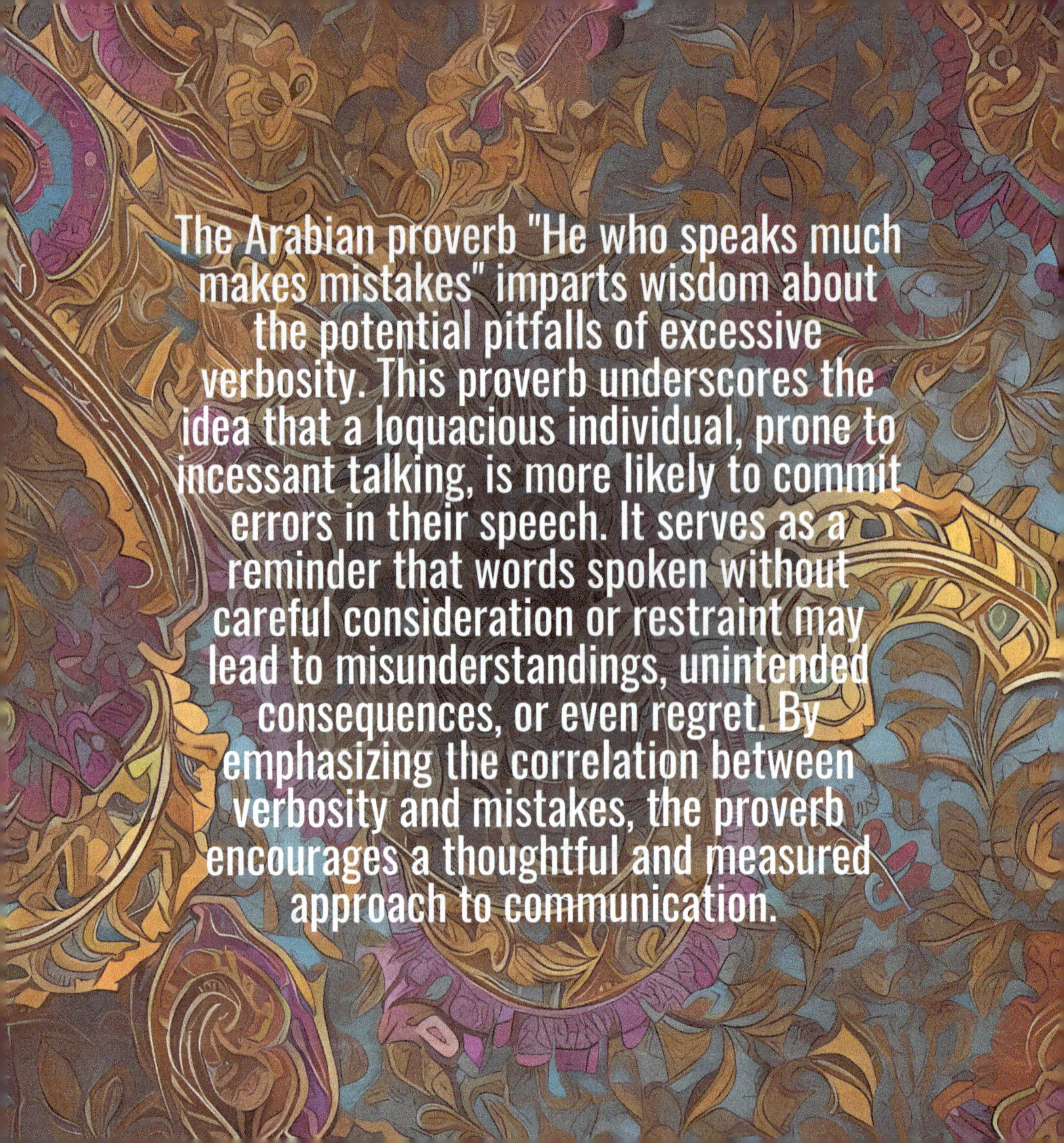
The Arabian proverb "He who speaks much makes mistakes" imparts wisdom about the potential pitfalls of excessive verbosity. This proverb underscores the idea that a loquacious individual, prone to incessant talking, is more likely to commit errors in their speech. It serves as a reminder that words spoken without careful consideration or restraint may lead to misunderstandings, unintended consequences, or even regret. By emphasizing the correlation between verbosity and mistakes, the proverb encourages a thoughtful and measured approach to communication.

TRUST IN GOD, BUT
TIE YOUR CAMEL.
Arabia

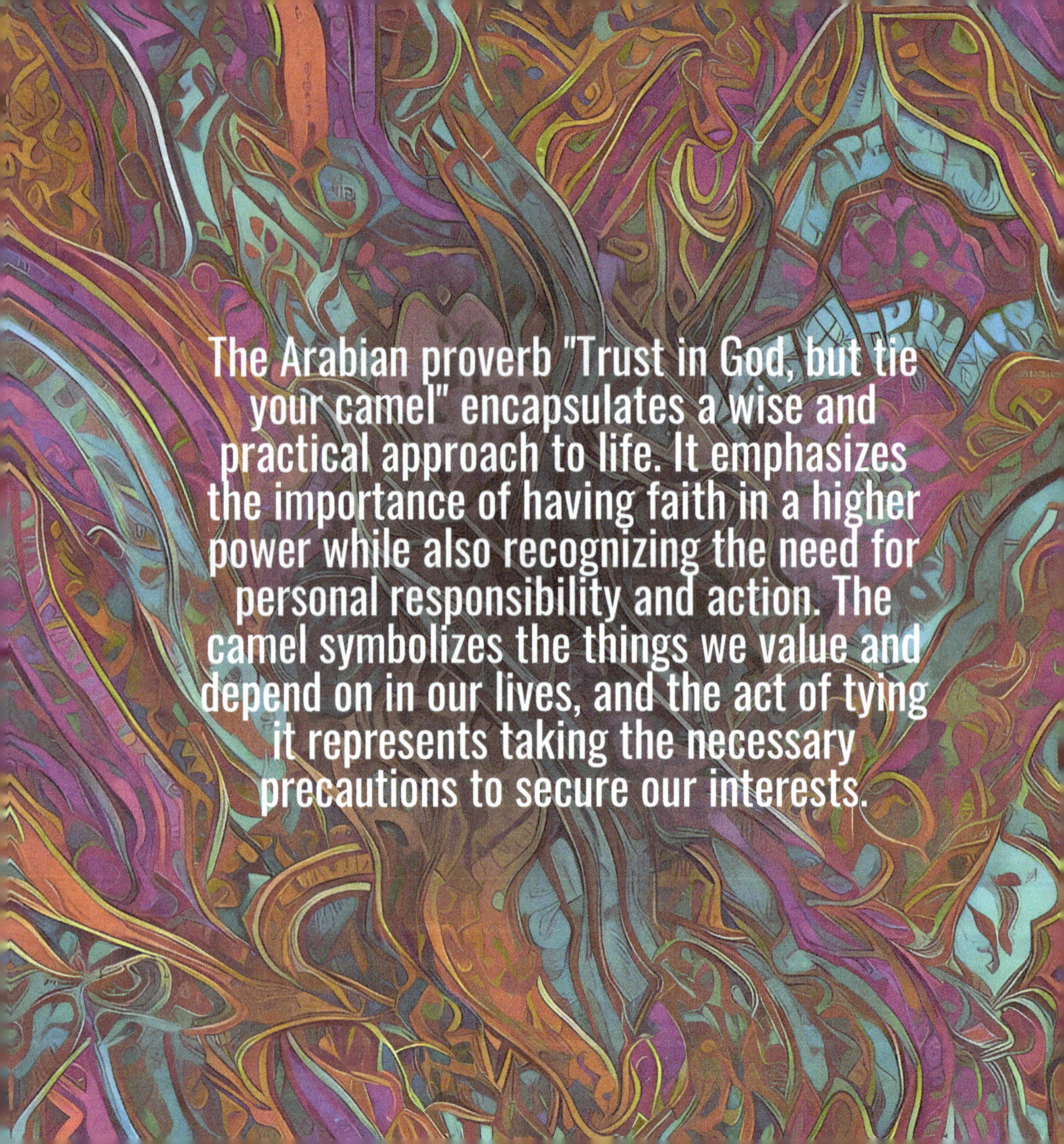
The Arabian proverb "Trust in God, but tie your camel" encapsulates a wise and practical approach to life. It emphasizes the importance of having faith in a higher power while also recognizing the need for personal responsibility and action. The camel symbolizes the things we value and depend on in our lives, and the act of tying it represents taking the necessary precautions to secure our interests.

BETTER YOUR
BELLY BURST THAN
GOOD FOOD WASTES.
Trinidad &
Tobago

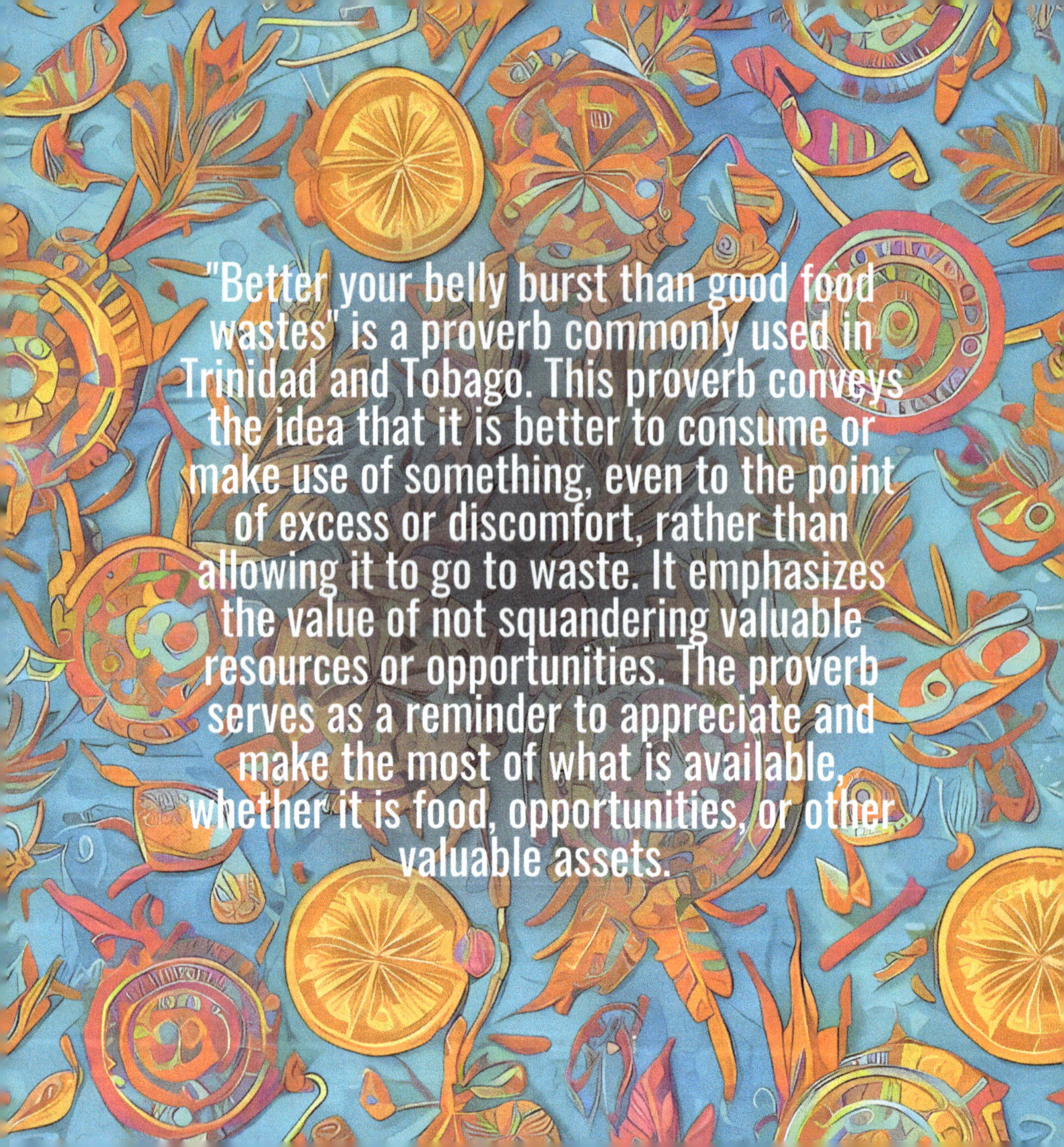
"Better your belly burst than good food wastes" is a proverb commonly used in Trinidad and Tobago. This proverb conveys the idea that it is better to consume or make use of something, even to the point of excess or discomfort, rather than allowing it to go to waste. It emphasizes the value of not squandering valuable resources or opportunities. The proverb serves as a reminder to appreciate and make the most of what is available, whether it is food, opportunities, or other valuable assets.

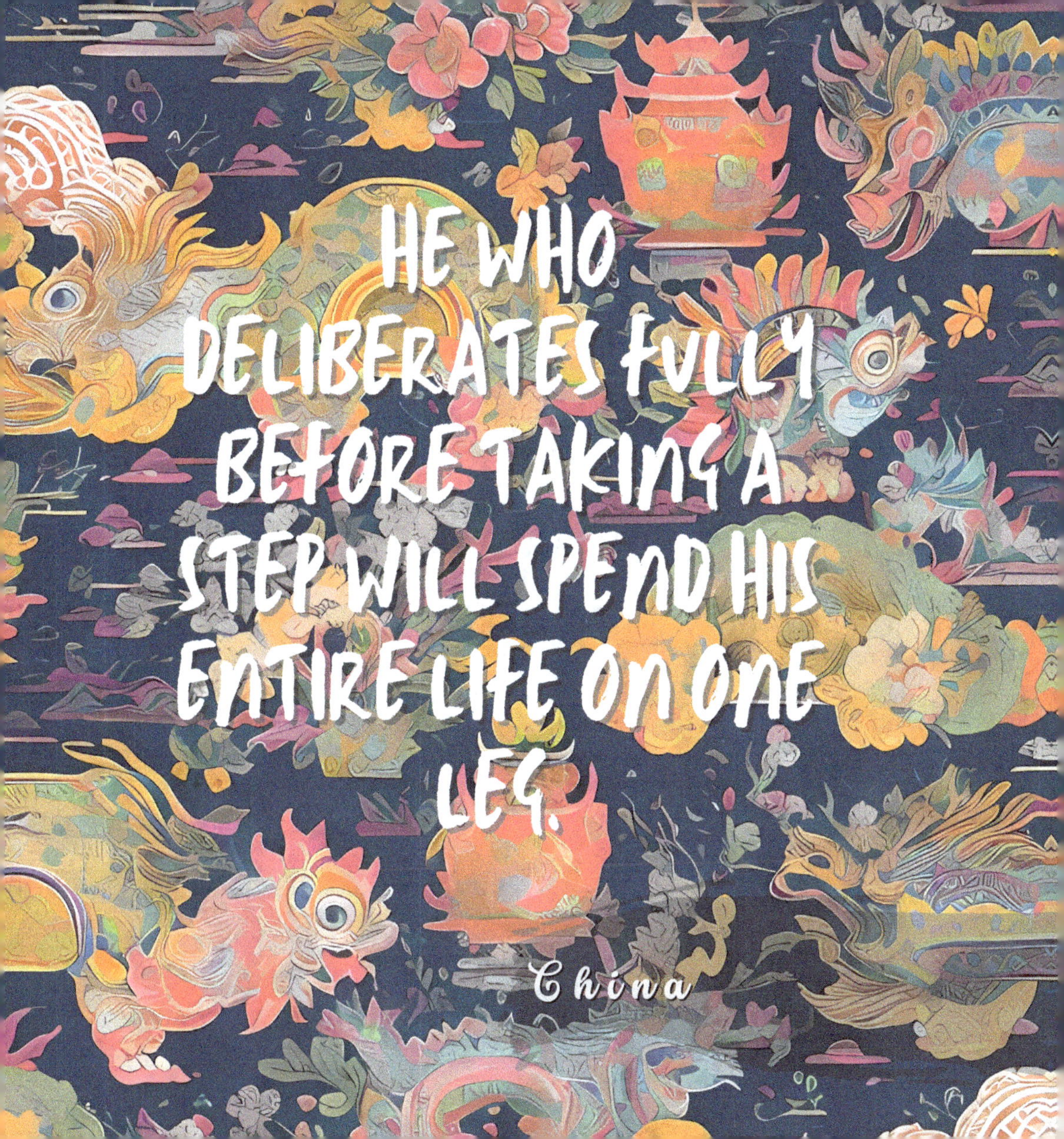
HE WHO
DELIBERATES FULLY
BEFORE TAKING A
STEP WILL SPEND HIS
ENTIRE LIFE ON ONE
LEG.
China

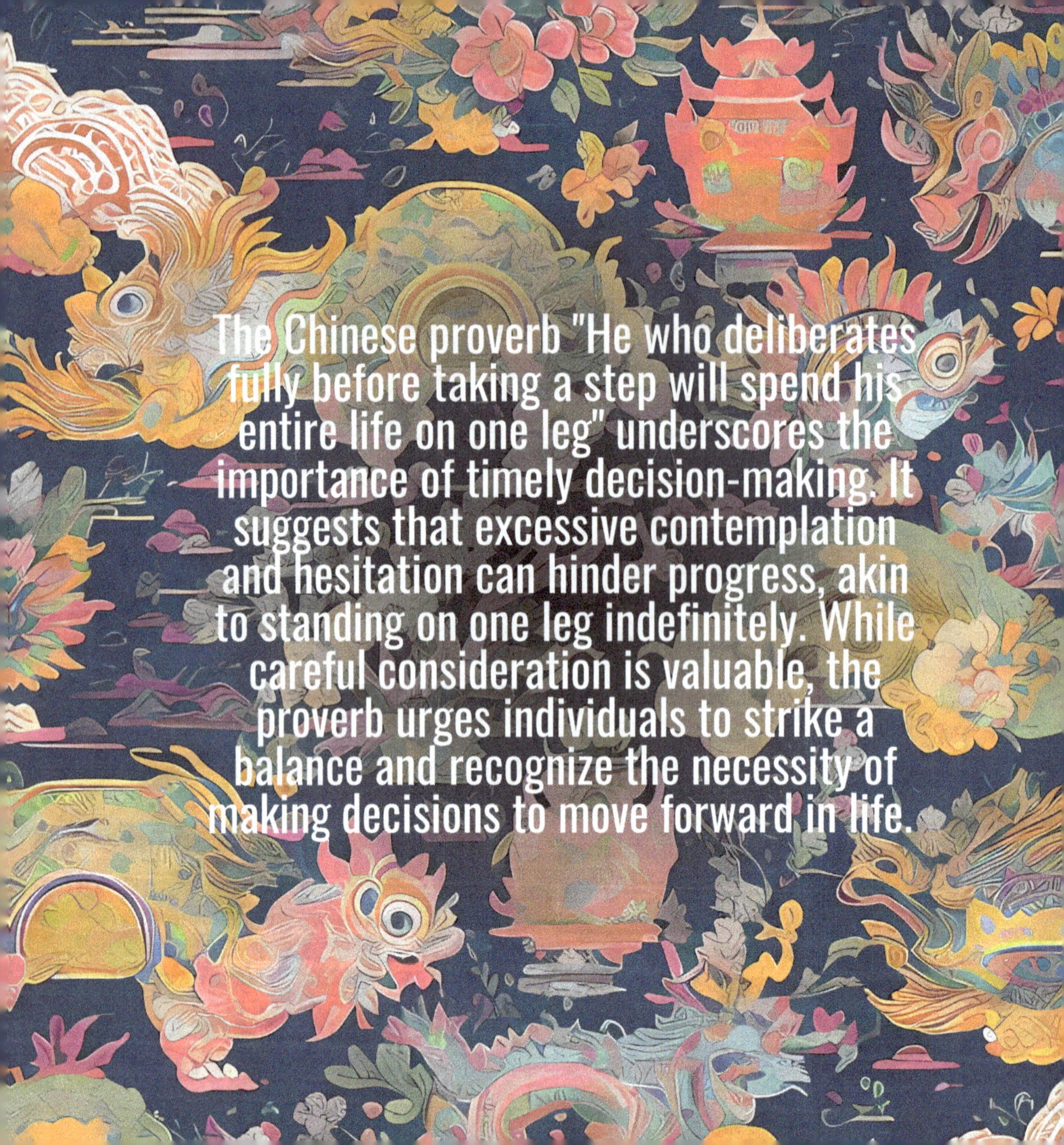

The Chinese proverb "He who deliberates fully before taking a step will spend his entire life on one leg" underscores the importance of timely decision-making. It suggests that excessive contemplation and hesitation can hinder progress, akin to standing on one leg indefinitely. While careful consideration is valuable, the proverb urges individuals to strike a balance and recognize the necessity of making decisions to move forward in life.

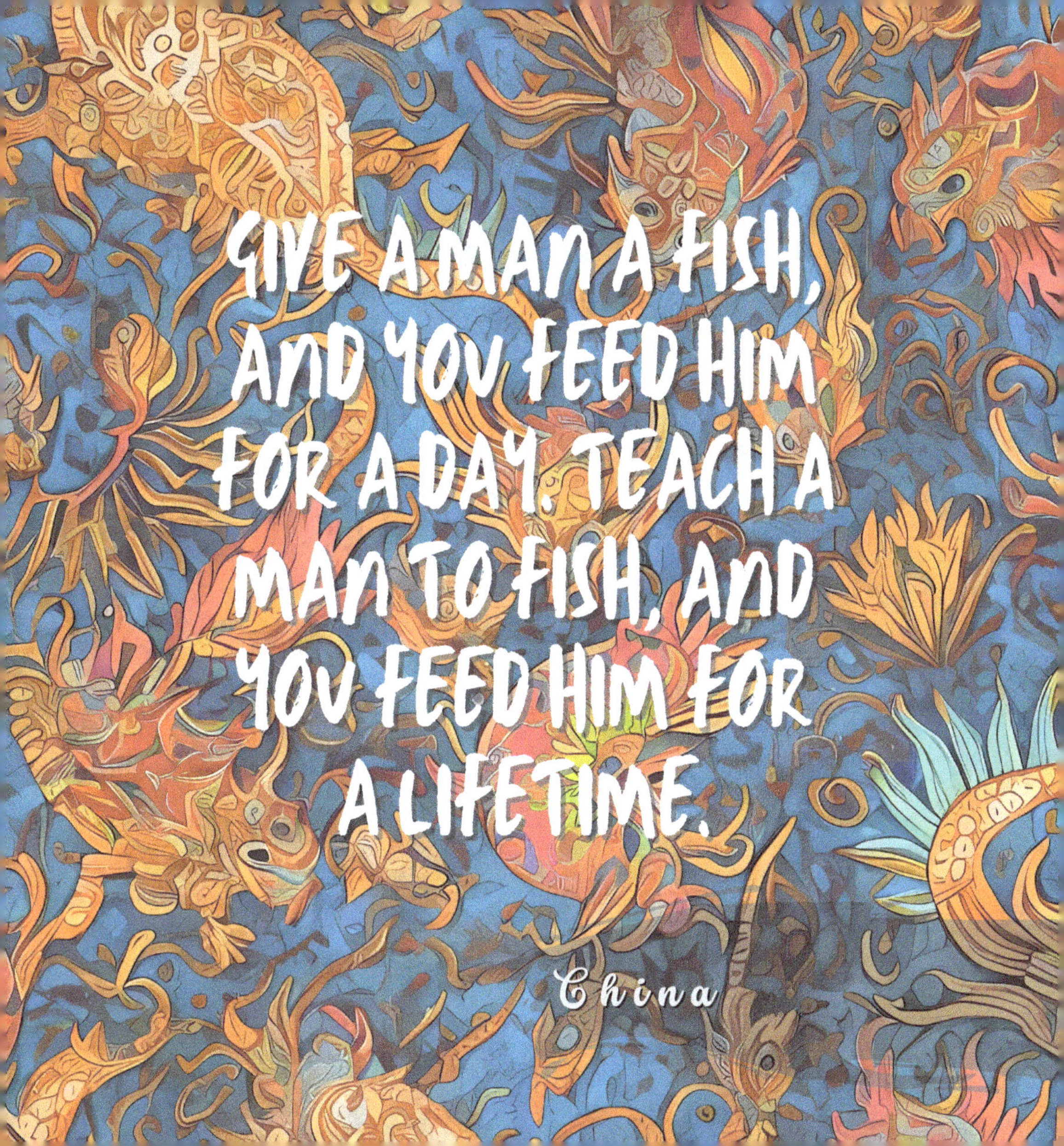
GIVE A MAN A FISH, AND YOU FEED HIM FOR A DAY. TEACH A MAN TO FISH, AND YOU FEED HIM FOR A LIFETIME.
China

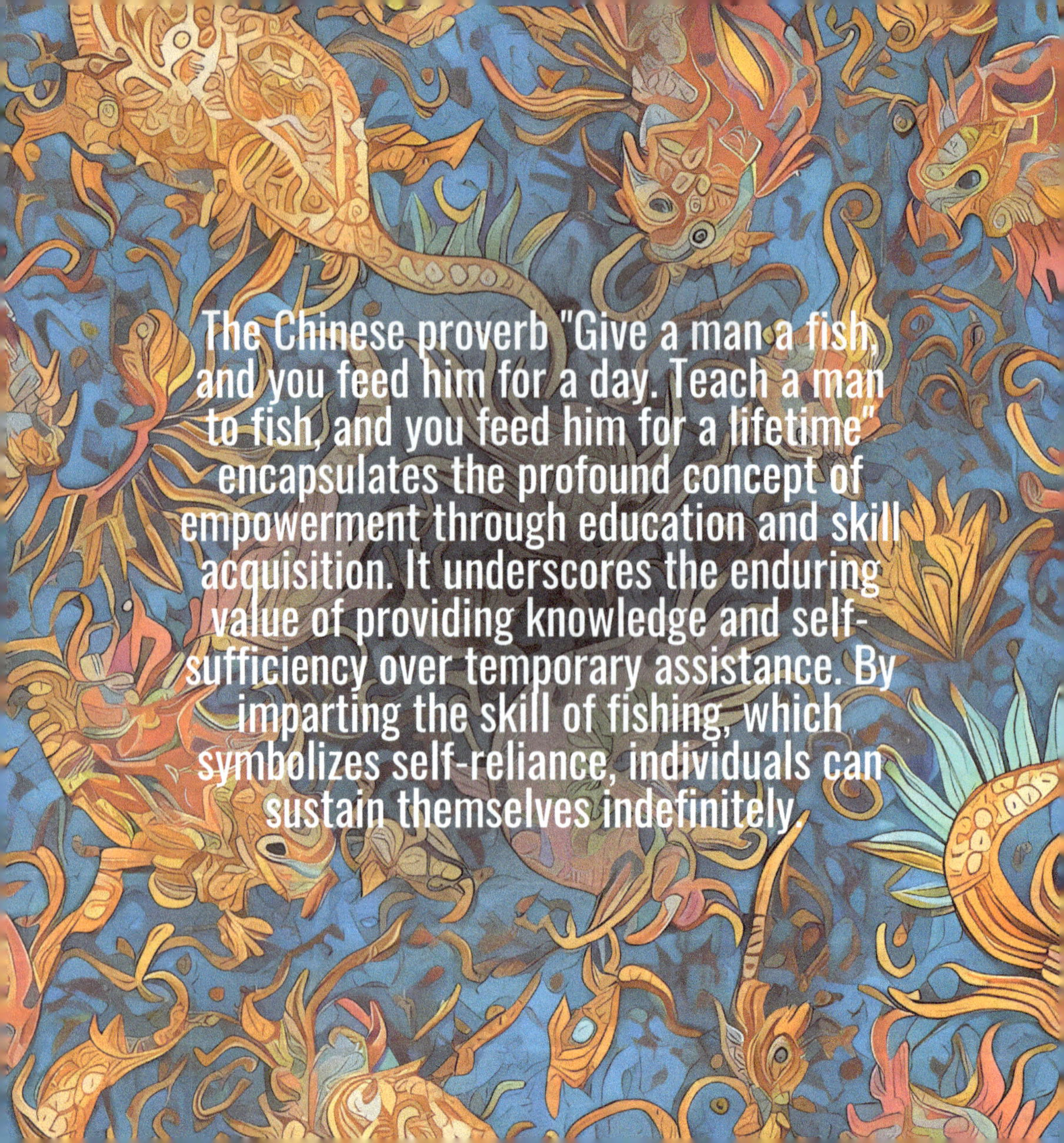
The Chinese proverb "Give a man a fish, and you feed him for a day. Teach a man to fish, and you feed him for a lifetime" encapsulates the profound concept of empowerment through education and skill acquisition. It underscores the enduring value of providing knowledge and self-sufficiency over temporary assistance. By imparting the skill of fishing, which symbolizes self-reliance, individuals can sustain themselves indefinitely.

FALL SEVEN TIMES,
STAND UP EIGHT.
Japan

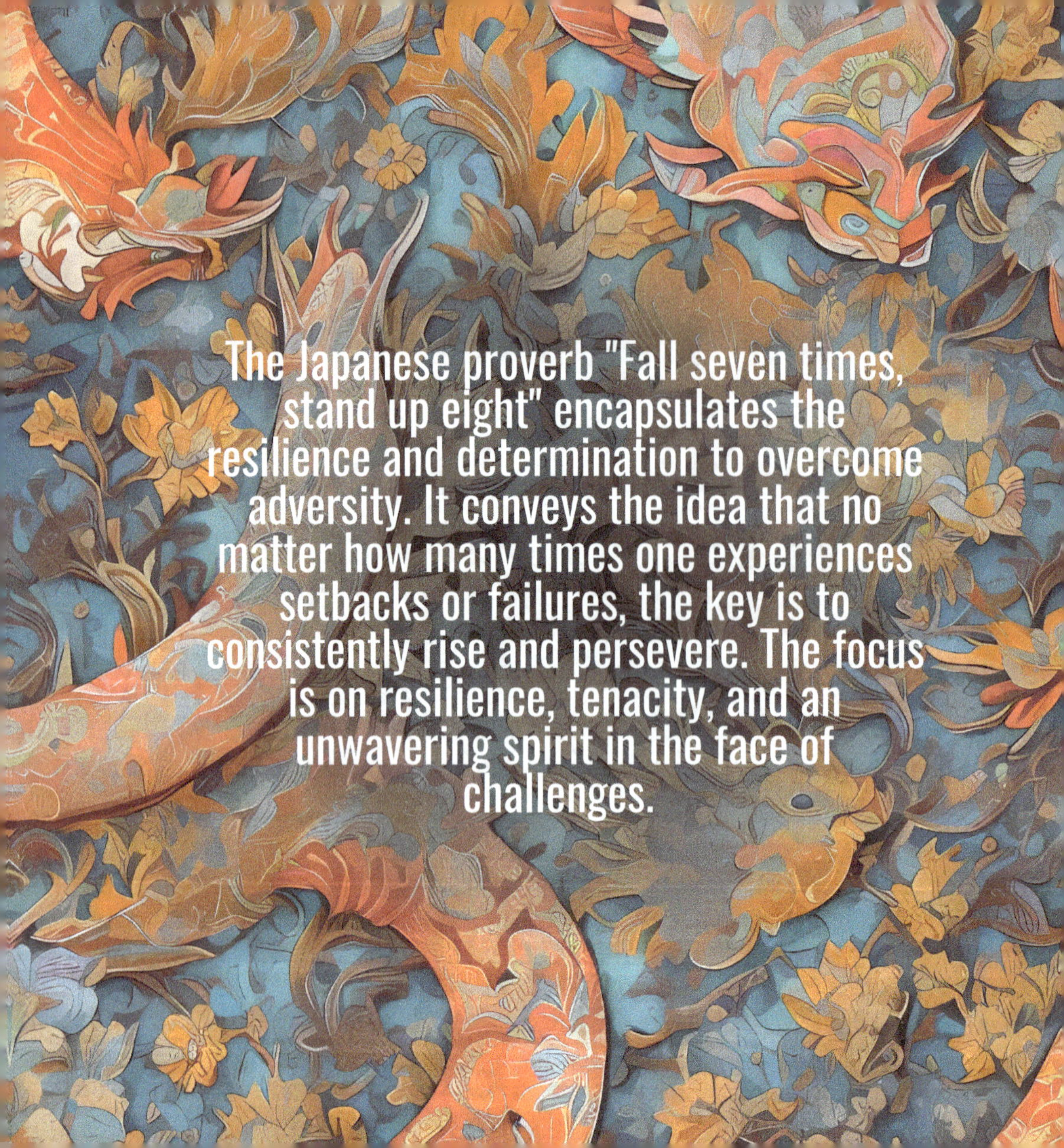

The Japanese proverb "Fall seven times, stand up eight" encapsulates the resilience and determination to overcome adversity. It conveys the idea that no matter how many times one experiences setbacks or failures, the key is to consistently rise and persevere. The focus is on resilience, tenacity, and an unwavering spirit in the face of challenges.

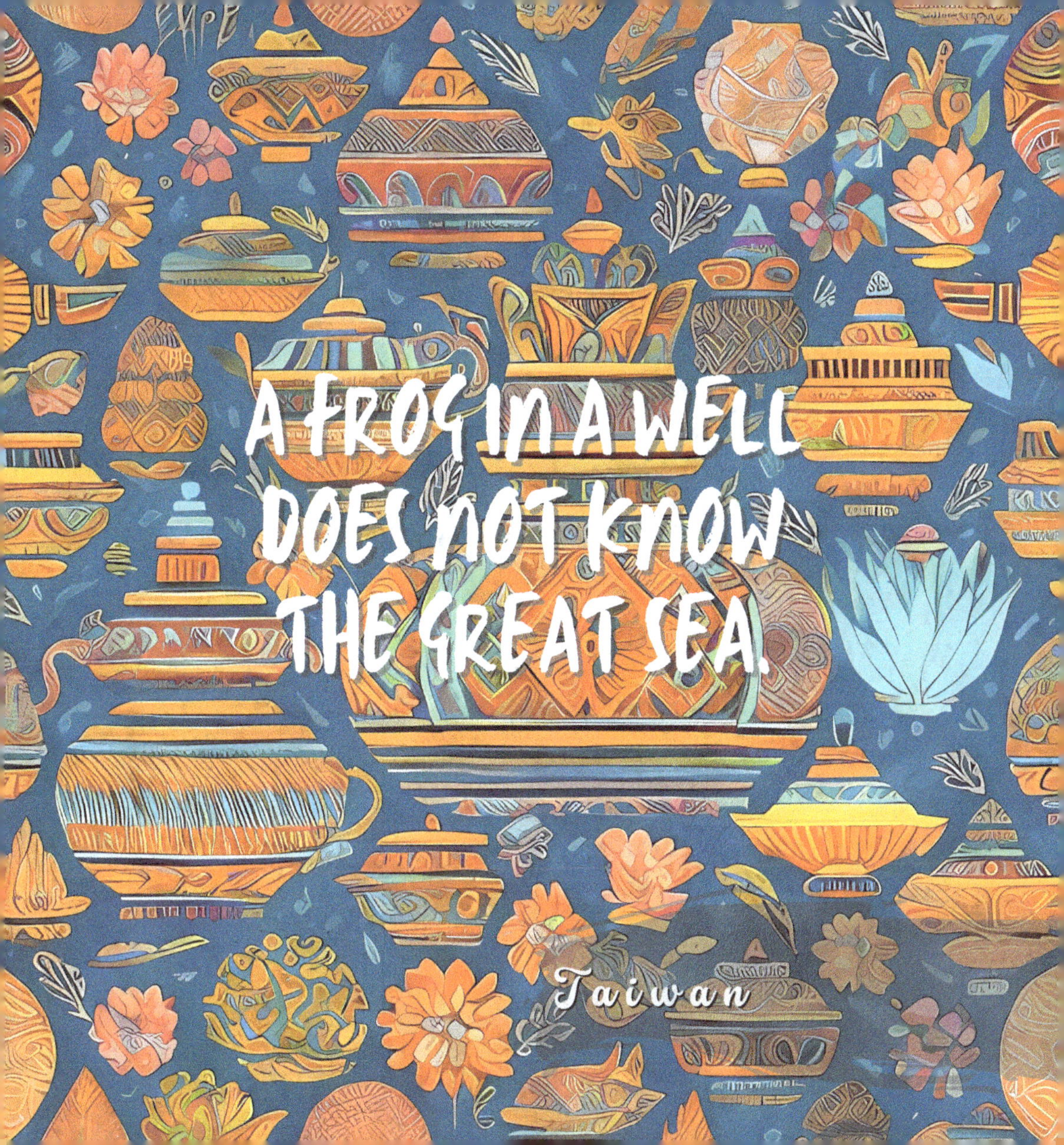
A FROG IN A WELL
DOES NOT KNOW
THE GREAT SEA.
Taiwan

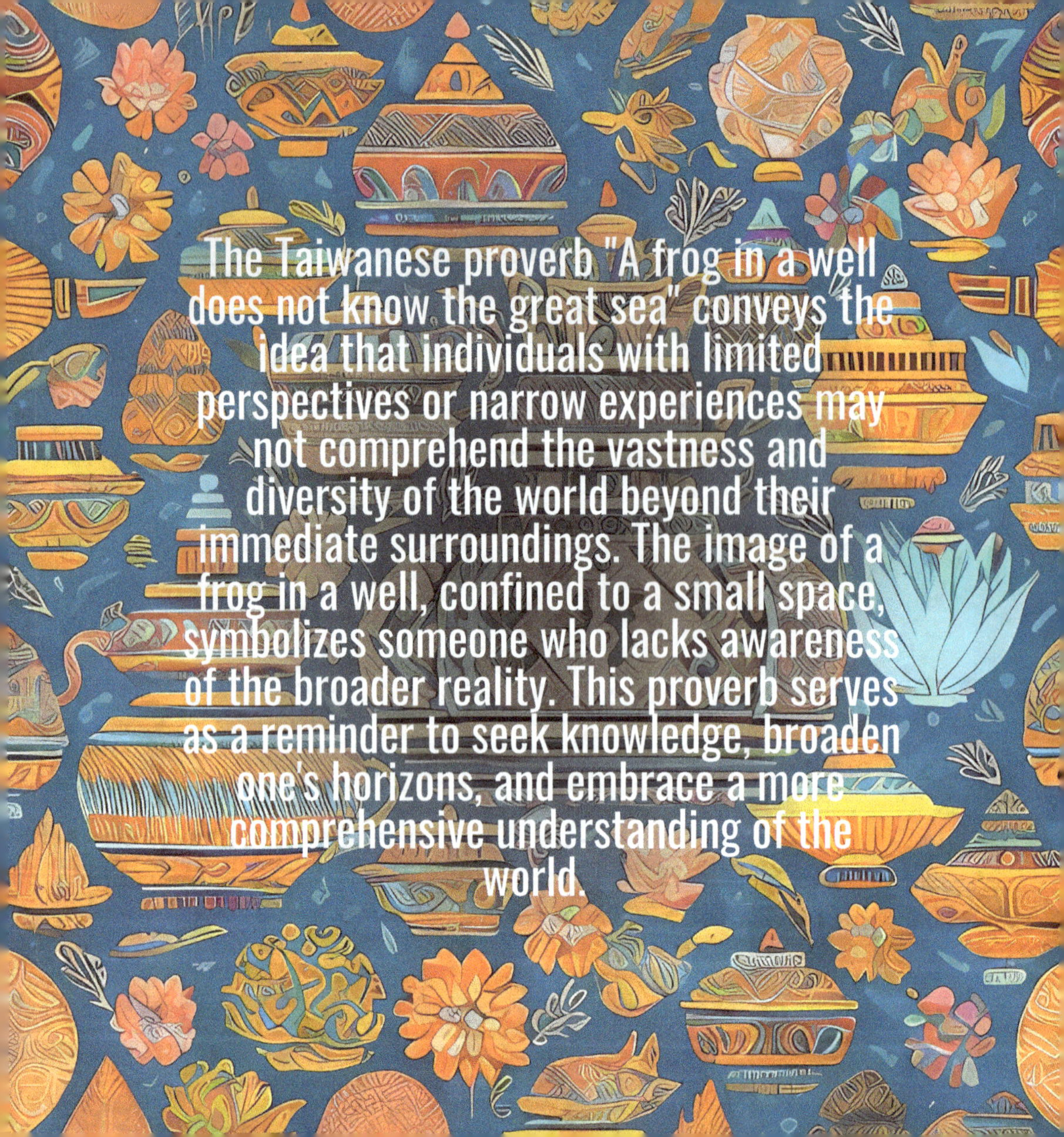
The Taiwanese proverb "A frog in a well does not know the great sea" conveys the idea that individuals with limited perspectives or narrow experiences may not comprehend the vastness and diversity of the world beyond their immediate surroundings. The image of a frog in a well, confined to a small space, symbolizes someone who lacks awareness of the broader reality. This proverb serves as a reminder to seek knowledge, broaden one's horizons, and embrace a more comprehensive understanding of the world.

THE CHAMELEON
CHANGES COLOR TO
MATCH THE EARTH,
THE EARTH
DOESN'T CHANGE
COLORS TO MATCH
THE CHAMELEON.
Cameroon

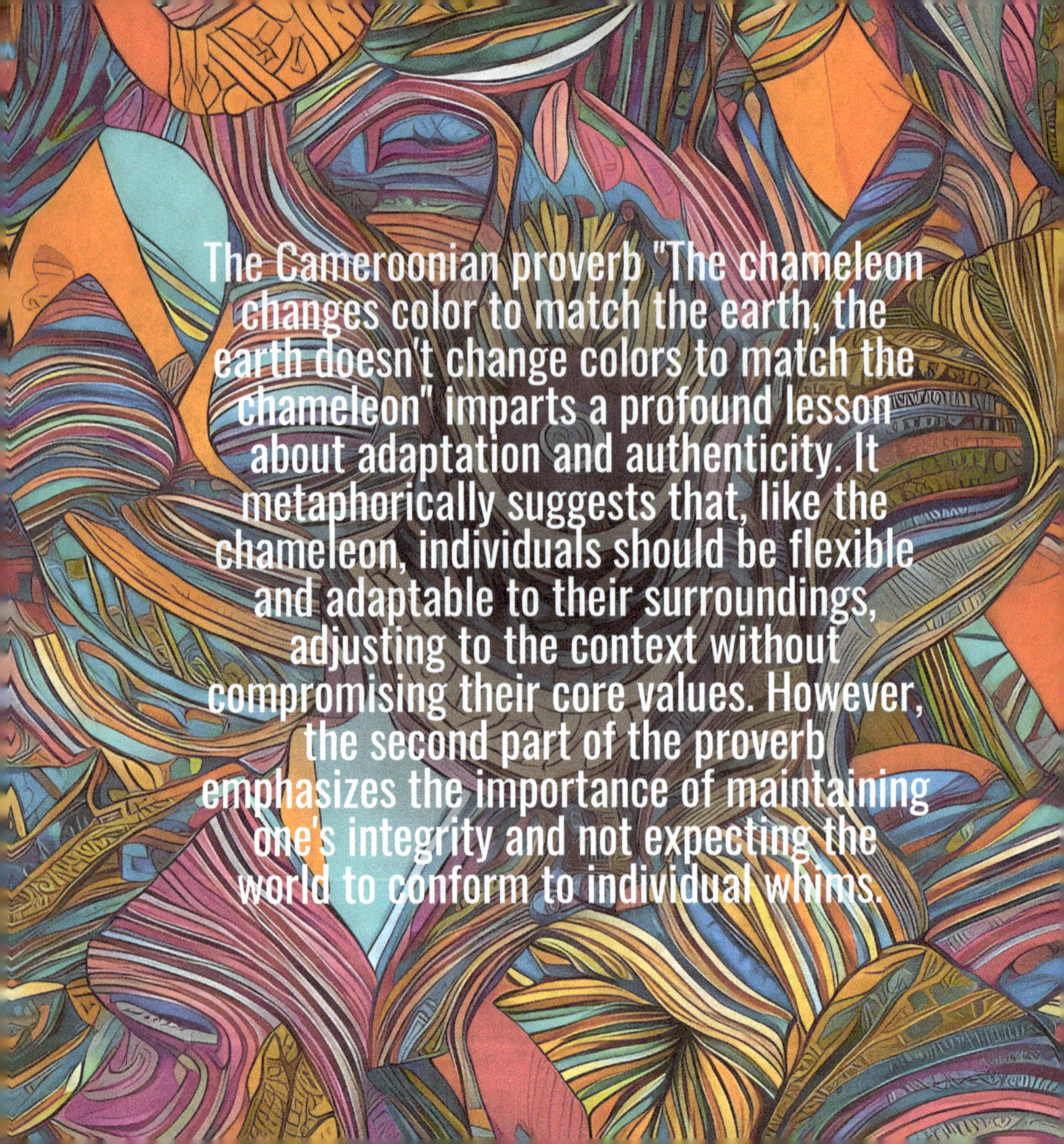

The Cameroonian proverb "The chameleon changes color to match the earth, the earth doesn't change colors to match the chameleon" imparts a profound lesson about adaptation and authenticity. It metaphorically suggests that, like the chameleon, individuals should be flexible and adaptable to their surroundings, adjusting to the context without compromising their core values. However, the second part of the proverb emphasizes the importance of maintaining one's integrity and not expecting the world to conform to individual whims.

THE CHILD WHO
LEARNS TO WASH
HIS HANDS
PROPERLY WILL
EAT WITH THE
ELDERS.
Ghana

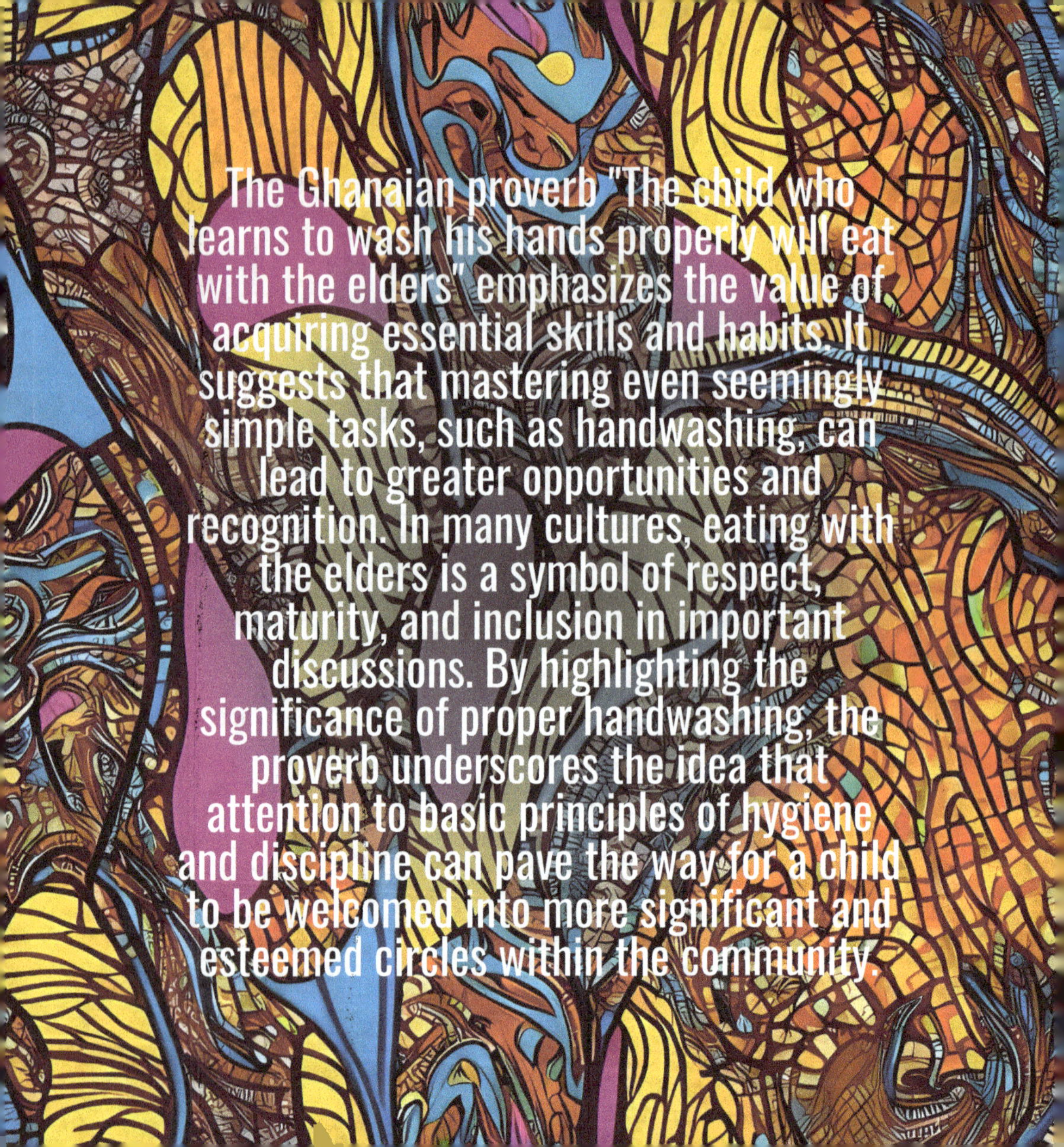

The Ghanaian proverb "The child who learns to wash his hands properly will eat with the elders" emphasizes the value of acquiring essential skills and habits. It suggests that mastering even seemingly simple tasks, such as handwashing, can lead to greater opportunities and recognition. In many cultures, eating with the elders is a symbol of respect, maturity, and inclusion in important discussions. By highlighting the significance of proper handwashing, the proverb underscores the idea that attention to basic principles of hygiene and discipline can pave the way for a child to be welcomed into more significant and esteemed circles within the community.

COMPARISON IS THE
THIEF OF JOY.
Swahili

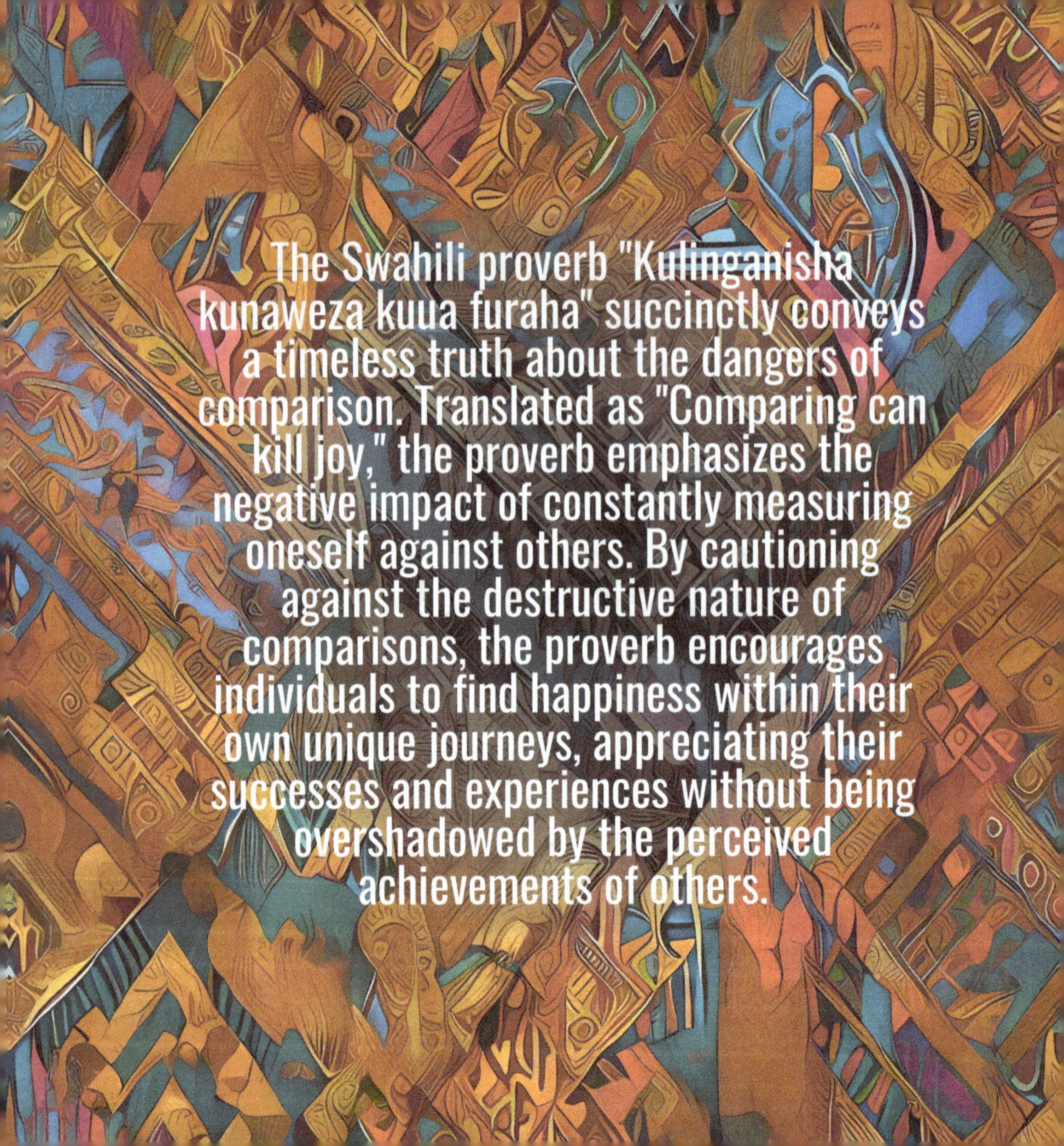

The Swahili proverb "Kulinganisha kunaweza kuua furaha" succinctly conveys a timeless truth about the dangers of comparison. Translated as "Comparing can kill joy," the proverb emphasizes the negative impact of constantly measuring oneself against others. By cautioning against the destructive nature of comparisons, the proverb encourages individuals to find happiness within their own unique journeys, appreciating their successes and experiences without being overshadowed by the perceived achievements of others.

HE WHO LOVES, LOVE YOU WITH YOUR DIRT.
South Africa

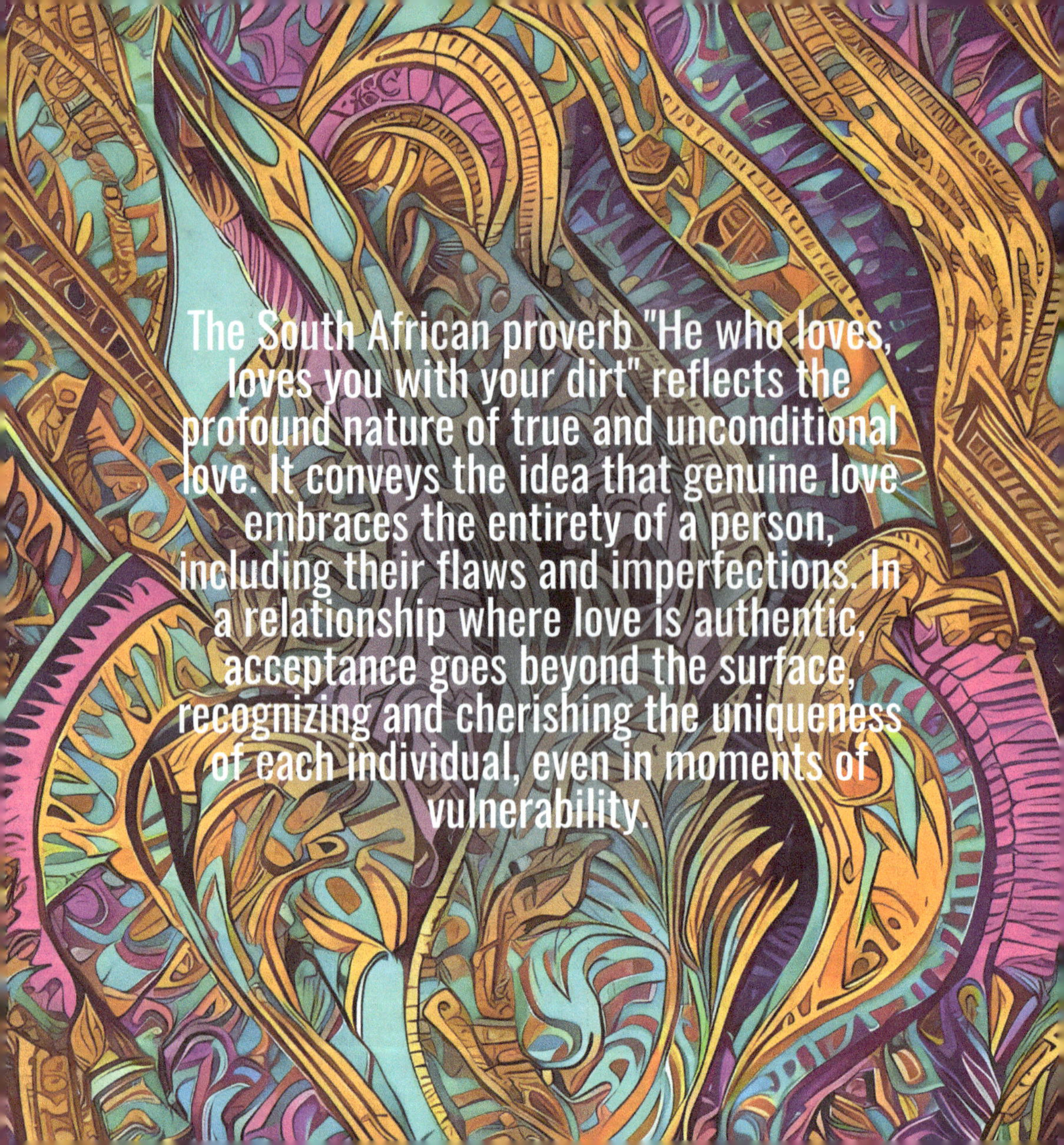
The South African proverb "He who loves, loves you with your dirt" reflects the profound nature of true and unconditional love. It conveys the idea that genuine love embraces the entirety of a person, including their flaws and imperfections. In a relationship where love is authentic, acceptance goes beyond the surface, recognizing and cherishing the uniqueness of each individual, even in moments of vulnerability.

WHEN THE MUSIC
CHANGES, SO DOES
THE DANCE.
Nigeria

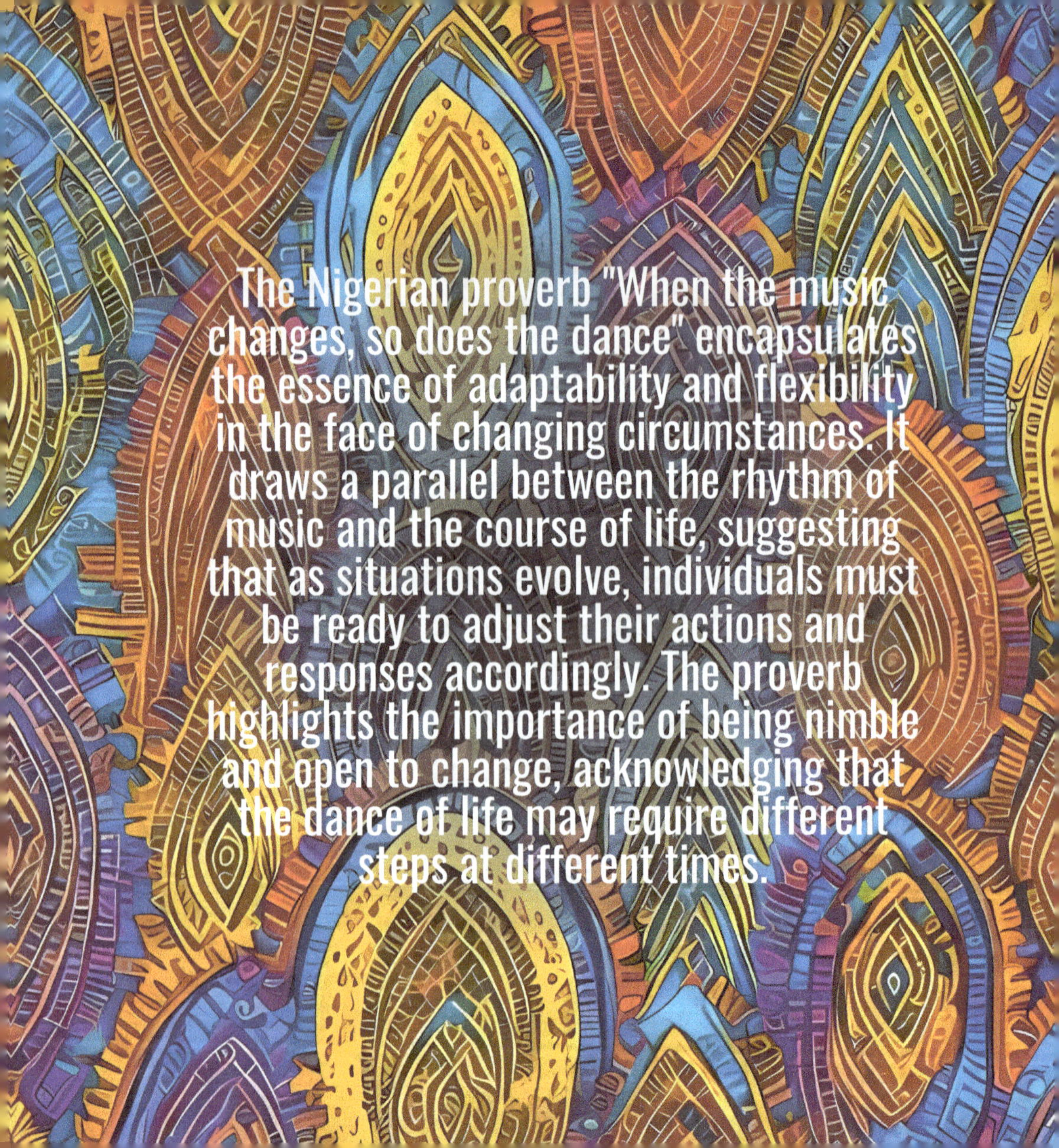

The Nigerian proverb "When the music changes, so does the dance" encapsulates the essence of adaptability and flexibility in the face of changing circumstances. It draws a parallel between the rhythm of music and the course of life, suggesting that as situations evolve, individuals must be ready to adjust their actions and responses accordingly. The proverb highlights the importance of being nimble and open to change, acknowledging that the dance of life may require different steps at different times.

YOU LEARN HOW TO
CUT DOWN TREES
BY CUTTING THEM
DOWN.
Zimbabwe

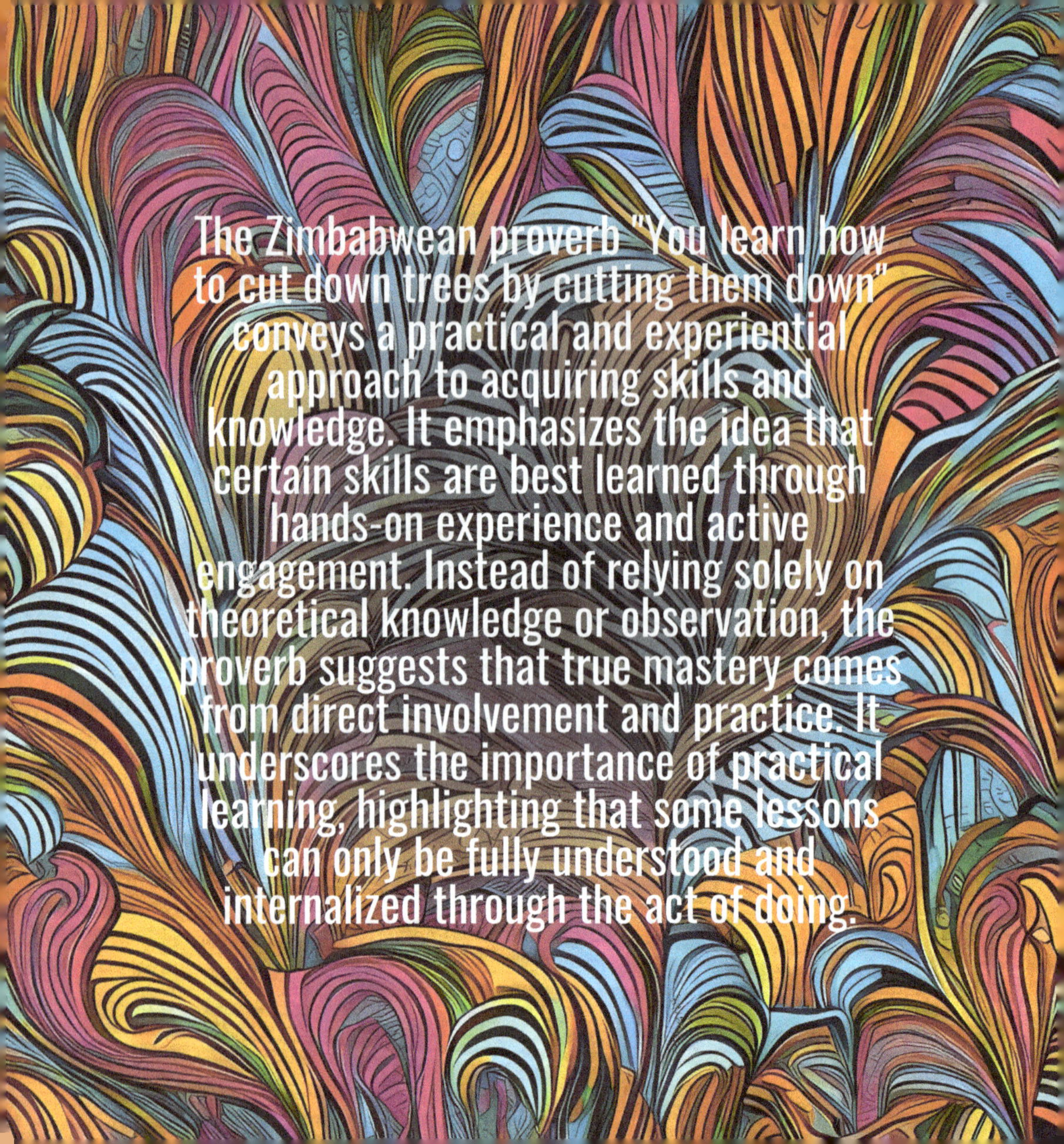
The Zimbabwean proverb "You learn how to cut down trees by cutting them down" conveys a practical and experiential approach to acquiring skills and knowledge. It emphasizes the idea that certain skills are best learned through hands-on experience and active engagement. Instead of relying solely on theoretical knowledge or observation, the proverb suggests that true mastery comes from direct involvement and practice. It underscores the importance of practical learning, highlighting that some lessons can only be fully understood and internalized through the act of doing.

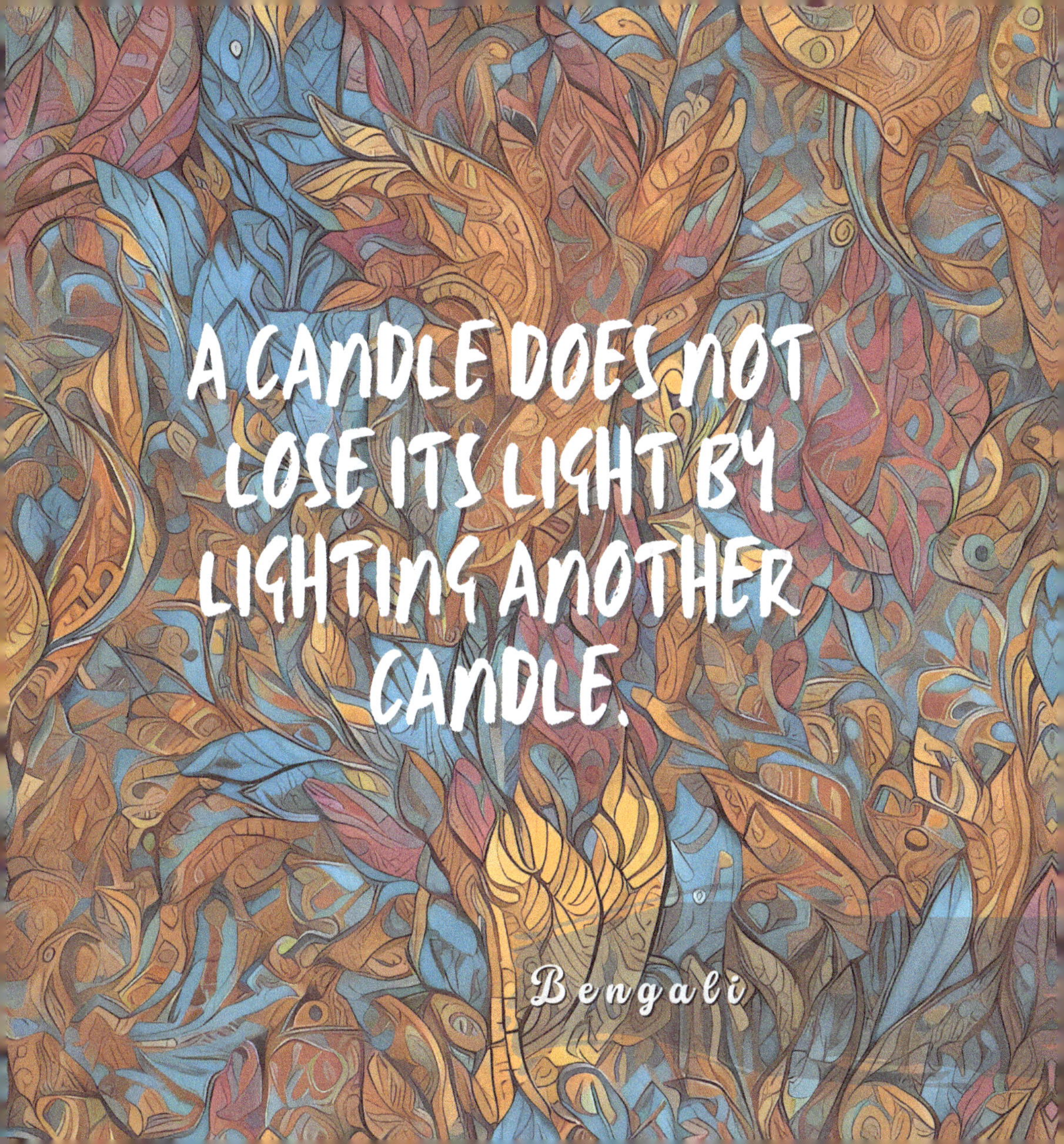
A CANDLE DOES NOT
LOSE ITS LIGHT BY
LIGHTING ANOTHER
CANDLE.
Bengali

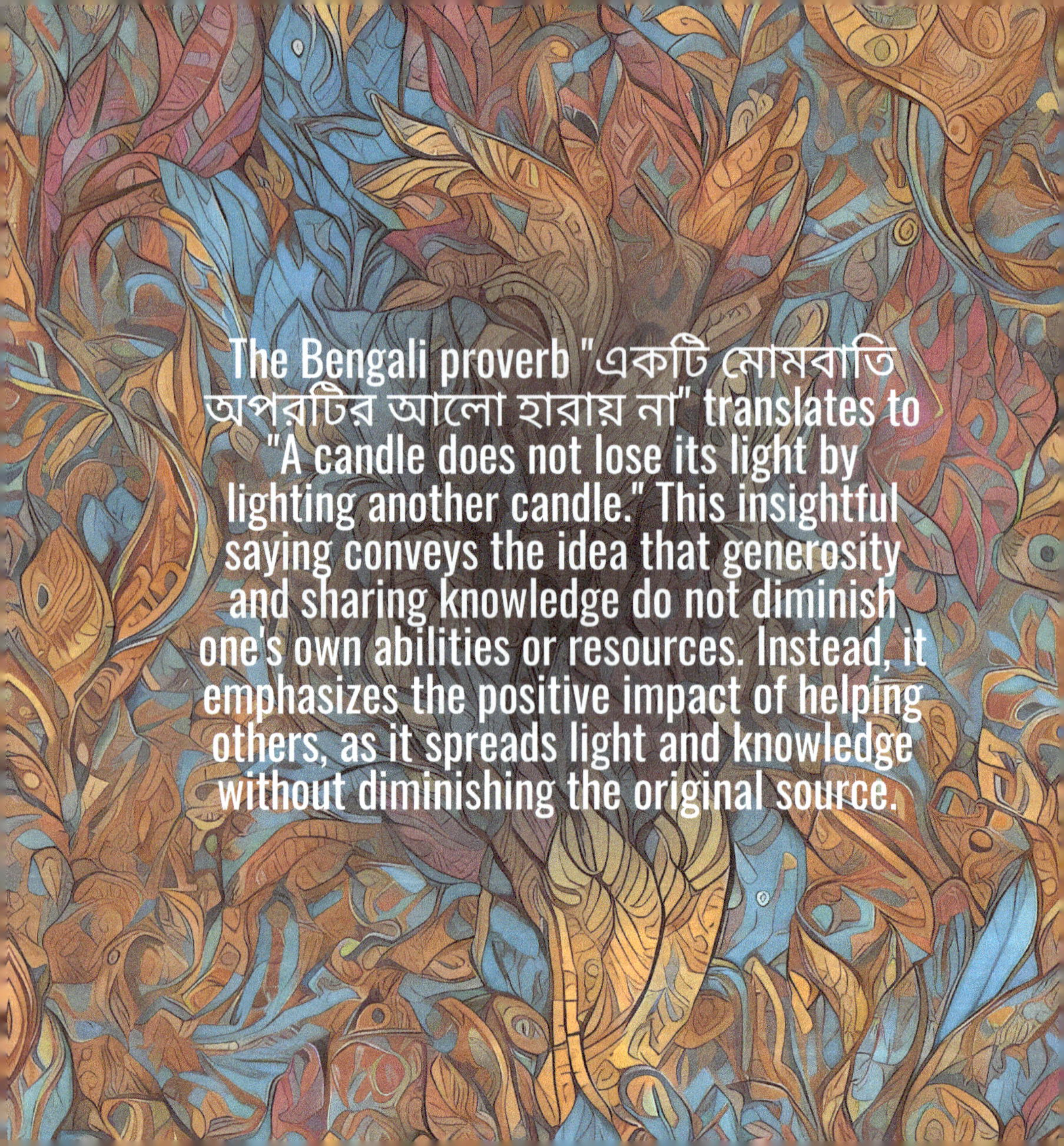
The Bengali proverb "একটি মোমবাতি অপরটির আলো হারায় না" translates to "A candle does not lose its light by lighting another candle." This insightful saying conveys the idea that generosity and sharing knowledge do not diminish one's own abilities or resources. Instead, it emphasizes the positive impact of helping others, as it spreads light and knowledge without diminishing the original source.

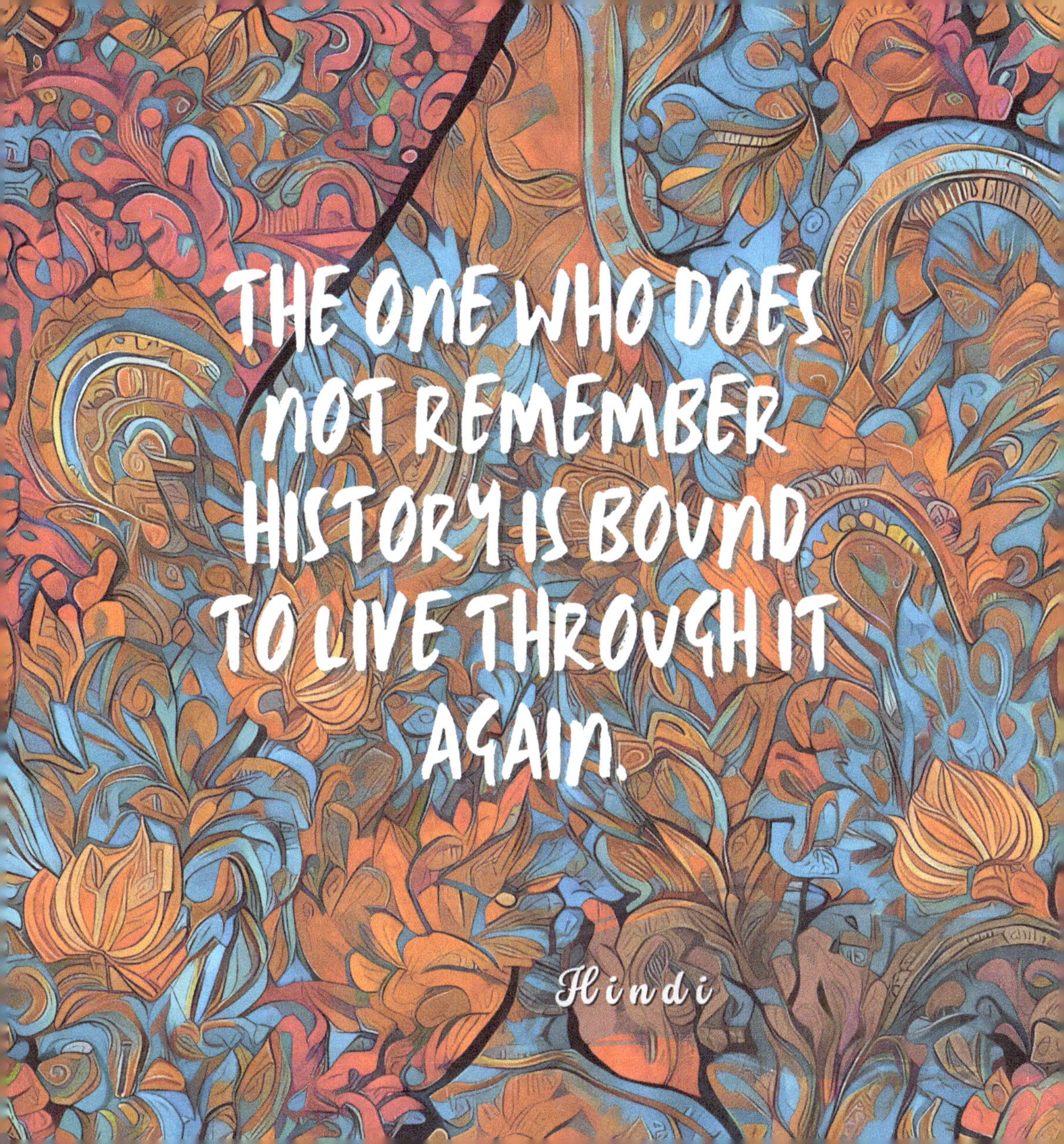
THE ONE WHO DOES
NOT REMEMBER
HISTORY IS BOUND
TO LIVE THROUGH IT
AGAIN.
Hindi

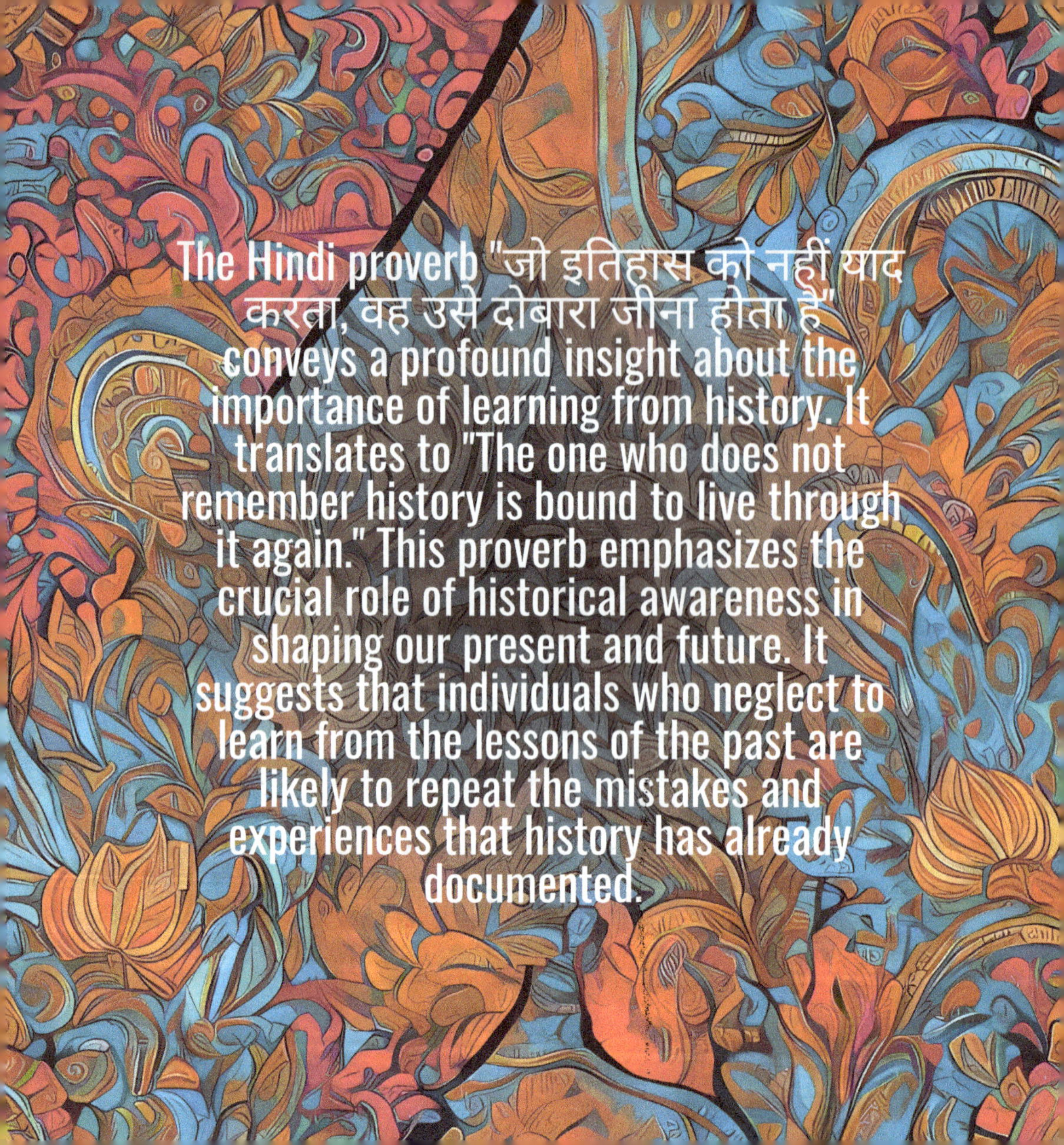
The Hindi proverb "जो इतिहास को नहीं याद करता, वह उसे दोबारा जीना होता है" conveys a profound insight about the importance of learning from history. It translates to "The one who does not remember history is bound to live through it again." This proverb emphasizes the crucial role of historical awareness in shaping our present and future. It suggests that individuals who neglect to learn from the lessons of the past are likely to repeat the mistakes and experiences that history has already documented.

THE COCONUT TREE
BENDS TO ITS OWN
WEIGHT.
Malayalam

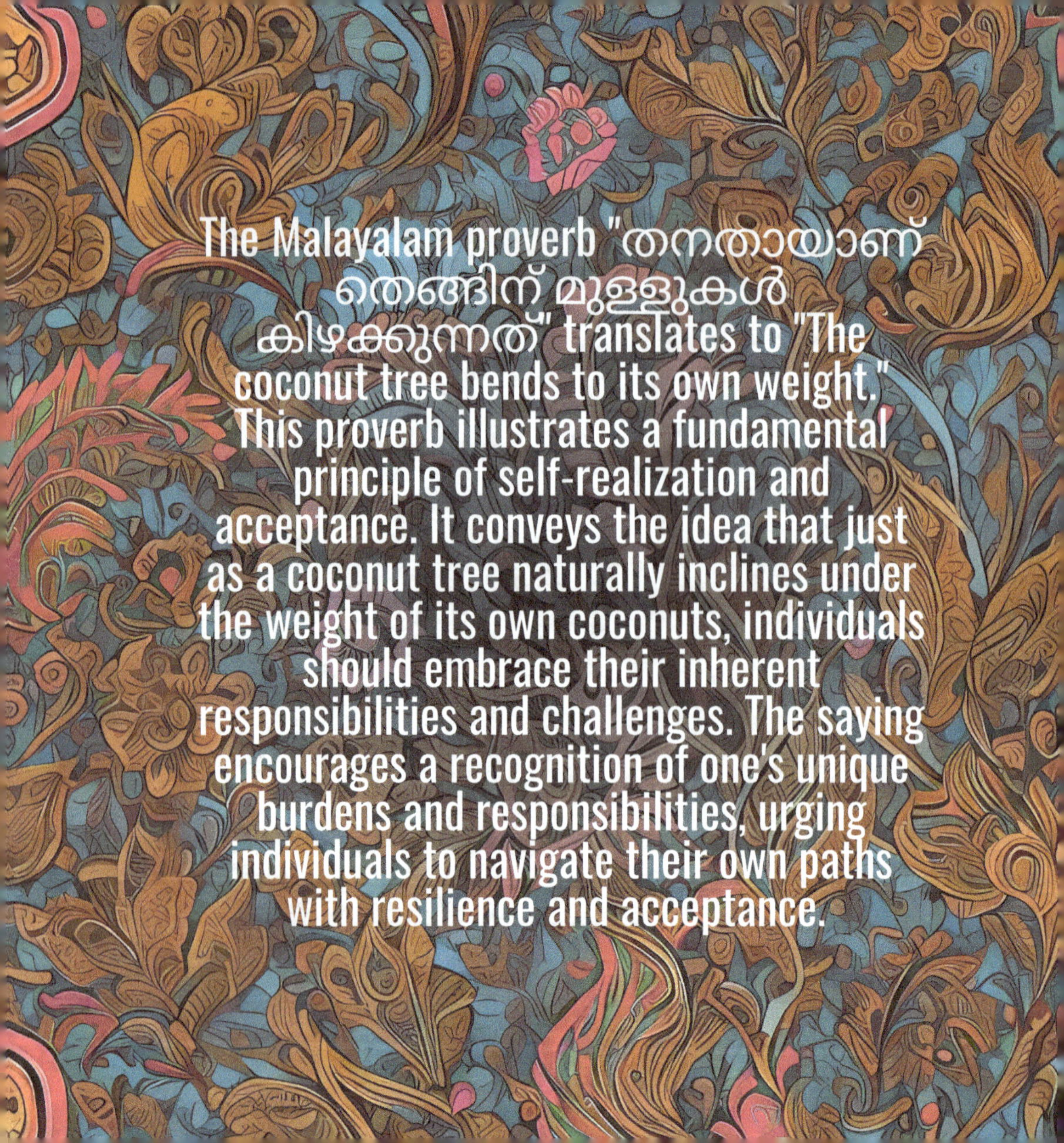

The Malayalam proverb "തനതായാണ് തെങ്ങിന് മുള്ളുകൾ കിഴക്കുന്നത്" translates to "The coconut tree bends to its own weight." This proverb illustrates a fundamental principle of self-realization and acceptance. It conveys the idea that just as a coconut tree naturally inclines under the weight of its own coconuts, individuals should embrace their inherent responsibilities and challenges. The saying encourages a recognition of one's unique burdens and responsibilities, urging individuals to navigate their own paths with resilience and acceptance.

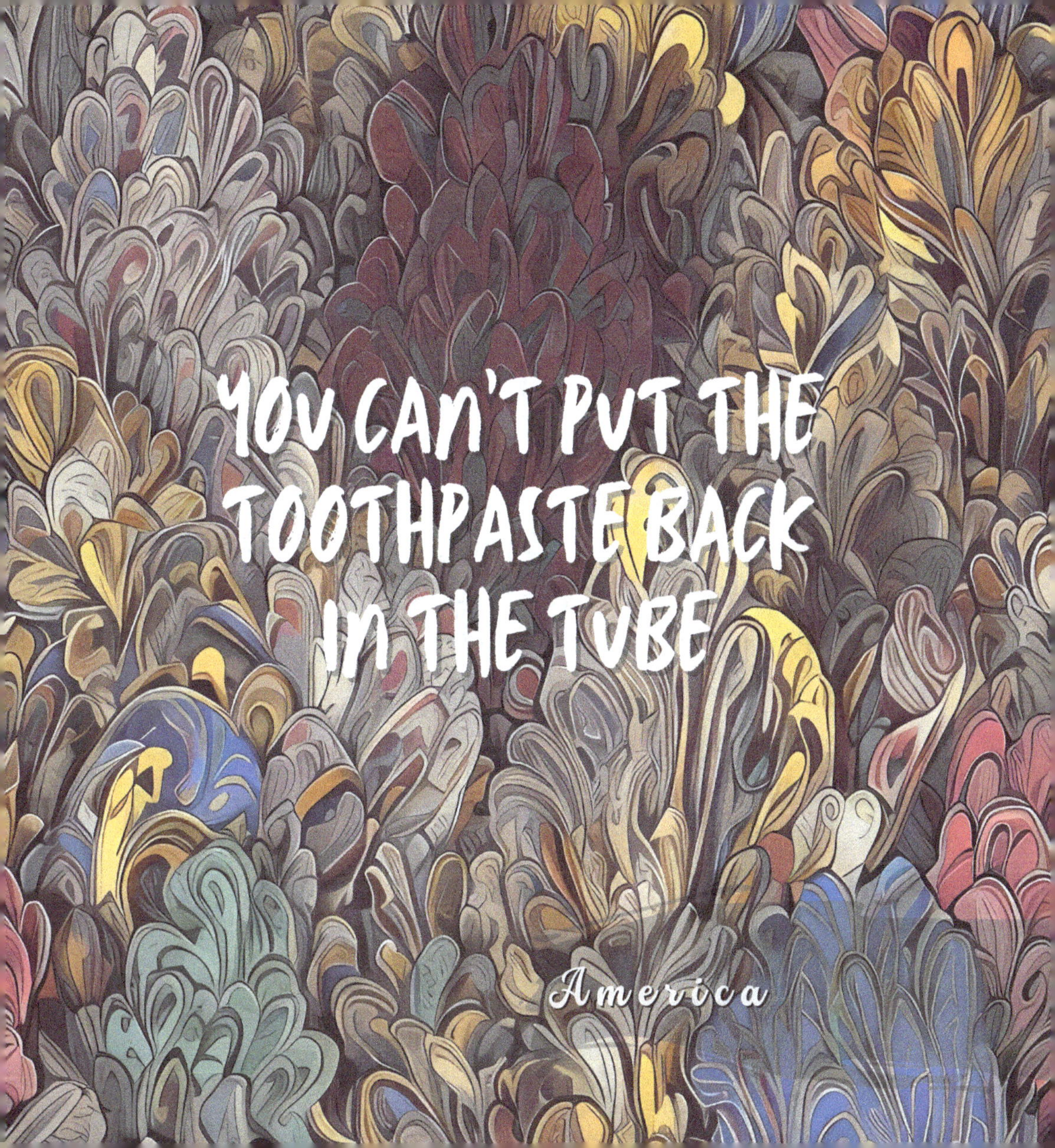
YOU CAN'T PUT THE TOOTHPASTE BACK IN THE TUBE
America

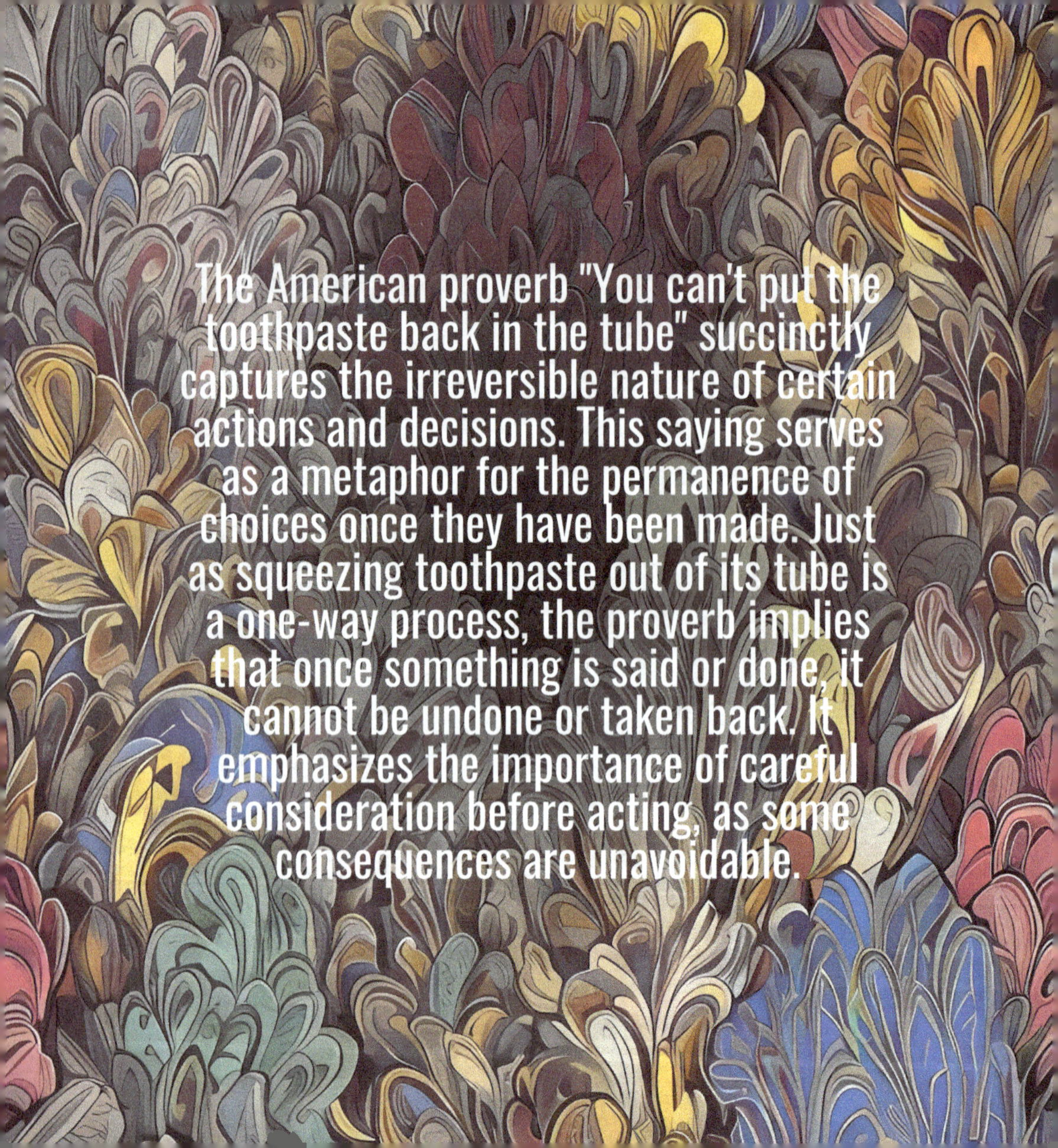

The American proverb "You can't put the toothpaste back in the tube" succinctly captures the irreversible nature of certain actions and decisions. This saying serves as a metaphor for the permanence of choices once they have been made. Just as squeezing toothpaste out of its tube is a one-way process, the proverb implies that once something is said or done, it cannot be undone or taken back. It emphasizes the importance of careful consideration before acting, as some consequences are unavoidable.

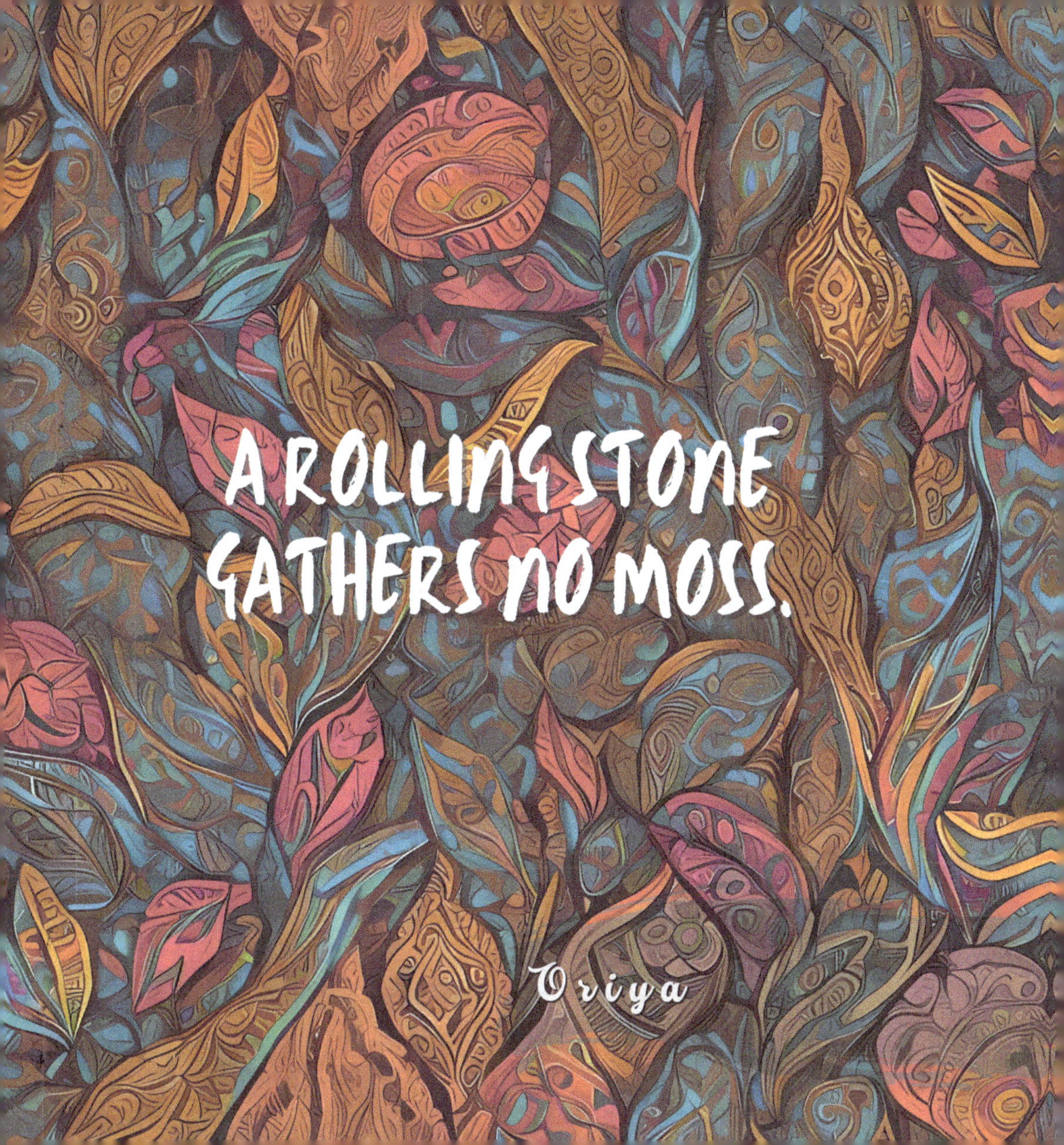
A ROLLING STONE
GATHERS NO MOSS.
Oriya

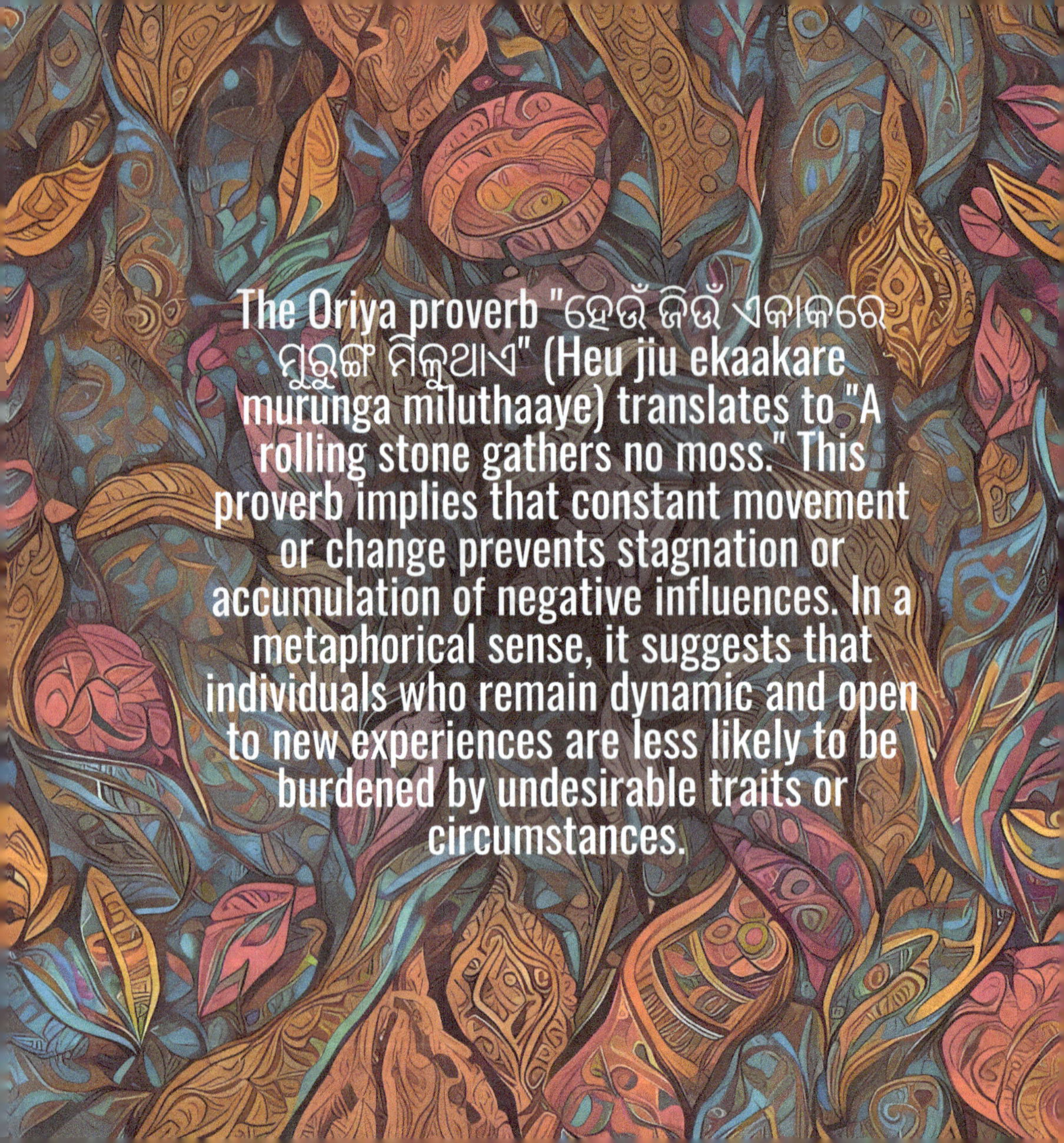
The Oriya proverb "ହେଉଁ ଜିଉଁ ଏକାକରେ ମୁରୁଙ୍ଗ ମିଳୁଥାଏ" (Heu jiu ekaakare murunga miluthaaye) translates to "A rolling stone gathers no moss." This proverb implies that constant movement or change prevents stagnation or accumulation of negative influences. In a metaphorical sense, it suggests that individuals who remain dynamic and open to new experiences are less likely to be burdened by undesirable traits or circumstances.

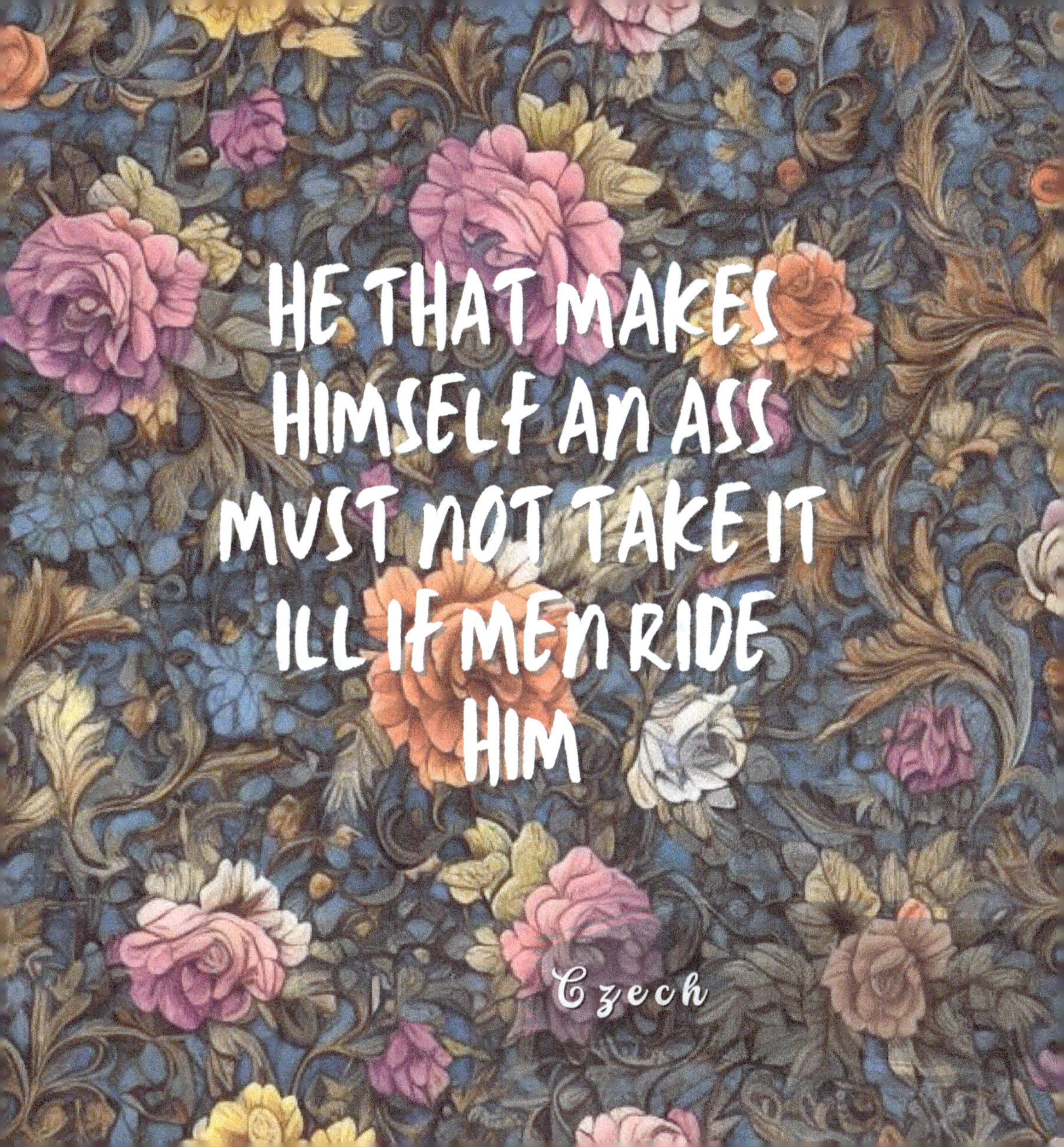
HE THAT MAKES
HIMSELF AN ASS
MUST NOT TAKE IT
ILL IF MEN RIDE
HIM
Czech

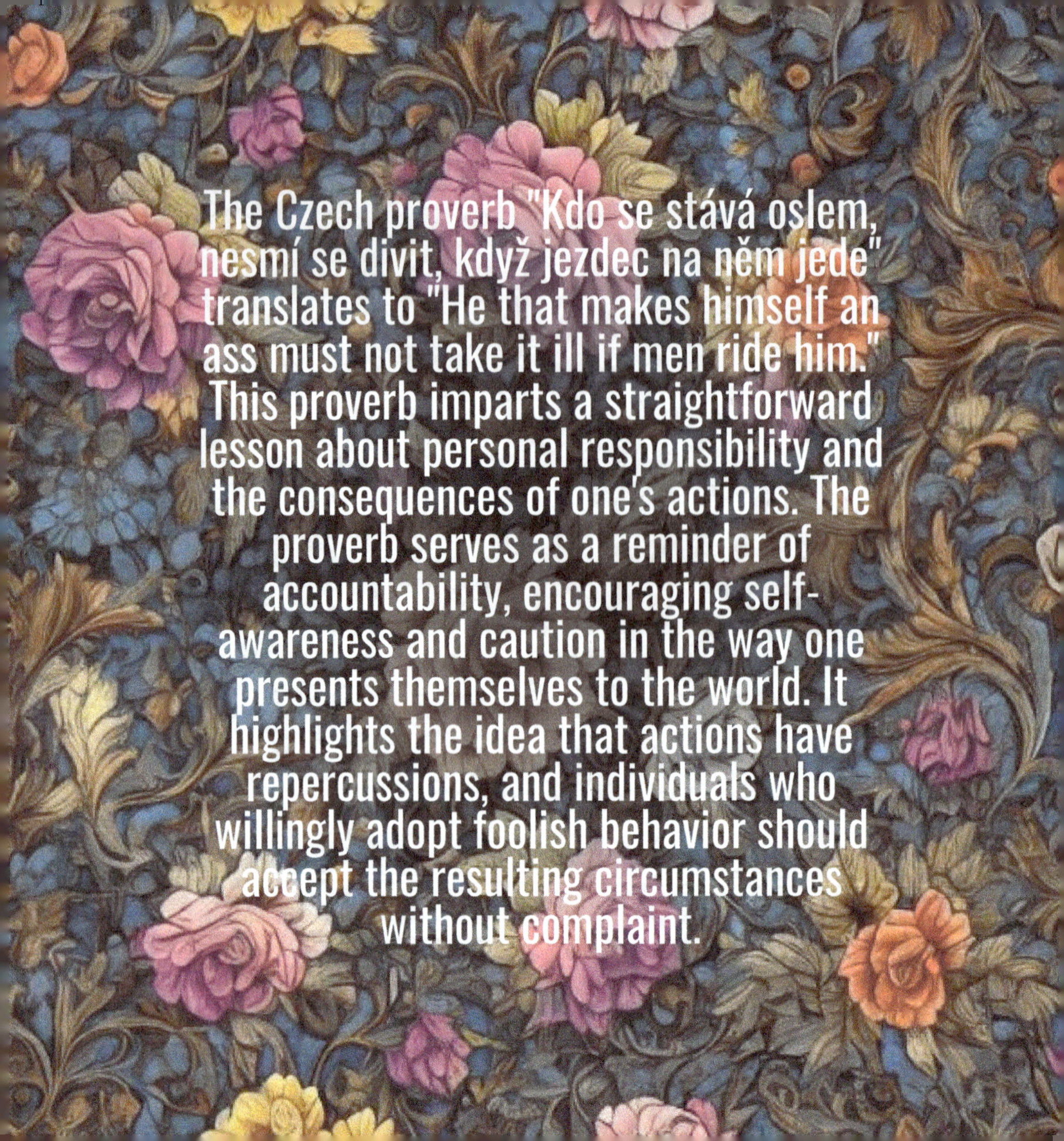
The Czech proverb "Kdo se stává oslem,
nesmí se divit, když jezdec na něm jede"
translates to "He that makes himself an
ass must not take it ill if men ride him."
This proverb imparts a straightforward
lesson about personal responsibility and
the consequences of one's actions. The
proverb serves as a reminder of
accountability, encouraging self-
awareness and caution in the way one
presents themselves to the world. It
highlights the idea that actions have
repercussions, and individuals who
willingly adopt foolish behavior should
accept the resulting circumstances
without complaint.

YOU CAN'T MAKE
AN OMELET
WITHOUT
BREAKING EGGS.
France

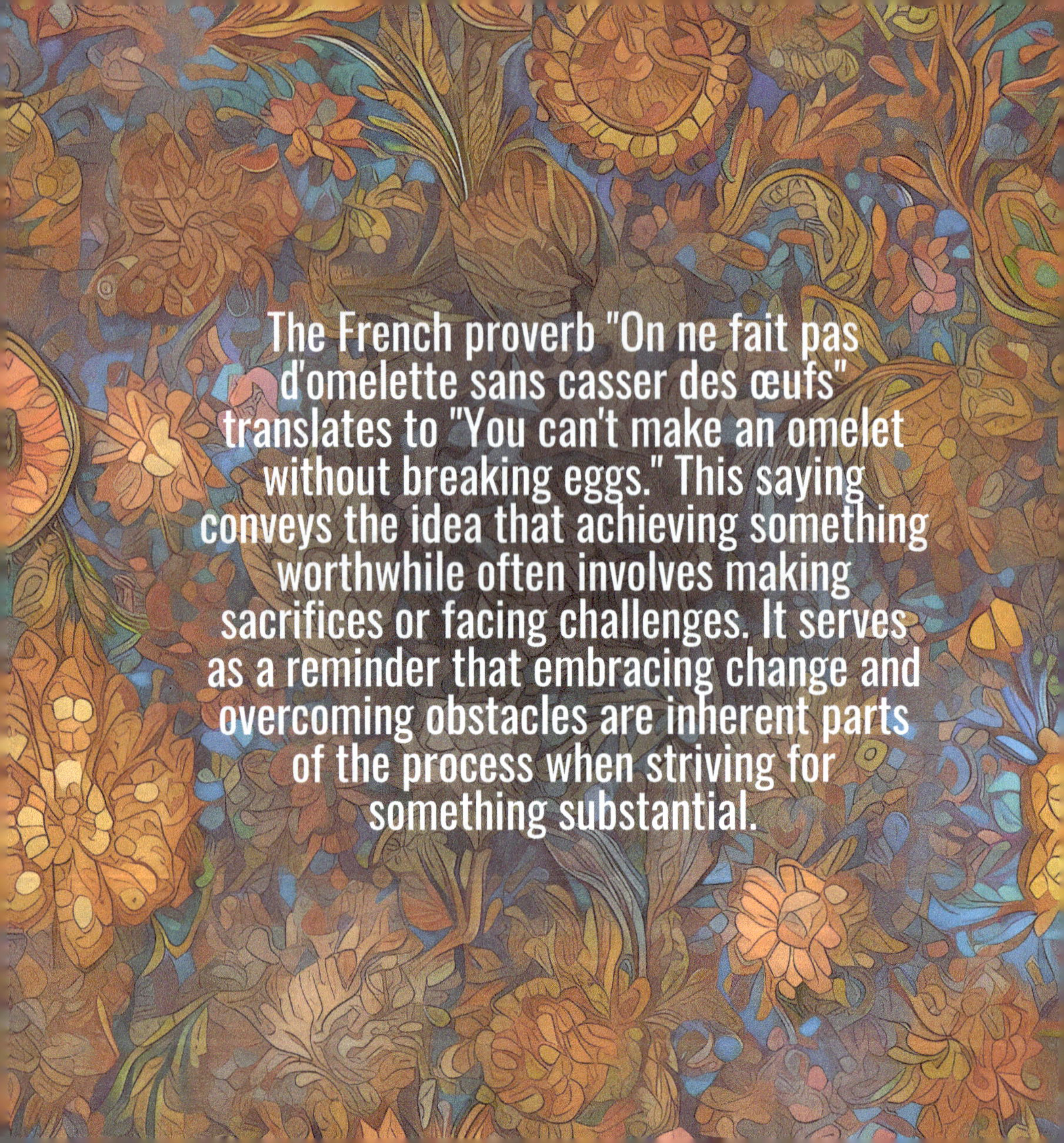
The French proverb "On ne fait pas d'omelette sans casser des œufs" translates to "You can't make an omelet without breaking eggs." This saying conveys the idea that achieving something worthwhile often involves making sacrifices or facing challenges. It serves as a reminder that embracing change and overcoming obstacles are inherent parts of the process when striving for something substantial.

WELL BEGUN IS
HALF DONE.
Italy

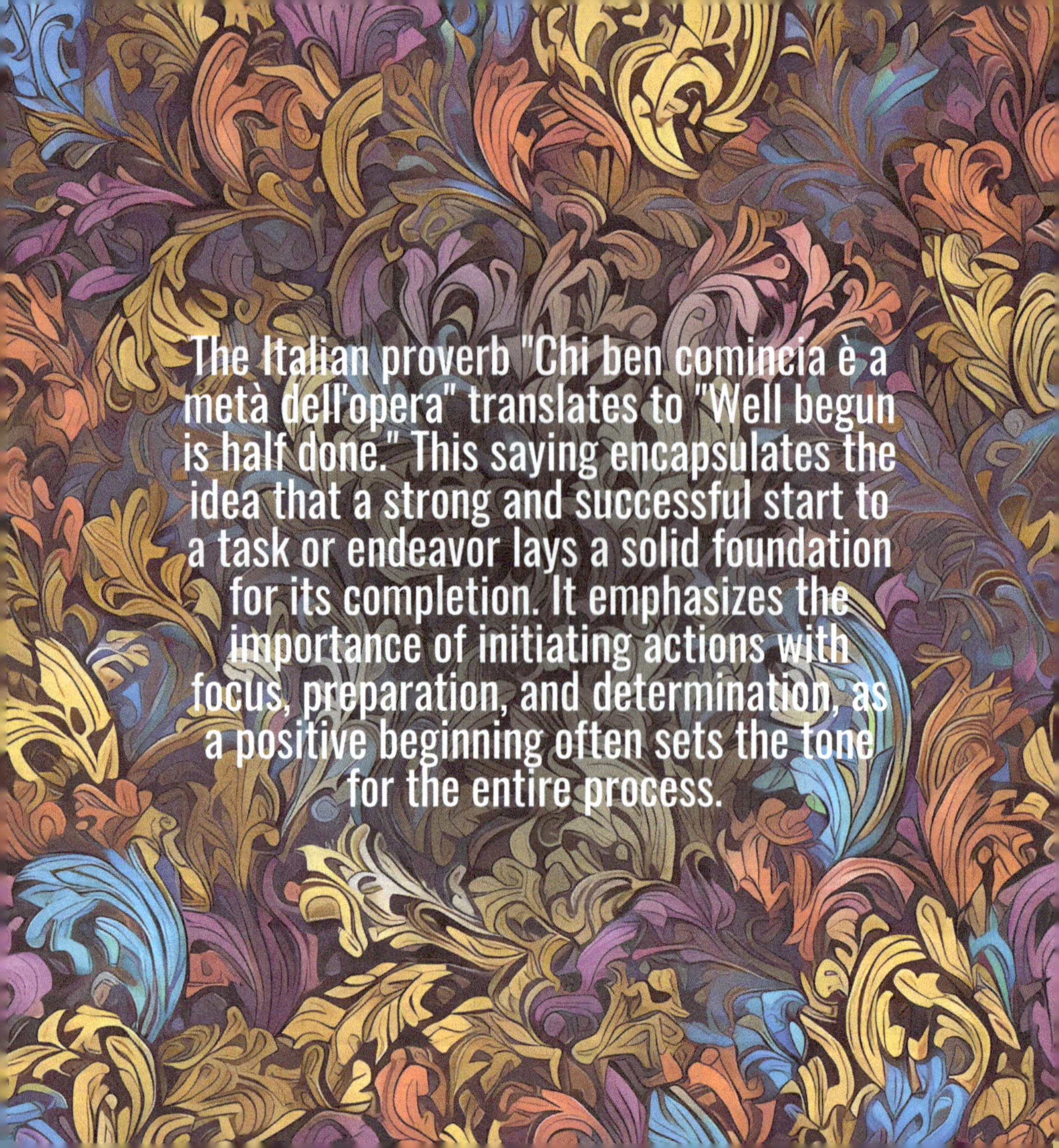

The Italian proverb "Chi ben comincia è a metà dell'opera" translates to "Well begun is half done." This saying encapsulates the idea that a strong and successful start to a task or endeavor lays a solid foundation for its completion. It emphasizes the importance of initiating actions with focus, preparation, and determination, as a positive beginning often sets the tone for the entire process.

FROM THE
CONCERT OF LIFE,
NO ONE GETS A
PROGRAM.
The
Netherlands

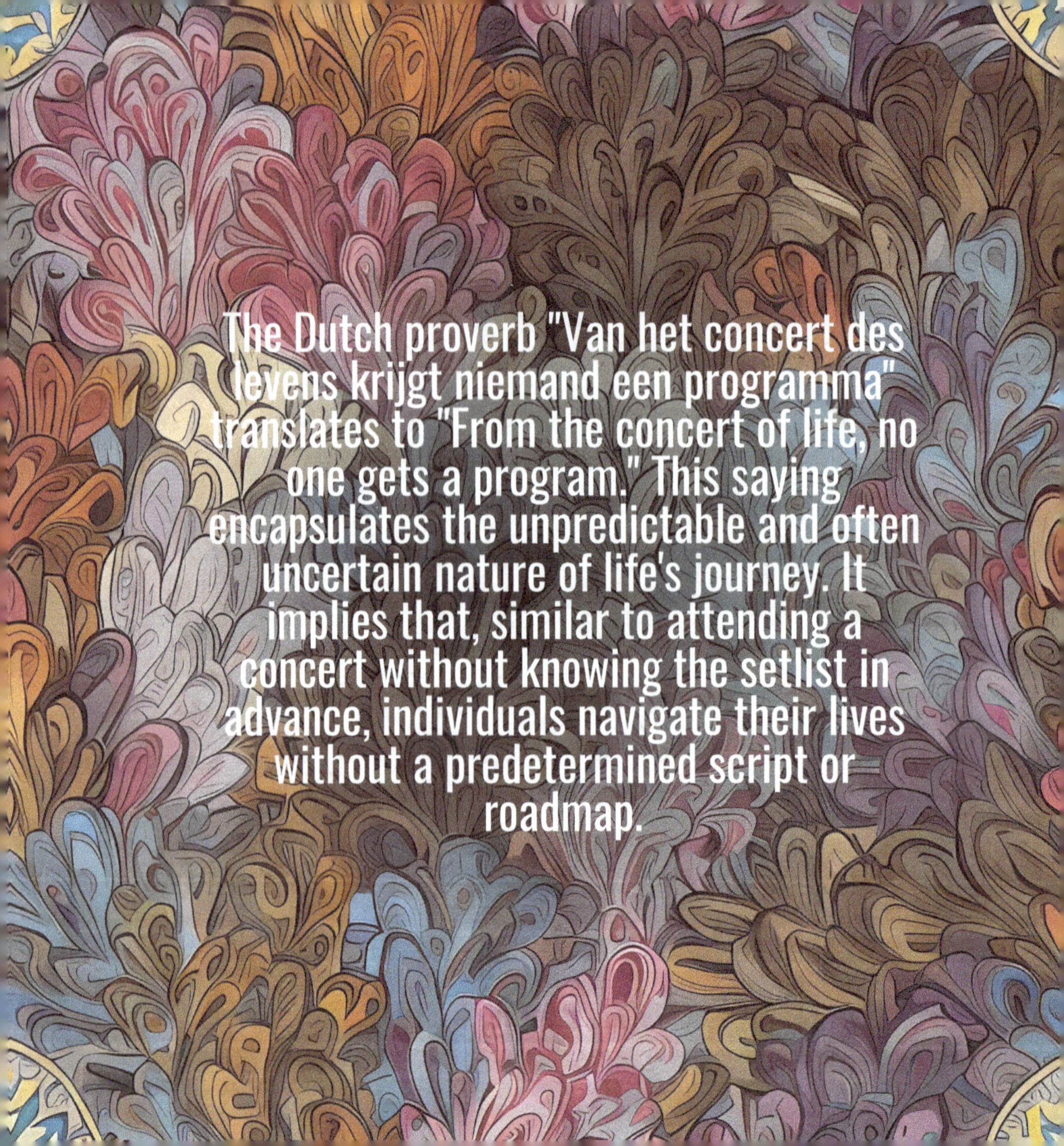

The Dutch proverb "Van het concert des levens krijgt niemand een programma" translates to "From the concert of life, no one gets a program." This saying encapsulates the unpredictable and often uncertain nature of life's journey. It implies that, similar to attending a concert without knowing the setlist in advance, individuals navigate their lives without a predetermined script or roadmap.

In a blacksmith's house, a wooden knife.
Latin American

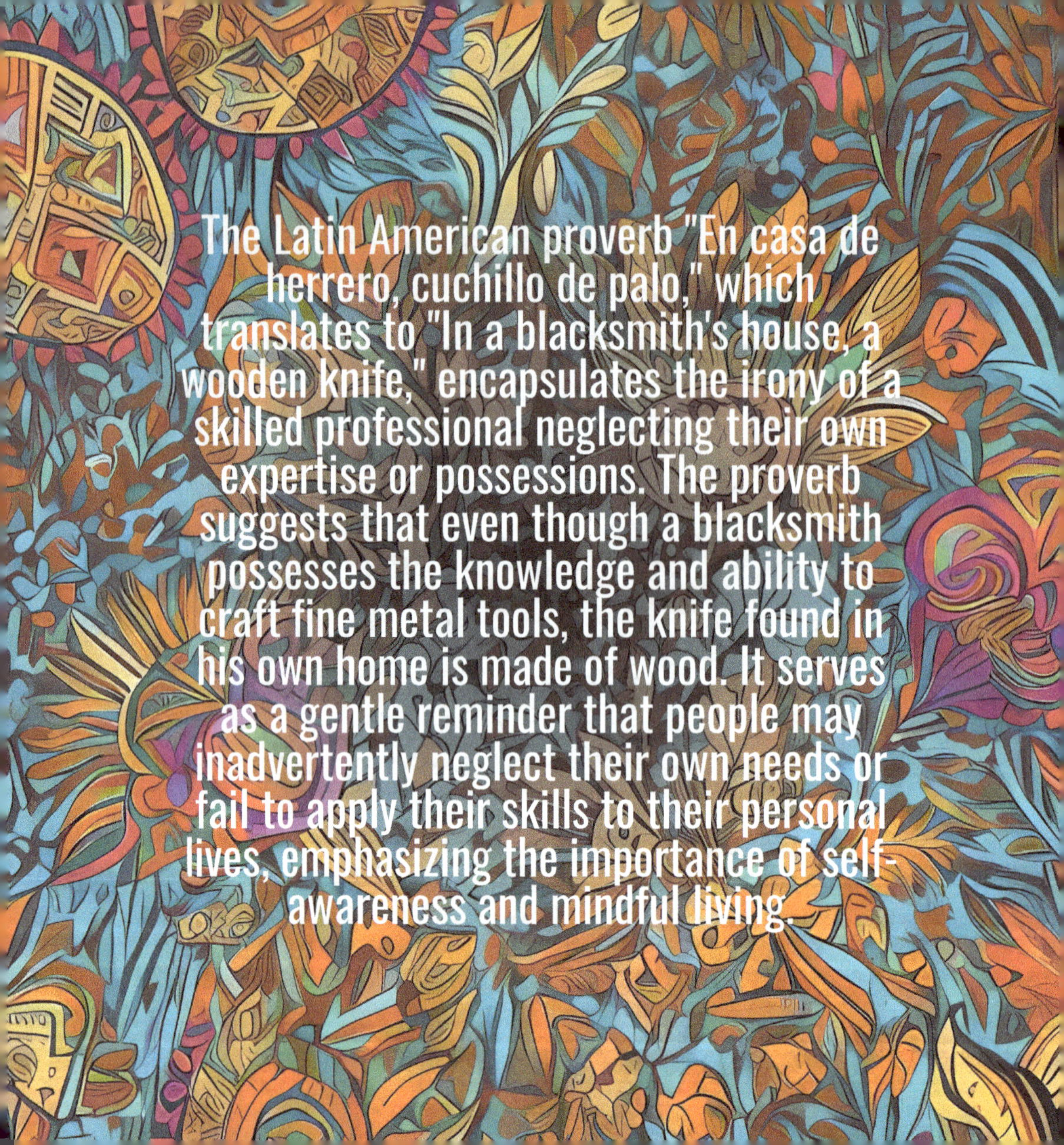

The Latin American proverb "En casa de herrero, cuchillo de palo," which translates to "In a blacksmith's house, a wooden knife," encapsulates the irony of a skilled professional neglecting their own expertise or possessions. The proverb suggests that even though a blacksmith possesses the knowledge and ability to craft fine metal tools, the knife found in his own home is made of wood. It serves as a gentle reminder that people may inadvertently neglect their own needs or fail to apply their skills to their personal lives, emphasizing the importance of self-awareness and mindful living.

HUNGER AND LOVE
ARE THE MOST
NORMAL THINGS.
Greece

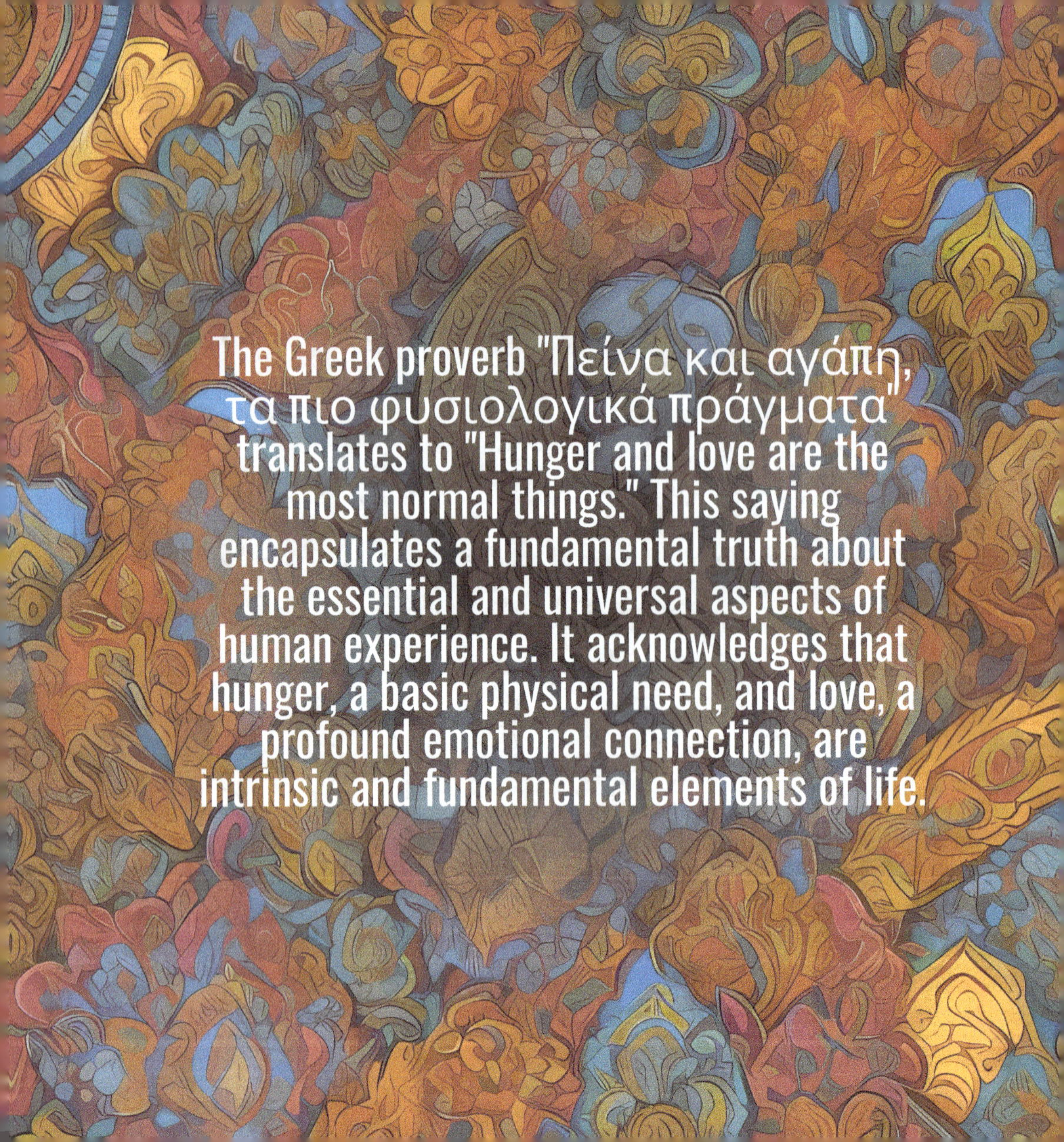
The Greek proverb "Πείνα και αγάπη, τα πιο φυσιολογικά πράγματα" translates to "Hunger and love are the most normal things." This saying encapsulates a fundamental truth about the essential and universal aspects of human experience. It acknowledges that hunger, a basic physical need, and love, a profound emotional connection, are intrinsic and fundamental elements of life.

EACH MONKEY TO
ITS BRANCH.
Latin American

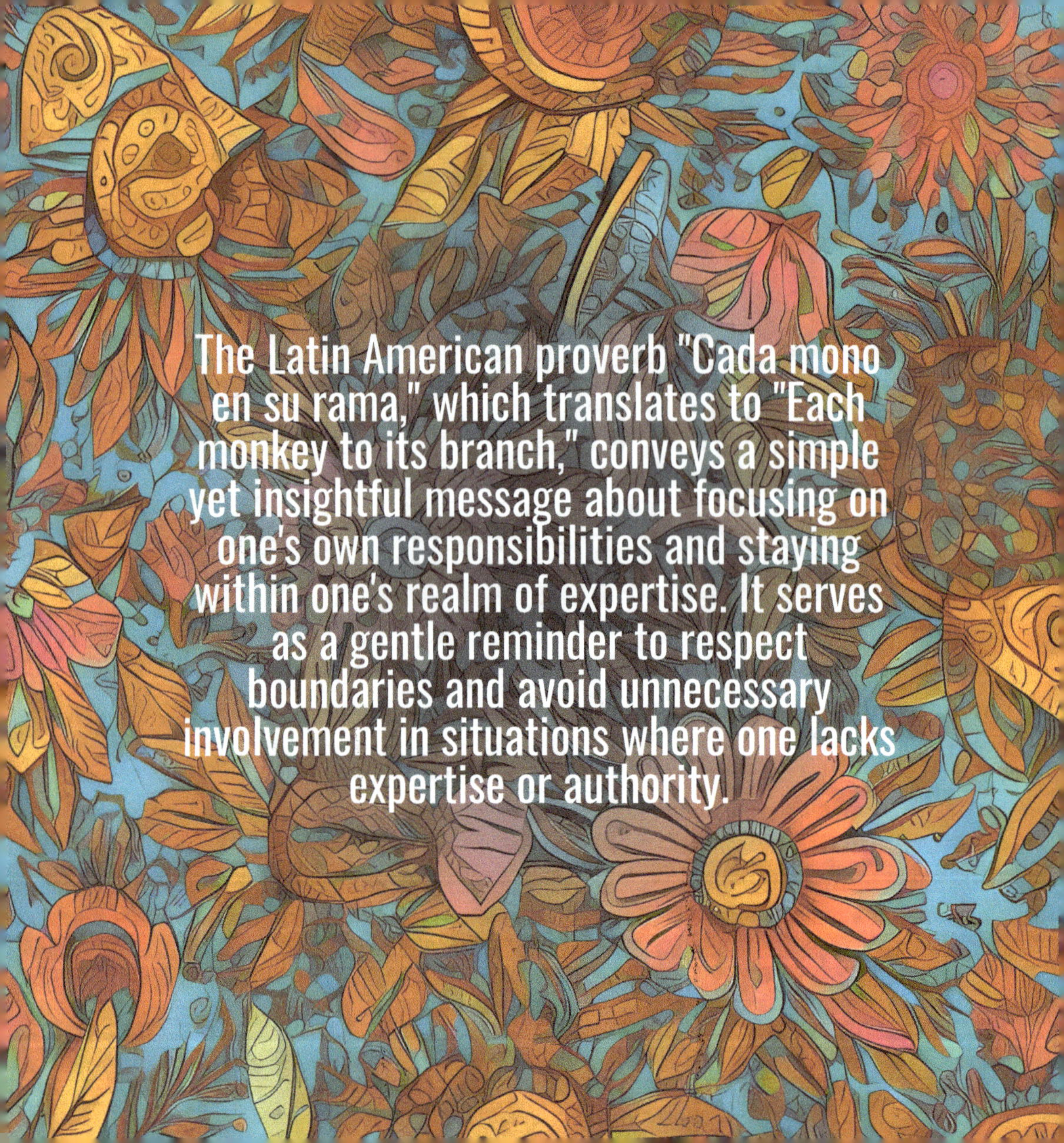

The Latin American proverb "Cada mono en su rama," which translates to "Each monkey to its branch," conveys a simple yet insightful message about focusing on one's own responsibilities and staying within one's realm of expertise. It serves as a gentle reminder to respect boundaries and avoid unnecessary involvement in situations where one lacks expertise or authority.

A DROP HOLLOWS
OUT THE STONE
NOT BY FORCE BUT
BY FALLING
CONSTANTLY.
Latin American

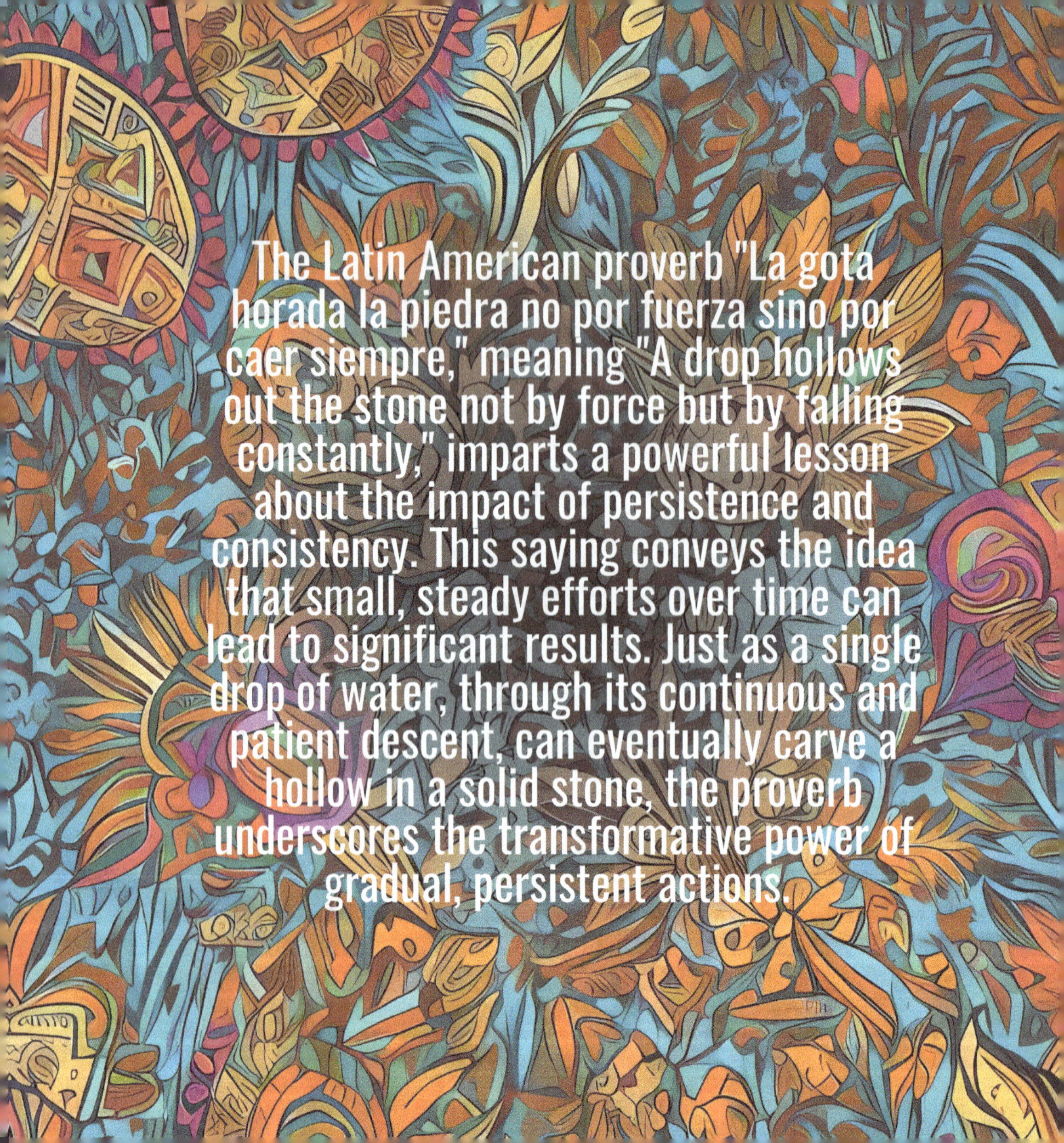

The Latin American proverb "La gota horada la piedra no por fuerza sino por caer siempre," meaning "A drop hollows out the stone not by force but by falling constantly," imparts a powerful lesson about the impact of persistence and consistency. This saying conveys the idea that small, steady efforts over time can lead to significant results. Just as a single drop of water, through its continuous and patient descent, can eventually carve a hollow in a solid stone, the proverb underscores the transformative power of gradual, persistent actions.

WHEN YOUR NEIGHBOR'S HOUSE IS ON FIRE, WET YOUR OWN
Bahamas

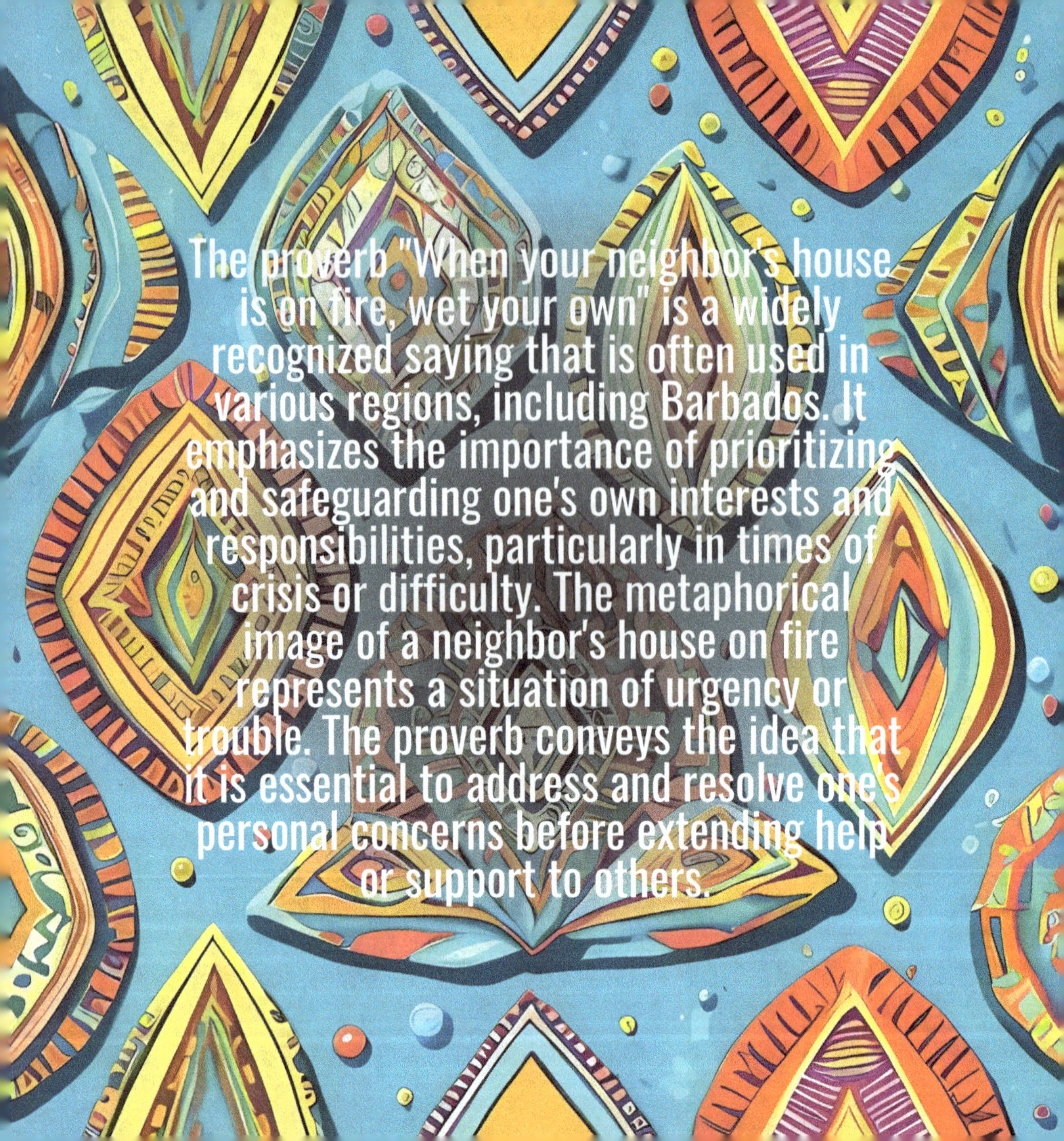

The proverb "When your neighbor's house is on fire, wet your own" is a widely recognized saying that is often used in various regions, including Barbados. It emphasizes the importance of prioritizing and safeguarding one's own interests and responsibilities, particularly in times of crisis or difficulty. The metaphorical image of a neighbor's house on fire represents a situation of urgency or trouble. The proverb conveys the idea that it is essential to address and resolve one's personal concerns before extending help or support to others.

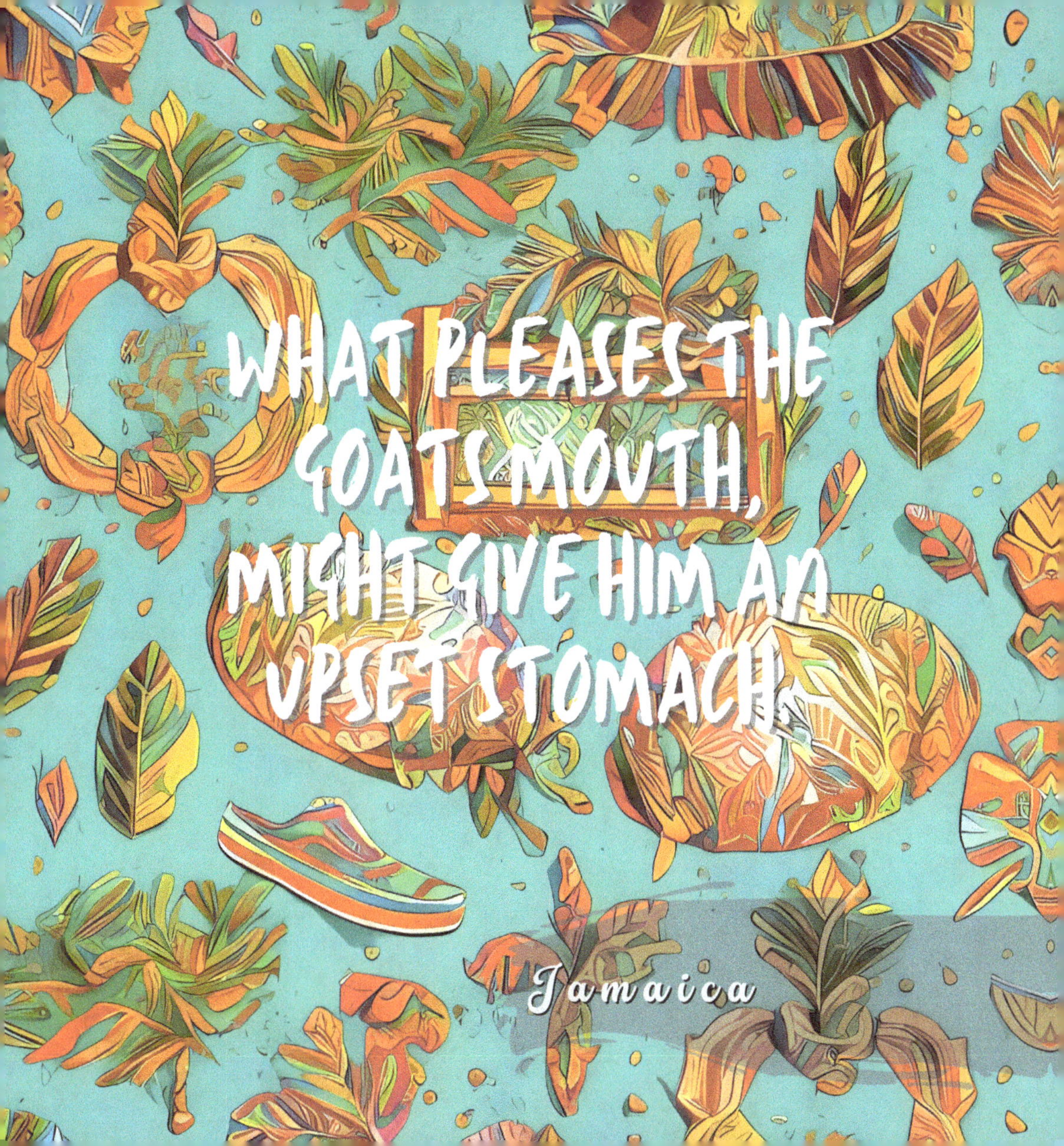
WHAT PLEASES THE GOATS MOUTH, MIGHT GIVE HIM AN UPSET STOMACH.
Jamaica

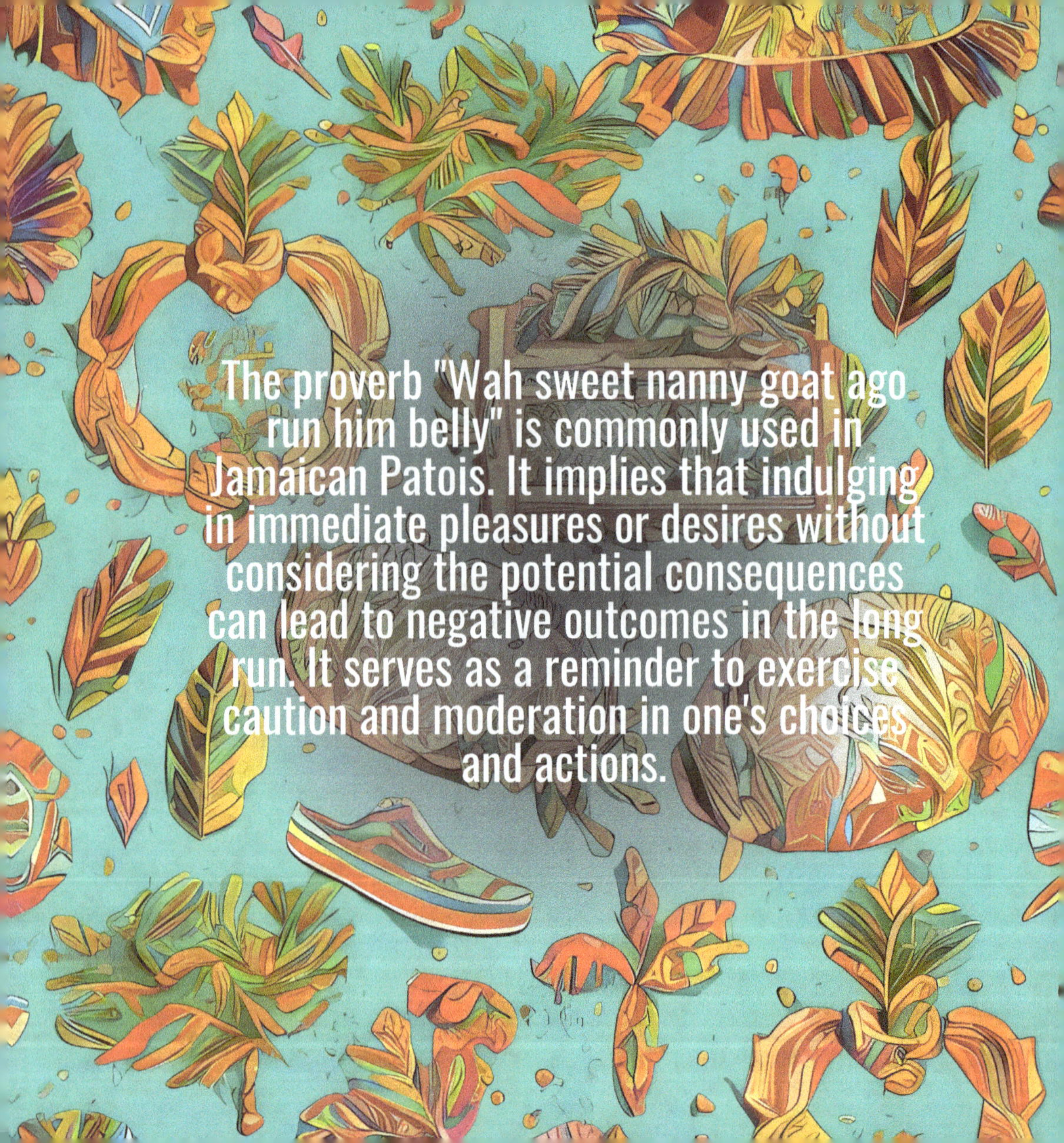
The proverb "Wah sweet nanny goat ago run him belly" is commonly used in Jamaican Patois. It implies that indulging in immediate pleasures or desires without considering the potential consequences can lead to negative outcomes in the long run. It serves as a reminder to exercise caution and moderation in one's choices and actions.

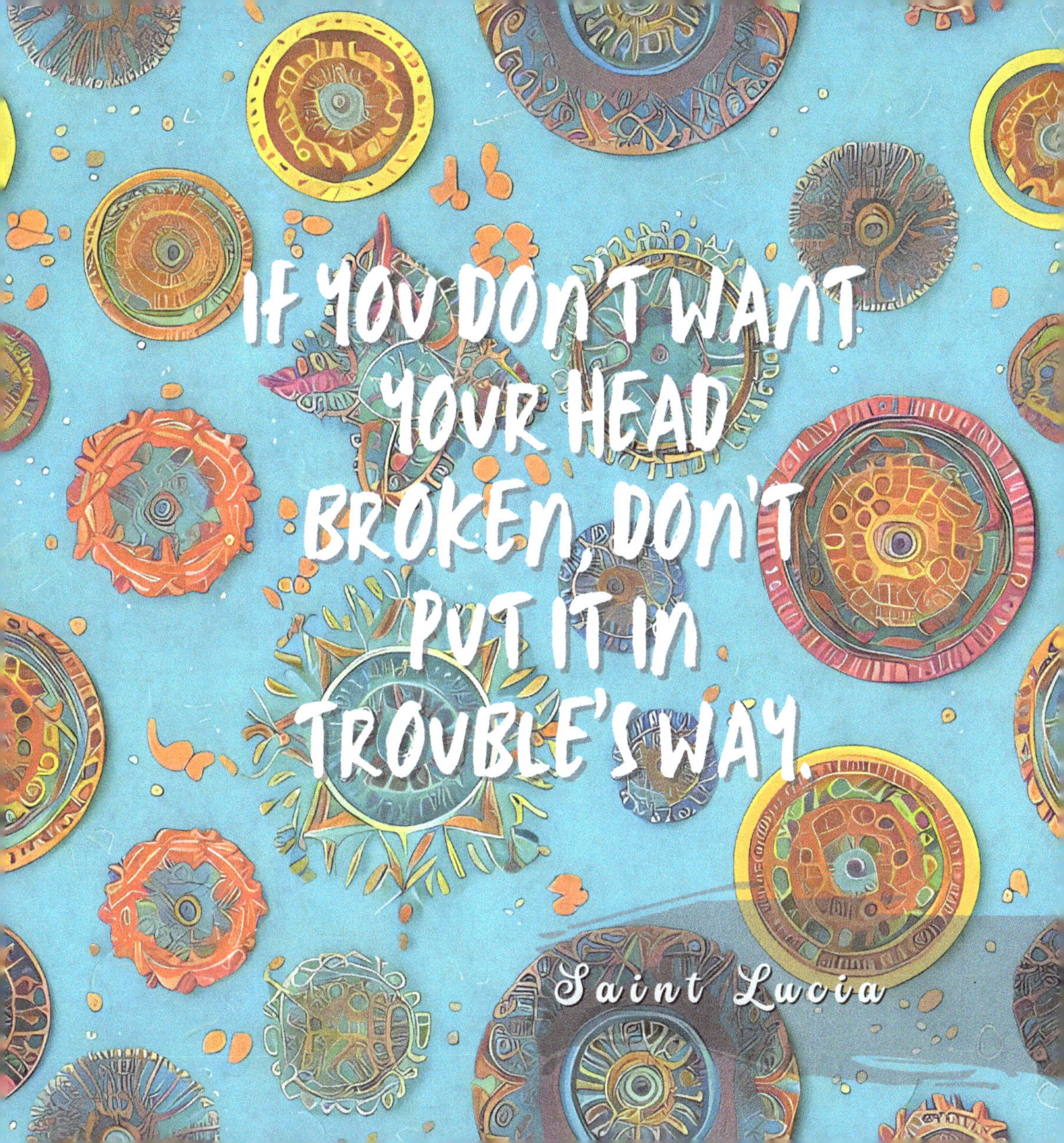
IF YOU DON'T WANT
YOUR HEAD
BROKEN, DON'T
PUT IT IN
TROUBLE'S WAY.
Saint Lucia

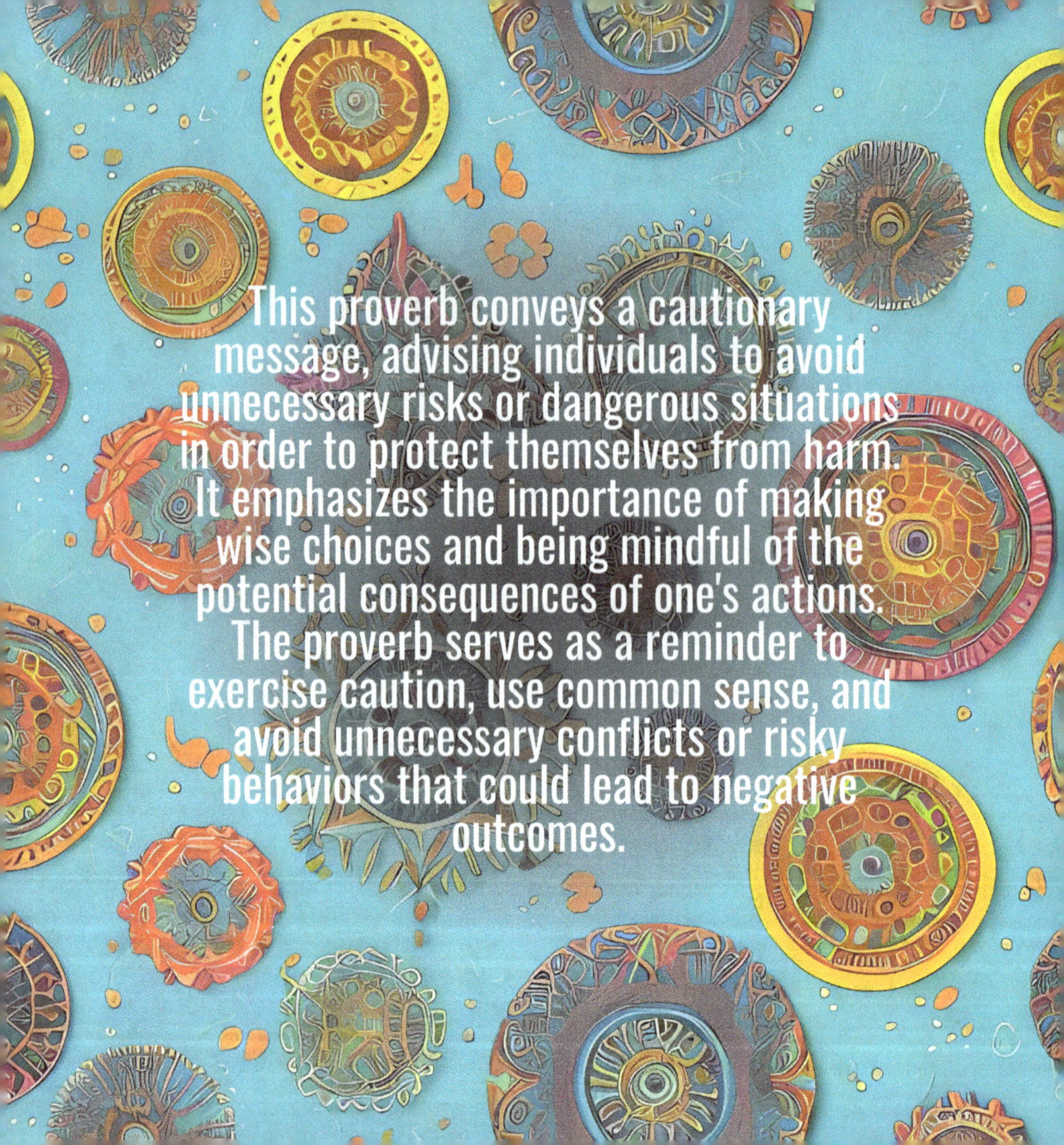
This proverb conveys a cautionary message, advising individuals to avoid unnecessary risks or dangerous situations in order to protect themselves from harm. It emphasizes the importance of making wise choices and being mindful of the potential consequences of one's actions. The proverb serves as a reminder to exercise caution, use common sense, and avoid unnecessary conflicts or risky behaviors that could lead to negative outcomes.

THE BEGINNING OF
ANGER IS MADNESS,
AND THE END OF IT
IS REGRET.
Arabia

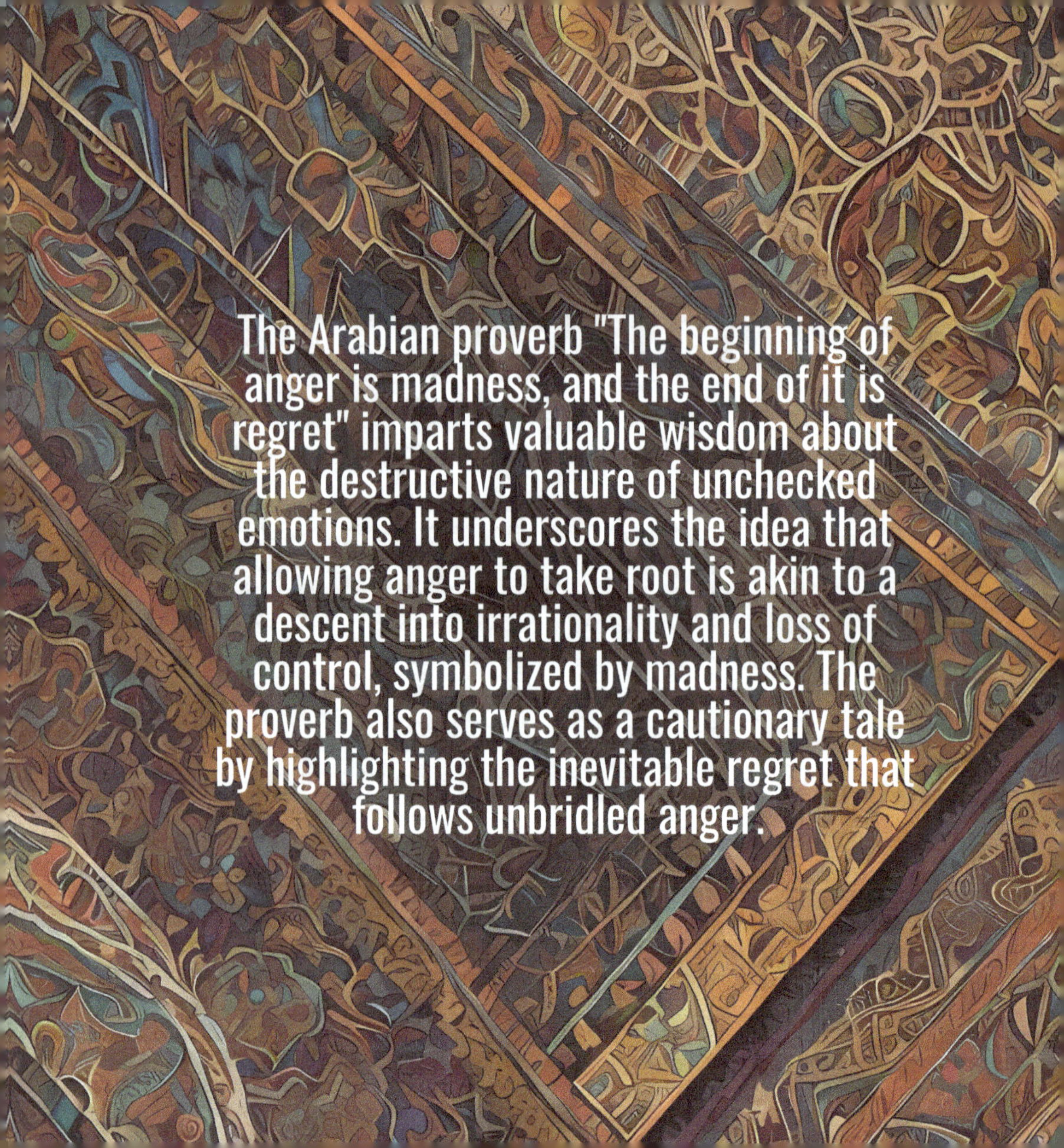

The Arabian proverb "The beginning of anger is madness, and the end of it is regret" imparts valuable wisdom about the destructive nature of unchecked emotions. It underscores the idea that allowing anger to take root is akin to a descent into irrationality and loss of control, symbolized by madness. The proverb also serves as a cautionary tale by highlighting the inevitable regret that follows unbridled anger.

AN OLD ROOSTER
DOESN'T LEARN
TO CROW.
Cuba

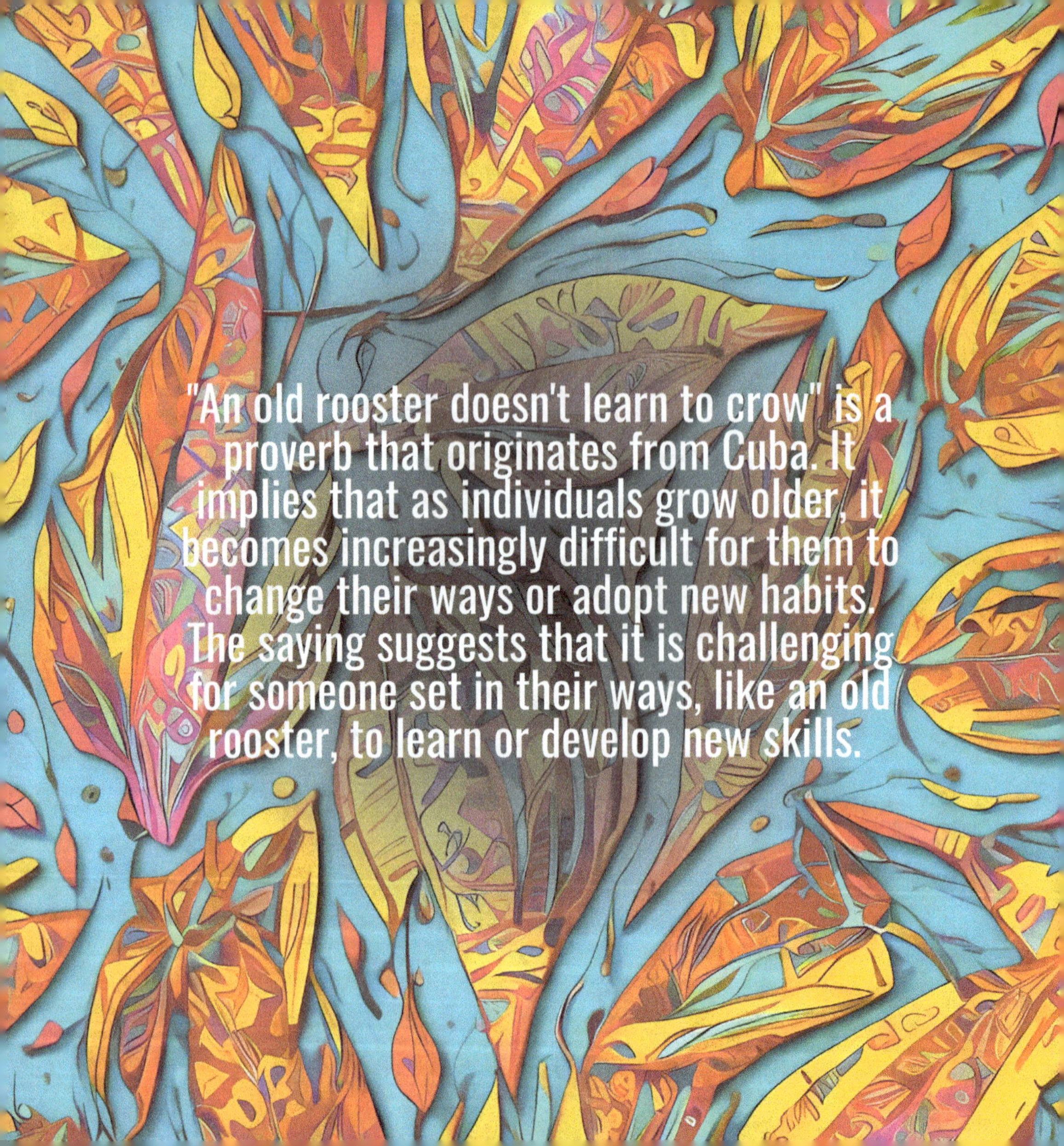

"An old rooster doesn't learn to crow" is a proverb that originates from Cuba. It implies that as individuals grow older, it becomes increasingly difficult for them to change their ways or adopt new habits. The saying suggests that it is challenging for someone set in their ways, like an old rooster, to learn or develop new skills.

WHEN YOU WANT TO
KEEP SOMETHING,
GIVE IT.
Arabia

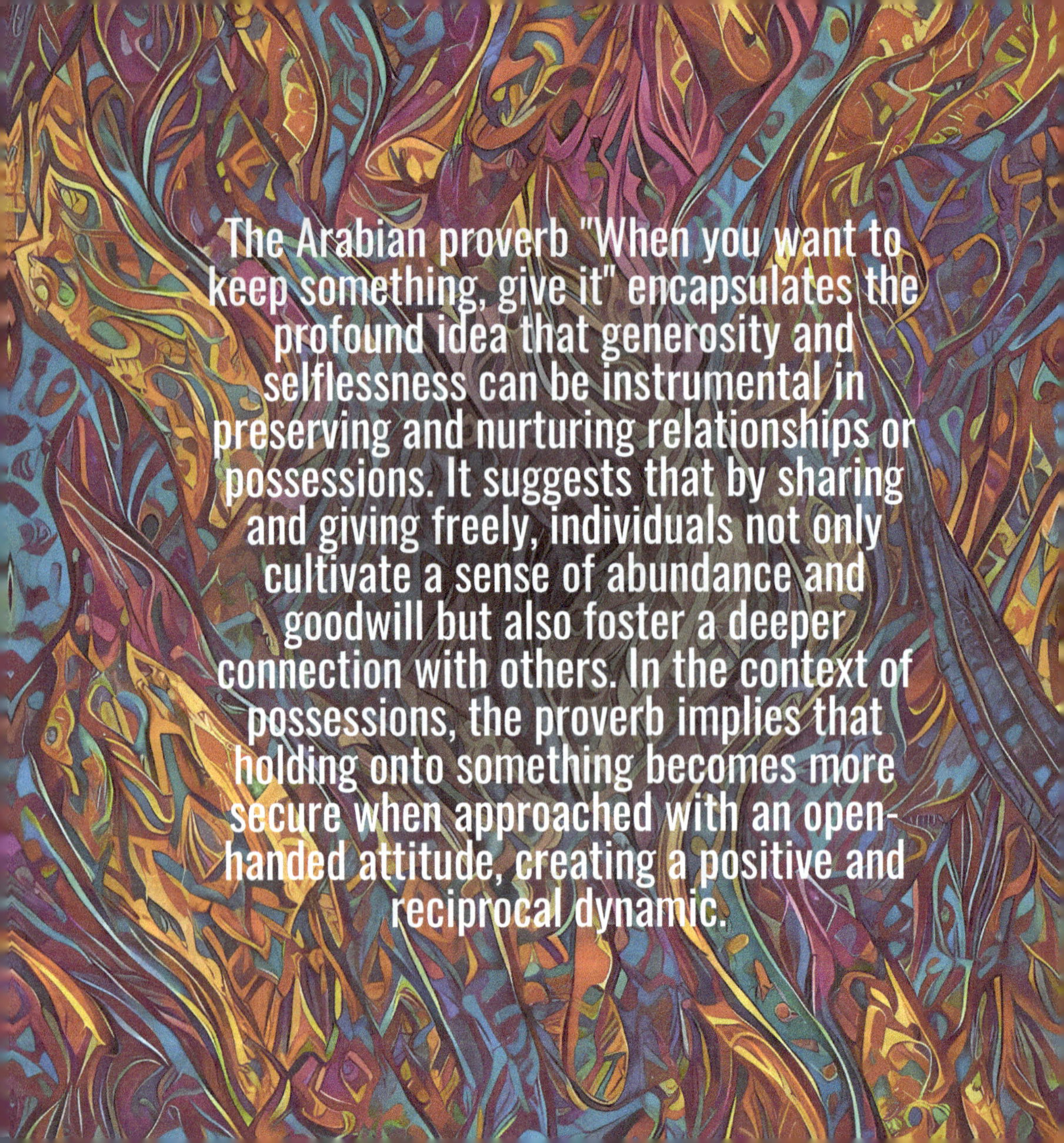

The Arabian proverb "When you want to keep something, give it" encapsulates the profound idea that generosity and selflessness can be instrumental in preserving and nurturing relationships or possessions. It suggests that by sharing and giving freely, individuals not only cultivate a sense of abundance and goodwill but also foster a deeper connection with others. In the context of possessions, the proverb implies that holding onto something becomes more secure when approached with an open-handed attitude, creating a positive and reciprocal dynamic.

A JOURNEY OF A
THOUSAND MILES
BEGINS WITH A
SINGLE STEP.
China

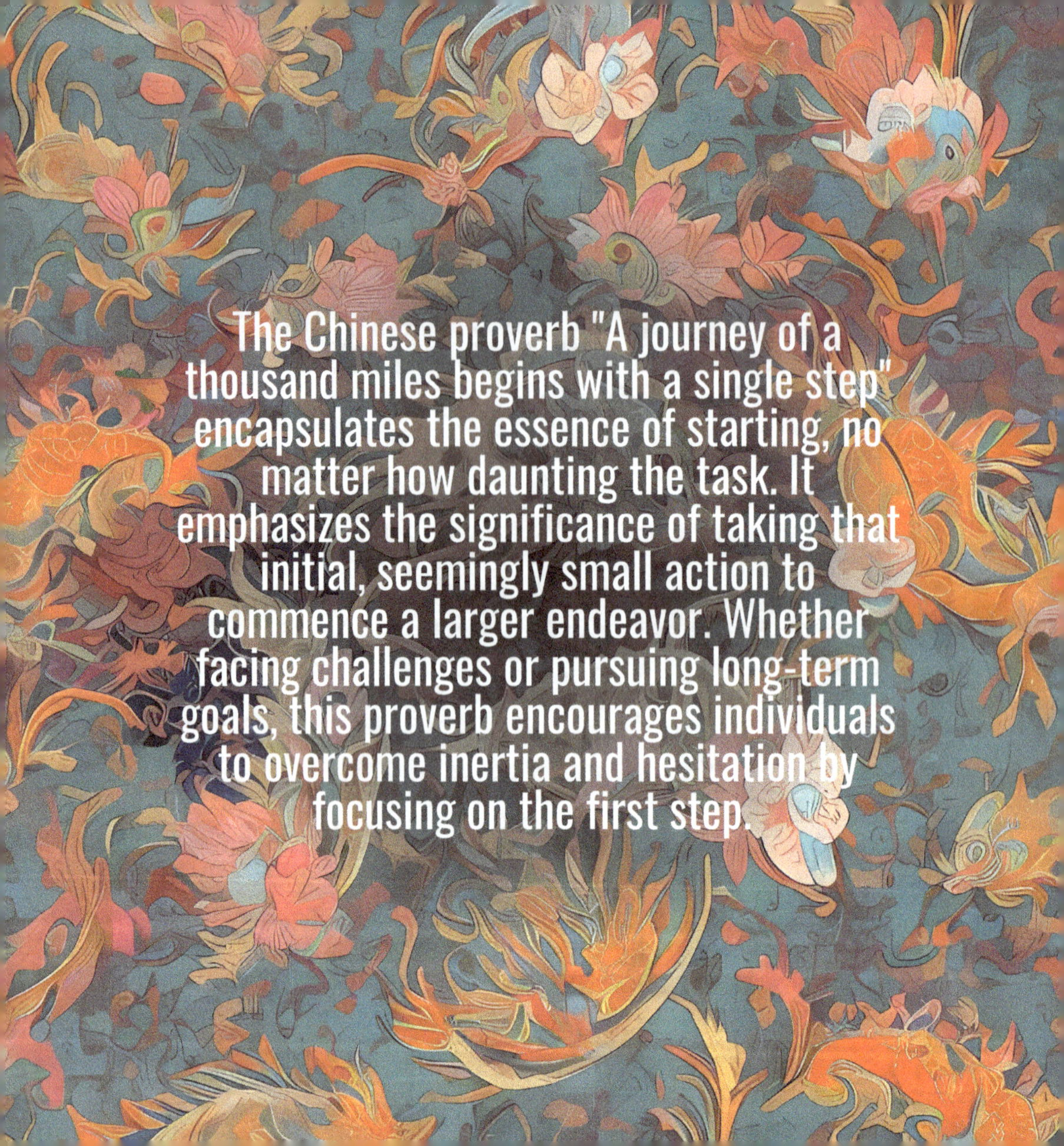

The Chinese proverb "A journey of a thousand miles begins with a single step" encapsulates the essence of starting, no matter how daunting the task. It emphasizes the significance of taking that initial, seemingly small action to commence a larger endeavor. Whether facing challenges or pursuing long-term goals, this proverb encourages individuals to overcome inertia and hesitation by focusing on the first step.

DON'T THINK THE GARDEN LOSES ITS ECSTASY IN WINTER. IT'S QUIET, BUT THE ROOTS ARE DOWN THERE RIOTOUS.
Taiwan

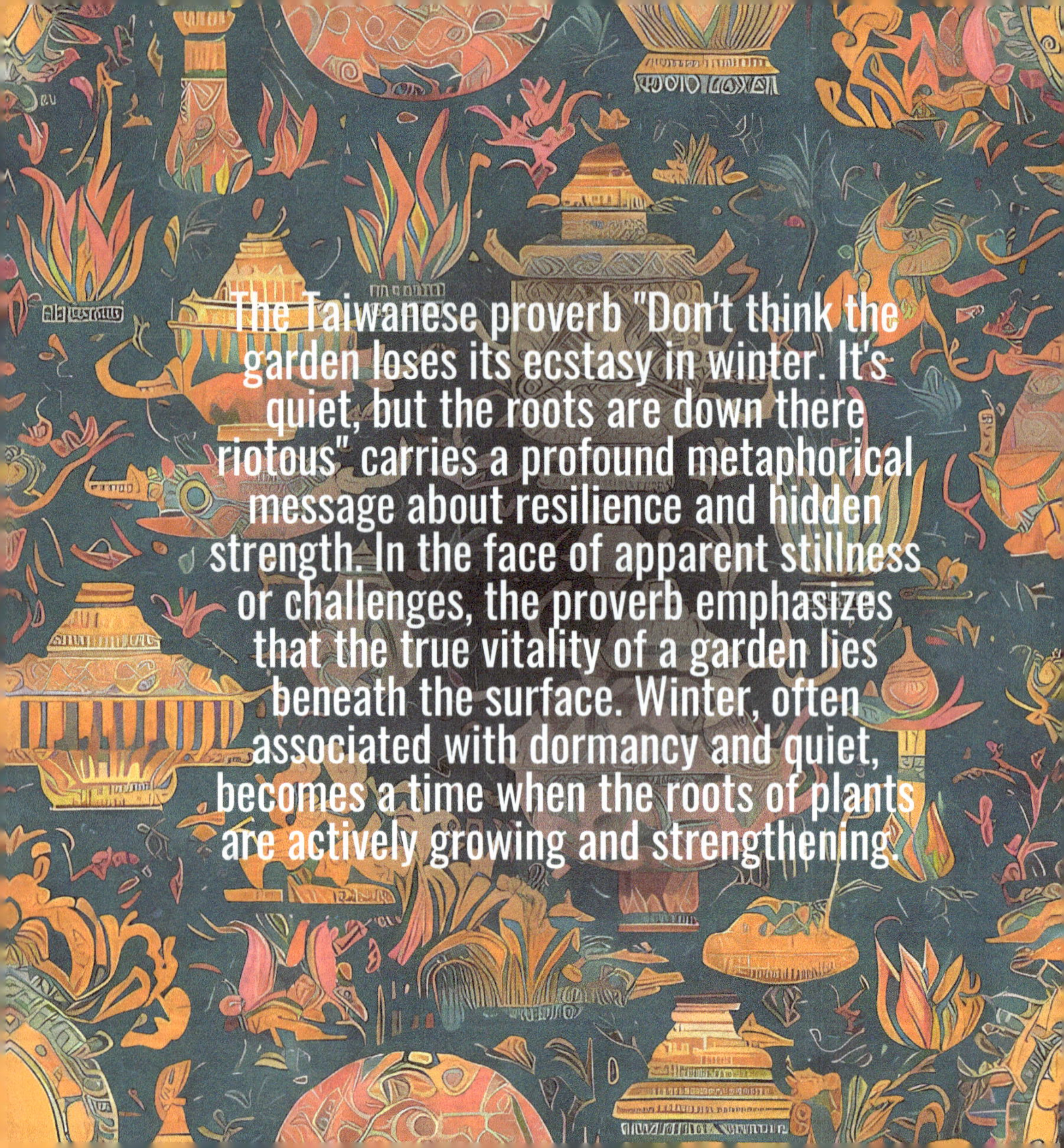

The Taiwanese proverb "Don't think the garden loses its ecstasy in winter. It's quiet, but the roots are down there riotous" carries a profound metaphorical message about resilience and hidden strength. In the face of apparent stillness or challenges, the proverb emphasizes that the true vitality of a garden lies beneath the surface. Winter, often associated with dormancy and quiet, becomes a time when the roots of plants are actively growing and strengthening.

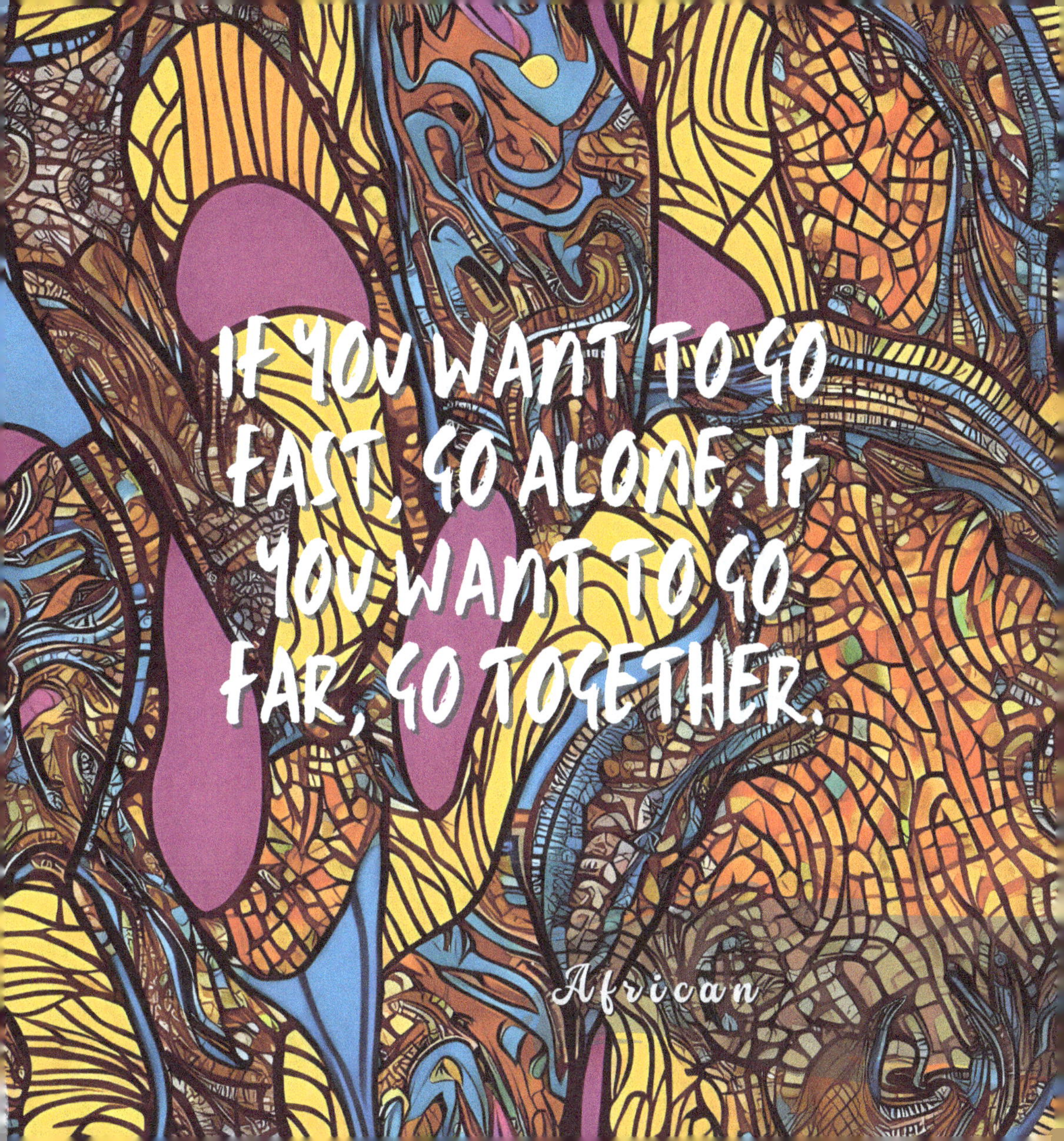
IF YOU WANT TO GO FAST, GO ALONE. IF YOU WANT TO GO FAR, GO TOGETHER.
African

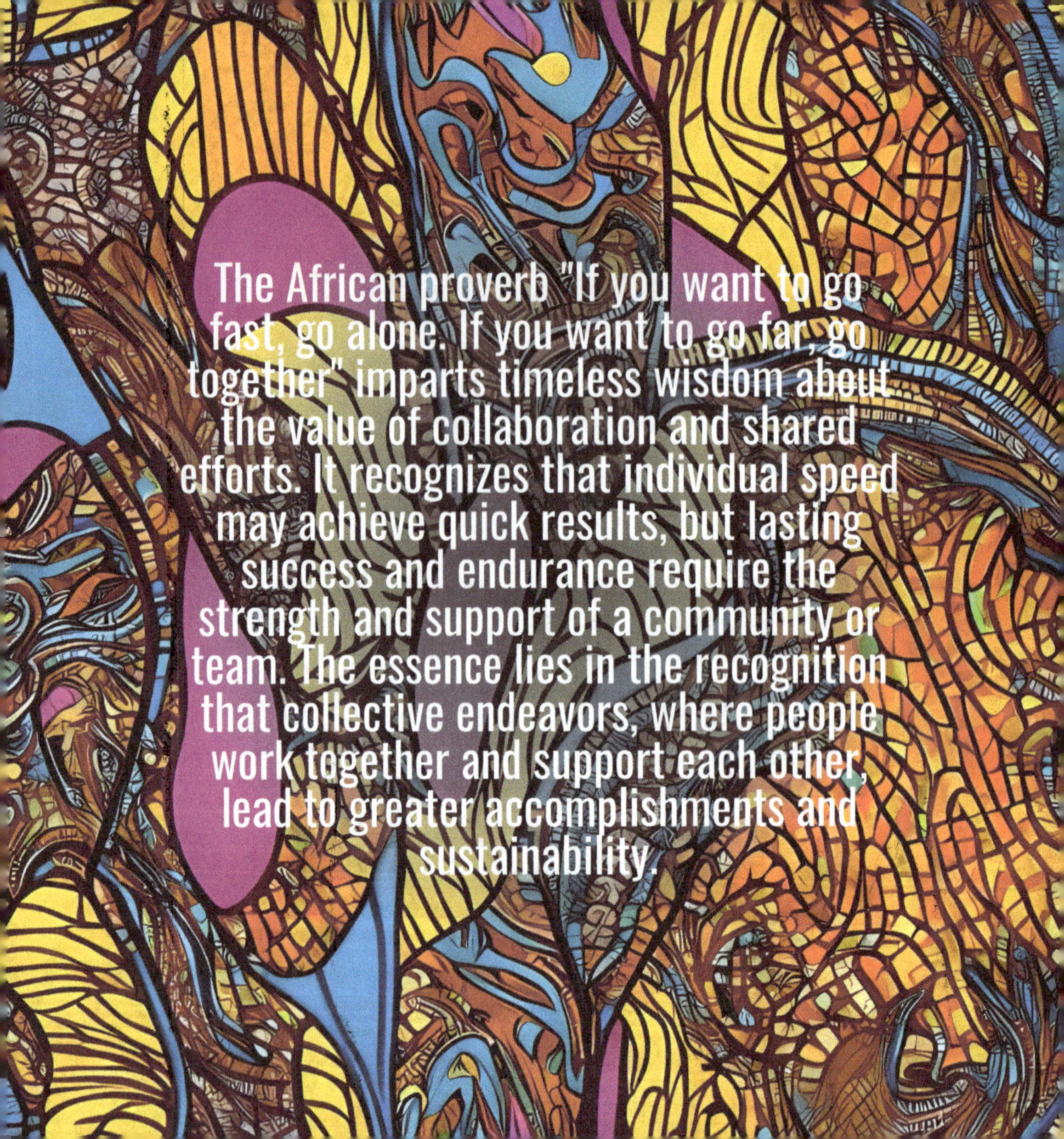

The African proverb "If you want to go fast, go alone. If you want to go far, go together" imparts timeless wisdom about the value of collaboration and shared efforts. It recognizes that individual speed may achieve quick results, but lasting success and endurance require the strength and support of a community or team. The essence lies in the recognition that collective endeavors, where people work together and support each other, lead to greater accomplishments and sustainability.

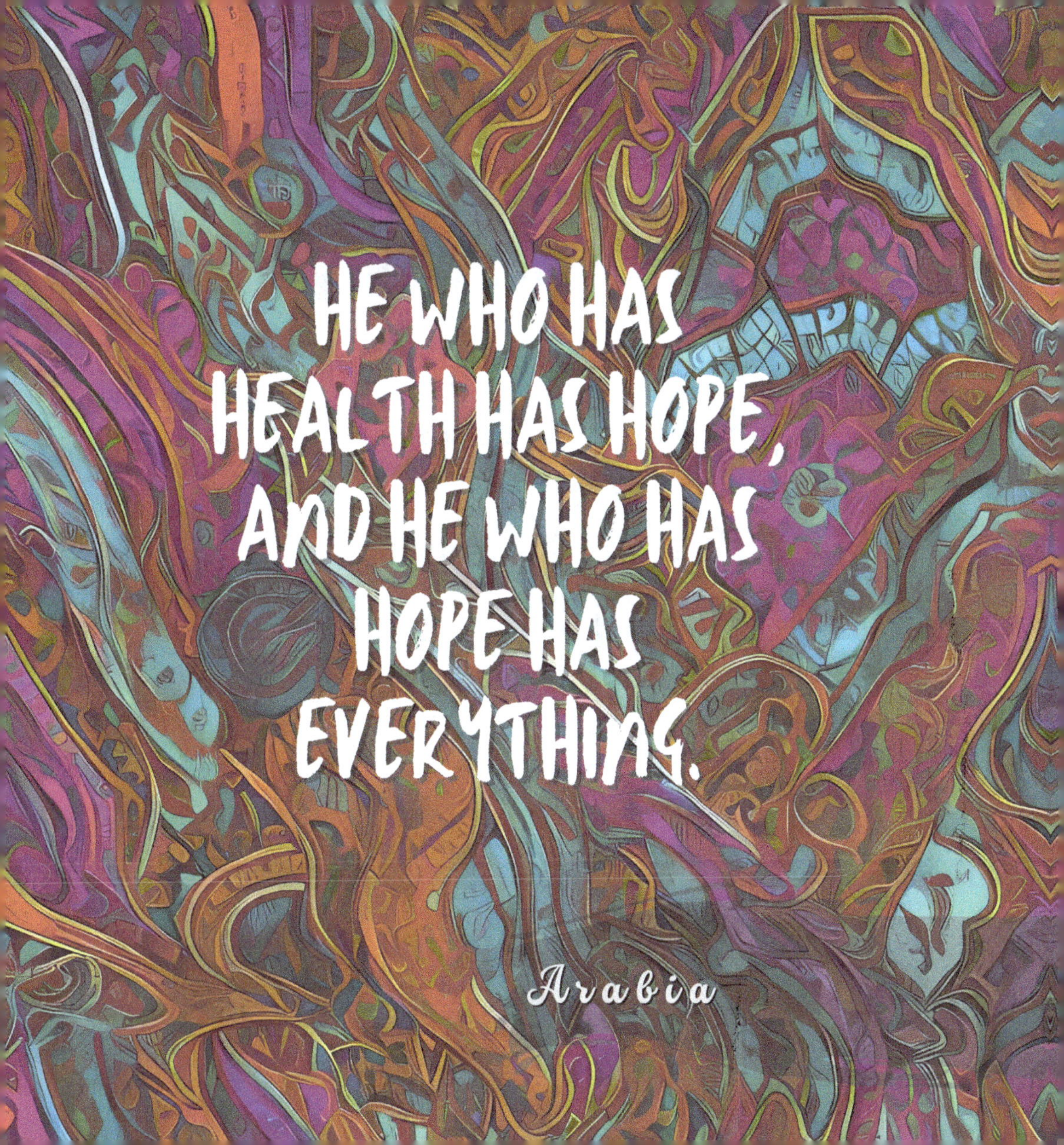
HE WHO HAS
HEALTH HAS HOPE,
AND HE WHO HAS
HOPE HAS
EVERYTHING.
Arabia

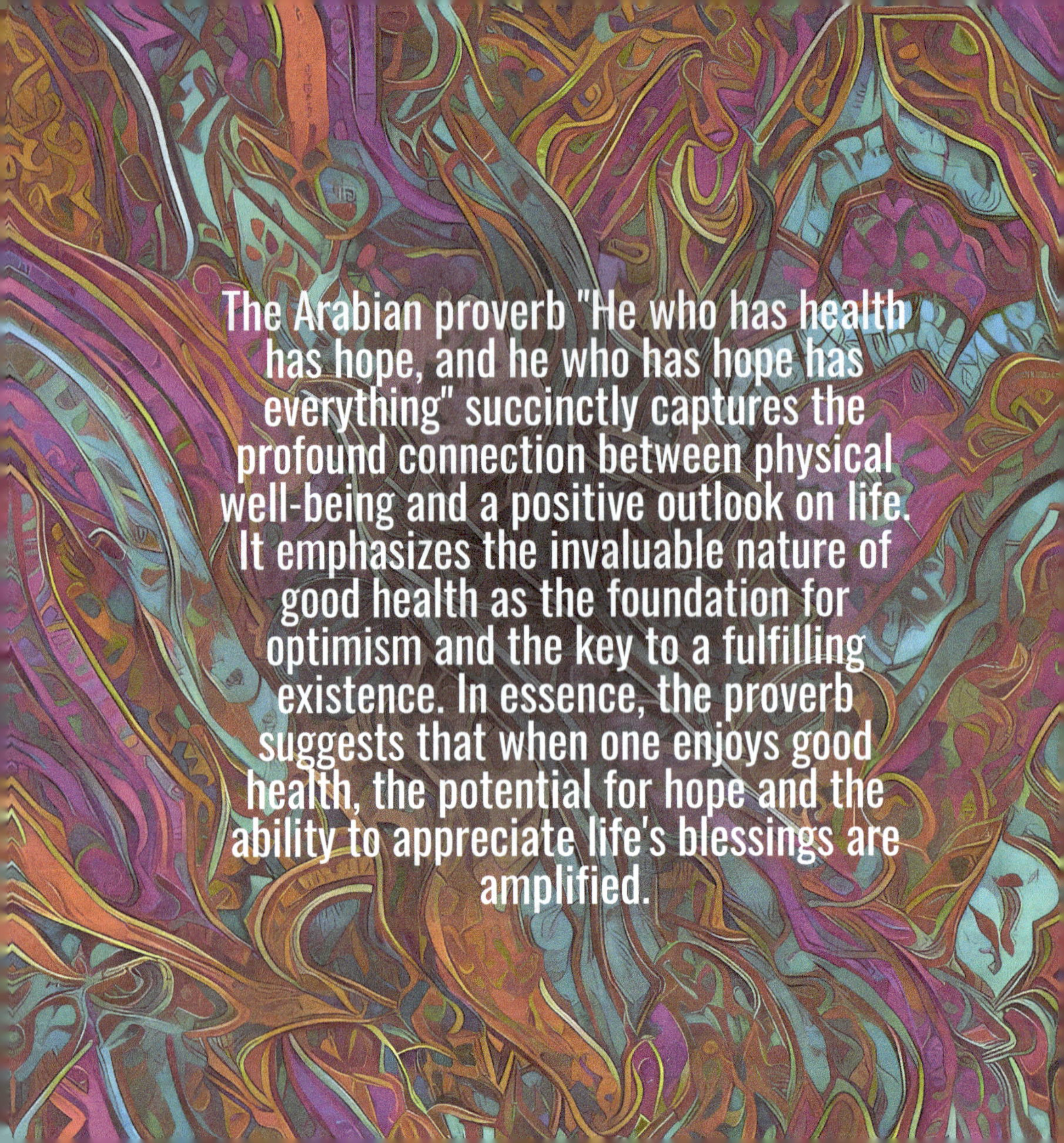

The Arabian proverb "He who has health has hope, and he who has hope has everything" succinctly captures the profound connection between physical well-being and a positive outlook on life. It emphasizes the invaluable nature of good health as the foundation for optimism and the key to a fulfilling existence. In essence, the proverb suggests that when one enjoys good health, the potential for hope and the ability to appreciate life's blessings are amplified.

PATIENCE IS THE MOTHER OF A BEAUTIFUL CHILD.
Ethiopia

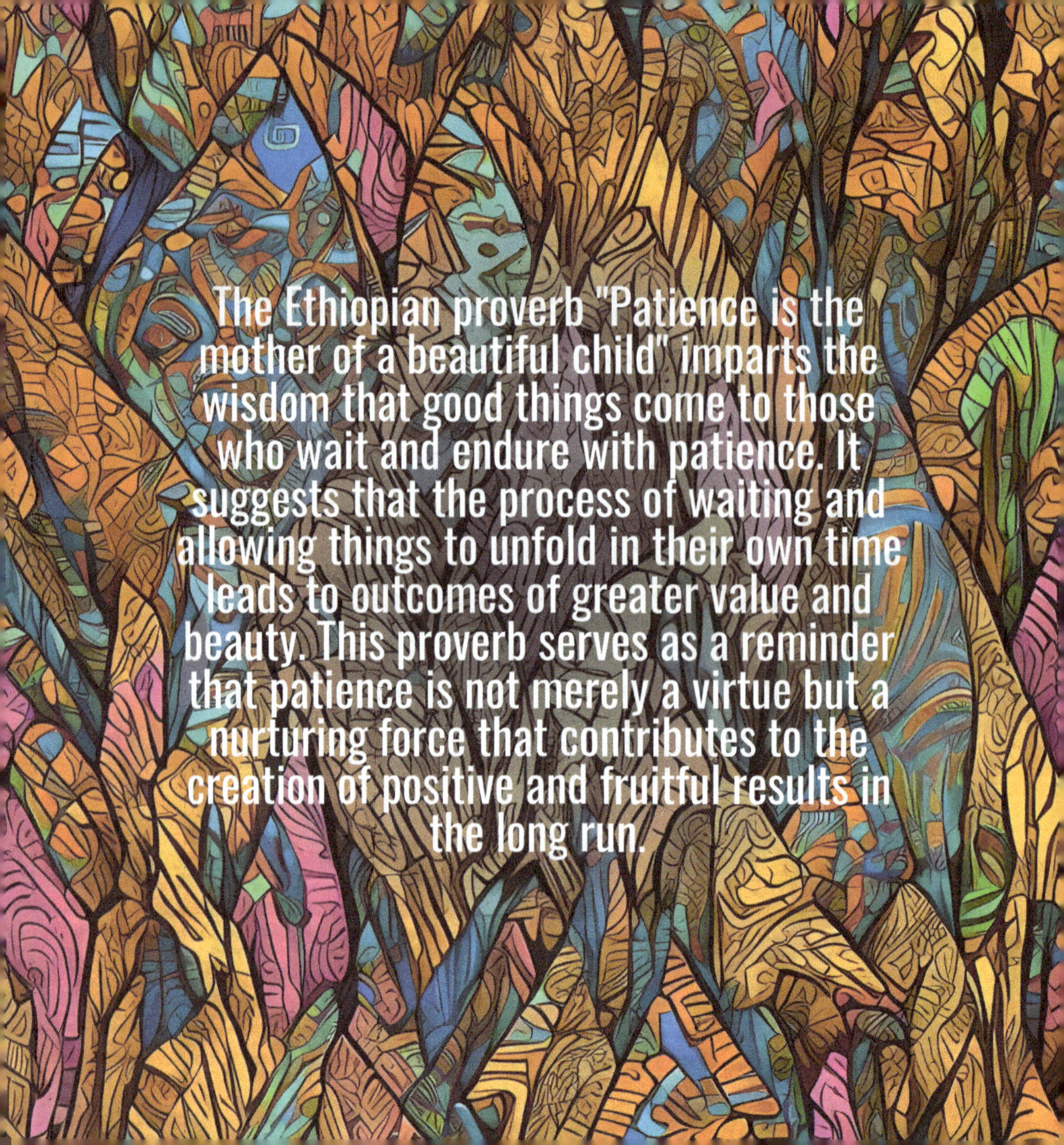
The Ethiopian proverb "Patience is the mother of a beautiful child" imparts the wisdom that good things come to those who wait and endure with patience. It suggests that the process of waiting and allowing things to unfold in their own time leads to outcomes of greater value and beauty. This proverb serves as a reminder that patience is not merely a virtue but a nurturing force that contributes to the creation of positive and fruitful results in the long run.

RAIN DOES NOT
FALL ON ONE ROOF
ALONE.
Ghana

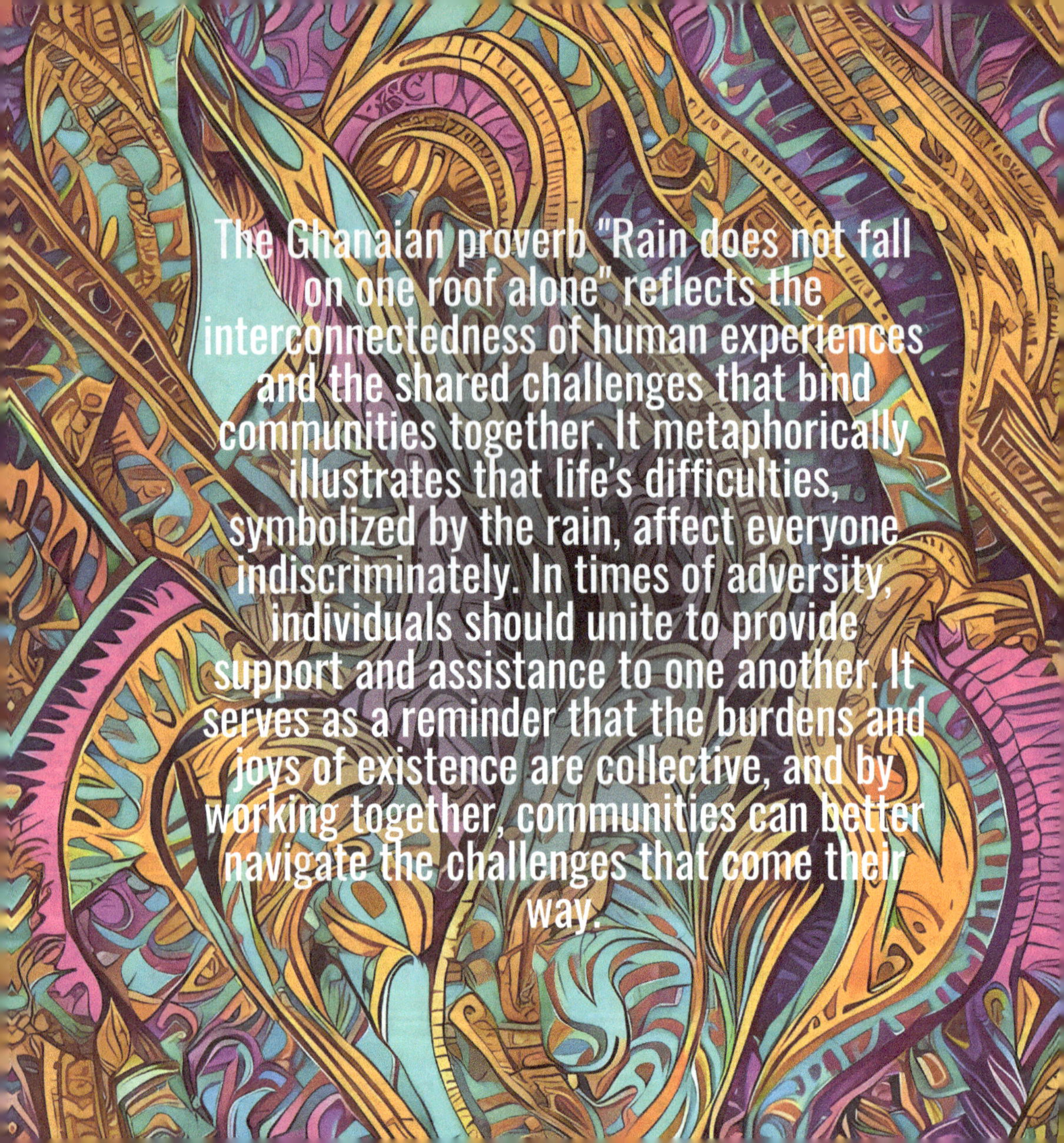
The Ghanaian proverb "Rain does not fall on one roof alone" reflects the interconnectedness of human experiences and the shared challenges that bind communities together. It metaphorically illustrates that life's difficulties, symbolized by the rain, affect everyone indiscriminately. In times of adversity, individuals should unite to provide support and assistance to one another. It serves as a reminder that the burdens and joys of existence are collective, and by working together, communities can better navigate the challenges that come their way.

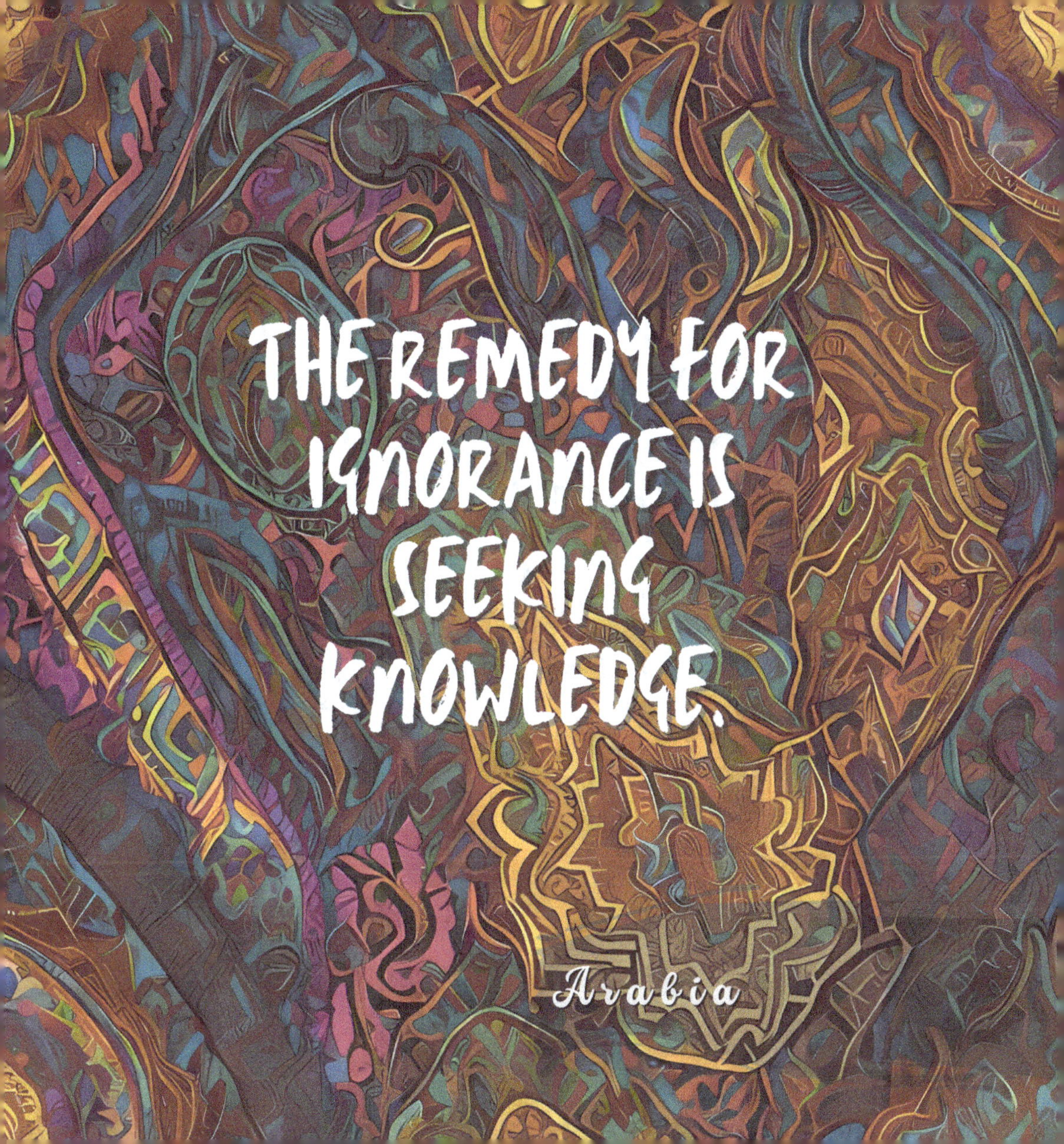
THE REMEDY FOR IGNORANCE IS SEEKING KNOWLEDGE.
Arabia

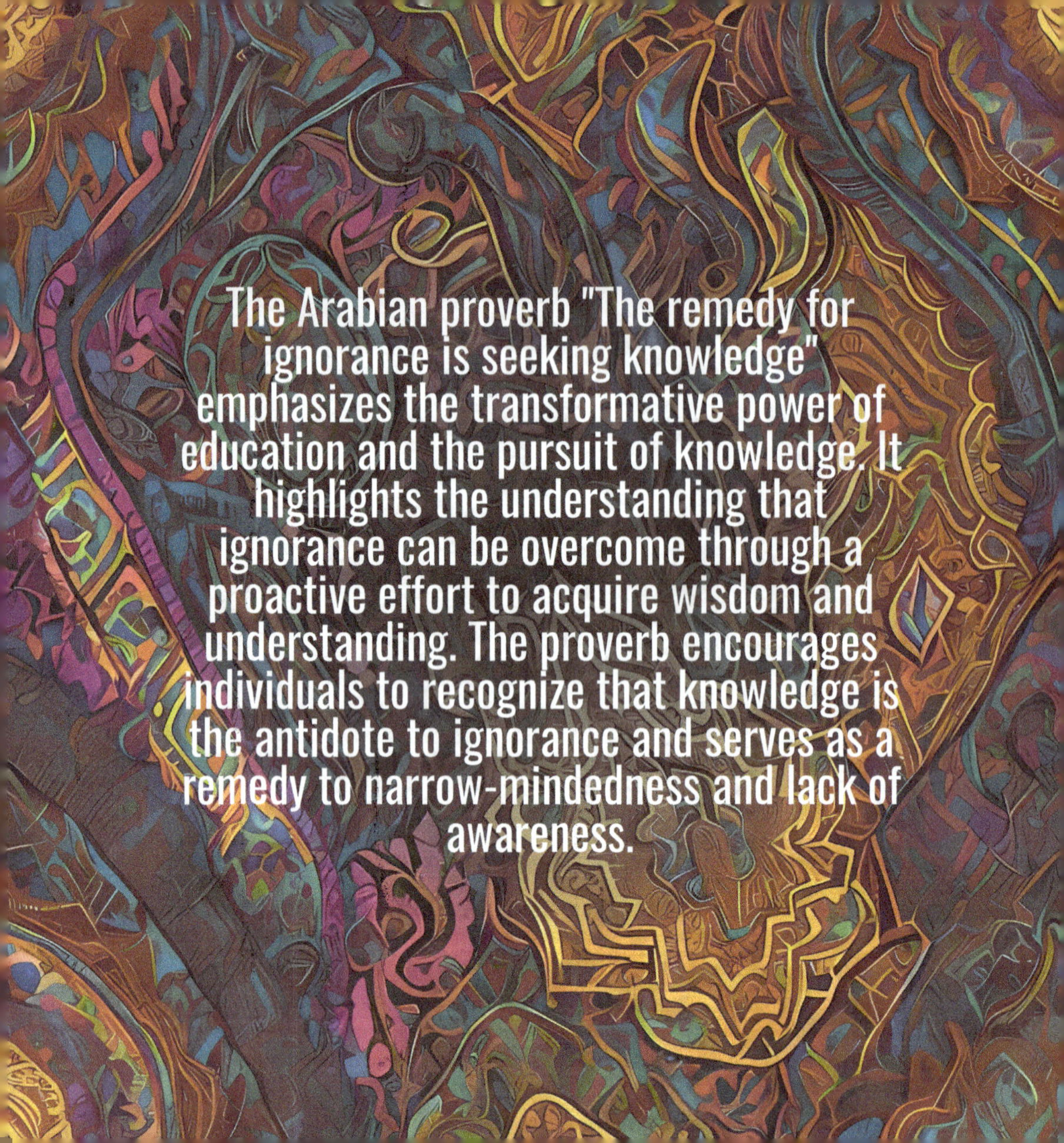

The Arabian proverb "The remedy for ignorance is seeking knowledge" emphasizes the transformative power of education and the pursuit of knowledge. It highlights the understanding that ignorance can be overcome through a proactive effort to acquire wisdom and understanding. The proverb encourages individuals to recognize that knowledge is the antidote to ignorance and serves as a remedy to narrow-mindedness and lack of awareness.

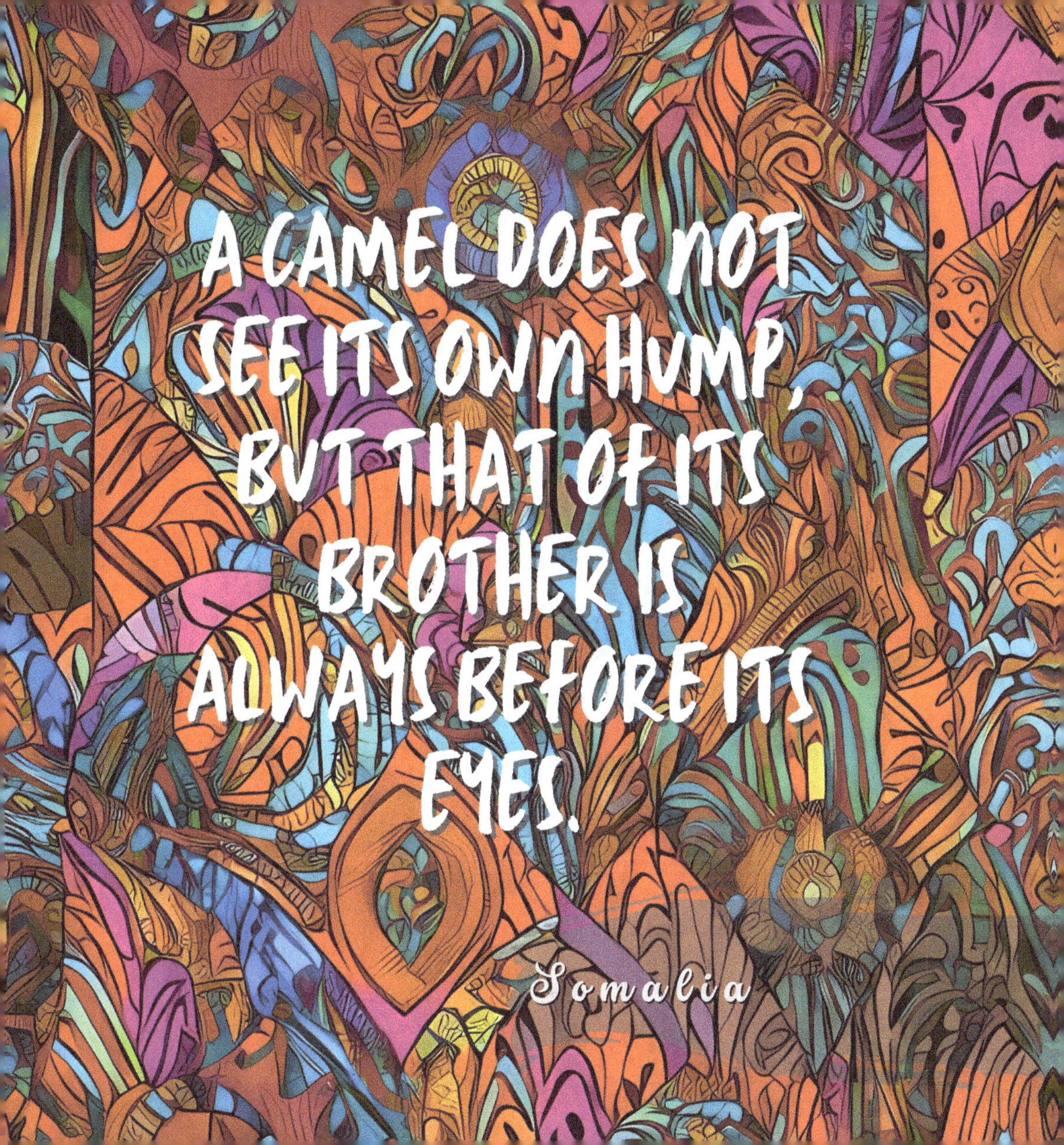
A CAMEL DOES NOT
SEE ITS OWN HUMP,
BUT THAT OF ITS
BROTHER IS
ALWAYS BEFORE ITS
EYES.
Somalia

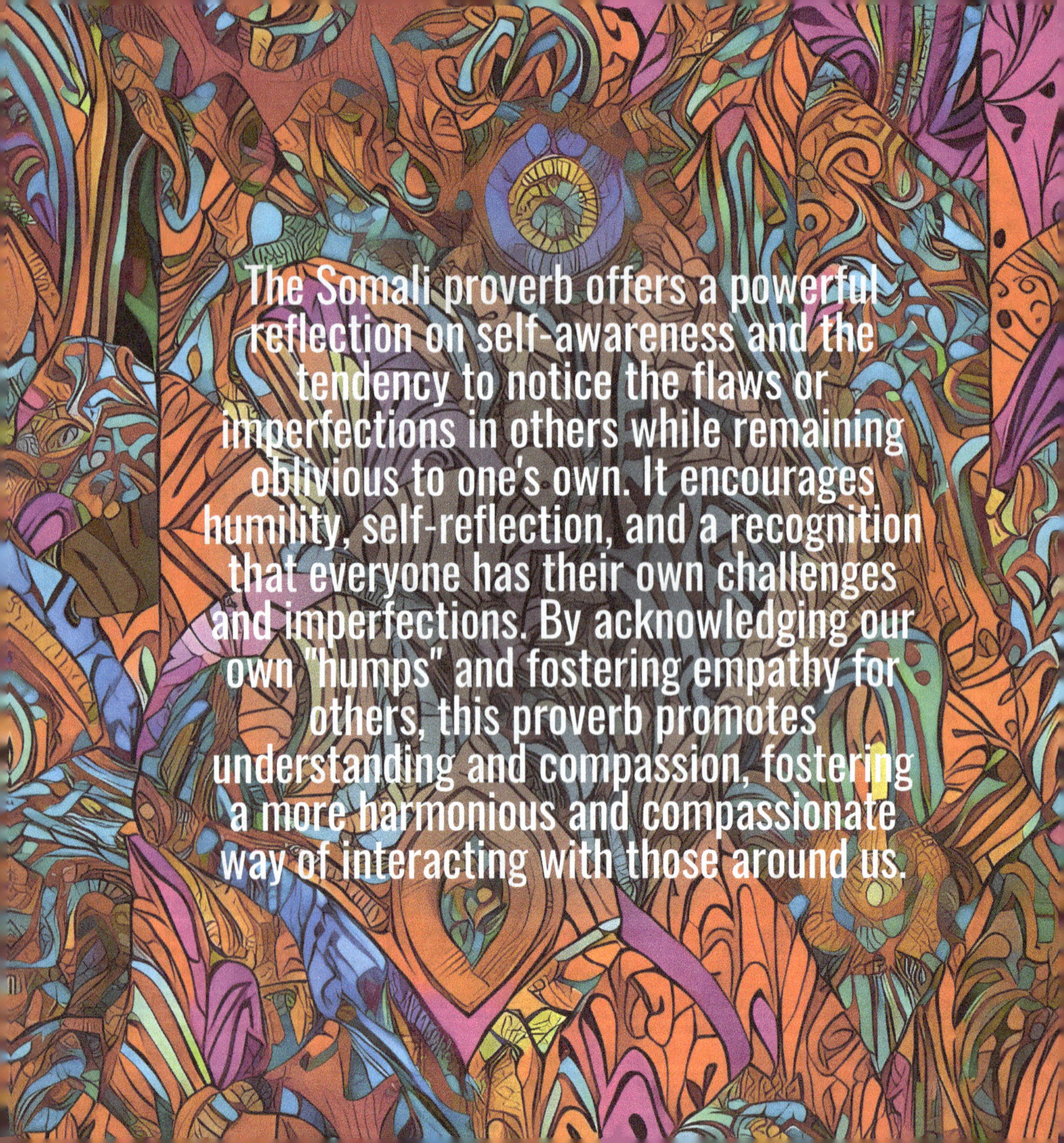

The Somali proverb offers a powerful reflection on self-awareness and the tendency to notice the flaws or imperfections in others while remaining oblivious to one's own. It encourages humility, self-reflection, and a recognition that everyone has their own challenges and imperfections. By acknowledging our own "humps" and fostering empathy for others, this proverb promotes understanding and compassion, fostering a more harmonious and compassionate way of interacting with those around us.

IF YOU CLOSE YOUR EYES TO FACTS, YOU WILL LEARN THROUGH ACCIDENTS.
Zimbabwe

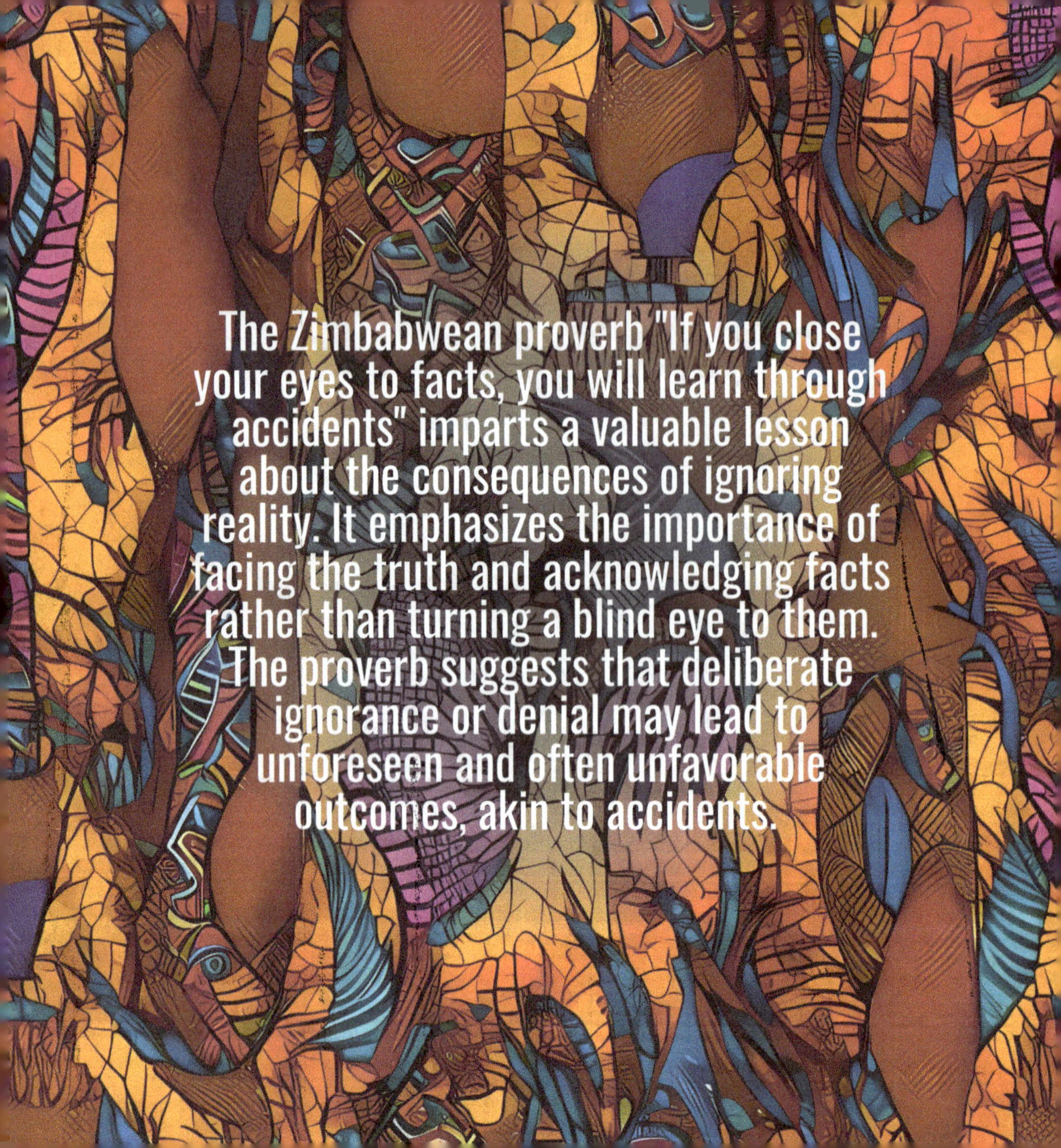

The Zimbabwean proverb "If you close your eyes to facts, you will learn through accidents" imparts a valuable lesson about the consequences of ignoring reality. It emphasizes the importance of facing the truth and acknowledging facts rather than turning a blind eye to them. The proverb suggests that deliberate ignorance or denial may lead to unforeseen and often unfavorable outcomes, akin to accidents.

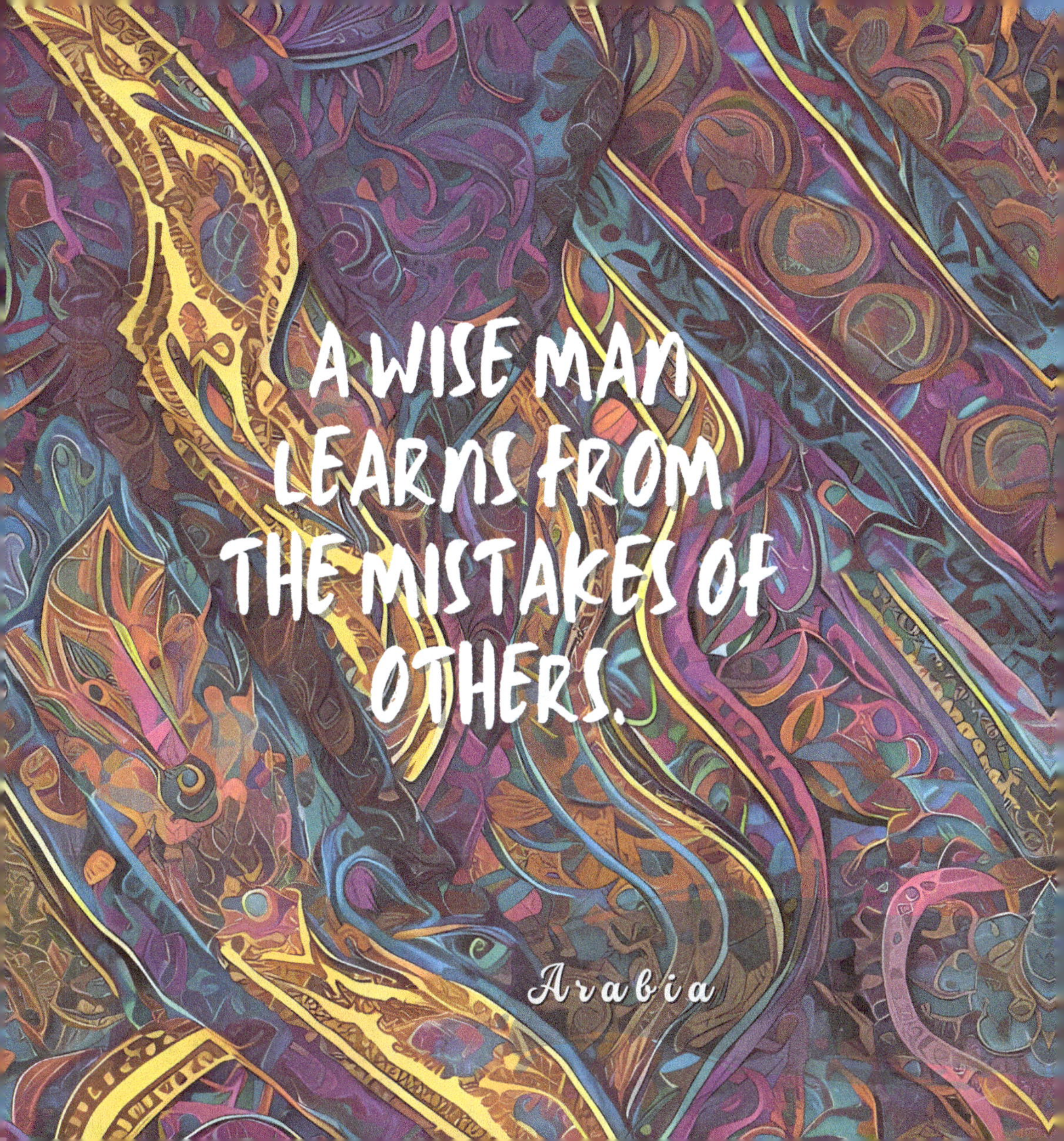
A WISE MAN LEARNS FROM THE MISTAKES OF OTHERS.
Arabia

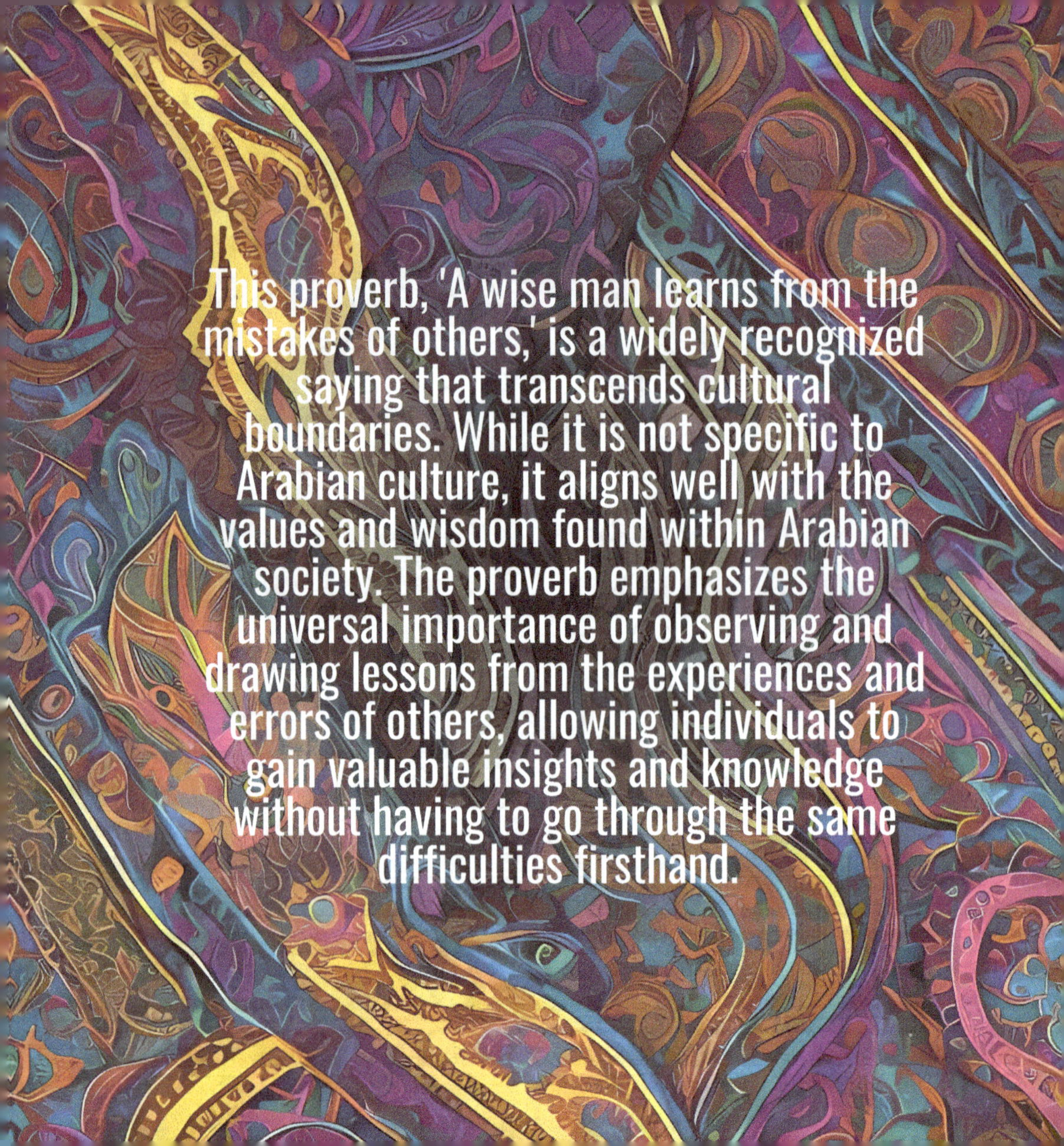

This proverb, 'A wise man learns from the mistakes of others,' is a widely recognized saying that transcends cultural boundaries. While it is not specific to Arabian culture, it aligns well with the values and wisdom found within Arabian society. The proverb emphasizes the universal importance of observing and drawing lessons from the experiences and errors of others, allowing individuals to gain valuable insights and knowledge without having to go through the same difficulties firsthand.

DRIVE AWAY NATURE, AND IT RETURNS AT A GALLOP.
France

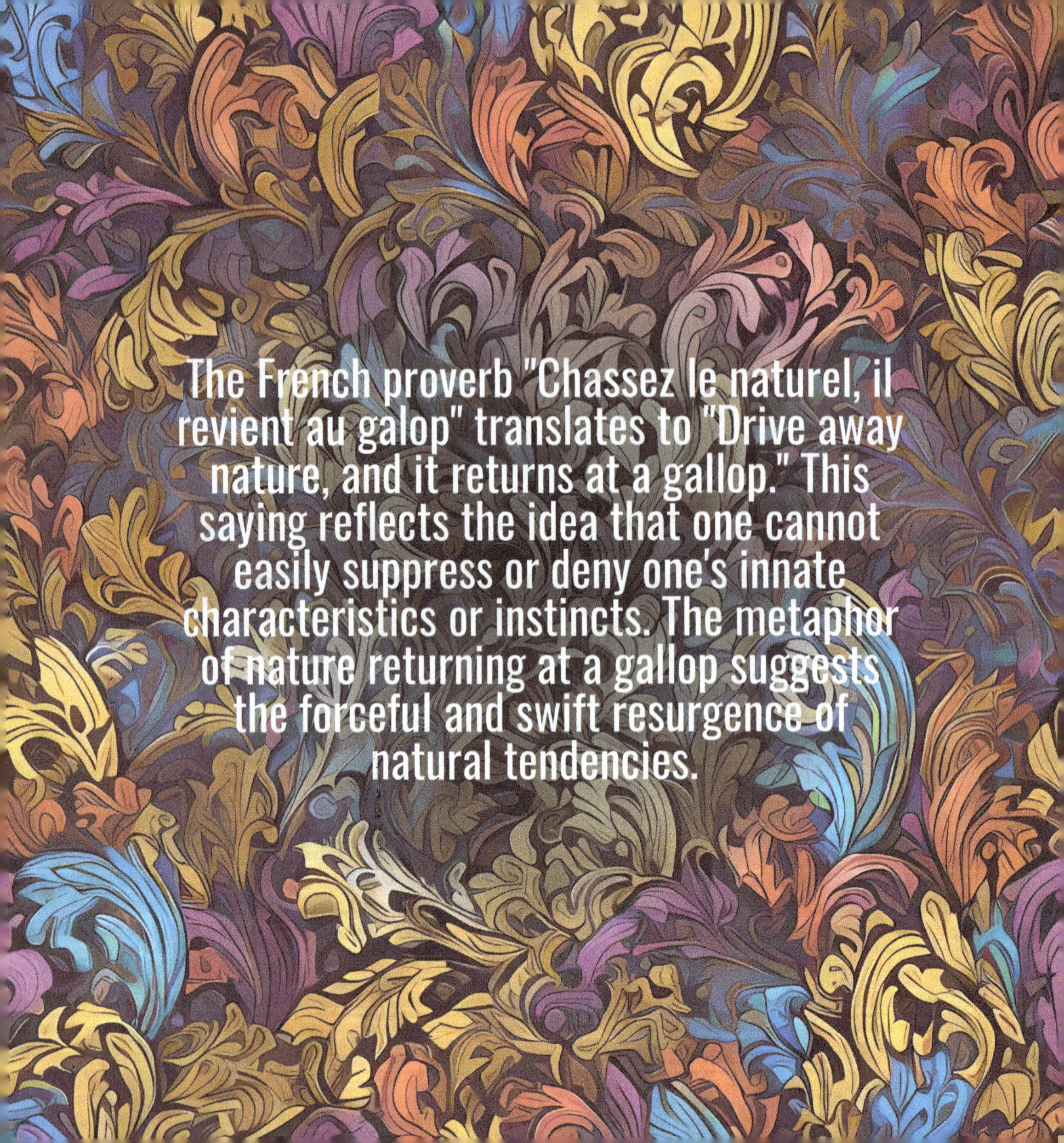

The French proverb "Chassez le naturel, il revient au galop" translates to "Drive away nature, and it returns at a gallop." This saying reflects the idea that one cannot easily suppress or deny one's innate characteristics or instincts. The metaphor of nature returning at a gallop suggests the forceful and swift resurgence of natural tendencies.

THE BEST WAY TO PREDICT THE FUTURE IS TO CREATE IT.
Germany

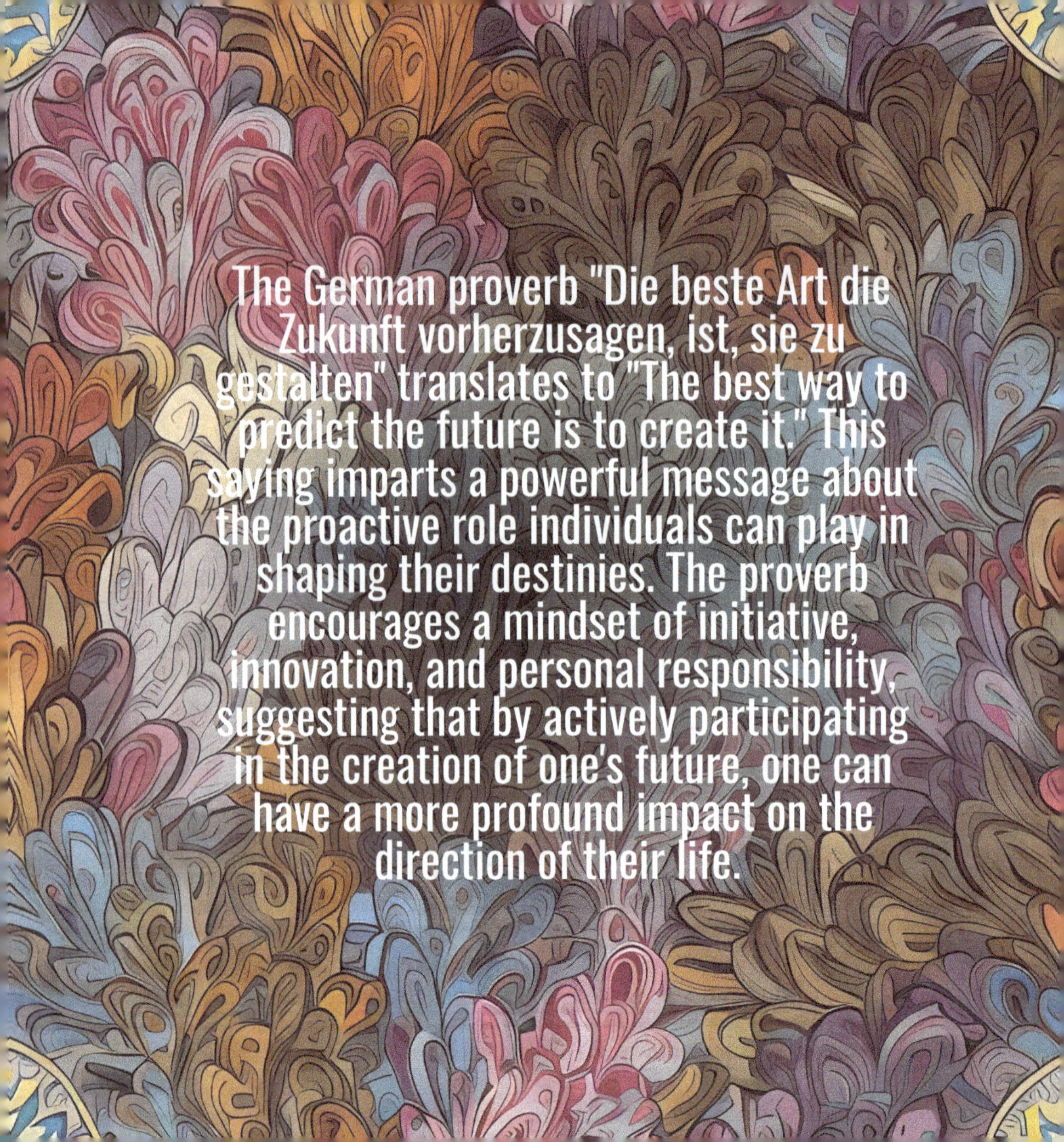

The German proverb "Die beste Art die Zukunft vorherzusagen, ist, sie zu gestalten" translates to "The best way to predict the future is to create it." This saying imparts a powerful message about the proactive role individuals can play in shaping their destinies. The proverb encourages a mindset of initiative, innovation, and personal responsibility, suggesting that by actively participating in the creation of one's future, one can have a more profound impact on the direction of their life.

AFTER THE GAME, THE KING AND THE PAWN GO INTO THE SAME BOX.
Italy

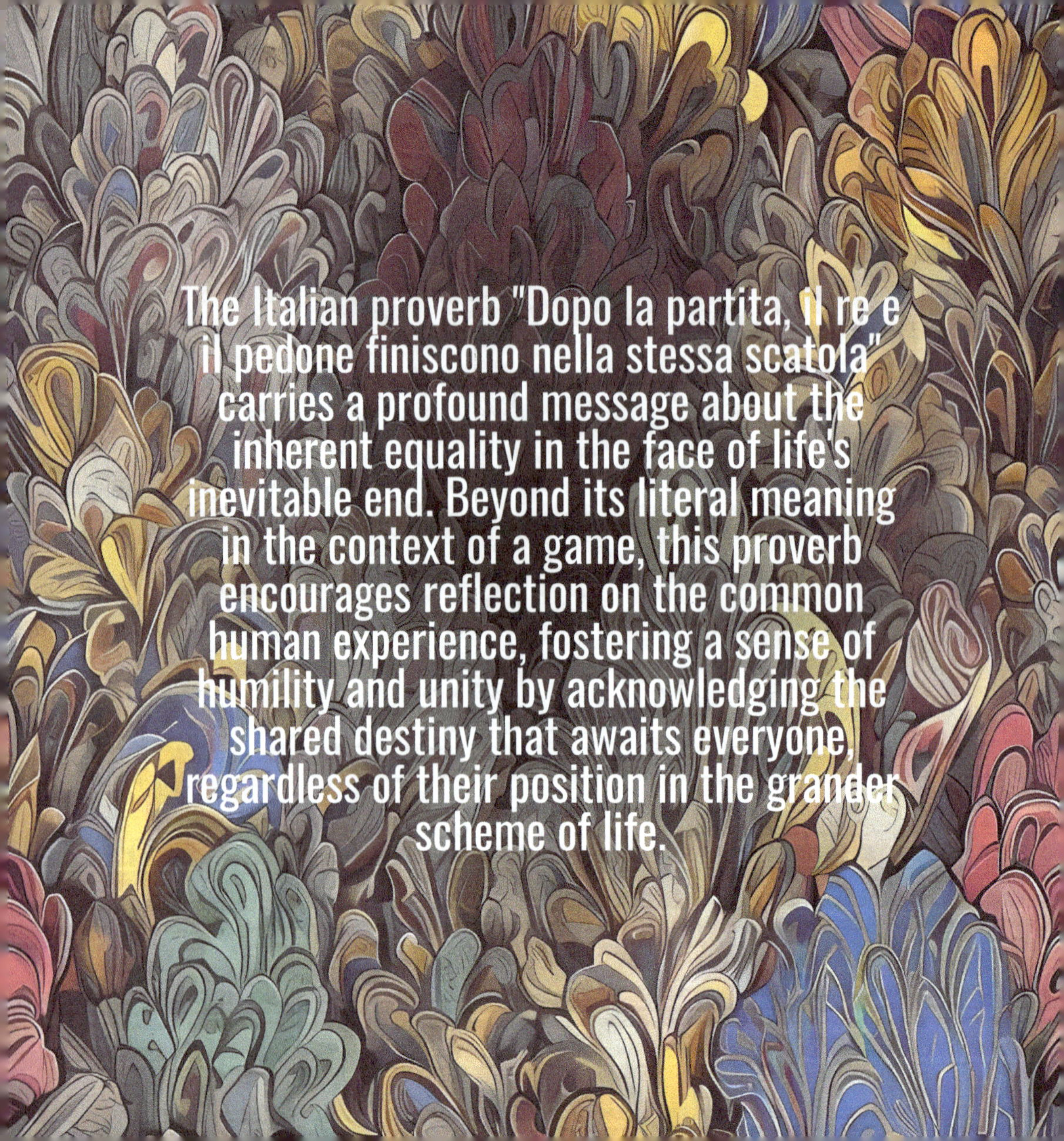

The Italian proverb "Dopo la partita, il re e il pedone finiscono nella stessa scatola" carries a profound message about the inherent equality in the face of life's inevitable end. Beyond its literal meaning in the context of a game, this proverb encourages reflection on the common human experience, fostering a sense of humility and unity by acknowledging the shared destiny that awaits everyone, regardless of their position in the grander scheme of life.

WHERE THE HEART INCLINES, THE FOOT FOLLOWS.
Latin American

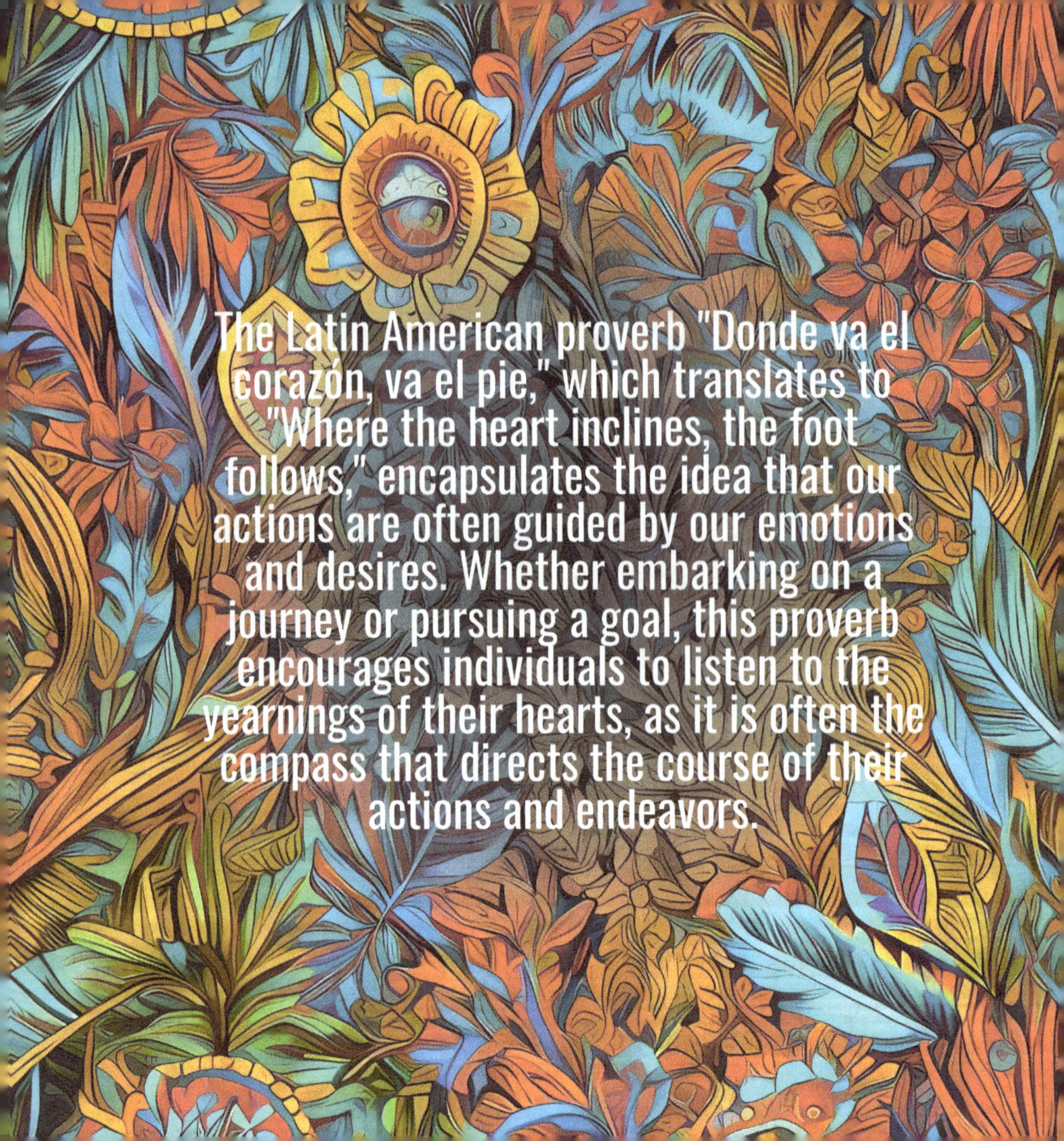
The Latin American proverb "Donde va el corazón, va el pie," which translates to "Where the heart inclines, the foot follows," encapsulates the idea that our actions are often guided by our emotions and desires. Whether embarking on a journey or pursuing a goal, this proverb encourages individuals to listen to the yearnings of their hearts, as it is often the compass that directs the course of their actions and endeavors.

SKILL IS BETTER THAN STRENGTH.
Latin American

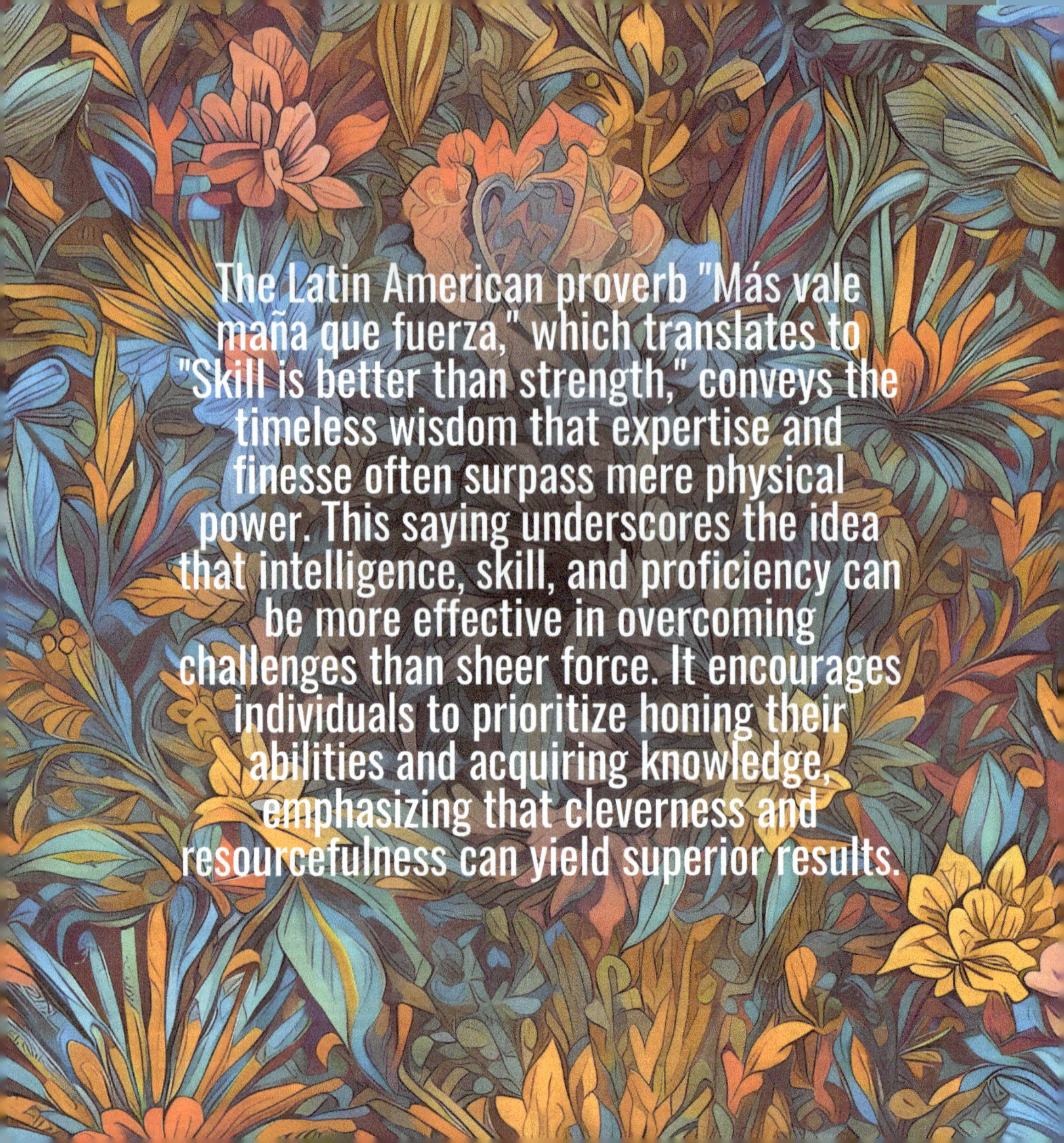

The Latin American proverb "Más vale maña que fuerza," which translates to "Skill is better than strength," conveys the timeless wisdom that expertise and finesse often surpass mere physical power. This saying underscores the idea that intelligence, skill, and proficiency can be more effective in overcoming challenges than sheer force. It encourages individuals to prioritize honing their abilities and acquiring knowledge, emphasizing that cleverness and resourcefulness can yield superior results.

YOU CAN'T WAKE A PERSON WHO IS PRETENDING TO BE ASLEEP.
Navajo

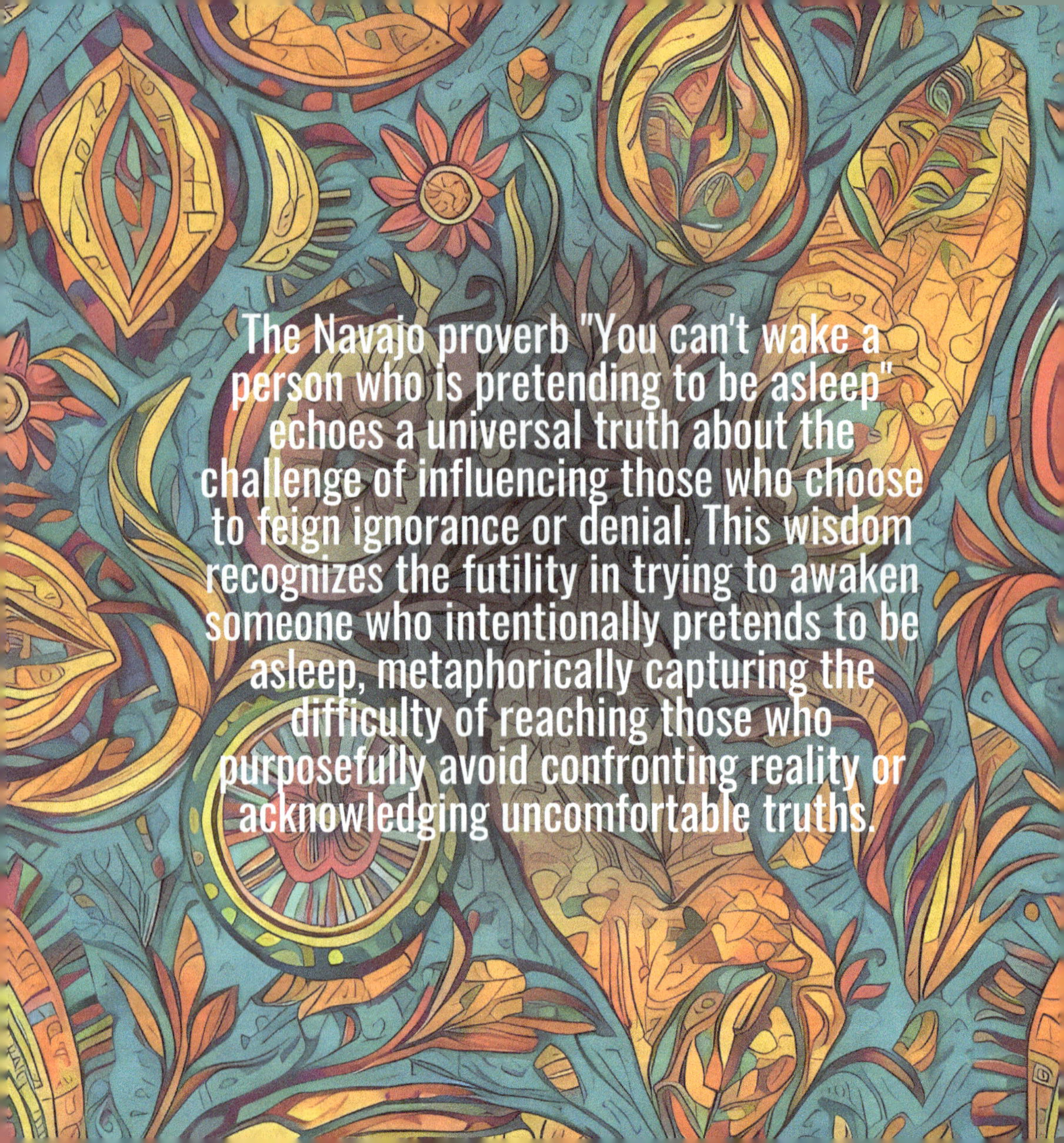
The Navajo proverb "You can't wake a person who is pretending to be asleep" echoes a universal truth about the challenge of influencing those who choose to feign ignorance or denial. This wisdom recognizes the futility in trying to awaken someone who intentionally pretends to be asleep, metaphorically capturing the difficulty of reaching those who purposefully avoid confronting reality or acknowledging uncomfortable truths.

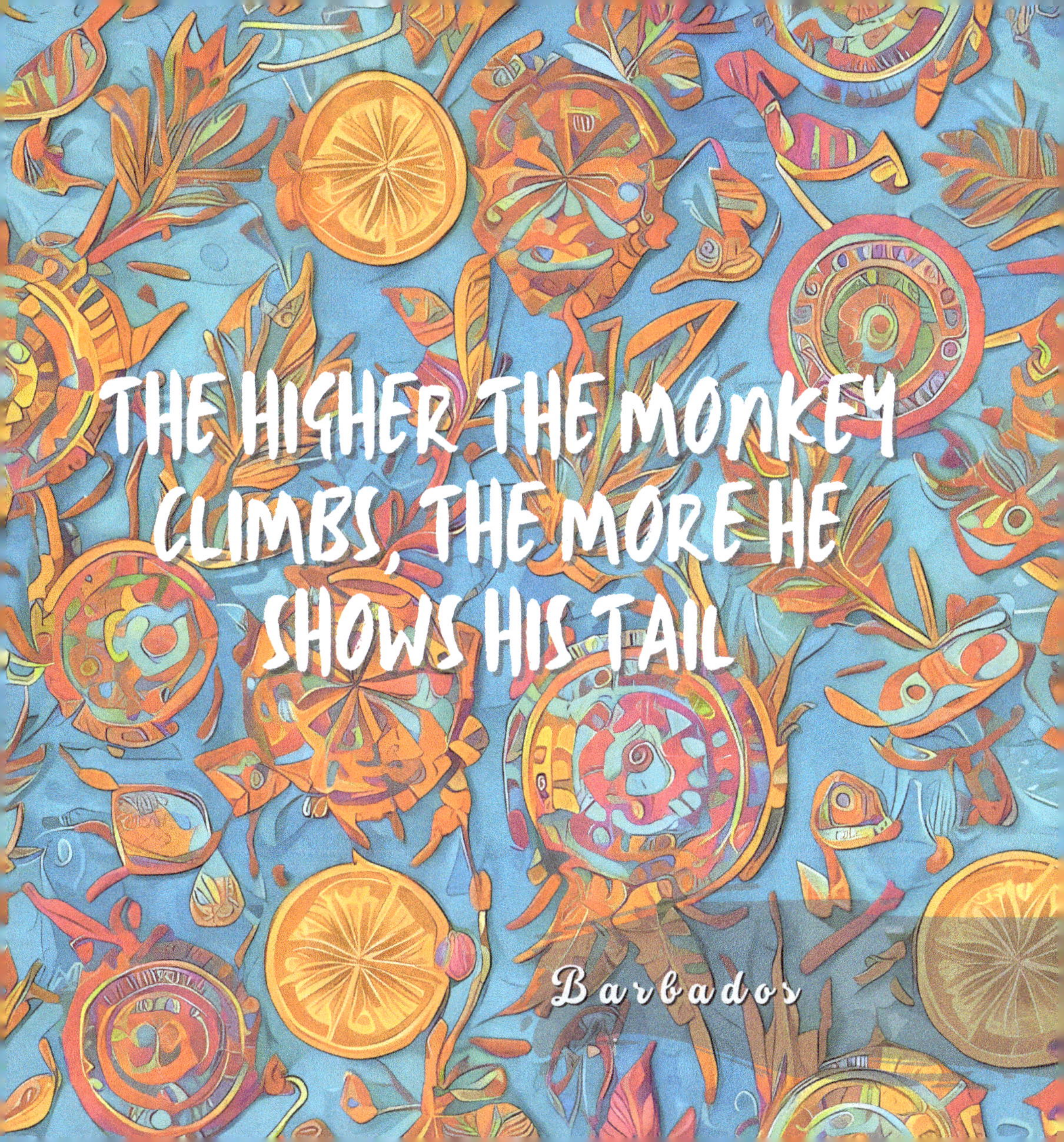
THE HIGHER THE MONKEY CLIMBS, THE MORE HE SHOWS HIS TAIL
Barbados

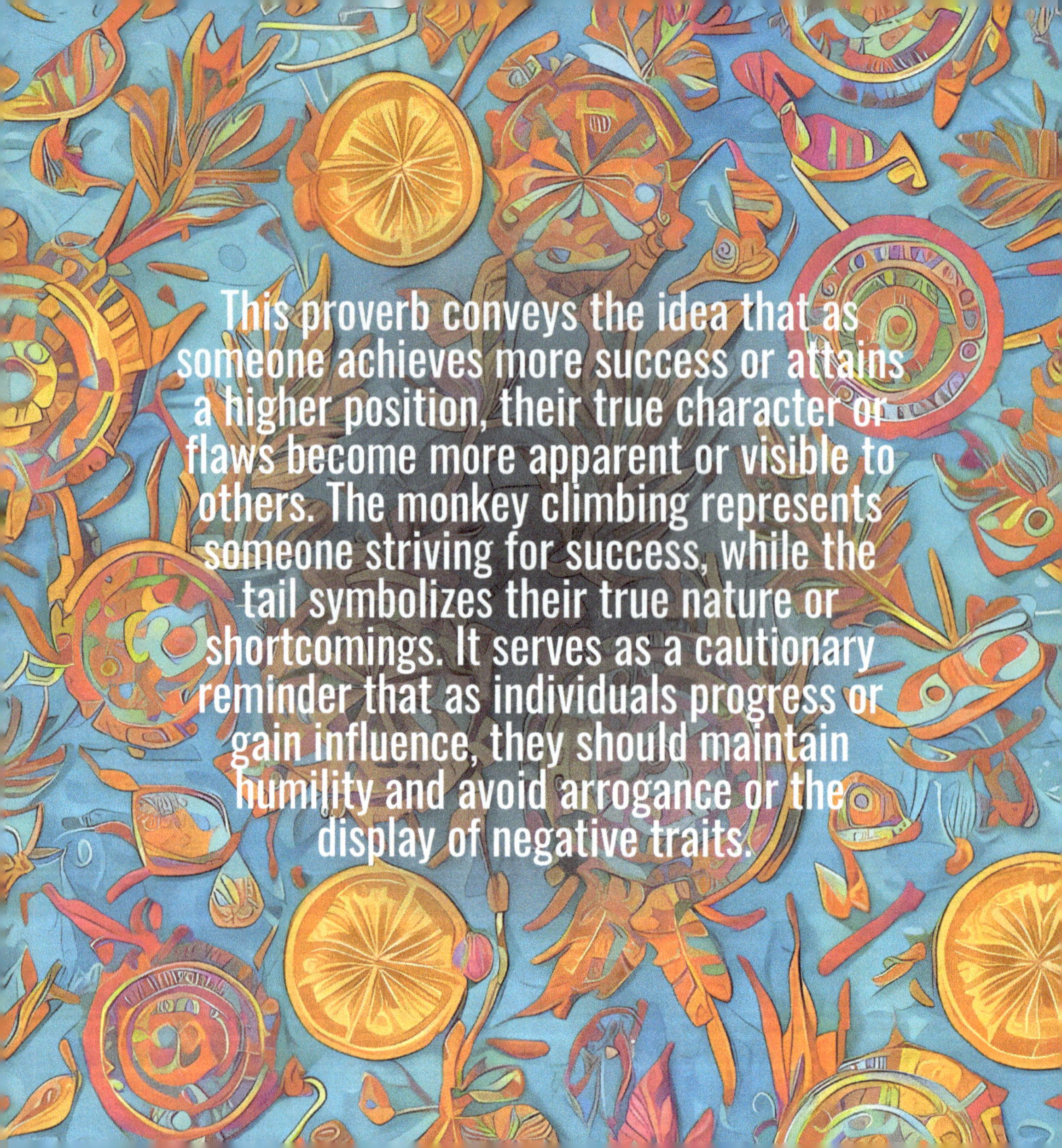
This proverb conveys the idea that as someone achieves more success or attains a higher position, their true character or flaws become more apparent or visible to others. The monkey climbing represents someone striving for success, while the tail symbolizes their true nature or shortcomings. It serves as a cautionary reminder that as individuals progress or gain influence, they should maintain humility and avoid arrogance or the display of negative traits.

BEHIND
MOUNTAINS,
THERE ARE MORE
MOUNTAINS.
Haiti

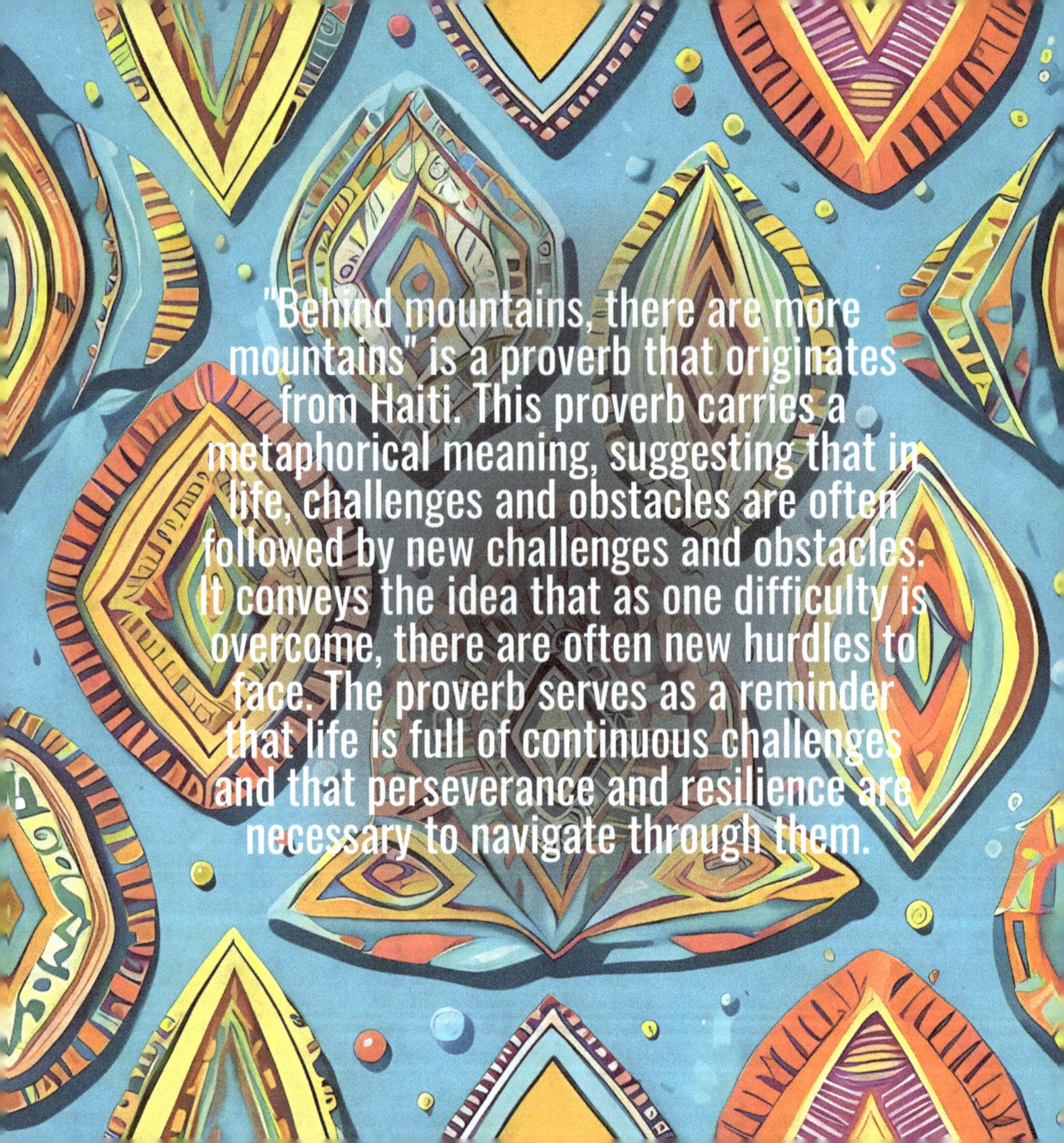

"Behind mountains, there are more mountains" is a proverb that originates from Haiti. This proverb carries a metaphorical meaning, suggesting that in life, challenges and obstacles are often followed by new challenges and obstacles. It conveys the idea that as one difficulty is overcome, there are often new hurdles to face. The proverb serves as a reminder that life is full of continuous challenges and that perseverance and resilience are necessary to navigate through them.

DON'T JUDGE EACH
DAY BY THE
HARVEST YOU REAP
BUT BY THE SEEDS
THAT YOU PLANT.
Scotland

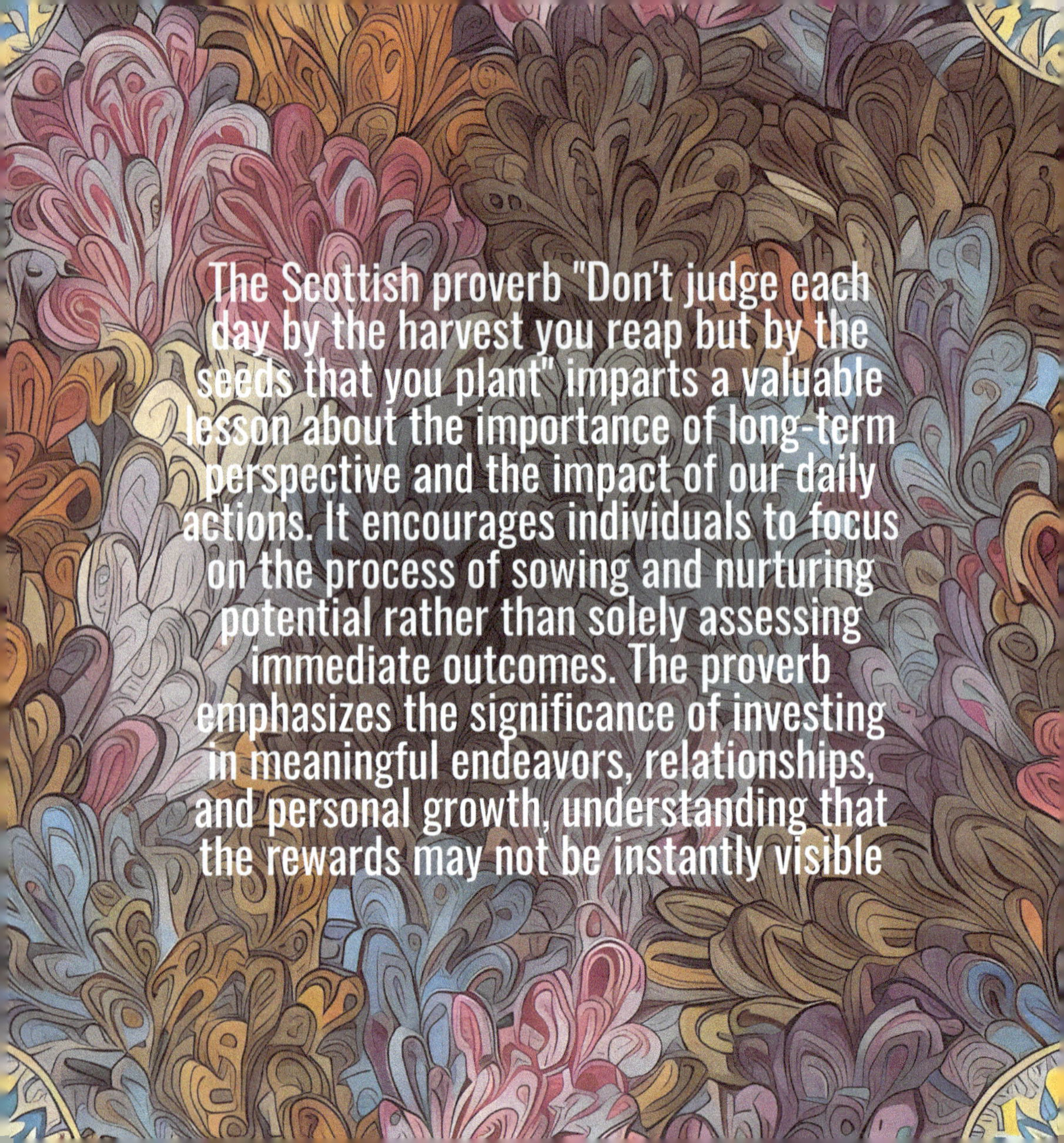
The Scottish proverb "Don't judge each day by the harvest you reap but by the seeds that you plant" imparts a valuable lesson about the importance of long-term perspective and the impact of our daily actions. It encourages individuals to focus on the process of sowing and nurturing potential rather than solely assessing immediate outcomes. The proverb emphasizes the significance of investing in meaningful endeavors, relationships, and personal growth, understanding that the rewards may not be instantly visible

PEOPLE MAY DUCK AND HIDE, BUT THEIR BUTTS ARE STILL ON SHOW.
St. Kitts & Nevis

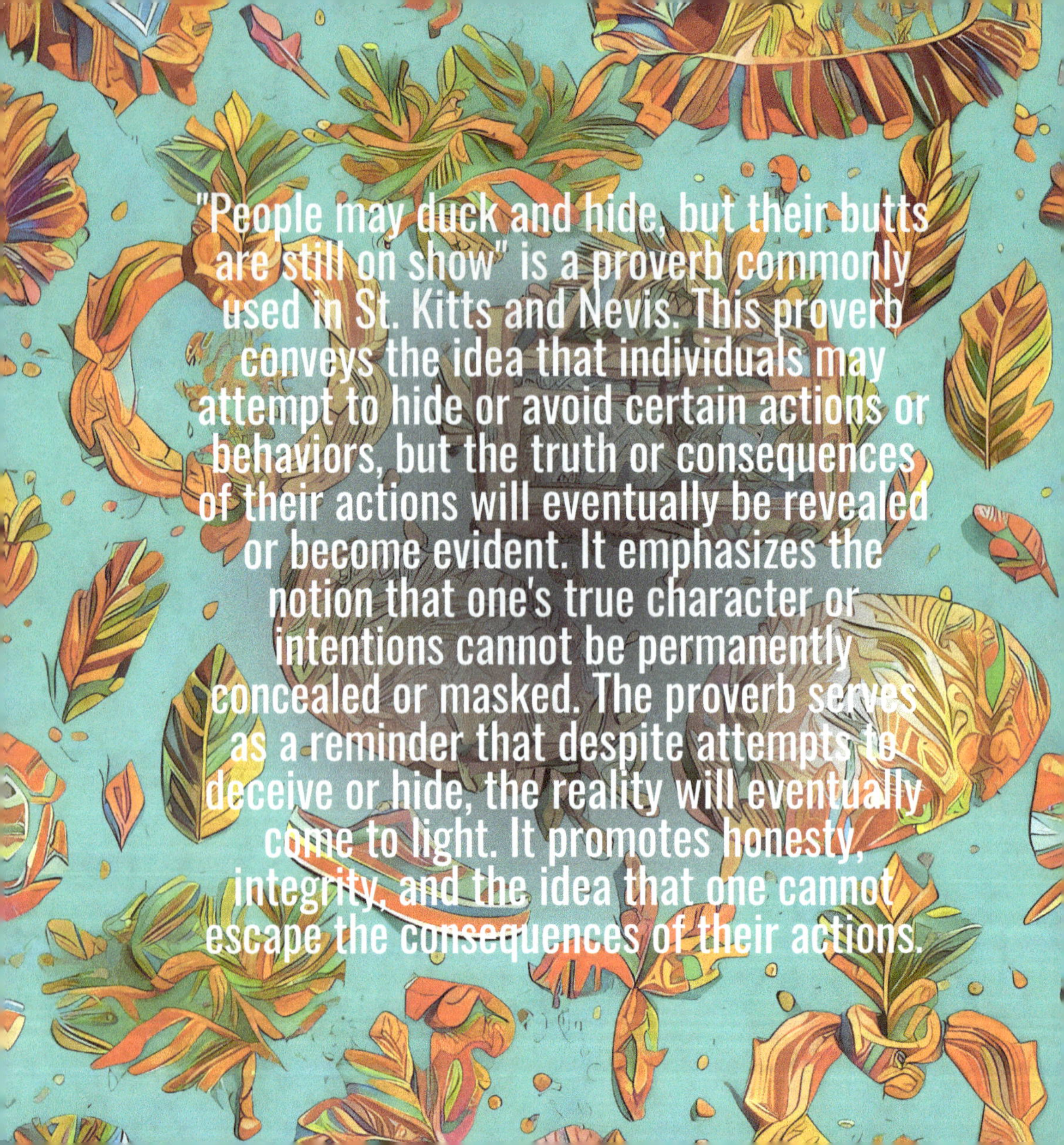
"People may duck and hide, but their butts are still on show" is a proverb commonly used in St. Kitts and Nevis. This proverb conveys the idea that individuals may attempt to hide or avoid certain actions or behaviors, but the truth or consequences of their actions will eventually be revealed or become evident. It emphasizes the notion that one's true character or intentions cannot be permanently concealed or masked. The proverb serves as a reminder that despite attempts to deceive or hide, the reality will eventually come to light. It promotes honesty, integrity, and the idea that one cannot escape the consequences of their actions.

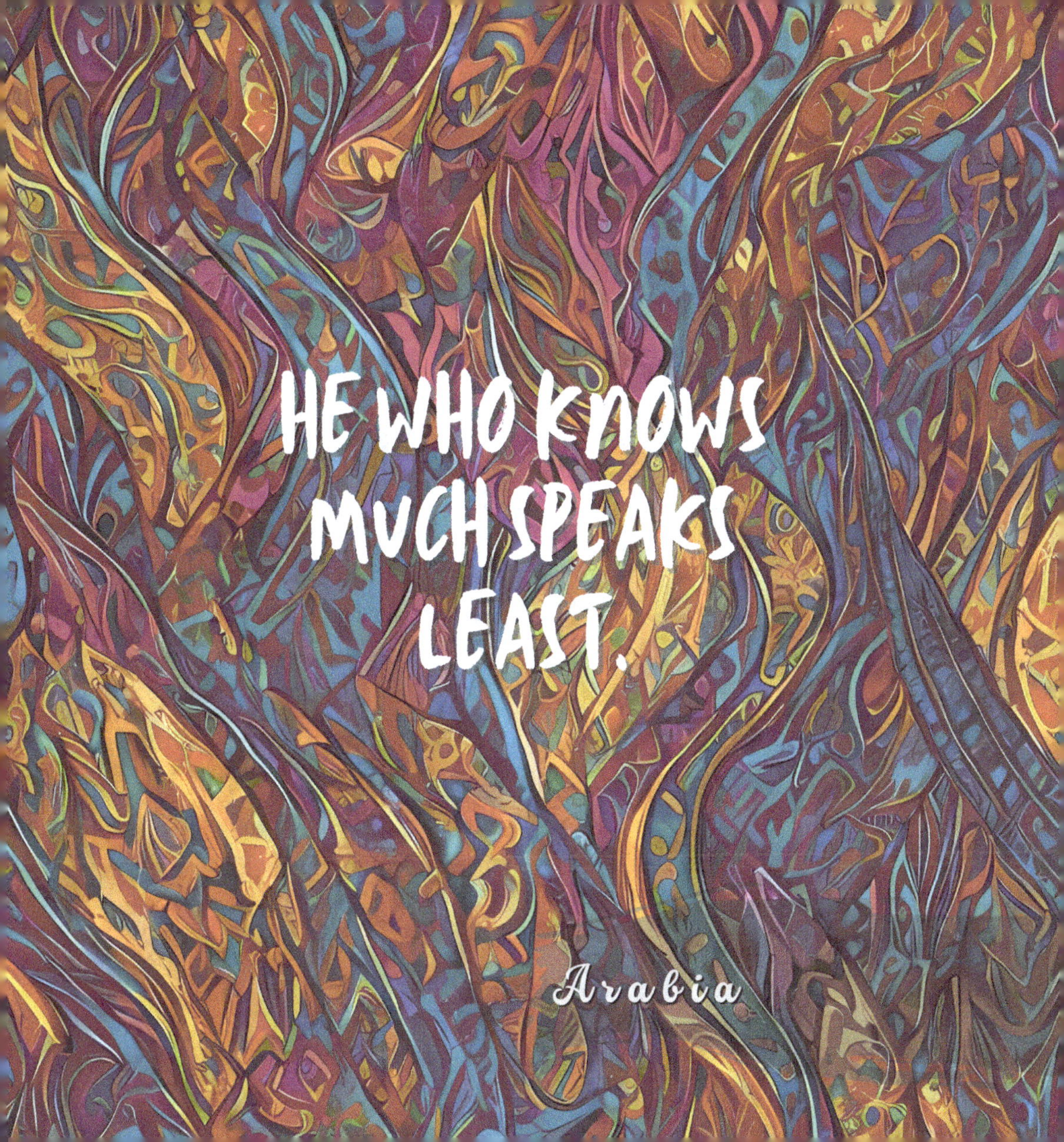
HE WHO KNOWS
MUCH SPEAKS
LEAST.
Arabia

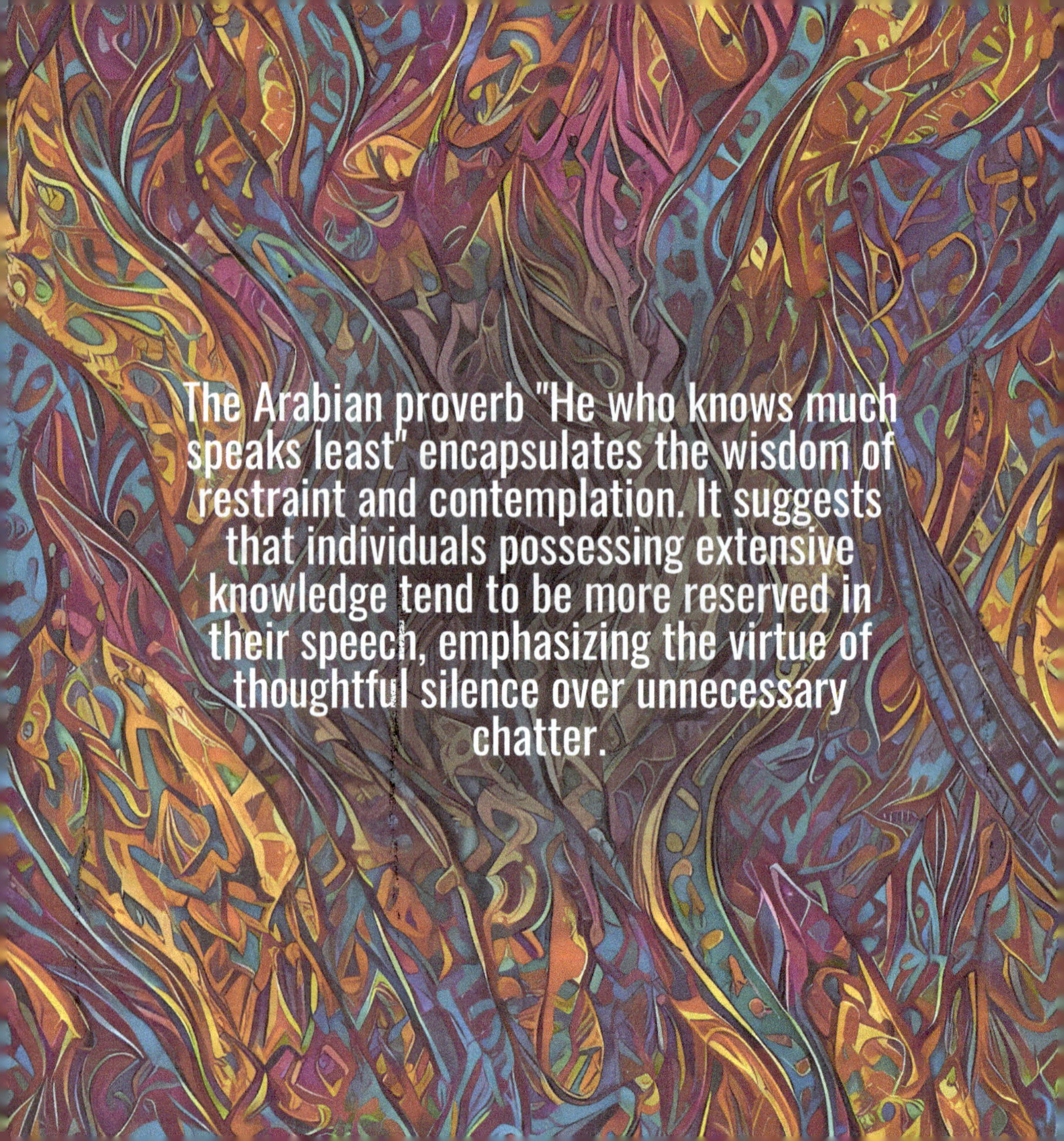
The Arabian proverb "He who knows much speaks least" encapsulates the wisdom of restraint and contemplation. It suggests that individuals possessing extensive knowledge tend to be more reserved in their speech, emphasizing the virtue of thoughtful silence over unnecessary chatter.

HE WHO LOOKS FOR
SEASHELLS WILL
FIND SEASHELLS; HE
WHO OPENS THEM
WILL FIND PEARLS.
Arabia

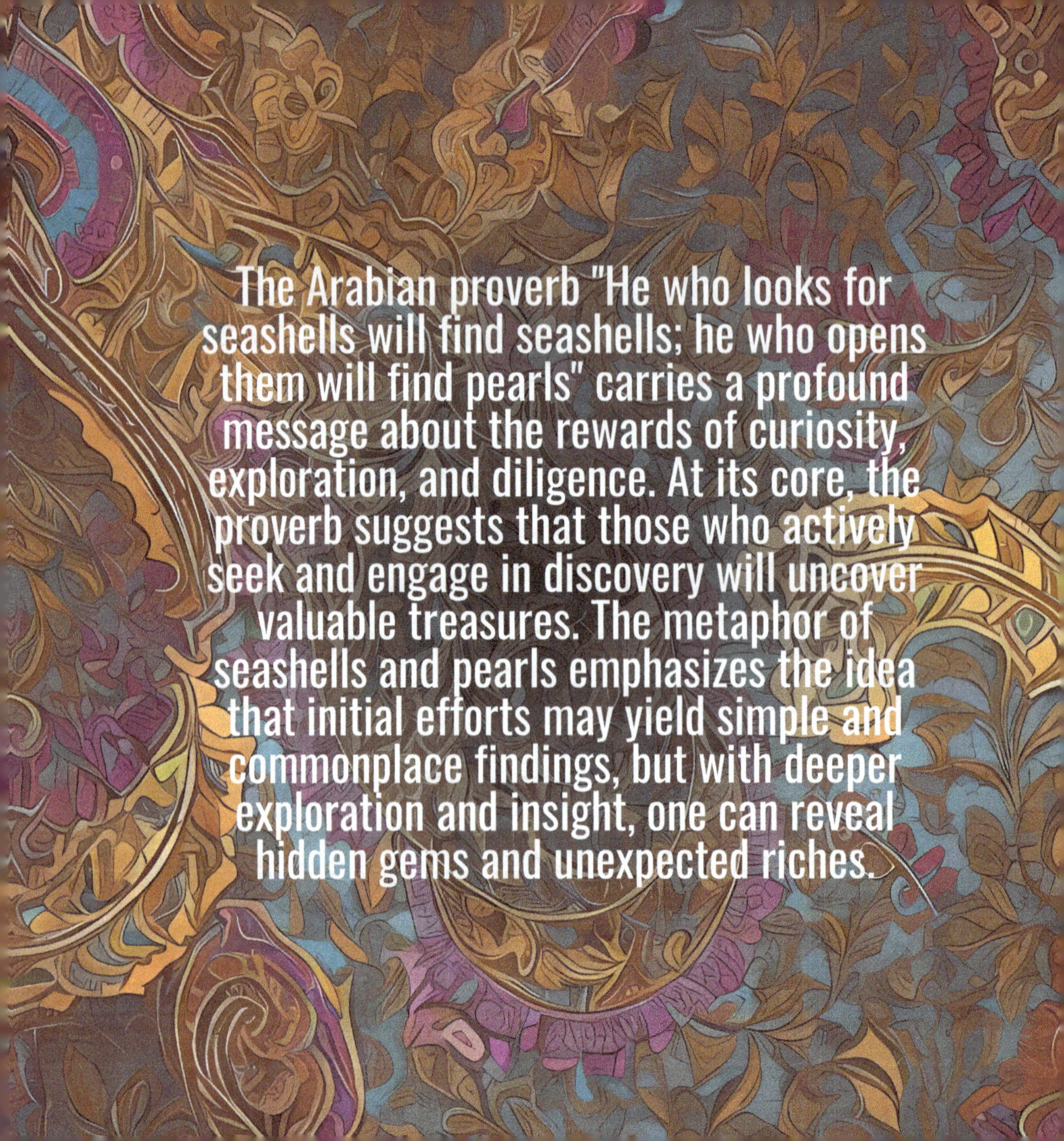

The Arabian proverb "He who looks for seashells will find seashells; he who opens them will find pearls" carries a profound message about the rewards of curiosity, exploration, and diligence. At its core, the proverb suggests that those who actively seek and engage in discovery will uncover valuable treasures. The metaphor of seashells and pearls emphasizes the idea that initial efforts may yield simple and commonplace findings, but with deeper exploration and insight, one can reveal hidden gems and unexpected riches.

HE WHO HAS A GOOD FRIEND DOESN'T NEED ANY MIRROR.
Arabia

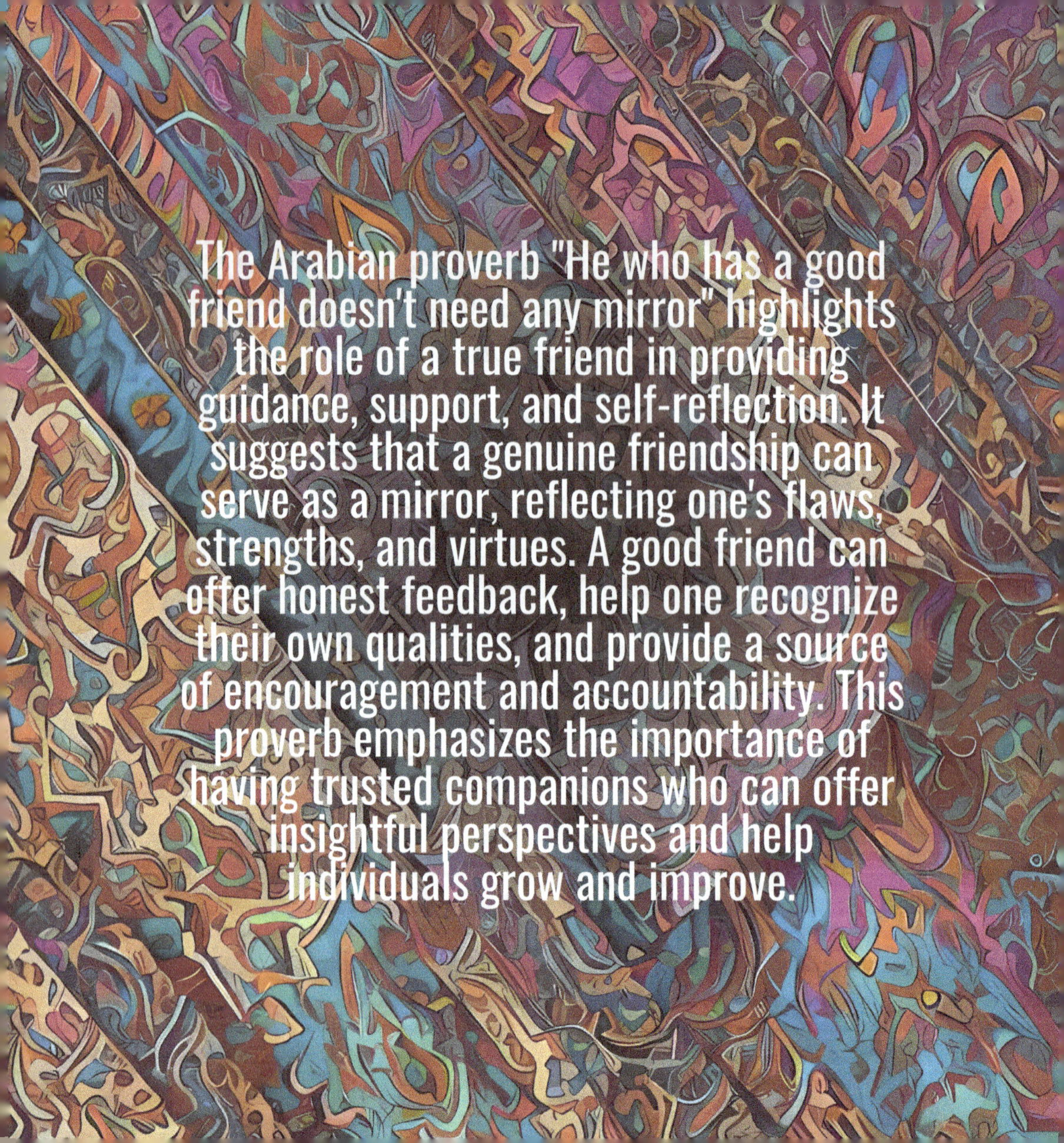
The Arabian proverb "He who has a good friend doesn't need any mirror" highlights the role of a true friend in providing guidance, support, and self-reflection. It suggests that a genuine friendship can serve as a mirror, reflecting one's flaws, strengths, and virtues. A good friend can offer honest feedback, help one recognize their own qualities, and provide a source of encouragement and accountability. This proverb emphasizes the importance of having trusted companions who can offer insightful perspectives and help individuals grow and improve.

THE BEST TIME TO
PLANT A TREE WAS
20 YEARS AGO. THE
SECOND BEST TIME
IS NOW.
China

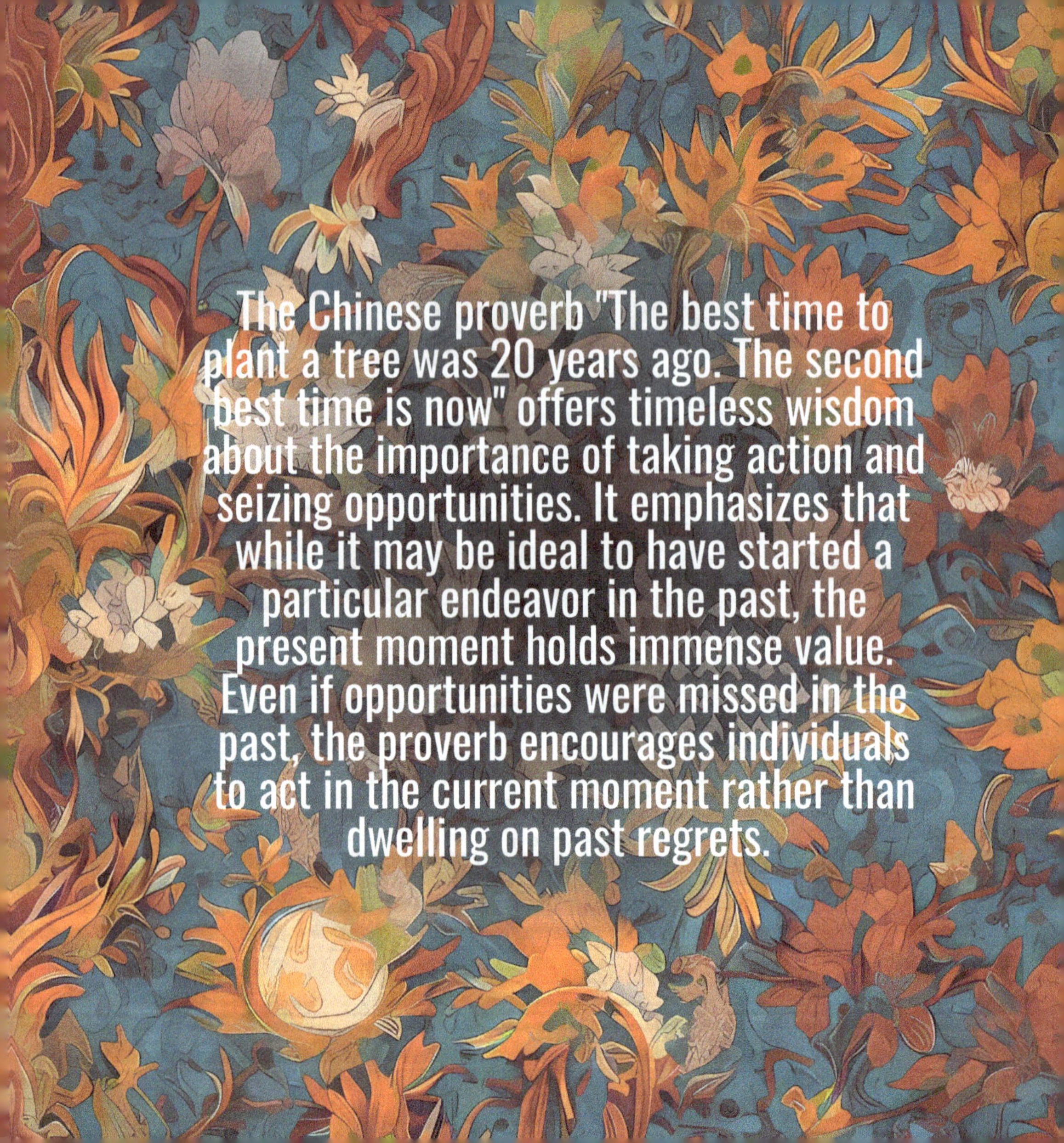
The Chinese proverb "The best time to plant a tree was 20 years ago. The second best time is now" offers timeless wisdom about the importance of taking action and seizing opportunities. It emphasizes that while it may be ideal to have started a particular endeavor in the past, the present moment holds immense value. Even if opportunities were missed in the past, the proverb encourages individuals to act in the current moment rather than dwelling on past regrets.

A BIRD DOES NOT SING BECAUSE IT HAS AN ANSWER, IT SINGS BECAUSE IT HAS A SONG.
China

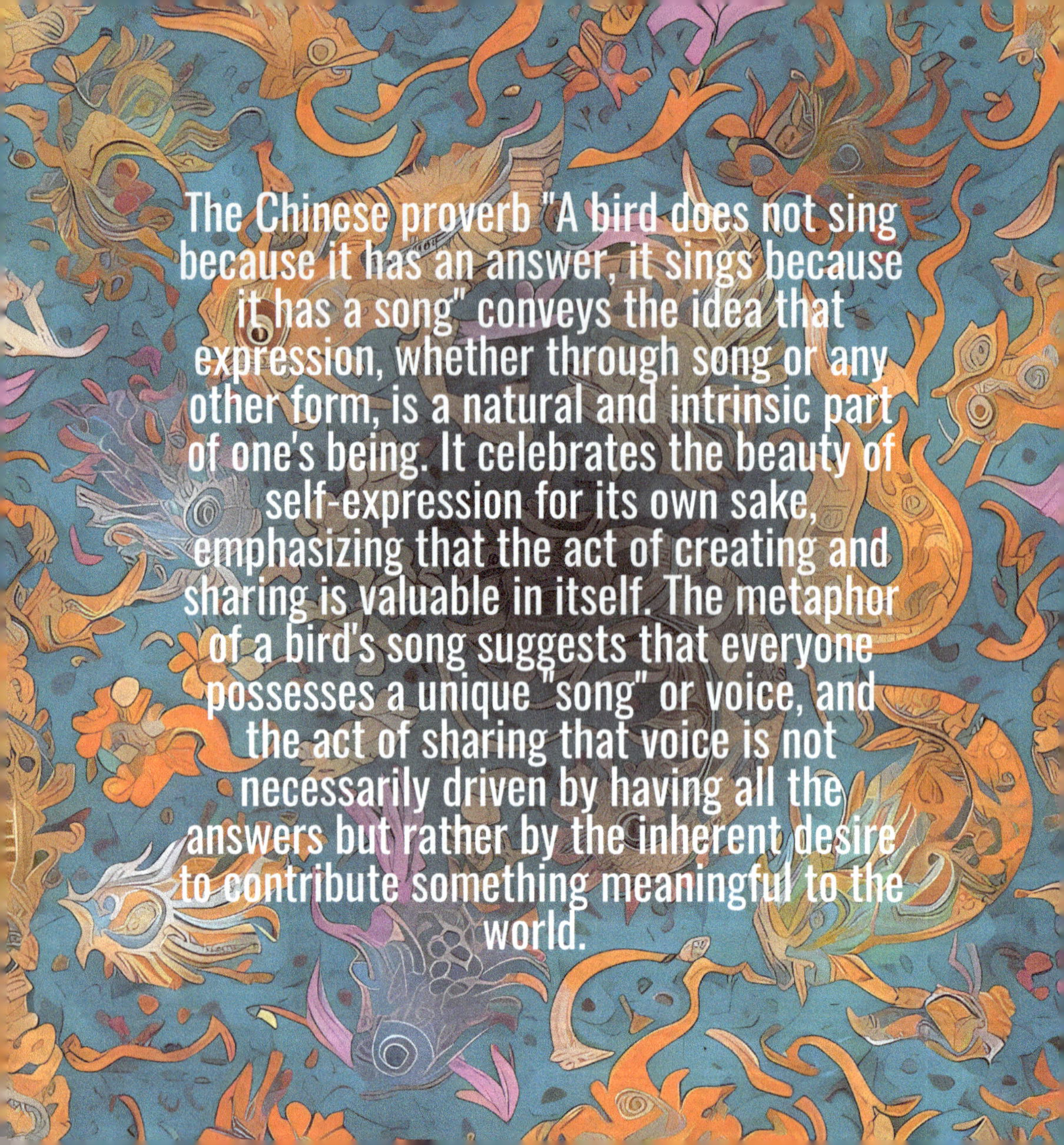

The Chinese proverb "A bird does not sing because it has an answer, it sings because it has a song" conveys the idea that expression, whether through song or any other form, is a natural and intrinsic part of one's being. It celebrates the beauty of self-expression for its own sake, emphasizing that the act of creating and sharing is valuable in itself. The metaphor of a bird's song suggests that everyone possesses a unique "song" or voice, and the act of sharing that voice is not necessarily driven by having all the answers but rather by the inherent desire to contribute something meaningful to the world.

YOU CANNOT CATCH
A FLEA WITH
GLOVES.
Korea

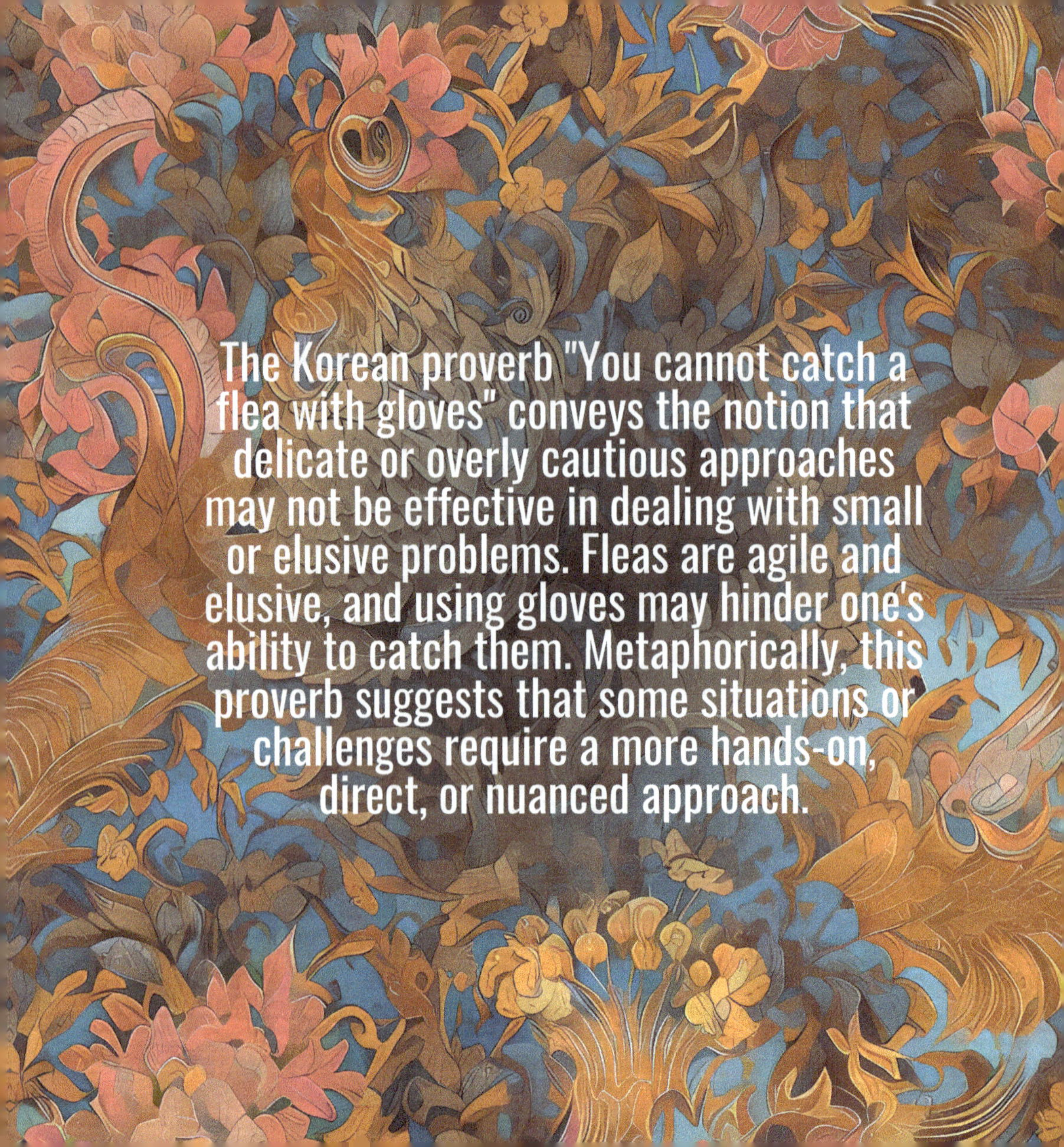
The Korean proverb "You cannot catch a flea with gloves" conveys the notion that delicate or overly cautious approaches may not be effective in dealing with small or elusive problems. Fleas are agile and elusive, and using gloves may hinder one's ability to catch them. Metaphorically, this proverb suggests that some situations or challenges require a more hands-on, direct, or nuanced approach.

A SINGLE ARROW IS
EASILY BROKEN,
BUT NOT TEN IN A
BUNDLE.
Mongolia

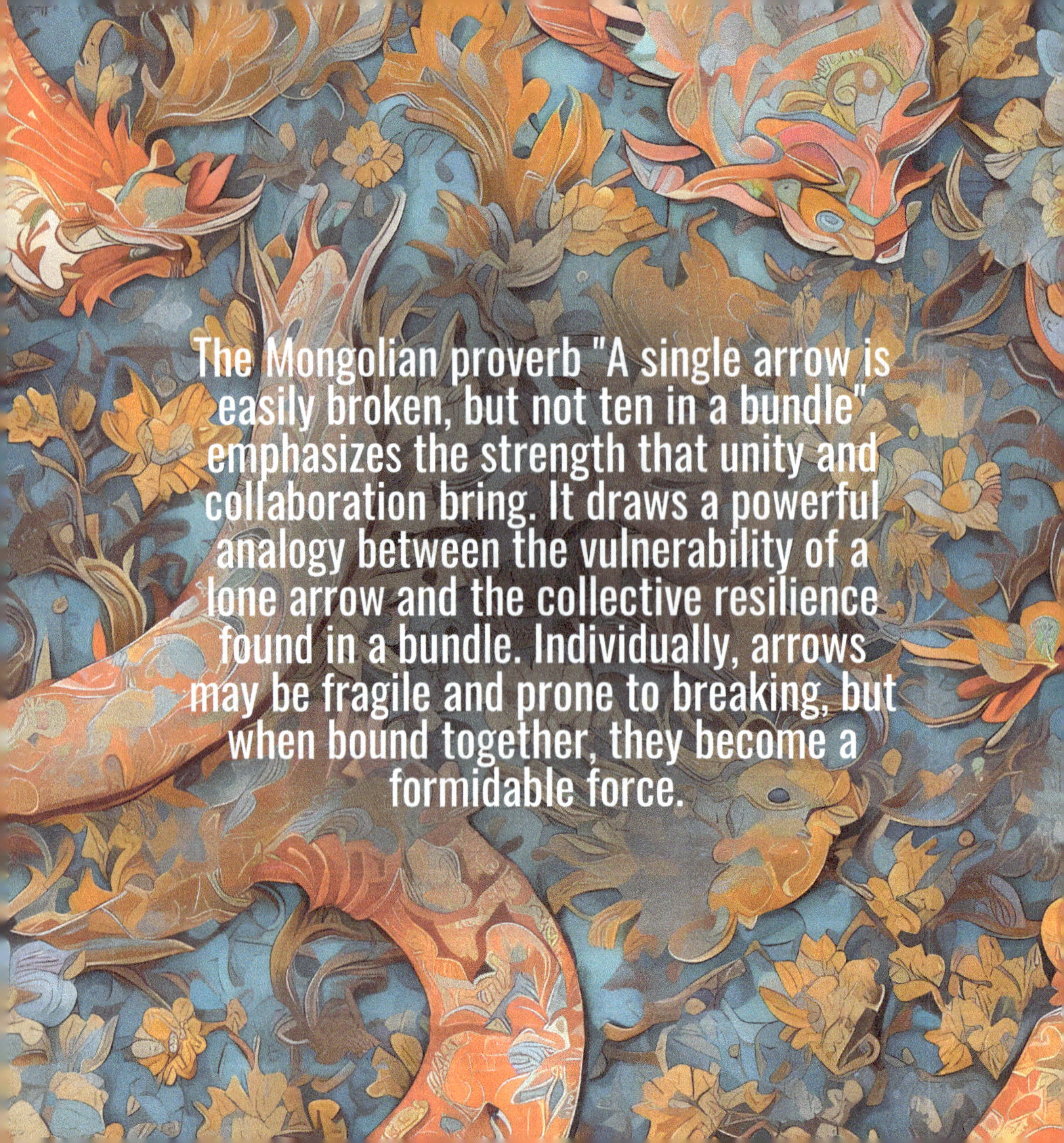
The Mongolian proverb "A single arrow is easily broken, but not ten in a bundle" emphasizes the strength that unity and collaboration bring. It draws a powerful analogy between the vulnerability of a lone arrow and the collective resilience found in a bundle. Individually, arrows may be fragile and prone to breaking, but when bound together, they become a formidable force.

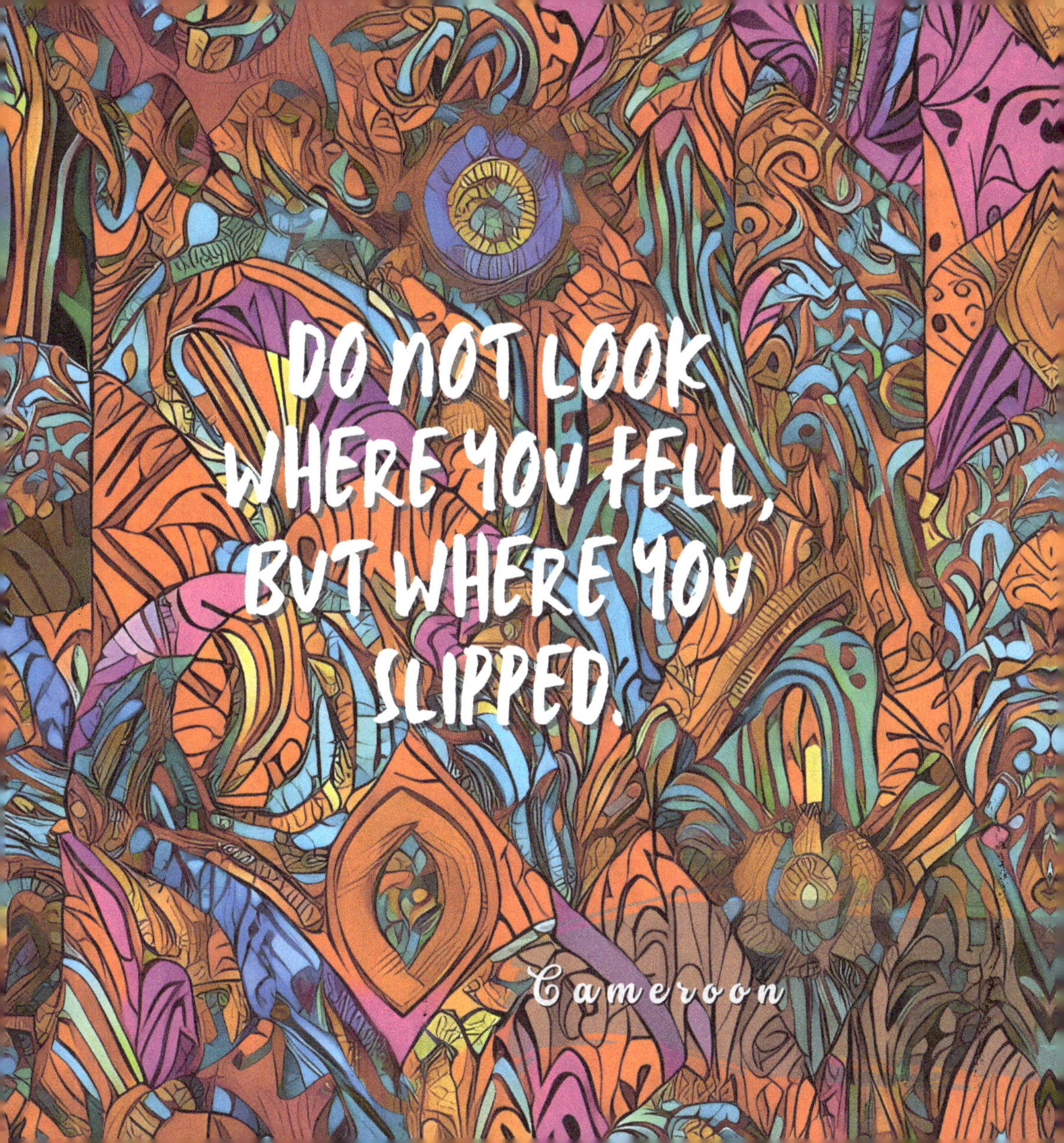
DO NOT LOOK
WHERE YOU FELL,
BUT WHERE YOU
SLIPPED.
Cameroon

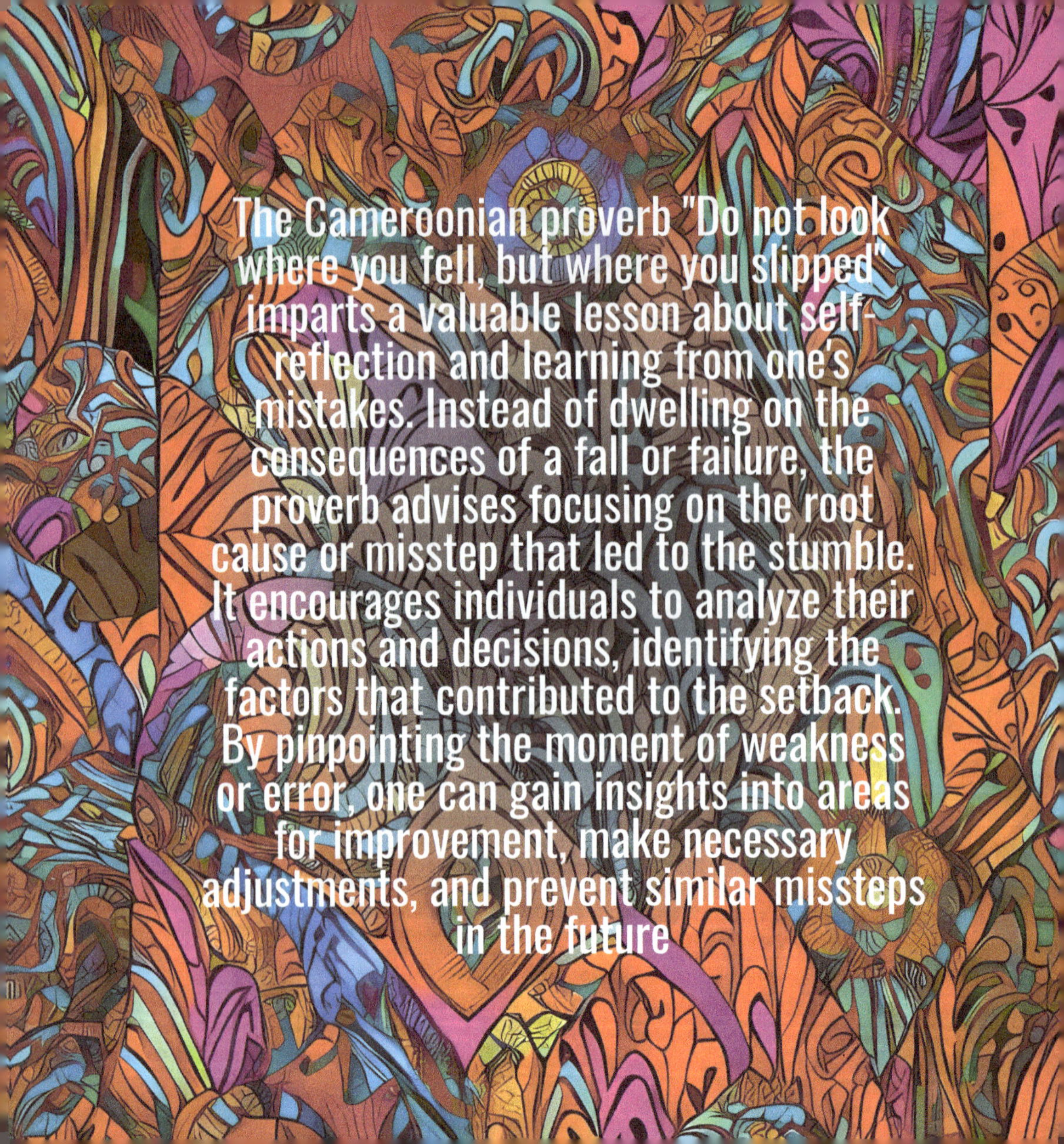
The Cameroonian proverb "Do not look where you fell, but where you slipped" imparts a valuable lesson about self-reflection and learning from one's mistakes. Instead of dwelling on the consequences of a fall or failure, the proverb advises focusing on the root cause or misstep that led to the stumble. It encourages individuals to analyze their actions and decisions, identifying the factors that contributed to the setback. By pinpointing the moment of weakness or error, one can gain insights into areas for improvement, make necessary adjustments, and prevent similar missteps in the future

DO NOT BLAME GOD FOR HAVING CREATED THE TIGER, BUT THANK HIM FOR NOT HAVING GIVEN IT WINGS.
Ethiopia

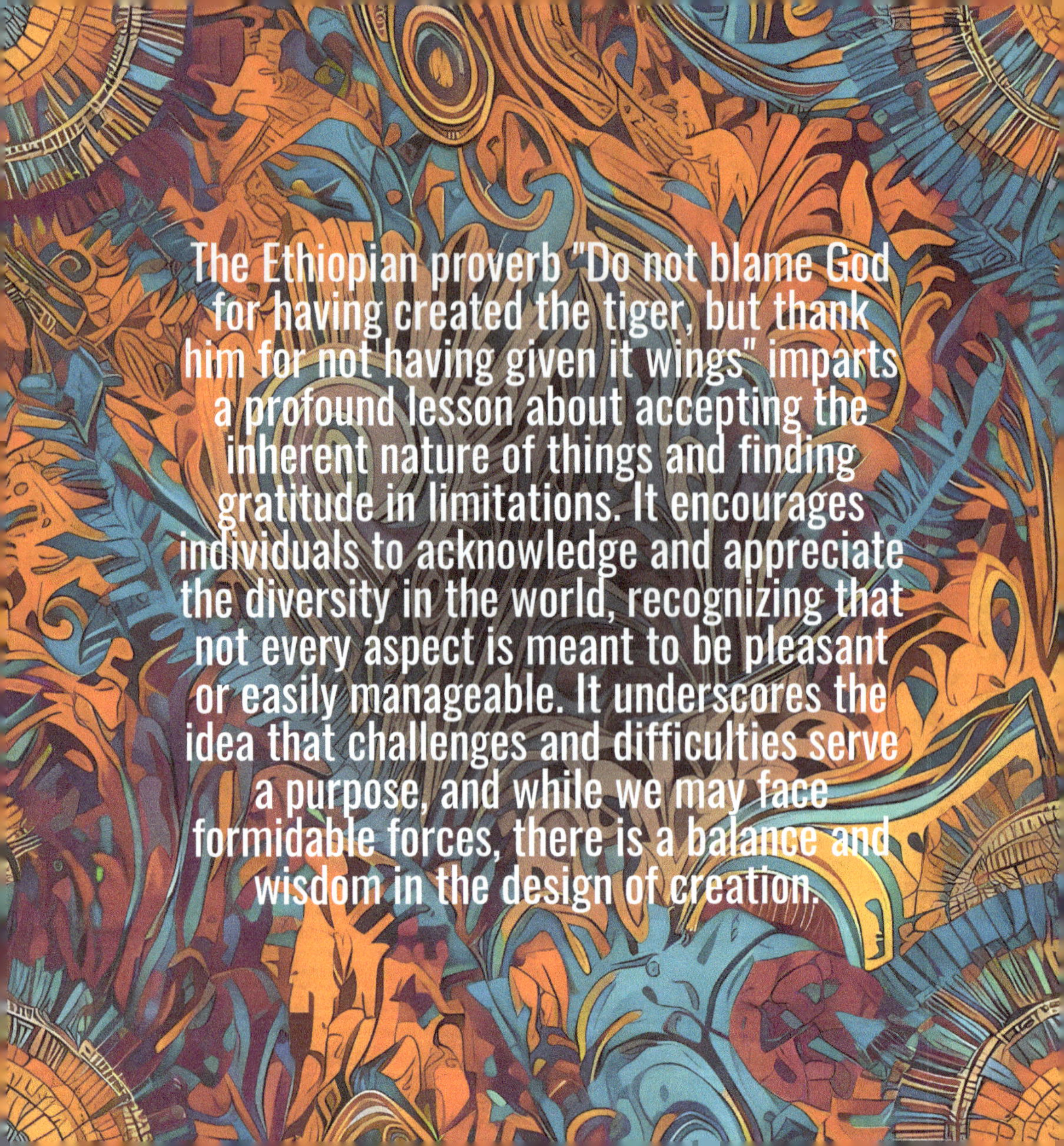

The Ethiopian proverb "Do not blame God for having created the tiger, but thank him for not having given it wings" imparts a profound lesson about accepting the inherent nature of things and finding gratitude in limitations. It encourages individuals to acknowledge and appreciate the diversity in the world, recognizing that not every aspect is meant to be pleasant or easily manageable. It underscores the idea that challenges and difficulties serve a purpose, and while we may face formidable forces, there is a balance and wisdom in the design of creation.

A MAN WHO USES
FORCE IS AFRAID OF
REASONING.
Kenya

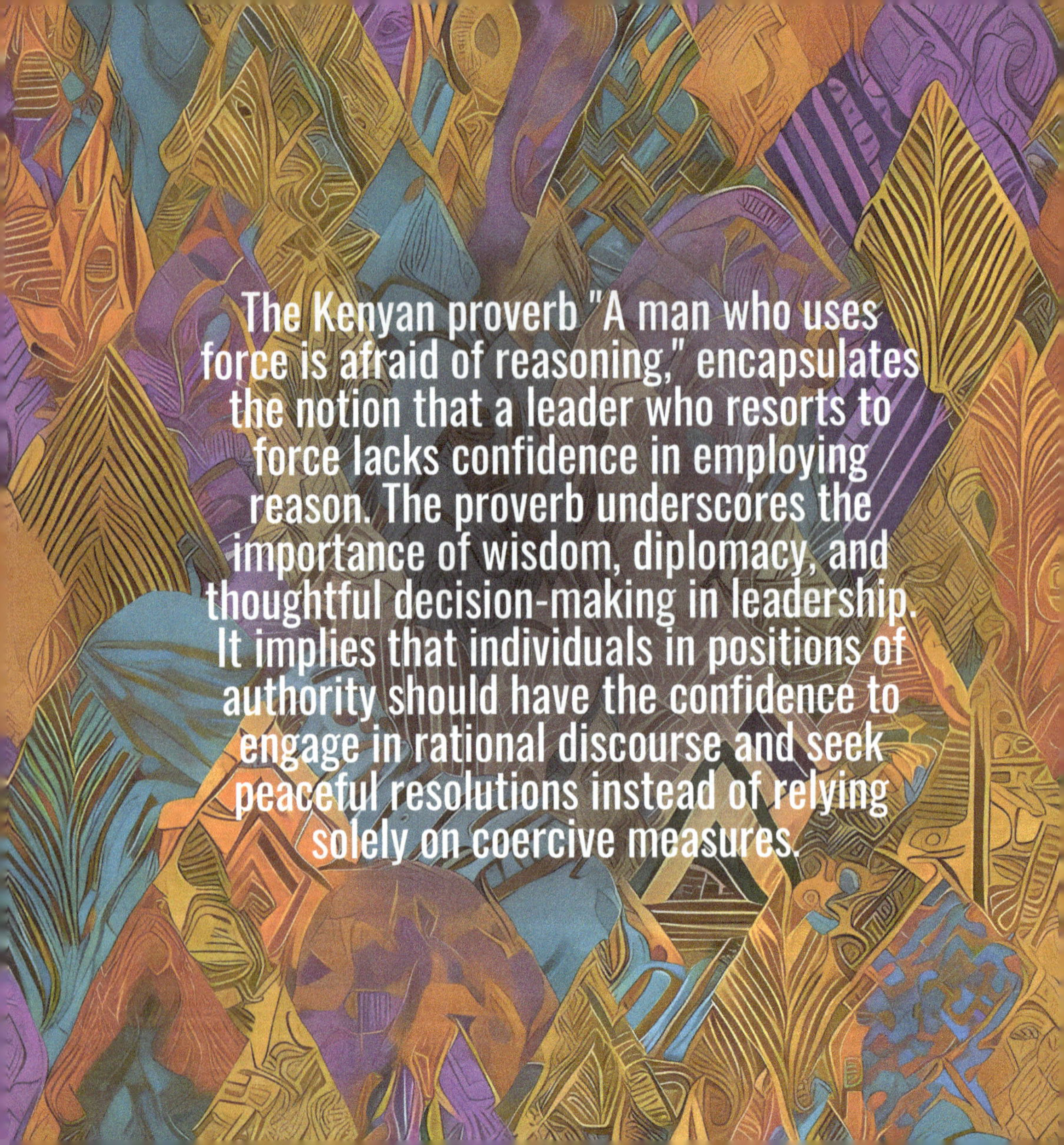

The Kenyan proverb "A man who uses force is afraid of reasoning," encapsulates the notion that a leader who resorts to force lacks confidence in employing reason. The proverb underscores the importance of wisdom, diplomacy, and thoughtful decision-making in leadership. It implies that individuals in positions of authority should have the confidence to engage in rational discourse and seek peaceful resolutions instead of relying solely on coercive measures.

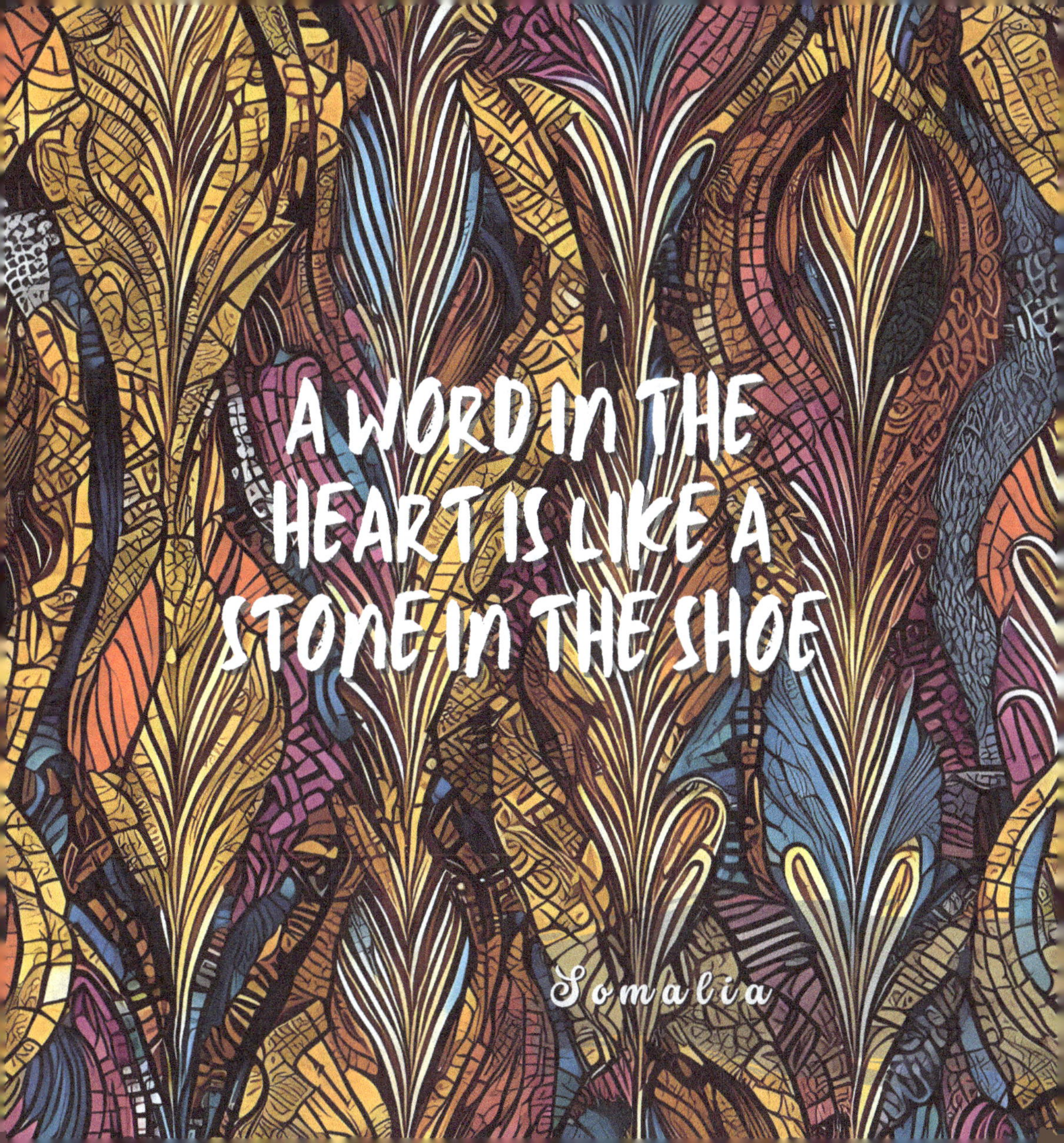
A WORD IN THE HEART IS LIKE A STONE IN THE SHOE
Somalia

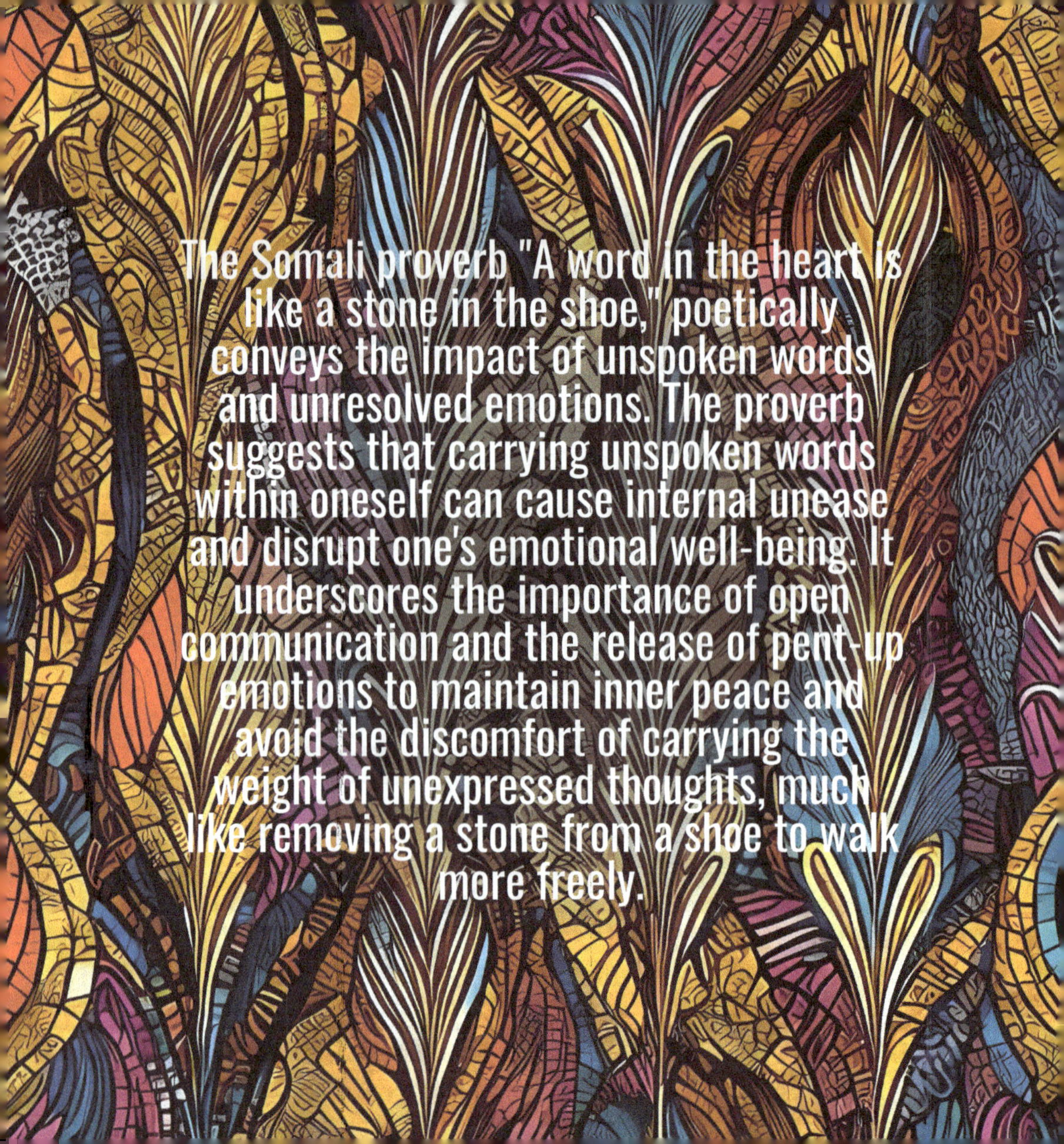

The Somali proverb "A word in the heart is like a stone in the shoe," poetically conveys the impact of unspoken words and unresolved emotions. The proverb suggests that carrying unspoken words within oneself can cause internal unease and disrupt one's emotional well-being. It underscores the importance of open communication and the release of pent-up emotions to maintain inner peace and avoid the discomfort of carrying the weight of unexpressed thoughts, much like removing a stone from a shoe to walk more freely.

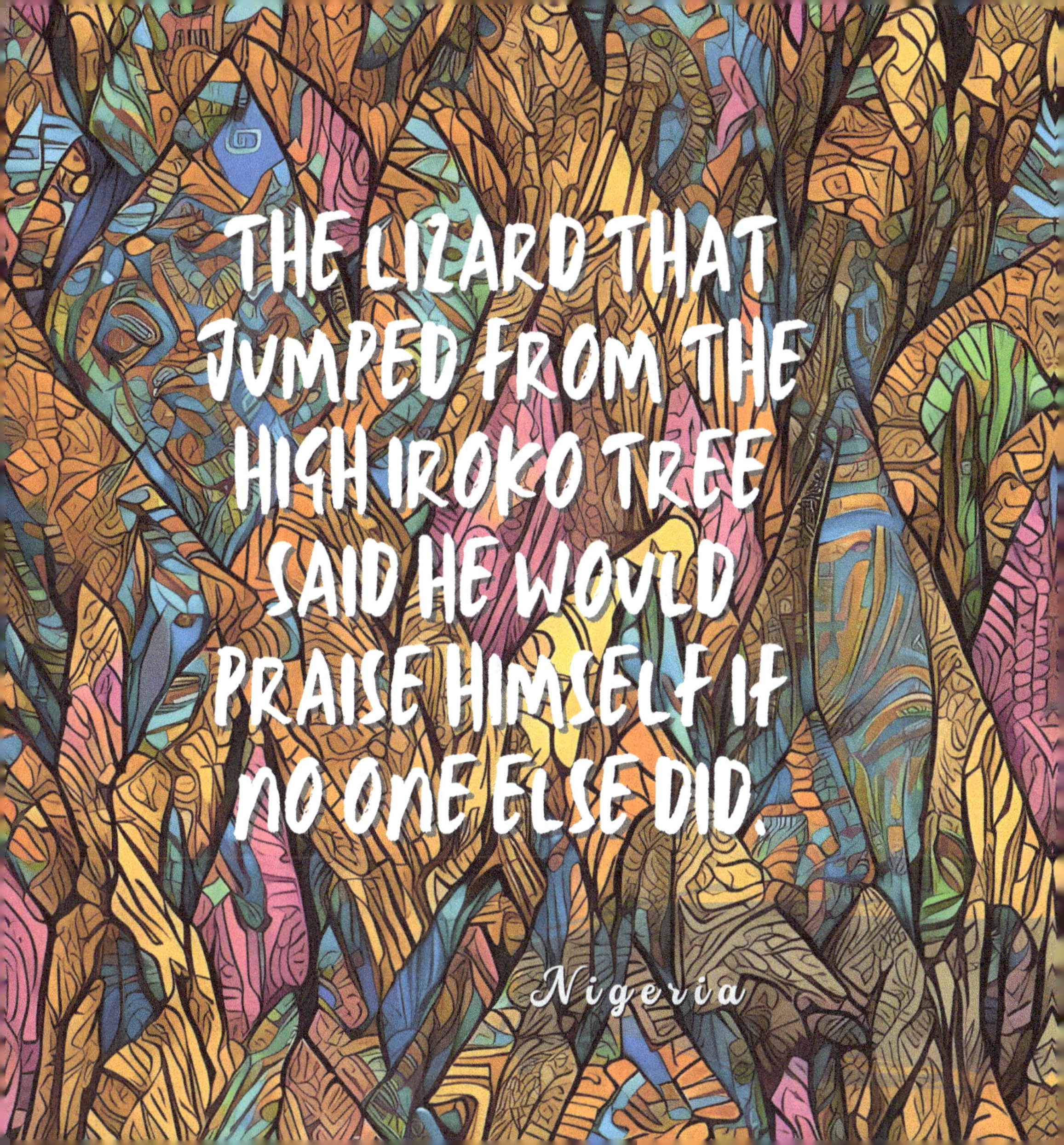
THE LIZARD THAT
JUMPED FROM THE
HIGH IROKO TREE
SAID HE WOULD
PRAISE HIMSELF IF
NO ONE ELSE DID.
Nigeria

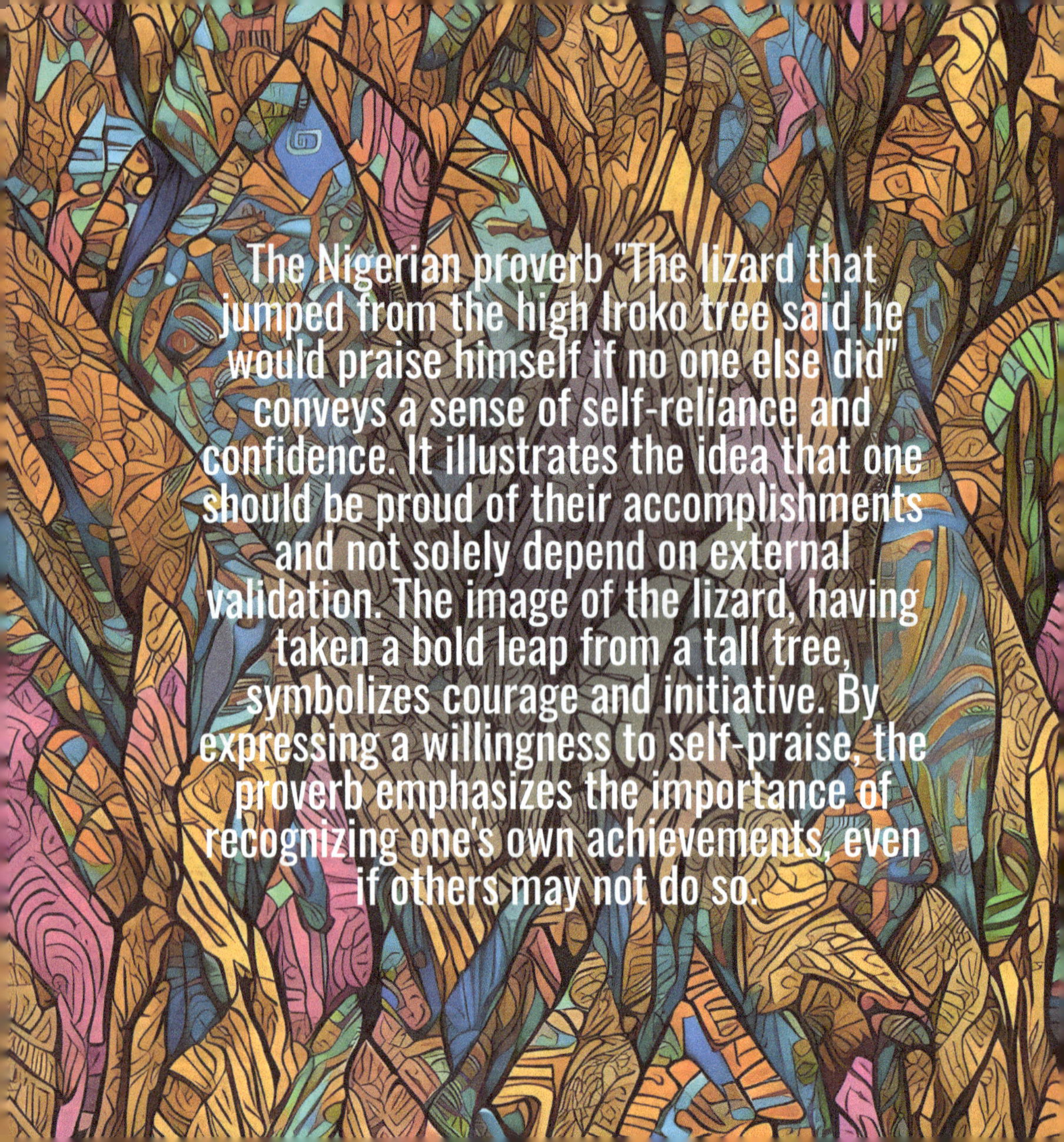
The Nigerian proverb "The lizard that jumped from the high Iroko tree said he would praise himself if no one else did" conveys a sense of self-reliance and confidence. It illustrates the idea that one should be proud of their accomplishments and not solely depend on external validation. The image of the lizard, having taken a bold leap from a tall tree, symbolizes courage and initiative. By expressing a willingness to self-praise, the proverb emphasizes the importance of recognizing one's own achievements, even if others may not do so.

HE WHO IS DAZZLED
BY THE SUN DOES
NOT SEE THE
STARS.
Arabia

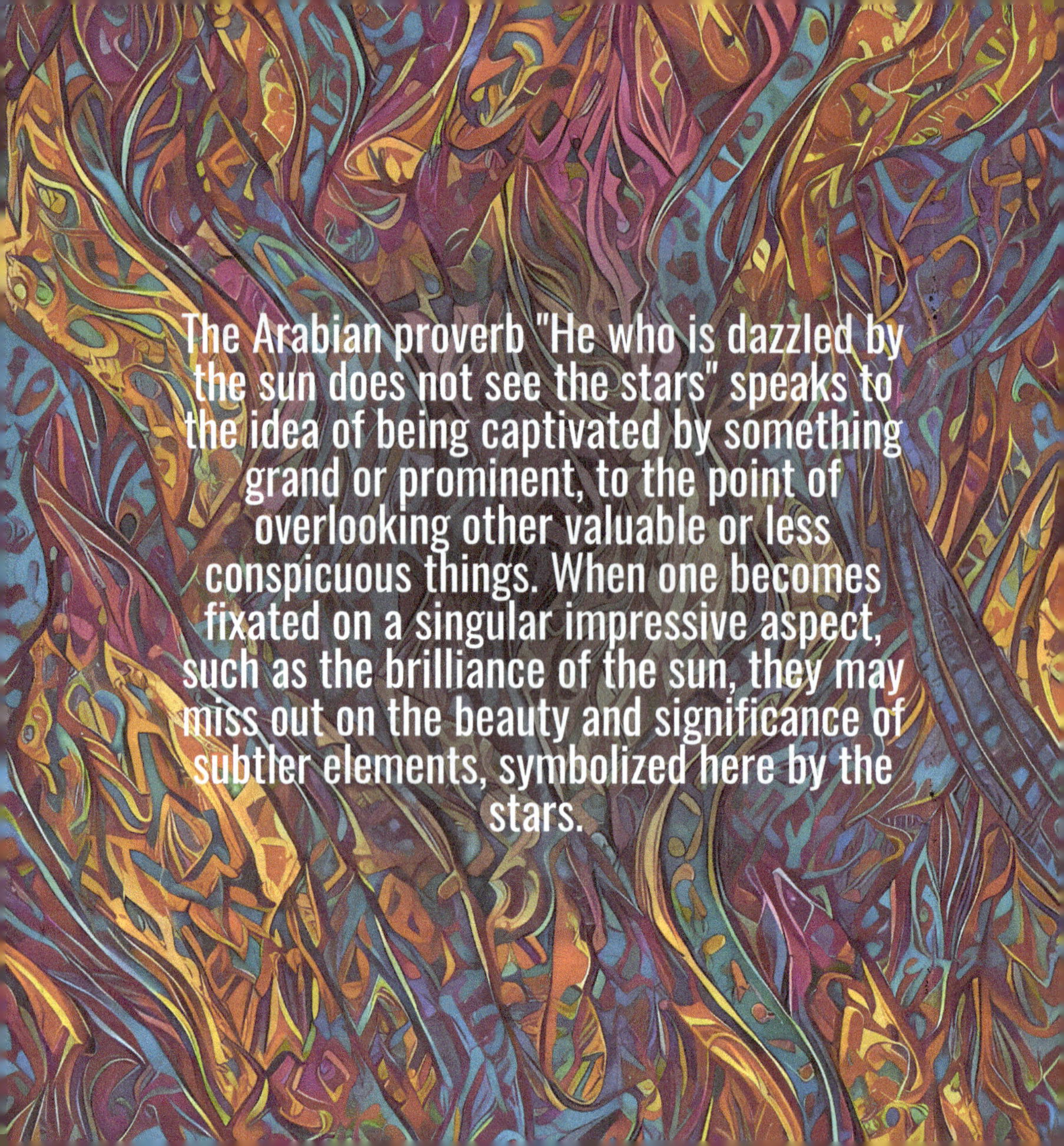

The Arabian proverb "He who is dazzled by the sun does not see the stars" speaks to the idea of being captivated by something grand or prominent, to the point of overlooking other valuable or less conspicuous things. When one becomes fixated on a singular impressive aspect, such as the brilliance of the sun, they may miss out on the beauty and significance of subtler elements, symbolized here by the stars.

STILL WATERS RUN
DEEP.
Urdu

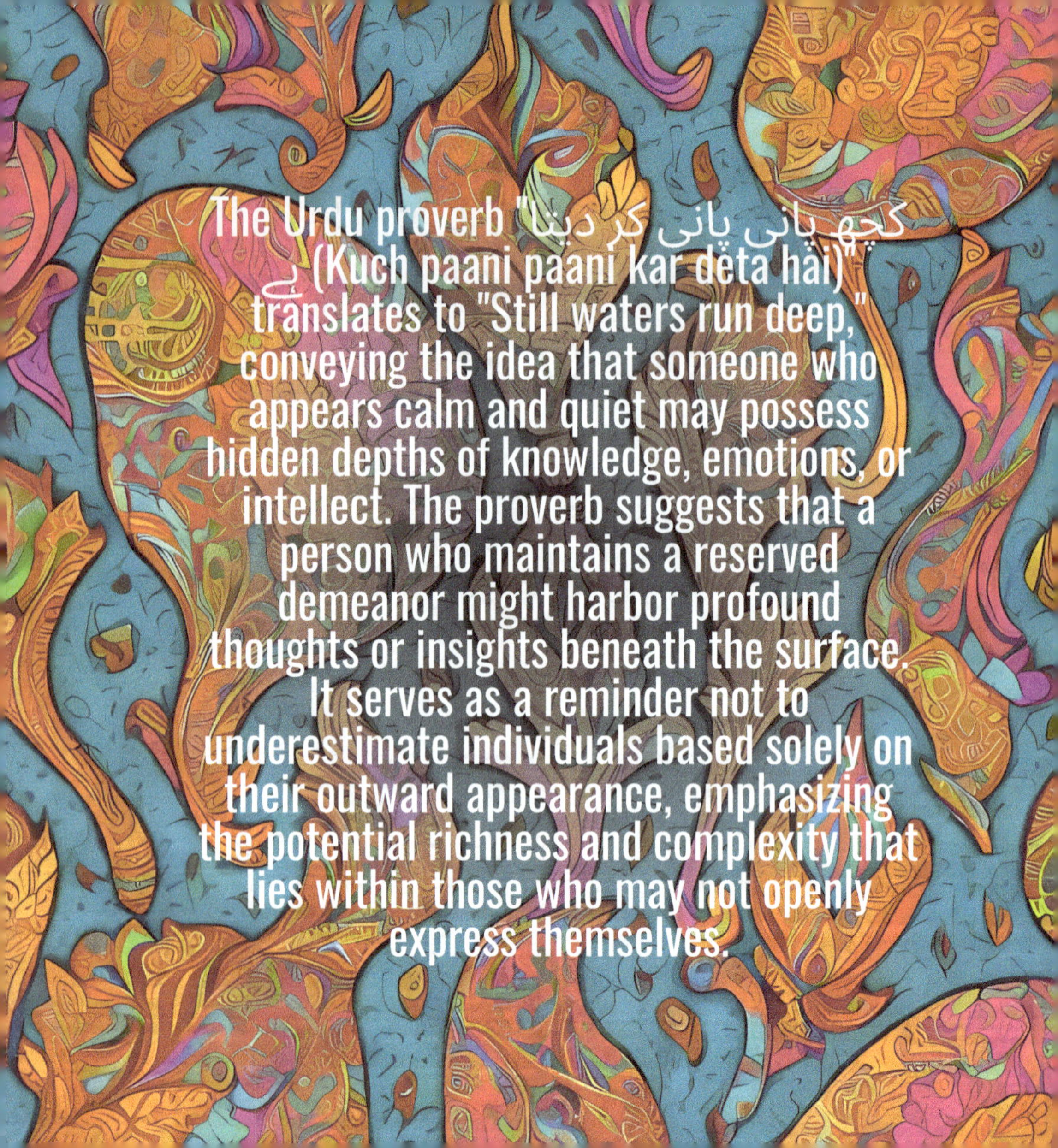
The Urdu proverb "کچھ پانی پانی کر دیتا ہے (Kuch paani paani kar dëta häi)" translates to "Still waters run deep," conveying the idea that someone who appears calm and quiet may possess hidden depths of knowledge, emotions, or intellect. The proverb suggests that a person who maintains a reserved demeanor might harbor profound thoughts or insights beneath the surface. It serves as a reminder not to underestimate individuals based solely on their outward appearance, emphasizing the potential richness and complexity that lies within those who may not openly express themselves.

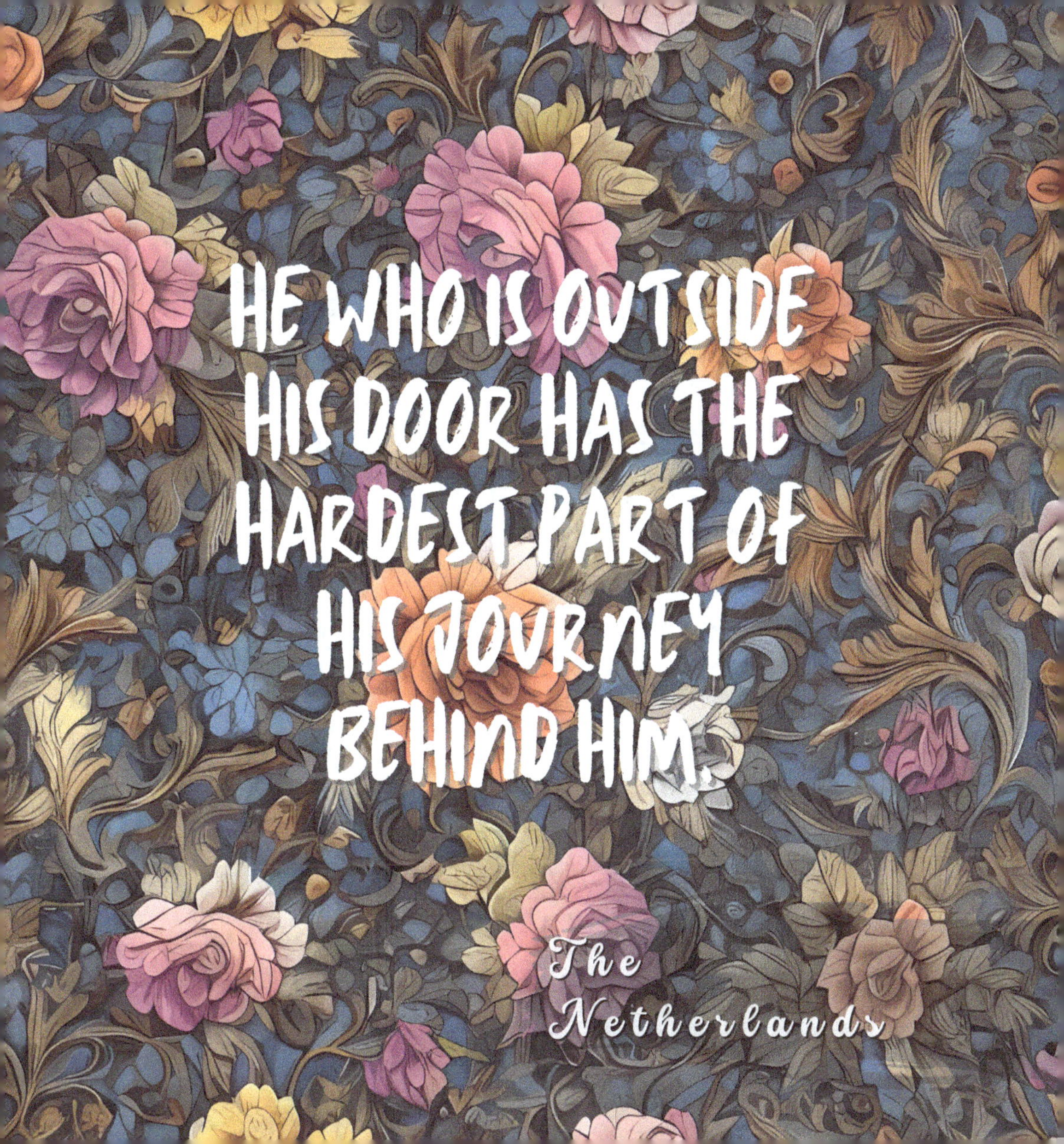
HE WHO IS OUTSIDE
HIS DOOR HAS THE
HARDEST PART OF
HIS JOURNEY
BEHIND HIM.
The
Netherlands

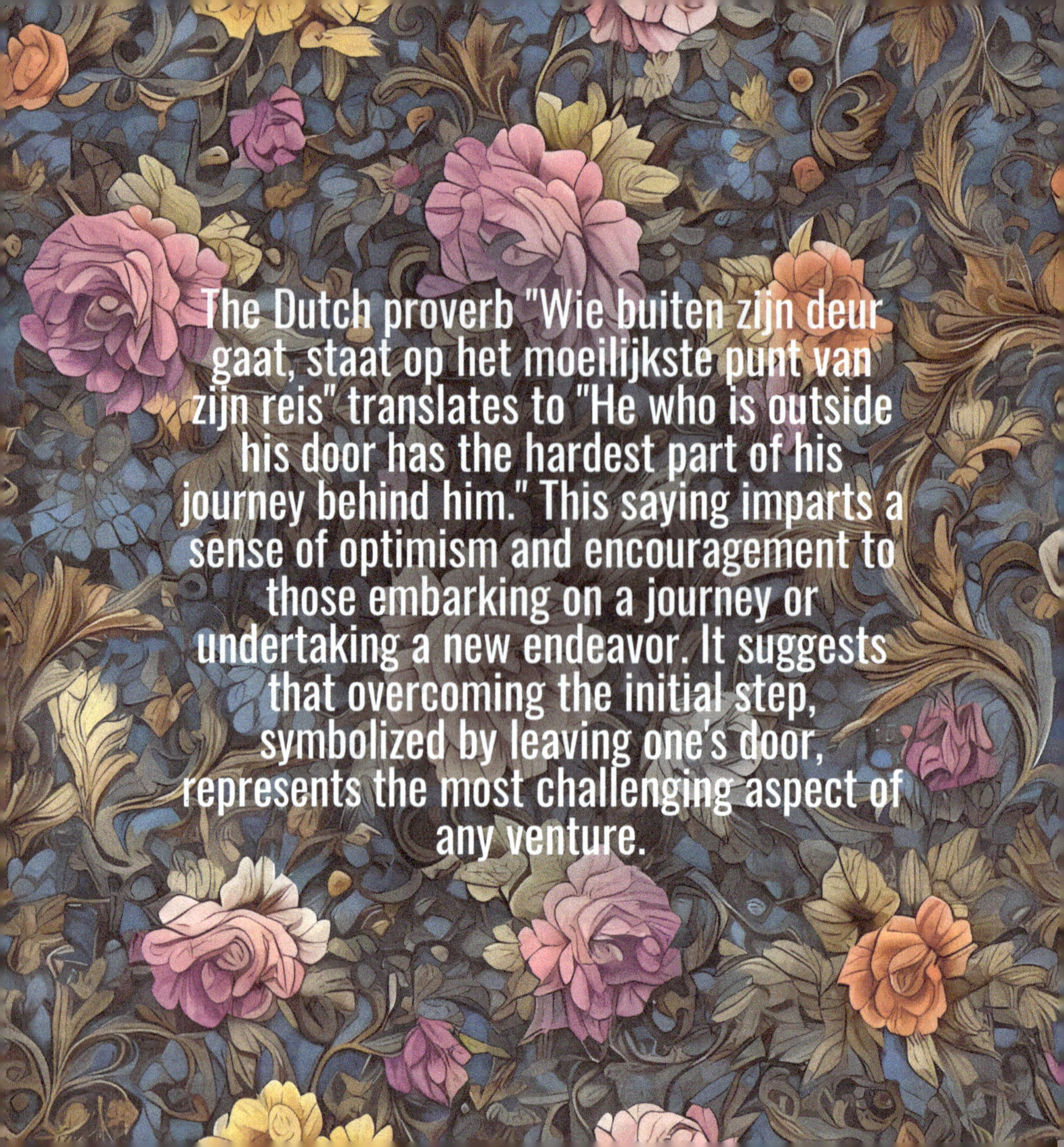

The Dutch proverb "Wie buiten zijn deur gaat, staat op het moeilijkste punt van zijn reis" translates to "He who is outside his door has the hardest part of his journey behind him." This saying imparts a sense of optimism and encouragement to those embarking on a journey or undertaking a new endeavor. It suggests that overcoming the initial step, symbolized by leaving one's door, represents the most challenging aspect of any venture.

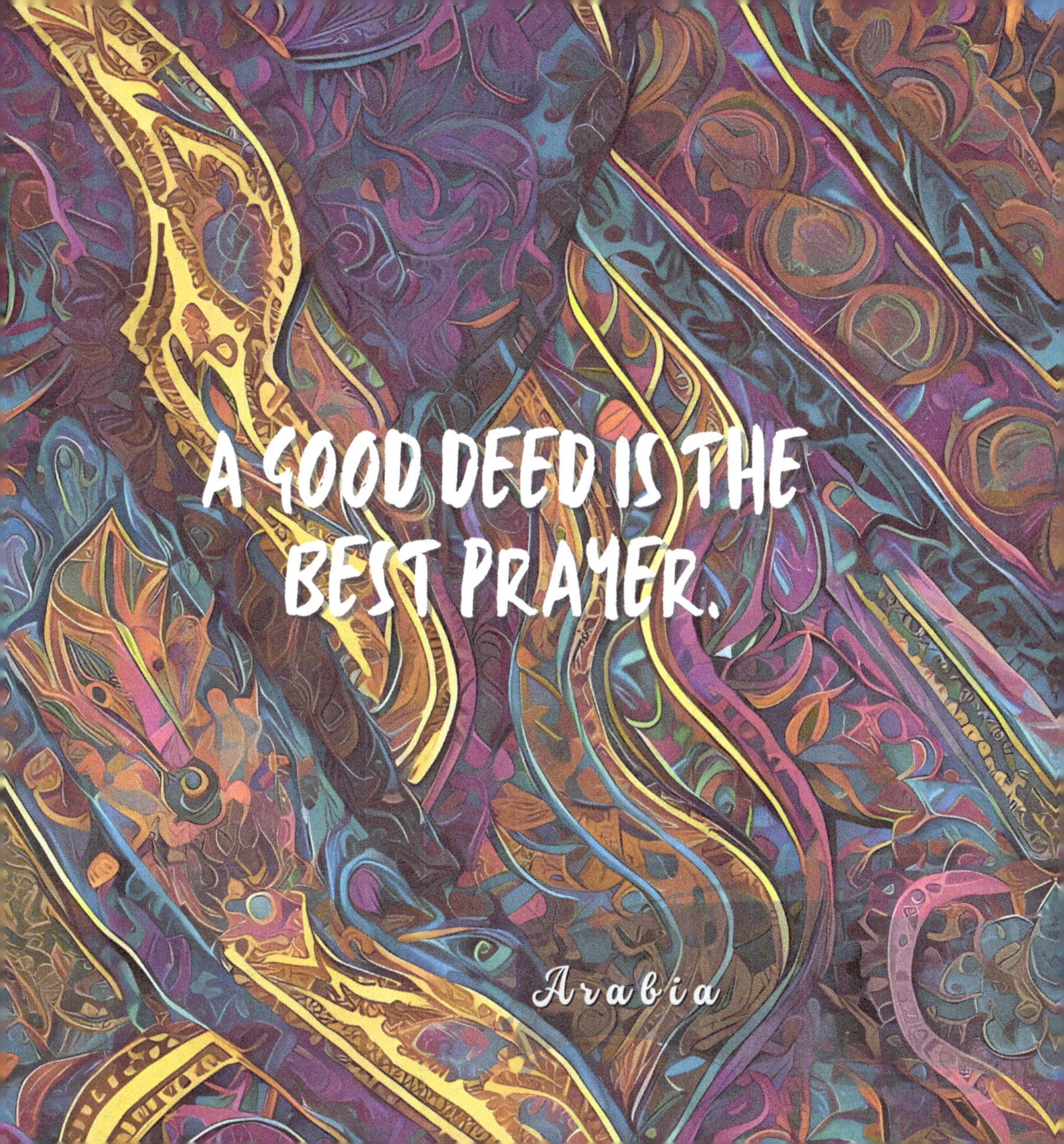
A GOOD DEED IS THE BEST PRAYER.
Arabia

The Arabian proverb "A good deed is the best prayer" highlights the significance of actions that benefit others as a form of spiritual devotion. It emphasizes the notion that performing acts of kindness, compassion, and selflessness can be more impactful and meaningful than words alone. This proverb suggests that our actions speak louder than our words and that genuine deeds of goodness and generosity are a powerful expression of our faith and spirituality. It encourages individuals to prioritize noble actions that positively impact others, recognizing that such deeds hold great value and are a profound way to connect with the divine.

EVEN A CLOCK
THAT DOES NOT
WORK IS RIGHT
TWICE A DAY.
Poland

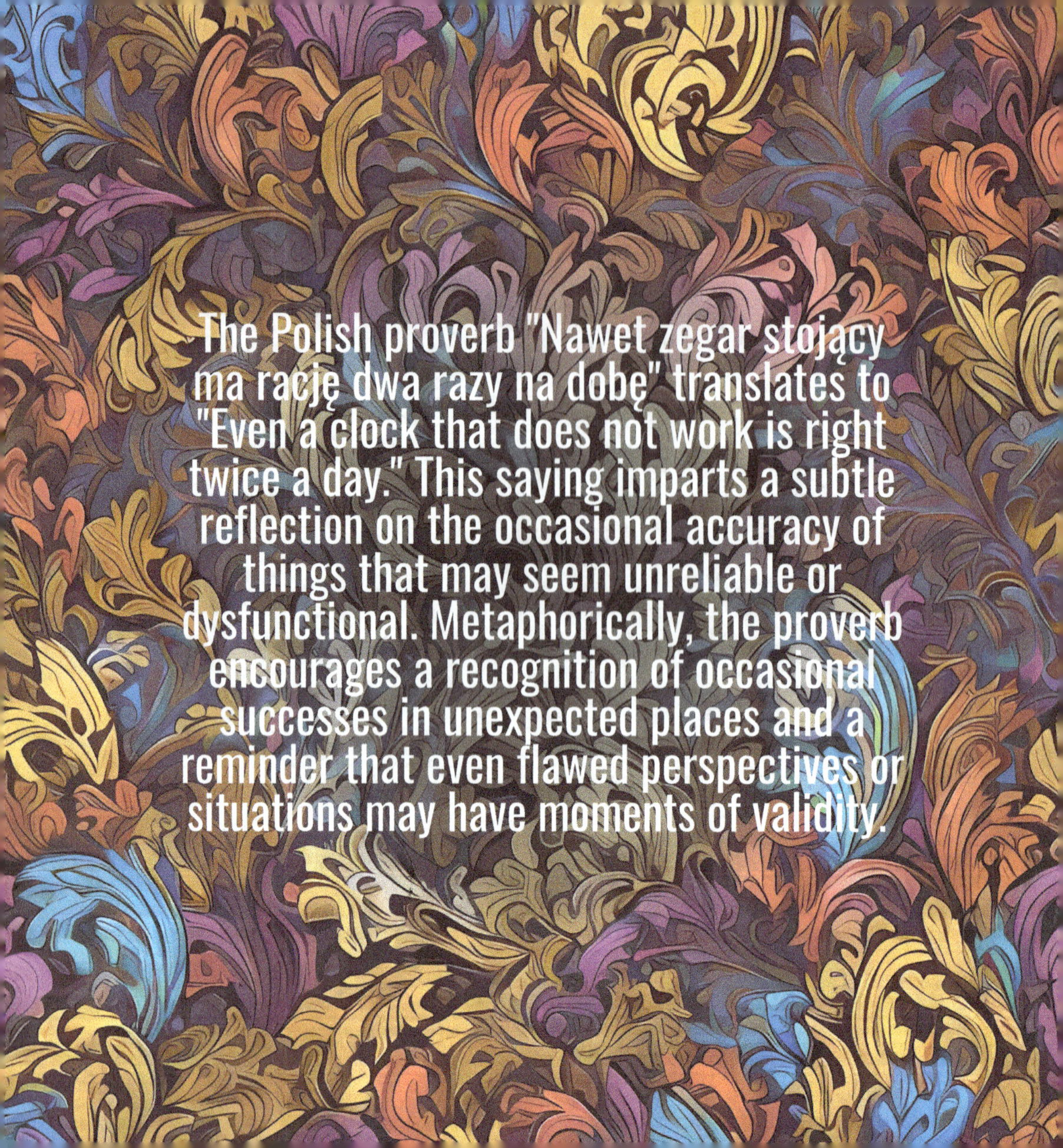

The Polish proverb "Nawet zegar stojący ma rację dwa razy na dobę" translates to "Even a clock that does not work is right twice a day." This saying imparts a subtle reflection on the occasional accuracy of things that may seem unreliable or dysfunctional. Metaphorically, the proverb encourages a recognition of occasional successes in unexpected places and a reminder that even flawed perspectives or situations may have moments of validity.

A MULE CARRIES CORN, BUT HE DOESN'T EVER EAT IT.
St. Kitts & Nevis

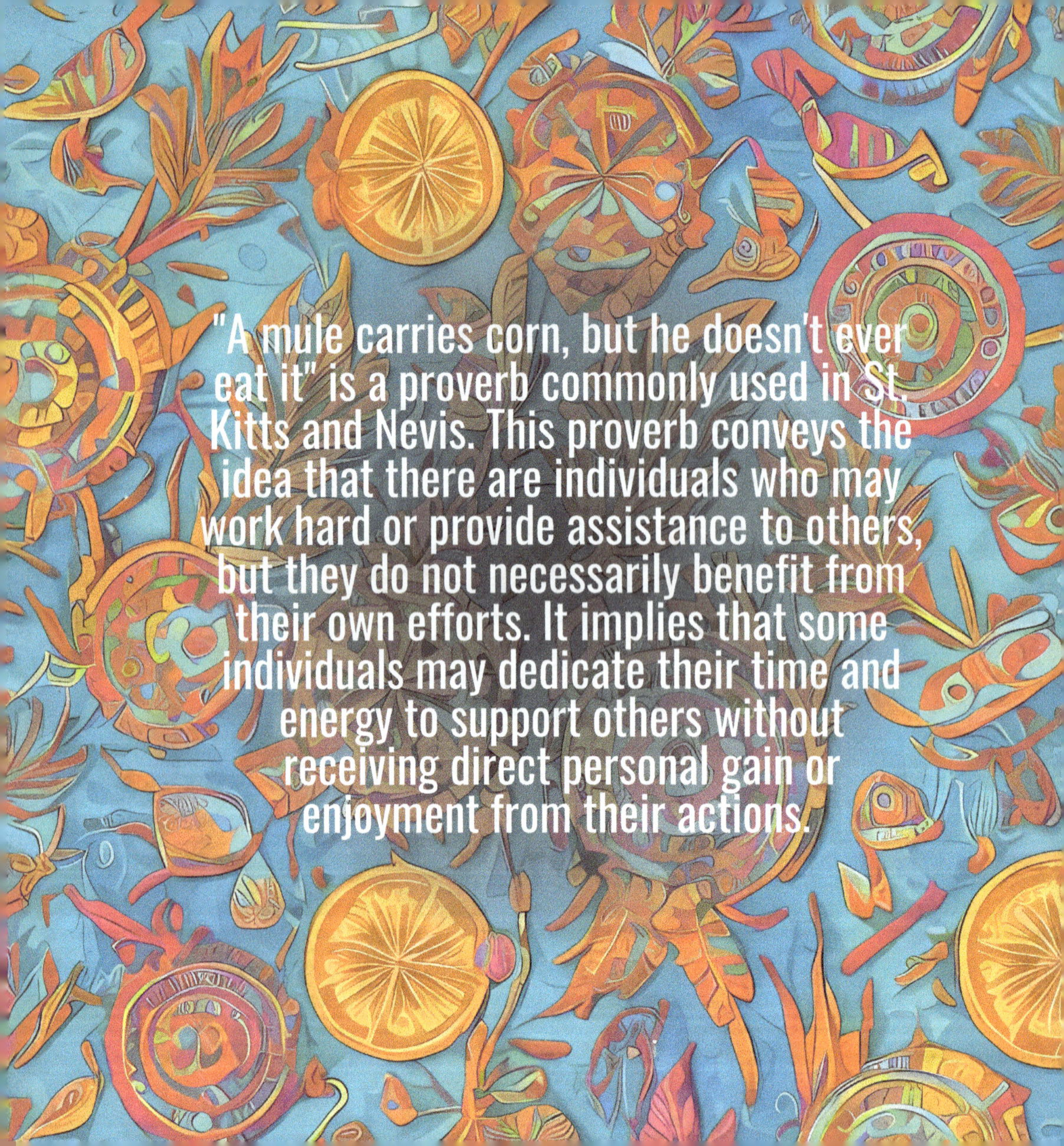
"A mule carries corn, but he doesn't ever eat it" is a proverb commonly used in St. Kitts and Nevis. This proverb conveys the idea that there are individuals who may work hard or provide assistance to others, but they do not necessarily benefit from their own efforts. It implies that some individuals may dedicate their time and energy to support others without receiving direct personal gain or enjoyment from their actions.

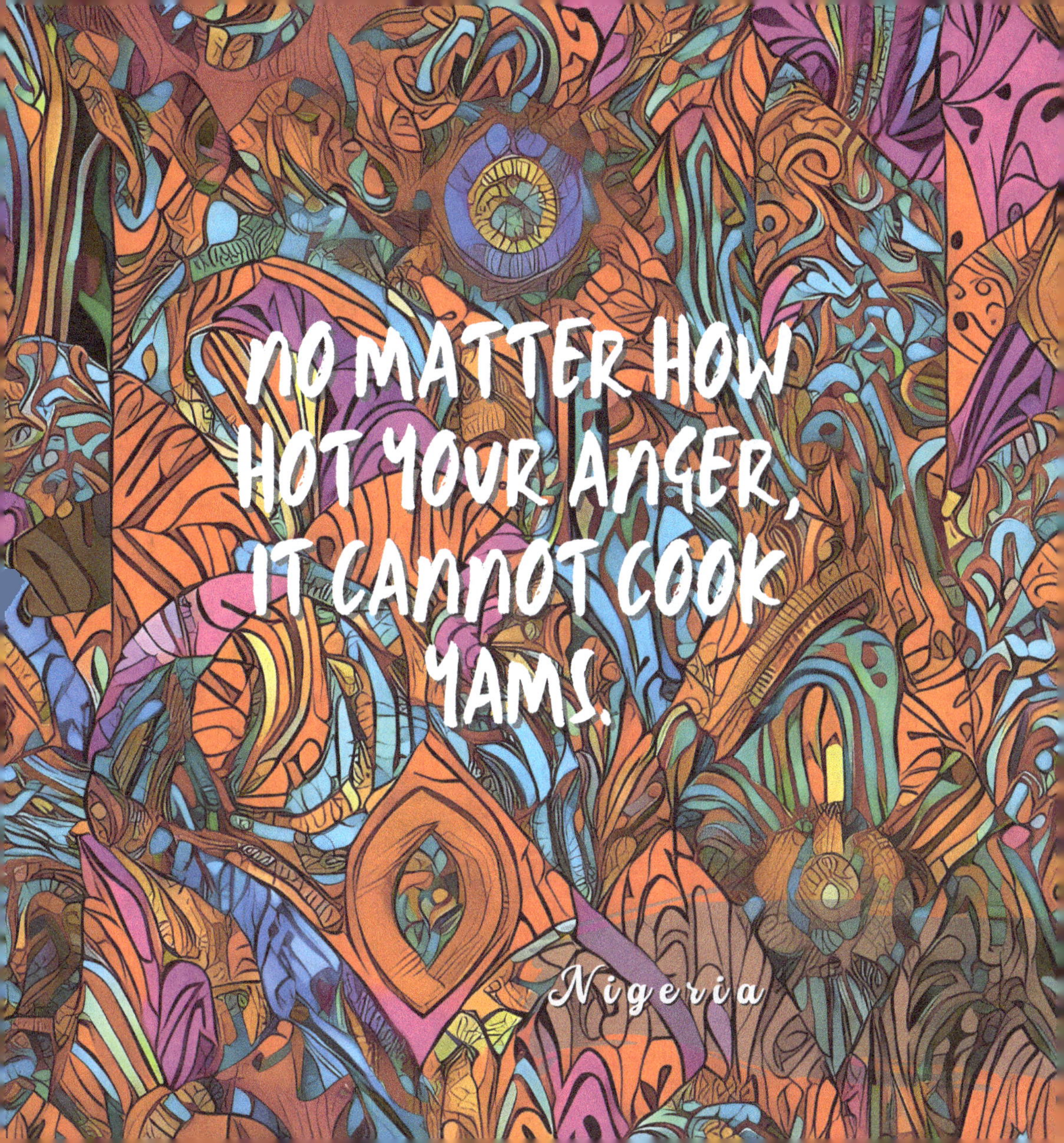
NO MATTER HOW
HOT YOUR ANGER,
IT CANNOT COOK
YAMS.
Nigeria

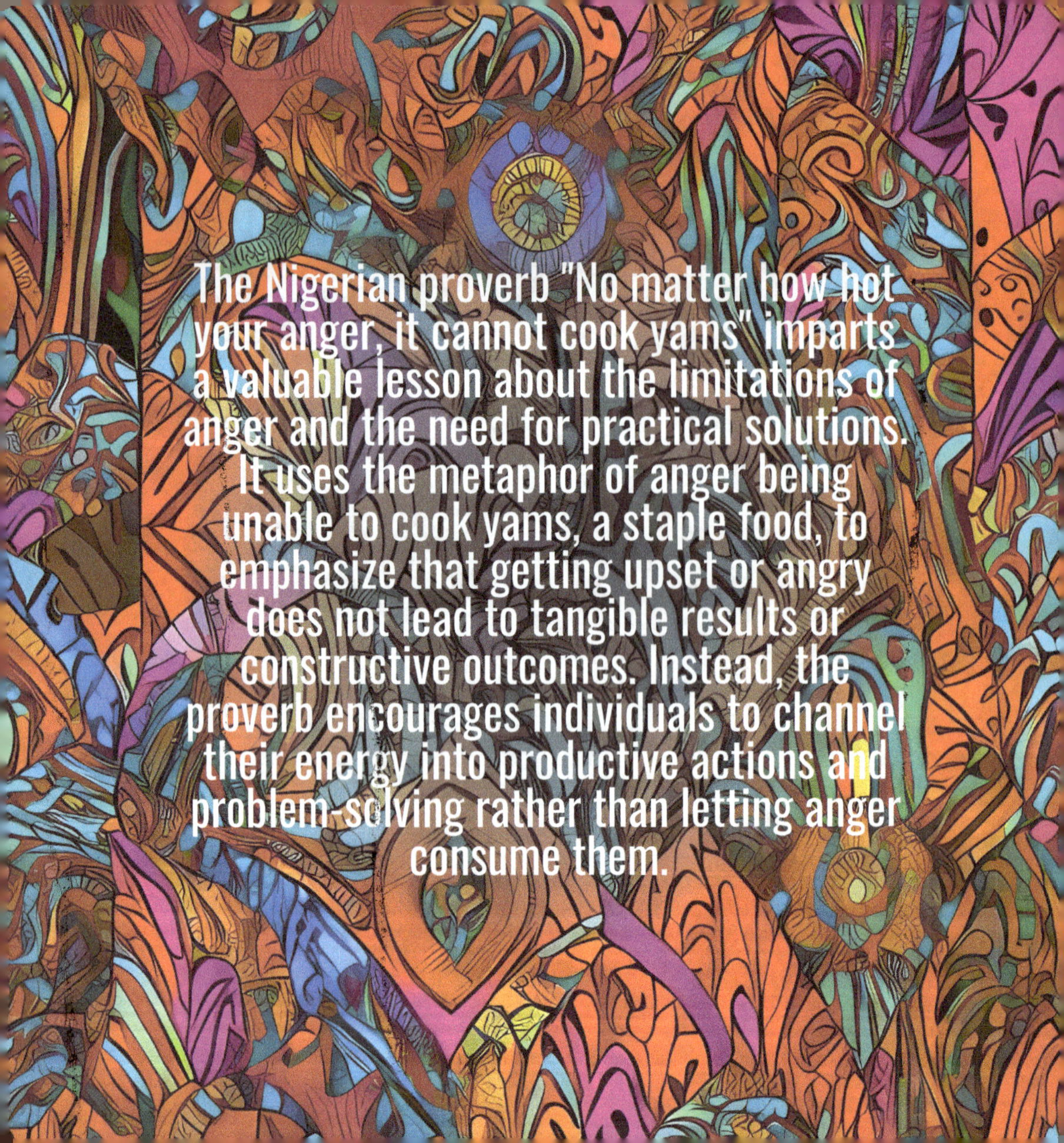

The Nigerian proverb "No matter how hot your anger, it cannot cook yams" imparts a valuable lesson about the limitations of anger and the need for practical solutions. It uses the metaphor of anger being unable to cook yams, a staple food, to emphasize that getting upset or angry does not lead to tangible results or constructive outcomes. Instead, the proverb encourages individuals to channel their energy into productive actions and problem-solving rather than letting anger consume them.

HUNGER IS THE
BEST SAUCE IN THE
WORLD.
Latin American

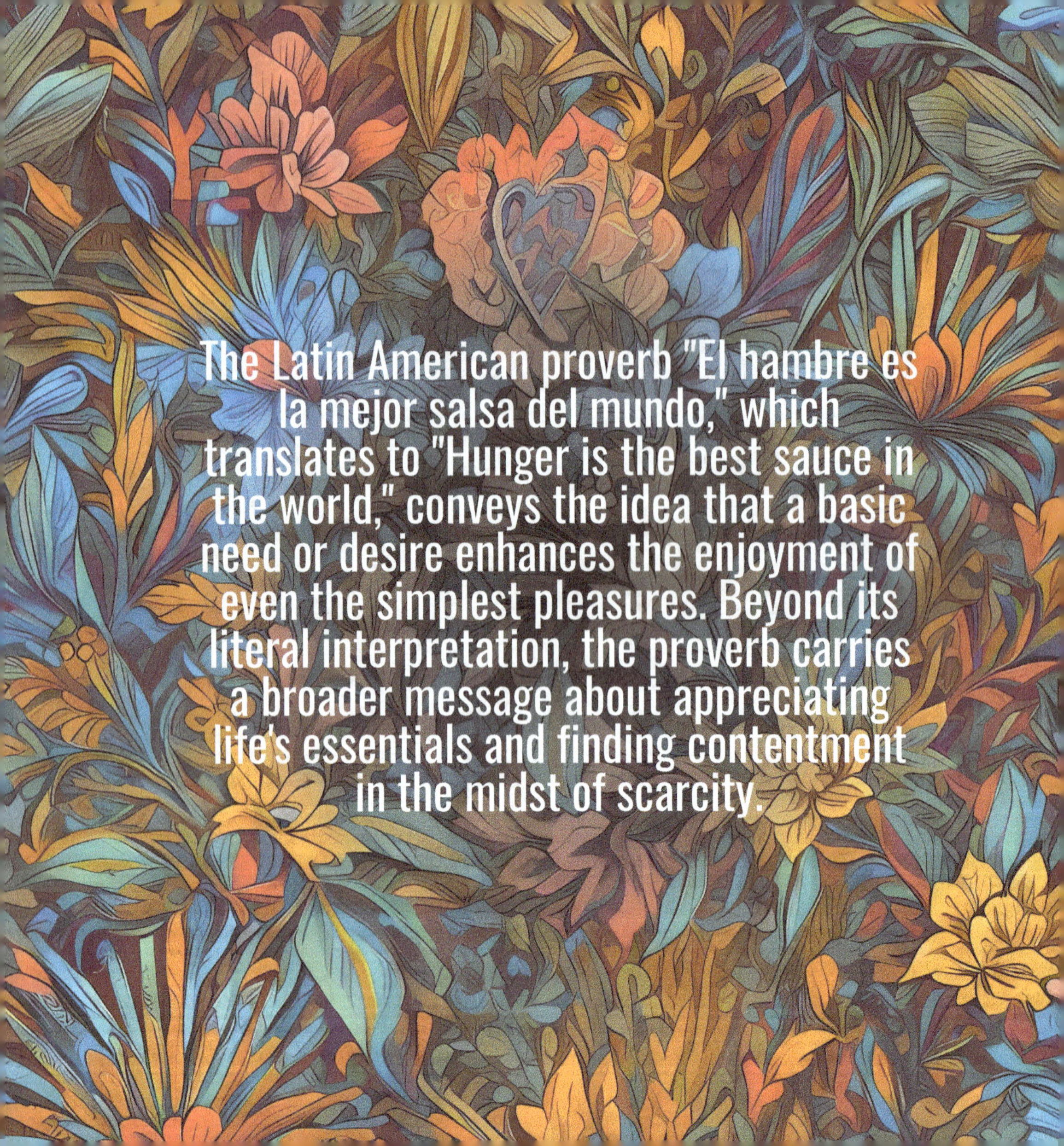
The Latin American proverb "El hambre es la mejor salsa del mundo," which translates to "Hunger is the best sauce in the world," conveys the idea that a basic need or desire enhances the enjoyment of even the simplest pleasures. Beyond its literal interpretation, the proverb carries a broader message about appreciating life's essentials and finding contentment in the midst of scarcity.

PATIENCE IS THE KEY TO PARADISE.
Arabia

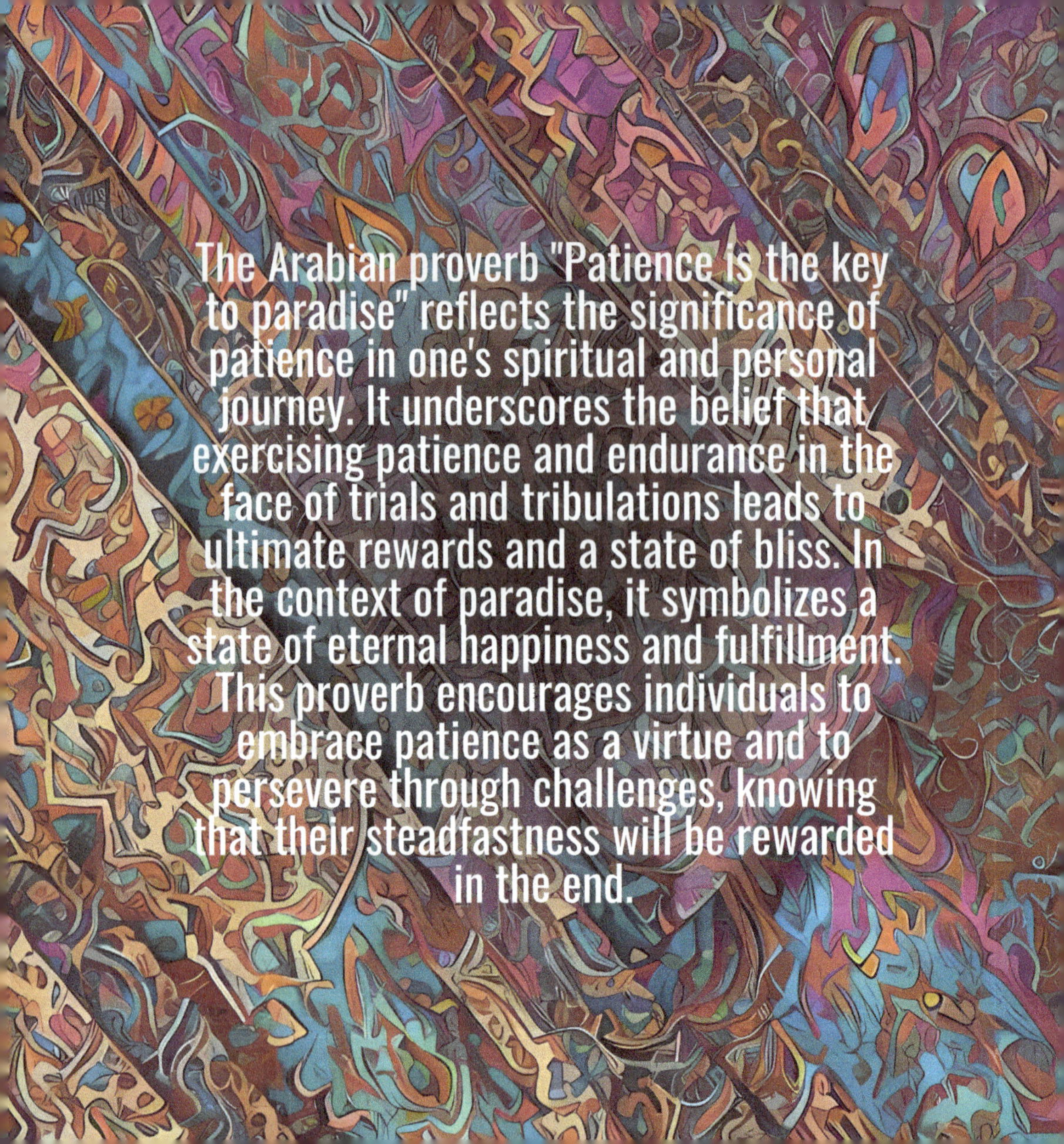
The Arabian proverb "Patience is the key to paradise" reflects the significance of patience in one's spiritual and personal journey. It underscores the belief that exercising patience and endurance in the face of trials and tribulations leads to ultimate rewards and a state of bliss. In the context of paradise, it symbolizes a state of eternal happiness and fulfillment. This proverb encourages individuals to embrace patience as a virtue and to persevere through challenges, knowing that their steadfastness will be rewarded in the end.

An inch of time is
an inch of gold,
but you can't buy
that inch of time
with an inch of
gold.
Taiwan

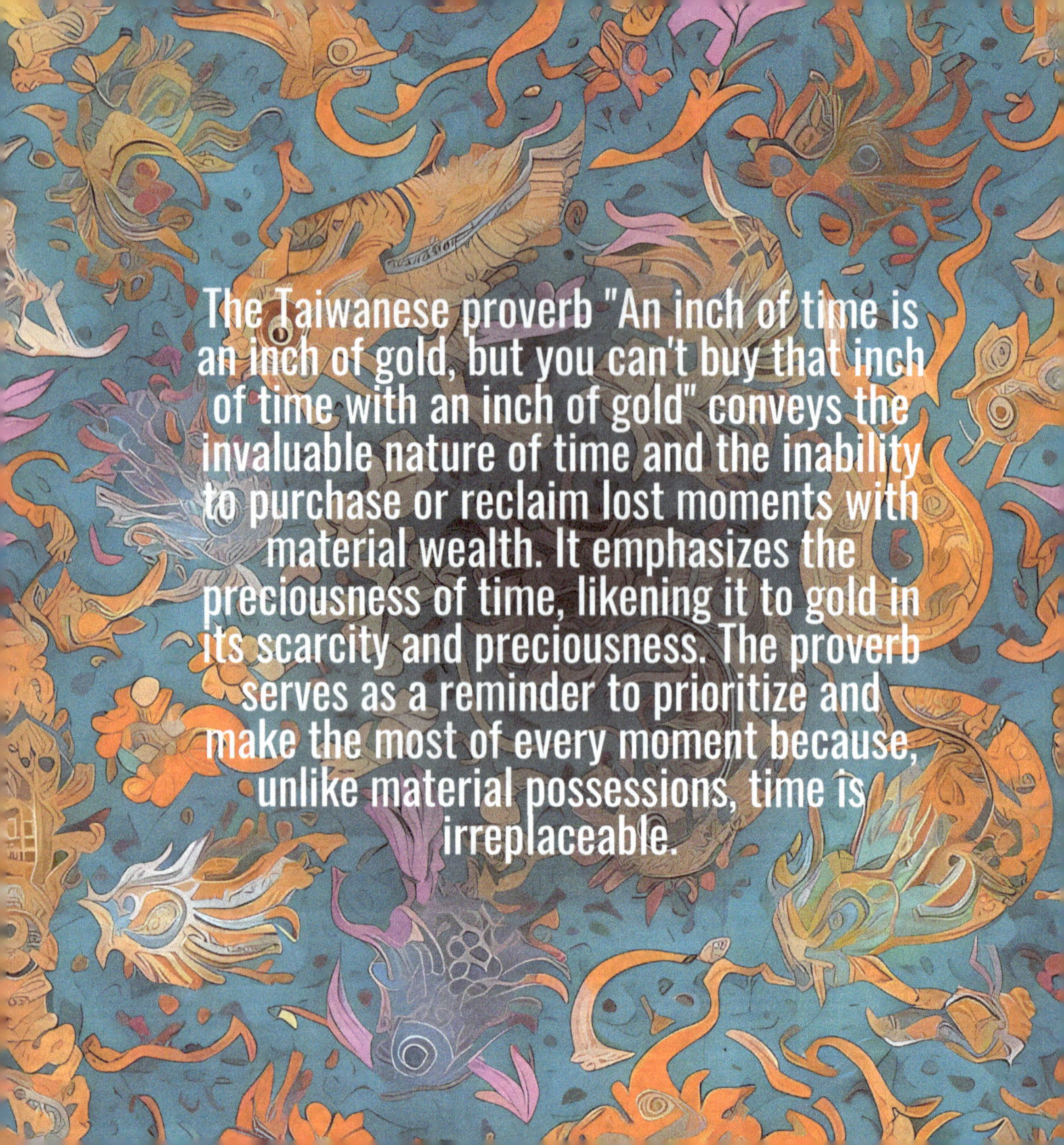

The Taiwanese proverb "An inch of time is an inch of gold, but you can't buy that inch of time with an inch of gold" conveys the invaluable nature of time and the inability to purchase or reclaim lost moments with material wealth. It emphasizes the preciousness of time, likening it to gold in its scarcity and preciousness. The proverb serves as a reminder to prioritize and make the most of every moment because, unlike material possessions, time is irreplaceable.

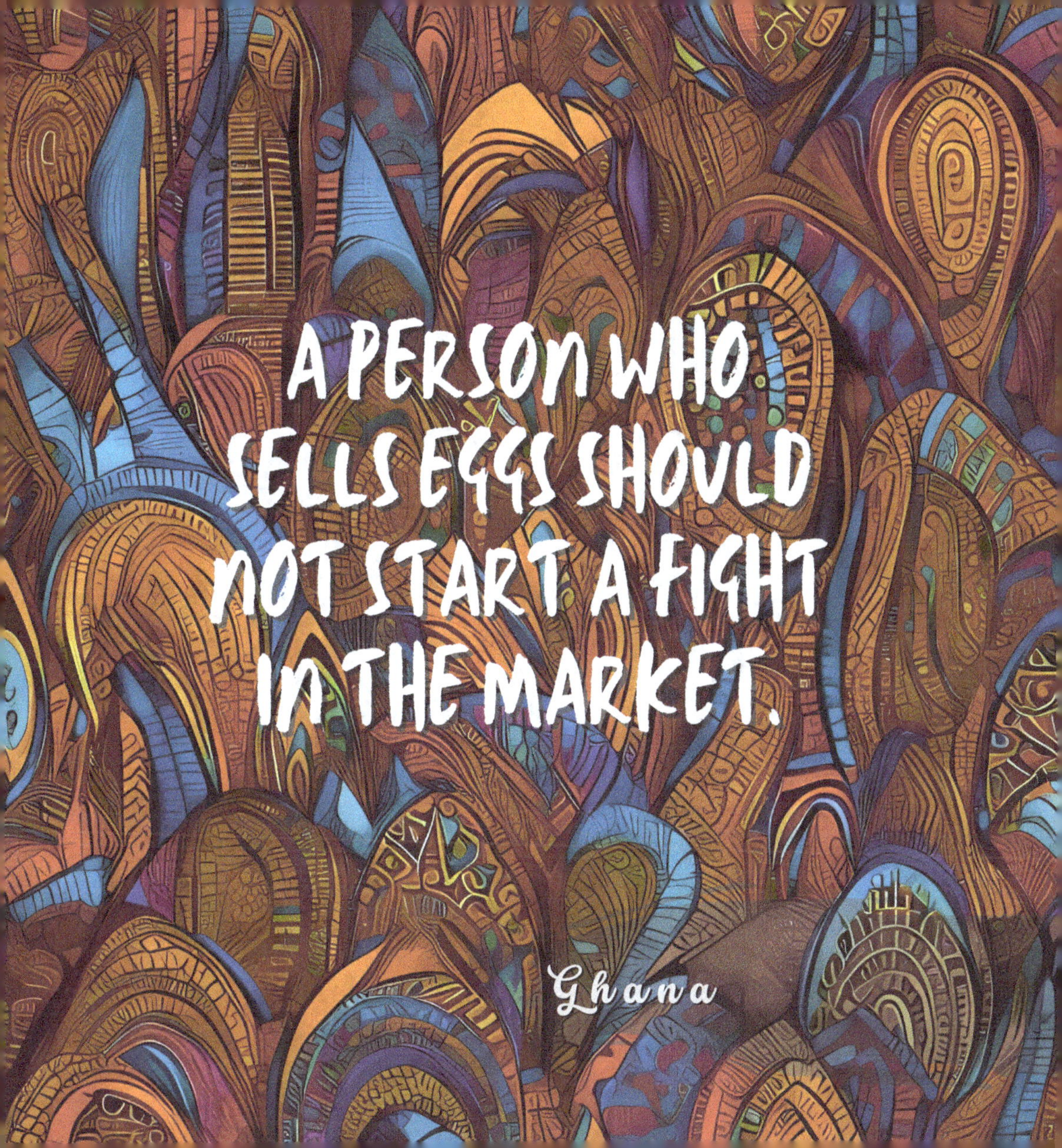
A PERSON WHO
SELLS EGGS SHOULD
NOT START A FIGHT
IN THE MARKET.
Ghana

This Ghanaian proverb suggests a practical piece of advice, emphasizing the importance of avoiding unnecessary conflicts, especially for someone engaged in a delicate or fragile occupation, such as selling eggs. Starting a fight in the market can lead to chaos and potential damage to one's own livelihood.

THE DOG BARKS,
BUT THE CARAVAN
MOVES ON.
Telugu

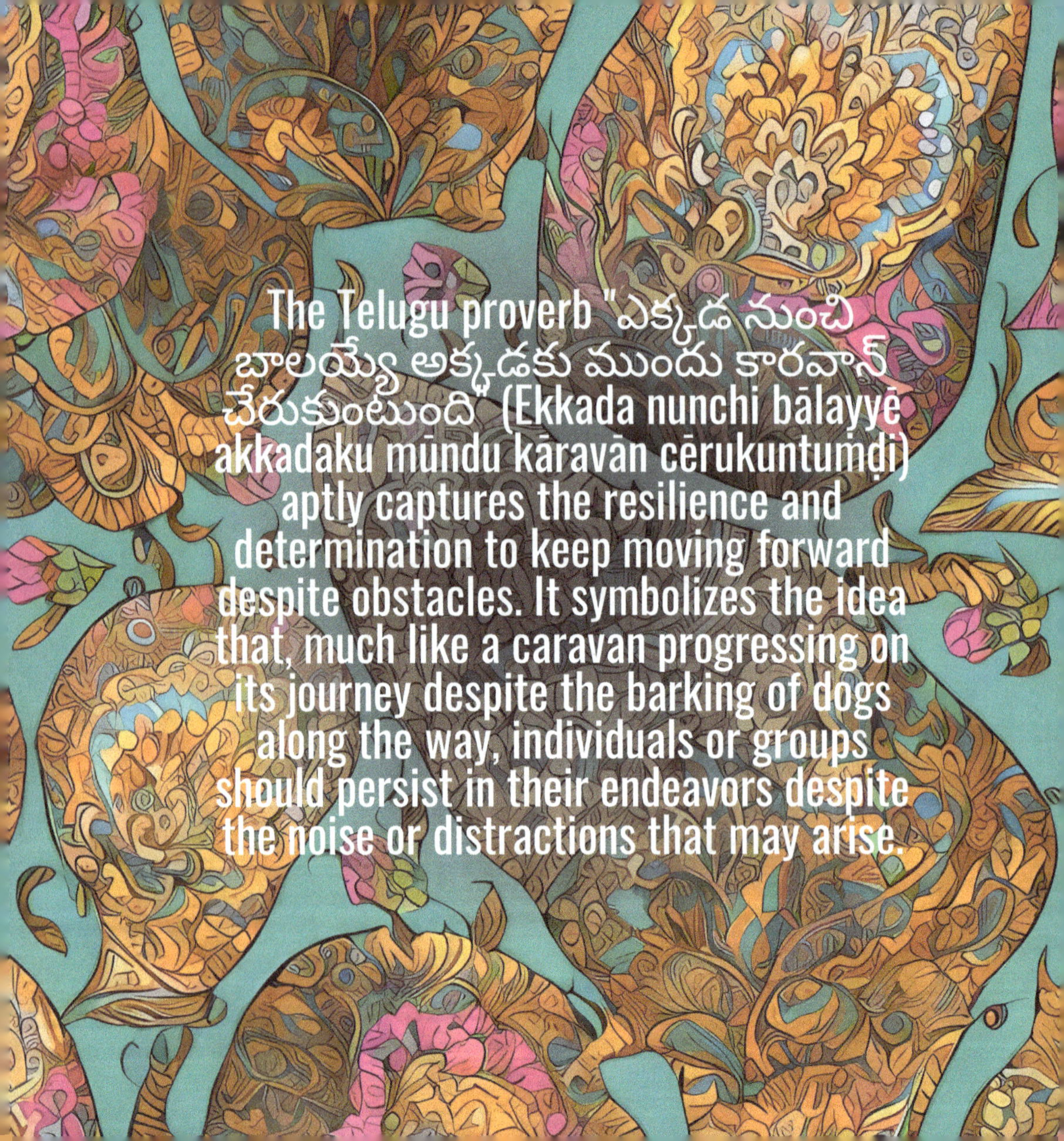

The Telugu proverb "ఎక్కడ నుంచి బాలయ్యే అక్కడకు ముందు కారవాన్ చేరుకుంటుంది" (Ekkada nunchi bālayyē akkadaku mūndu kāravān cērukuntuṁḍi) aptly captures the resilience and determination to keep moving forward despite obstacles. It symbolizes the idea that, much like a caravan progressing on its journey despite the barking of dogs along the way, individuals or groups should persist in their endeavors despite the noise or distractions that may arise.

PEOPLE LIVE IN EACH OTHER'S SHELTER.
Ireland

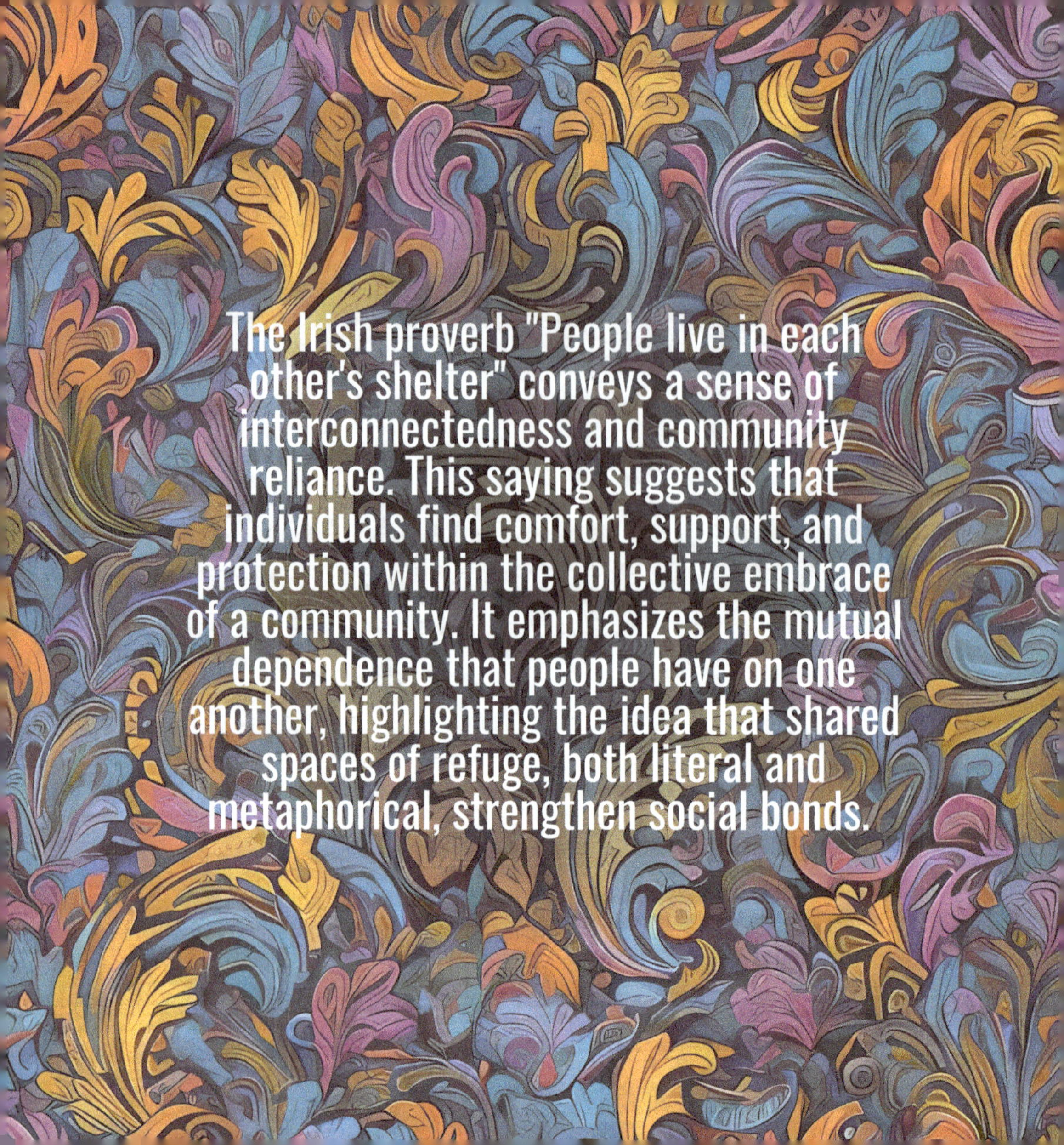
The Irish proverb "People live in each other's shelter" conveys a sense of interconnectedness and community reliance. This saying suggests that individuals find comfort, support, and protection within the collective embrace of a community. It emphasizes the mutual dependence that people have on one another, highlighting the idea that shared spaces of refuge, both literal and metaphorical, strengthen social bonds.

IT'S EASY TO FORGE
WHEN THE IRON IS
HOT.
Norway

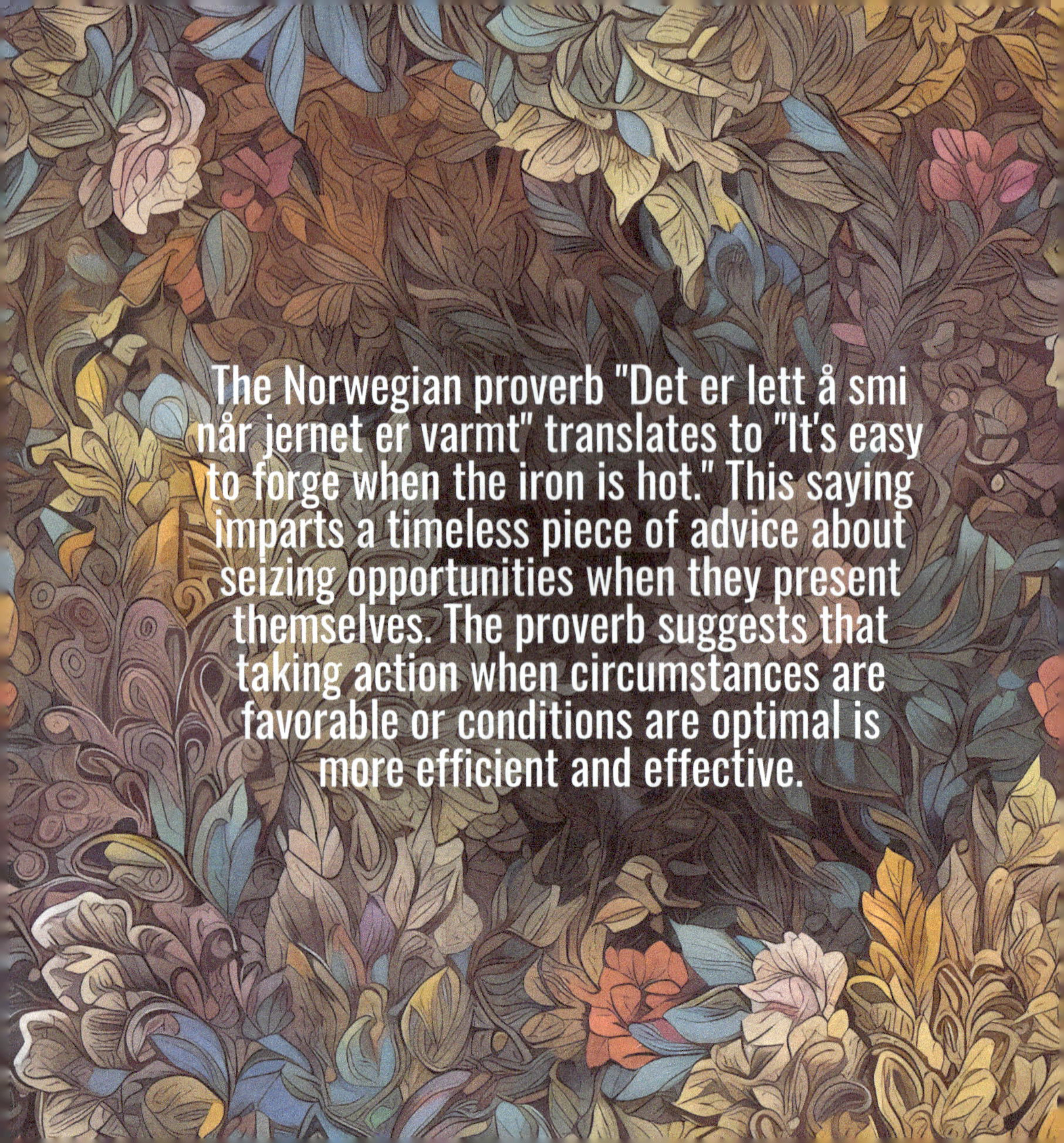
The Norwegian proverb "Det er lett å smi når jernet er varmt" translates to "It's easy to forge when the iron is hot." This saying imparts a timeless piece of advice about seizing opportunities when they present themselves. The proverb suggests that taking action when circumstances are favorable or conditions are optimal is more efficient and effective.

HOPE IS THE LAST THING TO BE LOST.
Latin American

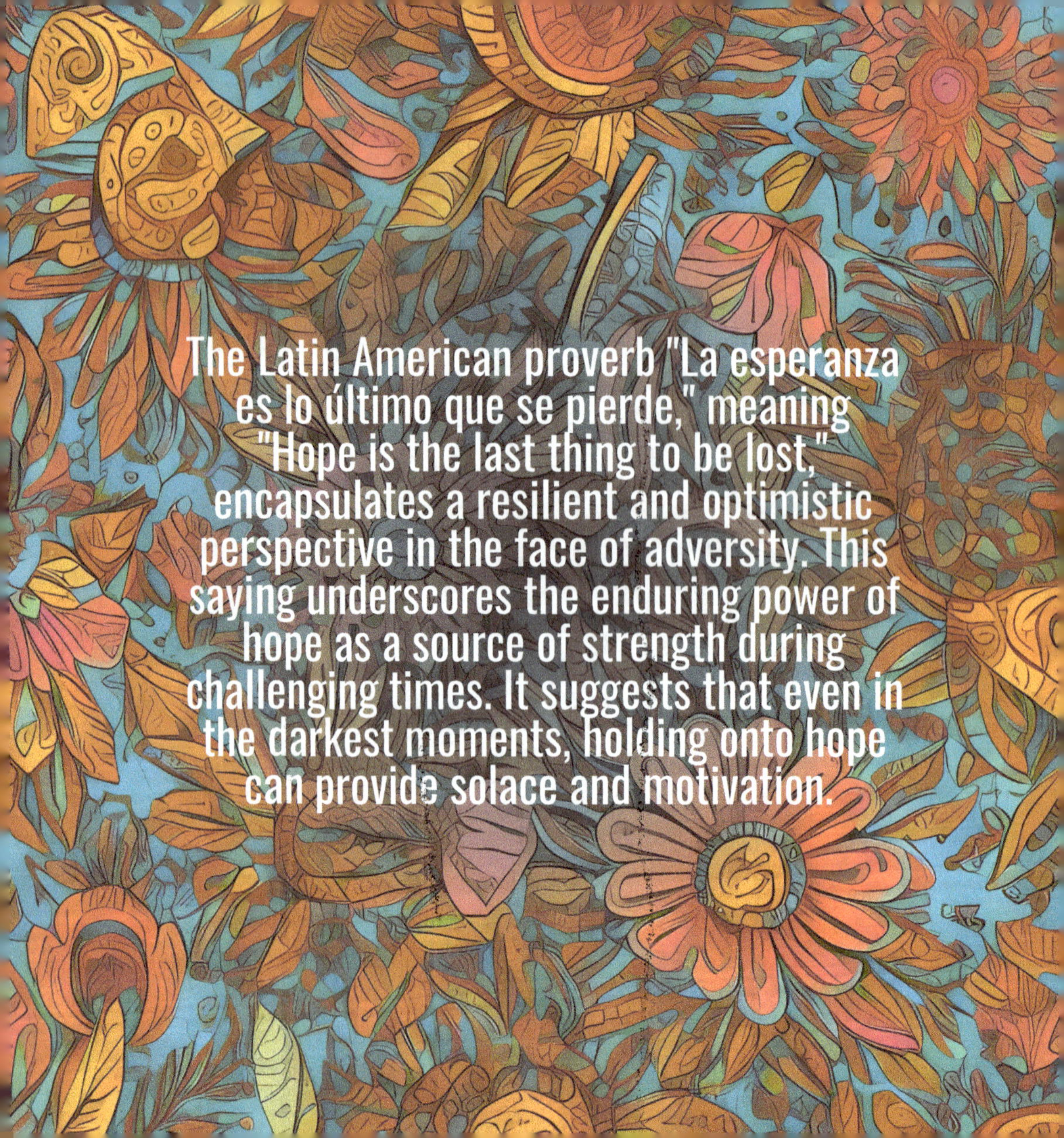

The Latin American proverb "La esperanza es lo último que se pierde," meaning "Hope is the last thing to be lost," encapsulates a resilient and optimistic perspective in the face of adversity. This saying underscores the enduring power of hope as a source of strength during challenging times. It suggests that even in the darkest moments, holding onto hope can provide solace and motivation.

A FOWL DOES FLY AS HIGH AS IT CAN.
Guyana

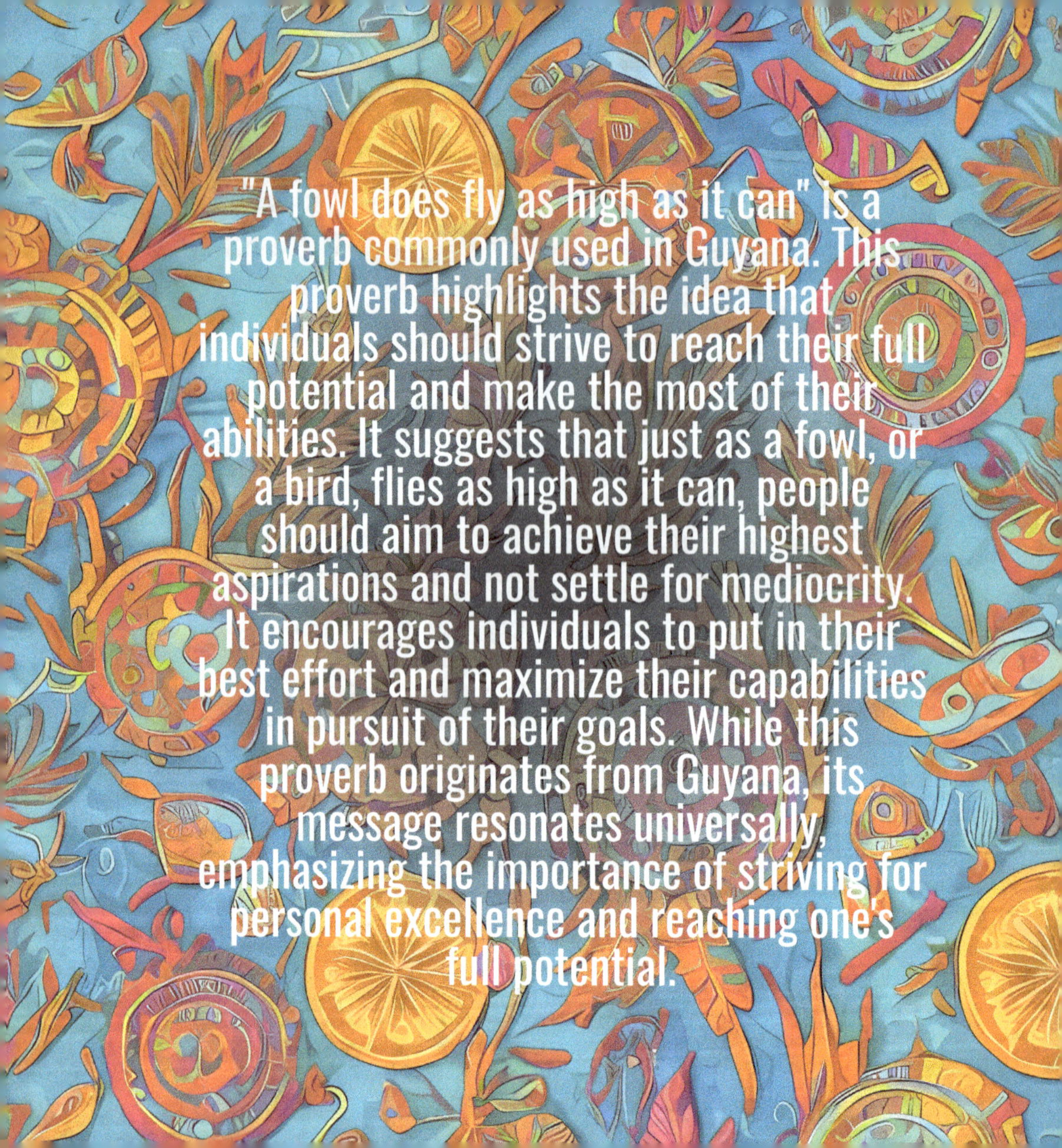
"A fowl does fly as high as it can" is a proverb commonly used in Guyana. This proverb highlights the idea that individuals should strive to reach their full potential and make the most of their abilities. It suggests that just as a fowl, or a bird, flies as high as it can, people should aim to achieve their highest aspirations and not settle for mediocrity. It encourages individuals to put in their best effort and maximize their capabilities in pursuit of their goals. While this proverb originates from Guyana, its message resonates universally, emphasizing the importance of striving for personal excellence and reaching one's full potential.

MONKEY'S CLIMB, AND
THEY NEVER FALL.
St. Kitts &
Nevis

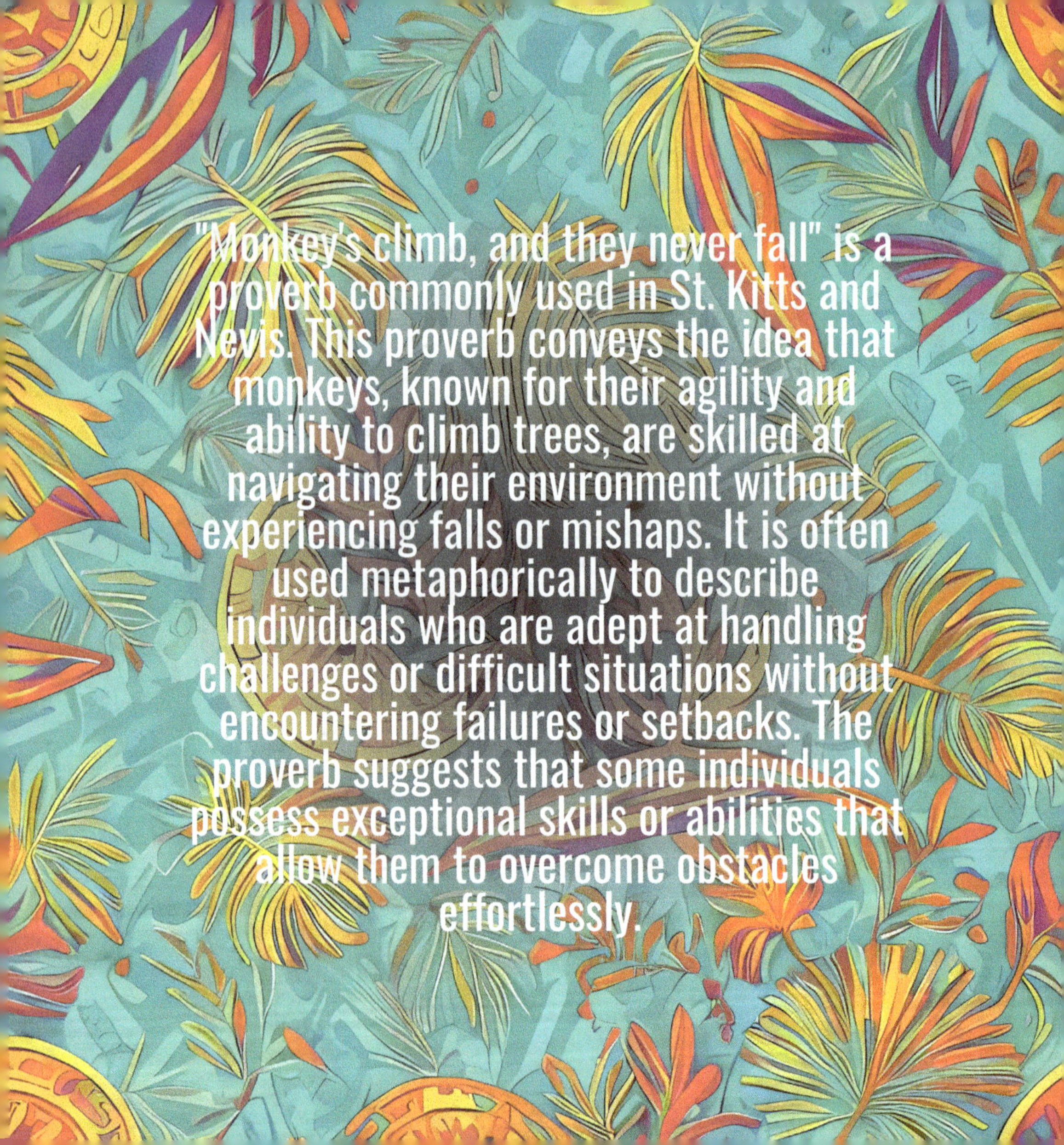

"Monkey's climb, and they never fall" is a proverb commonly used in St. Kitts and Nevis. This proverb conveys the idea that monkeys, known for their agility and ability to climb trees, are skilled at navigating their environment without experiencing falls or mishaps. It is often used metaphorically to describe individuals who are adept at handling challenges or difficult situations without encountering failures or setbacks. The proverb suggests that some individuals possess exceptional skills or abilities that allow them to overcome obstacles effortlessly.

A TREE BEGINS
WITH A SEED.
Arabia

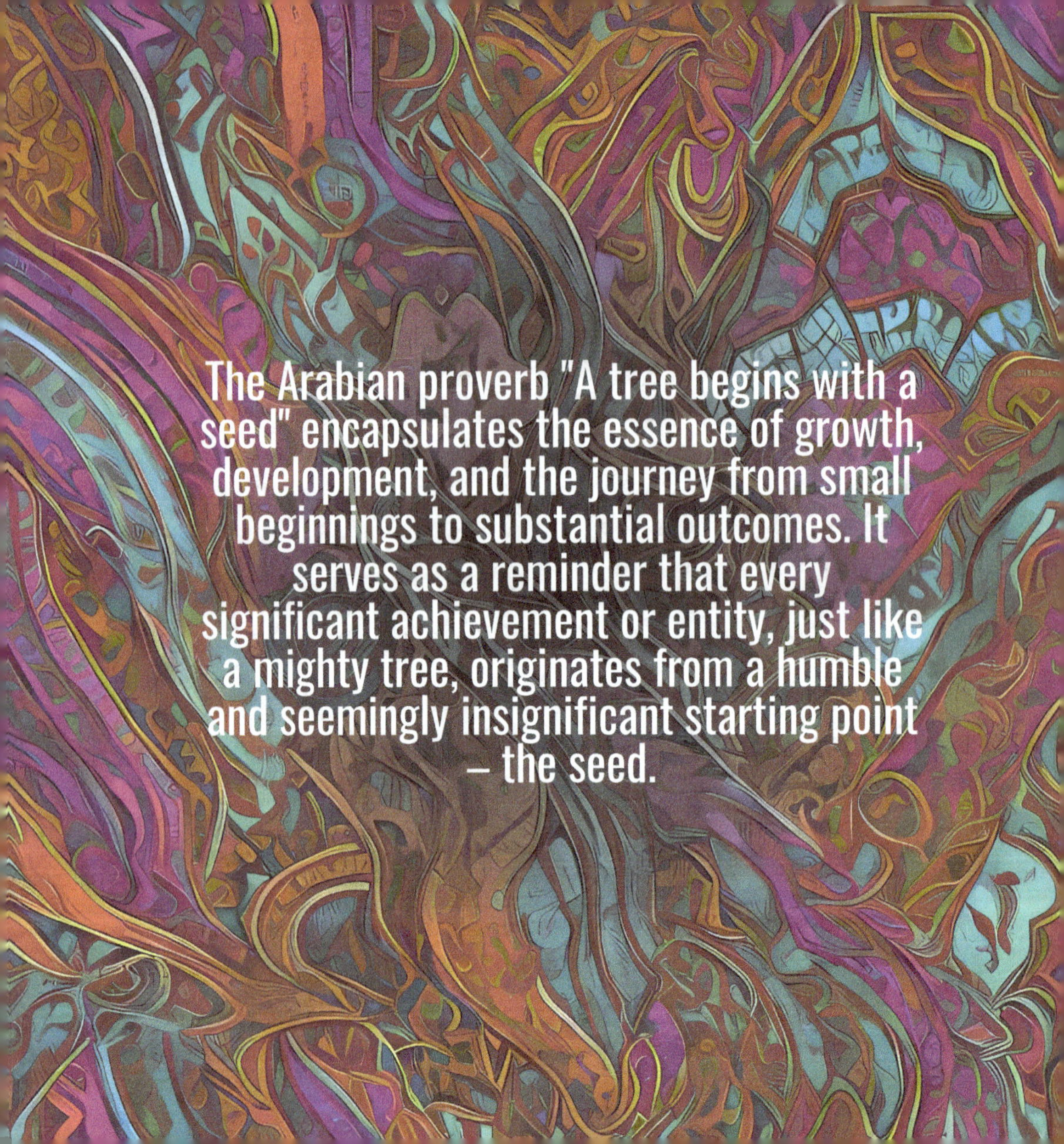

The Arabian proverb "A tree begins with a seed" encapsulates the essence of growth, development, and the journey from small beginnings to substantial outcomes. It serves as a reminder that every significant achievement or entity, just like a mighty tree, originates from a humble and seemingly insignificant starting point – the seed.

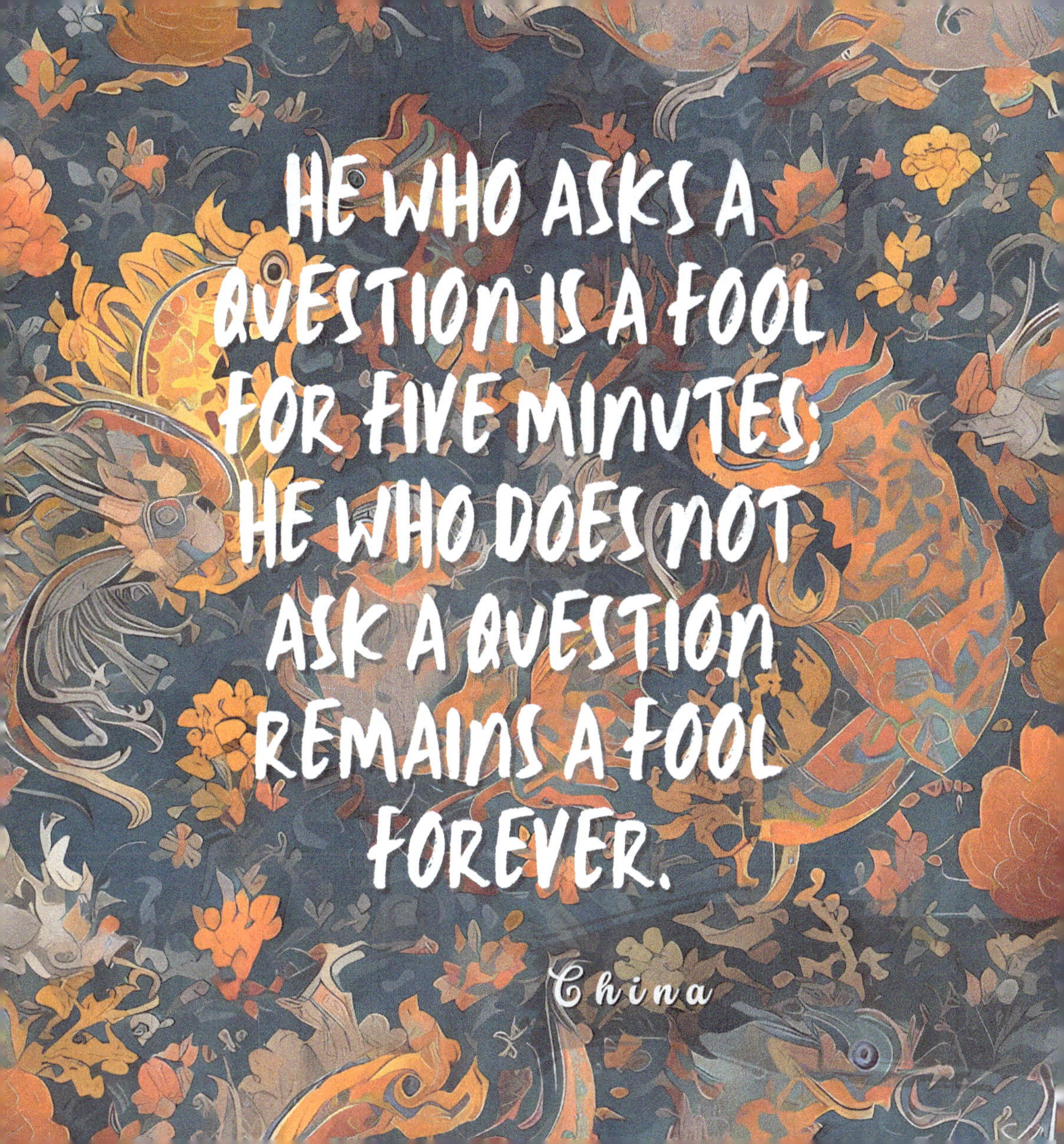
HE WHO ASKS A
QUESTION IS A FOOL
FOR FIVE MINUTES;
HE WHO DOES NOT
ASK A QUESTION
REMAINS A FOOL
FOREVER.
China

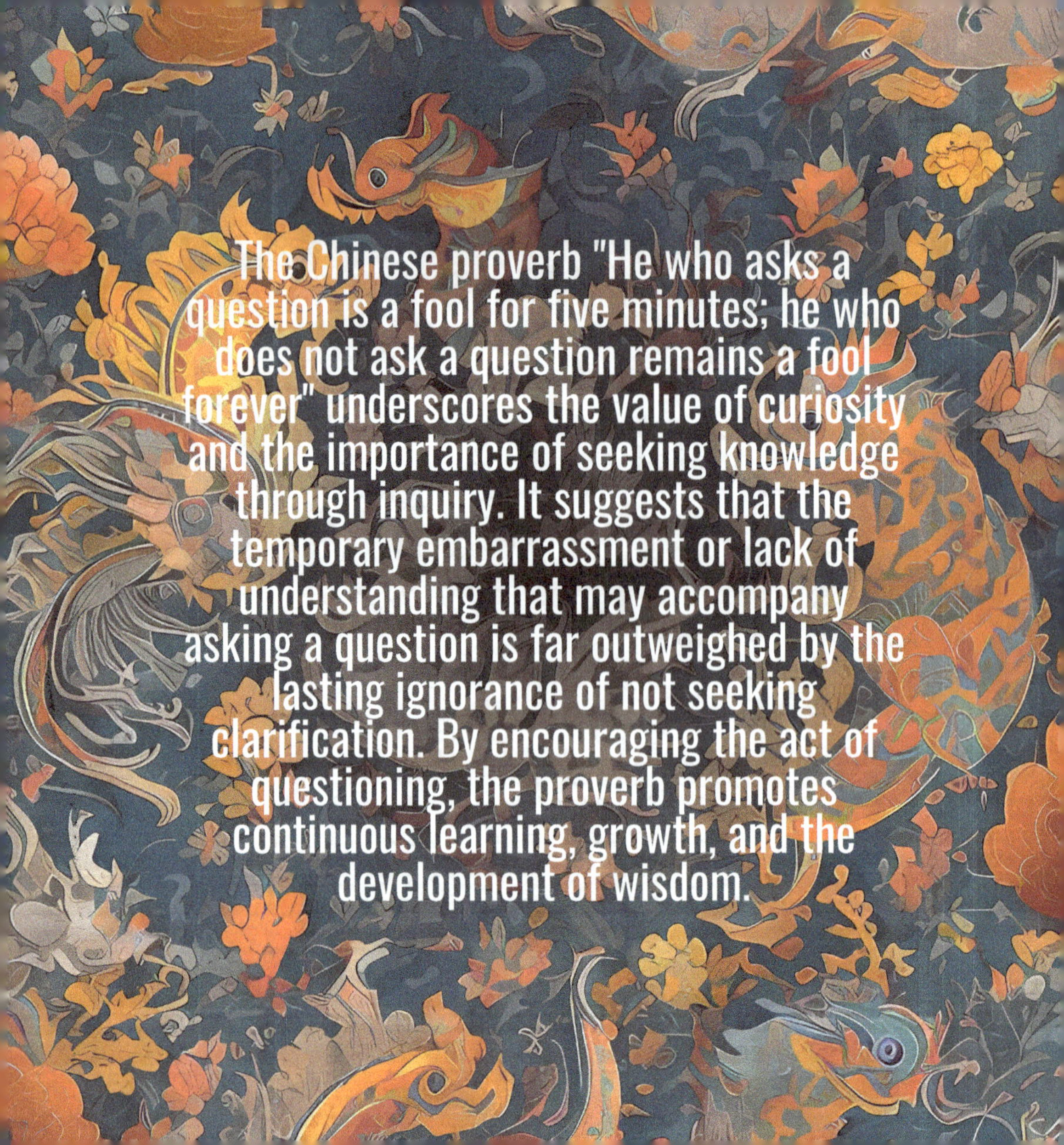
The Chinese proverb "He who asks a question is a fool for five minutes; he who does not ask a question remains a fool forever" underscores the value of curiosity and the importance of seeking knowledge through inquiry. It suggests that the temporary embarrassment or lack of understanding that may accompany asking a question is far outweighed by the lasting ignorance of not seeking clarification. By encouraging the act of questioning, the proverb promotes continuous learning, growth, and the development of wisdom.

A GUEST SEES MORE IN AN HOUR THAN THE HOST IN A YEAR.
Mongolia

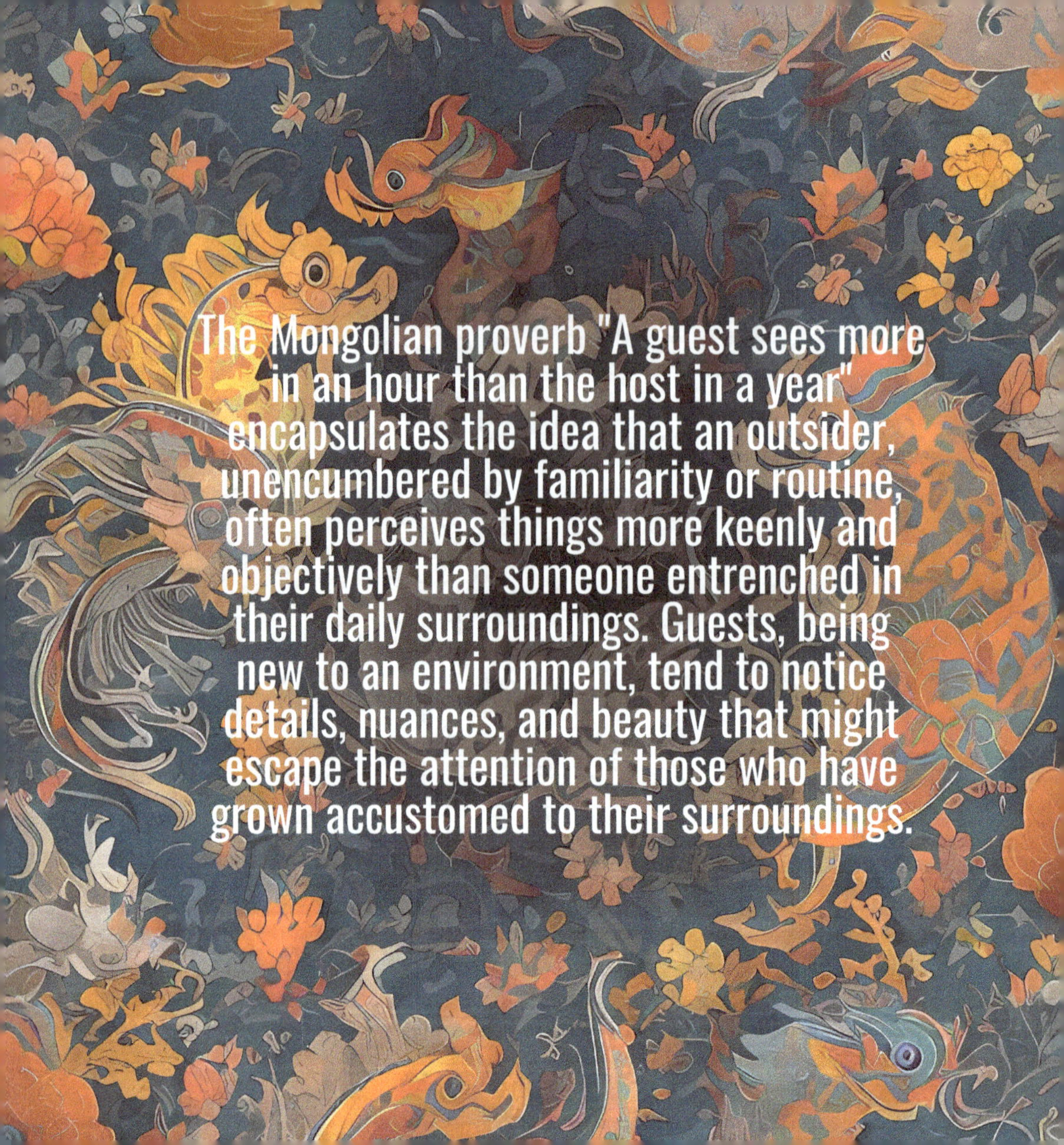

The Mongolian proverb "A guest sees more in an hour than the host in a year" encapsulates the idea that an outsider, unencumbered by familiarity or routine, often perceives things more keenly and objectively than someone entrenched in their daily surroundings. Guests, being new to an environment, tend to notice details, nuances, and beauty that might escape the attention of those who have grown accustomed to their surroundings.

WISDOM IS LIKE
FIRE. PEOPLE TAKE
IT FROM OTHERS.
Ivory Coast

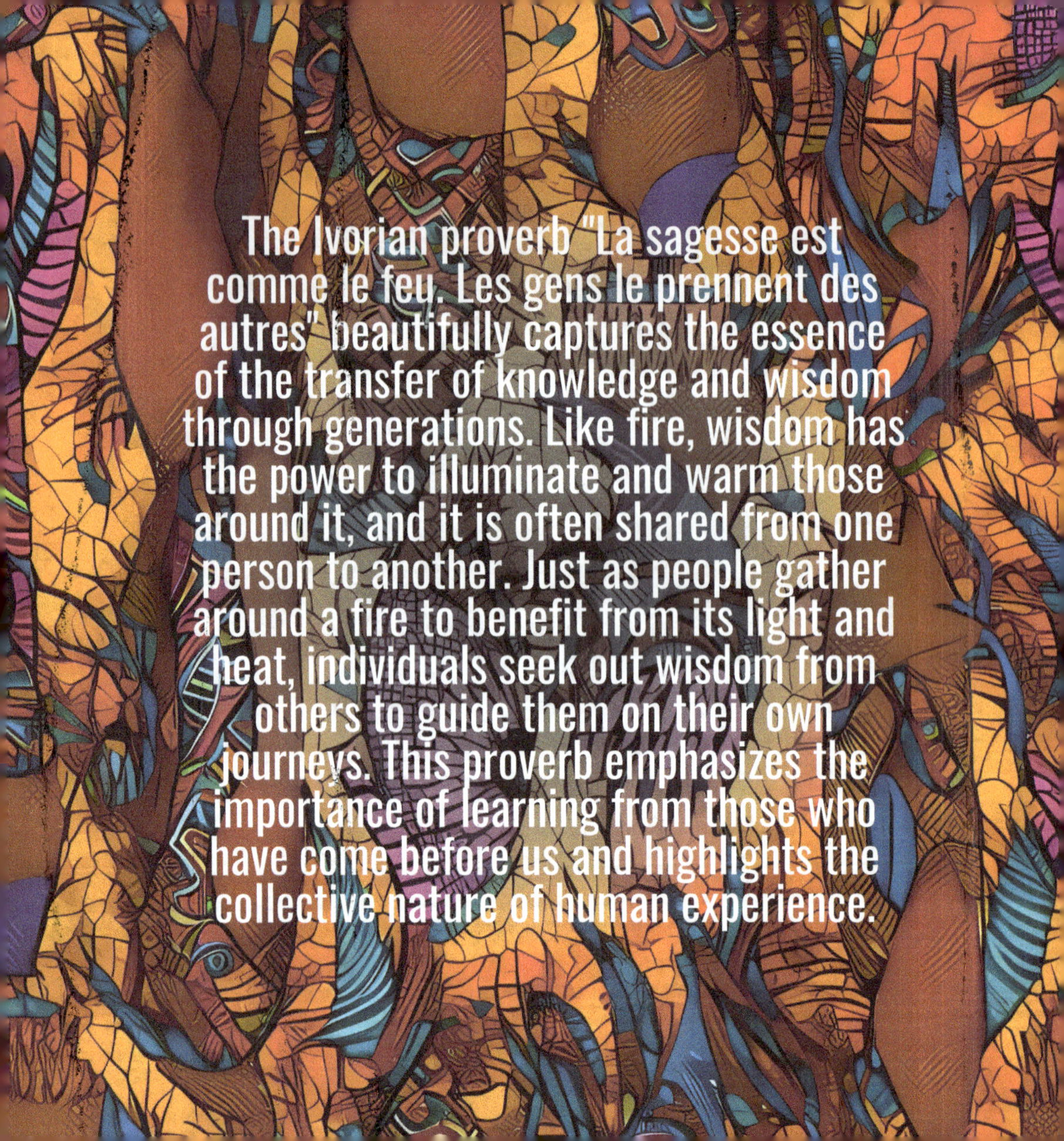

The Ivorian proverb "La sagesse est comme le feu. Les gens le prennent des autres" beautifully captures the essence of the transfer of knowledge and wisdom through generations. Like fire, wisdom has the power to illuminate and warm those around it, and it is often shared from one person to another. Just as people gather around a fire to benefit from its light and heat, individuals seek out wisdom from others to guide them on their own journeys. This proverb emphasizes the importance of learning from those who have come before us and highlights the collective nature of human experience.

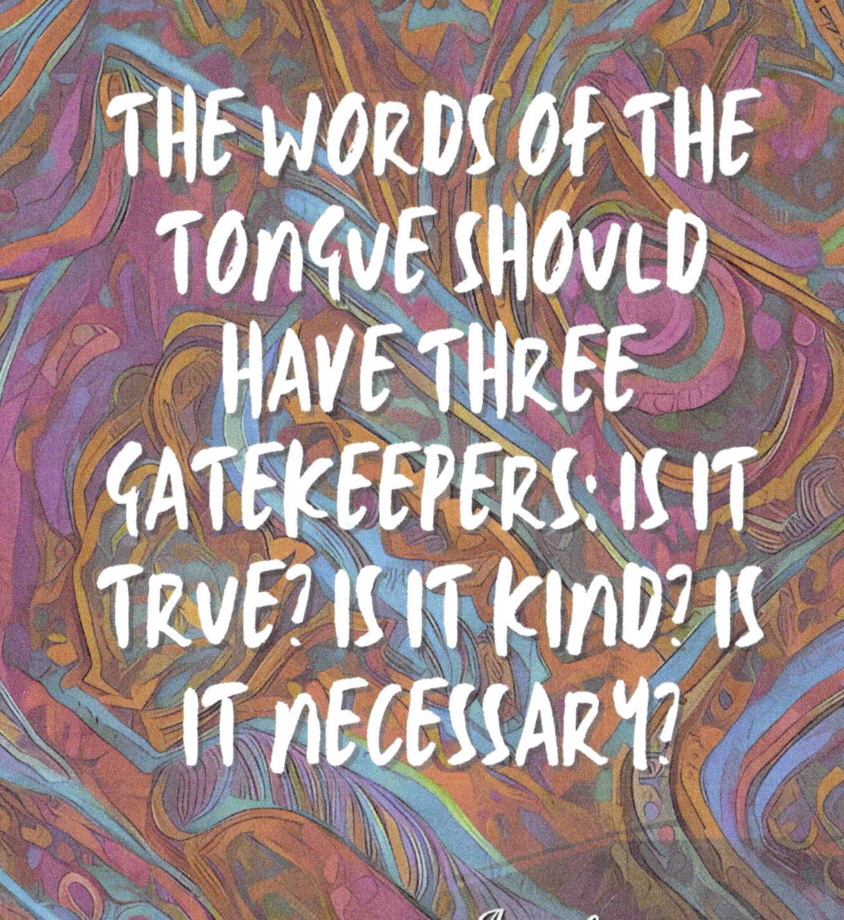
THE WORDS OF THE TONGUE SHOULD HAVE THREE GATEKEEPERS: IS IT TRUE? IS IT KIND? IS IT NECESSARY?
Arabia

The Arabian proverb "The words of the tongue should have three gatekeepers: Is it true? Is it kind? Is it necessary?" provides valuable guidance on the importance of mindful and responsible communication. It emphasizes the need for thoughtful consideration before speaking, highlighting three essential criteria for evaluating our words. The first gatekeeper, truth, encourages honesty and integrity in our speech, emphasizing the importance of conveying accurate information. The second gatekeeper, kindness, encourages us to choose words that are compassionate, empathetic, and considerate of others' feelings.

IT IS BETTER TO BE
RESPECTED THAN
LIKED.
Punjabi

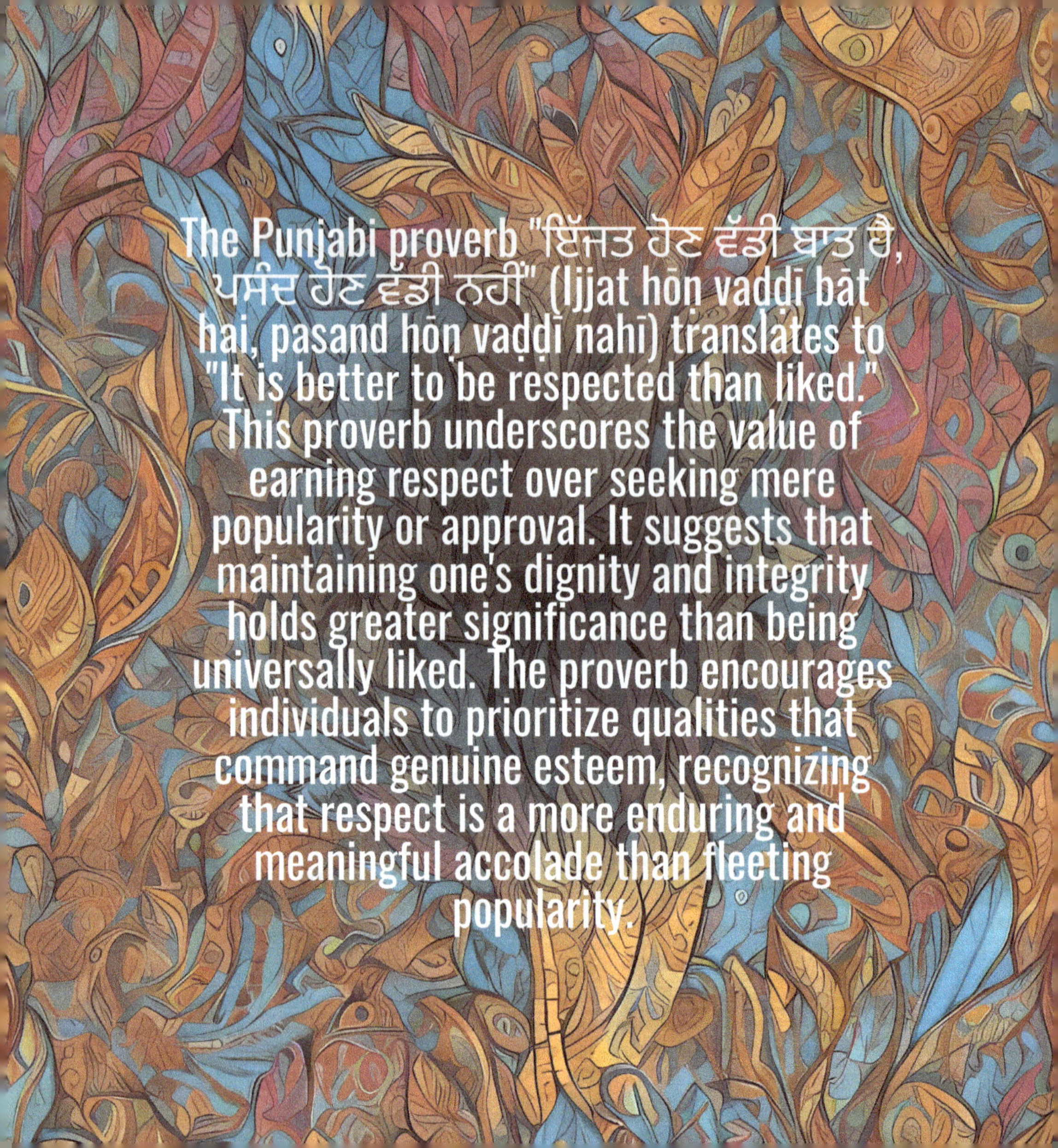
The Punjabi proverb "ਇੱਜਤ ਹੋਣ ਵੱਡੀ ਬਾਤ ਹੈ, ਪਸੰਦ ਹੋਣ ਵੱਡੀ ਨਹੀਂ" (Ijjat hōṇ vaddī bāt hai, pasand hōṇ vaḍḍī nahī) translates to "It is better to be respected than liked." This proverb underscores the value of earning respect over seeking mere popularity or approval. It suggests that maintaining one's dignity and integrity holds greater significance than being universally liked. The proverb encourages individuals to prioritize qualities that command genuine esteem, recognizing that respect is a more enduring and meaningful accolade than fleeting popularity.

WHERE YOU DIG A PIT, THERE YOU WILL FALL.
Czech

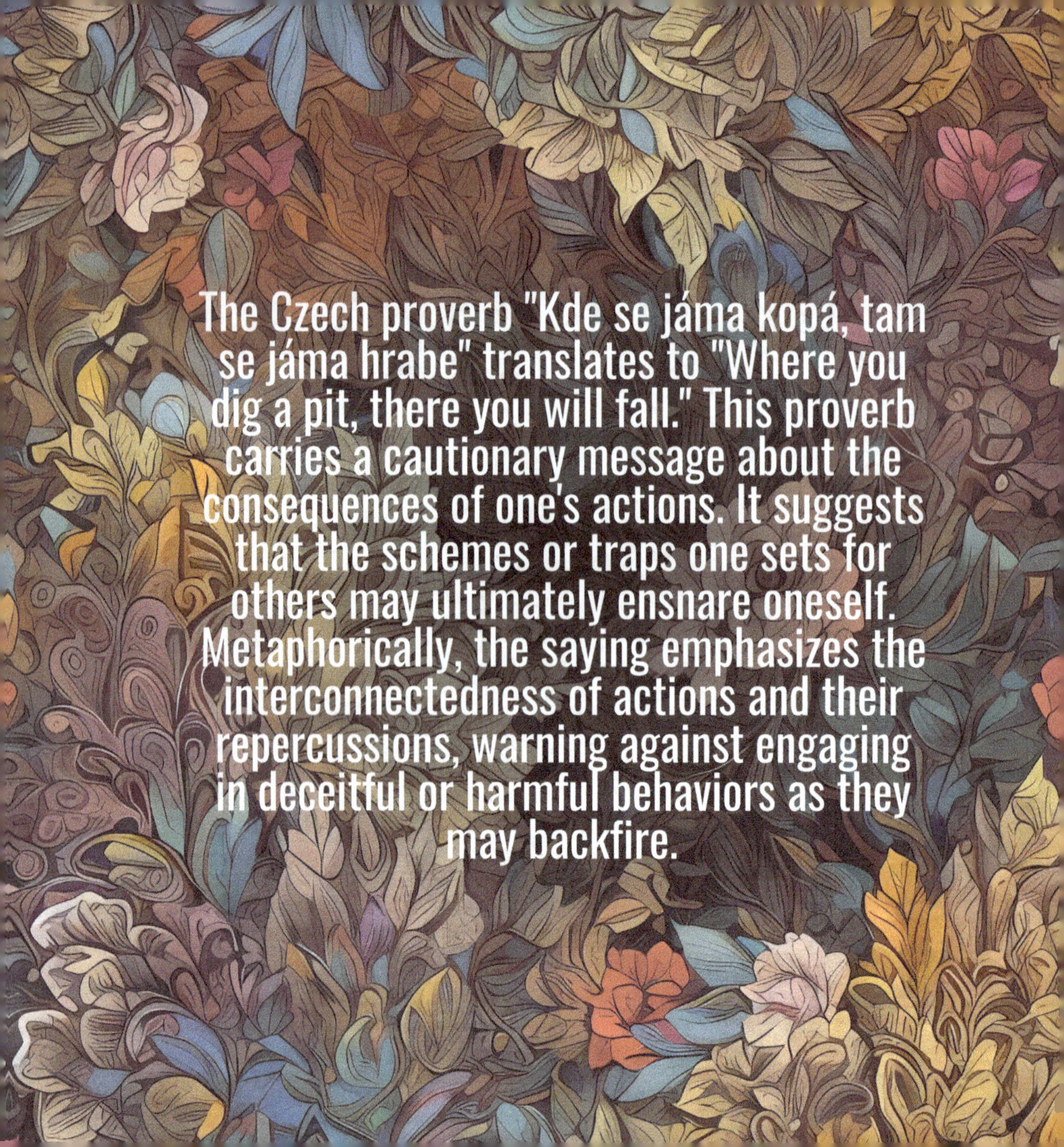

The Czech proverb "Kde se jáma kopá, tam se jáma hrabe" translates to "Where you dig a pit, there you will fall." This proverb carries a cautionary message about the consequences of one's actions. It suggests that the schemes or traps one sets for others may ultimately ensnare oneself. Metaphorically, the saying emphasizes the interconnectedness of actions and their repercussions, warning against engaging in deceitful or harmful behaviors as they may backfire.

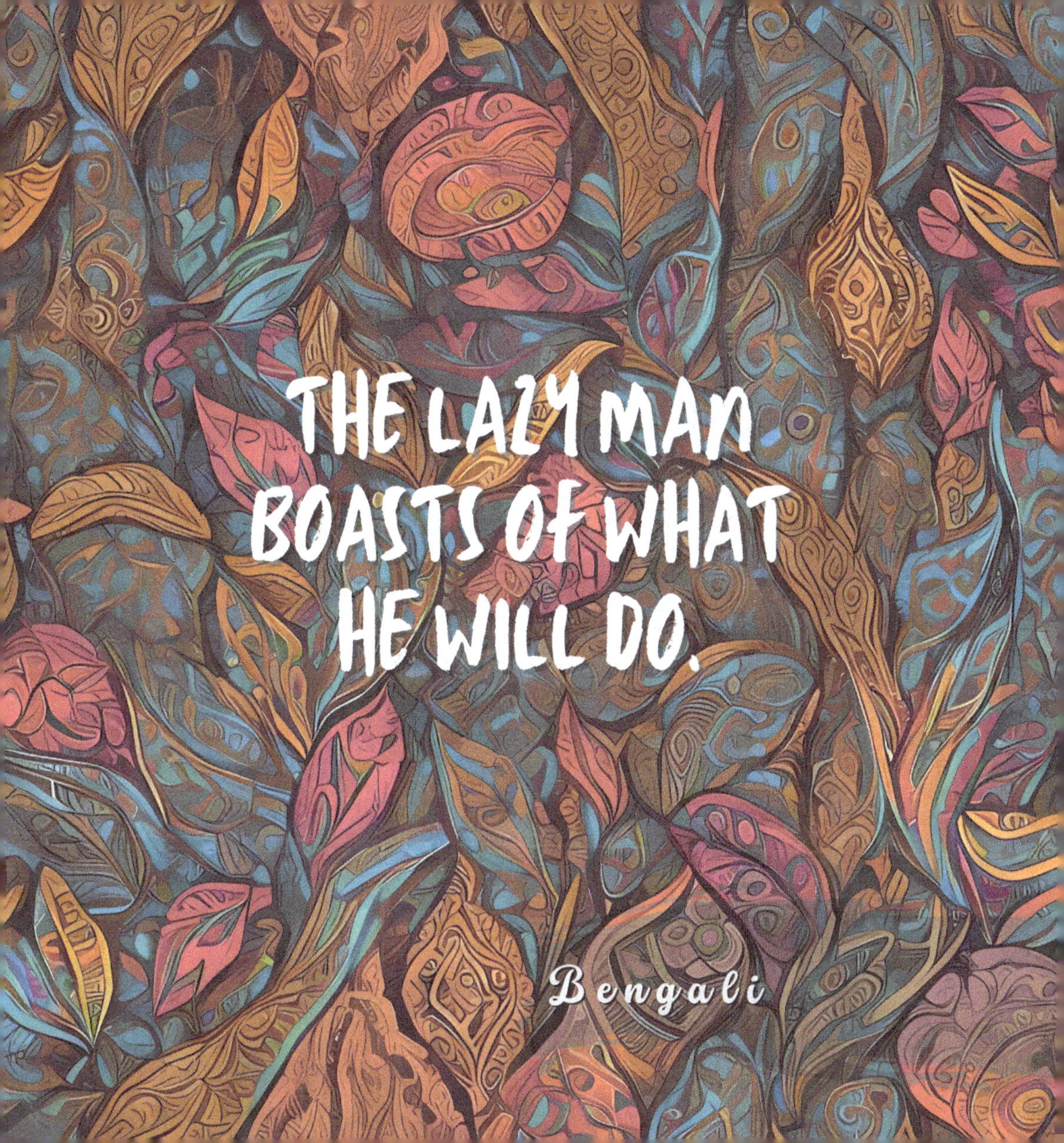
THE LAZY MAN BOASTS OF WHAT HE WILL DO.
Bengali

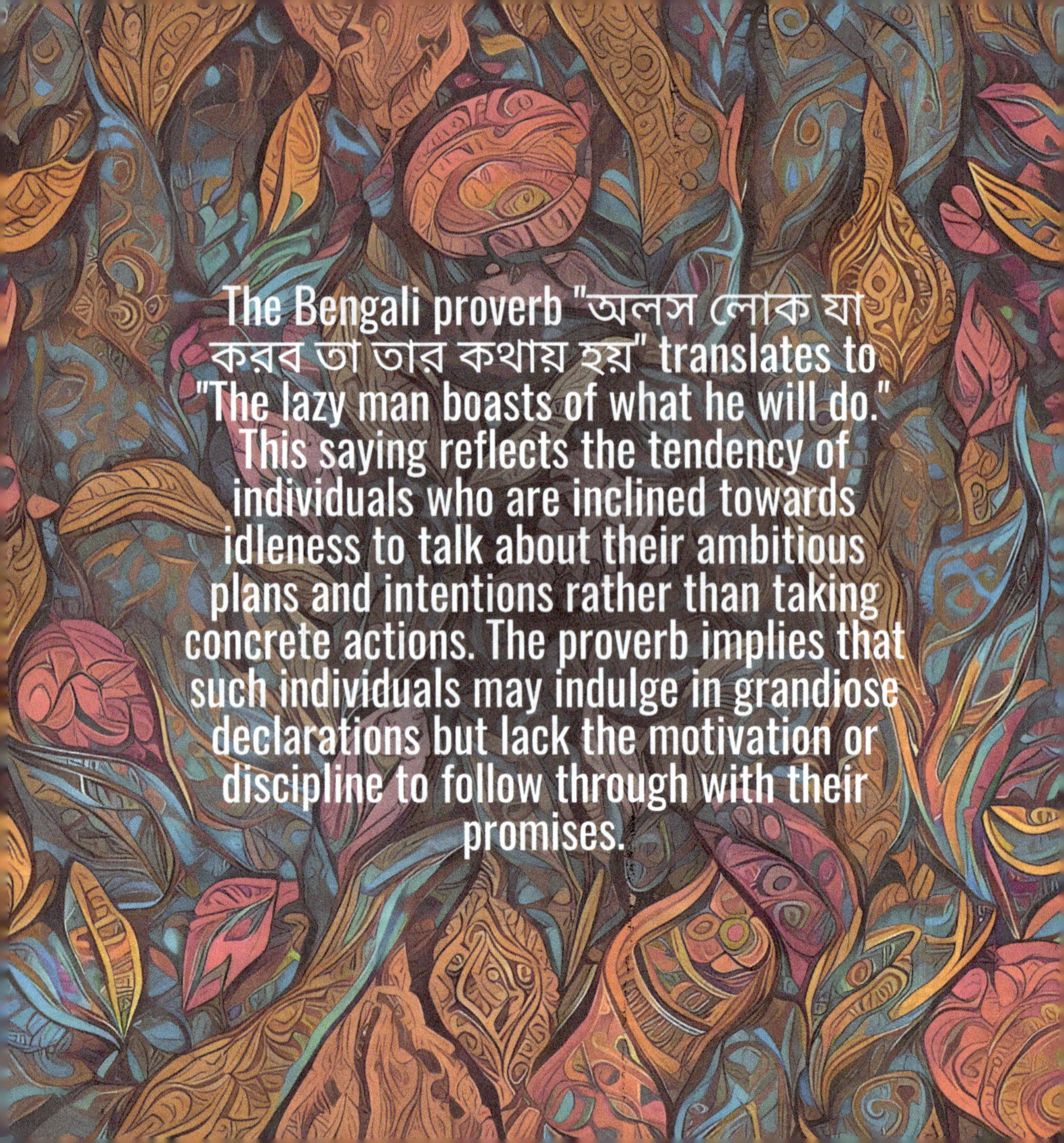
The Bengali proverb "অলস লোক যা করব তা তার কথায় হয়" translates to "The lazy man boasts of what he will do." This saying reflects the tendency of individuals who are inclined towards idleness to talk about their ambitious plans and intentions rather than taking concrete actions. The proverb implies that such individuals may indulge in grandiose declarations but lack the motivation or discipline to follow through with their promises.

A HOUSE DIVIDED
AGAINST ITSELF
CANNOT STAND.
Ireland

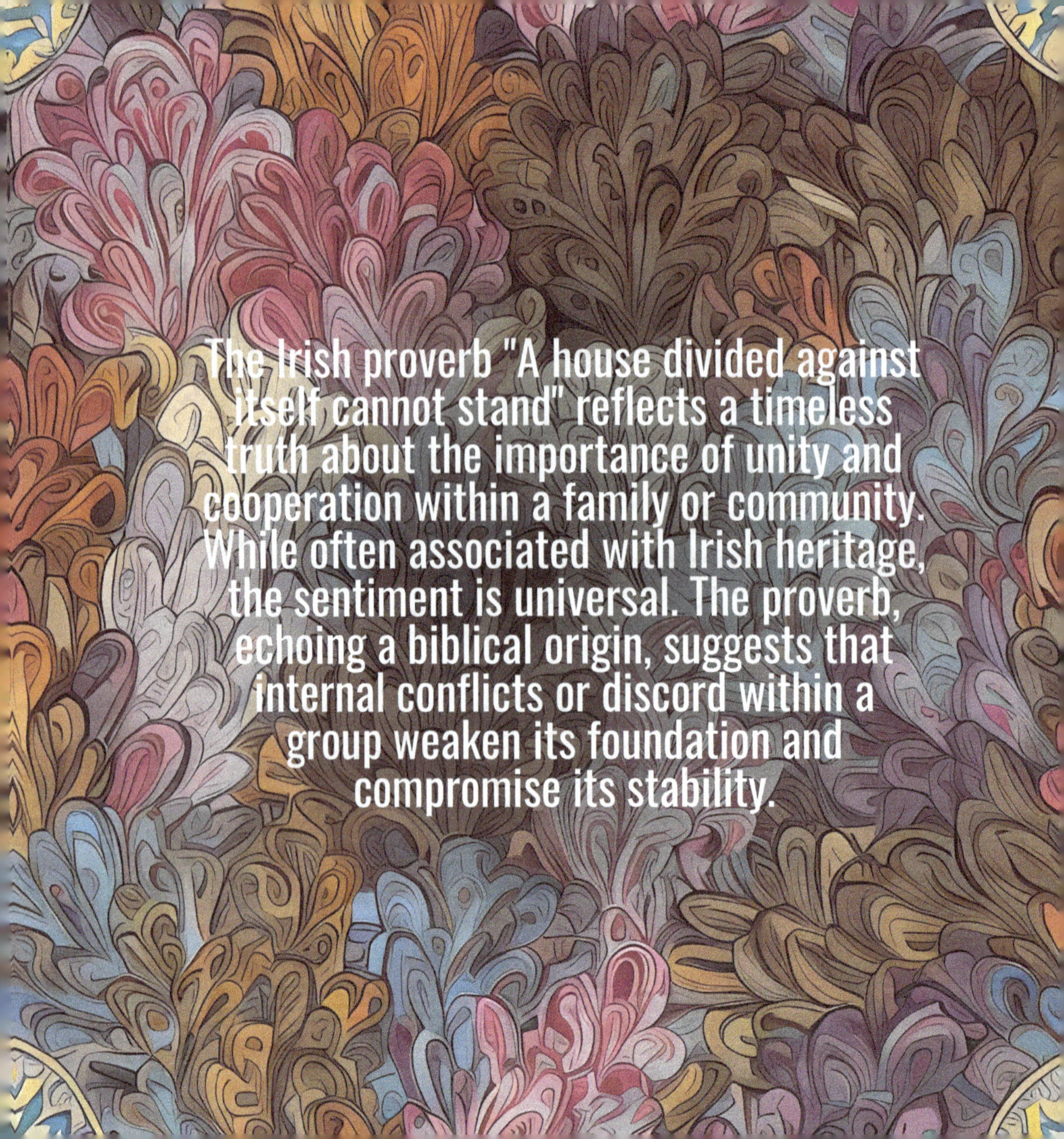

The Irish proverb "A house divided against itself cannot stand" reflects a timeless truth about the importance of unity and cooperation within a family or community. While often associated with Irish heritage, the sentiment is universal. The proverb, echoing a biblical origin, suggests that internal conflicts or discord within a group weaken its foundation and compromise its stability.

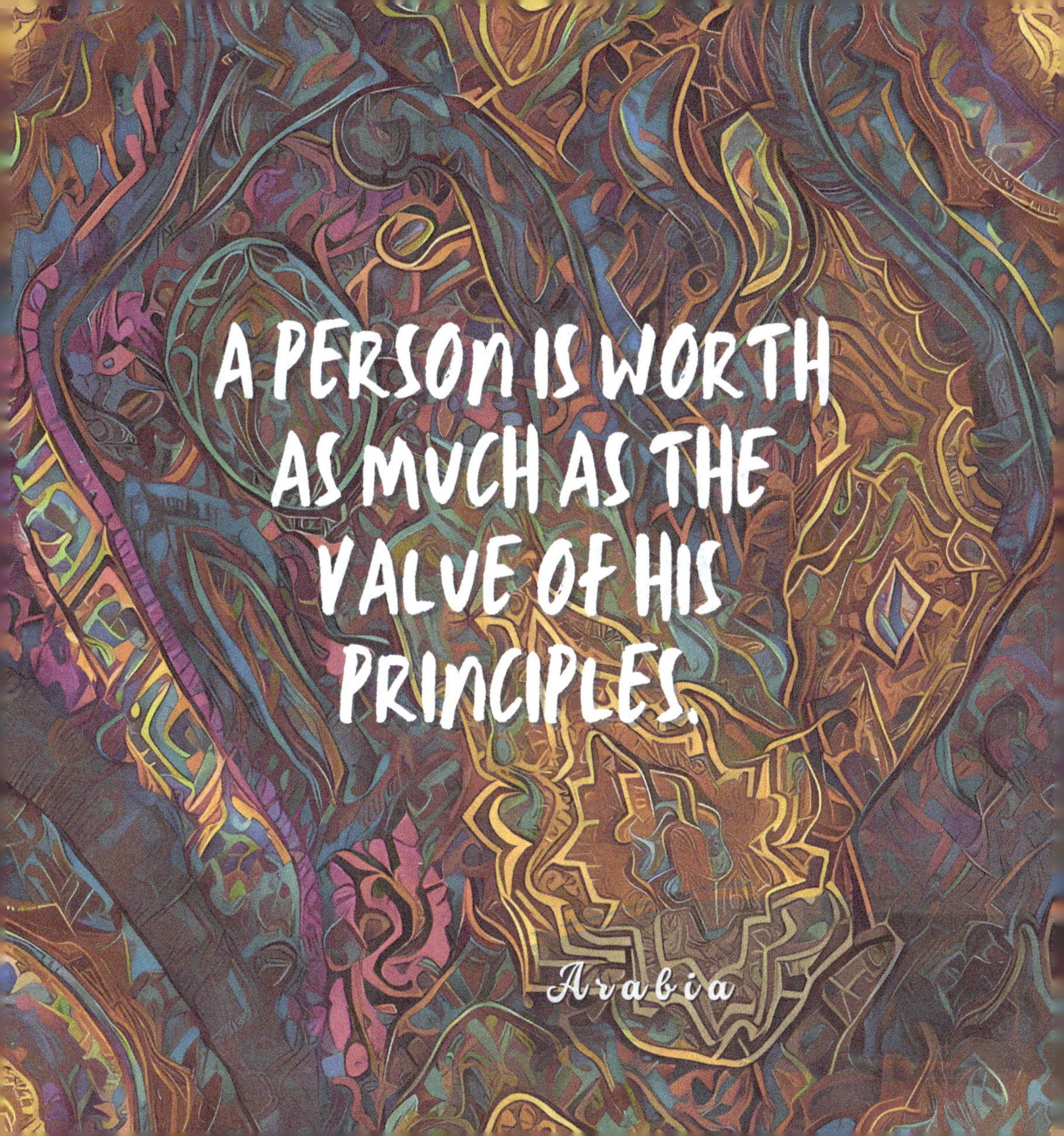
A PERSON IS WORTH AS MUCH AS THE VALUE OF HIS PRINCIPLES.
Arabia

The Arabian proverb "A person is worth as much as the value of his principles" emphasizes the importance of one's ethical foundation in determining their true worth. It suggests that an individual's character and intrinsic value are closely tied to the principles they uphold. In essence, the proverb encourages the recognition that personal integrity, moral standards, and adherence to ethical values are key factors in assessing an individual's true worth. It underscores the idea that material wealth or external achievements alone do not define a person; rather, it is the strength and integrity of their principles that contribute significantly to their overall value and character.

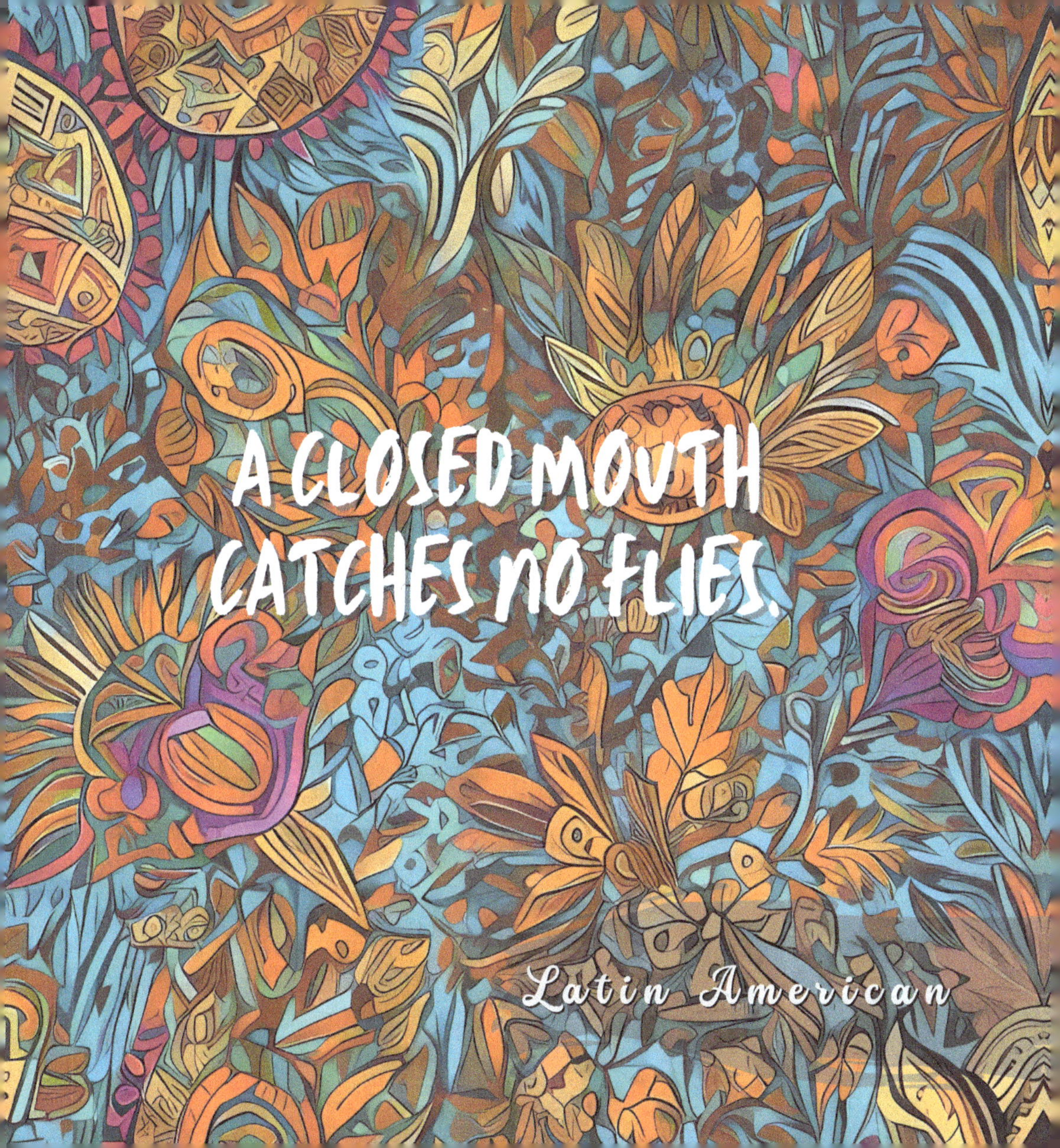
A CLOSED MOUTH
CATCHES NO FLIES.
Latin American

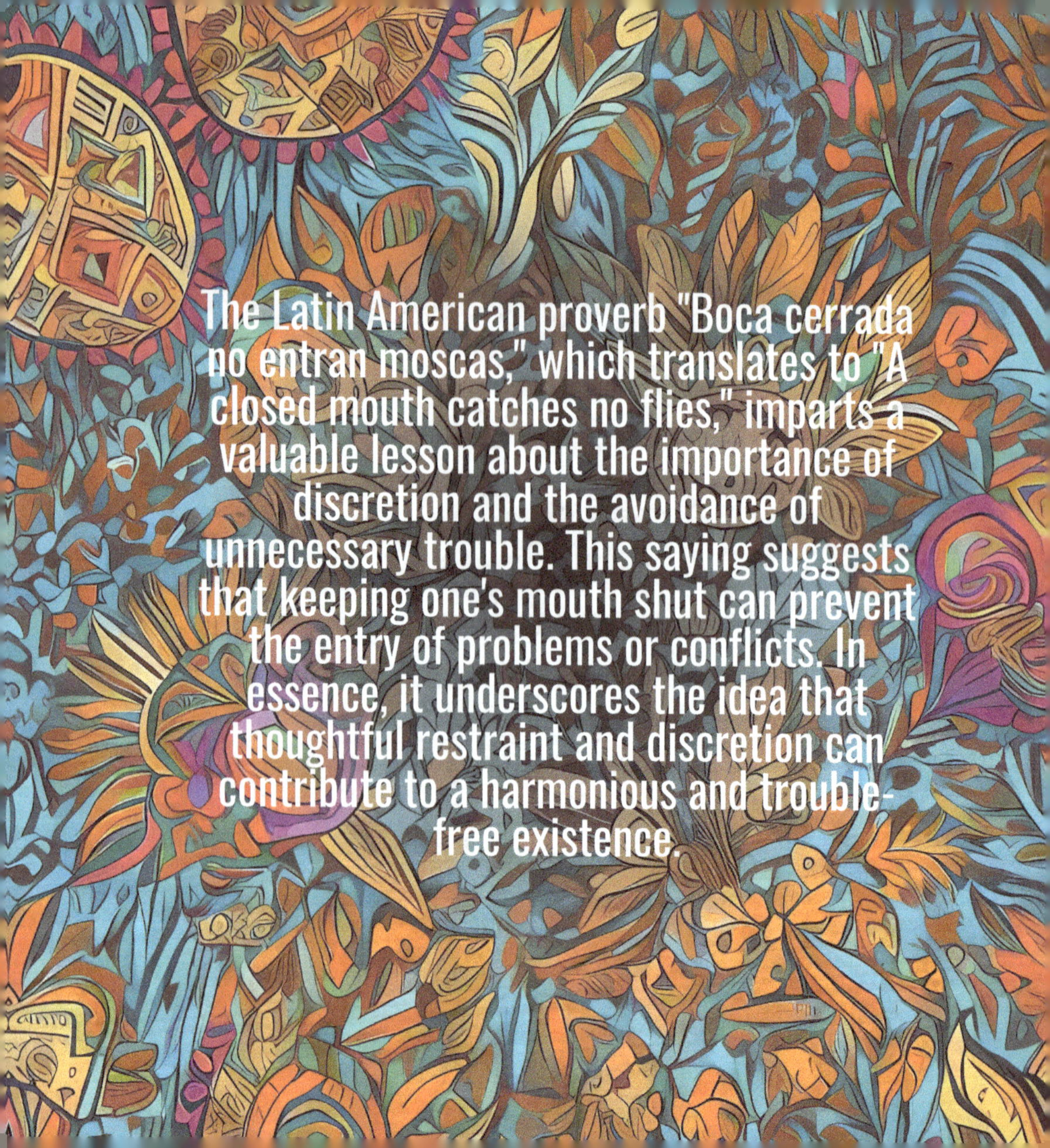

The Latin American proverb "Boca cerrada no entran moscas," which translates to "A closed mouth catches no flies," imparts a valuable lesson about the importance of discretion and the avoidance of unnecessary trouble. This saying suggests that keeping one's mouth shut can prevent the entry of problems or conflicts. In essence, it underscores the idea that thoughtful restraint and discretion can contribute to a harmonious and trouble-free existence.

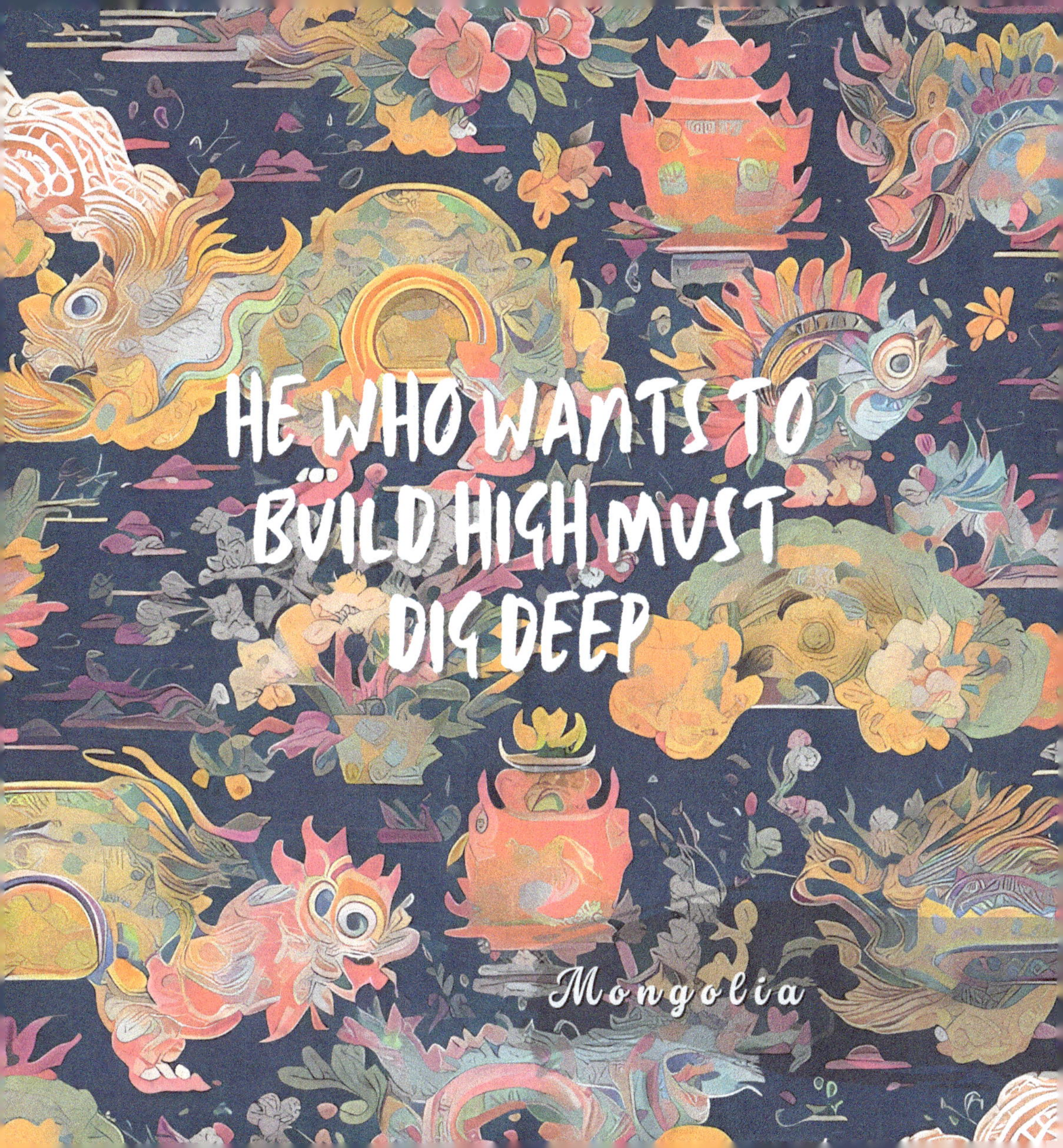
HE WHO WANTS TO BUILD HIGH MUST DIG DEEP
Mongolia

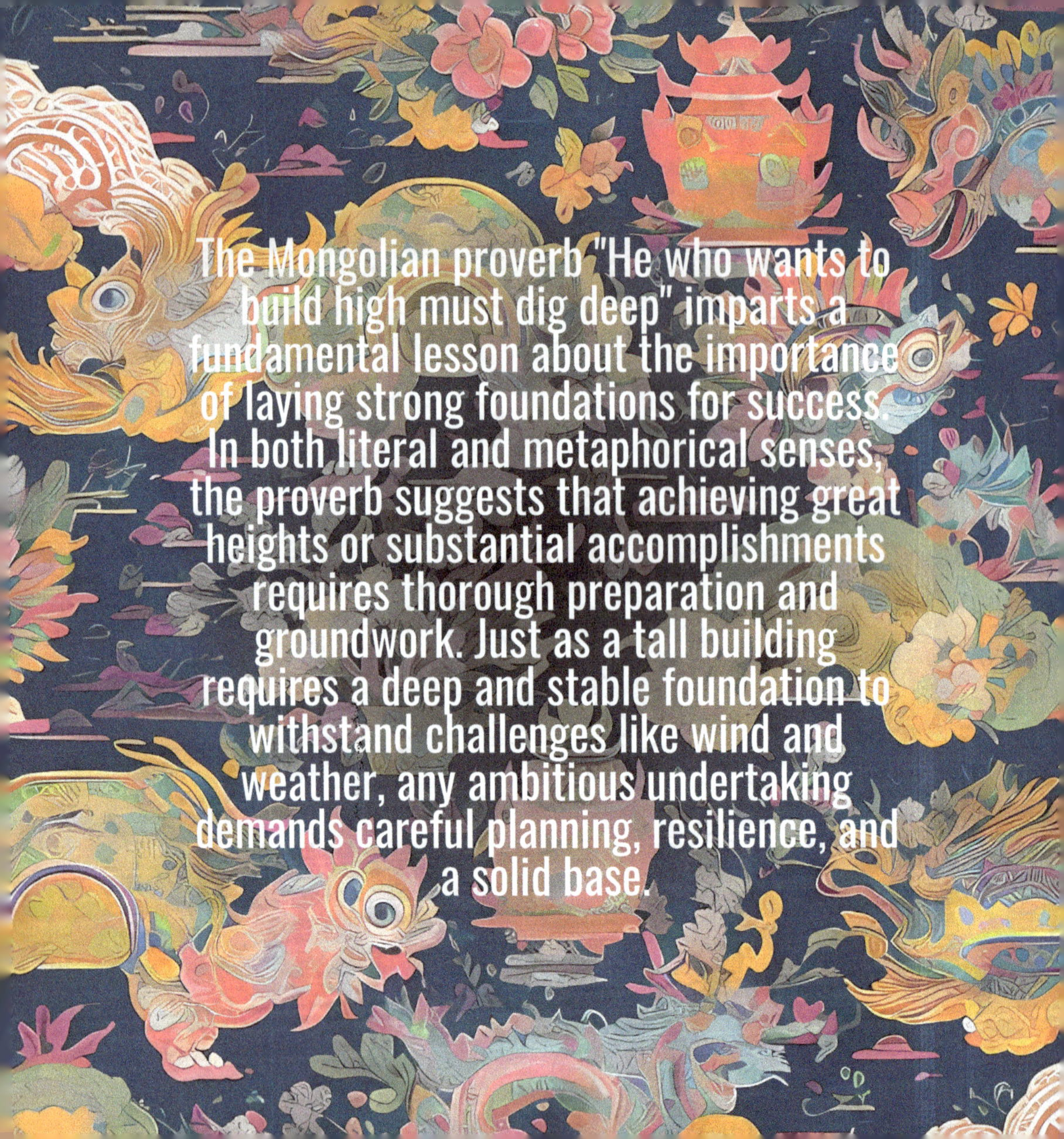
The Mongolian proverb "He who wants to build high must dig deep" imparts a fundamental lesson about the importance of laying strong foundations for success. In both literal and metaphorical senses, the proverb suggests that achieving great heights or substantial accomplishments requires thorough preparation and groundwork. Just as a tall building requires a deep and stable foundation to withstand challenges like wind and weather, any ambitious undertaking demands careful planning, resilience, and a solid base.

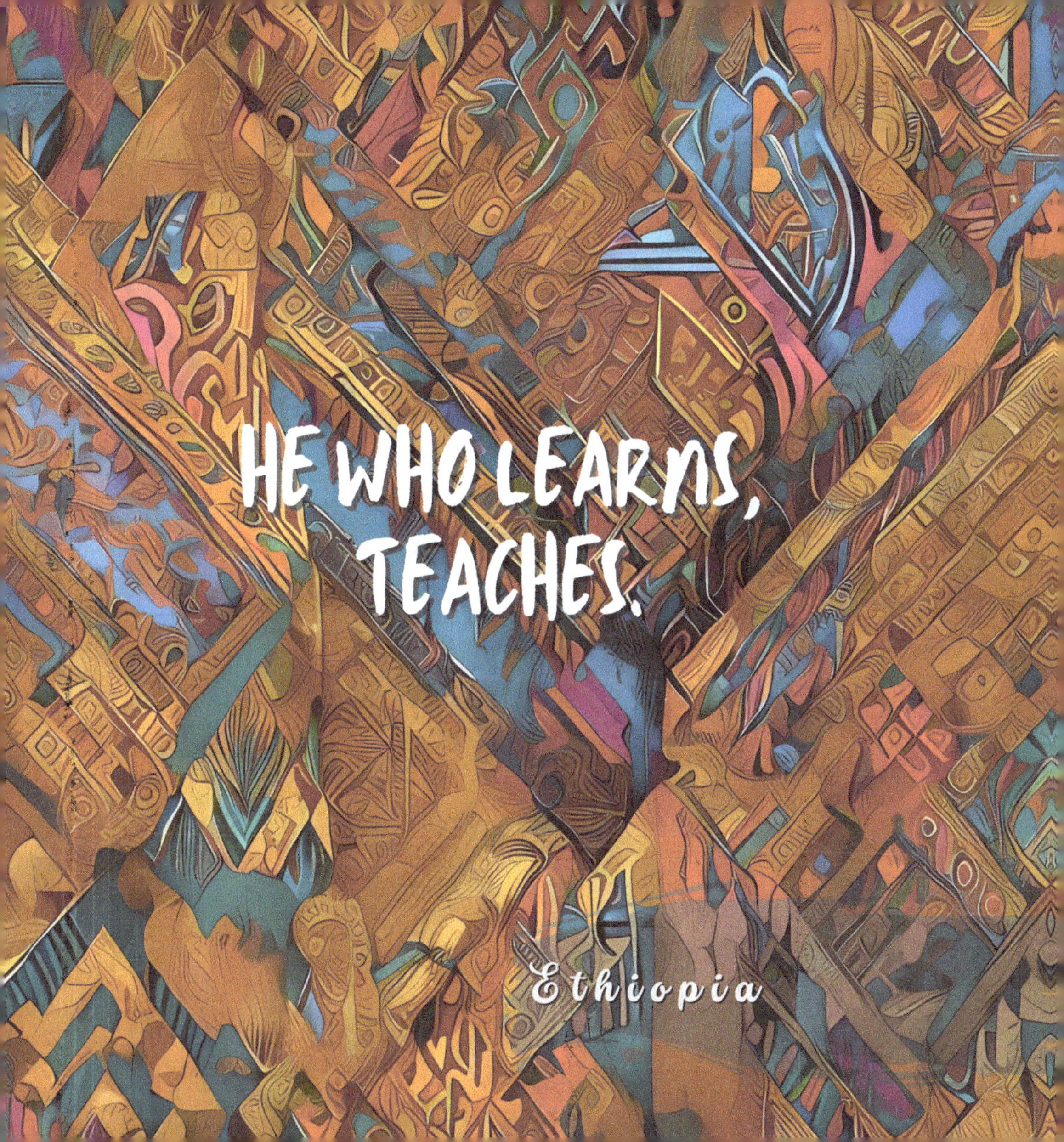
HE WHO LEARNS,
TEACHES.
Ethiopia

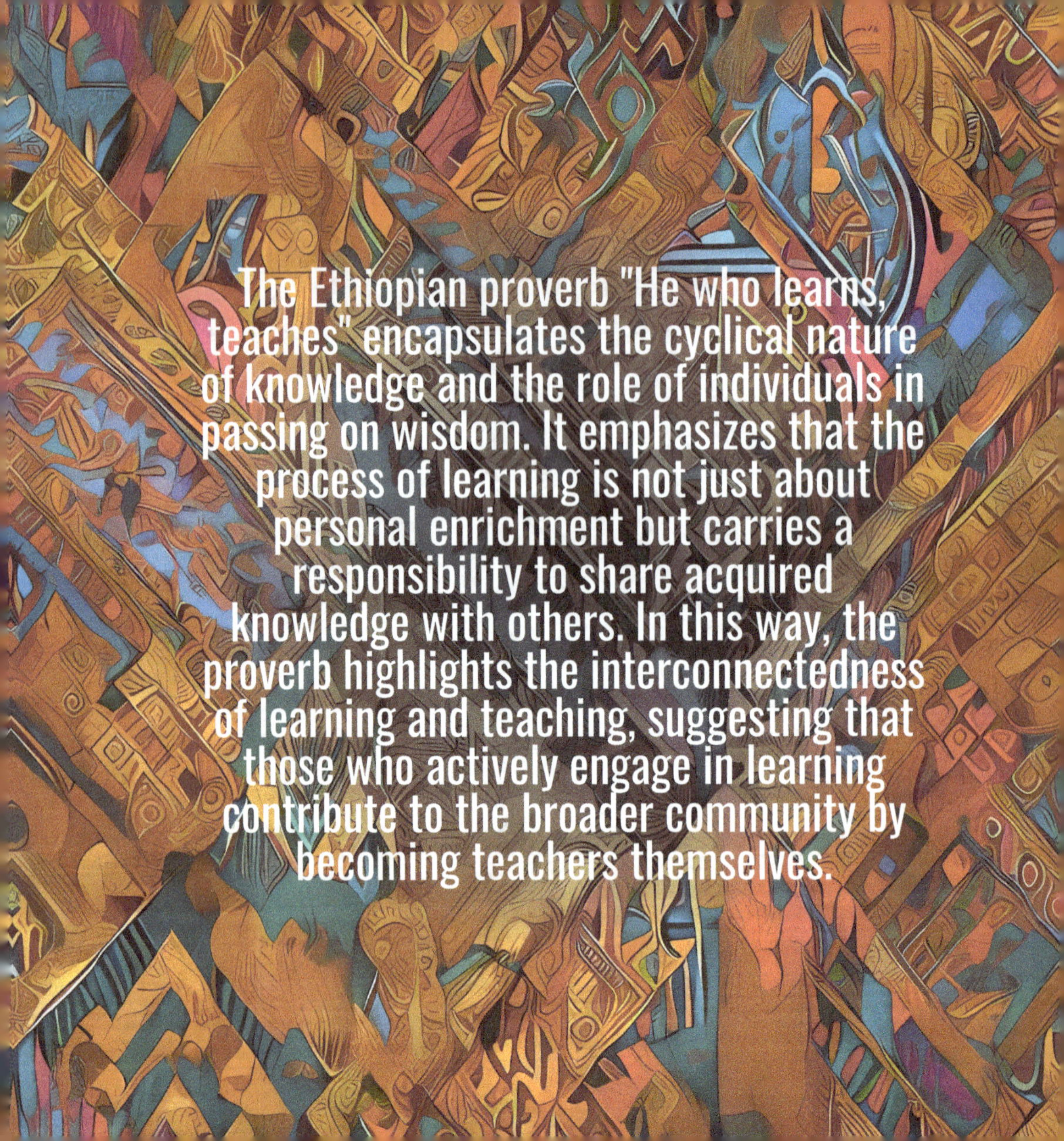
The Ethiopian proverb "He who learns, teaches" encapsulates the cyclical nature of knowledge and the role of individuals in passing on wisdom. It emphasizes that the process of learning is not just about personal enrichment but carries a responsibility to share acquired knowledge with others. In this way, the proverb highlights the interconnectedness of learning and teaching, suggesting that those who actively engage in learning contribute to the broader community by becoming teachers themselves.

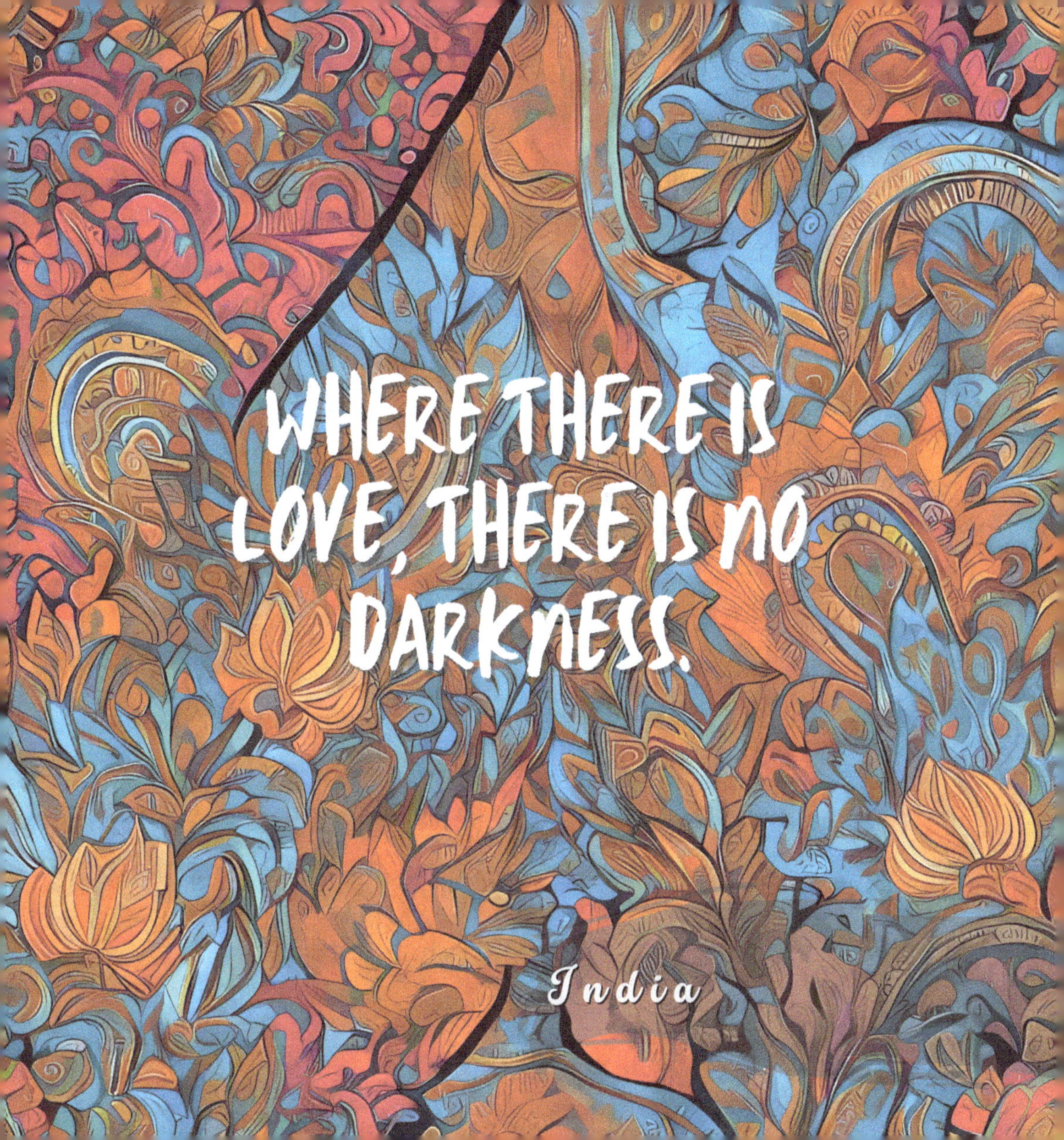
WHERE THERE IS LOVE, THERE IS NO DARKNESS.
India

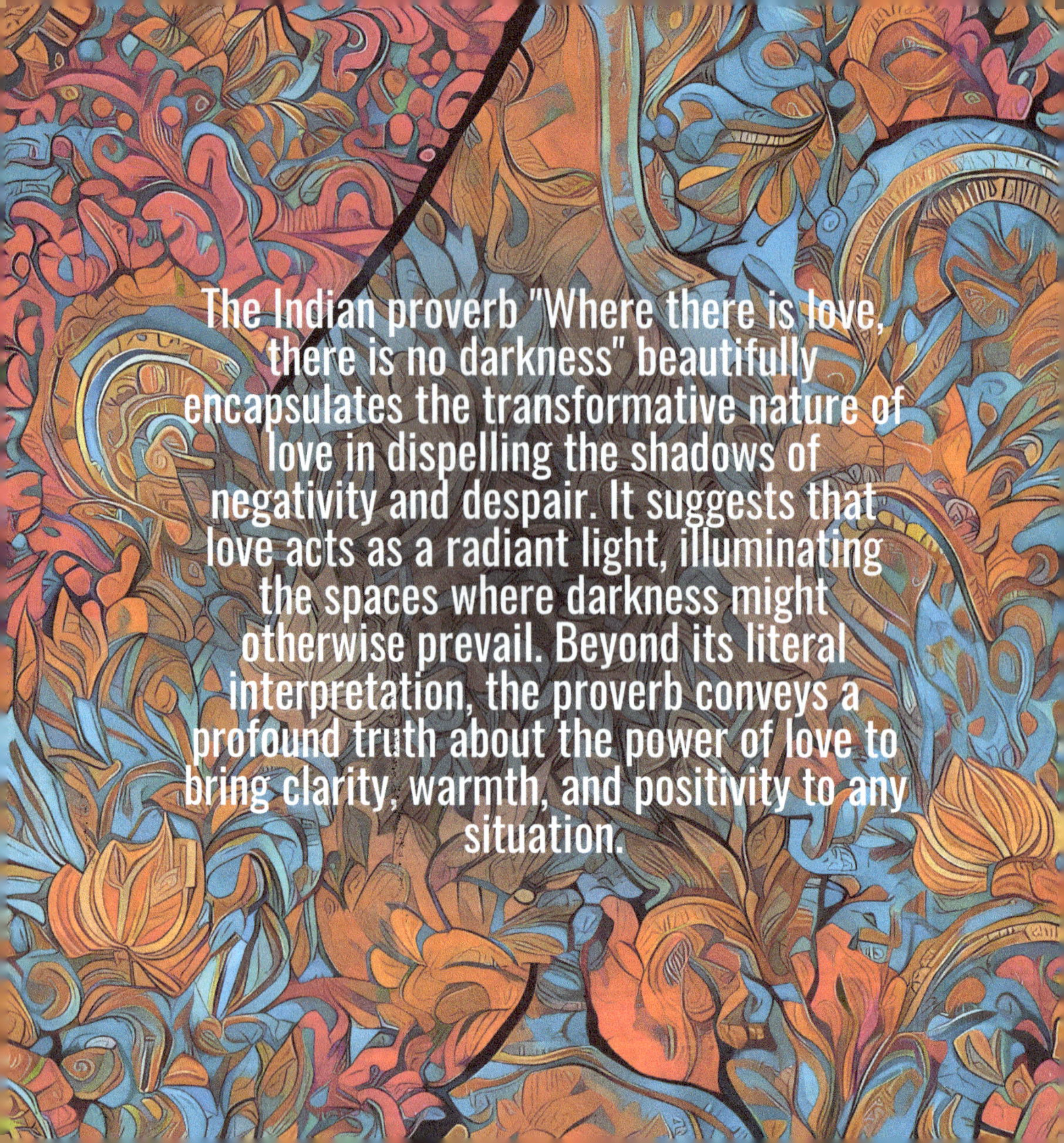

The Indian proverb "Where there is love, there is no darkness" beautifully encapsulates the transformative nature of love in dispelling the shadows of negativity and despair. It suggests that love acts as a radiant light, illuminating the spaces where darkness might otherwise prevail. Beyond its literal interpretation, the proverb conveys a profound truth about the power of love to bring clarity, warmth, and positivity to any situation.

NECESSITY IS THE
MOTHER OF
INVENTION.
England

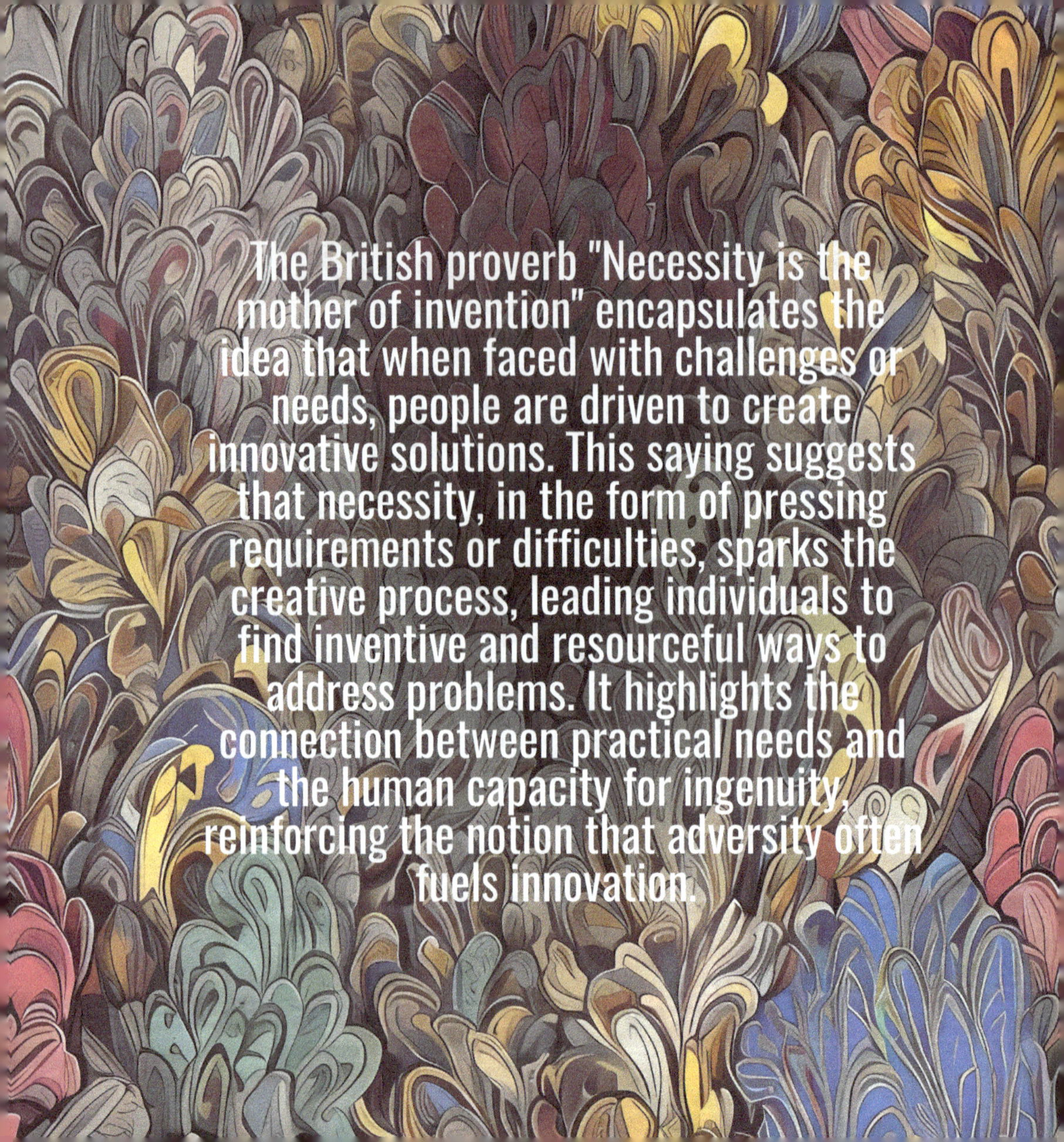
The British proverb "Necessity is the mother of invention" encapsulates the idea that when faced with challenges or needs, people are driven to create innovative solutions. This saying suggests that necessity, in the form of pressing requirements or difficulties, sparks the creative process, leading individuals to find inventive and resourceful ways to address problems. It highlights the connection between practical needs and the human capacity for ingenuity, reinforcing the notion that adversity often fuels innovation.

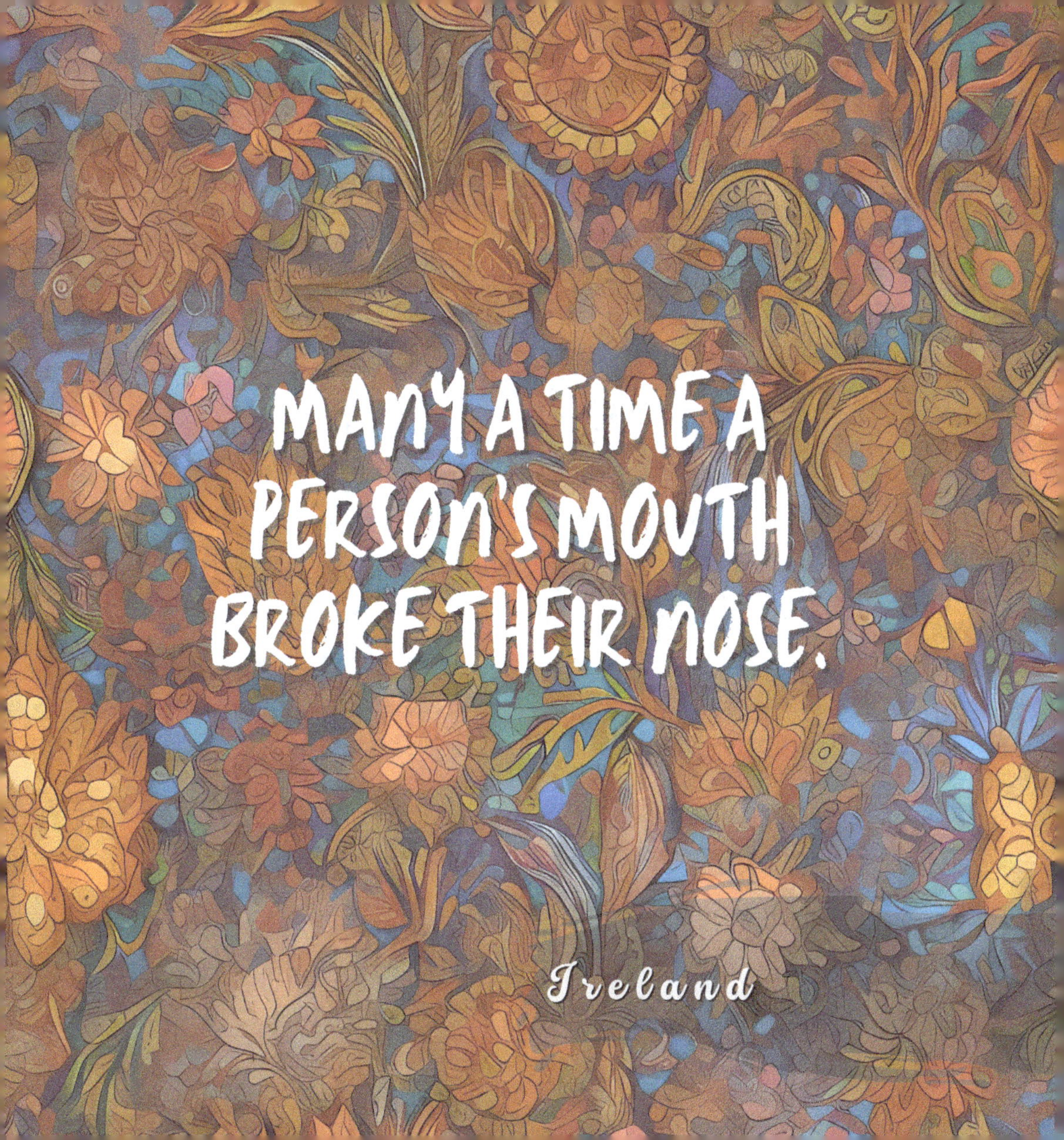
MANY A TIME A
PERSON'S MOUTH
BROKE THEIR NOSE.
Ireland

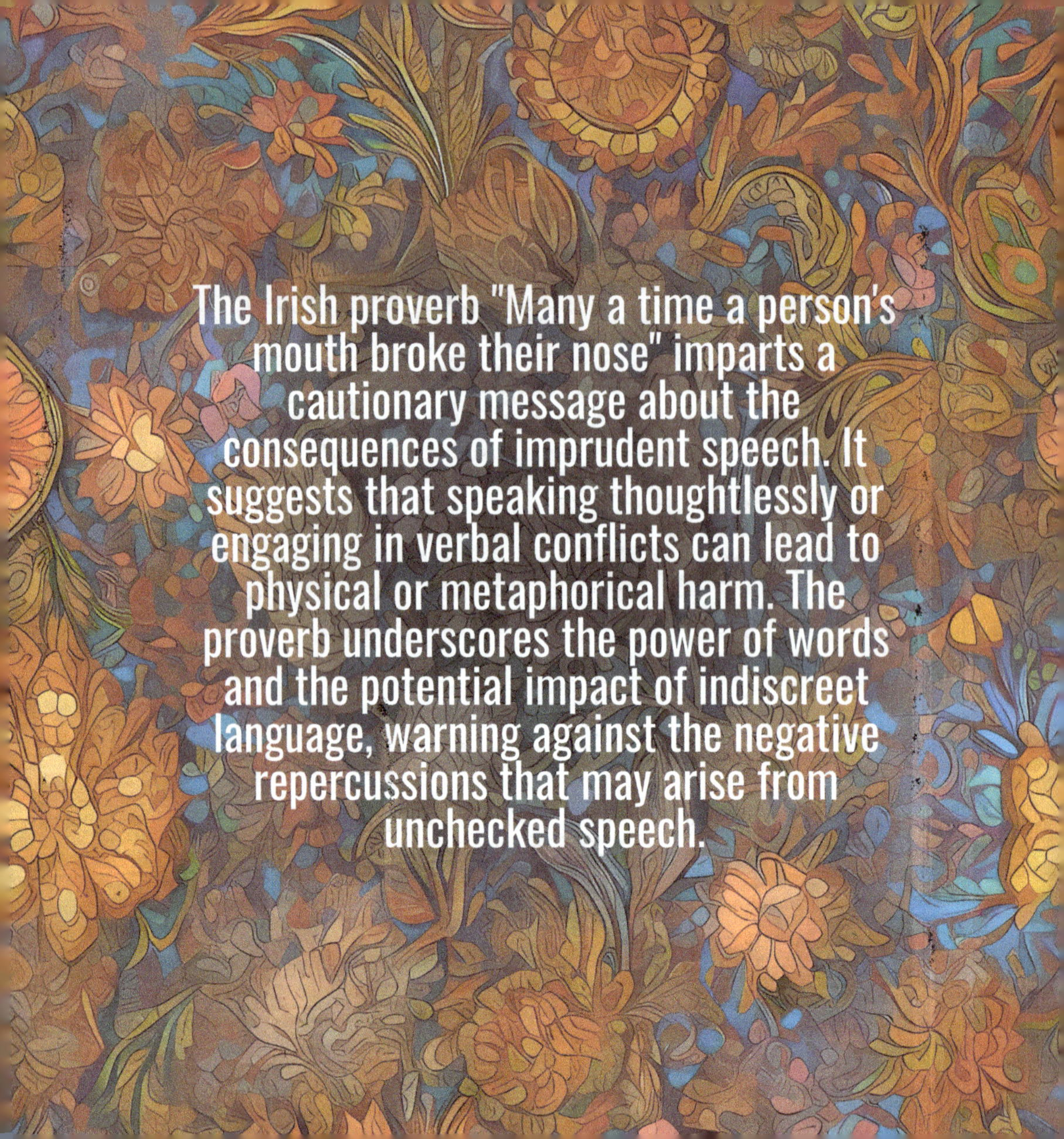

The Irish proverb "Many a time a person's mouth broke their nose" imparts a cautionary message about the consequences of imprudent speech. It suggests that speaking thoughtlessly or engaging in verbal conflicts can lead to physical or metaphorical harm. The proverb underscores the power of words and the potential impact of indiscreet language, warning against the negative repercussions that may arise from unchecked speech.

GETTING UP EARLY DOESN'T MAKE THE DAWN COME SOONER.
Latin American

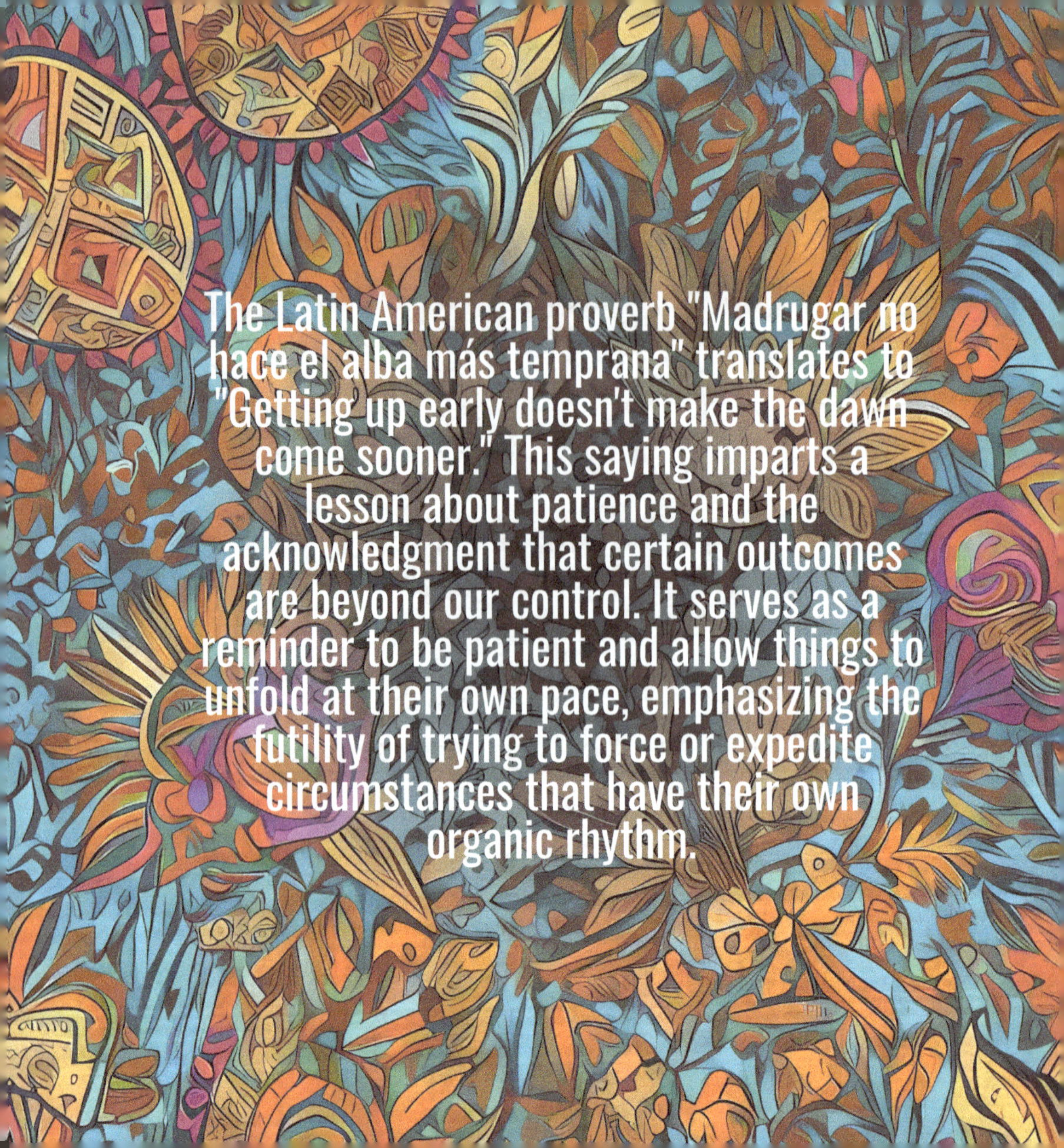

The Latin American proverb "Madrugar no hace el alba más temprana" translates to "Getting up early doesn't make the dawn come sooner." This saying imparts a lesson about patience and the acknowledgment that certain outcomes are beyond our control. It serves as a reminder to be patient and allow things to unfold at their own pace, emphasizing the futility of trying to force or expedite circumstances that have their own organic rhythm.

THE COW NEVER KNEW THE USE OF HIS OWN TAIL, UNTIL THE BUTCHER CUT IT OFF.
Jamaica

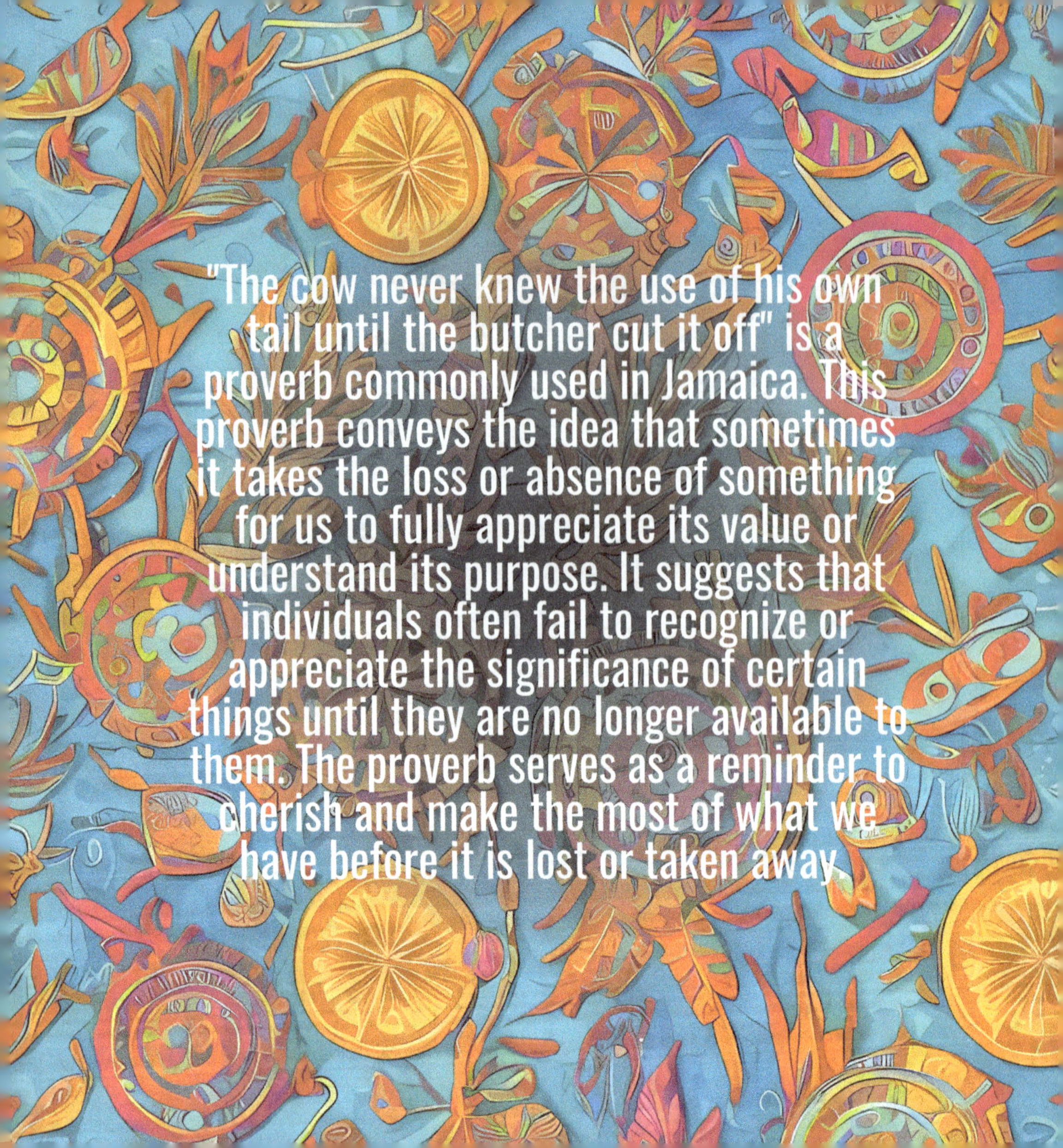

"The cow never knew the use of his own tail until the butcher cut it off" is a proverb commonly used in Jamaica. This proverb conveys the idea that sometimes it takes the loss or absence of something for us to fully appreciate its value or understand its purpose. It suggests that individuals often fail to recognize or appreciate the significance of certain things until they are no longer available to them. The proverb serves as a reminder to cherish and make the most of what we have before it is lost or taken away.

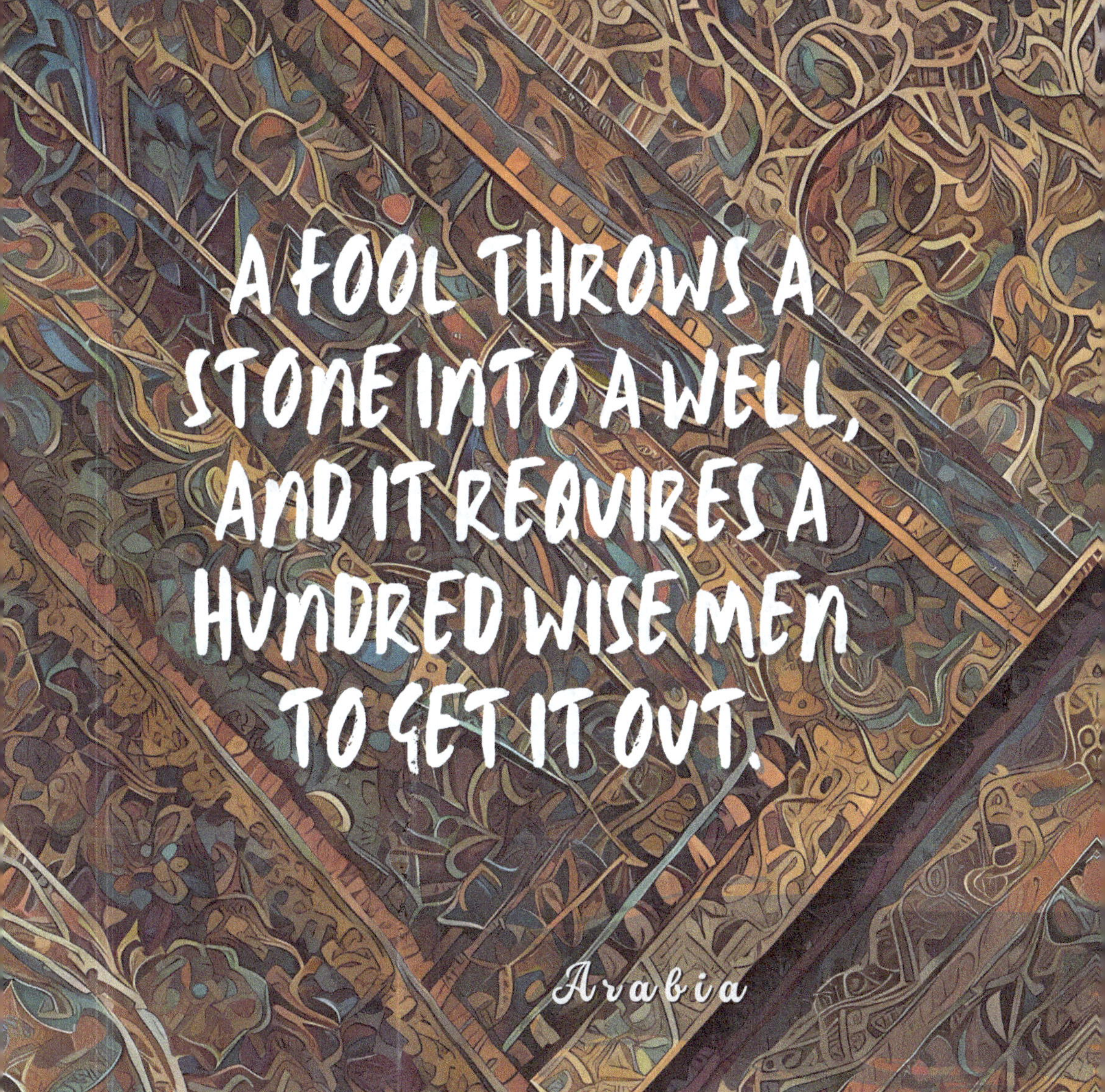
A FOOL THROWS A
STONE INTO A WELL,
AND IT REQUIRES A
HUNDRED WISE MEN
TO GET IT OUT.
Arabia

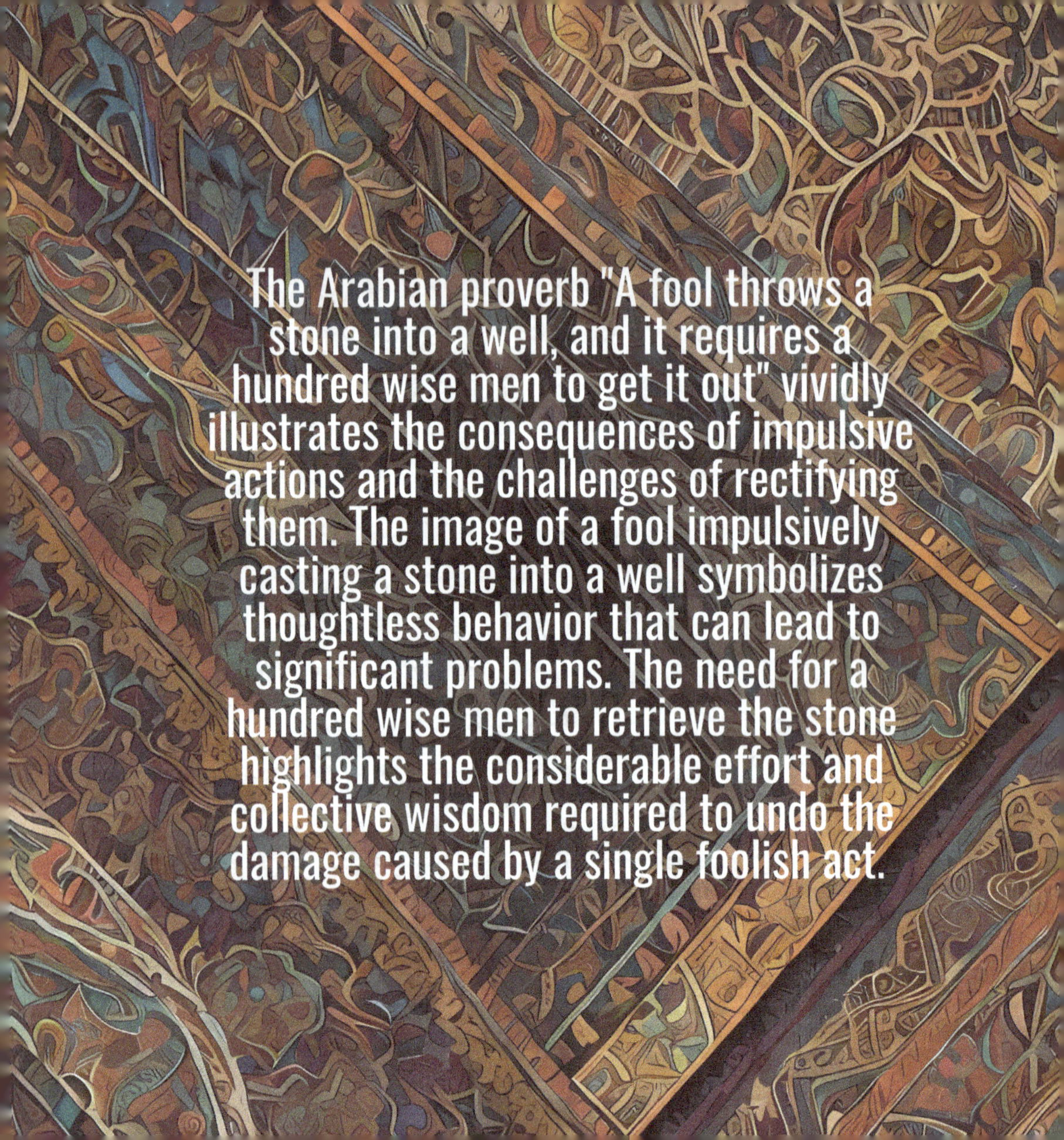
The Arabian proverb "A fool throws a stone into a well, and it requires a hundred wise men to get it out" vividly illustrates the consequences of impulsive actions and the challenges of rectifying them. The image of a fool impulsively casting a stone into a well symbolizes thoughtless behavior that can lead to significant problems. The need for a hundred wise men to retrieve the stone highlights the considerable effort and collective wisdom required to undo the damage caused by a single foolish act.

TIME SPENT
LAUGHING IS TIME
SPENT WITH THE
GODS.
Japan

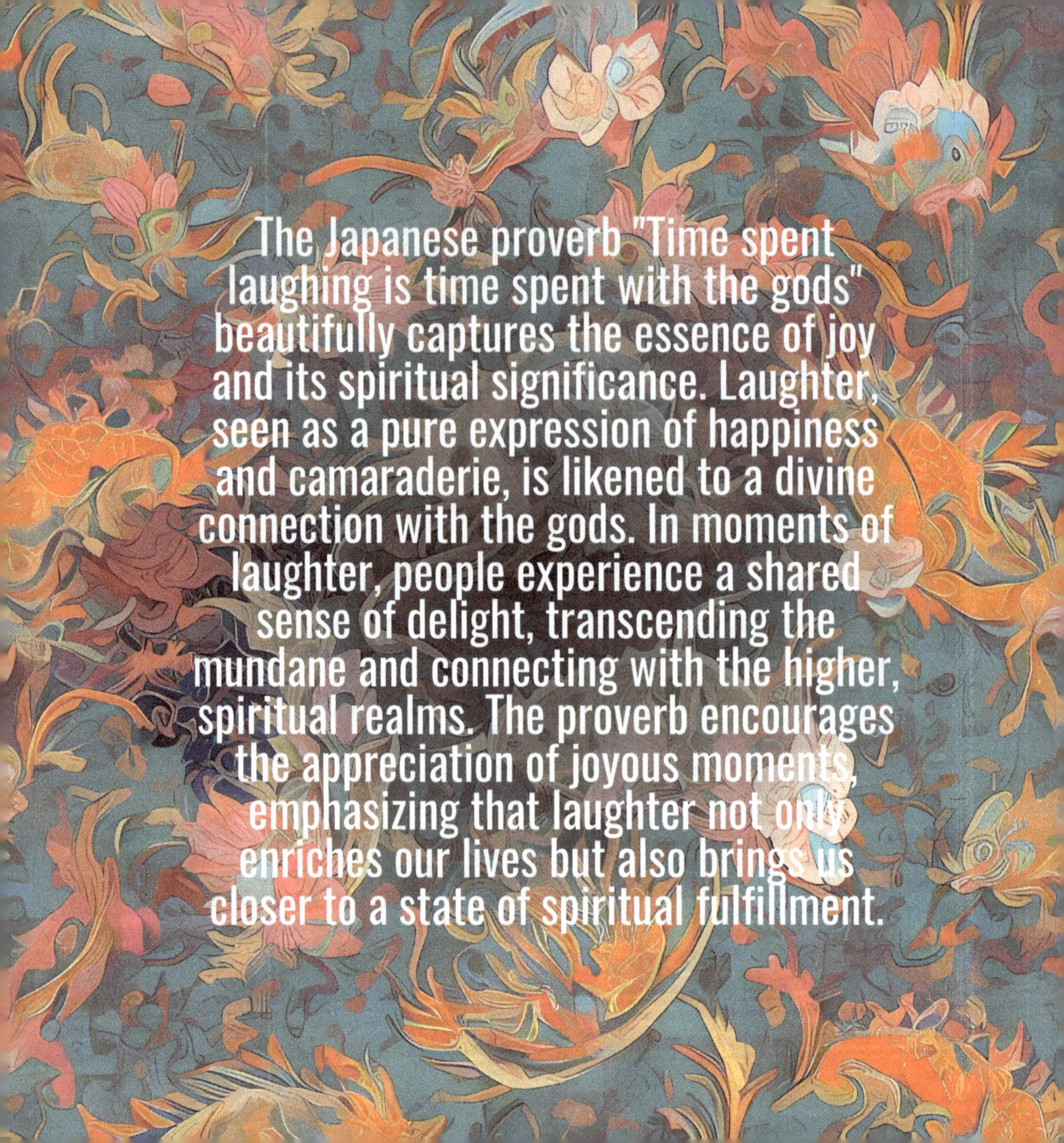

The Japanese proverb "Time spent laughing is time spent with the gods" beautifully captures the essence of joy and its spiritual significance. Laughter, seen as a pure expression of happiness and camaraderie, is likened to a divine connection with the gods. In moments of laughter, people experience a shared sense of delight, transcending the mundane and connecting with the higher, spiritual realms. The proverb encourages the appreciation of joyous moments, emphasizing that laughter not only enriches our lives but also brings us closer to a state of spiritual fulfillment.

A GOOD NEIGHBOR IS
BETTER THAN A
DISTANT RELATIVE.
Vietnam

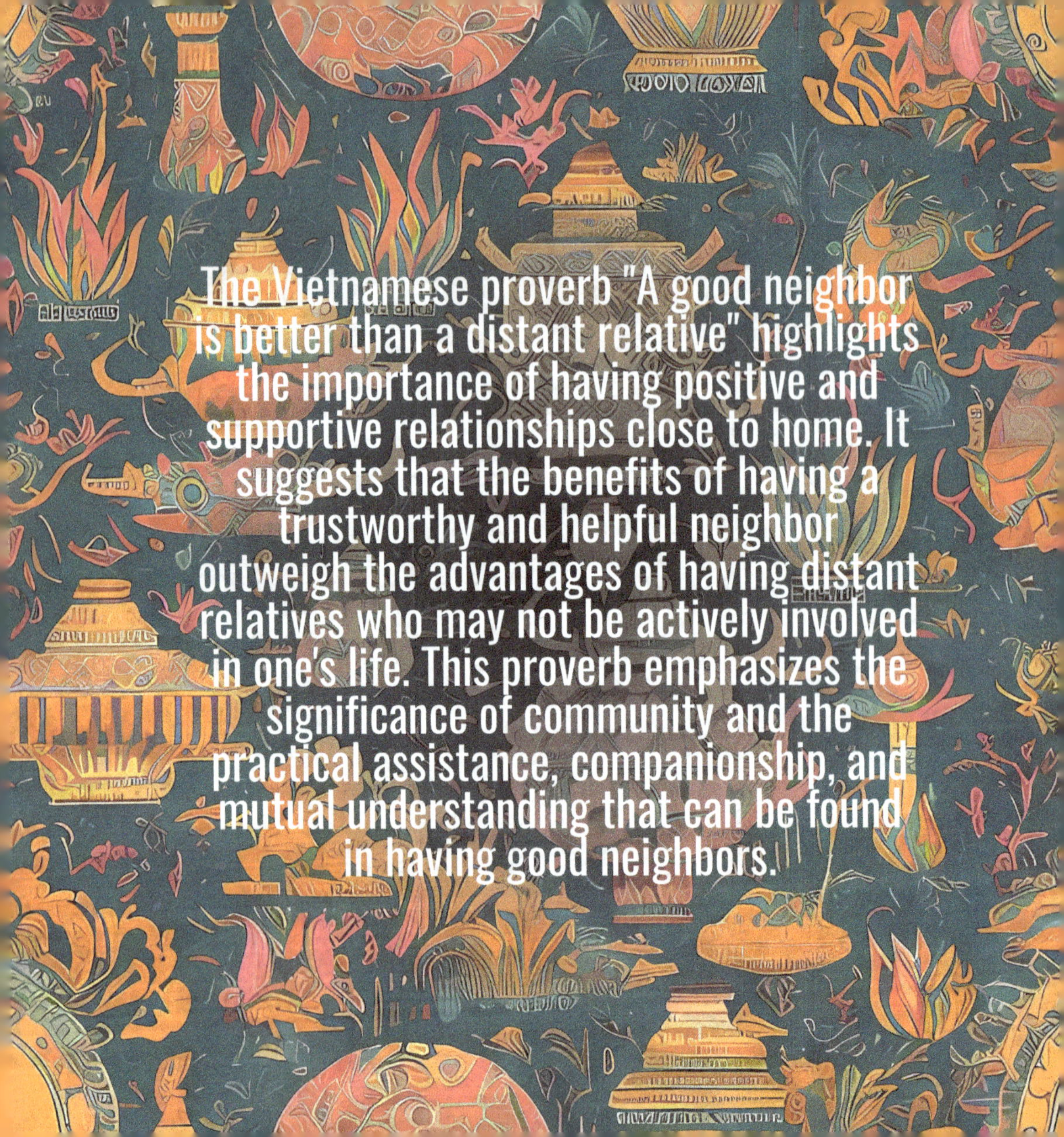

The Vietnamese proverb "A good neighbor is better than a distant relative" highlights the importance of having positive and supportive relationships close to home. It suggests that the benefits of having a trustworthy and helpful neighbor outweigh the advantages of having distant relatives who may not be actively involved in one's life. This proverb emphasizes the significance of community and the practical assistance, companionship, and mutual understanding that can be found in having good neighbors.

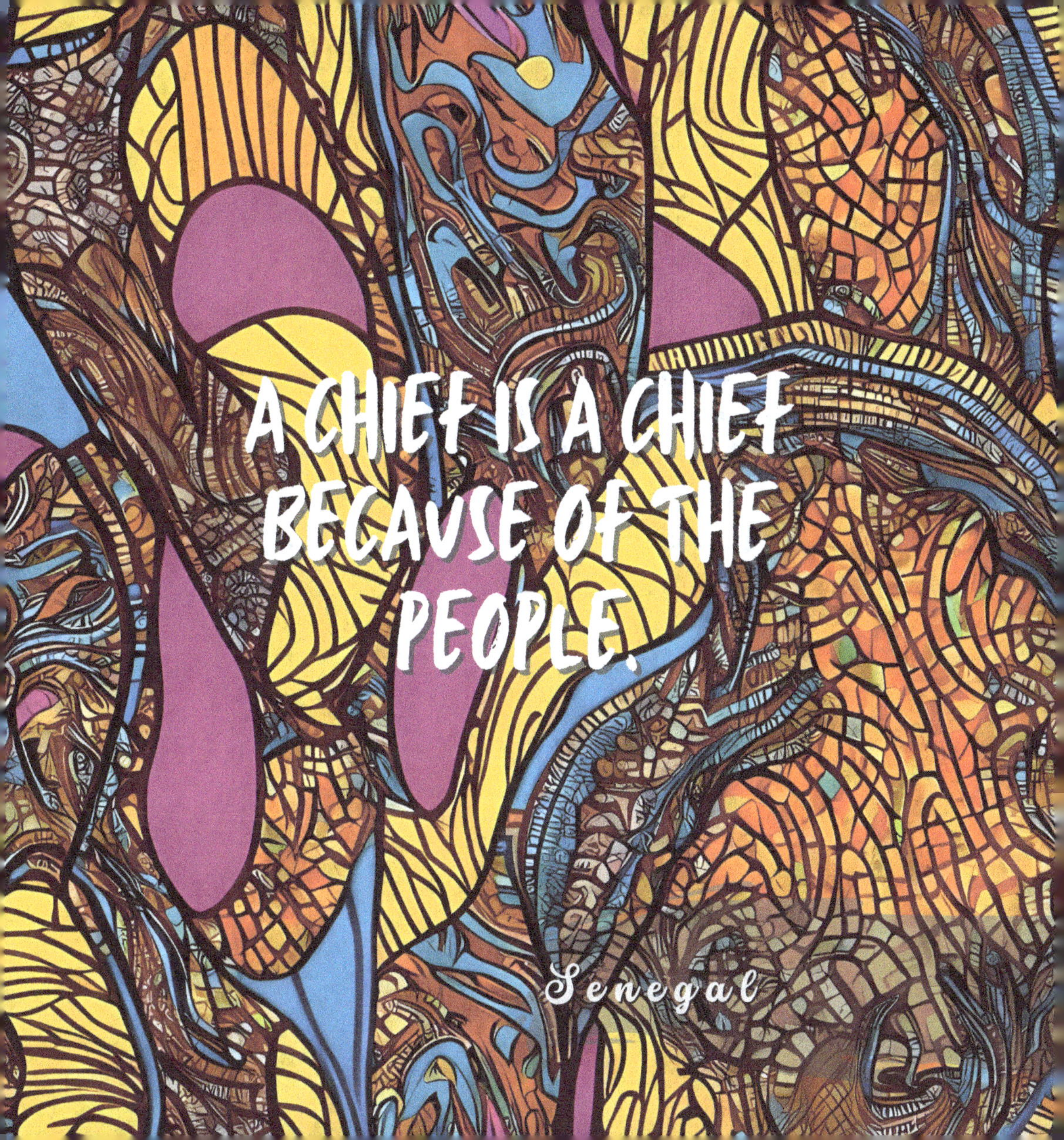
A CHIEF IS A CHIEF
BECAUSE OF THE
PEOPLE.
Senegal

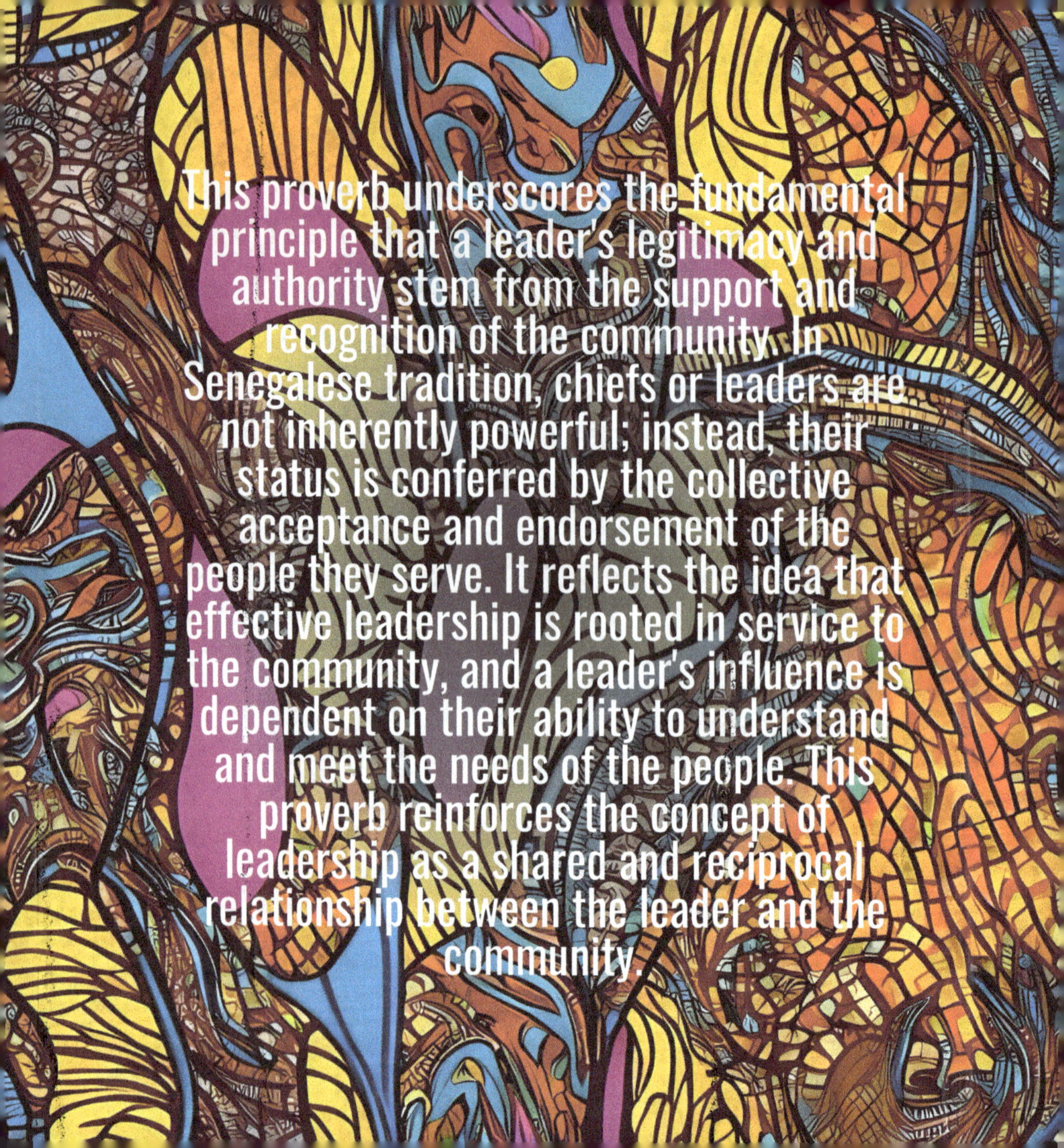

This proverb underscores the fundamental principle that a leader's legitimacy and authority stem from the support and recognition of the community. In Senegalese tradition, chiefs or leaders are not inherently powerful; instead, their status is conferred by the collective acceptance and endorsement of the people they serve. It reflects the idea that effective leadership is rooted in service to the community, and a leader's influence is dependent on their ability to understand and meet the needs of the people. This proverb reinforces the concept of leadership as a shared and reciprocal relationship between the leader and the community.

HE WHO TRAVELS
HAS STORIES TO
TELL.
Ireland

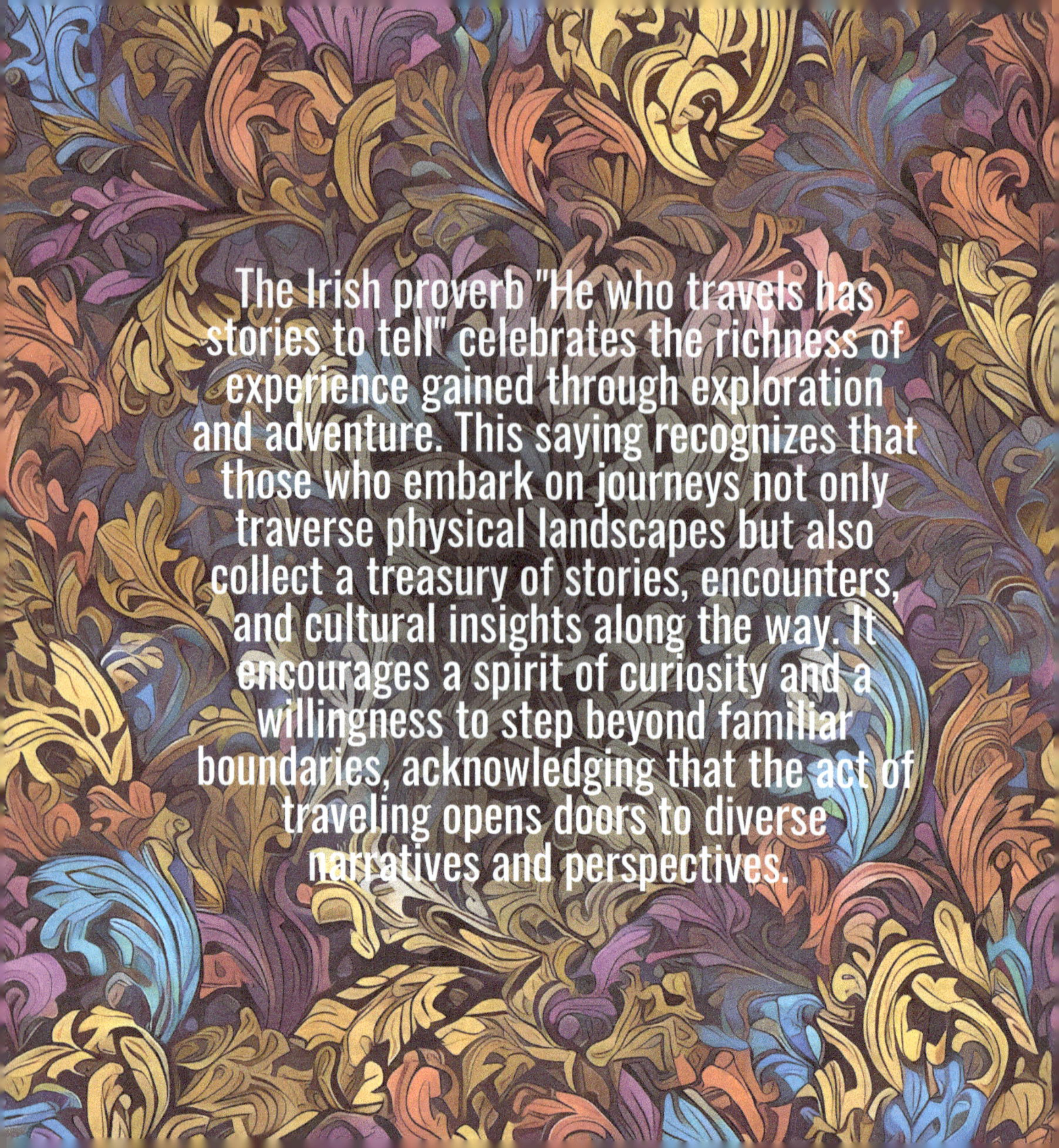

The Irish proverb "He who travels has stories to tell" celebrates the richness of experience gained through exploration and adventure. This saying recognizes that those who embark on journeys not only traverse physical landscapes but also collect a treasury of stories, encounters, and cultural insights along the way. It encourages a spirit of curiosity and a willingness to step beyond familiar boundaries, acknowledging that the act of traveling opens doors to diverse narratives and perspectives.

DON'T CRY OVER
SPILLED MILK.
Sweden

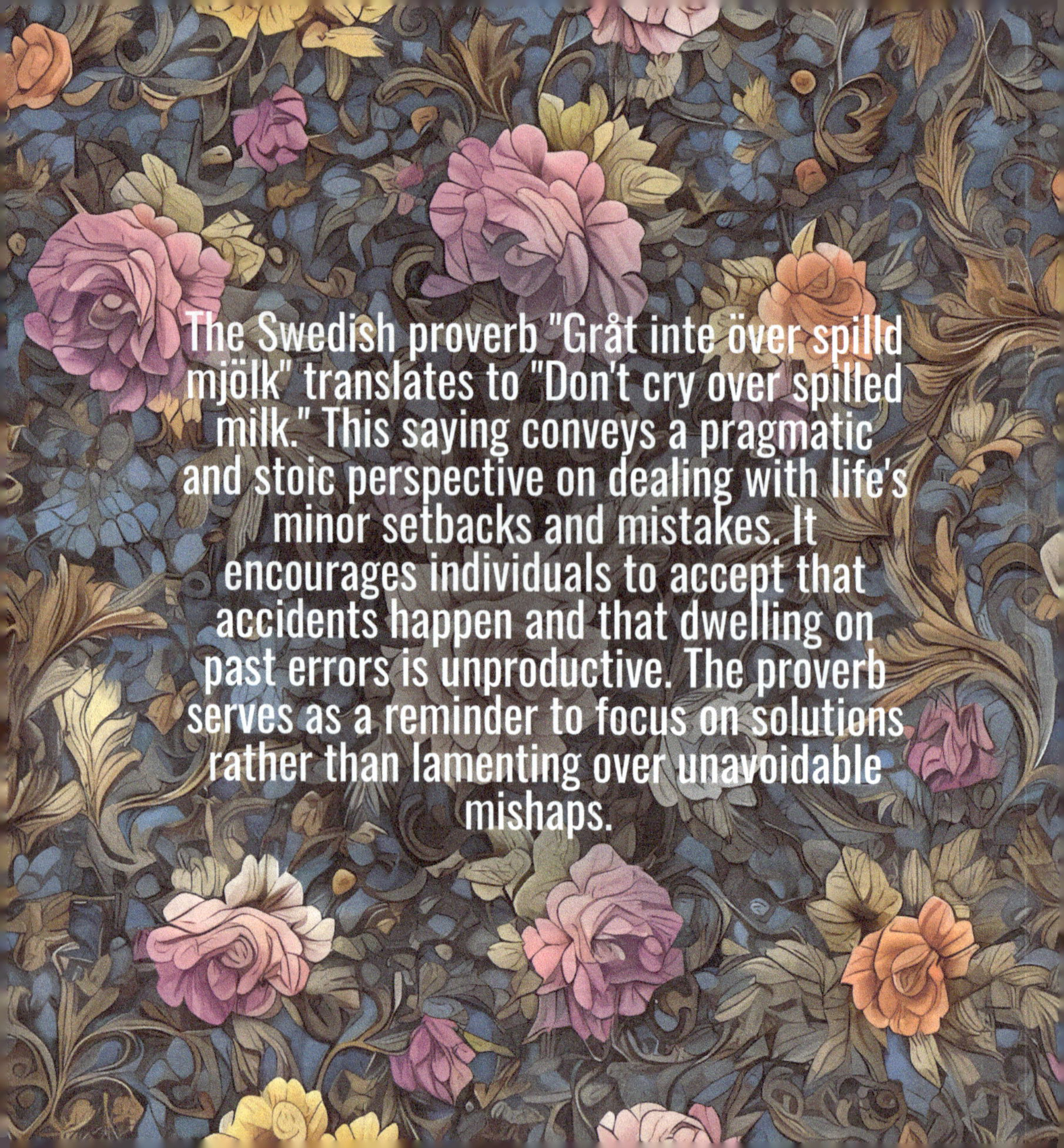

The Swedish proverb "Gråt inte över spilld mjölk" translates to "Don't cry over spilled milk." This saying conveys a pragmatic and stoic perspective on dealing with life's minor setbacks and mistakes. It encourages individuals to accept that accidents happen and that dwelling on past errors is unproductive. The proverb serves as a reminder to focus on solutions rather than lamenting over unavoidable mishaps.

IF YOU CAN'T HEAR,
YOU MUST FEEL.
Jamaica

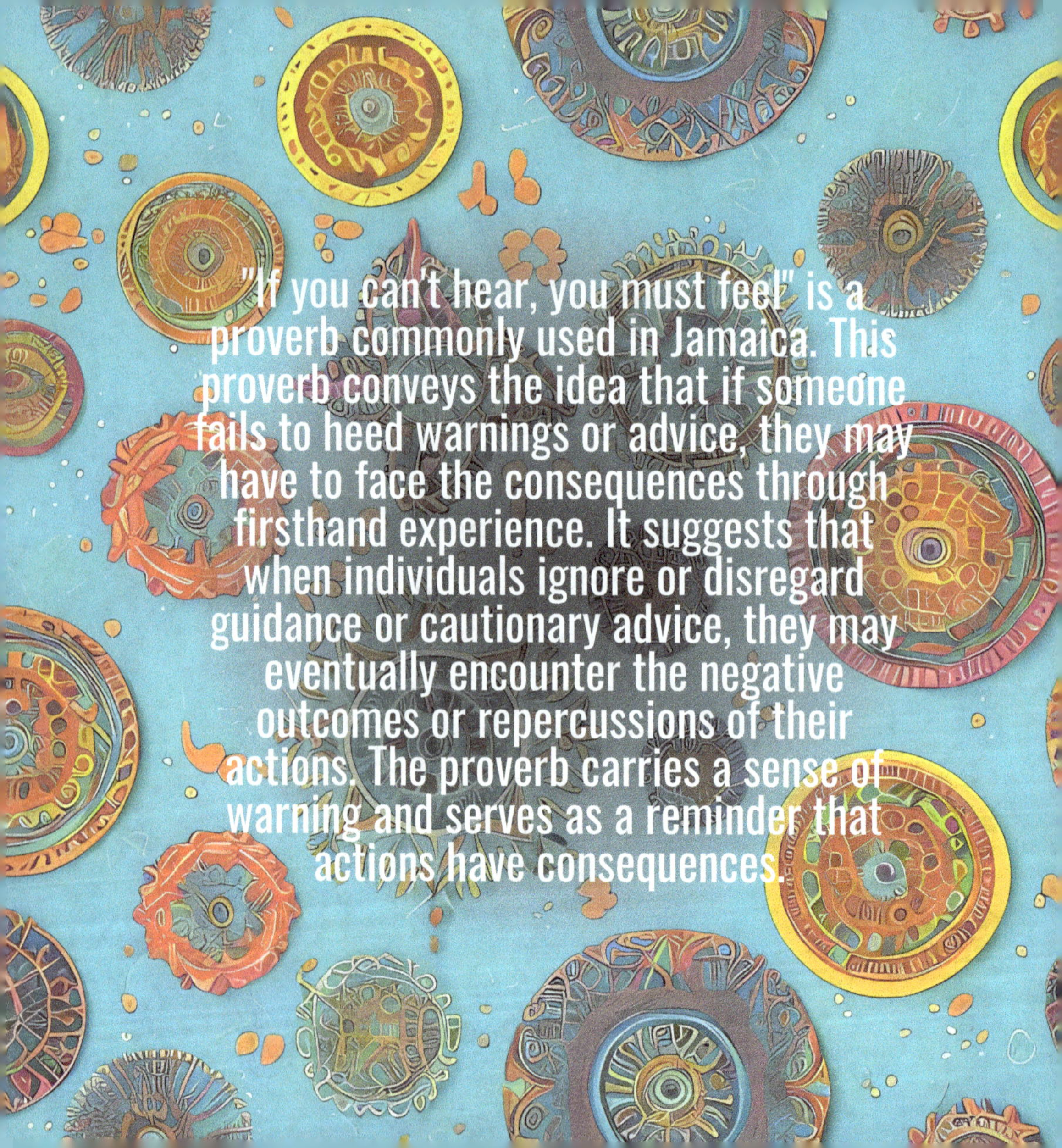
"If you can't hear, you must feel" is a proverb commonly used in Jamaica. This proverb conveys the idea that if someone fails to heed warnings or advice, they may have to face the consequences through firsthand experience. It suggests that when individuals ignore or disregard guidance or cautionary advice, they may eventually encounter the negative outcomes or repercussions of their actions. The proverb carries a sense of warning and serves as a reminder that actions have consequences.

A FOOL MAY BE KNOWN BY SIX THINGS: ANGER WITHOUT CAUSE, SPEECH WITHOUT PROFIT, CHANGE WITHOUT PROGRESS, INQUIRY WITHOUT OBJECT, PUTTING TRUST IN A STRANGER, AND MISTAKING FOES FOR FRIENDS.

Arabia

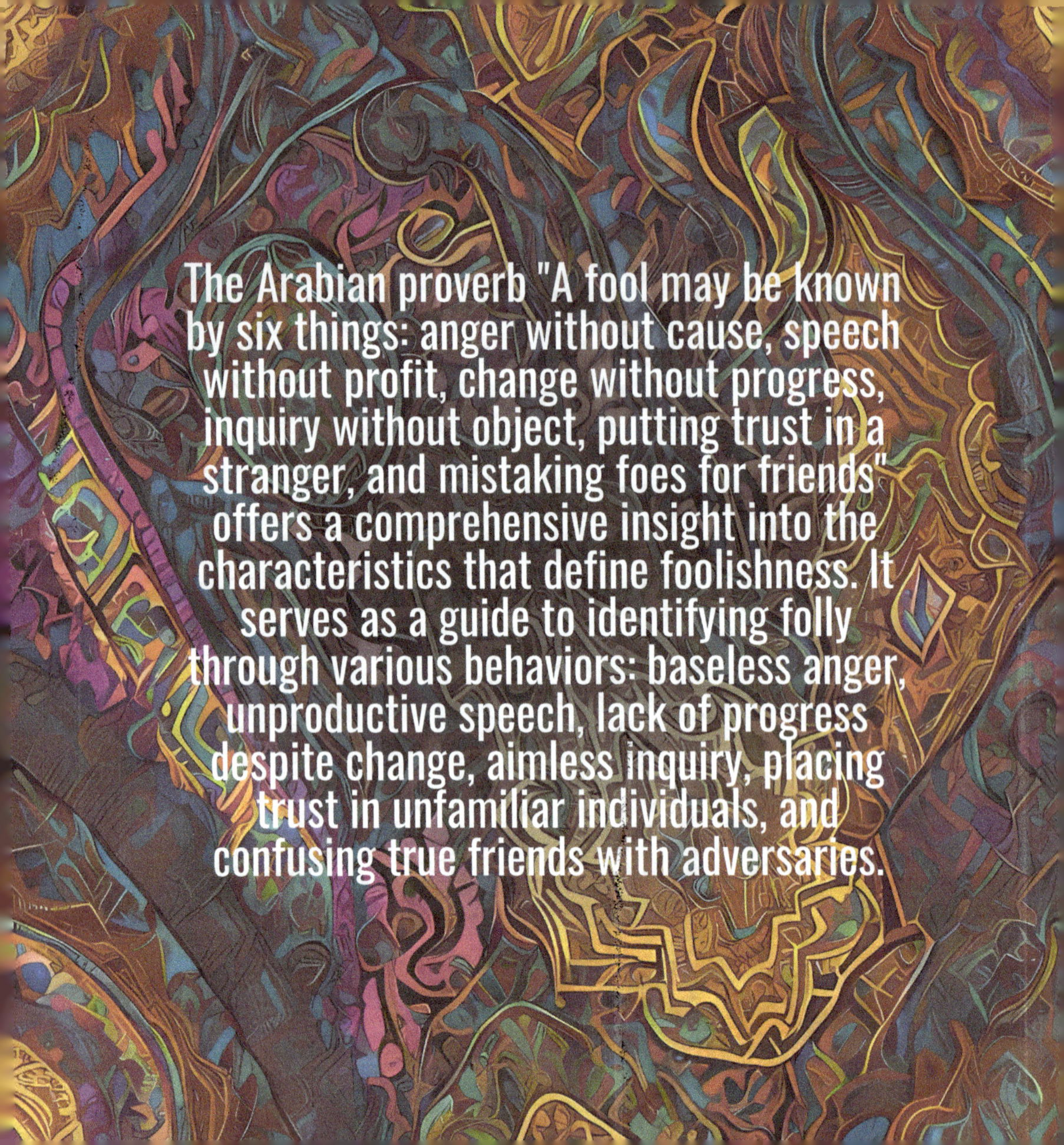

The Arabian proverb "A fool may be known by six things: anger without cause, speech without profit, change without progress, inquiry without object, putting trust in a stranger, and mistaking foes for friends" offers a comprehensive insight into the characteristics that define foolishness. It serves as a guide to identifying folly through various behaviors: baseless anger, unproductive speech, lack of progress despite change, aimless inquiry, placing trust in unfamiliar individuals, and confusing true friends with adversaries.

THE RAIN BEGINS
WITH A SINGLE
DROP.
Arabia

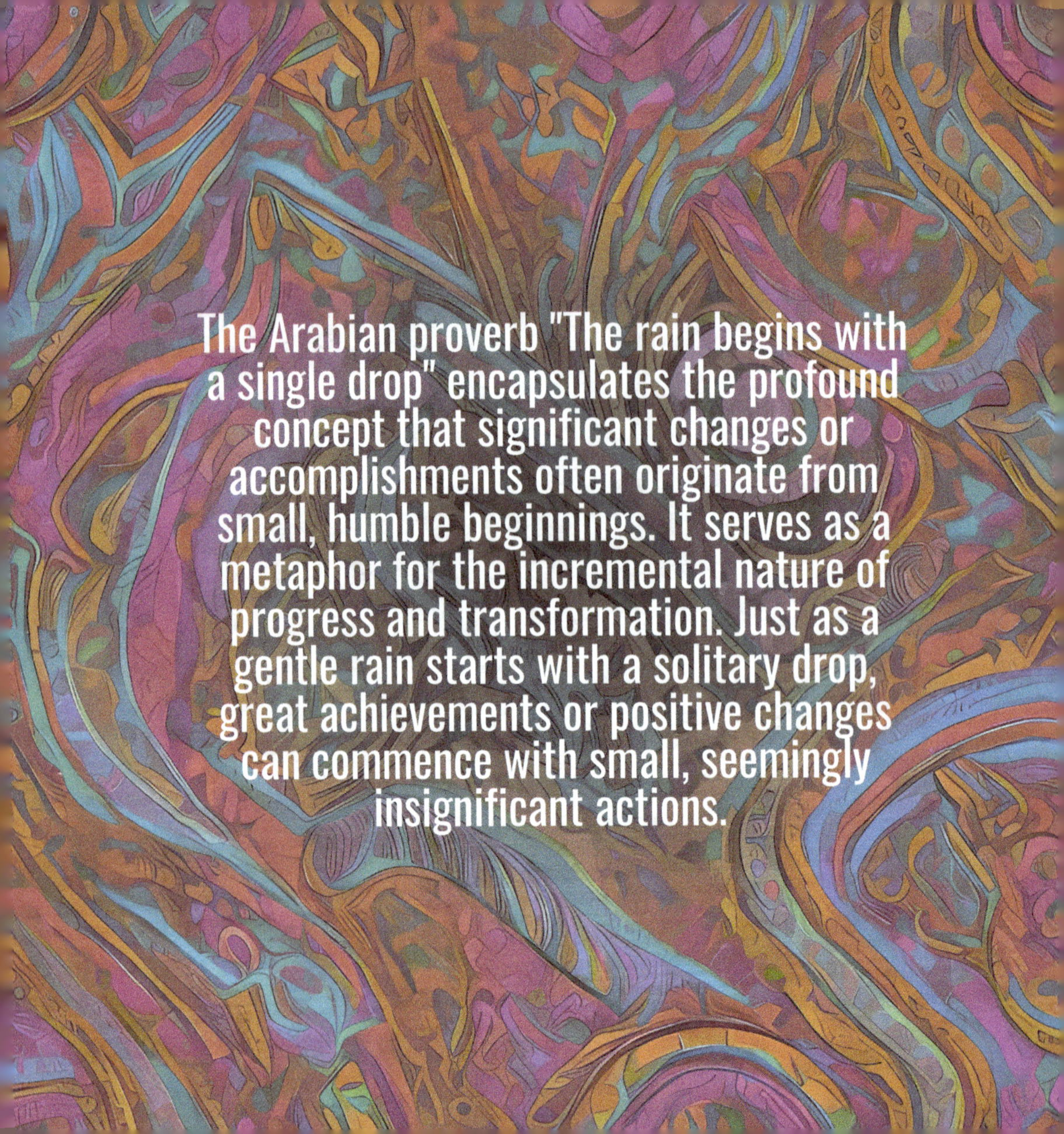

The Arabian proverb "The rain begins with a single drop" encapsulates the profound concept that significant changes or accomplishments often originate from small, humble beginnings. It serves as a metaphor for the incremental nature of progress and transformation. Just as a gentle rain starts with a solitary drop, great achievements or positive changes can commence with small, seemingly insignificant actions.

WHEN EATING FRUIT, REMEMBER THE ONE WHO PLANTED THE TREE.
Vietnam

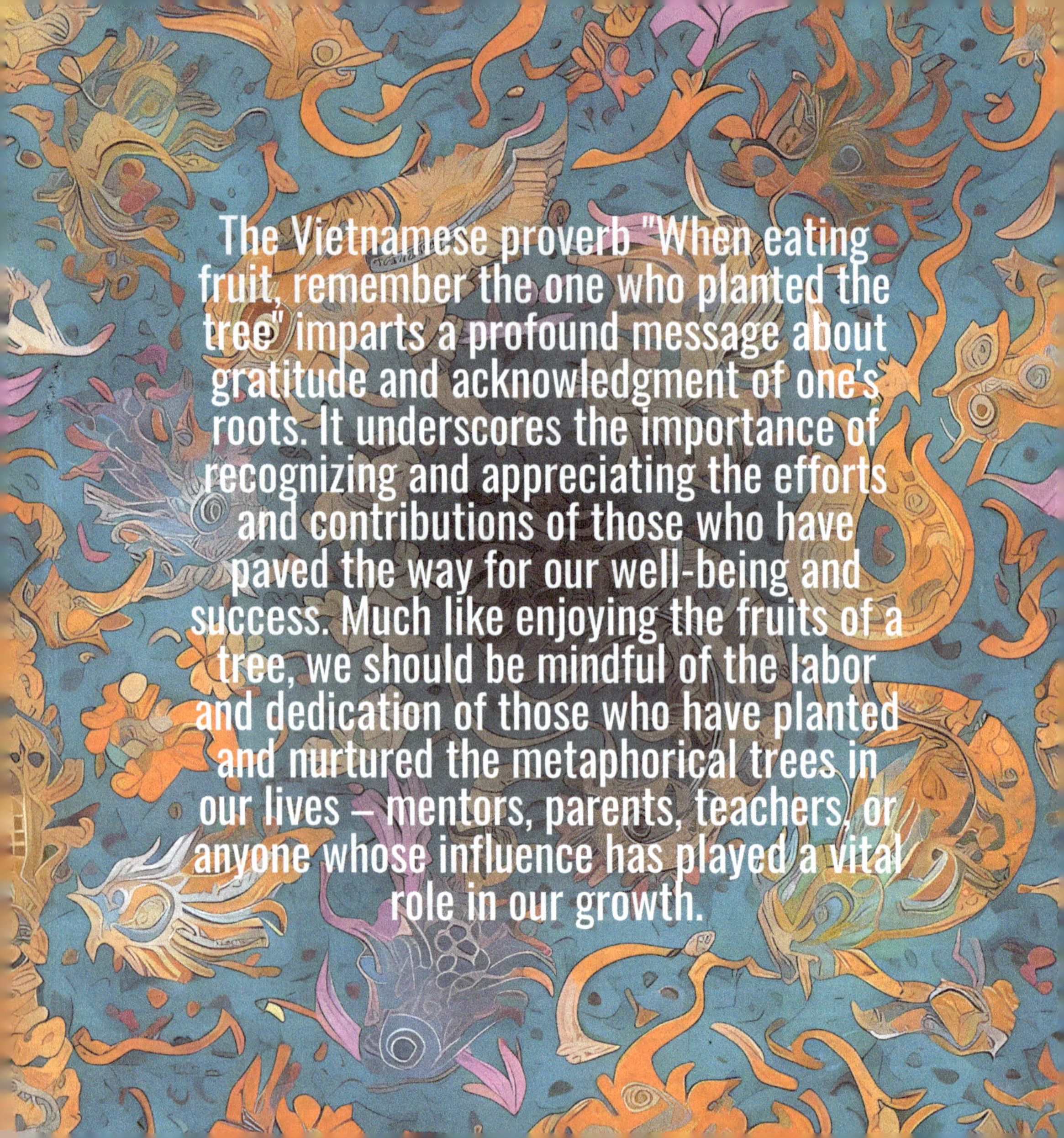
The Vietnamese proverb "When eating fruit, remember the one who planted the tree" imparts a profound message about gratitude and acknowledgment of one's roots. It underscores the importance of recognizing and appreciating the efforts and contributions of those who have paved the way for our well-being and success. Much like enjoying the fruits of a tree, we should be mindful of the labor and dedication of those who have planted and nurtured the metaphorical trees in our lives – mentors, parents, teachers, or anyone whose influence has played a vital role in our growth.

www.ingramcontent.com/pod-product-compliance
Lightning Source LLC
Chambersburg PA
CBHW082100090726
47910CB00008B/2541

* 9 7 8 1 3 9 9 9 7 8 3 0 9 *